O9-CFU-494

BEYOND BORDERS

BEYOND BORDERS
A Cultural Reader

Library Resource Center
Renton Technical College
3000 N.E. 4th St.
Renton, WA 98056

Randall Bass
Georgetown University

Joy Young
Georgetown University

HOUGHTON MIFFLIN COMPANY   *Boston   New York*

428
.64
BEYOND
2003b

Publisher: Patricia A. Coryell
Executive Editor: Suzanne Phelps Weir
Senior Development Editor: Sarah Helyar Smith
Editorial Assistant: Becky Wong
Senior Project Editor: Kathryn Dinovo
Cover Design Manager: Diana Coe
Senior Manufacturing Coordinator: Marie Barnes
Marketing Manager: Cindy Graff Cohen
Marketing Assistant: Sarah Donelson

Cover image: © The Stock Illustration Source, Inc.

photo credits:

Page 269, Courtesy of Mackinac State Historic Parks, Mackinac Island, Michigan; **Page 426–427,** © Art Spiegelman; **Page 454,** Christopher Columbus Chart, est. 1492; **Page 456,** Map by John Ferrar (1651); **Page 457,** Map by John Mitchell (1755) for the English Lords of Trade and Plantations; **Page 523–531,** © Jack Jackson; **Plates; 1,** © 2002, *www.odt.org;* **2,** Foolscap Map of the World, c. 1590; **3,** © Patricia Rodriguez; **4,** © Joel Sternfeld, Courtesy Pace/MacGill Gallery, New York; **5,** © Joel Sternfeld, Courtesy Pace/MacGill Gallery, New York; **6,** © Camilo Jose Vergara; **7,** © Eugene Richards; **8,** © Shooting Back/Charlene Williams; **9,** Street Arabs at Night (Riis #123), Museum of the City of New York; **10,** Courtesy Ribbon Rail Productions; **11,** © CORBIS; **12,** © Hulleah Tsinhahninnie; **13,** © Paul Fusco/Magnum Photos; **14,** © Judy Griesedieck; **15,** Courtesy of IBM; **16,** © Chris Woods/Diane Farris Gallery; **17 a–b,** © Pedro Meyer; **18 a–d,** © Catherine Opie; **19,** © Dana Fineman; **20 a,** Hulton-Deutsch Collection/CORBIS; **20 b,** © CORBIS; **21 a–b,** © Peter Menzel; **22 a–b,** © Peter Menzel; **23,** © Dang Ngo; **24,** © Peter Menzel; **25 a–b,** United Color of Benetton; **26,** © Martha Rosler.

Copyright © 2003 by Houghton Mifflin Company. All rights reserved.

No part of this work may be reproduced or transmitted in any form or by any means, electronic or mechanical, including photocopying and recording, or by any information storage or retrieval system without the prior written permission of the copyright owner unless such copying is expressly permitted by federal copyright law. With the exception of nonprofit transcription in Braille, Houghton Mifflin is not authorized to grant permission for further uses of copyrighted selections reprinted in this text without the permission of their owners. Permission must be obtained from the individual copyright owners as identified herein. Address requests for permission to make copies of Houghton Mifflin material to College Permissions, Houghton Mifflin Company, 222 Berkeley Street, Boston, MA 02116-3764.

Printed in the U.S.A.

Library of Congress Control Number: 2002105243

ISBN: 0-618-23497-7

123456789-QWF-06 05 04 03 02

CONTENTS

CHAPTER 3

NEGOTIATING BORDERS: *The Dynamics of Difference*   246

Image Portfolio

PREFACE

Beyond Borders: A Cultural Reader aims to help students become critical thinkers, readers, and writers by investigating the borders that construct our worlds. These borders are spaces—physical, social, or communicative—in which proximity and difference coincide, generating meaningful exchange. The book's critical essays, fiction, reportage, poetry, art, and graphics, organized thematically, raise issues about individual and collective identities, and how these arise, change, and proliferate in contact with other identities. In addition, *Beyond Borders* investigates the thematic and theoretical problems underlying the very notion of borders, including the usefulness of "border" as an analytical tool. Exposure to a range of views in a range of media helps students to develop analytical skills and an expressive repertoire, prompting them to think and write more precisely about how they construct—and are constructed by—their environments.

Exploring a Wide Variety of Texts

Beyond Borders' readings present a wide variety of subjects, styles, genres, voices, and disciplinary orientations. A large number belong to the "hybrid genres" that have proliferated in the last generation: essays that combine politics with autobiography or autobiography with cultural criticism. *Beyond Borders* also offers a variety of visual documents for interpretation, which helps students extend both their analytical skills and their definitions of the word "text." The array of texts in *Beyond Borders* encourages students to explore relationships among individuals, groups, nations, and international communities. Three fundamental and overlapping issues recur:

1. How persons derive and express individual identity.
2. How individuals form groups, and how groups express collective identity.
3. How groups interact with other groups, and how they exist either harmoniously or in tension within larger social units such as nations and international communities.

Questions at the end of each selection raise these issues in ways responsive to the unique concerns of the author or artist. On the Web site linked to *Beyond Borders* are questions that consider multiple selections and that raise the level of inquiry from chapter to chapter. The questions ask students to think about the many influences upon identity, the relationship between self-definition and the perception of others, and the ways that individuals and groups bridge or preserve differences. Recurring concerns create a balance between thematic coherence and flexibility.

An Intercultural and Interactive Book

The wide range of American voices in *Beyond Borders* represents all the power and perils of an open and heterogeneous society. The readings, prefaces, and appendices are designed to familiarize students with important issues and expressive modes of American interculturalism; in addition, questions and assignments ask students to respond actively at all stages of the reading and writing process. *Beyond Borders* assumes that students learn how to read and write critically when they can freely cross the border between textual consumer and producer. Because of this assumption, the book and the interactive Web site encourage interactivity in four ways:

1. By including different kinds of reading and writing activities designed to stimulate critical engagement and responsive writing.
2. By offering questions designed to stimulate discussion, as well as occasional collaborative writing projects.
3. By arranging selections to encourage meaningful comparison of texts.
4. By linking print and electronic resources and by asking students to consider how each medium shapes perception and communication.

Structure and Organization

The introduction sketches key concepts, problems, and terms related to borders and what they represent.

CHAPTER 1, Borders of Identity: Living Fictions, explores the influences that shape identity and the varied forms in which it is expressed.

CHAPTER 2, Borders of Community: Belonging and Alienation, focuses upon how groups derive and express a sense of identity, how they connect and clash with each other and with larger social entities.

CHAPTER 3, Negotiating Borders: the Dynamics of Difference, investigates how the notion of "border" itself may imply otherness and exclusion and how the creation of culture relies upon distinction.

BORDER VISIONS: An Image Portfolio, explores how images of various kinds can be read as cultural texts and how some images themselves act as "readings" of cultural meaning.

CHAPTER 4, Borders and Frontiers: Imagined and Virtual Communities, considers social identity in various conceptual realms, from model nations to cyberspace.

CHAPTER 5, The World's New Borders: Globalism versus Tribalism, pursues large questions of community as they relate to culture, geography, and politics.

CHAPTER 6, Border Visions: contains both prose and images and addresses visual rhetoric and strategies of looking.

Features

Each chapter adopts a similar structure with the following components:

- Critical Questions (at the beginning of each chapter)
- Framing Essay (at the beginning of each chapter)
- Working with the Text questions (after each reading)
- From Reading to Writing: Critical Questions Revisited (after each chapter)

CRITICAL QUESTIONS: Each chapter begins with a set of Critical Questions intended to frame students' reading and rereading of all the selections in the chapter and to provide a broad context for this writing.

FRAMING ESSAY: Each chapter opens with a brief framing essay that sketches the key issues of the selections to follow. The purpose of the essay is both to clarify some key terms and concepts for the chapter and to raise more fully the "problems" posed in the Critical Questions.

WORKING WITH THE TEXT: Each selection concludes with Working with the Text questions that ask students to focus on the ideas and writing in that section. Students' responses may range from personal narrative to a close rereading of the text looking at particular strategies employed by the author. Students' responses may be written, discussed, or both. The Working with the Text questions also ask students to engage in fieldwork (alone or in groups) or in electronic research on the Web.

FROM READING TO WRITING: CRITICAL QUESTIONS REVISITED: At the end of each chapter there are essay topics designed to help students pull together important themes and issues across the readings in the chapter. The questions reconsider the Critical Questions, as well as key points discussed in the introductory essays, framing these issues as writing topics. These questions have been written to name (1) a broad essay topic; (2) directions for shaping the paper overall and possible directions; and (3) suggested strategies for *building* the paper, moving from reading analysis to argument.

BEYOND BORDERS ONLINE—WORLD WIDE WEB SITE: *Beyond Borders* is also accompanied by an extensive World Wide Web site that serves as a source for critical thinking about cyberspace as well as for electronic fieldwork into issues of identity, community, place, and difference. It is also a platform for links to research and resources building on all topics in the book, and a hypertext guide to the integration of concepts across the book. The URL is http://www.hmco.com/hmco/college/english/bass/.

Experience shows that course-based materials become a resource for critical thinking and writing when they: (1) challenge students to consider new ideas or reconsider familiar ones; (2) offer them the means to pursue specific inquiries that they find compelling; and (3) present complex ideas in a coherent and recursive way. These goals—opening up important ideas and giving students a coherent environment in which to construct their own paths to understanding—have governed the creation of this book.

Acknowledgments

The road to revision was not an easy one, with many twists and turns, and the occasional sign ahead reading "Bridge Out." Nevertheless, with considerable help from those we love as well as those who would love to see us actually finish this thing, we were able to reach the goal.

We want to thank the people at Houghton Mifflin who made the project possible, especially those focused on the details of the revision, such as Katharine Glynn who pushed us along when we needed it, and Sue Howard who heroically tracked the photo permissions, Merrill Peterson and Eleanor Horner at Matrix, and Sarah Smith. And thanks to Suzanne

Phelps-Weir: at times the process wasn't pretty, but let's hope the baby's beautiful.

Our immense gratitude to Laura King for her excellent work on the reading pedagogy; our thanks also to Virginia Bell, for her work on the IRM and Web resources, and her longtime understanding and support for the book. We are particularly indebted to David Gewanter for his professional assistance in reshaping the end of chapter materials, and his generous interventions just when we needed it.

Thanks and love and hugs to Gail Solomon and David Gewanter for their support as our long suffering partners in this project.

RANDY BASS AND JOY YOUNG

BEYOND BORDERS

A Cultural Reader

INTRODUCTION

Beyond Borders is a book about the many borders that hold together the United States and its people. To say that our borders hold us together may seem a little odd. Normally, when we think of a border, we think of a division between two different places, such as a border between states, or countries. We usually think of borders as geographical lines—having some kind of physical presence and/or some political meaning. Indeed, that kind of geographical and dividing border is one of the many kinds of borders addressed in this book. But the idea of a "border" implies much more than a physical division.

A border in this book could be defined as *any place where differences come together,* whether these differences are national, cultural and social, differences in values or language, or differences in gender, family heritage, or economic status. The scope of this book includes all of the many borders that shape individual identity, and the cluster of identities we call "American." Whether individual or cultural, our identities are constructed by racial and ethnic borders; economic and class borders; borders of sexuality and gender; and the borders that separate different levels of community, such as family, neighborhood, and nation. Such borders are both real and imaginary, physical and symbolic. A border can be something you can see, such as the Rio Grande River that runs between the United States and Mexico; or a border can be unseen, such as the border of identity, the limit between self and other, "us" and "them." To say that borders are "places where differences come together" implies something beyond mere differences. Where differences come together, people or groups are rarely on an equal footing; there is almost always an imbalance—of power, resources, capital, trust, understanding, or desire. No matter who you are, you are

1

negotiating these borders continually, making transactions across boundaries and maneuvering among differences.

Yet the idea of *Beyond Borders* is that borders are not static dividing lines or barriers of difference, but *places* where something happens. *Borders are never neutral.* Borders always represent differences that mean *something:* differences in status, resources, power, ideas, values, hopes, history, language, or culture. Anywhere these differences find expression—whether in a poem, a photograph, an essay, a story, or a billboard—is what this book calls a "border text." Border texts express stress, energy, hope, and power—the creative tension sparked when differences meet. Although differences may often stand as the source of conflict, they are not necessarily destructive. What "happens" when differences meet is fundamental to social relationships, acts of communication, to the expression of one's own identity. In border texts and at "border crossings," exciting and difficult events take place. Indeed, the very concept of *borders* and *borderlands,* whether of geographic, political, or metaphorical realities, varies from selection to selection. Some texts challenge existing borders and reimagine them along different lines; others rethink the identity politics of the border, questioning the values and limits of the border as a cultural indicator and conceptual tool.

In any text there are always multiple levels of meaning: All texts are formed through a particular perspective, and all writers and texts are embedded in cultural contexts and therefore influenced by them. *Beyond Borders* encourages you to see how your own identity and perspective are shaped by cultural influences. Reflecting on those influences, you can be more thoughtful about the texts you read and what you write. It urges you to pay attention to how ideas travel through your cultural environment: through images and media, through politics and journalism, through music and fashion, through graffiti written on freeway abutments, and through home pages designed by college students. Finally, looking at texts as border texts is a way of looking in a new way at certain fundamental American issues, including what it means to be an American, and what it means for the United States of America to survive, given that it always has been and always will be a nation of diverse peoples. And it means thinking about the world as a whole, and whether it is coming together or breaking down into hostile, small pieces—or perhaps both.

Critical Reading Across Borders

As you begin to think about the concept of borders, it may be useful to start by thinking about maps, where traditional ideas of borders are most graphically represented. So, for starters, "here is a map of our

country." Actually it is not a map at all, but a poem about a map, by
Adrienne Rich. Adrienne Rich is one of the best known contemporary
American poets. This poem is part of a long poem called *An Atlas of the
Difficult World*.

An Atlas of the Difficult World

Here is a map of our country:
here is the Sea of Indifference, glazed with salt
This is the haunted river flowing from brow to groin
we dare not taste its water
This is the desert where missiles are planted like corns
This is the breadbasket of foreclosed farms
This is the birthplace of the rockabilly boy
This is the cemetery of the poor
who died for democracy   This is a battlefield
from a nineteenth-century war   the shrine is famous
This is the sea-town of myth and story   when the fishing fleets
went bankrupt   here is where the jobs were   on the pier
processing frozen fishsticks   hourly wages and no shares
These are other battlefields   Centralia Detroit
here are the forests primeval   the copper   the silver lodes
These are the Suburbs of acquiescence   silence rising fumelike from
     the streets
This is the capital of money and dolor whose spires
flare up through air inversions whose bridges are crumbling
whose children are drifting blind alleys pent
between coiled rolls of razor wire
I promised to show you a map you say but this is a mural
then yes let it be these are small distinctions
where do we see it from is the question

Now there might be a number of passages in Rich's poem that are suggestive, puzzling, or elusive. For now, let's focus on her conclusion. What do
you suppose Rich means when she maintains that her poem may be either
a "map" or a "mural"? (Think of a mural that you've seen, on a wall in
some public place or in a book, or look at the murals on the Web link in
the *Beyond Borders* site. Then look at the painting *American Progress,* by
John Gast, which is Plate 13—a painting that is like a mural.)
     What might Rich mean in saying that the differences between a map
and a mural are "small distinctions"?

What might she mean when she declares that "where do we see it from is the question"?

By saying this, she implies that "maps" may work with one set of rules, codes, and symbols, while "murals" work with another. Maps have one purpose and murals something else, just as maps are one kind of object and poems are another. One of those differences might be that maps are supposed to represent a place "objectively," while murals tell stories and perhaps tell them from a particular point of view. Rich, however, may be implying that even maps tell stories since "places" carry a certain history and certain cultural connotations. Maybe maps and murals are not all that different because places and their stories are hard to separate.

Now, let's try to put Rich's poem in perspective. One of the many ways to do this is to look at a few other maps. First, look at the two maps on pages 466 and 467 of Chapter 4. The map on page 466 is a conventional map of the world. The map on page 467 is called the "Peters projection" map. The Peters projection represents the countries of the world strictly according to their actual size in square miles. Traditional western projections (such as the Mercator projection and the more contemporary Robinson projection) correct for the curvature of the earth by exaggerating the size of areas near and above the equator. Consequently, the United States and Western Europe appear proportionally larger than they really are. The Peters projection de-emphasizes the U.S. and Western Europe. Many people feel that the Peters projection more accurately represents underdeveloped nations. Others think the Peters projection is misleading, unscientific, and mere "propaganda." (You can read more about the debate over the Peters projection map in the selection "Maps, Projections, and Ethnocentricity" in Chapter 4.)

Now look at a third map image, Plate 1 of the Image Portfolio. This map, created by Jesse Levine, is called the "Turnabout" Map. Unlike the Peters projection map, which was intended to help plan accurately for world economic development needs, the Turnabout Map was made strictly for rhetorical purposes. That is, it takes the convention of putting North America at the top of the map and purposely turns it on its head. What the Turnabout Map tries to show is how disorienting it can be to see something so familiar in reversed perspective. The Turnabout Map displaces the United States from its usual "superior" location on the map for special effect. Do you think that the effect of viewing the Turnabout map would be the same for everyone? Would someone from Latin America have the same feelings about the reversal as someone from the United States?

All of the texts we have looked at so far—the three maps, the mural, and the poem—in some way *represent* the United States. None of the texts *is* the United States itself. In other words, texts are not the things they talk about, but *representations* of the things they talk about. And each kind of text uses its own particular symbols and language to make its representation. Each text, then, requires that you know certain things in order to make sense of it. You have to know something about a map to read a map; and you have to know something about a poem to read a poem. (In this case you have to know something about a map—and something about geography and history—to make sense of the poem, too.) Perhaps this is one way to understand the final lines of Rich's poem. Here she says:

I promised to show you a map you say but this is a mural
then yes let it be   these are small distinctions
where do we see it from is the question

When you consider the three maps side by side, you can see that even maps are a matter of perspective and that each map tells a story about the context from which it is drawn. Even maps are made to serve particular interests, represent certain histories, and argue certain ideas. Similarly, Rich seems to be implying that maps and murals are not that different because all acts of representation are embedded in a particular context and cannot be separated from the perspective that produces or sees it.

What does this have to do with critical reading? We live in a world significantly shaped by texts: visual texts, written texts, printed texts, electronic texts, texts that tell stories, texts that try to inform, persuade, confuse, excite, and entertain. Each of these texts operates by different rules, using different languages, strategies, symbols, and styles. In order to live smartly in a world filled with texts and images, it is important to not just read, but read critically. Being a critical reader doesn't mean that you have to interpret and take apart every text you see, but that you can when you want to and need to. Furthermore, as much as we are shaped by texts, we can also shape ourselves through our own articulated texts. Every time we represent or express ourselves in writing, we actively exert a shaping influence on our immediate world. Becoming constructively critical about your own expression is as important as critical reading.

Being a critical reader and writer has a lot to do with this book's central theme of borders, not only in terms of content but in its approach to reading and writing. When you sit and examine a piece of writing or art—whether a work of fiction or poetry, a magazine article, a photograph, or another student's essay for a class assignment—you are standing at a border. To return to our original definition, if a border is a place where differences meet, then as a reader of a text, you are always at the border of someone else's meaning. On the other side of that page, on the other side of those words or images, is a whole set of ideas and experiences. To understand a writer's or artist's meaning you have to encounter that expression on its own terms—its language, its images, its points of tension, and its manner of combining parts into a whole. The process called critical reading involves learning how to cross that border and get into the text's world of experience and meaning. It is a means of understanding a text's influence or the ways that it has been shaped by the culture.

When you are critically reading a piece of writing, you're not just paying attention to what it says. You are also able to recognize and think about *how* it is saying things, able to read beyond surface meanings to the assumptions, arguments, and strategies behind them. Critical reading means learning about how texts work: how they express their meaning, how they appeal to your emotions and intellect, how they present arguments that are explicit and implicit, how they reason with you or try to persuade or even manipulate you.

One way to think of critical reading is to see it as the process of *slowing down* your reading. This doesn't mean you ought to read more slowly; it means that you need to read in such a way that you learn to be aware of a text's or image's various parts and processes. As your eye moves over the words on the page, for example, it is easy to think of any piece of writing as a smooth and coherent object. But all writing—whether a short story by a famous writer or a paper by one of your classmates—is the result of a process and the product of a context. Both the process and the context that produce a piece of writing are reflected in various ways in a text's parts and layers. When you slow down your reading you will see better the many components that come together in the writing process to make something that *seems* whole.

The Language of *Beyond Borders*

There is a very important and basic connection in this book between what it means to think critically about texts and the formation of individual and cultural identity. If all texts are formed by a perspective, constructed through a process, and embedded in cultural contexts, then something similar is true for the individuals and cultural contexts that produce them. Individuals have perspectives that have been shaped by the complexity of the contexts in which they've lived, just as a text is shaped by *its* context. Exploring the relationship between individuals and these contexts—their shaping power—is a central purpose of this book.

In fact, *Beyond Borders* focuses on three fundamental sets of ideas: (1) how individuals derive and express a sense of self-identity; (2) how individuals connect to each other through groups of various kinds and affiliations, such as cultures and communities; and (3) how groups define themselves, how groups interact with other groups, and how they exist in either harmony or tension in larger social units like nations and international communities. *Individuals* and *groups, identity* and *difference, community* and *conflict:* In many ways these form the book's subject matter. For each of these key ideas, we'll ask the same kinds of questions, regardless of whether we're looking at individuals, groups, or something larger, like the nation of the United States. We want to learn:

What are the many shaping influences on identity?

What is the relationship between the definition of self-identity and the perception of others?

What are the ways that individuals and groups connect and don't connect across their differences?

Let's look more closely at how these questions get raised across the chapters.

The first chapter of *Beyond Borders* emphasizes the self and self-identity. How do we come to be who we are? What are the shaping influences on our identity? In what ways do the stories, expectations, and rules of our immediate culture shape us? The focus here is on the self that is constructed by the social, spatial, and cultural elements of the environment. Our identity as individuals is not at all formed in some isolated or autonomous way. Although our sense of individuality is based very much on a feeling of freedom and autonomy, we derive all the aspects of our personality and beliefs (including the very belief that we're free and autonomous) from some shaping system.

Therefore the initial questions of this book revolve around self-identity: how we're shaped by and make connections to others. That is, when thinking about the influences on our self-identity, we should consider how we connect ourselves to larger contexts. How do we develop a sense of belonging? What makes us feel at home—or *not* feel at home? What creates a sense of alienation? How do we feel and express connections to community and to a culture? How does our belonging to a culture shape who we are? There are several layers of complexity to these questions of belonging because most of us belong to many different communities at once, and at times those communities conflict or exist in tension. There are, in addition, vast differences in the ways that people feel connected to each other: sometimes through shared values, sometimes through shared physical space, and sometimes just through a sense of interdependency or a network or interrelationships. Furthermore, equality is rarely found *within* social groups. Within communities and cultures there are usually imbalances among members: insiders and outsiders, those closer to the center and those at the margins, even those who resist fitting in but still play a vital role in the functioning and identity of the community.

Focusing on how individuals and groups define themselves leads inevitably to questions of how individuals and groups define *others*. How do
we define insiders and outsiders? Is it possible to have a sense of community without outsiders? Whereas Chapter 1 looks closely at individual identity and the ways individuals connect to each other, Chapters 2 and 3 look
at how definitions of community and cultural identity depend on the identification of differences and the construction of "otherness." How is "otherness" an ever-present factor in the way we construct culture? On what do
we base our sense of differences?

People perceive and act on their sense of differences from others in
many ways and for many reasons: out of fear, repulsion, disagreement, curiosity, fascination, attraction, indifference, habit, ignorance. Even if constructions of otherness are based on irrational motivations they can have
very real and significant ramifications. In what ways do we see constructions of otherness and images of difference all around us? In what ways do
our cultural values (i.e., the nature of identity within the groups to which
we belong) instill and reinforce images of difference? How do differences
drive us *together* as well as apart? How are differences appealing as well as
the source of tension? To what extent are differences "real" or "imagined"?

The purpose of raising these questions is not to pass judgment on
communities or groups that have a sense of self or of others. Human beings seek a sense of identity and belonging. In a heterogeneous society
that means the creation and maintenance of borders between groups.
What varies are the different strategies for negotiating those borders and
surviving what Mary Louise Pratt, in her essay in Chapter 3, calls "contact
zones." A "contact zone," according to Pratt, is any place where different
cultures come together with some "asymmetrical relations of power."
Whether this contact is at the level of cultural groups (as in the colonial situation she discusses) or at the level of individuals (for example, in a dating context that is potentially violent, as described in the essay by Mary
Gaitskill), a "contact zone" can be an important way to look at how people
communicate across their differences. What strategies do people use, either privately or publicly, to manage "asymmetrical relations of power"?
How do people appeal to each other across differences? Do they appeal to
fear, values, morality, shared destiny? When are "contact zones" positive
and productive places?

One of the questions raised by the readings in Chapter 3 is the extent
to which "contact zones" are about imagined power and perceived differences. Indeed, this echoes the place where the book began. How we see
ourselves, as well as how we see and interact with others, is based on a
whole *environment* of influences that are both real and imagined, physical

and symbolic, based in the world and at the same time based in language. If individual self-identity is shaped by physical and imagined forces—shaped by cultural ideas as much as by cultural places—then so, too, are cultures. That is, if individuals and groups both are shaped by an *environment* of forces, they are also shaped by a *geography* both physical and imagined.

Chapter 4 looks at the ways that cultures and communities imagine themselves as wholes, existing in a particular place. Another way to think of this is to imagine that individuals as well as groups construct for themselves a whole reality that is partially based on cultural values and partially based on physical place. In other words, who you are is shaped in part by where you are. Similarly, how you perceive where you are is significantly shaped by your beliefs and values.

This brings us back to the idea of *perspective* and *context*. Chapter 4 asks some of the book's most abstract or difficult questions: How are the perspectives of groups, cultures, communities, even nations formed by a context that could be characterized as an *imaginative reality*—a reality that is based on a geographical place yet developed in the mind? How is geographical space a cultural notion? For example, how was the notion of the American frontier both a description of a physical reality and a particular way of looking at cultural space—one that already had a sense of center and edge, of an old world and a new world, of a place where civilized peoples were settling in opposition to a wilderness? In what ways does physical environment shape cultural perceptions? Conversely, in what ways do cultural values shape our perceptions of geographical space and the physical environment?

Looking at the American notion of the frontier is useful because it is such a persistent and powerful myth in U.S. culture. The concept is also useful because it seems "natural" to people who grew up in the United States, so pervasive and ingrained are the images of frontier conquest and settlement. Yet, as more than one reading in Chapter 4 points out, thinking of a frontier as a *dividing line* between civilization and wilderness (or between culture and savagery) is not inevitable. It is possible, for example, to think of a frontier as a boundary or zone between two cultures. Along this divider there is not an inevitable sense of conquest or progress moving in a single direction (as in the movement of European civilization across the continent), but rather a more dynamic process of give-and-take across cultural boundaries. Whether one thinks of a frontier as a line or a zone brings us back to the book's most fundamental topics: the concept of borders and the human processes of self-definition and behavior that happen there. Borders, like frontiers, are places where something happens;

and the construction of reality that governs what that something is has as much to do with the cultural values of the people involved as it does with the place itself.

The discussion becomes more complicated when we shift our thinking from American frontiers to "electronic frontiers." Beginning with Columbus's "discovery of the new world," Chapter 5 begins with a look at "cyberspace," the current "new world" that is being discovered and settled. Why do we think of cyberspace as a "space"? Why do people think of places on the World Wide Web in spatial terms, as we maneuver among "home pages" and move between "sites"? Cyberspace is the ultimate expression of the conjunction of *border texts* and *border places:* After all, what are the places on the Internet but texts, and vice versa? And as a place built out of texts, cyberspace is nothing but constructed realities: homemade, online communities whose structures, participants, and environments are constructed in people's heads and played out in an imagined environment with new sets of rules and limits. What can these new communities and contexts tell us about the way we look at ourselves and others? How might online communication and interaction in virtual space shape new ways in which individual and communal identity are imagined in ways face-to-face communication cannot? How do these new communities relate to the ones we know? How will they interact or compete? Is there really the potential of new, unanticipated "border crossings" in cyberspace; can it open new forms of human understanding in terms of how we think about and identify ourselves and others?

The compelling questions about the shape of new communities and even new geographies occupy the book's final chapter, which looks at the "world's new borders." As we move into a world of interactive global technologies, is the world "getting smaller" and more connected? Or, as seems to be the case with the growing number of ethnic and group conflicts throughout the world, is the world becoming more fragmented? In Chapter 5, the major questions of the book come full circle. *Beyond Borders* begins by asking how individuals define themselves and connect with each other through groups. Chapter 5 looks at how groups define themselves and either connect or resist connection with some larger social identity, at either the national or the international level. Here we consider the issues of identity, community, and difference in terms of what Benjamin Barber calls "Jihad vs. McWorld": that is, the tension between the intense devotion to group identity (symbolized by the Islamic Jihad) and the phenomenon of an increasingly homogenized global culture, symbolized by the worldwide proliferation of McDonald's fast food restaurants, and other exports ("McWorld"). Our look at borders concludes, then, with the questions of the 21st century: What borders and boundaries compete for

Library Resource Center
Renton Technical College
3000 N.E. 4th St.
Renton, WA 98056

our attention? In what ways are differences increasing among us or decreasing? What will be the fate of individual self-definition and community rights as the world becomes both more coherent and more fragmented? Is it possible to move *beyond borders* and to explore alternative principles of identity that do not depend on difference, on inclusions and exclusions?

The image portfolio (which falls in the middle of the book) explores the borders of visual culture, examining the various ways that viewing and looking practices play such a central role in modern life. Visual culture, we discover, is not so much defined by medium—art, advertising, film, etc., as by the interaction between viewer and viewed. Despite the ever-increasing number of images that characterize our world, we still do not fully understand the relationship between image and language, nor how images operate on viewers and the word. In this section, spectatorship (the gaze, the practices of observation, surveillance) is shown to be as complex as various forms of reading (interpretation, analysis, etc.), as the images trace the ways in which visual experience is always expressed within the representational sensibilities of a wider "visible culture."

CHAPTER 1

BORDERS OF IDENTITY
Stories of the Self

Anon. Hopi: *The Hopi Boy and the Sun* [story]
Anna Deavere Smith: *Fires in the Mirror* [excerpt from play]
Robert Hass: *A Story About the Body* [prose poem]
Thomas King: *Borders* [story]
Joel Gilbert/Noel Ignatiev: *Who Lost an American?* [interview]
Abigail Trooboff: *The Gravity of Pink* [essay]
Amy Tan: *Mother Tongue* [essay]
Jim Mince: *The Begenning of the End* [essay]
Evelyn Lau: *Runaway: Diary of a Street Kid* [diary entry]
Tara Masih: *Exotic, or What Beach Do You Hang Out On?* [essay]
Frank Bidart: *Ellen West* [poem]

Critical Questions

Before reading   Where do we get our sense of self-identity? How does our family and community shape us? In what way can someone's identity be considered multiple identities?

Taking it further   Many other sources shape identity: our memories, the stories we tell and hear, the cultural myths around us, and our sense of being different from others. How is a sense of "otherness" and difference manifested through our language, stories, and images?

SELF-IDENTITY

In many ways, telling stories is one of our primary means for expressing borders and boundaries: the borders between right and wrong, between truth and fiction, between others and ourselves. All forms of stories, whether folktales, literary fiction, autobiography, history, or myths, are ways of expressing these borders, and of expressing cultural and social meaning. As Stuart Hall (a writer whose essay appears later in this book) puts it, "Identity is a narrative of the self; it's the story we tell about the self in order to know who we are." Exploring *the stories we tell to know who we are* is precisely what this chapter is all about. All of the texts in this chapter are stories about people trying to make sense of who they are in relationship to something: their family, their community, their past, their multiple roles and identities. These essays often invoke the idea of *cultural stories, symbols, and patterns* as influences that have significantly shaped their authors' behavior and beliefs. Stories and symbols can shape our lives by giving us ideal "plots" to which we would like our lives to adhere, or by luring us into a pattern—locking us into a narrative from which it is very difficult to escape.

Because stories are so important to our connections with the past, one of the persistent and important themes that runs through all of these selections is that of *memory:* Memories are stories that play important roles in our lives. And although we often talk about telling the difference between a true story and a false one, memories are a kind of story where the line between truth and fiction is not always easy to distinguish. Memories are in many ways images or snapshots placed back into a narrative or storied context. And indeed that is what a lot of these essays are about: trying to place recurrent and strong images—isolated but persistent moments—*from the past* into a larger context of meaning that makes sense to *the person's present.* That is, not only do we come to be who we are over time (rather than all at once), but we become who we are by developing a certain relationship to the past—not only our personal past, but our family's and culture's pasts, as well.

Just as it is sometimes difficult to tell the difference between truth and fiction in regard to the past, it is also the case that our everyday world is structured by all kinds of "fictions" that give certain meaning and shape to what we believe. The stories we see on television or in the movies, the underlying mythology of a country or culture, or stereotypes about certain kinds of people are all stories that exert power over how we act and what we believe. For example, even if we know that a television show is just a show, or a commercial is just a TV advertisement, that doesn't mean that their underlying stories and messages ("successful people look like this," "poor people act like that") don't help form our belief system. Many of the stories in this chapter explore the shaping power of everyday fictions, and the process by which people come to examine these fictions, sometimes to separate themselves from them, and sometimes to reject them.

In fact, self-discovery is the key theme of all these selections; but it is often not easy, simply because it often seems as though there is more than one "self" to be discovered. For many of these writers, exploring the self means exploring the multiple selves and roles that they have become as a result of their positioning within their families and cultures. Indeed, this is one of the key questions that so many of the writers in this chapter pose to us through their essays: How do we put our many selves together into a single self? What stories do we tell ourselves (and others) that help knit together the various pieces of our lives that are shaped by the roles we play, by the experiences we have, by the identities we are led to construct to survive each new situation or experience? Another facet of self-identity is crucial here: the connection between who we think we are and the people around us with whom we identify. To what extent is each of us our own self as well as a reflection for someone else? How fluid is our own identity, as it is shaped by the people around us as well as shaping others? How much is each of us an individual as well as a part of some collective identity with others in our shared contexts—our families, our places of work, our group of regular friends? In most western cultures, and especially in the United States, we are accustomed to think in terms of "individuality" as a critical concept of our identity. But in many ways, the idea of an autonomous, self-created individual is a "fiction" of our culture. That is, "self-identity" and a sense of individuality is a story we tell ourselves to feel whole in the context of the two shaping tendencies of our multiple selves: the fragmentation of the self into multiple roles and the fluidity of the self with those around us.

For many people, the process of managing these many roles and selves is not a problem; it is not even a matter of conscious reflection. People have work identities and home identities; people are one way with their families and another with friends. But for many of the writers in this chapter, feeling whole is problematic, in part because there is conflict among the multiple sources of identity. How is one to know and define oneself? From the inside—within a context that is self-defined from a grounding in community and a connection with culture and history that are comfortably accepted? Or from the outside—in terms of messages received from the media and people who are often ignorant? We are defined, and always defining ourselves, through some interaction between "inside" feelings and "outside" influences. What is self-identity, in the end, but the boundary between the two?

Our attempts to know and define ourselves inevitably involve defining others; and, in many cases, defining others means viewing them through the prejudice of a framework that casts them as the opposite or an antithesis of the defining perspective. When people define others rigidly as separate from or the opposite of a particular cultural identity, then they are engaging in the construction of *otherness*. Although people can feel this in very personal terms, in a larger sense individuals construct their sense of self based in part on the messages they receive from their culture. So this chapter is also very much concerned with some of the ways that the idea of otherness gets depicted in American culture, in both explicit and implicit (sometimes very subtle) ways. Here we will explore such images and ask what force images of otherness and difference have in our culture, how they get expressed, and what they have to do with creating and maintaining individual, communal, and cultural identity?

The Hopi Boy and the Sun

ANONYMOUS

Where cultures overlap—as in areas of the Southwest, with its mixture of Hispanic, Pueblo, and nomadic traditions—legends are often modified and reshaped in the retelling. This tale, related in 1920 by a Zuni elder who may have been part Hispanic, gives a curious twist to Hopi tales of the sun. Besides the traditional Hopi elements such as the trail of sacred cornmeal and the sun's fox skin, it embodies the fear and antagonism felt by the Pueblo farmers toward the marauding nomadic tribes. At the same time, it is full of things unknown to the Pueblos before the coming of the Spaniards, such as peaches, silver bracelets, and the ocean itself.

A poor Hopi boy lived with his mother's mother. The people treated him   1
with contempt and threw ashes and sweepings into his grandmother's house, and the two were very unhappy. One day he asked his grandmother who his father was.

"My poor boy, I don't know," she replied.　　2

"I must find him," the boy said. "We can't stay in this place; the people　3
treat me too badly."

"Grandchild, you must go and see the sun. He knows who your father is."　4

On the following morning the boy made a prayer stick and went out.　5
Many young men were sitting on the roof of the kiva, the underground ceremonial chamber. They sneered when they saw him going by, though one
of them remarked, "Better not make fun of him! I believe the poor little boy
has supernatural power."

The boy took some sacred meal made of pounded turquoise, coral,　6
shell, and cornmeal, and threw it upward. It formed a trail leading into the
sky, and he climbed until the trail gave out. He threw more of the sacred
meal upward, and a new trail formed. After he had done this twelve times,
he came to the sun. But the sun was too hot to approach, so the boy put
new prayers sticks into the hair at the back of his head, and the shadow of
their plumes protected him from the heat.

"Who is my father?" he asked the sun.　7

"All children conceived in the daytime belong to me," the sun replied.　8
"But as for you, who knows? You are young and have much to learn."

The boy gave the sun a prayer stick and, falling down from the sky,　9
landed back in his village.

On the following day he left home and went westward, hoping to begin　10
learning. When he came to the place where Holbrook, Arizona, now stands,
he saw a cottonwood tree and chopped it down. He cut a length of the
trunk to his own height, hollowed it out, and made a cover for each end.
Then he put in some sweet cornmeal and prayer sticks and decided he was
ready to go traveling. Climbing into the box, he closed the door and rolled
himself into the river.

The box drifted for four days and four nights, until finally he felt it strike　11
the shore at a place where two rivers join. He took the plug out of a peephole he had made and saw morning light. But when he tried to get out, he
couldn't open the door, no matter how hard he pushed. He thought he
would have to die inside.

In the middle of the afternoon a rattlesnake-girl came down to the river.　12
When she discovered the box, she took off her mask and looked into the
peephole. "What are you doing here?" she asked the boy.

"Open the door! I can't get out," he said.　13

The girl asked, "How can I open it?"　14

"Take a stone and break it."　15

So the girl broke the door, and when the Hopi boy came out, she took　16
him to her house. Inside he saw many people—young and old, men and
women—and they were all rattlesnakes.

"Where are you going? they asked him.   17

"I want to find my father," the boy replied.   18

The girl said, "You can't go alone; I'll go with you."   19

She made a small tent of rattlesnake skins and carried it to the river.   20
They crawled into the tent and floated for four days and four nights. Finally
they reached the ocean, and there they saw a meteor fall into the sea on its
way to the house of the sun. They asked the meteor to take them along.

In this manner they reached the sun's house, where they found an old   21
woman working on turquoise, coral, and white shell. She was the moon, the
mother of the sun.

"Where is my father?" the boy asked.   22

"He has gone out," the moon replied, "but he will be home soon."   23

The sun arrived in the evening, and the old woman gave him venison   24
and wafer bread. After he had eaten, he asked the boy, "What do you want
here?"

The boy replied, "I want to know my father."   25

"I think you are my son. And when I go into the other world, you shall   26
accompany me," the sun said this time. And early the next morning, he said,
"Let's go!" He opened a door in the ground, and they went out.

Seating himself on a stool of crystal, the sun took a fox skin and held it   27
up. Daylight appeared. After a while he put the fox skin down and held up
the tail feathers of a macaw, and the yellow rays of sunrise streamed out.
When at last he let them down, he said to the boy, "Now let's go!"

The sun made the boy sit behind him on the stool, and they went out   28
into another world. After traveling for some time, they saw people with long
ears, Lacokti inanenakwe. They used their ears as blankets to cover themselves when they slept. The sun remarked, "If bluebird droppings fall on
those people, they die."

"How is that possible?" the boy said. "How can people be killed that   29
way? Let me kill the birds!"

The sun said, "Go ahead! I'll wait."   30

The boy jumped down, took a small cedar stick, and killed the blue-   31
birds. Then he roasted them over a fire and ate them. The people shouted,
"Look at this boy! He's eating Navahos!"

"No," said the boy, "these aren't Navahos, they're birds." Then he went   32
back to the sun, and they traveled on.

About noon they came to another town. The sun said, "Look! The   33
Apache are coming to make war on the people."

The boy saw a whirlwind moving along. When wheat straw was blown   34
against the legs of the people, they fell dead. "How can people be killed by
wheat straw?" he said. "Let me go down and tear it up."

The sun said, "I'll wait."   35

The boy jumped down, gathered the wheat straw, and tore it up. The	36
people said, "Look at this boy, how he kills the Apache!"

"These aren't Apache," the boy replied, "they're wheat straws." Then he	37
went back to the sun.

They came to another town, where the Hopi boy saw people with very	38
long hair reaching down to their ankles. They had a large pot with onions
tied to its handles. Inside it thin mush was cooking and boiling over, and
when it hit a person, he died. The sun said, "Look at the Jicarilla Apache,
how they kill people!"

"No," said the boy, "that's not Jicarilla Apache; it's mush. I'll go down	39
and eat it."

The sun said, "I'll wait."	40

Then the boy jumped down, dipped the mush out of the pot, took the	41
onions from the handles, and ate the mush with the onions. The people
said, "Look how this boy eats the brains, hands, and feet of the Jicarilla
Apache!"

The boy said, "This isn't Jicarilla Apache! It's corn mush. Come and eat	42
with me!"

"No! they said. "We're not cannibals; we don't eat Apache warriors!"	43
Then the boy went back to the sun, and they traveled on.

Finally they came to the house of the sun in the east. There the sun's sis-	44
ter gave them venison stew for supper. After they had eaten, the sun said to
his sister, "Wash my son's head!"

The sun's sister took a large dish, put water and yucca suds into it, and	45
washed the boy's head and body. Then she gave him new clothing, the
same kind that the sun was wearing—buckskin trousers, blue moccasins,
blue bands of yarn to tie under the knees, a white sash and belt of fox skin,
turquoise and shell earrings, a white shirt, silver arm rings, bead bracelets,
and a bead necklace. She put macaw feathers in his hair and a *miha,* sacred
blanket, over his shoulder, and gave him a quiver of mountain lion skin.

Then the sun told him, "Go ahead! I'm going to follow you." The boy	46
opened the door in the ground and went out. He sat down on the crystal
stool, took the fox skin, and held it up to create the dawn. Then he put it
down and raised the macaw feathers, holding them up with the palms of his
hands stretched forward until the yellow rays of sunrise appeared. After that
he dropped his hands and went on into the upper world. As he did, the
people of Laguna, Isleta, and the other eastern pueblos looked eastward and
sprinkled sacred meal. The sun behind him said, "Look at the trails, the life
of the people! Some are short, others are long. Look at this one! He is near
the end of his trail; he's going to die soon." The boy saw an Apache coming, and in a short time the Apache had killed that man whose trail had been
so short. The Hopi boy said to the sun, "Let me go and help the people!"

"I'll wait," the sun replied.   47

The boy jumped down into the territory where the Laguna people were   48
fighting the Apache. He told the people to wet their arrow points with saliva
and hold them up to the sun, for this would help them in battle. The boy
himself killed ten Apaches, then went back to his father.

They traveled on, and when they saw a group of Navahos setting out to   49
make war on the Zuni, the boy killed them. He and his father crossed the
land of his own people, the Hopi, and then came to Mexican territory.

A Mexican was playing with his wife. When the sun saw them, he threw   50
the Mexican aside and cohabited with the woman. "I don't need a wife," he
told his son, "because all the women on earth belong to me. If a couple co-
habits during the daytime, I interfere as I just did. So I'm the father of all children conceived in the daytime."

In the evening the sun entered his house in the west. By then the boy   51
wanted to go back to his own people, so the sun's mother made a trail of
sacred flour, and the boy and the rattlesnake-woman went back eastward
over it. At noon they came to the rattlesnakes' home. The rattlesnake-
woman said, "I want to see my father and mother. After that, let's go on."
They entered the house, and she told her relatives that the Hopi boy was her
husband. Then they resumed their journey.

That evening they arrived in the Hopi village. The boy made straight for   52
his grandmother's house, but an old chief said, "Look at the handsome man
going into that poor home!" He invited the boy into his own house, but the
boy replied, "No, I'm going here." The war chief said, "We don't want you
in that dirty house."

"The house is mine," the boy replied, "so tell your people to clean it up.   53
When all of you treated me badly, I went up to the sun and he helped me."

On the following evening the boy appeared before a village council and   54
told all that had happened to him. "You must teach the people how to act
rightly. The sun says that you should forbid all bad actions." The people accepted his words, and everyone worked hard at cleaning his house. In return the boy gave peaches, melons, and wafer bread to the poor. Every
evening after sunset the women would come with their dishes, and he
would offer them venison stew and peaches. He said to the chief, "I teach
the people the right way to live. Even if you are my enemy, I must show you
how to behave well."

Twin children, a boy and a girl, were born to his wife. They had the   55
shape of rattlesnakes, but they were also humans.

—Based on a legend reported by Franz Boas in 1922.

Working with the Text

1. The Hopi boy in this story undertakes a quest to discover his paternity. Early in his search, the sun tells him, "All children conceived in the daytime belong to me"; he later witnesses such a conception, as he travels with his father across the sky. What does it mean to have the sun as a father and to share that father with all those conceived in the daytime? Why is it important that the sun demonstrates this principle in Mexican territory?

2. During the boy's journey through the other world, he pauses three times to rescue people from enemies that appear one way to him and another way to their victims. Why does the boy see the Navajo as bluebirds, the Apache as wheat straw, and the Jicarilla Apache as mush? Is his ability to vanquish them tied to his perceptions? Why does he eat the Navajo and the Jicarilla Apache?

3. The quest radically alters the boy's social identity, both during his journey and after he returns home. Describe the alterations, and consider possible reasons for them. What role do material signs (food, clothing, shelter) play in expressing identity?

4. Describe the roles of women in this tale. When are they active? For what purposes? When are they conspicuously absent? What is the significance of the last two sentences of the story: "Twin children, a boy and a girl, were born to his wife. They had the shape of rattlesnakes, but they were also humans"?

5. "The Hopi Boy" abounds with extraordinary material objects, from the meal the boy flings skyward to reach the sun to the crystal stool that transports him and his father. Choose one such object, and analyze its significance. Comment on materials, shape, size, function, and any other relevant features; then discuss how the object conveys cultural ideals. Next, choose an extraordinary object from the mythology of your own culture and perform a similar analysis.

Fires in the Mirror

ANNA DEAVERE SMITH

Fires in the Mirror is part of a series of performance pieces called On the Road: A Search for American Character. Smith's project is to interview people and later perform them in monologues of their own words. In August 1991, tensions in the Brooklyn neighborhood of Crown Heights erupted into riots after a black youth was killed by a car in a rabbi's motorcade and a Jewish student was slain by blacks in retaliation. Using verbatim excerpts from the interviews that she conducted, Smith provides a documentary portrait of urban race and class conflict, portraying more than two dozen Crown Heights adversaries, victims, and eyewitnesses on stage. Can language, asks Smith, be a photograph of what is unseen about society just as it reflects what is unseen in an individual? Smith's work demands that we examine critically our own complicity in cultural stereotypes that imprison our imaginations as she exposes the ordinary failings of the human response to this violent crisis.

Ntozake Shange

THE DESERT

(This interview was done on the phone at about 4:00 P.M. Philadelphia time. The only cue Ntozake gave about her physical appearance was that she took one earring off to talk on the phone. On stage we placed her upstage center in an arm chair, smoking. Then we placed her standing, downstage.)

Hummmm.
Identity—
it, is, uh . . . in a way it's, um . . . it's sort of, it's uh . . .
it's a psychic sense of place
it's a way of knowing I'm not a rock or that tree?   5
I'm this other living creature over here?
And it's a way of knowing that no matter where I put myself
that I am not necessarily
what's around me.
I am part of my surroundings   10

and I become separate from them
and it's being able to make those differentiations clearly
that lets us have an identity
and what's inside our identity
is everything that's ever happened to us.   15
Everything that's ever happened
to us as well as our responses to it
'cause we might be alone in a trance state,
someplace like the desert
and we begin to feel as though   20
we are part of the desert—
which we are right at that minute—
but we are not the desert,
uh . . .
we are part of the desert,   25
and when we go home
we take with us that part of the desert that the desert gave us,
but we're still not the desert.
It's an important differentiation to make because you don't know
what you're giving if you don't know what you have and you don't   30
know what you're taking if you don't know what's yours and what's
somebody else's.

George C. Wolfe

101 DALMATIONS

(The Mondrian Hotel in Los Angeles. Morning, Sunny. A very nice room. George is wearing denim jeans, a light blue denim shirt, and white leather tennis shoes. His hair is in a ponytail. He wears tortoise/wire spectacles. He is drinking tea with milk. The tea is served on a tray, the cups and teapot are delicate porcelain. George is sitting on a sofa, with his feet up on the coffee table.)

I mean I grew up on a black—
a one-block street—
that was black.
My grandmother lived on that street
my cousins lived around the corner.   5
I went to this
Black—Black—
private Black grade school
where

I was extraordinary.   10
Everybody there was extraordinary.
You were told you were extraordinary.
It was very clear
that I could not go to see *101 Dalmations* at the Capital Theatre
because it was segregated.   15
And at the same time
I was treated like I was the most extraordinary creature that had
been born.
So I'm on my street in my house,
at my school—   20
and I was very spoiled too—
so I was treated like I was this special special creature.
And then I would go beyond a certain point
I was treated like I was insignificant.
Nobody was   25
hosing me down or calling me nigger.
It was just that I was insignificant.
(Slight pause)
You know what I mean so it was very clear of
(Teacup on saucer strike twice on "very clear")   30
where my extraordinariness lived.
You know what I mean.
That I was extraordinary as long as I was Black.
But I am—not—going—to place myself
(Pause)   35
in relationship to your whiteness.
I will talk about your whiteness if we want to talk about that.
But I,
but what,
that which,   40
what I—
what am I saying?
My blackness does not resis—ex—re—
exist in relationship to your whiteness.
(Pause)   45
You know
(Not really a question, more like a hum)
(Slight pause)
it does not exist in relationship to—
it *exists*   50

it exists.
I come—
you know what I mean—
like I said, I, I, I,
I come from—   55
it's a very com*plex,*
con*fused,*
neu-rotic,
at times destructive
reality, but it is completely   60
and totally a reality
contained and, and,
and full unto itself.
It's complex.
It's demonic.   65
It's ridiculous.
It's absurd.
It's evolved.
It's all the stuff.
That's the way I grew up.   70
(Slight pause)
So that *therefore*—
and then you're White—
(Quick beat)
And then there's a point when,   75
and then these two things come into contact.

Aaron M. Bernstein

MIRRORS AND DISTORTIONS

(Evening, Cambridge, Massachusetts. Fall. He is a man in his fifties, wearing a sweater and a shirt with a pen guard. He is seated at a round wooden table with a low-hanging lamp.)

Okay, so a mirror is something that reflects light.
It's the simplest instrument to understand,
okay?
So a simple mirror is just a flat
reflecting   5
substance, like,
for example,

it's a piece of glass which is silvered on the back,
okay?
Now the notion of distortion also goes back into literature,   10
okay?
I'm trying to remember from art—
You probably know better than I.
You know you have a pretty young woman and she looks in a mirror
and she's a witch   15
(He laughs)
because she's evil on the inside.
That's not a real mirror,
as everyone knows—
where   20
you see the inner thing.
Now that really goes back in literature.
So everyone understood that mirrors don't distort,
so that was a play
not on words   25
but a concept.
But physicists do
talk about distortion.
It's a big
subject, distortions.   30
I'll give you an example—
if you wanna see the
stars
you make a big
reflecting mirror—   35
that's one of the ways—
you make a big telescope
so you can gather in a lot of light
and then it focuses at a point
and then there's always something called the circle of confusion.   40
So if ya don't make the thing perfectly spherical or perfectly
parabolic
then,
then, uh, if there are errors in the construction
which you can see, it's easy, if it's huge,   45
then you're gonna have a circle of confusion,
you see?
So that's the reason for making the

telescope as large as you can,
because you want that circle   50
to seem smaller,
and you want to easily see errors in the construction.
So, you see, in physics it's very practical—
if you wanna look up in the heavens
and see the stars as well as you can   55
without distortion.
If you're counting stars, for example,
and two look like one,
you've blown it.

Anonymous Girl

LOOK IN THE MIRROR

> *(Morning. Spring. A teen-age Black girl of Haitian descent. She has hair which is straightened, and is wearing a navy blue jumper and a white shirt. She is seated in a stairwell at her junior high school in Brooklyn.)*

When I look in the mirror . . .
I don't know.
How did I find out I was Black . . .
(Tongue sound)
When I grew up and I look in the mirror and saw I was Black.   5
When I look at my parents,
That's how I knew I was Black.
Look at my skin.
You Black?
Black is beautiful.   10
I don't know.
That's what I always say.
I think White is beautiful too.
But I think Black is beautiful too.
In my class nobody is White, everybody's Black,   15
and some of them is Hispanic.
In my class
you can't call any of them Puerto Ricans.
They despise Puerto Ricans, I don't know why.
They think that Puerto Ricans are stuck up and everything.   20
They say, Oh my Gosh my nail broke, look at that cute guy and
      everything.

But they act like that themselves.
They act just like White girls.
Black girls is not like that.
Please, you should be in my class.   25
Like they say that Puerto Ricans act like that
and they don't see that they act like that themselves.
Black girls, they do bite off the Spanish girls,
they bite off of your clothes.
You don't know what that means? biting off?   30
Like biting off somebody's clothes
Like cop, following,
and last year they used to have a lot of girls like that.
They come to school with a style, right?
And if they see another girl with that style?   35
Oh my gosh look at her.
What she think she is,
she tryin' to bite off of me in some way
no don't be bitin' off of my sneakers
or like that.   40
Or doin' a hairstyle
I mean Black people are into hairstyles.
So they come to school, see somebody with a certain style,
they say uh-huh I'm gonna get me one just like that uh-huh,
that's the way Black people are   45
Yea-ah!
They don't like people doing that to them
and they do that to other people,
so the Black girls will follow the Spanish girls.
The Spanish girls don't bite off of us.   50
Some of the Black girls follow them.
But they don't mind
They don't care.
They follow each other.
Like there's three girls in my class,   55
they from the Dominican Republic.
They all stick together like glue.
They all three best friends.
They don't follow nobody,
like there's none of them lead or anything.   60
They don't hang around us either.
They're
by themselves.

Rivkah Siegal

WIGS

(Early afternoon. Spring. The kitchen of an apartment in Crown Heights. A very pretty Lubavitcher woman, with clear eyes and a direct gaze, wearing a wig and a knit sweater, that looks as though it might be hand knit. A round wooden table. Coffee mug. Sounds of children playing in the street are outside. A neighbor, a Lubavitcher woman with light blond hair who no longer wears the wig, observes the interview at the table.)

Your hair
It only has to be—
there's different,
u h m,
customs in different 5
Hasidic groups.
Lubavitch
the system is
it should be two inches
long. 10
It's—
some groups
have
the custom
to shave their 15
heads.
There's—
the reason is,
when you go to the mikvah [bath]
you may, maybe, 20
it's better if it's short
because of what you—
the preparation
that's involved
and that 25
you have to go under the water.
The hair has a tendency to float
and you have to be completely submerged
including your hair.
So . . . 30
And I got married
when I was a little older,

and I really wanted to be married
and I really wanted to, um . . .
In some ways I was eager to cover my head.   35
Now if I had grown up in a Lubavitch household
and then had to cut it,
I don't know what that would be like.
I really don't.
But now that I'm wearing the wig,   40
you see,
with my hair I can keep it very simple
and I can change it all the time.
So with a wig you have to have like five wigs if you want to do that.
But I, uh,   45
I feel somehow like it's fake,
I feel like it's not me.
I try to be as much myself as I can,
and it just
bothers me   50
that I'm kind of fooling the world.
I used to go to work.
People . . .
and I would wear a different wig,
and they'd say I like your new haircut   55
and I'd say it's not mine!
You know,
and it was very hard for me to say it
and
it became very difficult.   60
I mean, I've gone through a lot with wearing wigs and not wearing
wigs.
It's been a big issue for me.

Angela Davis

ROPE

> *(Morning. Spring. Oakland, California. In reality this interview was
> done on the phone, with myself and Thulani Davis. Thulani and I were
> calling from an office at the Public Theatre. We do not know exactly
> what Angela was doing or wearing. I believe, from things she said, that
> she was sitting on her deck in her home, which overlooks a beautiful
> panorama of trees.)*

Race, um—
of course
for many years in the history
of African Americans in this country—
was synonymous with community.   5
As a matter of fact
we were race women and race men.
Billie Holiday for example
called herself a race woman
because she supported the community   10
and as a child growing up in the South
my assumptions were
that if anybody in the race
came under attack
then I had to be there   15
to support that person,
to support the race.
I was saying to my students just the other day,
I said,
if in 1970,   20
when I was
in jail,
someone had told me
that in 1991,
a Black man   25
who
said that his, um . . .
hero—
(Increased volume, speed, and energy)
one of his heroes   30
was Malcolm X—
would be nominated to the Supreme Court
I would have celebrated
and I don't think it would have been possible at that time
to convince me   35
that I would
be absolutely opposed,
a Black candidate—
I mean like absolutely—
(A new attack, more energy)   40
or that if anyone would have told me that

a *woman* . . .
finally be elected to the Supreme Court,
it would have been very difficult,
as critical as I am with respect to feminism,   45
as critical as I have always been with what I used to call,
you know, narrow nationalism?
I don't think
it would have been possible to convince me that things would have so
    absolutely
shifted that   50
someone could have evoked
the specter of lynching
on national television
and that specter of lynching would be used to violate our history.
And I still feel that   55
we have to point out the racism involved
in the razing of a Black man
and a Black woman
in that way.
I mean [Ted] Kennedy was sitting right there   60
and it had never occurred to anyone to bring him up
before
the world,
which is not to say that I don't think it should happen.
And it is actually a sign of how we,   65
in our various oppressed
marginalized communities,
have been able to turn
terrible acts of racism directed against us
into victory . . .   70
And therefore I think
Anita Hill did that,
and so it's very complicated,
but I have no problems aligning myself politically
against Clarence Thomas in a real passionate way,   75
but at the same time I can talk about the racism that led
to the possibility
of constructing those kinds of hearings
and
the same thing with Mike Tyson.   80
So I guess that would be,
um . . .

the way in which I would begin to look at community,
and would therefore think
that race has become, uh,   85
an increasingly obsolete way
of constructing community
because it is based on unchangeable
immutable biological
facts   90
in a very pseudo-scientific way,
alright?
Now
racism is entirely different
because see *racism,*   95
uh,
actually I think
is
at the origins of this concept of race.
It's not—   100
it's not the other way around,
that there were racists,
and then the racists—
one race came to dominate
the others.   105
As a matter of fact
in order for a European colonialist
to attempt
to conquer the world,
to colonize the world,   110
they had to construct this notion
of,
uh,
the populations of the earth being divided into certain,
uh,   115
firm biological, uh,
communities,
and that's what I think we have to go back and look at.
So when I use the word race now I put it in quotations.
Because if we don't transform   120
this . . . this intransigent
rigid
notion of race,
we will be caught up in this cycle

of genocidal   125
violence
that, um,
is at the origins of our history.
So I think—
and I'm   130
I'm convinced—
and this is what I'm working on in my political practice right now—
is that we have to find ways of coming together in a different way,
not the old notion of coalition in which we anchor ourselves very solidly
in our,   135
um,
communities,
and simply voice
our
solidarity with other people.   140
I'm not suggesting that we do not anchor ourselves in our communities;
I feel very anchored in,
um,
my various communities,
but I think that,   145
you know,
to use a metaphor, the rope
attached to that anchor should be long enough to allow us to move
into other communities
to understand and learn.   150
I've been thinking a lot about the need to make more intimate
these connections and associations and to really take on the responsibility
of learning.
So I think that we need to—
in order to find ways of working with   155
and understanding
the vastness
of our many cultural heritages
and ways of coming together without
rendering invisible all of that heterogeneity—   160
I don't have the answer,
you know
I don't know.
What I'm interested in is communities
that are not static,   165
that

can change, that can respond to new historical needs.
So I think it's a very exciting moment.

Working with the Text

1. A primary concern of *Fires in the Mirror* is perception and the experience that shapes it. This experience may be past or present, idea or event; it may inform, shape, or dominate a given portrait. Choose one character and discuss the relationship between experience and perception in his or her portrait. Is autobiography glancing or sustained? How clear is the relationship between the character's life and his or her understanding?

2. *Fires* is a sequence of dramatic monologues, yet, though the characters never converse, their performances often engage in dialogue, implicitly enlarging or qualifying or questioning one another's positions. Ntozake Shange and Anonymous Girl, for example, both consider the role of appropriation in forming identity, but the former's "taking" and the latter's "biting off" sketch subtly competing views. Analyze one or more local dialogues, then consider what kind of argument emerges from a series of such exchanges.

3. Consider the origin of this text in a one-woman performance. Given what the characters say, why might it be important that their voices and bodies occupy real time and real space? Why might it be important that a single actor play all the roles?

4. All of the monologues in our selection feature a central image (often reflected in the title): the desert, the street, the wig, the rope, and, of course, the mirror. Are these images literal, figurative, or both? What do they represent, and how do they help create the characters that use them?

5. Interview someone you admire, then write a dramatic monologue based on the interview. You may quote your subject directly, but you should strive to give your material shape and coherence through judicious editing. Be sure to include stage direction(s) and a compelling title.

A Story About the Body

ROBERT HASS

Robert Hass is the author of several highly regarded books of poems, including *Field Guide, Praise, Human Wishes,* and *Sun Under Wood*. He has produced several anthologies, a book of essays, and collaborates with Czeslaw Milosz on the translation of his poems. Hass is a former U.S. Poet Laureate, Yale Younger Poet, and MacArthur Fellow. He currently teaches at the University of California, Berkeley. His poems are sensitive to our fleeting, quietly passionate, and restorative encounters with the natural world and with each other. This poem testifies to the urgencies and fearfulness of erotic attraction, how two artists try to negotiate a single, troublesome art: physical love.

The young composer, working that summer at an artist's colony, had watched her for a week. She was Japanese, a painter, almost sixty, and he thought he was in love with her. He loved her work, and her work was like the way she moved her body, used her hands, looked at him directly when she made amused and considered answers to his questions. One night, walking back from a concert, they came to her door and she turned to him and said, "I think you would like to have me. I would like that too, but I must tell you that I have had a double mastectomy," and when he didn't understand, "I've lost both my breasts." The radiance that he had carried around in his belly and chest cavity—like music—withered very quickly, and he made himself look at her when he said, "I'm sorry. I don't think I could." He walked back to his own cabin through the pines, and in the morning he found a small blue bowl on the porch outside his door. It looked to be full of rose petals, but he found when he picked it up that the rose petals were on top; the rest of the bowl—she must have swept them from the corners of her studio—was full of dead bees.

Working with the Text

1. Why can't the composer accept the altered contours of the artist's body? How is surgical alteration distinct from other forms of difference in the poem: age, gender, experience, and (presumably) nationality? How is it similar?

2. Why did the artist answer the composer with a material gesture, rather than in language or in painting? What does her answer mean?

3. Why does Hass title this poem "A Story About the Body"? Whose body is indicated by the definite article ("the")? Why is this poem designated a story? Why are the protagonists simply designated "he" and "she"?

4. In a brief essay, analyze the bowl of dead bees covered with petals. Consider each element of the assembly, its full range of significance and its typical context. Then consider the meaning that emerges when these separate meanings collide and/or complement one another.

5. Write a brief dialogue in which one character finds a boundary he or she cannot cross. Alternatively, write a brief dialogue in which the final statement is nonverbal: for example, a gesture, image, musical passage, or mode of dress.

Borders

THOMAS KING

Born in California, novelist Thomas King has spent most of his life teaching and writing in Canada and the Upper Midwest. He is currently on the faculty at the University of Minnesota. Of Cherokee as well as German and Irish decent, King has used much of his work to explore the diversity of Native American life today. Feeling no strong tie to any particular native culture, King has said that he feels "free to ask some of the really nasty questions that other writers may not want to ask . . . One of the questions that's important to ask is, 'Who is an Indian? How do we get this idea of Indianness'"? King's recent work includes the novels *Medicine River* (1990) and *Green Grass, Running Water* (1993). "Borders," the following short story, raises interesting questions about citizenship, community, and identity as a Blackfoot woman refuses to claim Canadian citizenship in order to cross the border into the United States.

When I was twelve, maybe thirteen, my mother announced that we were going to go to Salt Lake City to visit my sister who had left the reserve, moved across the line, and found a job. Laetitia had not left home with my mother's blessing, but over time my mother had come to be proud of the fact that Laetitia had done all of this on her own.

"She did real good," my mother would say.   2

Then there were the fine points of Laetitia's going. She had not, as my   3
mother liked to tell Mrs. Manyfingers, gone floating after some man like a balloon on a string. She hadn't snuck out of the house, either, and gone to Vancouver or Edmonton or Toronto to chase rainbows down alleys. And she hadn't been pregnant.

"She did real good."   4

I was seven or eight when Laetitia left home. She was seventeen. Our   5
father was from Rocky Boy on the American side.

"Dad's American," Laetitia told my mother, "so I can go and come as   6
I please."

"Send us a postcard."   7

Laetitia packed her things, and we headed for the border. Just outside of   8
Milk River, Laetitia told us to watch for the water tower.

"Over the next rise. It's the first thing you see."   9

"We got a water tower on the reserve," my mother said. "There's a big   10
one in Lethbridge, too."

"You'll be able to see the tops of the flagpoles, too. That's where the   11
border is."

When we got to Coutts, my mother stopped at the convenience store   12
and bought her and Laetitia a cup of coffee. I got an Orange Crush.

"This is real lousy coffee."   13

"You're just angry because I want to see the world."   14

"It's the water. From here on down, they got lousy water."   15

"I can catch the bus from Sweetgrass. You don't have to lift a finger."   16

"You're going to have to buy your water in bottles if you want good   17
coffee."

There was an old wooden building about a block away, with a tall sign   18
in the yard that said "Museum." Most of the roof had been blown away. Mom told me to go and see when the place was open. There were boards over the windows and doors. You could tell that the place was closed, and I told Mom so, but she said to go and check anyway. Mom and Laetitia stayed by the car. Neither one of them moved. I sat down on the steps of the museum and watched them, and I don't know that they ever said anything to each other. Finally, Laetitia got her bag out of the trunk and gave Mom a hug.

I wandered back to the car. The wind had come up, and it blew Laeti-   19
tia's hair across her face. Mom reached out and pulled the strands out of Laetitia's eyes, and Laetitia let her.

"You can still see the mountain from here," my mother told Laetitia in 20
Blackfoot.

"Lots of mountains in Salt Lake," Laetitia told her in English. 21

"The place is closed," I said. "Just like I told you." 22

Laetitia tucked her hair into her jacket and dragged her bag down the 23
road to the brick building with the American flag flapping on a pole. When
she got to where the guards were waiting, she turned, put the bag down,
and waved to us. We waved back. Then my mother turned the car around,
and we came home.

We got postcards from Laetitia regular, and, if she wasn't spreading jelly 24
on the truth, she was happy. She found a good job and rented an apartment
with a pool.

"And she can't even swim," my mother told Mrs. Manyfingers. 25

Most of the postcards said we should come down and see the city, but 26
whenever I mentioned this, my mother would stiffen up.

So I was surprised when she bought two new tires for the car and put 27
on her blue dress with the green and yellow flowers. I had to dress up, too,
for my mother did not want us crossing the border looking like Americans.
We made sandwiches and put them in a big box with pop and potato chips
and some apples and bananas and a big jar of water.

"But we can stop at one of those restaurants, too, right?" 28

The border was actually two towns, though neither one was big enough 29
to amount to anything. Coutts was on the Canadian side and consisted of the
convenience store and gas station, the museum that was closed and boarded
up, and a motel. Sweetgrass was on the American side, but all you could see
was an overpass that arched across the highway and disappeared into the
prairies. Just hearing the names of these towns, you would expect that
Sweetgrass, which is a nice name and sounds like it is related to other places
such as Medicine Hat and Moose Jaw and Kicking Horse Pass, would be on
the Canadian side, and that Coutts, which sounds abrupt and rude, would
be on the American side. But this was not the case.

Between the two borders was a duty-free shop where you could buy 30
cigarettes and liquor and flags. Stuff like that.

We left the reserve in the morning and drove until we got to Coutts. 31

"Last time we stopped here," my mother said, "you had an Orange 32
Crush. You remember that?"

"Sure," I said. "That was when Laetitia took off." 33

"You want another Orange Crush?" 34

"That means we're not going to stop at a restaurant, right?" 35

My mother got coffee at the convenience store, and we stood around 36
and watched the prairies move in the sunlight. Then we climbed back in the

car. My mother straightened the dress across her thighs, leaned against the wheel, and drove all the way to the border in first gear, slowly, as if she were trying to see through a bad storm or riding high on black ice.

The border guard was an old guy. As he walked to the car, he swayed 37
from side to side, his feet set wide apart, the holster on his hip pitching up and down. He leaned into the window, looked into the back seat, and looked at my mother and me.

"Morning, ma'am." 38

"Good morning." 39

"Where you heading?" 40

"Salt Lake City." 41

"Purpose of your visit?" 42

"Visit my daughter." 43

"Citizenship?" 44

"Blackfoot," my mother told him. 45

"Ma'am?" 46

"Blackfoot," my mother repeated. 47

"Canadian?" 48

"Blackfoot." 49

It would have been easier if my mother had just said "Canadian" and 50
been done with it, but I could see she wasn't going to do that. The guard wasn't angry or anything. He smiled and looked towards the building. Then he turned back and nodded.

"Morning, ma'am." 51

"Good morning." 52

"Any firearms or tobacco?" 53

"No." 54

"Citizenship?" 55

"Blackfoot." 56

He told us to sit in the car and wait, and we did. In about five minutes, 57
another guard came out with the first man. They were talking as they came, both men swaying back and forth like two cowboys headed for a bar or a gunfight.

"Morning, ma'am." 58

"Good morning." 59

"Cecil tells me you and the boy are Blackfoot." 60

"That's right." 61

"Now, I know that we got Blackfeet on the American side and the Cana- 62
dians got Blackfeet on their side. Just so we can keep our records straight, what side do you come from?"

I knew exactly what my mother was going to say, and I could have told 63
them if they had asked me.

"Canadian side or American side?" asked the guard. 64

"Blackfoot side," she said. 65

It didn't take them long to lose their sense of humor, I can tell you that. 66
The one guard stopped smiling altogether and told us to park our car at the side of the building and come in.

We sat on a wood bench for about an hour before anyone came over to 67
talk to us. This time it was a woman. She had a gun, too.

"Hi," she said. "I'm Inspector Pratt. I understand there is a little misun- 68
derstanding."

"I'm going to visit my daughter in Salt Lake City," my mother told her. 69
"We don't have any guns or beer."

"It's a legal technicality, that's all." 70

"My daughter's Blackfoot, too." 71

The woman opened a briefcase and took out a couple of forms and be- 72
gan to write on one of them. "Everyone who crosses our border has to declare their citizenship. Even Americans. It helps us keep track of the visitors
we get from the various countries."

She went on like that for maybe fifteen minutes, and a lot of the stuff 73
she told us was interesting.

"I can understand how you feel about having to tell us your citizenship, 74
and here's what I'll do. You tell me, and I won't put it down on the form.
No one will know but you and me."

Her gun was silver. There were several chips in the wood handle and 75
the name "Stella" was scratched into the metal butt.

We were in the border office for about four hours, and we talked to al- 76
most everyone there. One of the men bought me a Coke. My mother
brought a couple of sandwiches in from the car. I offered part of mine to
Stella, but she said she wasn't hungry.

I told Stella that we were Blackfoot and Canadian, but she said that that 77
didn't count because I was a minor. In the end, she told us that if my mother
didn't declare her citizenship, we would have to go back to where we came
from. My mother stood up and thanked Stella for her time. Then we got
back in the car and drove to the Canadian border, which was only about a
hundred yards away.

I was disappointed. I hadn't seen Laetitia for a long time, and I had 78
never been to Salt Lake City. When she was still at home, Laetitia would go
on and on about Salt Lake City. She had never been there, but her boyfriend
Lester Tallbull had spent a year in Salt Lake at a technical school.

"It's a great place," Lester would say. "Nothing but blondes in the 79
whole state."

Whenever he said that, Laetitia would slug him on his shoulder hard 80
enough to make him flinch. He had some brochures on Salt Lake and some

maps, and every so often the two of them would spread them out on the table.

"That's the temple. It's right downtown. You got to have a pass to get in."   81

"Charlotte says anyone can go in and look around."   82

"When was Charlotte in Salt Lake? Just when the hell was Charlotte in Salt Lake?"   83

"Last year."   84

"This is Liberty Park. It's got a zoo. There's good skiing in the mountains."   85

"Got all the skiing we can use," my mother would say. "People come from all over the world to ski at Banff. Cardston's got a temple, if you like those kinds of things."   86

"Oh, this one is real big," Lester would say. "They got armed guards and everything."   87

"Not what Charlotte says."   88

"What does she know?"   89

Lester and Laetitia broke up, but I guess the idea of Salt Lake stuck in her mind.   90

The Canadian border guard was a young woman, and she seemed happy to see us. "Hi," she said. "You folks sure have a great day for a trip. Where are you coming from?"   91

"Standoff."   92

"Is that in Montana?"   93

"No."   94

"Where are you going?"   95

"Standoff."   96

The woman's name was Carol and I don't guess she was any older than Laetitia. "Wow, you both Canadians?"   97

"Blackfoot."   98

"Really? I have a friend I went to school with who is Blackfoot. Do you know Mike Harley?"   99

"No."   100

"He went to school in Lethbridge, but he's really from Browning."   101

It was a nice conversation and there were no cars behind us, so there was no rush.   102

"You're not bringing any liquor back, are you?"   103

"No."   104

"Any cigarettes or plants or stuff like that?"   105

"No."   106

"Citizenship?"   107

"Blackfoot."   108

"I know," said the woman, "and I'd be proud of being Blackfoot if I 109
were Blackfoot. But you have to be American or Canadian."

When Laetitia and Lester broke up, Lester took his brochures and maps with 110
him, so Laetitia wrote to someone in Salt Lake City, and, about a month later,
she got a big envelope of stuff. We sat at the table and opened up all the
brochures, and Laetitia read each one out loud.

"Salt Lake City is the gateway to some of the world's most magnificent 111
skiing.

"Salt Lake City is the home of one of the newest professional basketball 112
franchises, the Utah Jazz.

"The Great Salt Lake is one of the natural wonders of the world." 113

It was kind of exciting seeing all those color brochures on the table and 114
listening to Laetitia read all about how Salt Lake City was one of the best
places in the entire world.

"That Salt Lake City place sounds too good to be true," my mother 115
told her.

"It has everything." 116

"We got everything right here." 117

"It's boring here." 118

"People in Salt Lake City are probably sending away for brochures of 119
Calgary and Lethbridge and Pincher Creek right now."

In the end, my mother would say that maybe Laetitia should go to Salt 120
Lake City, and Laetitia would say that maybe she would.

We parked the car to the side of the building and Carol led us into a small 121
room on the second floor. I found a comfortable spot on the couch and
flipped through some back issues of *Saturday Night* and *Alberta Report*.

When I woke up, my mother was just coming out of another office. She 122
didn't say a word to me. I followed her down the stairs and out to the car. I
thought we were going home, but she turned the car around and drove
back towards the American border, which made me think we were going to
visit Laetitia in Salt Lake City after all. Instead she pulled into the parking lot
of the duty-free store and stopped.

"We going to see Laetitia?" 123

"No." 124

"We going home?" 125

Pride is a good thing to have, you know. Laetitia had a lot of pride, and 126
so did my mother. I figured that someday, I'd have it, too.

"So where are we going?" 127

Most of that day, we wandered around the duty-free store, which wasn't 128
very large. The manager had a name tag with a tiny American flag on one

side and a tiny Canadian flag on the other. His name was Mel. Towards evening, he began suggesting that we should be on our way. I told him we had nowhere to go, that neither the Americans nor the Canadians would let us in. He laughed at that and told us that we should buy something or leave.

The car was not very comfortable, but we did have all that food and it   129
was April, so even if it did snow as it sometimes does on the prairies, we wouldn't freeze. The next morning my mother drove to the American border.

It was a different guard this time, but the questions were the same. We   130
didn't spend as much time in the office as we had the day before. By noon, we were back at the Canadian border. By two we were back in the duty-free shop parking lot.

The second night in the car was not as much fun as the first, but my   131
mother seemed in good spirits, and, all in all, it was as much an adventure as an inconvenience. There wasn't much food left and that was a problem, but we had lots of water as there was a faucet at the side of the duty-free shop.

One Sunday, Laetitia and I were watching television. Mom was over at Mrs.   132
Manyfingers's. Right in the middle of the program, Laetitia turned off the set and said she was going to Salt Lake City, that life around here was too boring. I had wanted to see the rest of the program and really didn't care if Laetitia went to Salt Lake City or not. When Mom got home, I told her what Laetitia had said.

What surprised me was how angry Laetitia got when she found out that   133
I had told Mom.

"You got a big mouth."   134

"That's what you said."   135

"What I said is none of your business."   136

"I didn't say anything."   137

"Well, I'm going for sure, now."   138

That weekend, Laetitia packed her bags, and we drove her to the border.   139

Mel turned out to be friendly. When he closed up for the night and found   140
us still parked in the lot, he came over and asked us if our car was broken down or something. My mother thanked him for his concern and told him that we were fine, that things would get straightened out in the morning.

"You're kidding," said Mel. "You'd think they could handle the simple   141
things."

"We got some apples and a banana," I said, "but we're all out of ham   142
sandwiches."

"You know, you read about these things, but you just don't believe it.   143
You just don't believe it."

"Hamburgers would be even better because they got more stuff for energy." 144

My mother slept in the back seat. I slept in the front because I was smaller and could lie under the steering wheel. Late that night, I heard my mother open the car door. I found her sitting on her blanket leaning against the bumper of the car. 145

"You see all those stars," she said. "When I was a little girl, my grandmother used to take me and my sisters out on the prairies and tell us stories about all the stars." 146

"Do you think Mel is going to bring us any hamburgers?" 147

"Every one of those stars has a story. You see that bunch of stars over there that look like a fish?" 148

"He didn't say no." 149

"Coyote went fishing, one day. That's how it all started." We sat out under the stars that night, and my mother told me all sorts of stories. She was serious about it, too. She'd tell them slow, repeating parts as she went, as if she expected me to remember each one. 150

Early the next morning, the television vans began to arrive, and guys in suits and women in dresses came trotting over to us, dragging microphones and cameras and lights behind them. One of the vans had a table set up with orange juice and sandwiches and fruit. It was for the crew, but when I told them we hadn't eaten for a while, a really skinny blonde woman told us we could eat as much as we wanted. 151

They mostly talked to my mother. Every so often one of the reporters would come over and ask me questions about how it felt to be an Indian without a country. I told them we had a nice house on the reserve and that my cousins had a couple of horses we rode when we went fishing. Some of the television people went over to the American border, and then they went to the Canadian border. 152

Around noon, a good-looking guy in a dark blue suit and an orange tie with little ducks on it drove up in a fancy car. He talked to my mother for a while, and, after they were done talking, my mother called me over, and we got into our car. Just as my mother started the engine, Mel came over and gave us a bag of peanut brittle and told us that justice was a damn hard thing to get, but that we shouldn't give up. 153

I would have preferred lemon drops, but it was nice of Mel anyway. 154

"Where are we going now?" 155

"Going to visit Laetitia." 156

The guard who came out to our car was all smiles. The television lights were so bright they hurt my eyes, and, if you tried to look through the windshield in certain directions, you couldn't see a thing. 157

"Morning, Ma'am."   158

"Good morning."   159

"Where you heading?"   160

"Salt Lake City."   161

"Purpose of your visit?"   162

"Visit my daughter."   163

"Any tobacco, liquor, or firearms?"   164

"Don't smoke."   165

"Any plants or fruit?"   166

"Not any more."   167

"Citizenship?"   168

"Blackfoot."   169

The guard rocked back on his heels and jammed his thumbs into his   170
gun belt. "Thank you," he said, his fingers patting the butt of the revolver.
"Have a pleasant trip."

My mother rolled the car forward, and the television people had to   171
scramble out of the way. They ran alongside the car as we pulled away from
the border, and, when they couldn't run any farther, they stood in the middle
of the highway and waved and waved and waved.

We got to Salt Lake City the next day. Laetitia was happy to see us, and,   172
that first night, she took us out to a restaurant that made really good soups.
The list of pies took up a whole page. I had cherry. Mom had chocolate.
Laetitia said that she saw us on television the night before and, during the
meal, she had us tell her the story over and over again.

Laetitia took us everywhere. We went to a fancy ski resort. We went to   173
the temple. We got to go shopping in a couple of large malls, but they
weren't as large as the one in Edmonton, and Mom said so.

After a week or so, I got bored and wasn't all sad when my mother said   174
we should be heading back home. Laetitia wanted us to stay longer, but
Mom said no, that she had things to do back home and that, next time, Laetitia
should come up and visit. Laetitia said she was thinking about moving
back, and Mom told her to do as she pleased, and Laetitia said that
she would.

On the way home, we stopped at the duty-free shop, and my mother   175
gave Mel a green hat that said "Salt Lake" across the front. Mel was a funny
guy. He took the hat and blew his nose and told my mother that she was an
inspiration to us all. He gave us some more peanut brittle and came out into
the parking lot and waved at us all the way to the Canadian border.

It was almost evening when we left Coutts. I watched the border   176
through the rear window until all you could see were the tops of
the flagpoles and the blue water tower, and then they rolled over a hill and
disappeared.

Working with the Text

1. The narrator says that he and his mother dress up for the trip because his mother doesn't want them "crossing the border looking like Americans." What does this suggest about the mother's views of American culture?

2. In refusing to identify herself as Canadian, do you think the mother is making a political statement, intending to become a "cause"? Or is she following her heart? Or is she simply being stubborn? Do you agree with Mel that she is "an inspiration to us all"?

3. This whole incident is related from the perspective of the young boy. How does this narrative voice contribute to the effect of the story? How does the fact that the boy is willing to tell the authorities that he and his mother are "Blackfoot and Canadian" color the issue?

4. There are three "places" in this story: Canada, the United States, and the space in between. To whom does this middle space belong? How does it relate to the mother's identity as Blackfoot? What does it suggest about the nature of borders generally? Do borders always force choices? Can you think of other examples where people are asked to make an either/or choice where an alternative or more complicated response is appropriate or desirable?

5. Look at the Web exercise at the *Beyond Borders* site called "How many sides does a border have?" Are there other examples linked there of border situations where identity is not simply a matter of one thing or another?

Who Lost an American?

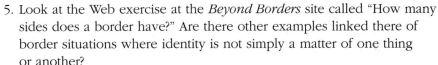

JOEL GILBERT, AS TOLD TO NOEL IGNATIEV

This interview first appeared in the anti-race, anti-racism journal *Race Traitor* (1993). Noel Ignatiev, one of its founding editors, identifies his writings, political activism, and publishing efforts as part of "white skin privilege politics"—the conviction, states Ignatiev, that "the key to fundamental social change in the U.S. is the challenge to the system of race privilege that embraces all whites, including the most downtrodden." Ignatiev is the author of *How the Irish Became White* and teaches at Harvard. The subject of the interview, twenty-year-old Joel Gilbert, tells of his abusive childhood, his early fascination with Hitler and skinheads, and his political turnaround in becoming a "race traitor" who seeks to "destroy this so-called white society" through grassroots campaigns against racism. Gilbert works as a cook and bicycle messenger in Boston.

Race Traitor

NOEL IGNATIEV & JOHN GARVEY, [Eds.]

I was born in 1973, and grew up in Port Huron, Michigan, a town of thirty thousand people. The north end of town was pretty much for the wealthy or the upper class, and the south end, where I grew up, was mostly white, working-class people. There were some black folks, some Hispanic folks, but not many. I have one older brother, a younger sister, and a younger brother.   1

One of the first things I can remember is my father beating my mother. My father had a good job as a truck driver for the local dairy, and he was making pretty good money. He was trying to establish a middle-class life, and he just couldn't deal with the pressures, so he would take it out on my mother.   2

We had a big family and we ate a lot. My mother went shopping and spent a lot on groceries. My father was upset at her because she bought this four-dollar box of cereal. It was sugar-coated and he had this thing about sugar. She came home, and he saw this box of cereal, and took the box of cereal and smashed it and threw it down the stairs, and then beat my mother, screaming that we couldn't afford it, and that us kids shouldn't have that kind of cereal. The next morning when we woke up, we saw him sitting at the table. He had gone to the basement and got out the cereal box and was eating the cereal. Seeing that just twisted my insides. It made me hurt so much.   3

When I was in first grade, my mom got a divorce and we moved to a different house. My father would come around and bug her and demand that they get married again. I remember coming into the room from my bedroom and he was standing above her and she was sitting there with tears running down her face. He had a monstrous grimace, and she told me to go back to bed. One night he came to the house when my mother was listening to the stereo, and she wouldn't let him in. He forced his way in and threw the stereo out the window. I heard all this, but I was too scared to get out of bed.   4

My mom got a court order to keep him away, and the police would come and sympathize with my father. Those policemen weren't out to protect us. The courts wouldn't do anything. He owed my mother a lot of money that we could have used to eat.   5

My mom knew she had to get away and we moved to Ann Arbor, two   6
hours from Port Huron. There was no way he could drive down there the
way he used to. We would visit him every other week, and he would buy
us clothes and toys, but he wouldn't let us take them home when we left.

While we lived in Ann Arbor, my mom had two different jobs. She   7
worked at an insurance company and also at a bar. We lived in a two-
bedroom apartment, not much space or privacy, not too much to eat. We
had good times, though. Our family got really close, and my older brother
and I looked after each other, and after our younger brother and sister. We
didn't have a television so we went garbage-picking and found one. When
we wanted snacks we would scrounge up change in the house and buy
candy. We entertained each other, and would go for walks together. I
learned to cook and scrub pots and pans when I was eight years old. My
mom was always good to us when she could be. But she started drinking
and developed a problem with alcohol. We lived with her in Ann Arbor for
about two years, and then she couldn't afford to keep us any more. At that
time my father owed my mother about five thousand dollars in child support, and she essentially traded us to him. They worked it out with the court
so that she wouldn't have to pay any child support but would get us back
after two years. A lot of this I found out later.

So we moved back from our mother to our father, and that's when things   8
got really bad. When we moved in with him, he was working a lot too, so the
system we had set up when we lived with our mother continued. My brothers, sister, and I were all very close. We had to watch over each other. We
cooked, we cleaned, we entertained each other. I looked up to my brother
more than I did my father. I had little respect for my father. He had never been
able to control us when we were all together and we thought he had no right
to now. So he beat us. Most of it was directed against my older brother and
me, because we knew what was going on and hated him. My younger brother
and sister were too young to understand and he left them alone.

He'd beat me every day, for anything from not cleaning a dish properly   9
to not getting a grade in school. After the physical beating was over, the
emotional abuse would start. He would tell me that he loved me and that I
was a bad kid, and that he didn't want to do what he had to do, but he did
it because he loved me. So I was very confused about myself, and what this
man represented to me. I didn't understand who gave him the authority to
treat me the way he did. And that whole time he was taking us to church
each week. He was a devout Christian. To this day he seems like the nicest
person you could meet, in public. But behind closed doors, he's a monster.

I had always been rebellious in school. When I moved in with my father   10
that rebellion continued. I was in a new school, and I didn't like the situation

I was living in, and so I was a troublemaker. I was an outcast because I was a little on the weird side. Essentially I went on my own, and did my own things and stayed to myself. My brother had a paper route and I would help him with that. I would hang with some of the older people on the route, and talk to them.

The friends I had were all into playing war games. We'd go and get plastic guns and play in the woods, and talk about military strategies. I started getting interested in World War II. I read a lot about it. Reading was an escape for me. I think it was history that drew me to reading, because I loved to go into another time. I started reading about Nazis, and the more I got into that the less I focused on the other parts of the War. I got interested in the different things Hitler was doing. The more I read about Hitler the more powerful he seemed to me. I could relate to that power. I felt helpless, like I had no power, and I felt that through this message I could get power.   11

I knew that Germany and the U.S. had fought on opposite sides in the War, but that didn't matter. I didn't like the American way of life. I was unhappy with what I saw. At that age I had realized that my father was working a lot. He would come home from the day's work and wanted to see things clean. And if they weren't clean he would take it out on us. I didn't understand why my father had to work so much, and why whatever happened at work made him angry enough to come home and hit me and my older brother. Also I didn't like being pushed around and humiliated by my teachers because I was different. I had trouble learning and they called me dumb. I realized that school wasn't going to do anything for me, my father and mother weren't going to do anything for me, the community I lived in wasn't going to do anything. So I looked to other places. I would watch TV documentaries on Hitler and they would talk about how he built the autobahns, and how he and Dr. Porsche produced the Volkswagen bug, which really fascinated me because I liked that type of car. They were able to put everybody to work, and give everybody a car, and build themselves up to the point where eventually they could take on the whole world in a war. I studied about how they went into Russia, and how they were able to roll in there until the cold and the Russian fighters fought them back. It seemed like they had so much power. Like at the Nuremberg rallies, where it seemed that they had hundreds of thousands of people doing the same thing—their right hands to Hitler, and he was able to command them to do anything he wanted. I would daydream about that being me, here in America, about being Hitler or somebody of his strength and power.   12

I realized through my studies that he had killed six million Jews. But at that point I was starting to get connected with the grandfather of one of my friends. He lived alone a few blocks away from my house, and I'd go over and talk with him. He was an anti-Semite. He had a whole room full   13 of books and magazines of different white-supremacist and anti-Semitic groups. Even though he didn't claim to be a Nazi—he actually disliked the Nazis—he liked to read up on what they were doing. He talked about the Establishment, by which he meant international Jewry controlling the world through capital. He said that there weren't six million Jews killed. He gave me a pamphlet that said there was no Auschwitz, that during the War it was a factory that produced clothes for soldiers, and that towards the end of the War Hollywood flew into Germany and turned this wrecked factory into a filmset with gas chambers to make it look like six million Jews were killed. I was thirteen or fourteen and I didn't know what to believe. This guy said that the Jews controlled Hollywood and had faked the whole thing. He sculpted a lot of my ideas to what the Nazi Party believed, that the capitalist system was created by the Jews and that they were doing that to get rich. He started giving me books about the Rockefellers, and he traced how DuPont was all Jews, and I went along with it because I wanted something to believe in.

This period of my life developed over two years of living with my father   14
and being beat around by him, and the school, and just fed up. I thought this was a way out. I had only one other friend who was into Nazism. He was a kid in high school in the ninth grade, and he was from a worse situation than mine. He would come to school dirty, with his hair messed up— so did I, but not like this kid. He had only one pair of pants. His father beat him openly, black and blue marks. My father was always smart enough not to leave any marks. This kid and I started talking. He liked to use the word n-i-g-g-e-r more often than I did, and he hated Jews, even though he didn't know any Jews either, and he said that his uncle was a white supremacist. He was a lot like me: he hated his folks, he hated school, he hated the town we had to grow up in.

I watched Oprah Winfrey on TV and there were skinheads on her show   15
and I was cheering them on. In the back of my mind I realized that they were fools, but I wanted to get in touch with them. I didn't have any names or addresses of people to contact, but if I did I would have. At that point in my life I could have become a full-fledged Nazi. I was ready for it. If there had been some group around I could have joined, I would have.

What turned me around? At the time I was getting interested not only in   16
the Nazis but in other things, like the Weathermen and the Chicago Seven. People were telling me about SDS (Students for a Democratic Society), because I grew up in Port Huron and people knew that the founding statement of SDS was adopted there, in the park my family used to go to in the summer for picnics. I knew I was radical, that I disliked the system, that I disliked my parents and the school system. I got interested in Charles Manson, because I knew he was radical, and killed people, and wanted to tear down the system.

I was looking for alternatives to the Nazis, because there was something inside me that told me it was wrong. A lot of that was my Christian beliefs, that asked me why would I hate black people? I mean, my next-door neighbor was black, and he was a good guy. And then I didn't know any Jews, so why would I hate them? Even if the world was run by Jews, what did that have to do with me?

I bought *Soul on Ice* by Eldridge Cleaver, and read that, and I was start-   17
ing to get into the Black Power movement, and my mom asked me if I had ever read Malcolm X. And she asked, why didn't I get a copy of that? And so I saved up some money and bought a copy. This was before the whole Malcolm X craze, and I sat down and read it. I read about the white su- premacists who burned down his house, and killed his father, and tore apart his family, and I thought, if these folks could do that just because of his skin color, then that couldn't be the answer at all, no way. The more I read about Malcolm X and his life, the more I identified with him. I felt so bad that whites had treated him the way they did, but at the same time I knew that whites were treating me the same way. The funny thing is, at that time I didn't finish the book. Since then I've read the whole thing, but at that time I had the habit of starting books and not finishing them, and I didn't get past the part where he returns from Mecca.

From there I considered myself a black nationalist. I started looking for   18
people who were like Malcolm X. Maybe I could hook up with them, and find a way to escape from the oppression I felt. I hated whites. I would talk about the goddamn honkies, or whatever. I hated the little town I grew up in, and I thought that when I grew up I would move to Detroit or Chicago and join up with some people and come back and wipe the place out.

I was always in trouble, and my father didn't know how to handle it.   19
When we were still living in Ann Arbor, my mom wanted to help us deal with everything that was happening, so she started taking us to family ther- apy. When I moved in with my father he took me to the school therapist and then he took me to psychologists. I would tell them what was happening. And then they would organize family sessions, and I would sit in the room, with the therapist in the middle and my father on the other side, and they would make me repeat what I had told them in private. And I would do it, and my father would just shake his head, and they would believe him and not me. And so I was this rebellious kid who was making up lies. And after the sessions he would scream at me for saying things that were not true. He was in his own denial. I knew I didn't want to be a man like my father. He wasn't a man, he was a coward. I later found out that his father did the same thing to him, and who knows what *his* father did to him. This is the kind of thing that goes on and society just doesn't see it. And the thing is, I had sev- eral different friends in school who had the same problems. I knew one kid who killed himself because his father beat him.

I moved back with my mother when I was about sixteen. I switched   20
schools and had to make new friends. I was a complete outcast because I
was different. I tried to fit in but I couldn't. People would make fun of me
and I was depressed all the time. I stopped going to school. I began seeing
a new therapist. Finally I put myself into the hospital. I told the therapist that
I needed a place where I could be safe. So she worked it out so that I could
go to a mental hospital in Detroit.

I was there for three weeks and that screwed me up worse than before,   21
because they put me on all kinds of medications—the first one was prozac,
then they put me on lithium, then on haldol, and another drug. The drugs
gave me neck spasms, and I couldn't swallow, and I could hardly breathe.
Just recently have I learned that these drugs have killed people. They were
about to send me to a bigger institution where I would have been for at least
a year, where I would have been doped up more on their shit. I cleaned up
my act and played straight for a couple of days, and then I went to my
psychiatrist and said I was ready to go home. I promised to continue taking
my drugs, and he let me go home. I went back home and kept getting more
depressed.

I was suicidal from age twelve on. My older brother actually attempted   22
suicide when he was seventeen. And then he went into the army and that
really fucked him up. So there were all kinds of things that could have happened to me. I could have killed myself, I could have become a Nazi, I
could have been in a mental institution for the rest of my life.

I dropped out of school and was working at different jobs which didn't   23
last. I was still living with my mom, but I would spend a lot of time at
friends' houses, staying drunk and getting high. We were living on the north
side at that time, where a lot of the rich kids lived, and I would see them
driving Mercedes, and wearing expensive clothes, and that didn't make any
sense to me, because I had only three or four outfits and got most of my
clothes from the Goodwill. Finally, when I was just turning seventeen I decided I couldn't go on like this anymore, and that I was going to understand
why my life was so fucked up, and do what I needed to do to destroy the
church, to destroy the family, to destroy the cops, the courts, the schools,
and to destroy psychiatry. I turned vegetarian, because I realized that the
meat I was eating represented so much of the system. People beat their
wives, beat their children, and kill animals and eat them. When the Gulf War
was building up, I marched together with some people from the local community college, on a peaceful march from the town hall to the local recruit-
ing station. Looking back, I wish I had stormed a cop the way I wanted to.
At the same time I was scared, because I knew that seventeen-year-olds
could be drafted, and I didn't want to go to the army or have anything to do
with that war.

When the War ended I didn't have anything more to rant about, so I got   24
in touch with the local drug scene, and with some local Deadheads, and began hanging out with them. I began to travel, and towards the end of the
summer I came to Boston, and my friend from Ann Arbor was living there,
and he introduced me to my now-girlfriend. I went back to Michigan, but
she and I stayed in touch, and I decided to move to Boston. I moved with
four goals: the first was to have a relationship with my girlfriend; the second
was to get a job; the third was to find a place to live; and the fourth was to
go to college.

It was winter. I don't know why I choose winters to move. I slept on the   25
street in Harvard Square. There was a strong group of kids who would go
garbage-picking together, and chip in for food, and take care of each other.
Even while I was homeless I had a job, but I would go in to work tired every
day. It was a tough time, and I asked my mother to send me money for a
train ticket home. She sent it to me, but just as I was about to go back I found
an apartment, and so I gave the ticket money to the people I moved in with.
And then I found another job, temping for good money, and I found a better place to live, and my relationship with my girlfriend got better.

I still wanted to go to college. I enrolled in Roxbury Community College,   26
expecting to find the black radicals I was looking for, so we could work together and smash the system. I am one of a handful of "white" students at
Roxbury. I enrolled in some really good classes, but unfortunately I didn't
find the people I wanted to hook up with. It wasn't as radical as I was hoping. In fact, there are hardly any radicals.

I went in with the idea that no matter what happened, I was going to   27
educate myself, and I was going to make friends. I think I've done both of
those things. At first I was a little scared. I didn't know how people would
take to me, but I went in with a respectful attitude. I never tried to act in any
special way, but just to be myself. After a while, people could see that, and
started to return the respect. This year I'm on the student government association, and I know a lot of the students and faculty. I spend a lot of time
and energy integrating myself into the community. There are people there
from all different parts of the Caribbean, from Central and South America,
from all parts of Africa, and those are people you can learn from. I don't
think I represent the normal whites they see. Most of the kids there come
from economic backgrounds similar to mine, and we have a lot in common.
Never has anyone told me to get out because I didn't belong, or anything like
that. People take their time and try to get to know me before they judge me.

I've lived in a lot of different parts of Boston. I lived in Somerville for a   28
while, which is pretty white, and I noticed a lot of racist tendencies from
people there, and I didn't like living there at all. I lived for a while in
Dorchester, with two roommates. One was from Zimbabwe, the other was

from here. He had both black and white family, and had to deal with the white part of his family. I learned a lot from that. I lived for six months on the line between Roxbury and the South End. It's a very poor area, a lot of drugs, with a lot of Puerto Ricans and other Hispanic people. I took the same approach there that I took at RCC. I'd sit on the stoop and smoke with the guys, and shoot the shit. I found we liked the same type of music, and had a lot in common. It got a little too rough for my girlfriend and me, so we moved. I live with my girlfriend now in Jamaica Plain, in a very mixed area—a lot of blacks, a lot of Hispanics, and the whites who live there tend to be cool. It's as much of a community as I've experienced in Boston. Other parts of J.P. have been gentrified, but I'm not part of that. I don't represent whiteness any more, and so there's no way I can gentrify anything. For the most part I feel at home with black people. I've got plenty of black inside me. And I think most of the whiteness I grew up with has washed away.

One of the reasons my girlfriend and I were able to come together is 　29 that she saw I'm not like the average white male. I don't want to boast on myself, but I think I'm more mature, because of my experiences, than the average person my age. She isn't as political as I am, but we share a way of looking at the world. I hope that as I evolve politically we can grow together.

I want to destroy this so-called white society. I don't want any more kids 　30 to grow up like I did. I don't want to see psychiatry being used to hurt people. I don't want to see cops beating down anybody, black or white. I don't want to see families destroyed the way mine was. The kid this society gave birth to and tried to socialize has rebelled.

Working with the Text

1. "Who lost an American?" asks the title of this interview with a self-professed young radical. What does "lost" mean in the context of Joel Gilbert's life story? Why does the title seek to establish culpability for the loss? Does it succeed? Why or why not?

2. The narrator clearly believes that experience shapes political identity, yet he demonstrates how easily his experience could have produced, not a "race traitor," but a racist. What exactly tipped the scale away from white supremacy? What values do "race treachery" and racism share?

3. An important border for Gilbert is that between public and private. In his youth, the border was marked by the closed front door of his home, behind which "the nicest person you could meet," his father, became "a monster." How does the domestic frontier change as the interview progresses? Is there a realignment of public and private space?

4. Describe the narrator's "voice" and its role in shaping reception of his story. Pay particular attention to diction, sentence structure, and the choice of illustrative detail. Consider alternatives (bitter? sardonic? exhibitionist?), and discuss why Gilbert and Ignatiev chose to work in a different tonal register.

5. Working with a partner, give an oral account of an experience that shaped a current political conviction. Do not seek to be as comprehensive as Gilbert, but do include relevant information and anecdotes. Try to proceed in chronological order, though you may need to circle back, if your partner has questions. Then, exchange roles and interview your partner. Both narratives should be recorded, if possible. Finally, take your partner's interview and make a transcript of it, cutting and reordering to promote clarity. Try to preserve your partner's "voice"; better yet, try to enhance it by pruning false starts, redundancy, and clumsy phrasing.

The Gravity of Pink (Student Essay)

EDEN ABIGAIL TROOBOFF

Eden Abigail Trooboff was a sophomore at Columbia University, in New York City, when she wrote this essay. In the essay, she tries to reconcile messages she receives from others about her sense of femininity and identity as a woman with her own feelings and memories. In the piece she tries to model how a personal essay might also make use of academic material.

But if I wish to define myself, I must first of all say: "I am a woman"; on this truth must be based all further discussion (de Beauvoir xv).

In Hebrew School we were asked to decide whether we would fight for the   1
Americans or the Israelis if the U.S. and Israel ever went to war. We were choosing our identities and loyalties, examining those parts of ourselves that the school considered most complex in the context of faith and religion. They needed us to decide how our Americanism and Judaism would mesh, to deal with questions of assimilation at a young age. I didn't get too involved in this question, partly because my father said such a war would

never happen, but also because the notions of religious and national self-definition seemed so distant and open; there were lots of choices to be made, and none of them had to be made anytime soon.

I wonder why we never addressed questions that now seem so much   2
more urgent and problematic; why we didn't deal particularly with the given identities, especially sexual identity, which may not be a directly religious issue, but which becomes problematic in the context of Biblical gender roles and particularly Eve in the Garden of Eden. Perhaps we didn't discuss these problems because we had no choice about who ate the apple. When I considered the fall out of Eden spurred by Eve, being female and feminine seemed horrifyingly up-in-the-air, in that I was born into this role of temptress and scapegoat without any say. I negotiated early on, if not in so many words, how my moral weight would be taken from me.

Some parts of the self are up for grabs. Others are identities that we   3
cannot transcend, regardless of our choices and of the questions well-intentioned teachers ask us to ponder. Who am I before all else? Jewish? American? female? Can I form my identity like a grocery list, putting certain items first as the staples in the refrigerator of myself?

Aristotle believed that "the female is a female by virtue of a certain lack   4
of qualities" (de Beauvoir xvi). If traditionally I am an emptiness to be filled, life formed as an addendum rather than as an initial creative idea, identifying myself means adding parts of myself to a void. It means encountering the body that I am born in, and considering it perhaps not just as a passive, unavoidable identity, but as a vital dwelling place. How will I come to understand this home?

> Anatomy is a woman's destiny, say the theorists of femininity; the identity of woman is determined by her biology (Friedan 79).

I don't know if this strange man with gray in his hair wanted me to feel   5
flirted with. Really he was coming on to our leggy, blonde Dutch houseguest who was traveling with my family through New England for the summer. But I was wearing a pink dress with a big V in back and I felt too female to be a child. He danced extravagantly with all three of us, my sister, Anna, and me, maybe just to cross that line which exists in every wedding reception between the adults and the children. I was twelve, flattered and amused to be feeling the silly tingles of flirtation. With him leaning over to put his arm around my back, I felt my body for the first time in relation to a man's. At the end of the song, he scooped up my legs and twirled me around. With the myopic vision one adopts of childhood memories, I remember everyone turning around to watch this little pink girl get picked up so easily by this charming man. I was unable or unwilling to show my anger

at being lifted without being asked. I smiled a little uncontrollably, conscious that any other response would betray the sensitivity that my parents reminded me I had far too much of.

I have become protective of my gravity. I feel sick to my stomach when   6
I wear pink, as though my insides had lost the weight that keeps them together. When friends try to lift me up, I sit down, keeping my weight as earth-bound as I can. I keep my back covered. I try to be more mind than body. I've swallowed the pink in me. I am thrown off kilter when I am made aware that I have a body at times when I have nearly forgotten.

Gravity is taken from women. My friends have told me slowly of their   7
weightlessness, not saying the R-word that they know applies to their loss of themselves. How can I form an allegiance to a group that is victimized? Why would I want to belong? How can I think about my female consciousness when I am forced to feel it every time girl friends get together and talk about mistrust, loss of power, and violence? The process of finding identity becomes emotional rather than intellectual when the loss of control means abuse.

Women are bound together psychologically by a fear of the dark, by the   8
impulse to check the backseat before driving off, by the inability to walk through an unlit place alone, by the subtle suggestions of how small you are compared to him, how easily he could lift you or hold you down. Maybe the real fear is of floating, feeling your body out of your own control, fearing it is less your own than that of those who may take it from you. I wonder if there is an experience of fear or loss of self that bonds men together. Or are they connected by an awareness of their gravity? I find my femininity wrapped in vulnerability. I wonder if masculinity is wrapped in strength.

I seek to see my body as my own, as the place that I dwell in which remains mine even if it is victimized. The fear of our weightlessness causes   9
me to hunker down with other women, to keep each other from floating away.

> The closest I've ever come to myth was that favorite game in college—we called it Earliest Memory, my friends sprawled out in someone's living room. Moonlight on the bedroom floor we'd say or oh god, that fall down the steep back stairs . . . (Boruch, "The Quiet House").

Physical memories seem the oldest to me; I can't remember when pain   10
seemed unfamiliar. My mom tells me the most interesting time to watch infants is when they first discover their body parts, seizing at their toes and fingers, developing the strange physical habits that stay with us for life, establishing the bodies that won't feel quite so new again. And since this joy-

ful time which my mom remembers for me, physical realization is what brings me down to earth, what gives me weight when sleep or distraction has all but removed me from my body: falling out of bed the night my sister did too and broke her collar bone; tripping on an acorn and scarring my knee; the tingly feeling of a fever. When I realize my sexuality, I am replaying that physical discovery that began with belly buttons and wrists.

Bodily weight can become symbolic and spiritual. In an Eastern Religions class, I learned how Buddhist writings merge the idea of physical temporality with nirvana. They embrace the body in its ability to experience pleasure, but also believe that pleasure to be far from the enlightenment experience that can be reached only by divorcing the self from the body. In The Unbearable Lightness of Being, Milan Kundera discusses the relationship of body and soul through his character Tereza, who stares at herself in the mirror in the hopes of seeing her soul show itself in her body. Her body becomes a way to keep anonymity at bay. The physical is what keeps us near the ground and nearer to ourselves. 11

Coming to terms with my body and my relationship to it means considering my hands. I try to see myself in them. I am a heavily left-handed lefty, and my left hand has very dry skin that cracks in the winter and gets red in the summer. I am very self-conscious about my hands, but also very proud of how used and unkempt my left hand looks—the leathery writer's bump, the guitar calluses, the nails cut below the quick. 12

As a feminist and inheritor of Betty Friedan's philosophy of womanhood, I wonder if her ideology dictates that I should separate my mind from my body, believe that my anatomy is neither my destiny nor an essential part of my identity. But I need to know my body to understand where exactly I live, to consider it the basis of my identity for no other reason than that the physical is the first and last thing I will know. 13

In elementary school, I was often asked what my favorite place in the world is. We don't associate our bodies as a place because it is the ultimate mobile home, the place we cannot leave. But when we have nowhere else to go, the body is our being's only shelter. I seek to understand that body enough to know that it has enough spiritual weight and pulsation not to float away. 14

WORKS CITED

de Beauvoir, Simone. *The Second Sex*. New York: Alfred A. Knopf, 1953.

Friedan, Betty. *The Feminine Mystique*. New York: Bantam Doubleday Dell Publishing Group, 1983.

Kundera, Milan. *The Unbearable Lightness of Being*. New York: Harper & Row, 1984.

Working with the Text

1. In "The Gravity of Pink," Trooboff plays with the term "gravity" in several ways and uses the idea of weight and weightlessness metaphorically as well as literally. How does her use of gravity and weight contribute to her meaning about her sense of self? How does she link the idea of weight and weightlessness to a feeling of control?

2. Trooboff says that "physical memories seem the oldest to me." But are her memories strictly physical? Can you clearly separate the border between the physical and the emotional in her essay?

3. How do you respond to her depiction of her body as a place, or even a home? In what ways do you think of your body as a place you inhabit?

4. Explore the ways that a sense of control or loss of control is tied to gender roles in this essay. How are boundaries of personal space, touch, and control scripted into our environments as matters of social convention? To what extent, for example, is identity constructed in part by a sense of one's "weightlessness," or conventions of interaction?

Mother Tongue

AMY TAN

Chinese American novelist Amy Tan is the author of two best-selling novels: *The Joy Luck Club*, which was made into a motion picture directed by Wayne Wang, and *The Kitchen God's Wife* (1991). "Mother Tongue" first appeared in *The Threepenny Review* (1990), and was selected for *The Best American Essays 1991*. In the essay Tan describes living with a private "English" at home and a "different English" in public, an experience that she feels was creatively enabling to her as a writer.

I am not a scholar of English or literature. I cannot give you much more than   1
personal opinions on the English language and its variations in this country
or others.

I am a writer. And by that definition, I am someone who has always   2
loved language. I am fascinated by language in daily life. I spend a great
deal of my time thinking about the power of language—the way it can

evoke an emotion, a visual image, a complex idea, or a simple truth. Language is the tool of my trade. And I use them all—all the Englishes I grew up with.

Recently, I was made keenly aware of the different Englishes I do use. I was giving a talk to a large group of people, the same talk I had already given to half a dozen other groups. The nature of the talk was about my writing, my life, and my book, *The Joy Luck Club*. The talk was going along well enough, until I remembered one major difference that made the whole talk sound wrong. My mother was in the room. And it was perhaps the first time she had heard me give a lengthy speech, using the kind of English I have never used with her. I was saying things like, "The intersection of memory upon imagination" and "There is an aspect of my fiction that relates to thus-and-thus"—a speech filled with carefully wrought grammatical phrases, burdened, it suddenly seemed to me, with nominalized forms, past perfect tenses, conditional phrases, all the forms of standard English that I had learned in school and through books, the forms of English I did not use at home with my mother.

Just last week, I was walking down the street with my mother, and I again found myself conscious of the English I was using, the English I do use with her. We were talking about the price of new and used furniture and I heard myself saying this: "Not waste money that way." My husband was with us as well, and he didn't notice any switch in my English. And then I realized why. It's because over the twenty years we've been together I've often used that same kind of English with him, and sometimes he even uses it with me. It has become our language of intimacy, a different sort of English that relates to family talk, the language I grew up with.

So you'll have some idea of what this family talk I heard sounds like, I'll quote what my mother said during a recent conversation which I videotaped and then transcribed. During this conversation, my mother was talking about a political gangster in Shanghai who had the same last name as her family's, Du, and how the gangster in his early years wanted to be adopted by her family, which was rich by comparison. Later, the gangster became more powerful, far richer than my mother's family, and one day showed up at my mother's wedding to pay his respects. Here's what she said in part:

"Du Yusong having business like fruit stand. Like off the street kind. He is Du like Du Zong—but not Tsung-ming Island people. The local people call putong, the river east side, he belong to that side local people. That man want to ask Du Zong father take him in like become own family. Du Zong father wasn't look down on him, but didn't take seriously, until that man big like become a mafia. Now important person, very hard to inviting him. Chinese way, came only to show respect, don't stay for dinner. Respect for making big celebration, he shows up. Mean gives lots of respect. Chinese custom. Chinese social life that way. If too important won't have to stay too long. He come to my wedding. I didn't see, I heard it. I gone to boy's side, they have YMCA dinner. Chinese age I was nineteen."

You should know that my mother's expressive command of English be-   7
lies how much she actually understands. She reads the *Forbes* report, listens to *Wall Street Week,* converses daily with her stockbroker, reads all of Shirley MacLaine's books with ease—all kinds of things I can't begin to understand. Yet some of my friends tell me they understand 50 percent of what my mother says. Some say they understand 80 to 90 percent. Some say they understand none of it, as if she were speaking pure Chinese. But to me, my mother's English is perfectly clear, perfectly natural. It's my mother tongue. Her language, as I hear it, is vivid, direct, full of observation and imagery. That was the language that helped shape the way I saw things, expressed things, made sense of the world.

Lately, I've been giving more thought to the kind of English my mother   8
speaks. Like others, I have described it to people as "broken" or "fractured" English. But I wince when I say that. It has always bothered me that I can think of no way to describe it other than "broken," as if it were damaged and needed to be fixed, as if it lacked a certain wholeness and soundness. I've heard other terms used, "limited English," for example. But they seem just as bad, as if everything is limited, including people's perceptions of the limited English speaker.

I know this for a fact, because when I was growing up, my mother's   9
"limited" English limited *my* perception of her. I was ashamed of her English. I believed that her English reflected the quality of what she had to say. That is, because she expressed them imperfectly her thoughts were imperfect. And I had plenty of empirical evidence to support me: the fact that people in department stores, at banks, and at restaurants did not take her seriously, did not give her good service, pretended not to understand her, or even acted as if they did not hear her.

My mother has long realized the limitations of her English as well. When   10
I was fifteen, she used to have me call people on the phone to pretend I was she. In this guise, I was forced to ask for information or even to complain and yell at people who had been rude to her. One time it was a call to her stockbroker in New York. She had cashed out her small portfolio and it just so happened we were going to go to New York the next week, our very first trip outside California. I had to get on the phone and say in an adolescent voice that was not very convincing, "This is Mrs. Tan."

And my mother was standing in the back whispering loudly, "Why he   11
don't send me check, already two weeks late. So mad he lie to me, losing me money."

And then I said in perfect English, "Yes, I'm getting rather concerned. You had agreed to send the check two weeks ago, but it hasn't arrived." 12

Then she began to talk more loudly. "What he want, I come to New York tell him front of his boss, you cheating me?" And I was trying to calm her down, make her be quiet, while telling the stockbroker, "I can't tolerate any more excuses. If I don't receive the check immediately, I am going to have to speak to your manager when I'm in New York next week." And sure enough, the following week there we were in front of this astonished stockbroker, and I was sitting there red-faced and quiet, and my mother, the real Mrs. Tan, was shouting at his boss in her impeccable broken English. 13

We used a similar routine just five days ago, for a situation that was far less humorous. My mother had gone to the hospital for an appointment, to find out about a benign brain tumor a CAT scan had revealed a month ago. She said she had spoken very good English, her best English, no mistakes. Still, she said, the hospital did not apologize when they said they had lost the CAT scan and she had come for nothing. She said they did not seem to have any sympathy when she told them she was anxious to know the exact diagnosis, since her husband and son had both died of brain tumors. She said they would not give her any more information until the next time and she would have to make another appointment for that. So she said she would not leave until the doctor called her daughter. She wouldn't budge. And when the doctor finally called her daughter, me, who spoke in perfect English—lo and behold—we had assurances the CAT scan would be found, promises that a conference call on Monday would be held, and apologies for any suffering my mother had gone through for a most regrettable mistake. 14

I think my mother's English almost had an effect on limiting my possibilities in life as well. Sociologists and linguists probably will tell you that a person's developing language skills are more influenced by peers. But I do think that the language spoken in the family, especially in immigrant families which are more insular, plays a large role in shaping the language of the child. And I believe that it affected my results on achievement tests, IQ tests, and the SAT. While my English skills were never judged as poor, compared to math, English could not be considered my strong suit. In grade school I did moderately well, getting perhaps B's, sometimes B-pluses, in English and scoring perhaps in the sixtieth or seventieth percentile on achievement tests. But those scores were not good enough to override the opinion that my true abilities lay in math and science, because in those areas I achieved A's and scored in the ninetieth percentile or higher. 15

This was understandable. Math is precise; there is only one correct answer. Whereas, for me at least, the answers on English tests were always a judgment call, a matter of opinion and personal experience. Those tests 16 were constructed around items like fill-in-the-blank sentence completion, such as, "Even though Tom was———, Mary thought he was———." And the correct answer always seemed to be the most bland combinations of thoughts, for example, "Even though Tom was shy, Mary thought he was charming," with the grammatical structure "even though" limiting the correct answer to some sort of semantic opposites, so you wouldn't get answers like, "Even though Tom was foolish, Mary thought he was ridiculous." Well, according to my mother, there were very few limitations as to what Tom could have been and what Mary might have thought of him. So I never did well on tests like that.

The same was true with word analogies, pairs of words in which you were supposed to find some sort of logical, semantic relationship—for example, "*Sunset* is to *nightfall* as——— is to———." And here you would be presented with a list of four possible pairs, one of which showed the same kind of relationship: *red* is to *stoplight, bus* is to *arrival, chills* is to *fever, yawn* is to *boring.* Well, I could never think that way. I knew what the tests were asking, but I could not block out of my mind the images already created by the first pair, "*sunset* is to *nightfall*"—and I would see a burst of colors against a darkening sky, the moon rising, the lowering of a curtain of stars. And all the other pairs of words—red, bus, stoplight, boring—just threw up a mass of confusing images, making it impossible for me to sort out something as logical as saying: "A sunset precedes nightfall" is the same as "a chill precedes a fever." The only way I would have gotten that answer right would have been to imagine an associative situation, for example, my being disobedient and staying out past sunset, catching a chill at night, which turns into feverish pneumonia as punishment, which indeed did happen to me.

I have been thinking about all this lately, about my mother's English, about achievement tests. Because lately I've been asked, as a writer, why there are not more Asian Americans represented in American literature. Why are there few Asian Americans enrolled in creative writing programs? Why do so many Chinese students go into engineering? Well, these are broad sociological questions I can't begin to answer. But I have noticed in surveys—in fact, just last week—that Asian students, as a whole, always do significantly better on math achievement tests than in English. And this makes me think that there are other Asian-American students whose English spoken in the home might also be described as "broken" or "limited." And perhaps they also have teachers who are steering them away from writing and into math and science, which is what happened to me.

Fortunately, I happen to be rebellious in nature and enjoy the challenge of disproving assumptions made about me. I became an English major my first year in college, after being enrolled as pre-med. I started writing nonfiction as a freelancer the week after I was told by my former boss that writing was my worst skill and I should hone my talents toward account management.

But it wasn't until 1985 that I finally began to write fiction. And at first I wrote using what I thought to be wittily crafted sentences, sentences that would finally prove I had mastery over the English language. Here's an example from the first draft of a story that later made its way into *The Joy Luck Club,* but without this line: "That was my mental quandary in its nascent state." A terrible line, which I can barely pronounce. [20]

Fortunately, for reasons I won't get into today, I later decided I should envision a reader for the stories I would write. And the reader I decided upon was my mother, because these were stories about mothers. So with this reader in mind—and in fact she did read my early drafts—I began to write stories using all the Englishes I grew up with: the English I spoke to my mother, which for lack of a better term might be described as "simple"; the English she used with me, which for lack of a better term might be described as "broken"; my translation of her Chinese, which could certainly be described as "watered down"; and what I imagined to be her translation of her Chinese if she could speak in perfect English, her internal language, and for that I sought to preserve the essence, but neither an English nor a Chinese structure. I wanted to capture what language ability tests can never reveal: her intent, her passion, her imagery, the rhythms of her speech and the nature of her thoughts. [21]

Apart from what any critic had to say about my writing, I knew I had succeeded where it counted when my mother finished reading my book and gave me her verdict: "So easy to read." [22]

Working with the Text

1. Describe the various "Englishes" that Amy Tan grew up with and later adapted for fiction. Which of these does she use in "Mother Tongue"? What are the powers and resources of each? Why does she call her mother's English "limited," and how does she complicate the notion of limitation in language?

2. In what ways does "Mother Tongue" link language, culture, and perception? How does language mark cultural difference? How does language mark social bonds?

3. Why was Tan pleased when her mother pronounced her first novel "So easy to read"? Why, earlier, did her mother's presence make Tan "keenly aware of the different Englishes" she uses? What is the role of the audience in understanding how language functions?

4. Why do you suppose Tan cut the sentence, "That was my mental quandary in its nascent state," from an early draft of what would become *The Joy Luck Club?* Describe the language of that sentence, and speculate about the authorial identity that it helps to create. Then compare it to the following sentences: "Not waste money that way"; "Even though Tom was shy, Mary thought he was charming"; and "Fortunately, I happen to be rebellious in nature and enjoy the challenge of disproving assumptions made about me." Which stylistic features mark identity most strongly?

5. Choose one of the following means of studying the "Englishes" you are immersed in. (1) Observe and record the different ways that you speak and write over the course of a single day, noting specific sentences characteristic of each. How does your language vary? What roles do medium, setting, purpose, and audience play? (2) Observe and record differences among speakers in a single setting, such as a café. Note how these differences produce different responses among listeners. (3) Observe and record differences among writers in an Internet setting such as a newsgroup, listserv, or chat room. What role do modes of expression play in marking inclusion and exclusion online?

The Begenning of the End

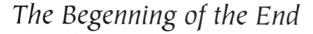

JIM MINCE

Jim Mince is a day laborer and self-described "Willy Nelson look-alike" who plays the guitar and sings. He wrote the following essay while a resident at Matthew 25, a short-term facility for homeless men in Nashville, Tennessee. The essay became part of a collection of homeless people's writings entitled *An American Mosaic: Prose and Poetry by Everyday Folk,* edited by Robert Wolf. Wolf explains that because Mince spoke with a Texas accent and spelled phonetically, his spelling was left intact in order to provide readers with an idea of Mince's speech.

An American Mosaic

ROBERT WOLF, ED.

In China recently there was supposed to be a gathering of students and scol-   1
lars. They gathered to protest the way the government was being run. They
wonted to see a better government. They were for democracy.

The government let them have the meeting, then when things were in   2
full swing, the government sent troops in, killing and mutulating hundreads.
They had obsurvers, so that later they could round up the ring leaders. Education is good, but this is what they ment when they said a little nollage
can be dangerous.

I have been in Nashville little over a year. I came here to see what I   3
could do with my songs. Shortley after I arrived my truck was stolen along
with ever thing else I owned. So I was forced to live on the street. Being a
construction worker and having a good traid, most of what I had saw in life
was the good life. I never saw people haf to stand in doorways to stay out
of the rain, or sleep under vidock's on hard concreat, some time with cord-
bord under them to keep the cold of the concreat from coming through. Get
up at five in the morning to go to the mission for breekfest and by six go to
the labor sourse to be sent out on all sorts of jobs from carring sheat rock to
shingles at a meager wage of three thirty-five. And then only three to four
days a week. How in heaven's name dose suciety expect these people to get
off the street? They don't. This world is ruled by five percent.

When I grew up, times were good. If you would work it didn't take long   4
to get ahead. And I have been up and down the hill a couple times so I can't
complain. I look around and see the drunks on Broadway and from time to
time I've found myself down there. Now these people in the barrooms, that
I talk to, some run a scam while others tell the trooth.

I beleave in God and Christ and from the turn of events that put me on   5
the street I beleave I was ment to see theas things. And I try my best to stand
for what is right.

I am now fifty years old and God has been good to me. Hard work and   6
persurverance has kept me strong, and on my fiftieth birthday I climbed
over the peek of the Ryman Auditorium. And I'm grateful to God to feel
this good.

But what I've seen and hurd since I hit Nashville hurts a body way down   7
deep inside. I was drinking beer one night at Nashburl last fall when a man
I never met came up to me. He told me how he had contracted agent orange while in Viet Naum and that he was dying.

I bought him a drink and stood up and drank to him. As we left the bar   8
a cop car came up. And two cops jumped out. He was only about eight to

ten feet ahead of me and before I knew it they had his hands behind him and had hit him on the right side of the fore head three times.

At this I stepped up and told the cops that I had just gotten out of jail an   9
didn't wont to go back again. But if they hit him one moor time they were going to give me a reason to do so. I also told them if that be the case they had better call for some back up.

At that they arested him and took him to the hospital. Another man that   10
was with us let me sleep in the back of his pick up that night. And when I woke up the next day he brought me back to town. I went up to the mission and there I met the man who had been beet up. And he invitet me out to his brothers house, gave me a sheep skin vest and three pair of cordoroy britches. I had a nice hot bath, and a large soft bed to sleep in that night.

And shortley after that the cops beet a man so suverely that he died in   11
the hospital that night, so I was told. I talked to men on the street who said that the cops had his hands behind his back before they ever started beating him. It don't take much to figure out who was right.

So one week after New Yeres I walked up to the mission some time   12
shortley after ten. I had been drinking and the administrator told me I was bared for life. I've been back since so I guess that waren't true. I had saw men come in to the mission with a countinance that gload. A smile and how you doing coming from them. And they stay a month or to for meager wages. I'm talking five bucks a week or less.

Then they hit Broadway one night for a laff or two. Well they mess up,   13
and the mission kicks them out. Theas same men I've saw mope around like zombies.

So when I was told that I was barred for life I said, Then I might as well   14
nock your head off. I went through the door and hit the man in the nose.

At that a large black man who I had no quarrel with came at me. Not   15
really wanting to hurt him, for I knew he didn't know the reason, I through a punch and hit him in the chest. He picked me up and through me through the door. And as I hit the wall on the other side I saw three cop cars pull up. I scrambled to my feet and hit the side walk. Two cops stood three feet in frunt of me.

They had there sticks helt high and were waring green wool sweaters.   16
The one on my left said run for it. At that I replied I'm not running. But I knew at the best I was in for a whopping. And I said the hell I won't and headed down the hill.

When I got to where the red cross sign was across from salvacion army   17
I turned a bit to find out where they were. A club hit me across the throat and well I hit the ground. They hit me across the throat one moor time.

I balled up and prayed Lord forgive then for they don't know what they do. Thinking they had done there job, they put there handcuffs on me. And then I lay in jail tell the next morning. 18

The charge was short and simple. I was charged with staggering outside the mission. And a man came by the drunk tank and said plead guilty and youl be releasead. Thinking what they might do if I spent a week in there I pleadead guilty to the charge. 19

Now I'm a working man and I eurn my money. I don't steel and I don't cheat. But I had goten off from work at the Ryman. And as I started up the hill at Fift and Broadway I met a friend who said let's have a beer. We were setting in the Turf just he and I. At a table right next to the door. At six thirty a cop came in placed his self about twenty feet from where I sat and comminsed to stare at me. Well I stared back. And after a few seconds he pointed toward the door. 20

Well he arrested me. No rights did he read. So I set in a van on Broadway for a while. Now I don't thank the cop was bad, but I was mad so I pissed right in his van down on Broadway. They took us all to jail. And he said he still like me. Even though I pissed right in his van. 21

It was turist season and he had his orders. Arrest any one that looks supicious. Now how high up theas orders came I do not know. But the charges all seem to be the same thing, drunk. 22

The next day was a work day and I should have been at work by seven. Scared I might loose my job I pleadead guilty. They releasead me. And I was back down at the job by ten. 23

Now the night of the Summer Lights came around. And I was staying with some frinds at Tooter Inn. And they had all took off earley. And I was by my self. 24

So I desidead to check out the Summer Lights. I had barely got up town. And I started across the street when a car hit me in the left leg just below the crouch. It threw me across the hood onto the windshield. And I rolled on to the side walk on my back. It seamed like just seconds tell the ambulance arrived and the cops were standing over me. The driver was a young man with his girlfriend. From the way he shook, I knew that he was scared. 25

So I checked out all my limbs and I knew that they weren't broken. And I told the cops to let him go, it was my falt. 26

So instead of letting me go they wontead to arrest me. So I said take me to the hospittle. When I arrived at the hospittal I was met by theas same cops, who said with a smurk, You mean you took up an ambulance when some one could have been dying. When they get done with you, well get you yet. 27

I gave the reseptionest my name. And when she went in to the back I 28
looked around and they were gone. So I got outside the door. And the closest thing I saw where I could hide was a dompster. So I spent the night in
there and walked back to town the next day.

I didn't work Monday or Tuesday. For I was in no shape to clime 29
the hights.

This land was built on freedom and liberty and justice for all. Like the 30
people over in China, I wonder where it went when so few can tell so
menny what to do.

If a person's doing rong then arrest him. But don't arrest a man cause he 31
wares a red bandanna, or because of what you think that he might do.
He must do the crime before he dose the time, or let me ask you, is this little China?

The last thing I have to say is about a friend of mine I asked to hold a 32
couple hundread bucks. He went out to find some grass and they cought
him with a couple of dime bags. Now he had my money and two week's
wages of his owne. So he spent two weeks in jail on suspission of dealing.

Now he has to go to court to prove his innosence of a charge that 33
should not have been to begin with. Let liberty prevail. And keep us out of
jail and who know we might be suciety to.

Working with the Text

1. Mince begins his essay by invoking the Tien An Men Square massacre
   of 1989, in which government troops attacked unarmed demonstrators,
   and closes it by asking whether the Nashville streets are "little China."
   Why does he frame the essay with such a comparison? What does China
   represent in the essay, and what views of the world are adumbrated in
   the comparison?

2. "I try my best to stand for what is right," says the author. What does he
   mean by that assertion? Does it apply more to personal conduct or to
   social policy? What is the relationship between these two domains, in
   the essay?

3. For those who suffer it, homelessness redraws the border between
   private and public space, often to the point of nearly annihilating
   the private. How does the geography of Mince's essay reflect this
   altered border?

4. The author's religious faith informs his narration at many points, never
   more than when he is clubbed by police outside the mission that has
   ejected him. Quoting Jesus Christ as he is crucified, Mince prays, "Lord
   forgive then for they don't know what they do." What is the effect of
   this citation? How does it influence our perception of the narrator and

the story he tells? What events at the mission either enhance or perturb the allusion?

5. Write a short account of an altercation you either witnessed or helped cause. The dispute need not be physical or heated; any clash of wills should suffice. As you are writing, try to spell some of the words phonetically. Put the account away for a day or two, then reread it, reflecting upon how the altered spelling affects your narrative. Write an additional paragraph describing the effects.

Runaway: Diary of a Street Kid

EVELYN LAU

Asian Canadian author Evelyn Lau was born in Vancouver in 1971. She is the youngest author ever to be shortlisted for the Governor General's Award for poetry. She has written several volumes of stories, including *Choose Me* and *Fresh Girls* (1993), poetry—*In the House of Slaves* and *Oedipal Dreams*—and the novel *Other Women* (1995). Her work explores the disturbing and often brutal relations between men and women, and the abuses of urban life. Her first published work, *Runaway* (1989), is her disturbing memoir of having left the home of her strict Chinese immigrant parents at the age of fourteen only to find drugs, sexual violence, and misery on the streets of Vancouver. While living on the streets for two years Lau kept a journal detailing her experiences. In it Lau at times struggles to differentiate herself from the "other" drug addicts, prostitutes, and teenage runaways, hoping that her writing will help her create a new sense of self. At other times, seeing herself as the "same" as the others, she experiences devastating bouts of uncertainty and depression. A similar sense of ambivalence and incertitude underlies her sense of place. Lau seems to run both "to" the city of Vancouver and "away" from it, unsure why she is running, where she is going *to,* and what exactly she is running *away* from.

Runaway: Diary of a Street Kid

MINERVA, 1996

September 20

Sitting again in the Dairy Queen, one of the few places in Calgary open for twenty-four hours, watching the hands of the clock creep towards midnight. I'm exhausted. Isn't the night going to end? It can't be even midnight yet. Tomorrow it'll be six months since I left home, and here I am waiting in the Dairy Queen for morning to come, yet realizing that it won't bring safety or shelter. It won't bring warmth.

My brain doesn't feel capable of functioning anymore. I'm scared. The streets are empty and black, and police cars comb the downtown area. Afraid of the aloneness, needing someone, somewhere. Afraid of getting caught. I miss Dr. Graham's jewels of eyes instilling strength, Dr. Hightower's good-natured chuckle spreading warmth.

There's just all this sadness, pulling me down and away from hope. Oh God, this can't be happening to me, can it? Too much pride and no money.

September 21

Autumn was sneaking into Calgary, breathing lemon over the trees, scattering carpets of leaves over the pavement. I walked and walked. Midnight found me shivering and trying to stay awake in a restaurant about to close. Two men came in and sat down near me, so I went over and asked if they knew which bus would take me to Emergency Services. They glanced at each other, chuckling—they were cab drivers, and offered me a free ride if I wanted to sit around while they had dinner. I joined them and we started talking. I didn't go into my background but admitted I needed a place to stay. This startled Henry into ruminating about times when he'd been poor and people had gone out of their way to help—a hippie had taken him in and dispensed bowls of Trail Mix; a hotel manager had given him a room for two nights out of the storm and made him meals. He looked thoughtful. I sighed and promised myself not to be drawn like a magnet back to the warmth of the YWCA. The workers there had made it clear that I should 'shit or get off the pot.' 'Sometimes you have to be cruel to be kind,' Sparky had stated bluntly, stubbing out another cigarette.

We got into Henrys friend's cab and began driving towards Emergency Services. Henry lifted the curtain of darkness by turning towards me suddenly, the street lamps illuminating his face, and saying, 'I wasn't sure before, but I'm going to take you home for a few days. It'll be my way of paying those guys back.'

I was really grateful—a bed! Sleep. Yes, there must be a God up there, 6
looking after His kids. I was going to be safe.

The driver turned dubiously to Henry and asked if he really wanted to 7
do this; he nodded resolutely. They began talking about where they could
pick up some drugs, waving to several guys hanging outside a convenience
store. Henry motioned me into his car, an old cab, parked in the lot. His friend
rolled down his window and regarded me with big, serious brown eyes.

'Henry is a very good friend of mine, and I'm sure you'll be safe with 8
him. But if anything goes wrong, talk to me about it, okay?'

I would have dropped to my knees right there and thanked God, except 9
then I would probably have fallen asleep.

Henry was a different person when we drove home together. He had 10
problems that were making him angry, but he wouldn't talk about them, de-
spising people who unburdened themselves on others. So instead we talked
about drugs—he dropped acid once or twice a year, snorted coke at Christmas, but drank and smoked pot and took downers a lot. Drugs had, I felt certain, fallen into their appropriate place in my life—as recreation, not escape.

Henry lived alone in a cluttered basement suite—Kurt Vonnegut novels 11
were piled high on the floor, and cereal boxes spilled their contents onto the
carpet. He pulled out the Hide-Away bed, switched on the radio, and
speeded off to work. I unpacked some of my clothes and sank into bed, into
a sleep undisturbed by dreams, waking only once. I was safe, safe!

Henry was shaking me at eight the next morning, after five hours of 12
sleep. Pouting, I rolled over and attempted to hide under the pillow, but he
was adamant.

'Get up! We're going out to look for a job for you.' 13

I crept reluctantly out of bed and splashed cold water on my face. Henry 14
was hovering restlessly around; actually, it's pretty hard to describe a man
over six feet and weighing two hundred pounds as 'hovering' anywhere.
Henry was smoking, drinking coffee and combing the Classifieds, flexing his
enormous muscles. Not somebody you'd pick a fight with. He waited for me
to get ready, pacing.

Our first stop was Manpower. While he went to the bar for 'a few 15
drinks,' I collected the necessary info for a birth certificate and SIN card and
jotted down job possibilities from the bulletin boards. We met at the bar,
where he was sitting by the window, gulping rye and beer. We sat there
until he ran out of money, drinking and getting to know each other. The
alcohol haze took the sharp edges away. We argued about politics—the theory of anarchism, white supremacy, poverty. When we started on the topic
of suicide, Henry shoved his big, tanned arms onto the table. Both wrists
and most of the lower arms were badly scarred. I stared out the window.

Our next stop was a youth employment center, where I made an appointment. Henry and I went back home, smoked hash and got more money for booze. After the appointment, I found him in a strip joint. Center stage was illuminated by scarlet spotlights; a naked woman gyrated to the music, sucking her breasts, spreading her legs. I shrugged, chalked it up as another experience and wove around the tables looking for Henry, finding him very drunk and depressed. He was singing loudly and smacking the tabletop, but he wouldn't talk about what was bothering him (at least it wasn't me). 16

The naked woman sprawled across the stage, holding out her breasts to the whistling men, arching and strutting, doing splits and spread-legged rolls. I wondered if she felt soiled, and wanted helplessly to change things. 17

As another girl, a blonde in glittering pink mini, high heels and tight blouse, began twirling and caressing herself, Henry growled in a slurred voice, 'Let's split,' and somehow he managed to drive us home. 18

September 23

Today is Tuesday. After we came home from the strip joint yesterday afternoon, Henry and I both went to sleep—the racket the people upstairs were making woke me up less than an hour later. Henry had set his alarm for 7:30 P.M.; when it rang for five minutes, I went in and set it to ring again in five minutes. I did this half a dozen times, asking him each time if he were awake, whereupon he'd murmur 'yes' and then be dead to the world. Realizing the clock wouldn't work, I alternated between talking to Henry, shaking him, and threatening to turn on the lights—in short, playing the role of too-nice group home parent or something. I was really trying. I spent an hour and a half attempting to wake him up—after all, he'd helped me. 19

Unexpectedly, a pissed-off man came stumbling out of bed at 9:00, claiming that it was my fault that he hadn't gotten up at 7:30 in time to buy dope from his friend before going to work. We got into an argument. I was hurt, but count on yours truly to end up apologizing and inviting Henry to share his feelings. He marveled at how he could kill me with one punch, then spun around and went back to bed. 20

This morning Henry kicked me out. I thanked him for the two nights over, said I understood and left. 21

Evelyn, you bitch. One thing's for sure: I'm not going to be nice like that again. 22

The Emergency Services worker blew his chance. He accused me of being paranoid about trusting him, then went right ahead and called my parents. He also filed a Missing Persons. No more understanding or empathy. 23

Henry. You think that pot is going to help me forget? (You knew, though, didn't you, that I would just toke and smile and say, I understand.) You know something, I liked you a lot. I liked your voracious reading, your 24 brilliant memory, your honesty. I liked your showing me the scars on your wrists, and your drinking that made you vulnerable. I liked how you looked like a teddy bear in your mustard-colored sweater, how you looked responsible, fatherly and strong.

I came to Calgary searching for something better but found the same things happening over again. I felt surprisingly close to someone, and was essentially laughed at. God, I feel like shit. Henry, I hate you for what you promised and then grabbed back. I hate you for pretending to be Mr. Macho Rescuer and then turfing me out on the streets. I grew very fond of you in two days, maybe because under that huge frame of yours you were a baby needing affection and were afraid to admit that yes, you had a drinking problem; yes, just because you could put a guy in hospital for six months didn't mean you couldn't be hurt.   25

I went to the Food Bank after two days without food, hating myself for it. Hated sharing a table with a block of moldy cheese, swatting away half a dozen flies. How could people set up a food bank in an unheated, boarded-up old store with shelves packed with bags of food spilling onto the floor and still pretend to care about the broken people shuffling through its doors? What kind of respect is that?   26

September 25

I was clear on just one thing: going home to Vancouver. It wasn't a matter of failure or losing face anymore. Aside from the Food Bank stint, I hadn't eaten for days, or slept properly either. And I was very cold. The cold seemed to have seeped through my flesh and be residing gleefully inside. I'd bottomed out.   27

The next morning I went to a drop-in center. I managed to march in without running into the walls, set down my bags and proclaim loudly, 'I need a place to sleep. Don't tell me you can't do anything—I'm going to sleep now.' Go ahead, bastards, call the cops, do anything you want. I added to the threat by surveying the dirty floor with lascivious eyes.   28

The staff immediately brought in a counsellor, and the kitchen people hustled in tea, coffee and sandwiches. After listening to my story, the counsellor called in a minister connected with a group home for prostitutes. The minister was a cute little man, improbable in black preacher's clothes, with hair that frizzled below his shoulders. He was impatient with my story (I was rambling by now) but asked a lot of questions, mostly about drugs. The counsellor said how one of the girls she'd been seeing had a pimp who told her to do something she didn't want to; when she refused, he went straight for her face, slicing diagonally from left to right from cheekbone to chin.   29

The minister decided to drive me to the group home. We went out into the main dining area of the drop-in, where over a hundred people, mostly   30 men, sprawled around tables eating handouts. They had stringy hair and bloated faces, puffed bodies huddled in someone else's discarded clothing. I would have reached out to them if things had been different . . .

On the way the minister had to stop at a hospital to pray over a dying man; in the meantime I slept in the back seat of his car. He picked up the counsellor—when they got into the car they said I'd been talking in my sleep and had asked one clear, urgent question: 'Are we in Vancouver yet?' They thought it was funny, but I needed to go home. Rising out of sleep, discovering that it was still Calgary, I felt depression drop its cloak over me.   31

The group home, which had been in operation for only a few months, was in an old house that had been boarded up and had furniture collecting dust on its sagging porch, The daytime staff person (whom I later learned with astonishment was a volunteer), immediately gave me a hug, surprising me so much that I stumbled against him, extricating myself as soon as possible. I wanted a goddamn bed, not love or understanding.   32

The worker and I had a meeting in the living room, with the minister and the counsellor in attendance. I tried to make it clear from the start that I hadn't come here to live, just to sleep for the night, but the worker wouldn't accept that. Neither would the minister or the counsellor. More questions, then the girls who lived in the house filtered in. They hugged and kissed the worker, said 'I love you' to him and did the same to each other.   33

My jaw must have dropped a foot. The worker sat very close to me and explained that the home was run on love and spirituality—genuine rather than physical love, which had often led to pain for the girls. In answer to this I shrank into my corner of the couch, wrapped my arms around myself and stared. It had to be a put-on. A Jamaican girl in tight jeans climbed right on top of the worker and began hugging and stroking him.   34

The minister looked at his watch. He had offered to lend me the money for the bus ticket, 'if that's what you really want,' and the bus to Vancouver was leaving soon. The girls were sprawled all over the living room, on the couches, on the floor, comforting each other, asking me to stay. The minister watched with his liquid brown eyes; the worker squeezed my shoulder.   35

A native Indian with faintly simian features who was twenty-one but looked no older than sixteen motioned me to her and pleaded with me to stay.   36

'Come on, just try this place for a few days,' she offered, her brown eyes growing serious. The worker had described her as the life of the house, but she was quiet now. Panic gripped me and wouldn't let go. A voice droned: THIS IS YOUR CHANCE AT HAPPINESS. TAKE IT, EVELYN. Months ago these same kids had been prostitutes with pimps, getting knifed and beaten up. Months ago they had been angry and unreachable . . .   37

GO BACK, EVELYN, TO WHERE YOU BELONG. GO BACK TO VANCOUVER, WHERE YOU   38
CAN GET ALL THE ACID YOU WANT; GO BACK TO THE STREETS, GO BACK TO TRYING TO
KILL YOURSELF AGAIN. WHAT HAVE YOU DONE TO DESERVE THIS LOVE? IT'S TOO GOOD
TO BE TRUE. BE STRONG, EVELYN—YOU CAN DO IT ON YOUR OWN.

I shook my head. The worker's eyes sank into holes above his check-   39
bones and suddenly he looked very tired. The light faded from the minister's face. The counsellor simply looked pissed off. I felt somehow as if I'd
failed, as we climbed into her car and the native Indian girl stood alone on
the porch, waving to me.

We drove to the bus depot in silence. Then, standing in line for the bus,   40
I turned back to the minister. 'Why do you think I've failed?'

He didn't smile or anything, just said, 'Maybe the girl made you feel that   41
way. Maybe she knew what was in store for you—working the streets—and
that's why she looked so sad. She's got knife scars all over her, and . . . well,
she doesn't tell many people this, but she's got a bullet mark on her too,
from working downtown.'

Then he and the counsellor were gone and I was standing there hold-   42
ing my ticket and feeling more dead than ever.

You complain of being betrayed, Evelyn. You claim that Calgary is a   43
write-off because people turned you in, disappointed you, failed you. How
many people have you disappointed? Think about that, for once.

Reality is tough, isn't it?   44

So here I am, back in Vancouver—where's all the wonderful things you   45
claimed to be coming back to, Evelyn? I don't see you rushing to the youth
newspaper house, or giving your beloved doctors a call—instead, you're sitting penniless in a library, considering going to the Hare Krishnas for dinner
and a bed to sleep in, after a day spent hunting for a meaningless and elusive job. What was it that the group home worker had said? 'I can just
see you in five or ten years. You'll be a bag lady, wandering the streets.' At
the time I'd scoffed, but just because I'm not pushing a shopping cart, what's
the difference?

The world catches a person by surprise . . . No, Evelyn, that's not right.   46
You knew what was going to happen all along, didn't you?

Working with the Text

1. One essential feature of life as a runaway is the need to keep moving,
   if only because offers of charity are often limited in scope or attached
   to unacceptable conditions. How does Lau's continual movement
   shape her sense of geography? Where are the borders in her world?
   What communities, values, beliefs, ideals come together there? How

does the young Lau—and the people she meets during her travels—
negotiate the conflicts that arise at these borders?

2. Why does Lau refuse the invitation of the group home in Calgary?
What does her refusal suggest about how institutional refuge is
perceived by runaways? Do you see implications for social policy in
her refusal?

3. Atop the hierarchy of needs that Lau describes is sleep, more precious
even than food, also in short supply. Though the value of sleep to one
without a secure bed may seem obvious, in Lau's journal sleep takes
on additional importance and, occasionally, symbolic value. How
does sleep express identity in Lau's writing? What is its relationship
to related states of consciousness? To wakefulness? What is the significance of her loudly proclaiming "I'm going to sleep now" in the drop-
in center?

4. The first words of *Runaway* (not included in the selection above) are
"I decided to become a writer when I was six years old." Lau goes on
to explain that she hoped to do for readers what writers had done for
her: help them to lose themselves for a while in an alternate world.
Which features of Lau's writing seem most devoted to letting readers
"open one of my books and disappear for a while"? Does her writing
have other goals as well? Do these goals complement one another—
or collide?

5. Keep a journal for one week. Though you may wish to use Lau's as a
model, you may also choose a different approach, if you prefer. The
journal need not be particularly dramatic, introspective, or socially
relevant; still, events, however commonplace they seem to you, should
be rendered concretely, with details that appeal to the senses. In short,
strive for careful observation, rather than extensive reflection.

Exotic, or "What Beach Do You Hang Out On?"

TARA MASIH

In the following essay, Tara Masih reflects on what it means to be called "exotic." A woman of mixed-race parentage, Masih suggests that the label, while perhaps intended positively, has several not-so-positive connotations. Part of Masih's point is also that words like "exotic" can have multiple meanings simultaneously, and that sometimes it is the complex of all those meanings that conveys the total sense of a term, even if the user has a narrower intention in mind. This essay is from *Two Worlds Walking,* eds. Diane Glancy and C.W. Truesdale (New Rivers Press, 1994).

When you are of mixed parentage—one parent dark-skinned, one light— you come out looking like café au lait. You become one of those gray areas people struggle with; they struggle with their compulsion to categorize you, label you, and place you neatly on the shelf in a safe spot, safe because the species is one that has already been identified. Yet while humans have always feared the unfamiliar and foreign, times are forcing us to change.

"Your look is in," I'm told by friends. "I like exotic-looking women," I'm told by men. I still have not learned how to react to these well-meaning comments. I bite my lip, smile, and nod vaguely, hoping they'll take my expression as a thank you.

What that expression really reflects is a reaction to my own struggle, a reluctance to be placed in any category to satisfy the comfort of others. Now I am labeled, and they can rest easy. Everything's safe.

Fear of the stranger goes back centuries. In her essay, Susan Sontag uses this metaphor to explain the fear of AIDS victims: "The fact that illness is associated with the poor—who are, from the perspective of the privileged, aliens in one's midst—reinforces the association of illness with the foreign: with an *exotic* place" [my italics].

There is no doubt that words have power, or rather, we imbue them with power. As the Bible proclaims, the word is flesh and dwells among us. Like humans, words are either accepted or rejected, synthesized into culture or banished. For instance, during the McCarthy era, the term *communist,* like the person it labeled, was claimed to be evil and therefore every effort was made to eradicate it from the American vocabulary.

79

What many people may not realize is that the word *exotic* is derived   6
from the Greek word *exō,* meaning "outside." "Exotic" itself carries several
meanings in modern times, and as cultural and collective views change
terms and phrases, chameleon-like, are made to reflect and adapt. (*Communism* is no longer an evil word, communists no longer exist in an "evil
empire.") According to *Webster's Ninth Collegiate,* there are four modern
definitions of *exotic.*

1. Introduced from another country: not native to the place where found

It is amazing what a short-term memory we Americans have. Our history   7
begins with the discovery, by Italian explorer Cristofero Colombo, of this
land and its exotic American Indians (and we all know he was looking for
a quicker trade route to my ancestors, those other exotics in India proper).
But by definition it was Colombo and his followers, religious refugees and
convicts, who were the exotics. In essence, all Americans are exotic. Our
history, riddled with convenient lapses in memory, takes a great leap to the
American Revolution, discounting the fact that the nonnative Europeans,
with "savage-like" enthusiasm, slaughtered the natives (now rightly referred
to as Native Americans). Our fear of foreigners is no doubt a projection of
our fear of ourselves.

2. archaic: outlandish, alien

By this definition, *exotic* is hardly a compliment. The word again addresses   8
the fear of the unfamiliar. (The *Oxford English Dictionary* uses the words
barbarous, strange, uncouth as synonymous with foreigners.) It's why we
seek to erase differences in this culture. By covering our bodily smells with
the same scents, by following the current trends in hair styles (witness all the
media coverage recently devoted to *Friends* star Jennifer Aniston's retro haircut) by spending all our energy/time/money to wear the same clothes during
the same season, and by keeping up with the latest profanity, we are saying
to our compatriots: "Hey, I'm just like you, therefore I'm *safe* and *familiar.*"
(Note how these two adjectives are often paired.) It is no accident that most
of the women and men accused of witchcraft during the hysteria of the seventeenth and eighteenth centuries were citizens who lived by themselves,
outside of the community—social lepers. In our own century, Michael Jackson is the epitome of one who has tried, literally, to erase his exotic features,
even going so far as to erase his gender—he is generic in every sense,
and therefore can be marketed to a broader audience. His attempts, nevertheless, backfired. In erasing all differences he has become that which
he tried to avoid. A true alien, living a solitary life away from society, he is
like the witches of old—a target for outlandish rumors and supernatural
speculation.

3. Strikingly or excitingly different or unusual

The word's own definitions contradict each other. While the unfamiliar can   9
be frightening, it can also be exciting. As psychologists have discovered,
love and lust are heightened in the presence of fear. Now we know how to
make someone fall in love with us—take them on a walk over a shaky
bridge. And as fear and excitement appear to be in opposition, so do different cultures' concepts of beauty. In the States it is considered an asset to
be tan, though the tan shouldn't be natural. It should be achieved through
leisurely hours of sunning on tropical beaches or through the assistance of
artificial means. Americans brave melanoma, carcinoma, early aging for this
brief stain of color. I enjoy being the barometer every summer for my friends
to measure their tan by. With what glee some of them greet their achieved
goal—to be darker than I am. But only in the summer, when it's acceptable.
Or if they've been to Florida. I went to the beach once with a friend. "Look
how everyone's staring at me," she said. "Black people aren't supposed to
go to the beach, it's only for whites trying to look black!"

I find it ironic that meanwhile, on the other side of the earth, people are   10
doing their best to appear light-skinned. Hindu gods are rendered by artists
with a blue tint to their skin, and Indian movie stars are lighter than many
Europeans. I was appalled to find my own cousin, in preparation for her
wedding, spreading hair bleach all over her amber-tinted face and neck.
"I'm too dark," she said. "It's not pretty."

If we go beyond the outward schizophrenia of these opposing ideals,   11
we find a sad explanation—it is class related. In the States, a tan is a sign of
wealth. It takes money and leisure time to be able to noticeably tan—not
burn, but tan, like the model in the Bain de Soleil advertisements.

But in equatorial countries such as India, a tan is a sign of the lower   12
caste. The wealthy stay indoors, cooling themselves under rotating ceiling
fans, while the rest of society works beneath a branding sun.

4. of or relating to striptease

This meaning is so repugnant it's comical. Is an exotic woman expected to   13
dance her version of the seven veils for the edification (or destruction) of
men? Visions of Salome arise, and again that fear of what is different, or
man's fear of woman. As Jung noted, we give women all the characteristics
that "swarm in the male Eros." Because of the sexual connotations, it has become de rigueur for a man to be seen with a foreign-looking woman. The
advertising community, taking note of this, has littered their ads with exotic
women, the cosmetics industry is cashing in on their growing number, and
the film industry is giving more roles to women who don't look like Cindy
Crawford, beautiful as she is.

Which brings me to the real definition of *exotic*.   14

A growing segment of the U.S. population being targeted for consumerism

As the discussions of the previous definitions reveal, in our society industry   15
and consumerism build the foundation from which change evolves. The
foundation for consumerism began with the colonists' revolt against taxa-
tion. A growing consumerism held our country together, forcing a civil war:
according to some social historians, the North didn't want to lose the South's
textile or agricultural contributions, which fed the Northern industries. It met
the demands of the civil rights and the women's movement during the
sixties, when the work force was in dire need of replenishment. Today, consumerism is behind the efforts to manufacture environmentally safe products, fake fur, and to provide dolphin-safe nets.

And it now causes publishers to compete against each other so that they   16
may proudly announce that thirty-five percent of their authors are minorities; it causes politicians to include minority policies in their political platforms; it's behind the slight darkening of the skin and rearranging of models'
features; and it drives fashion designers to steal other cultures' traditional attire, reproduce it, and sell it for a criminal price. Are women aware that
they're wearing a mini sarong from Africa? Or *shalwars* from India? These
pants cost as much as $200 in the States, but in India, depending on how
well you can bargain, you can get them for $5. Westerners don't see the
women sitting cross-legged in dark rooms and on thin mats, a useless protection from damp floors, embroidering or weaving their own fallen hair
into the materials. And they never haggle with a street vendor for 5 rupees
(the equivalent of about 25¢), until the boy says earnestly, with that tilt of
the head peculiar to Indians, "Look, miss, to you 5 rupees is nothing—to me
it is everything." True.

The melting pot is recognized as an anachronistic term. The new buzz-   17
word for the nineties is *multicultural* or *multinational,* because we know
that soon minorities will be the majority. They are gaining economic independence and buying their way into acceptance. So out of fear, our culture
is adopting their clothing and jewelry, eating their foods in restaurants with
purple decors, and taking up their causes to the point where we will forget
who it all really belongs to. But I hope that we will fight the desire to have
these groups assimilate, and that the prefix *multi* will begin to take power,
allowing this country to exist as many rather than as one generic, incestuous
mass. May the words of *M*A*S*H*'s Frank Burns be banished to an unen-
lightened past: "Individuality is fine. As long as we do it together."

No one should be labeled and shelved. I hope that we open our minds   18
to learn from other cultures, accept what each has to offer, not because we
can make a profit from them but because it will enrich our own culture. As

Richard Rodriguez writes, "Diversity which is not shared is no virtue. Diversity which is not shared is a parody nation."

Perhaps the real definition of *exotic* should be "A recognition of that which is especially unique to each culture." For if someone calling me exotic meant a recognition of a proud people who persevere in the face of terrible poverty and disease, if they saw in me even a spark of Paul, a disfigured leper who, every evening, sits on the leprosarium stairs to take in the beauty of the Himalayan foothills during sunset, with no bitterness at his lot, then I would smile widely and say, "Thank you."   19

Working with the Text

1. Why does Masih devote so much attention to the word "exotic" itself? What does this attention imply about the relationship between words and social attitudes? What does she mean when she says that "the word is flesh and dwells among us"? What is the relationship among the four dictionary definitions of "exotic"? Between the first "real definition"?

2. What are some examples in the media (print or broadcast) that express the meanings Masih finds in "exotic"? Do these examples treat exoticism in a way that—while not overtly negative—does cast it as marginal or outside the mainstream? Bring an example to class.

3. Masih concludes by promoting a new definition based on Richard Rodriguez's concept of shared diversity: "Exotic" should be to cultures what "unique" is to individuals. What is gained and what is lost in such a redefinition?

4. The essay ranges widely through history for its illustrations; McCarthy, Columbus, and Michael Jackson all make fleeting appearances in support of specific assertions. The author also draws heavily on the comments and behavior of her friends as evidence. Why does the essay draw on so many disparate sources? Does it use different kinds of evidence for different purposes? Finally, look at the whole structure of the essay. Is there a connection between the cultural diversity Masih promotes and her pattern of organization?

5. Choose a word with significance both to you and to a larger cultural group, and look up the word in a comprehensive dictionary, such as you will find in the reference room of a library. Note the three or four most prominent definitions, and free-write for fifteen or twenty minutes on each one. Then, craft a new definition of the word, one that improves upon the old definitions but that does not pull completely away from them.

Ellen West

FRANK BIDART

Frank Bidart writes in poetical forms that can appear "nonpoetical." In so doing, he captures the speaking voice, often in anguish, raised to protest a seeming inevitability. "Ellen West" is a dramatic meditation that includes the language of doctors' reports and a haunting monologue spoken by a woman who will not eat. The poem is built around the difficulty of accepting or coping with one's own body; though the solution that the speaker finds is disturbing, it nonetheless incorporates feelings inherent to us all. Frank Bidart has published several books of poems, including *The Book of the Body* (1977), which contains "Ellen West," *In the Western Night: Collected Poems 1965–90,* and *Desire* (1997). He teaches at Wellesley College.

I love sweets,—
                    heaven
would be dying on a bed of vanilla ice cream . . .

But my true self
is thin, all profile   5

and effortless gestures, the sort of blond
elegant girl whose
                    body is the image of her soul.

—My doctors tell me I must give up
this ideal;   10
            but I
WILL NOT . . . cannot.

Only to my husband I'm not simply a "case."

But he is a fool. He married
meat, and thought it was a wife.   15

                    •   •   •

Why am I a girl?

I ask my doctors, and they tell me they
don't know, that it is just "given."

But it has such
implications—;   20
        and sometimes,
I even feel like a girl.

      •   •   •

Now, at the beginning of Ellen's thirty-second year, her physical condition
has deteriorated still further. Her use of laxatives increases beyond measure.
Every evening she takes sixty to seventy tablets of a laxative, with the result   25
that she suffers tortured vomiting at night and violent diarrhea by day, often
accompanied by a weakness of the heart. She has thinned down to a skele-
ton, and weighs only 92 pounds.

About five years ago, I was in a restaurant,
eating alone   30
        with a book. I was
not married, and often did that . . .

—I'd turn down
dinner invitations, so I could eat alone;

I'd allow myself two pieces of bread, with   35
butter, at the beginning, and three scoops of
vanilla ice cream, at the end,—

            sitting there alone
with a book, both in the book
and out of it, waited on, idly   40
watching people,—

        when an attractive young man
and woman, both elegantly dressed,
sat next to me.
        She was beautiful—;   45
with sharp, clear features, a good
bone structure—;
        if she took her make-up off
in front of you, rubbing cold cream
again and again across her skin, she still would be   50
beautiful—
      more beautiful.

And he,—
      I couldn't remember when I had seen a man

so attractive. I didn't know why. He was almost   55

a male version
        of her,—

I had the sudden, mad notion that I
wanted to be his lover . . .

—Were they married?   60
          were *they* lovers?

They didn't wear wedding rings.

Their behavior was circumspect. They discussed
politics. They didn't touch . . .

—How could I discover?   65
         Then, when the first course
arrived, I noticed the way

each held his fork out for the other

to taste what he had ordered . . .

           They did this   70
again and again, with pleased looks, indulgent
smiles, for each course,
        more than once for *each* dish—;
much too much for just friends . . .

—Their behavior somehow sickened me;   75

the way each *gladly*
put the *food* the other had offered *into his mouth*—;

I knew what they were. I knew they slept together.

An immense depression came over me . . .

—I knew I could never   80
with such ease allow another to put food into my mouth:

happily *myself* put food into another's mouth—;

I knew that to become a wife I would have to give up my ideal.

        •   •   •

Even as a child,
I saw that the "natural" process of aging   85

is for one's middle to thicken—
one's skin to blotch;

as happened to my mother.
And her mother.
                    I loathed "Nature."   90

At twelve, pancakes
became the most terrible thought there is . . .

I shall *defeat* "Nature."

In the hospital, when they
weigh me, I wear weights secretly sewn into my belt.   95

                    •   •   •

January 16. The patient is allowed to eat in her room, but comes readily with
her husband to afternoon coffee. Previously she had stoutly resisted this on
the ground that she did not really eat but devoured like a wild animal. This
she demonstrated with utmost realism. . . . Her physical examination showed
nothing striking. Salivary glands are markedly enlarged on both sides.   100
    January 21. Has been reading *Faust* again. In her diary, writes that art is
the "mutual permeation" of the "world of the body" and the "world of the
spirit." Says that her own poems are "hospital poems . . . weak—without
skill or perseverance; only managing to beat their wings softly."
    February 8. Agitation, quickly subsided again. Has attached herself   105
to an elegant, very thin female patient. Homo-erotic component strikingly
evident.
    February 15. Vexation, and torment. Says that her mind forces her al-
ways to think of eating. Feels herself degraded by this. Has entirely, for the
first time in years, stopped writing poetry.   110

                    •   •   •

Callas is my favorite singer, but I've only
seen her once—;

I've never forgotten that night . . .

—It was in *Tosca,* she had long before
lost weight, her voice   115
had been, for years,
                    deteriorating, half itself . . .

When her career began, of course, she was fat,

enormous—; in the early photographs,
sometimes I almost don't recognize her . . .   120

The voice too then was enormous—
healthy; robust; subtle; but capable of
crude effects, even vulgar,
                              almost out of
high spirits, too much health . . .   125

But soon she felt that she must lose weight—
that all she was trying to express

was obliterated by her body,
buried in flesh—;
                    abruptly, within   130
four months, she lost at least sixty pounds . . .

—The gossip in Milan was that Callas
had swallowed a tapeworm.

But of course she hadn't.

                    The *tapeworm*   135
was her *soul* . . .

—How her soul, uncompromising,
insatiable,
              must have loved eating the flesh from her bones,

revealing this extraordinarily   140
mercurial; fragile; masterly creature . . .

—But irresistibly, nothing
stopped there; the huge voice

also began to change: at first, it simply diminished
in volume, in size,   145
                    then the top notes became
shrill, unreliable—at last,
usually not there at all . . .

—No one knows *why*. Perhaps her mind,
ravenous, still insatiable, sensed   150

that to struggle with the *shreds* of a voice

must make her artistry subtler, more refined,
more capable of expressing humiliation,
rage, betrayal . . .

—Perhaps the opposite. Perhaps her spirit   155
loathed the unending struggle

to *embody* itself, to *manifest* itself, on a stage whose

mechanics, and suffocating customs,
seemed expressly designed to annihilate spirit . . .

—I know that in *Tosca,* in the second act,   160
when, humiliated, hounded by Scarpia,
she sang *Vissi d'arte*
                —"I lived for art"—

and in torment, bewilderment, at the end she asks,
with a voice reaching   165
               harrowingly for the notes,

"Art has *repaid* me LIKE THIS?"

                    I felt I was watching
autobiography—
            an art; skill;   170
virtuosity

miles distant from the usual soprano's
athleticism,—
            the usual musician's dream
of virtuosity *without* content . . .   175

—I wonder what she feels, now,
listening to her recordings.

For they have already, within a few years,
begun to date . . .

Whatever they express   180
they express through the style of a decade
and a half—;
            a style *she* helped create . . .

—She must know that now
she probably would *not* do a trill in   185
exactly that way,—
            that the whole sound, atmosphere,
dramaturgy of her recordings

have just slightly become those of the past . . .

—Is it bitter? Does her soul   190
tell her

that she was an *idiot* ever to think
anything
       material wholly could satisfy? . . .

—Perhaps it says: *The only way*   195
to escape
the History of Styles

is not to have a body.

           •   •   •

When I open my eyes in the morning, my great
mystery   200
       stands before me . . .

—I *know* that I am intelligent; therefore

the inability not to fear food
day-and-night; this unending hunger
ten minutes after I have eaten . . .   205
                 a childish
dread of eating; hunger which can have no cause,—

half my mind says that all this
is *demeaning* . . .

          Bread   210
for days on end
drives all real thought from my brain . . .

—Then I think, No. The ideal of being thin

conceals the ideal
not to have a body—;   215
           which is NOT trivial . . .

This wish seems now as much a "given" of my existence

as the intolerable
fact that I am dark-complexioned; big-boned;
and once weighed   220
one hundred and sixty-five pounds . . .

—But then I think, *No.* That's too simple,—

without a body, who can
know himself at all?
         Only by   225

acting; choosing; rejecting; have I
made myself—
        discovered who and what *Ellen* can be . . .

—But then again I think, *NO.* This *I* is anterior
to name; gender; action;   230
fashion;
      MATTER ITSELF,—

. . . trying to stop my hunger with FOOD
is like trying to appease thirst
            with ink.   235

      •   •   •

March 30. Result of the consultation: Both gentlemen agree completely with
my prognosis and doubt any therapeutic usefulness of commitment even
more emphatically than I. All three of us are agreed that it is not a case of
obsessional neurosis and not one of manic-depressive psychosis, and that
no definitely reliable therapy is possible. We therefore resolved to give in to   240
the patient's demand for discharge.

      •   •   •

The train-ride yesterday
was far *worse* than I expected . . .

           In our compartment
were ordinary people: a student;   245
a woman; her child;—

they had ordinary bodies, pleasant faces;
              but I thought

I was surrounded by creatures

with the pathetic, desperate   250
desire to be *not* what they were:—

the student was short,
and carried his body as if forcing
it to be taller—;

the woman showed her gums when she smiled,   255
and often held her
hand up to hide them—;

the child
seemed to cry simply because it was
small; a dwarf, and helpless . . .   260

—I was hungry. I had insisted that my husband
not bring food . . .

After about thirty minutes, the woman
peeled an orange

to quiet the child. She put a section   265
into its mouth—;
                    immediately it spit it out.

The piece fell to the floor.

—She pushed it with her foot through the dirt
toward me   270
several inches.

My husband saw me staring
down at the piece . . .

—I didn't move; how I wanted
to reach out,   275
                    and as if invisible

shove it in my mouth—;

my body
became rigid. As I stared at him,
I could see him staring   280
at me,—
            then he looked at the student—; at the woman—; then
back to me . . .

I didn't move.

—At last, he bent down, and   285
casually
            threw it out the window.

He looked away.

—I got up to leave the compartment, then
saw his face,—   290

his eyes
were red;
            and I saw

—I'm sure I saw—

disappointment.   295

•   •   •

On the third day of being home she is as if transformed. At breakfast she
eats butter and sugar, at noon she eats so much that—for the first time in
thirteen years!—she is satisfied by her food and gets really full. At afternoon
coffee she eats chocolate creams and Easter eggs. She takes a walk with her
husband, reads poems, listens to recordings, is in a positively festive mood,   300
and all heaviness seems to have fallen away from her. She writes letters, the
last one a letter to the fellow patient here to whom she had become so attached. In the evening she takes a lethal dose of poison, and on the following morning she is dead. "She looked as she had never looked in life—calm
and happy and peaceful."   305

•   •   •

Dearest.—I remember how
at eighteen,
            on hikes with friends, when
they rested, sitting down to joke or talk,

I circled   310
around them, afraid to hike ahead alone,

yet afraid to rest
when I was not yet truly thin.

You and, yes, my husband,—
you and he   315

have by degrees drawn me within the circle;
forced me to sit down at last on the ground.

I am grateful.

But something in me *refuses* it.

—How eager I have been   320
to compromise, to kill this *refuser,*—

but each compromise, each attempt
to poison an ideal

which often seemed to *me* sterile and unreal,

heightens my hunger. 325

I am crippled. I disappoint you.

Will you greet with anger, or
happiness,

the news which might well reach you
before this letter? 330

       Your *Ellen*.

Working with the Text

1. The poem begins by distinguishing the "I" who loves sweets from the ideal "true self," writing about the former in the first person and the latter in the third. It ends with another distinction, this time between the "I" who seeks compromise with the tyrannical ideal and the "refuser." What other forms of self-division does "Ellen West" reveal, and how are they manifest? Are the borders between conflicting principles clear and stable or shifting and obscure? How do they relate to her eating disorder?

2. Some anthropologists claim that the most important border to human beings is the one between the body and the world, which shifts from culture to culture but is always strictly monitored. Activities that breach this border—food, sex, and elimination are the most common—must be strictly regulated by custom, though most people don't perceive the regulation, assuming, for example, that it's "natural" to eat pigs but not cats. What kinds of relationships between the body and the world does "Ellen West" make visible, and how does eating (or not eating) express them? Is the speaker's illness a distortion or a repudiation of normal customs?

3. Through the course of the poem, the speaker struggles to understand the relationship between body, soul, and art, as expressed in her eating disorder. At the end of the section explicitly devoted to this "great mystery," she cries "trying to stop my hunger with FOOD/ is like trying to appease thirst/ with ink." Why does she use an analogy here? What does it mean? Why does her discharge from treatment immediately follow this statement?

4. Discuss the structure of this poem and how that structure contributes to the poem's meaning. Why does it alternate between free verse and prose? Between present and past tense? Between narration and analysis?

Why is the imaginative biography of Maria Callas at the center of the poem? Why does it end with a letter to a fellow sufferer?

5. "Ellen West" abounds in startling pronouncements, some aphoristic, some paradoxical, some perverse. Choose one ("the *tapeworm*/was her *soul,*" for example), and write a brief essay on its meaning and its resonance in the poem. Pay careful attention to context and to language; use a good dictionary and, if necessary, an encyclopedia for challenging terms ("tapeworm" and "soul"). Acknowledge multiple meanings and ambiguity, but do take a position on how the line functions in the poem.

Critical Questions Revisited: From Reading to Writing

Essay Topic 1: How do competing influences help shape a sense of self-identity?

YOUR PAPER: Based on evidence from one or more works in this chapter, analyze how competing influences help form identity. You might consider, for example, the ways that family or cultural contexts compete with received messages and outside perceptions, or how innate, community, and cultural identity seem at odds. Or you might consider the competing tensions between a "private" and a "public" self. How are such conflicts negotiated? Are they (and must they be) resolved?

SUGGESTED STRATEGIES

- Find passages from your readings that present the idea of a multiple or fractured sense of self.
- What kinds of conflicts are shown? How do they prompt the development of the self? What is gained and lost in this development?
- From these examples, how is a single person formed from a multitude of sources?

Essay Topic 2: How do violence, alienation, and fantasy work to shape a present sense of the self?

YOUR PAPER: Show how writers use past moments of alienation, violence, and desire as influencing the present sense of self. You might, for example, show how some writers portray the past as characterized by moments of pain or alienation, and the reactions that those moments trigger. Do these "wounds" seem to come from inside or outside? How do they complicate questions of what it means to be innocent or a victim?

SUGGESTED STRATEGIES

- Why do some writers use violent or painful memories to characterize the past? Discuss specific examples.
- How do their experiences influence the present?
- In these texts, how do authors respond to alienation and violence? Do these feelings compete with fantasies or idealized notions of what life ought to be? What alternatives can you offer?

Essay Topic 3: How do stories shape our self-identity? In what ways do people "live out" stories or cultural myths, by choice or unconsciously?

YOUR PAPER: Explore how stories influence people's sense of their lives. Using two or three examples, characterize how stories prompt people's beliefs and decisions—how they become in some ways the creation of a text.

SUGGESTED STRATEGIES

- Analyze passages that show stories prompting people's beliefs and decisions.
- How do people "live out" stories even when trying to free themselves from their grip? Why do stories carry such power?
- Compare these with specific moments when this has happened to you. Characterize the power of stories.

Essay Topic 4: What influences and challenges our ways of expressing differences between ourselves and others?

YOUR PAPER: Analyze how writers explore the ways perception of an "other" shapes one's own self-perception. You might consider some of the ways social or cultural categories help define a sense of self. How do some writers portray their journey toward a sense of identity by recognizing and breaking out of these categories?

SUGGESTED STRATEGIES

- Identify passages in your readings where an author is grappling with the perception of difference between oneself and others.
- How do these moments of representing difference get connected to identity in the readings? Are there different ways that identity and difference (or otherness) can be linked?
- From these examples, can you begin to make some general claims about the relationship of a sense of oneself and the perception of difference from others?

CHAPTER 2

BORDERS OF COMMUNITY:
Difference and Otherness

Critical Questions

Before reading: What factors give us a feeling of communal identity? How is our sense of communal identity based on difference?

Taking it further: Sometimes we feel both inside and outside a community simultaneously. How does a community provide an implicit sense (or code) of what it means to be "normal"? Can there be a community in

which individual differences somehow make no difference? How do we
think about and express distinctions between ourselves and others? Are
these differences—the sense of an "us" versus a "them"—inevitable?

BELONGING TO A CULTURE

A crucial concept related to belonging is *culture*. Culture is a complicated
term, in part because of its different usages. Culture can be understood
generally as the totality of socially transmitted behaviors, beliefs, and institutions that constitute a "system" or "way of living" for a particular people.
Although we might refine this definition, the common view is that the "system" we call "culture" connects people to their surrounding world.

When Americans speak of their culture, they often refer to two or
more things simultaneously. First, they suggest a national culture, one that
is generated by a combination of media, economics, and the dominant political and social ideals. At the same time, many people belong to one or
more smaller social and economic groups that coexist within American society, groups socially complex enough to constitute a culture. Certainly, individuals can live within more than one definition of "my culture"; many
people feel the *doubleness* of cultural belonging very strongly. For others,
there is only a sense of being "an American." Nonetheless, all of us in one
way or another in the United States belong to both a national culture and
at least one culture that is defined by our class, "race," religion, gender or
sexuality, or other influences. Whether or not one's own personal cultural
orientation shows affinity or friction with the national culture varies from
group to group and person to person.

"Culture" is a complex idea used in the most sweeping and abstract
ways, yet each of us experience our own culture(s) every day in the smallest and most familiar things: in the food we eat, the clothes we wear, the
rituals we practice. Many aspects of culture are invisible to us in the sense
that they constitute the habitual way we see the world. Oftentimes, we
think of that way as "normal" and other ways as different. This, then, is
one of the links between culture and identity.

WHAT IS A COMMUNITY?

Surely, though, we feel a sense of belonging at more than one level at a
time. A connection to a culture is just one level. Another critical level of
personal connection is *community*. Like culture, the term "community" has

various usages. Community often refers to a place where people share a common identity through their physical proximity, such as a city, town, or neighborhood. Many uses of community have this idea of a group of people living in the same locality, even if the implications of community consciousness go beyond mere geographical bonding. Community can also mean a social group having common interests and affinities—ethnic or racial, sexual preference, linguistic, religious, etc.

One useful way to think about the relationship between culture and community is to consider *culture* a network of beliefs, customs, practices, behaviors, and values, and to understand *community* as the more immediate network of human relationships. The two together—culture and community—go a long way toward defining how people understand and express a sense of belonging and connection to their surroundings, how they define their own identities and that of others.

DIFFERENCE AND OTHERNESS

If a culture is about a particular social system and community is about interdependence of people who share resources or values, then who are the people in those contexts who do not share in those practices or values? Do concepts like culture and community necessarily imply "insiders" and "outsiders"? Is "belonging" founded upon exclusion?

Individuals construct their sense of self based in part on the messages they receive from the general culture at large. As Stuart Hall puts it in his essay in this chapter, a "critical thing about identity is that it is partly the relationship between you and the Other. Only when there is an Other can you know who you are." When we speak of constructions of "otherness," we are speaking not only of an attitude or belief, but also of the embodiment of that belief in language and images that make up the cultural environment. To speak of culture and community is to speak of "us" and "them," "self" and "other." Accordingly, this chapter also concerns some of the ways that the idea of "otherness" gets depicted in American culture, in both explicit and subtly implicit ways. Several of the essays explore such ideas and analyze the force that ideas of difference and otherness have in our culture—the ways they get expressed, and the means by which they create and maintain individual, communal, and cultural identity.

Some people are believed to belong to the "core" of American society; others belong in different ways—perhaps as guests, or as aliens, or as residents on the periphery, but forever *outside* the center. All cultures have norms; consequently, they vary in their capacity to accommodate differences. What the selections in this chapter explore is how **difference** is constructed as **otherness,** in the United States. More specifically, what are the aspects of expression and thinking in the United States in which a dominant core culture is used as a standard for labeling, judging, and treating people?

Robert Berkhofer Jr. finds in the "discovery" of the so-called "new world" an America that from its inception defined itself via shifting sets of dichotomies between European/Indian, white/dark, civilized/savage, cultured/primitive. Essays by David Sibley, Peter Marin, Leonard Kriegel, Ruben Martinez, Kai Erickson, and Jacob Riis reveal that people considered "outside" the core of American society—either as an overt threat or as a necessary but marginalized underclass—have changed according to region and period. What is notable, as the selection from Stuart Hall suggests, is that in most instances there is a sense of difference, of otherness, and even, Elizabeth Bishop shows, a sense of fear and shame.

One of the key concerns in this chapter, and throughout the book, is the relationship between intra- and intercultural difference. Randall Balmer, Daniel Kemmis, and John Hartigan depict multicultural communities where the borders between cultures are often blurred. Such borders may elide differences within the community, yet they may also promote a compensatory distinction between inside and outside. Can a community with multicultural or liberal notions of difference, they ask, maintain its identity without a sense of cultural outsiders or others?

Going Up in LA

RUBEN MARTINEZ

A native of Los Angeles, Ruben Martinez is an Emmy-award-winning journalist as well as a poet and performance artist. He currently serves as the U.S.–Mexico correspondent for the Pacific News Service, cohosts the PBS cultural and political series *Life and Times,* and acts as a guest commentator on National Public Radio's (NPR's) *All Things Considered.* His 1992 book, *The Other Side: Notes from the New LA, Mexico City, and Beyond,* includes a number of personal reports focusing on Hispanic American life and identity. The following chapter from that book looks at the thriving culture of graffiti artists in Los Angeles and its relation to adolescent solidarity, gang warfare, individual expression, and possible escape from poverty and crime.

Los Angeles, April 1989

The stain on the old couch that sits in the empty lot has already turned brown, a dark flower spread out upon the grimy fabric. Although it's a school day and only 10:30 in the morning, about a dozen teenagers stand about, passing around a quart of Colt 45 Malt Liquor. Some of the faces show fear; others are hardened into stony stares. "We know who did it, but we're not going to tell you," says one of the younger boys. His hair is cropped stubby short, and he wears dark jeans and a plain T-shirt. "We're not going to spell it out, but you can pretty much guess what's going to happen tonight."

At approximately seven o'clock the previous evening, these kids had been seated on or standing around the couch. Among the group was Prime, a seventeen-year-old homeboy. A few days earlier, Prime was sitting in his family's living room, which doubles as a bedroom, in a neighborhood not far from the empty lot. It is a crime-ridden area to be sure, dominated by one of the city's oldest Latino gangs. This is where Prime grew up, and where his two unemployed parents try to scrape by on welfare.

Although Prime admitted that he'd been "in the wrong place at the wrong time" on more than one occasion, he saw himself less as a gangster, more as a "writer" (as graffiti artists call themselves), one of the best-known among the city's thousands of young, spraycan-wielding "bombers."

Prime shook hands gingerly that day. His right hand still bore the chalky plaster stains from a cast that had been removed the day before, the bones in his right—and writing—hand having been broken in a fist fight.

As soon as I entered the room, he began to show off his canvases. After years of doing complex, colorful works on walls across the city, Prime had begun experimenting with acrylics, airbrush, oils, washes. It was Valentine's Day, and he'd done a piece for his girlfriend—a brightly colored Cupid surrounded by soft pink roses, with a dedication that read, "José and Nery, *por vida.*" He pointed to a larger work dominated by grays, blacks and silvers, titled *Dazed and Confused,* an ambitious circular composition centered on a pair of dice that become a large syringe, then a huddled, shadowy figure and, finally, a large, wicked-looking skull.

Prime sat down on the sagging bed, the plaster wall behind him bulging with cracked paint. At the age of eight, he tells me, he snatched his sister's goldfleck hairspray and wrote "Little Joe, 18 Street" in the back yard. Soon afterward his initials were "up" in the neighborhood alleys.

"I never got really crazy," he told me. But as gang violence in the inner city increased dramatically in the mid-1980s, he was busted for various misdemeanors, including "vandalism" (i.e., spraypainting), and he once almost did time for armed robbery. It wasn't until about 1984 that Prime graduated from gang-writing to more original and complex forms of graffiti. He

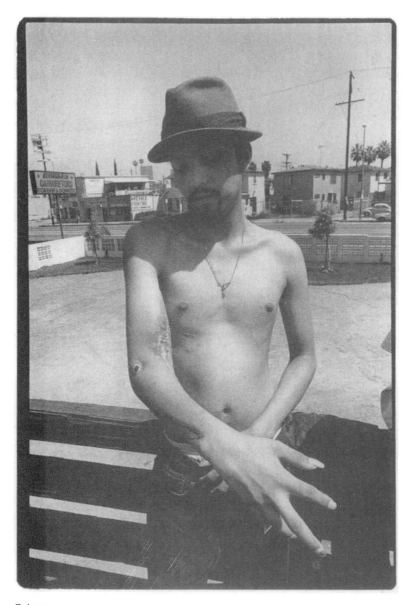

Prime

The Belmont Tunnel

developed a style that set him apart from other graffiti artists, working closely with several colleagues in the K2S—STN ("Kill To Succeed—Second To None") crew, one of the first to appear on the city's Eastside.

The glory days of the nascent L.A. scene came in 1984, when a youth club named Radio-Tron opened its doors. "It was a cultural center where people could go practice breaking and drawing," recalls Moda (the tag is Spanish for "fashion"), a founding member of the Bomb Squad. Housed in a building in the Westlake *barrio* near MacArthur Park, Radio-Tron was akin to an established artist's studio, a haven from the streets where writers always ran the risk of a bust. Soon, every inch of the site was covered with tags and pieces. "All the guys I knew were being thrown in jail or getting killed," says Primo D, also of the Bomb Squad. "Radio-Tron was an alternative."

The center's curriculum, according to founder and director Carmelo Al- varez, a longtime inner-city youth activist, included deejaying, scratch and rap, and "advanced graffiti." "I just took what they had and structured it." But the experiment didn't last long. Wrangles with the city (Alvarez balked when the Department of Parks and Recreation made a move to take over the center), as well as a Fire Marshall's citation (for storage of "hazardous chemicals"—aerosol cans), led to its being closed. "When Radio-Tron shut down, everybody started getting into the gang thing," says Primo D. "There was nothing else to do."

Not long after the Bomb Squad's tags and cartoonlike "characters" first appeared in the downtown area, a group of mostly middle-class Anglo Westside teens took note and founded WCA (West Coast Artists), soon the biggest crew in the city with an active membership of about thirty-five, plus a subsidiary crew (BC, or Beyond Control) of a dozen or so. Today, on any given weekend morning, you can see WCA at work, along with other Westside crews like KSN (Kings Stop at Nothing), at one of their favorite spots, the Motor Yard in West Los Angeles.   10

    Everything in the yard, including the rails, the ties, the torched wrecks of cars, has been tagged, pieced, bombed—as the writers say, "terrorized." The thousands of discarded spraycans testify to the countless generations of pieces that have gone up, one on top of another, on the half-mile stretch of concrete retaining wall that flanks the railroad tracks.   11

    Carrying in dozens of Krylon spraycans in backpacks or milk crates, the crews usually arrive early in the day and work alongside the railroad tracks that run parallel to the Santa Monica freeway near National Boulevard. A box will invariably be blasting Eazy E's "Boys-N-the-Hood" or Boogie Down Production's "My Philosophy" as the writers, ranging in age from six to their early twenties, fish sketches out of their back pockets, [open] the cans, press down customized nozzles ("fat tips" culled from small Testor's spraycans, which allow for a thicker, smoother line) and begin the sweeping rhythmic motions that trace the skeleton of a new piece.   12

    Phoe of BC, a wiry, clean-cut teenager of Hawaiian–Filipino ancestry, is there one weekend, wearing a dark blue baseball cap embroidered with the name of his crew. His tag, he tells me, is an intentional misspelling of "foe," which, according to him, means "society's enemy." He works on a three-dimensional wildstyle piece that is typical of Westside work. The edges of the letters are sharp as shards of glass, but serif-like cuts and arrows make the composition virtually unreadable to the untrained eye.   13

    "Writing is, like, a different community," says Phoe, yelling to be heard over the freeway roar that almost drowns out his high-pitched voice. "It's communication with other writers throughout the city." Wherever he goes ("even when I go out to dinner with my parents"), the tools of the trade—markers or spraycans—are at his disposal.   14

    As with many Westside writers, Phoe's response to the city's anti-graffiti forces, or to those sympathetic adults who encourage him to professionalize his talent, is lackadaisical. "Yeah, yeah, yeah. They're telling me to go out   15 and sign up for scholarships and art classes, and get paid for writing, and I'm, like, well, I don't really need the money because I work." Yet some WCA writers do take "legal" jobs now and then, pounding the streets in search of sympathetic business owners who'll pay them to paint storefront signs and the like. Risk, one of WCA's premier writers, recently did backgrounds for a Michael Jackson video.

Still, there's an allure to the "illegal" work. And, since most writers lack studio space, sites like the Motor Yard are indispensable. "They just don't understand," says Ash, another respected WCA writer. "We need this place to paint, or else we're going to bomb the streets more, straight up." 16

Although a few Westside writers are friendly with their Eastside counterparts, interaction between the two groups is limited. Indeed, the rivalry between WCA and K2S—STN dates back to the origins of the L.A. writing scene. Like breakdancers, writers "battle" each other. The spoils of victory may include several dozen spraycans, or the appropriation of a writer's tag. 17

As soon as WCA and K2S—STN each became aware of the other, the stage was set for the East–West battle, which took place at the Belmont Tunnel in 1985. WCA went up with the bigger production in their trademark flashy style, featuring a pastel-yellow/clover-green/pastel-aqua, black-outlined, white-highlighted, hot-pink-and-avocado-bordered piece by Risk. Next to it was a character by fellow writer Cooz, of a Japanese-animation-style buxom woman wearing shiny wraparound shield glasses, a cascade of auburn hair spilling over her shoulders. 18

K2S—STN countered with a shocker from Prime. Employing an abstract, futuristic style, he wrote his tag with an altered color scheme and composition: triangles and squares of hot pink, white, true blue and baby blue produced a new kind of three-dimensional effect. Next to it he drew a robot character he'd found in a comix mag. 19

Some West Coast writers congratulated Prime afterward in an apparent admission of defeat. By the next morning, however, all of the WCA productions, as well as a substantial part of Prime's, had been "dissed" (painted over) by unknown writers, and the bad blood began. To this day, some WCA writers maintain that Prime was the culprit, although he always denied the allegation. 20

There are substantial stylistic differences between East and West Los Angeles writers. WCA writers are sensitive to the charge that they are "biting" (the writer's term for plagiarism) New York styles. "We took the New York styles and made them into our own style," says Wisk, the crew's most prolific writer, a little defensively. Using thin letters with stylized swirls and blends of color accented with arrows and sparkles, West Coast's work often achieves a slick magazine look—the New York stamp is unmistakable. 21

K2S—STN, on the other hand, while sometimes drawing on the same influences, produces more readable block- or bubblelike letters that echo old gang-writing styles updated with the wildstyle. The result is aesthetically analogous to the split between the Anglo and ethnic art worlds of the 1960s and 1970s—playful abstraction on the one hand, Socialist Realism-flavored work on the other.

But the stylistic differences between the two groups hide deeper tensions. The Eastside writers, who lay claim to being the original Los Angeles bombers, feel that WCA has received a disproportionate share of media attention, including articles in the *Los Angeles Times* that have largely ignored the Eastside writers in favor of Westsiders.   22

"It was only when white people started doing graffiti that they said it was art," Prime once said bitterly. "We were doing it before them, but [the media] were blaming us for vandalism." These sentiments are echoed by most Eastside writers, and their resentment is obviously both class- and race-based.   23

"Most of the West Coast writers are from middle-class families," says Moda of the original L.A. Bomb Squad. "On this side of town, you're faced with the gang problem and graffiti at the same time. It affects the writers from poor neighborhoods: because they have the distraction of gangs, they might not be able to pursue it all the way. Like Prime—he's stuck between gangs and graffiti."   24

Prime's father approaches the bed slowly. An oxygen mask all but hides the son's incipient beard and mustache. Dried blood is still encrusted on his forehead and temples. The father takes his son's bloody hand into his own, leans down and whispers something into his ear. Prime tries to speak, but the words are mumbled, delirious. His father lifts back the white sheet and peers at Prime's right arm, swathed in bandages. After two major operations, the doctors are finally willing to predict that Prime is going to make it.   25

Over the next few days, Prime's fellow writers will visit his bedside in an endless procession. Among them is Duke, twenty years old, a native of Guatemala and a seven-year writing veteran of K2S—STN. Like Prime, Duke has been involved in gangsterism. When he heard the news about the shooting, his first impulse was "to go out and take care of shit," but he checked himself. "The art took me out of the trip," says Duke, who is dressed in his trademark smoke-gray jeans, his boyish face showing a spotty beard. "It helped me to look at this world in a more positive sense."   26

Initiated into gangs at an early age, Duke says his first spraycan escapade involved simple tagging. But after some heavy violence on the streets—he was once tied to a car bumper by rival gang members and dragged for two blocks—he decided to try to "clean up his act." When the   27

Kings stop at nothing

first wave of graffiti art hit L.A., he began devoting more and more of his time to piecing.

"I wanted to kick back," Duke says of the early days of graffiti. At that time, when he was in tenth grade, "jungle football" clubs were sprouting up all over the inner city. The emphasis at first was on sports, but soon fights were breaking out between the rival groups. Then guns were brandished, and the club Duke had helped to organize quickly became one of the largest gangs in the Pico-Union area, a *barrio* that is home to over a quarter of a million central Americans.

Early one morning in October 1985, a shotgun blast tore Duke's stomach open as he was walking to school. The doctors later told him it was a miracle that he had survived. Then came family problems and a difficult separation from his girlfriend. He gave up writing for months and found himself at a crossroads, uncertain as to which path to follow. But today he's back in the writing scene, and serious about moving up from the streets to a "legal" career by painting storefront signs and doing everything he can to set up his own art studio at home.

Prime, like Duke, had begun to distance himself from the gang world before he was shot. "He wasn't the kind to go out and say, 'Let's take care of these dudes,'" says Duke after visiting Prime one day. "Thank God he's not gone. And I hope he never goes." Like Geo, who was shot for yelling out the wrong gang name when they asked him, "Where you from?" Or Sine, who was stabbed when he tried to defend a younger kid from a gangster wielding a switchblade. Or Risko, who died in a car that tumbled off a Harbor Freeway overpass as he and another friend fled from the police after a gang outing. All were writers associated with K2S—STN.

Government agencies in Los Angeles County spend some $150 million annually in the war against graffiti. Sandblasters are available for heavy-duty "buffing" across the city, and a city-run warehouse doles out free paint to any citizen who asks for it. (30,000 gallons, enough to cover 6 million square feet of graffiti, have been given away since 1986.) A legal offensive is also in the works. Daniel Ramos, a.k.a. Chaka, probably the most prolific writer in the history of graffiti (some 10,000 tags up and down the state), was busted by the LAPD and the City Attorney threw the proverbial book at him. He languished in jail for months and was recently assigned to a special reformatory "boot camp." Anti-graffiti forces, springing from well-to-do and generally conservative home-owners' associations nationwide, have lobbied for special anti-graffiti legislation—a ban on the sale of spraycans, for example.

"We're really deterring them," says LAPD spokesperson William Medina, who coordinates a neighborhood cleanup effort in the Rampart *barrio* area of L.A. For the LAPD, even the elaborate pieces that have gone up at the various "yards" around town are considered illegal. "We view it as graffiti," says Medina. "The only things we don't consider illegal are [city-] organized and approved murals."

Community meetings focusing on graffiti typically draw standing-room-only audiences. Responding to an increasingly vociferous public, Mayor Tom Bradley formed the Mayor's Committee for Graffiti Removal and Prevention. The chairman of the committee, Stuart Haines, is the owner of Textured Coatings of America, a profitable paint manufacturing company. "It's like a guy who works in a weapons manufacturing plant being named head of a task force to stop a war," said one supporter of graffiti art.   33

The adult response, then, has placed top priority on eradication and enforcement of anti-vandalism statutes. Only a pittance has been funnelled into public mural programs, which gave youngsters the opportunity to refine their talents under the tutelage of established artists. "The real answer is to pass tougher laws to punish the graffiti artists who deface public property, along with the gang members who are identifying their turf," says Stuart Haines.   34

Among the adults searching for alternatives to this deadlock is Adolfo V. Nodal, the general manager of the city's Cultural Affairs Department and a longtime supporter of public arts, via endeavors like the MacArthur Arts Project, which featured art by local writers on the park's amphitheater. "Arresting kids and abatement through paint-outs is not the only way to do it," says Nodal. "It has to be an issue of implementing cultural programs for kids. We've been fighting a losing battle on this issue."   35

"We haven't looked at *why* they're painting," says Mary Trotter of the Vernon Central Merchants Association, which is sponsoring a graffiti art contest that offers a cash prize of $1,200, plus wall space donated by neighborhood businesses. "They want to communicate something to us, and we're not listening."   36

"Hollywood should understand," says independent filmmaker Gary Glaser, who produced a documentary on the L.A. writing scene called *Bombing L.A.* "This is hype town Number One. The kids can't get on television, so they tag."   37

Beneath the visor of a baseball cap that barely contains his shock of bushy red hair, the sea of parking lights is reflected in Wisk's glasses. It's about nine in the evening, and we are driving east on the Santa Monica Freeway.   38

One of the most famous taggers in town, Wisk is a founding member of WCA. His simple but undeniably attractive tag consists of a butterfly-like *W*. He numbers every one of them, as would an artist producing a limited   39 edition of serigraphs. The *W*s are visible as far west as Venice Beach, north to the San Fernando Valley, south to Watts and east to Pomona. After two years of almost nightly "bombing" runs, Wisk broke the 2,000 mark this week.

Blowing bubbles and snapping his wad of chewing gum, Wisk directs me to exit the Santa Monica Freeway at Crenshaw Avenue, and we park near an overpass. He opens the door a crack and shakes each of his cans, pressing the nozzles a touch to make sure they're in working order.   40

"Ready?" asks Wisk. He pushes his glasses back up on his nose.   41

We walk, real cool and slow, across the overpass to a spot of fence already bent from previous bombing raids. We slow down, even walk in place until no more cars are passing by. After a glance left and right to make sure nobody's around, Wisk says, "Go!" and we hop over the fence.   42

Like soldiers on maneuvers, we run low alongside the freeway wall, Wisk shaking his can all the way. We zip past sooty ivy and sickly palm trees, the roar of traffic all around us. Wisk stops about two hundred yards down from the overpass, before a spot of wall clear of bushes and trees. "Stay low, dude! Look out for 5–0s and if you see one, yell out, 'Cops!'"   43

The can hisses as Wisk moves up and down, arcs around, outlining his throw-up in black. Then comes the fill-in, rapid back-and-forth motions with white or silver. *W*s number 2021, 2022, 2023 are up in a matter of minutes.   44

"Everybody takes the freeways," says Wisk, pausing before beginning *W* number 2024. "Everybody, *everybody* and their mother sees this! This is like the subways in New York, except you move past it instead of having it move past you."   45

Wisk, getting greedy and perhaps a bit reckless, risks a bust by going up with *W* number 2025. He's already covered fifty yards. Whatever aerosol mist doesn't make it onto the wall rises up in a cloud that is gilded by the amber street lamp above us. Wisk notices me looking at the sight. "I love it!" he exclaims, satisfaction sweeping over his freckled face.   46

Later, driving back down the freeway, westbound, Wisk tells me, "Look at that shit that we did the other night," pointing excitedly to his and a fellow WCA writer's tags. "Look! *W, W, W, W, J-A, J-A, J-A!* Look at all them *W*s lined up, bro'! Boom! Boom! Boom! Boom! Boom!"   47

"We were just kickin' it up there, drinking beer," says Skept, his freckled face and light green eyes showing the strain of the days since Prime was shot. His usual gregarious demeanor is subdued. "We were sitting down on the couch. Then, *chk, chk,* BOOM! BOOM! BOOM!"   48

Skept (short for "Skeptical"), a Japanese-American who grew up in a mostly Latino *barrio,* is another veteran of K2S—STN. Like Duke and Prime, he's been leading a double life for years now, although he's long since left the old 'hood and now lives in a comfortable downtown loft with his father,   49

Library Resource Center
Renton Technical College
3000 N.E. 4th St.
Renton, WA 98056

a well-known abstract expressionist. We walk into the ample, brightly lit studio. His father sits near the southernmost wall, smoking a pipe, poring over papers. Skept's room is at the northern end. We enter and he closes the door behind him, revealing a poster of the heavy metal group Iron Maiden.

He pops a Jungle Brothers rap tape into the player and brings out some   50
photo albums. There's a piece by Prime, in his trademark color-patch style. And there's a photo of Geo standing before a piece, a shot taken not long before he died. He was a good-looking, slightly overweight Latino kid with a bright, adolescent smile. "Lots of friends have passed away in the last couple of years," says Skept, staring at the photo.

Then he shows me his recent work, "psychedelic" paintings on small art   51
boards, pieces that "even my dad was surprised by." Multicolored circles, squares and bubbles appear to float in a primordial miasma. He plans on doing such a piece soon, up on a wall, perhaps here, downtown.

The question that is running through my mind as we kick back and talk   52
about writing is, Why did Skept have to go back to the neighborhood the night the shooting took place, knowing that there was a possibility of yet another drive-by killing?

Instead I ask, "You know what adults would tell you about all this, don't   53
you?"

"'You shouldn't go, this and that.' My dad doesn't even know I was there   54
when they shot him. I haven't even told anybody in my family about Prime. I didn't want to hear it. I already know what they'll say."

Skept will sometimes ensconce himself in the studio, drawing for days   55
on end. Or he'll go out piecing at the yards. Then there'll be the urge to do a daring, illegal piece on the streets. Then he'll go back and "kick it" in the old gang neighborhood. "But the shooting," I remind him.

"It's happened so many times already, I'm getting used to it," he says,   56
then pauses. "But—I don't know why—this time it seems so different. Maybe because I was there, I was so close . . ."

"You'll go back even though you know this might happen again?" I ask.   57
"Probably."   58

A few days earlier, I had accompanied Skept, who was unshaven and   59
had sleepless circles under his eyes, on a writing excursion to the Belmont Tunnel. Several writers were out that day, but Skept wandered off by himself to an out-of-the-way spot in the shadow of the old trolleycar station. There, he did a quick throw-up. With a baby-blue outline and a dark gray fill-in, he wrote his crew's name. The fat, blocklike letters seemed to collapse upon each other, as though plummeting through the air. In gold he wrote the names of Geo and Sine. He knelt before the piece in silence for several minutes.

*   *   *

Prime is sitting up in bed, flanked by two *cholos* in dark glasses. He offers   60
his left hand in greeting. The doctors, he says, have told him that he's doing
all right, "so far." He's kind of worried about their emphasis on the "so far,"
but says he's already going stir-crazy. He wants to go home.

He reminisces about the writing binges of the early days, when he and   61
Skept and Geo would "walk from the Beverly Center Mall all the way downtown, tagging up all the way." They'd go all night sometimes, catching a
wink wherever they could rather than go home. At dawn, they'd search for
an apartment building with a swimming pool for a makeshift bath, then
warm up at a local laundromat.

Prime stops suddenly. A grimace of pain crosses his face, and his right   62
shoulder twitches involuntarily. I ask him about his arm. "I don't know, ey.
I don't know," he says, looking away.

On my way out of Prime's room, I run into Duke and Radio-Tron   63
founder Carmelo Alvarez, who continues to work closely with many of the
K2S—STN writers. Duke stays with me in the hallway, leaning against the
yellow wall under the bad fluorescent lights. He's working on a storefront
for a neighborhood residents' association, he tells me. And he's recently
been talking with Frank Romero, the famous Chicano artist. "I tripped out
when he said that I could work with him on a project," says Duke, flashing
a quick grin. For now, everything's "fresh."

I recall a photo Duke once showed me of Prime. It was taken on the day   64
they worked together on a big piece near Belmont High, not far from where
Prime was shot. The photo was taken looking down from the top of the
wall, showing Prime frozen in mid-stroke—his right arm raised, a look of
tremendous concentration on his face.

The piece they worked on that day is the one Duke is proudest of. He   65
drew his "Dream Lady," with a soft, sensuous aqua face and windborne orange hair. Prime contributed a Cerebus-like character, K2S—STN's mascot,
in baby blue, with touches of clover green and turquoise. The piece is long
gone, but has been immortalized in Duke's photo album.

"If Prime comes out not being able to draw with his right hand, he'll do   66
it with his left," Duke says with almost desperate conviction. "And if he
comes out not being able to move his left hand, he'll do it with his feet."

It is difficult not to be impressed by Duke's determination. At the same   67
time, I find myself doubting. Graffiti art is temporal, fragile. It has a lifespan
of only a week or two before another writer goes over a piece, or the city
buffs it out. How far can the kids really go with it? The New York gallery
scene's fascination with street art only directly affected a few writers in the
short time it lasted. And even if some do make it into the L.A. galleries, will
their work lose its power in that context?

And what of the inner-city black hole that threatens to swallow all the   68
colors and deny every escape route? One well-known Eastside writer was
awarded a scholarship to a prestigious local art school, which he attended
for three years. He's now doing time for murder. Art doesn't always save,
but here's Duke before me, all enthusiasm and faith, and who's to say that
he and Prime and Skept can't realize their dreams?

Later, Prime's visitors are walking out of County together, past the emer-   69
gency entrance, where two paramedic trucks and a sheriff's patrol car are
parked. The sun has just set and high, dark gray clouds streak across the
sky, creating a dark canvas. Duke stops and stares. He has caught something
we hadn't noticed: a small, baby-blue aperture in the gray.

"It's like a gateway to a new world," he says.   70

Working with the Text

1. In paragraph 21, Martinez quotes the graffiti artist Phoe as saying,
   "Writing is, like, a different community." What are some features of this
   community? Who is included, and who is not? Are the borders of this
   community stable or shifting? What is the role of geography? Of skill?
   Of class? Of artistic lineage?

2. Describe the relationship between writing and other forms of self-
   expression in the United States. Do you agree with Gary Glaser when
   he asserts, "The kids can't get on television, so they tag"? What cultural
   values do television and writing share? How do the two media and
   their values diverge? What social and aesthetic values does writing
   share with more traditional painting? Why has there been only limited
   assimilation of writers into main stream art?

3. Why does Martinez begin the essay with the image of a bloodstained
   couch? Think about what a couch normally represents and where it
   is normally found, then consider how its significance alters when it
   appears in a vacant lot and becomes the site of a shooting. Why
   does the author describe the stain as "a dark flower"? More generally,
   why does the attack on Prime open and close the essay? What is the
   relationship between the violent lives of Martinez's artists and the work
   they produce?

4. Analyze the terminology Martinez cites—"write," "bomb," "piece,"
   "tag," "wildstyle," "crew," "throw-up," "terrorize," "battle," "dis"—and
   the names adopted by his artists. What do these reveal about the
   nature and purposes of graffiti artistry?

5. The Internet offers several important sites on graffiti, the most
   extensive of which is ART CRIMES. Starting at the *Beyond Borders* Web

site, look at some of the examples of graffiti from cities around the world contained there. How are these similar to or different from the graffiti discussed in "Going Up in LA"? Look closely at one section and consider how the examples there express violence, anger, alienation, and specific political statements. Does graffiti writing look the same on the street as it does on the Web?

Tunnel Notes of a New Yorker

LEONARD KRIEGEL

A life-long resident of New York City, Leonard Kriegel taught English for many years at the City University of New York (CUNY), a school system known for its large percentage of immigrant students. His writings include a novel and, most recently, a collection of autobiographical essays, *Falling into Life.* The following essay originally appeared in *American Scholar,* a publication of the Phi Beta Kappa Society. In it, Kriegel argues that the kind of graffiti one finds in urban environments today expresses a savage sense of alienation, "an urban statement whose ultimate end is nothing less than the destruction of urban life" and community.

When I was eight, I loved to run with my friends through the tunnel leading   1
into Reservoir Oval in the North Central Bronx. The Oval occupied the site of a former city reservoir dredged by the WPA and then landscaped with playgrounds, wading pools, softball fields, a quarter-mile dirt track, and some of the finest tennis courts in the city—all ringed by attractive bush- and tree-lined walks that provided a natural shield for the sexual probings of early adolescence. Nothing else that bordered our neighborhood—not the wilds of Bronx Park or the chestnut trees of Van Cortlandt Park or the small camel-humped rock hill in Mosholu Parkway down which we went belly-whopping on American Flyer sleds in winter—fed us so incontrovertible a sense that America's promise now included us as did the long green and gray sweep of Reservoir Oval.

We would run through that entrance tunnel like a pack of Hollywood   2
Indians on the warpath, our whoops echoing off the walls until we emerged from its shadows into the lush green lawns and brick walks and playing fields. Our portion of the Bronx was an ethnically mixed stew of immigrant families and their children, many of whom had fled Manhattan's crowded

Lower East Side tenements for the spacious, park-rich green borough where Jonas Bronck had followed his cow across the Harlem River three hundred years earlier. The Bronx was still the city's "new" borough in 1941. Sparsely settled until after World War I, our neighborhood contained typical New York working- and lower-middle-class families on the rise in an America emerging from the Depression.

We children had already been assimilated into the wider American 3 world. All of us—Irish and Italian Catholic as well as Eastern European Jew—believed we could ride the dream of success to a singular destiny. We were not yet of an age where we could physically journey into that wider America the books we read and the movies we saw told us was ours for the taking. The Oval was where we played together. It was also where we sometimes fought each other over myths that grew increasingly foreign and more raggedly European with each passing day. (Not that we were unaware of our parents' cultural baggage: marriage between Italian and Irish Catholics was still considered "mixed" in 1941.)

Occasionally, I would chance the Oval alone, in search of more solitary 4 adventure. A curious metamorphosis would envelop me at such times: the entrance tunnel seemed darker and more threatening, the shadows warning me to move cautiously past walls peppered with graffiti. Alone, I let loose no war whoops to echo through that emptiness. Instead, I picked my way carefully through that dark half-moon of enclosed space, as if the graffiti scrawled on its surface held the clue to my future. There was something menacing about words scrawled on walls. Like an archaeologist probing ru- ins, I might turn in terror at any moment and run back to the security of my apartment three blocks south of the Oval.

Most of the graffiti was of the "John loves Mary!" kind, no different from 5 the scribbled notes we passed one another in the P.S. 80 school yard down the hill. But it was also on that tunnel's walls that I first read the rage and fury of those who stained the world with conspiratorial fantasies. As rage ex- ploded like bullets, words burrowed into my consciousness. "Roosevelt Jew Bastard!" "Unite Unite / Keep America White!" "Father Coughlin Speaks Truth!" "Kill All Jews!" In the raw grasp of age-old hatreds, politics was plot and plot was history and that reality seemed as impregnable as it was inescapable.

Like adults, children learn to shape anger through the words they con- 6 front. The graffiti on that tunnel wall mobilized my rage, nurturing my need for vengeance in the midst of isolation. It wasn't simply the anti-Semitism I wanted vengeance upon; it was my own solitary passage through that entrance tunnel. As I moved through it alone, the tunnel was transformed into everything my budding sense of myself as embryonic American hated. Walking through it became an act of daring, for graffiti had converted its emptiness into a threat that could only be taken the way it was offered—a threat that was distinctly personal.

In no other part of that huge complex of fields and walks was graffiti   7
in great evidence. Other than the occasional heart-linked initials carved into the green-painted slats of wooden benches, I remember nothing else defacing the Oval. One emerged from that tunnel and the graffiti disappeared—all of it, "John loves Mary!" as well as "Kill All Jews!" It was as if an unwritten compact had been silently agreed upon, allowing the tunnel leading to the Oval to be scrawled over (despite occasional whitewashing, the tunnel was dark and poorly lit) while the rest of that huge recreation complex remained free of the presence of graffiti. Running that tunnel alone was an act of purgation, rewarded when one was safely home with the illusion (and occasionally the reality) of ethnic harmony.

Other than that tunnel, the presence of graffiti was localized to a few al-   8
leys and subway stations and public urinals in the New York I remember from the forties and fifties. Until the sixties, even chalk and paint adhered to the unwritten laws of proportion in neighborhoods like mine. Buildings had not yet been crusted over with curlicued shapes and exploding slashes, zigzagging to a visual anarchy that testified to a love of color and line overwhelmed by hatred of the idea that color and line do not dictate the needs of community. Even the anti-Semitic graffiti of that tunnel remains in my memory as less the product of hatred than an expression of the distance existing between groups struggling to claim a portion of the American past.

In an essay published in 1973, Norman Mailer labeled graffiti a "faith," a   9
word that struck me even back then as an odd use of language when applied to what a graffiti writer does. From the perspective of that eight-year-old child moving through that tunnel entrance, graffiti was the very antithesis of faith. It embodied a poetics of rage and hatred, a syntax in which anyone could claim the right, if he possessed the will, to impose his needs on others. But rage is not faith, as even an eight-year-old knew. It is simply rage.

In today's New York—and in today's London and Paris and Amsterdam   10
and Los Angeles—the spread of graffiti is as accurate a barometer of the decline of urban civility as anything else one can think of. Paradoxically, even as it spread, graffiti was hailed as one of the few successful attempts the voiceless in our nation's cities made to impose their presence on urban culture. If graffiti is now the most obvious form of visual pollution city landscapes are forced to endure (even more polluting than those paste-up false windows with flower pots that grow like urban ivy on the deserted apartment houses fronting the Major Deegan Parkway in the East Bronx), it has assumed for New Yorkers the shape and frame of this city's prospects.

Where expectation is confused with coherence, those savage slashes on brick and sidewalk embody our idea of all that city life is and all that we can now expect it to be.

In books and photographic essays, graffiti is heralded as the art structuring the real urban landscape that the poor confront in their daily lives. "Graffiti makes a statement!" is the rallying cry of those who defend its presence. True enough—even if one believes that the statement graffiti makes chokes the very idea of what a city can be. One can argue that it is not what the statement says but the style the statement employs that lends graffiti its insistent singularity. But the evidence of the streets insists that graffiti is an urban statement whose ultimate end is nothing less than the destruction of urban life. Regardless of whether it is considered art or public nuisance, graffiti denies the possibility of an urban community by insisting that individual style is a more natural right than the communitarian demands of city life.

Defenders of graffiti may insist that its importance lies in the voice it gives to anger and that its triumph resides in the alternative it offers to rage. Perhaps so. But anyone who walks through the streets of today's New York understands that the price graffiti demands is an emotional exhaustion in which we find ourselves the victims of that same rage and anger supposedly given voice—*vented* is today's fashionable word—by these indiscriminate slashes of color plastered against brick and wall and doorway and telephone booth.

Contemporary graffiti is not particularly political—at least not in New York. On those few times when one spots graffiti that does seek to embrace a message, the politics seem prepubescent sloganeering. Few openly political sayings are lettered onto these buildings and walls. Even the huge graffiti-like wall mural of a small Trotskyite press that one sees driving north on West Street in lower Manhattan speaks not of politics but of a peculiar Third World clubbiness more characteristic of the early 1970s than of our time. Malcolm X, Che Guevara—originally offered as a pantheon of Third World liberators, the faces over the years have taken on the likeness of the comic-book superheroes in whose image one suspects they were originally conceived and drawn. The future they appeal to is curiously apolitical, as if the revolution they promise lies frozen in a nineteenth-century photograph in which reality assumes the proportions of myth. One has the impression that these are icons that have been hung on the wall for good luck, like a rabbit's foot or one of those plastic Jesuses one sees hanging from the rearview mirrors of battered old Chevys.

The single most effective political graffito I have seen over the past few years was not in New York. Last summer, as I drove through streets filled with the spacious walled-in homes and immaculate concrete driveways of a wealthy Phoenix suburb, on my way to visit Frank Lloyd Wright's Taliesin West, I came across "Save Our Desert" slashed in large dripping red letters across a brown sun-drenched adobe wall surrounding one of the huge sun palaces that root like cacti in the nouveau riche wilds of Goldwater Country. Here was a graffito in which politics was central, a gauntlet thrown at the feet of developers for whom the Arizona desert is mere space to be acquired and used and disposed of for profit.

Perhaps because it is more traditional, political graffiti seems more understandable than these explosions of line and color and ectoplasmic scrawl now plastered like dried mucus against New York's brick and concrete. "Save Our Desert!" may be simplistic, but at least it expresses a desire to right a balance deemed unjust and unnecessary. Political graffiti intrudes on privacy by voicing a specific protest. This alone serves to distinguish it from the public stains New Yorkers now assume are as natural as blades of grass growing between the cracks in a sidewalk.   15

In 1972, I lived with my family in London. What little graffiti I saw in an England that had discovered the mod was still an expression of class and caste. It did not yet encrust London like a multi-colored scab. I remember no initials or words slashed across public monuments or statue pedestals.   16

On weekend afternoons, my wife and I and our two young sons would wander from stall to stall at the Portobello Road flea market. On one of those Saturdays, as my sons hopped from one seller hawking medals and military insignia to another, I walked off alone and found myself staring up at huge white letters spray-painted across a large gray Dickensian wall: "BOGSIDE OR CLYDESIDE," the letters read, "Support the Angry Side!"   17

A bitter strike was in progress at the Clyde River Ship Works in Scotland, while the struggle between Catholic and Protestant in the Bogside of Derry had already turned as murderous and self-righteous as, invariably, religious wars do. As my sons searched for military treasures, I stood transfixed before that rage of identity shaped by men unwilling to suffer indignities without trying to right the balance and even the score.   18

In 1972, I still thought of myself as in good part a product of my social class. The anger of Clydeside was easy enough for me to identify with. An allegiance to trade unionism—at times, a blind allegiance—was as much political religion as I could muster back then. But during the four months I had spent in London, I watched in bewilderment as the events in Northern Ireland were regurgitated on the nightly television news. The cool English accents of the BBC announcer served to make the Bogside more politically confusing than I could afford to acknowledge. I wanted a politics simple enough to fit the cut of ideology. Yet even after trips to Southampton to seek   19 out dockworkers with whom I could discuss what was taking place in Ulster, I couldn't figure out which side I should be on: If anger and rage were the criteria, both sides seemed eminently worthy of support.

A few weeks later I, along with the rest of the world, would witness the murder of Israeli athletes at the Munich Olympics. That was an easier religious war for me to understand, one that echoed and re-echoed with the tremors of the tunnel graffiti of my childhood. Birth and history told me very clearly which side I was on in the struggle between Arab and Jew. But between Ulster Protestant and Ulster Catholic, I knew nothing other than the boundaries of my ignorance. Not even that BBC voice calmly reciting the day's casualties made the struggle in Derry anything other than a free-fall of demands and counterdemands. 20

Why do these two images—the shadowy entrance tunnel to the playing fields of my childhood and the gray Dickensian wall in London—spring from the sheath of memory when I think about graffiti today? And I think about graffiti a great deal. For to live in my New York and not think about graffiti is to make oneself either purposefully blind or oblivious. Why is it that I find both "Death for Christ Killers!" and "Support the Angry Side!" somehow preferable to the curlicued shapes and exploding stars and slashing initials slapped like overturned garbage cans at curbside against the walls and trucks, the steel gates and red brick, the subway entrances and superb nineteenth-century cast-iron architecture of a city that grows more and more fragile with each passing day? Why does today's New York graffiti seem even more ominous than that 1941 scrawl "Kill All Jews!"? And why does the current state of this city seem to me more accurately captured by these wordless dispatches from rootless souls than by all the statistics about street crime and drug abuse and white flight to the suburbs in the *New York Times?* 21

Until about five years ago, I used to go back to my old neighborhood in the Bronx. Occasionally, I would drift through the decaying tunnel entrance to the Oval. The smells had grown more sour than when I was eight, and the faces of the children in the playground had grown darker. But those darker faces merely indicated that the ethnic successions that had been taking place in this city for the past hundred and fifty years were still taking place. Far more striking was how the graffiti had changed. No longer did the words echo with pent-up hatreds or speak of adolescent romance. Instead, the tunnel walls, along with the playing fields and playgrounds, were crusted over with color and line. In a city seething with the raucous claims of victimization hurled against counter-victimization, few privileges were demanded by that graffiti. As if in some huge art gallery, the focus was on color, line, ubiquitous form and curlicued signal. Like an avalanche, line and 22 color moved toward an ultimate disintegration that would not violate the demands of those who had created these graffiti waves. In this New York, art now rode even the artists, while the new beckoned to the bored Columbus in each American soul.

We live in a culture in which the cartoon explosions of the graffiti artist   23
Basquiat are heralded as the work of a Renoir or a Van Gogh. An Andy Warhol toy, taken up and then discarded by the whims of fashion. Basquiat's death by a heroin overdose is transmogrified into a mirror image of city life. Like Van Gogh's ear, it is the artist's physical presence, not the work, on which we are expected to concentrate. Even as art rides the artists, artists are transformed into what our conception of what city life should be demands.

On the surface, style has never been in greater demand than in today's   24
New York. From an art in which performance is defined as a nude body covered by chocolate and music is the sound of silence, the culture reverberates to the beat of the contemporary. Curlicues and initials and slashes against conventional surfaces scream to be noticed. Claim is splashed against counter-claim. It is not talent but defiance that is sold as a commodity. From doorway and mailbox, from truck and metal store guards, from telephone booth and statue pedestal, Kilroy is here, there, and everywhere. Only this Kilroy is no mere democratic signature. This Kilroy is not a name anchored to an idea of a country. This Kilroy stands before us in spasms of color, initialed explosions of red on white, black on red. And what, we ask as we listen to a boom box in some passing car in the street below, is more attractive than style in a city so intent on creating itself anew?

Over and over, voices insist that graffiti proves that behind the rage of   25
urban poverty there remains an endurance of aspiration. Perhaps. But why should rage become so prevalent at a moment in history when style has been deemed so ubiquitous? That question speaks tellingly of the true politics of this "tough" city as it spins like a gyroscope out of control through our fashion-conscious age. Lured by myths celebrating their endemic toughness ("If you can make it here," Sinatra sings—and we New Yorkers echo him, even as we nervously glance over our shoulders to see who or what is coming up behind us—"you'll make it anywhere"), New Yorkers crave absolution through symbols: Bella Abzug's hats, Felix Rohatyn's suits, Al Sharpton's hairdo, the electric signs blinking through the cash-and-carry hustler's moment in Times Square, the graffiti scrawls on our streets.

The truth, of course, is that people in this city are anything but tough.   26
New Yorkers endure conditions that would be unacceptable in most Third World cities. Even the city's millionaires live with a fatalism one might logically expect to find in illiterate Latin American peasants or Bosnian Muslims shunted from place to place to the horrible music of "ethnic cleansing." The

real truth is that we New Yorkers more and more sound like people so used to being beaten over the head that our primary instinct is to hunker down and ride out any storm, burdened by the knowledge that another catastrophe is just around the corner. And so we try to turn a blind eye to these graffiti initials jumbled together like alphabet soup, plastered against wall and kiosk, public telephone and public urinal, staining our aspirations and our lives.

In 1973, when he wrote "The Faith of Graffiti," Mailer was able to view those wall stains as an urban stamp of vitality, the shifting emblems of a New York underclass alive and vibrant with the tremor of its inability to rest. But Mailer should have known better. Mailer was, after all, raised in Brooklyn. And he must have known that, in this chameleon of a city, the new quickly becomes the old, the lived-with, the used-by. Lacking substance, the new grows boring. And we begin to remember the not-new with a nostalgia that breeds a breakdown of confidence in what it is we actually do see. How long can one love the idea of New York at the cost of the actual city's reality? Not a question to be asked lightly in the physical and intellectual squalor in which we New Yorkers live now. 27

How unusually clear New York seems in black-and-white newsreels from the forties and fifties. Not that the streets were so much cleaner than they are today (they were somewhat cleaner, but New Yorkers have always been slobs and garbage has long since been among the city's badges). Not that one longs for the kitsch of double-decker buses on Fifth Avenue. But how solid and enduring the stone buildings appear in black and white, how singularly they command our affection. Yes, empty paper cups were discarded in the streets back then, too, and traffic bottlenecked into impregnable jams. But where are those savage strokes of line and color demanding recognition of rage as actuality? Why are the walls quiet with the grain of brick and granite instead of explosive with the desecration of graffiti? Did no one in that New York belong to the angry side? Did no one see his function in life as spray-painting red and black and orange initials on any surface that had the temerity to remain ignorant of his singular presence? 28

To deny this city's painful decline over the past three decades is to deny the obvious. One can measure that decline through the spread of graffiti. The process began with the insistence that these mindless blotches and savage strokes embodied a legitimate, if admittedly different, sense of fashion, that they could be viewed—indeed, they had to be viewed—as a "natural" expression of the new and daring. This is the gist of the argument Mailer makes, and it is not an argument we can afford to ignore even today. We certainly could not afford to ignore it back in 1973, as we witnessed graffiti's spectacular rise as a New York growth industry. Only today the vision has 29 rubbed down, like overwatered brick that soon chips and crumbles, and these savage slashes of color fill us with a weary disgust at their seeming omnipresence. An ocean of painted initials laps in growing waves against brick and concrete, even as we pretend it isn't there.

Like everything else in this city, graffiti demands an emotional invest- 30 ment from those who defend it. One can only vindicate these slashes and blobs of color because their presence is so overwhelming. What choice do we have but to demand that the world recognize the "art" in these urban voices? Anything else forces us to examine the consequences of what we have allowed through the intimidating fear of not being in fashion. Even as acceptance is demanded, graffiti continues to pound against the city, having grown as mechanical and fixed as the sound of the boom boxes in the streets below our windows. We label graffiti "real," we label it "authentic," we label it "powerful." Like true pedants, we discuss the nuances of these different voices. We create graffiti martyrs from Keith Haring, dead of AIDS, and from Basquiat, dead of a drug overdose. In their deaths, we tell our-selves, our city lives. For their art is "urban." And urban counts. Urban must count. If not, why have we permitted what has been done to this city we claim to love?

If the graffiti plastered first on subway cars and then on billboard and 31 doorway and brick truly constitutes an art form, then it is an art that seeks to rip out the root idea of what supposedly created it—the idea that a specif-ically urban culture exists. Defended as a creative act in which the city itself becomes the artist's canvas, the paradox of graffiti is the extent to which its existence connotes an implicit hatred of what a city is and what it can offer its citizens. At the core of graffiti's spread lurks the dangerously romantic no-tion that the city is a place of such overwhelming evil that it must be torn apart, savaged into its own death, its residents given a "voice" in the irra-tional hope that in this way its more urbane voices will be stilled. Graffiti slashes at the heart of New York, the heart of urbanity, by attacking the city's splendid nineteenth-century monuments of cast-iron architecture in the res-urrected Soho neighborhood of lower Manhattan as indifferently as it attacks the playful 1930s art deco apartment house façades that once made the now-dingy Grand Concourse in the Bronx so singularly playful an example of urban aspiration.

New Yorkers stand like helpless mannequins before the onslaught. Graf- 32 fiti does not, after all, destroy lives. It is not like the scourge of crack, or the horrendous spread of AIDS, or the rising tension in our neighborhoods be-tween blacks and Jews and between blacks and Asians. Graffiti is no more than a background for the homeless who cage themselves in makeshift cardboard boxes or laundry baskets at night or the crazies who walk the streets engaged in heated dialogues with Jesus or Lenin or Mary Baker Eddy or George Steinbrenner or the dead yet still-celebrated Basquiat. Graffiti is innocent, or so we continue to tell ourselves even in the face of powerful evidence to the contrary. "No one ever died from graffiti!" a friend impatiently snaps, as I point out a deserted bank on the northwest corner of Fourteenth Street and Eighth Avenue, its once-attractive façade gouged and stabbed by slashes of black spray paint. "There are more important problems in this city."

Of course, there *are* more important problems in this city. Yet none speak more directly to the true state of affairs in this New York than the mushrooming graffiti in our streets. And nothing traces the actual state of those streets better than the insistence graffiti makes that there are neither rules nor obligations for the survival of urban hope and aspiration. The prospect of a voice for the voiceless illuminates every dark alley in the New Yorker's mind, like the reflection of one of those stars already extinguished millions and millions of light years away. But is that to be all those of us who claim to love this city are finally left with, these dead light gleanings of one false revolution after another, beneath whose costly illusions—in the name of fashion—we have bent this great and wounded metropolis out of time and out of function and perhaps even out of its future?

33

Working with the Text

1. Though Kriegel acknowledges that most of the graffiti in his childhood tunnel "was of the 'John loves Mary!' kind," he nonetheless argues that all graffiti embodies "a poetics of rage and hatred." Why? Is this seeming contradiction a paradox? And why does the author prefer "Death to the Christ Killers" over the brightly colored shapes and initials of contemporary graffiti?

2. In paragraph 11, Kriegel writes that "graffiti is an urban statement whose ultimate end is nothing less than the destruction of urban life. Regardless of whether it is considered art or public nuisance, graffiti denies the possibility of an urban community by insisting that individual style is a more natural right than the communitarian demands of city life." What assumptions is Kriegel making about the values that should prevail in cities and about the urban features that express them? Is the relationship between individual and community necessarily competitive? Is the urban landscape as legible as the author suggests?

3. Much of the argument in this essay depends upon figurative language, metaphors and similes linking graffiti to distasteful images such as

dried mucus, scabs, and lacerations. Moreover, provocative adjectives, such as "savage," seek to link graffiti with violence. Why does Kriegel use such verbal strategies? With which readers are they likely to be most successful? Why does Kriegel address his audience in the first person plural? Who are "we" and "us," and who are not "we" and "us"? How can you tell?

4. Compare Kriegel's essay with Ruben Martinez's "Going Up in LA." Does either essay reveal deficiencies in the other, or are they simply the products of irreconcilable perspectives? Do they agree on any topic—for example, art? Consider each essay's rhetorical strategies as a function of its purpose. How does each writer position himself in relation to his material? What kinds of evidence does he use? Describe differences in diction, sentence structure, and organization, then discuss how those differences serve the essays' different argumentative goals.

5. Imagine Prime or Duke or Wisk (from the Martinez selection) accompanying Kriegel through his tunnel, as it appears today (see the description in paragraph 22). Write a short dialogue they might have, striving to reflect both their positions and their mode of expression.

Collective Trauma: Loss of Communality

KAI ERIKSON

The work of Kai Erikson, a renowned sociologist and professor at Yale University, has been considered among the most innovative and influential in the field. His numerous books include *Wayward Puritans* (1966), and *A New Species of Trouble: Explorations in Disaster, Trauma, and Community* (1994). The following essay is a chapter from his groundbreaking 1976 book *Everything in Its Path: Destruction of Community in the Buffalo Creek Disaster*. In the aftermath of a devastating flood that killed 125 people in a rural West Virginia community and left as many as 5,000 people homeless, Erikson painstakingly interviewed survivors in order to assess the impact of such a disaster on individuals and their sense of community. Erikson suggests that within so tightly knit a community as Buffalo Creek, where most residents spent their lives without ever leaving, the sense of self was so closely tied to a sense of belonging to the community as a whole that loss of community meant loss of personal identity.

The disaster stretched human nerves to their outer edge. Those of us who did not experience it can never really comprehend the full horror of that day, but we can at least appreciate why it should cause such misery and why it should leave so deep a scar on the minds of those who lived through it. Our imagination can reach across the gulf of personal experience and begin to re-create those parts of the scene that touch the senses. Our eyes can almost see a burning black wave lashing down the hollow and taking everything in its path. The ears can almost hear a roar like thunder, pierced by screams and explosions and the crack of breaking timbers. The nostrils can almost smell the searing stench of mine wastes and the sour odor of smoke and death and decay. All this we can begin to picture because the mind is good at imagery.

But the people of Buffalo Creek suffered a good deal more that day, for they were wrenched out of their communities, torn from the human surround in which they had been so deeply enmeshed. Much of the drama drains away when we begin to talk about such things, partly because the loss of communality seems a step removed from the vivid terror of the event itself and partly because the people of the hollow, so richly articulate when describing the flood and their reaction to it, do not really know how to express what their separation from the familiar tissues of home has meant to them. The closeness of communal ties is experienced on Buffalo Creek as a part of the natural order of things, and residents can no more describe that presence than fish are aware of the water they swim in. It is just there, the envelope in which they live, and it is taken entirely for granted. In this chapter, then, . . . I will use quotations freely, but one must now listen even more carefully for the feelings behind the words as well as registering the content of the words themselves.

I use the term "communality" here rather than "community" in order to underscore the point that people are not referring to particular village territories when they lament the loss of community but to the network of relationships that make up their general human surround. The persons who constitute the center of that network are usually called "neighbors," the word being used in its Biblical sense to identify those with whom one shares bonds of intimacy and a feeling of mutual concern. The people of Buffalo Creek are "neighbor people," which is a local way of referring to a style of relationship long familiar among social scientists. Toennies called it "gemeinschaft," Cooley called it "primary," Durkheim called it "mechanical," Redfield called it "folk," and every generation of social scientists since has

found other ways to express the same thought, one of the most recent being Herbert Gans's concept of "person orientation."

What is a neighbor? When you ask people on Buffalo Creek what the 4
term means, they try to remember that you come from the city and they illustrate their answer with the kind of concrete detail that makes mountain
speech so clear and direct.

What's a neighbor? Well, when I went to my neighbor's house on Satur- 5
day or Sunday, if I wanted a cup of coffee I never waited until the lady of the
house asked me. I just went into the dish cabinet and got me a cup of coffee
or a glass of juice just like it was my own home. They come to my house, they
done the same. See?

We was like one big family. Like when somebody was hurt, everybody 6
was hurt. You know. I guess it was because it was the same people all the
time. I don't know how to explain it. It's a good feeling. It's more than friends.
If someone was hurt, everybody was concerned, everybody. If somebody lost
a member of their family, they was always there. Everybody was around
bringing you something to eat, trying to help. It's a deeper feeling.

Here, if you have a neighbor, it's somebody you know, it's somebody that 7
maybe you take them to the store. I mean, to us neighbors are people that we
have. We just know each other, that's all.

Neighbor? It means relationship. It means kin. It means friends you 8
could depend on. You never went to a neighbor with a complaint that they
didn't listen to or somebody didn't try to help you with. That's a neighbor.
When you wanted a baby-sitter you went next door and they'd baby-sit. Or
you did something for them. They'd either need something or we'd need
something, you know. When you see somebody going down the road, it's
"Where are you going?" "To the store." "Well, bring me back such and such."

A neighbor, then, is someone you can relate to without pretense, a fa- 9
miliar and reliable part of your everyday environment; a neighbor is someone you treat as if he or she were a member of your immediate family. A
good deal has been said in the literature on Appalachia about the clannish-
ness of mountain life, but on Buffalo Creek, as in many coal camps, this
sense of tribal attachment reaches beyond linkages of kin to include a wider
circle, and the obligations one feels toward the people within that circle are
not unlike the obligations one normally feels toward one's own family.

In good times, then, every person on Buffalo Creek looks out at the 10
larger community from a fairly intimate neighborhood niche. If we were to

devise a map representing the average person's social world, we would capture at least the main contours by drawing a number of concentric circles radiating out from the individual center—the inner ring encompassing one's immediate family, the next ring encompassing one's closest neighbors, the third encompassing the familiar people with whom one relates on a regular basis, and the fourth encompassing the other people whom one recognizes as a part of the Buffalo Creek community even though one does not really know them well. Beyond the outermost of those rings is the rest of the world, the terrain populated by what an older generation called "foreigners." Given the size of Buffalo Creek, it is obvious that the community contained people who were relative strangers to one another. Yet there was a clear sense of kinship linking even those relative strangers together— although, as we shall see shortly, that sense of kinship turned out to depend to a greater degree than people realized on the security of one's neighborhood niche.

Communality on Buffalo Creek can best be described as a state of mind   11 shared among a particular gathering of people, and this state of mind, by definition, does not lend itself to sociological abstraction. It does not have a name or a cluster of distinguishing properties. It is a quiet set of understandings that become absorbed into the atmosphere and are thus a part of the natural order. The remarks below, for example, are separate attempts by a husband and wife to explain the nature of those "understandings."

Braeholm was more like a family. We had a sort of understanding.   12 *If someone was away, then we sort of looked after each other's property. We didn't do a lot of visiting, but we had a general understanding. If we cooked something, we would exchange dishes. It was sort of a close-knit type of thing.*

Before the disaster, the neighbors, we could look out and tell when one   13 *another needed help or when one was sick or something was disturbing that person. We could tell from the lights. If the lights was on late at night, we knew that something unusual was going on and we would go over. Sometimes I'd come in from work on a cold day and my neighbor would have a pot of soup for me. There was just things you wouldn't think about. I would look forward to going to the post office. If my car wouldn't start, all I'd have to do is call my neighbors and they would take me to work. If I was there by myself or something, if my husband was out late, the neighbors would come over and check if everything was okay. So it was just a rare thing. It was just a certain type of relationship that you just knew from people growing up together and sharing the same experiences.*

*   *   *

And the key to that network of understandings was a constant readiness to   14
look after one's neighbors, or, rather, to know without being asked what
needed to be done.

If you had problems, you wouldn't even have to mention it. People would   15
just know what to do. They'd just pitch in and help. Everyone was concerned
about everyone else.

I don't think there was a better place in the world to live. People was there   16
when you needed them. You got sick, they helped you. If you needed help of
any kind, you got it. You didn't even have to ask for it. Now I'm a person that
didn't make friends easy. I wasn't hard to get along with, I just didn't mix.
But I knew everybody, and—Well, I just don't know no way to explain it to
you, to make you see it.

You'd just have to experience it, I guess, to really know. It was wonderful.   17
Like when my father died. My neighbors all came in and they cleaned my
house, they washed my clothes, they cooked. I didn't do nothing. They knew
what to do. I mean it's just like teamwork, you know. If one of the kids was
sick, they'd drop every what they were doing, take the kid to the hospital or sit
up all night with him. It was just good. How did they know when you needed
help? I don't know how to explain it, really. The morning my daddy died—he
died in Logan—my aunt called me and told me on the phone at about ten
o'clock in the morning, and I had just got time to get off the phone and go set
on the bed and in come three of my neighbors. They knew it that quick. I
don't know how. They just knew.

The difficulty is that when you invest so much of yourself in that kind   18
of social arrangement you become absorbed by it, almost captive to it, and
the larger collectivity around you becomes an extension of your own personality, an extension of your own flesh. This means that not only are you
diminished as a person when that surrounding tissue is stripped away, but
that you are no longer able to reclaim as your own the emotional resources
you invested in it. To "be neighborly" is not a quality you can carry with you
into a new situation like negotiable emotional currency; the old community
was your niche in the classic ecological sense, and your ability to relate to
that niche is not a skill easily transferred to another setting. This is true
whether you move into another community, as was the case with the first
speaker [who follows], or whether a new set of neighbors moves in around
your old home, as was the case with the second.

Well, I have lost all my friends. The people I was raised up and lived with, 19
they're scattered. I don't know where they're at. I've got to make new friends,
and that's a hard thing to do. You don't make new friends and feel towards
them like you did the people you lived with. See, I raised my family there. We
moved there in '35 and stayed there. I knew everybody in the camp and
practically everybody on Buffalo, as far as that is concerned. But down here,
there ain't but a few people I know, and you don't feel secure around people
you don't know.

Neighbors. We used to have our children at home, we didn't go to hospi- 20
tals to have children. The one on this side of me, them two in back of me, this
one in front of me—they all lived there and we all had our children together.
Now I've got all new neighbors. I even asked my husband to put our home up
for sale, and he said, "What do you think we're going to do? We're old people,
we can't take to buy another home." And I said, "I don't care what you do
with it. I'm not staying here. I can't tell you in words what's the matter." I
said, "I don't care if we go to the moon, let's just get out of here. I'm just not
interested enough anymore. You go out the back door here and there's a new
neighbor. In front of me is a new neighbor and on the other side of me is a
new neighbor. It's just not the same home that I've been living in for thirty-
five years. It's just not the same to me."

A community of the sort we are talking about here derives from and de- 21
pends on an almost perfect democracy of the spirit, where people are not
only assumed to be equal in status but virtually identical in temperament
and outlook. Classes of people may be differentiated for certain purposes—women from men, adults from children, whites from blacks, and so
on—but individual persons are not distinguished from one another on the
basis of rank, occupation, style of life, or even recreational habits. This is not
hard to understand as a practical matter. The men all work at the same jobs;
the women all command domestic territories of roughly the same original
size and quality; the children all attend the same schools as an apprentice-
ship for the same futures; and everybody buys the same goods at the same
stores from equivalent paychecks. Yet the leveling tendency goes even beyond that, for the people of the hollow, like the people of Appalachia generally, do not like to feel different from their fellows and tend to see status
distinctions of any kind as fissures in the smooth surface of the community.
Good fences may make good neighbors in places like New Hampshire,
where relationships depend on cleanly marked parcels of individual space,
but they are seen as lines of division in places like Buffalo Creek.

In most of the urban areas of America, each individual is seen as a sep-   22
arate being, with careful boundaries drawn around the space he or she occupies as a discrete personage. Everyone is presumed to have an individual
name, an individual mind, an individual voice, and, above all, an individual
sense of self—so much so that persons found deficient in any of those qualities are urged to take some kind of remedial action such as undergoing psy-
chotherapy, participating in a consciousness-raising group, or reading one
of a hundred different manuals on self-actualization. This way of looking at
things, however, has hardly any meaning at all in most of Appalachia. There,
boundaries are drawn around whole groups of people, not around separate
individuals with egos to protect and potentialities to realize; and a person's
mental health is measured less by his capacity to express his inner self than
by his capacity to submerge that self into a larger communal whole.

It was once fashionable in the social sciences generally to compare hu-   23
man communities to living organisms. Scholars anxious to make the kind of
distinction I am wrestling with now would argue that persons who belong
to traditional communities relate to one another in much the same fashion
as the cells of a body: they are dependent on one another for definition,
they do not have any real function or identity apart from the contribution
they make to the whole organization, and they suffer a form of death when
separated from that larger tissue. Science may have gained something when
this analogy was abandoned, but it may have lost something, too, for a
community of the kind being discussed here *does* bear at least a figurative
resemblance to an organism. In places like Buffalo Creek, the community
in general can be described as the locus for activities that are normally
regarded as the exclusive property of individuals. It is the *community*
that cushions pain, the *community* that provides a context for intimacy,
the *community* that represents morality and serves as the repository for
old traditions.

Now one has to realize when talking like this that one is in danger of   24
drifting off into a realm of metaphor. Communities do not have hearts or
sinews or ganglia; they do not suffer or rationalize or experience joy. But the
analogy does help suggest that a cluster of people acting in concert and
moving to the same collective rhythms can allocate their personal resources
in such a way that the whole comes to have more humanity than its constituent parts. In effect, people put their own individual resources at the dis-
posal of the group—placing them in the communal store, as it were—and
then draw on that reserve supply for the demands of everyday life. And if
the whole community more or less disappears, as happened on Buffalo
Creek, people find that they cannot take advantage of the energies they
once invested in the communal store. They find that they are almost empty
of feeling, empty of affection, empty of confidence and assurance. It is as if

the individual cells had supplied raw energy to the whole body but did not have the means to convert that energy back into a usable personal form once the body was no longer there to process it. When an elderly woman on Buffalo Creek said softly, "I just don't take no interest in nothing like I used to, I don't have no feeling for nothing, I feel like I'm drained of life," she was reflecting a spirit still numbed by the disaster, but she was also reflecting a spirit unable to recover for its own use all the life it had signed over to the community.

I am going to propose, then, that most of the traumatic symptoms experienced by the Buffalo Creek survivors are a reaction to the loss of communality as well as a reaction to the disaster itself, that the fear and apathy and demoralization one encounters along the entire length of the hollow are derived from the shock of being ripped out of a meaningful community setting as well as the shock of meeting that cruel black water. The line between the two is difficult to draw, as one survivor suggested: 25

> We can't seem to put it all together. We try, but it just isn't there. It may be the shock of the disaster or the aftermath of it all. I don't know. It's hard to separate the two. . . . 26

Loss of Connection

It would be stretching a point to imply that the neighborhoods strung out along Buffalo Creek were secure nests in which people had found a full measure of satisfaction and warmth, but it is wholly reasonable to insist that those neighborhoods were like the air people breathed—sometimes harsh, sometimes chilly, but always a basic fact of life. For better or worse, the people of the hollow were enmeshed in the fabric of their community; they drew their being from it. When that fabric was torn away by the disaster, people found themselves exposed and alone, suddenly dependent on their own personal resources. 27

And the cruel fact of the matter is that many survivors, when left to their own mettle, proved to have meager resources, not because they lacked the heart or the competence, certainly, but because they had always put their abilities in the service of the larger community and did not know how to recall them for their own individual purposes. A good part of their personal strength turned out to be the reflected strength of the collectivity—on loan from the communal store—and they discovered that they were not very good at making decisions, not very good at getting along with others, not very good at maintaining themselves as separate persons in the absence of neighborly support. 28

Words like "lonely" and "lonesome" appear again and again in local   29
conversations.

I can't get used to the way it is. It is very lonesome and sad. I'm disgusted.   30
I'm moving out of this valley.

A lot has changed. Nothing is the same. It is just a big lonesome hollow to   31
me, and I hope I don't ever have to go back up there.

People are "lonely" in the sense that old and trusted neighbors have   32
moved away, leaving them isolated; but the word "lonesome" means something else as well. The people of the hollow are lone some-ones, left to
themselves, out of touch even with those they see every day. Despite the
obvious fact that most of them are surrounded by other people, they feel as
if they have been cast on a distant beach, drenched and bruised and frightened beyond measure, but suffering mainly from the feeling that they are in
a land of strangers, with no one to talk to about the past, no one to share
what is left of the future, and no one from whom to draw a sense of who
they are. One elderly woman who moved several miles from Buffalo Creek
into a nearby town crowded with people has already been quoted: "It is like
being all alone in the middle of a desert." And a man of about the same age
who continued to live in his damaged home after the flood put it:

Well, there is a difference in my condition. Like somebody being in a   33
strange world with nobody around. You don't know nobody. You walk the
floor or look for somebody you know to talk to, and you don't have anybody.

Many survivors fear that they are beginning to suffer the kind of dis-   34
orientation and even madness that can come from prolonged stretches
of isolation.

I just stay mad. Sometimes I think they have brighter people in the nut   35
house than I am. I haven't had a real good night's sleep in nine months.
Sometimes I wake up and have a big fear inside of me. It feels like something
has chased me for miles. I feel numb, my heart feels like it is jumping out of
me. My mind is just a blank.

One result of this fear is that people tend to draw farther and farther into   36
themselves and to become even more isolated. This is the behavior of
wounded animals that crawl off to nurse their hurts. It is also the behavior
of people who string rough coils of barbed wire around their lonely out-
posts because they feel they have nothing to offer those who draw near.

I don't know. I'm a different person since the disaster. People get on my 37
nerves. They irritate me. People that I always liked prior to the flood, I've
alienated myself from them now. I like to be in seclusion. I seldom have a
civil word for people now. I'm rather sarcastic and sometimes I'm a bit too
smart. It's mostly because I don't want to fool with anyone.

I took nervous fits all the time. I went crazy. I got real upset and started 38
shaking all over, and I would just forget about everybody. I couldn't remem-
ber nobody. I didn't want nobody around me. I didn't want nobody to speak
to me or even to look at me. I wanted nobody even ten miles around me to
call my name, I got like that. I just wanted to hit them and make them leave
me alone.

Seems like everything in you just curls up in knots and you want to ex- 39
plode. I've always been an easygoing man all my life and good to everybody.
But here lately I'm as ill as a copperhead. I'm just ready to explode on any-
body right there.

Well, I can't hold a conversation like I once could, I can't give people a 40
good word. I was always a quiet-termed man, you know, but I could always
hold a conversation with any man I met. But I ain't been able to do that since
this thing has happened. I'm just a different man. I don't have the same at-
titude towards people that I had. It used to be that I cared for all people, but
anymore I just keep myself alive. That's the only thing I study about.

So the lonesomeness increases and is reinforced. People have heavy 41
loads of grief to deal with, strong feelings of inadequacy to overcome,
blighted lives to restore, and they must do all this without very much in the
way of personal self-confidence. Solving problems and making decisions,
those are the hard parts.

Yes, I think the whole society of Buffalo Creek has changed. The people 42
are more depressed and despondent. Uncertainty seems to rule their lives.
They aren't sure of how to make decisions. If they make a decision, they
aren't sure they have done the right thing. My parents can't decide whether
they want to move somewhere else, whether they want to build on their lot.
They don't know what to do. They don't know what is going to happen. And
I know my in-laws have already purchased one house and sold it because
they didn't like it. They are in the process of buying another, which they
aren't sure they want to buy. That's the type of thing. People don't know
where to go.

* * *

Well, I'm disorganized. It's like I lost my life and I've never been able to   43
find it again. That's the way I feel. I want to find it. I try to find it, but I don't
know how. In a way, I gave my life up in the flood, and it's like I'm not re-
pented. Since then, everything has been disorganized. I can't organize any-
thing anymore. If I pound a nail, I'll scar myself all up. Anything I do, I do it
wrong. I wanted to get away from people, so I thought I'll get me some ani-
mals or something to raise. So I got me some dogs to take care of and chick-
ens to take care of and the damned dogs killed my chickens. It's all simple,
but I can't seem to solve the problems. I mean there are so many problems I've
got to look at and try to solve, but I can't seem to solve any of them. I used not
to make mistakes in decisions, and I do today on about everything. . . .

One result of all this is that the community, what remains of it, seems to   44
have lost its most significant quality—the power it generated in people to
care for one another in times of need, to console one another in times of distress, to protect one another in times of danger. Looking back, it does seem
that the general community was stronger than the sum of its parts. When the
people of the hollow were sheltered together in the embrace of a secure
community, they were capable of extraordinary acts of generosity; but when
they tried to relate to one another as individuals, separate entities, they
found that they could no longer mobilize whatever resources are required
for caring and nurturing. This story is certainly not a new one. Daniel Defoe
wrote of the London plague:

> Indeed the distress of the people at this seafaring end of the town was very
> deplorable, and deserved the greatest commiseration: but alas! this was a time
> when every one's private safety lay so near them, that they had no room to pity
> the distresses of others; for every one had death, as it were, at his door, and
> many even in their families, and knew not what to do, or whither to fly. . . . It is
> not indeed to be wondered at; for the danger of immediate death to ourselves
> took away all bowels of love, all concern for one another.

And that is what happened on Buffalo Creek—a loss of concern, a loss   45
of human trust. "It seems like the caring part of our lives is over," one elderly
woman said, and this thought was echoed over and over again by persons
of all ages. The following speakers are, in order, a teen-age boy, a woman
in her middle years, and a man in his seventies.

It used to be that everyone knew everyone. When you were hitchhiking,   46
you just put out your thumb and the first car along would pick you up. But
it's not like that now. They just don't care about you now. They got problems
of their own, I guess.

* * *

The changes I see are in the people. They seem to be so indifferent toward 47
their fellow man. I guess it's because they had to watch a whole lifetime go
down the drain.

I'm getting old, too, and I can't get no help. Nobody'll help you do noth- 48
ing. You have to pay somebody, and they'll come and start a project for you,
but then they'll walk off and leave you. It's just too much.

Behind this inability to care is a wholly new emotional tone on the 49
creek—a distrust even of old neighbors, a fear, in fact, of those very persons
on whom one once staked one's life. A disaster like the one that visited Buffalo Creek makes everything in the world seem unreliable, even other survivors, and that is a very fragile base on which to build a new community.

I've just learned that you don't trust nobody. I just feel that way. You 50
don't put no confidence in nobody. You believe nothing you're told. I don't
know, you could have come along before the flood and told me you was go-
ing to give me the moon, and I'd have believed you.

That's it. Nobody trusts anybody anymore. You know, when we moved 51
back home I was so scared I went out and bought a pistol. I don't know
whether it was the place or the house or the people or what I was so scared of.
And I'm still scared. I don't know what of, either. Why, my husband and I
used to go to bed at night and leave our front door open, but now, of a day,
those doors are locked. I'm scared to death.

This emptiness of concern, although he did not say so directly, may 52
have been what a young miner had in mind when he said:

Well, it seems like everything just don't go right no more. There's a part 53
of you gone and you can't find it. You don't know what part it is. It's just a
part that's gone.

Working with the Text

1. What are the characteristics of communality, according to Erikson?
   Why is the term so difficult to define in the abstract? How does the
   accumulation of concrete detail in the stories of the Buffalo Creek
   survivors help to define the term?

2. Erikson contrasts Appalachian communities, in which "boundaries are
   drawn around whole groups of people," with urban America, where
   "each individual is seen as a separate being, with careful boundaries

drawn around the space he or she occupies as a discrete personage." What does the essay understand as the costs and benefits of individualism versus communality? On the basis of your own experience, how would you qualify, augment, or challenge Erikson's insights, either about the costs and benefits of his two social models or about the prevalence of urban individualism?

3. In the opening paragraph, Erikson invites readers to imagine the disaster at Buffalo Creek, offering a sequence of vivid sensory details, then concluding, "All this we can begin to picture because the mind is good at imagery." What purpose does this introduction serve? How does the reader's imagination further the essay's social and intellectual goals?

 4. Explore some of the links to Buffalo Creek and Appalachia on the *Beyond Borders* Web site. How have matters changed since 1972? Is the physical environment the same? Is the cultural environment the same?

 5. Reflect upon a time when you lost an important community, either by relocating or by some other means. Write informally about what that community was like and what its loss meant to you, in terms of everyday perceptions and activities. Then bring that writing to class, where you will collate it with similar writing by your peers and consider as a group what the collection reveals about your views on community. If time allows, collaborate on a draft essay modeled, both structurally and thematically, upon Erikson's.

 6. Research a disaster that seriously affected a community like Buffalo Creek outside the United States. Choose one aspect of the disaster and compare it to the Buffalo Creek disaster.

The Last Best Place: How Hardship and Limits Build Community

DANIEL KEMMIS

Born in Fairview, Montana, Daniel Kemmis has spent his life in the state, except for the years he spent away at law school. A long-term Montana state representative, Kemmis was the Democratic mayor of the city of Missoula. His books include *Community and the Politics of Place* (1990) and *The Good City and the Good Life* (1995). In the following, which was originally delivered as a speech, Kemmis posits that in the future the idea of belonging to a "community" in the United States will be strongly influenced by whether or not we can come to some shared goals concerning the rights of individual property owners versus the right of the government to serve what it sees as the interests of the citizenry as a whole. Communities, suggests Kemmis, are held together by "limits."

While the spirit of democracy sweeps eastward across Europe, over the Urals, whistling through the cracks in the Great Wall, America stands bemused, with no hint of any awareness, at least in official policy, of what all this might mean. Schiller's words and Beethoven's music resound in Berlin and will again, I believe, in Beijing. But in Boston or Boise a self-satisfied smugness resembling a hypnotic slumber holds the world spirit at bay.

Watching all of this, I can't help but recall certain words of Hegel, whose articulation of the idea of a spirit of history seems indispensable to capturing what is happening to the world. In 1820 Hegel set out to write his *Philosophy of History*, seeking to identify those forces that had made and would make real human history. Hegel paused for a moment at the starting gate to dispose of one nagging question, namely whether America had any prospect of contributing anything worthwhile to the history of human civilization. His answer, delivered without hesitation, was "no." His reason speaks still to America, and especially to the American West.

In a nutshell, Hegel predicted that America would not begin to contribute to civilization until it had confronted its own limits. Specifically, he argued that the safety valve of the frontier had prevented and would continue to prevent the development of a truly civil society. In making his case,

Hegel took a position diametrically the opposite of Jefferson's. Jefferson had argued that civic culture was essentially rooted in agriculture and threatened by the growth of cities. He therefore assigned to the Western frontier a crucial and at the same time foredoomed role, which he repeated over and over in a standard Jeffersonian formula that went like this: Civic culture would remain strong in America as long as agriculture expanded faster than cities grew, which would happen as long as there was "vacant" Western land into which agriculture could expand. That this pattern could not recur indefinitely—that there had to be an end, sometime, to the filling in of what white Americans called vacant land—was a reality that Jefferson chose to suppress. In doing so, he contributed very substantially to the Myth of the West—specifically, to the myth that it was somehow a place without limits.

Hegel, as I have said, argued that civic culture, far from depending on   4
the existence of the frontier, could only be achieved once the frontier was closed. More specifically, he turned Jefferson on his head by assuming that civic culture was an essentially urban phenomenon—something that really only occurred when significant numbers of people were forced to stop farming and to gather in cities. He agreed with Jefferson that the Western frontier allowed agriculture to outpace urbanization. His conclusion was simply the exact opposite of Jefferson's; he wrote that until Americans began facing each other in cities, they would not become a truly civil society and would not make a substantial contribution to the history of civilization.

Now, one hundred years after the 1890 census, which led the Census   5
Bureau and then Frederick Jackson Turner to declare the frontier closed, we stand, here in the West, at a cross-wiring of historical currents that almost forces us to ask who we are and where we are going. We mark the centennial of the closing of the frontier just as world history turns Karl Marx on his head, which presumably might mean that Hegel has again landed on his feet. If Hegel were here at this conference, along with Thomas Jefferson, what would he say now about the West and about the possibility of its contributing to the history of civilization?

I'm going to use the challenge of this occasion to propose an answer to   6
that question. I believe the world spirit is alive in Western valleys and to the leeward side of Western cutbanks where people claimed by this landscape have gathered to carry out the business of living well in hard country. I believe that there is, native to this soil, a politics of truly human proportions. It is a politics that we have not yet been bold enough to propose to ourselves. But the hour of its being proposed is drawing near. When that proposition is articulated in a genuinely Western voice, the West will respond, and its response will make its mark on the course of history.

Now, predictions like these deserve to be subjected to a variety of tests,   7
the chief one being, of course, the test of time. Beyond that, anyone mak-

ing such predictions might be asked to warrant in some way his or her standing to make predictions. In America, we can always make the grand claim of citizenship; we can remind our listeners that it is, after all, a free country, and I can predict anything I want to. Since I hope to deal with a more meaningful form of citizenship, I had better pass up that way of backing my claim. Others can warrant predictions by their training in the discipline of history, but while I deeply admire the discipline, I am certainly not trained in it. It is, rather, as a politician that I make my predictions about the near future of the West. And I think that is fitting enough, since my predictions are about the political future of the region.

I have long believed that places select people. Portland selects people who like rain. Having grown up in Montana in a pioneer family that settled four generations ago in eastern Montana, I have observed over the years how frequently recurring the pattern of my own ancestors was in the settlement of the high plains of the state. My great-grandparents tried Oregon in the early 1880s, but the rain and the overcrowding finally drove them away, and they moved east, back across the Rockies, to the open country that could be cursed in an almost infinite variety of ways but could never be accused of being too wet. Over time, the place of my upbringing came to be peopled by folks whose words were as sparse as rain and whose humor was as dry as the hills out of which they eked a living. 8

The shaping of a people by the land they inhabit takes time, and in America it has taken longer, simply because we have never been quite sure that we were here to stay. Wendell Berry begins his book *The Unsettling of America* by observing that Americans have never quite intended to be where they were—that they have always thought more in terms of where they would go, rather than of where they actually were. But Berry also identifies a second strain in the pattern of settlement—what he calls a tendency to stay put, to say, "No further—this is the place." One peculiarity of the settlement of the West is that it attracted—it selected—people who were more given than others to escape settlement. Only they would be willing to put up with the harshness, the inhospitality of the land, which grew more inhospitable the nearer they came to inhabiting the last of the frontier. 9

So the West drew to itself more than its share of unsettlers, of people whose essential relation to place was the denial of place. And yet the places that they came to, being the last place to go, finally took hold of them, drew them down into their flinty soil, rooted them, claimed them, shaped them the way they shaped sagebrush. Over the generations, these people increasingly came to recognize themselves and to recognize their neighbors in the forms the land produced. And the selection process did not stop at some point; it goes on still. People still are drawn here not just in spite of but because of the hardness of the land. 10

Gradually, a culture grew out of the land, a group of storytellers and im-   11
agemakers capable of holding this people up to itself. In Montana we relied
on people like Joseph Kinsey Howard and K. Ross Toole to show us who
we were, and in each locality there were similar voices. But there have been
regional voices as well, not least that of Wallace Stegner, and now a new
generation including voices like Bill Kittredge's. Bill and Annick Smith have
proven, dramatically, how deep and powerful the common culture of place
is by producing for Montana's centennial an exceptional and exceptionally
popular collection of voices entitled *The Last Best Place.*

Let me touch now for just a moment on democracy—about what, at   12
least from the perspective of a practicing politician, democracy is or might
be. There is an unsettling premonition, as we watch East Berliners pouring
through the breached wall to go shopping in West Berlin, that democracy
may in the end not reach very far beyond some notion of equal access to all
good things, especially blue jeans and cheeseburgers. As a politician, I have
had my fair share of exposure to the behavior, and the fundamental insatia-
bility, of the citizen as consumer. I am convinced that democracy is steadily
diminished, just as the earth's capital is steadily diminished, by this version
of democracy. It is a democracy that cannot endure, and all true democrats
must warn against its dangers.

In the age of fast food and pervasive fingertip convenience, we have   13
come to believe that democracy is a birthright that is as easy to practice as
a precooked microwave dinner is to heat and serve. But it has never been
so, and it will not be so for the coming generation of world democrats.
Here, at least, Frederick Jackson Turner still speaks in a voice of Jeffersonian democracy to which we need to attend if we are to understand what
makes democracy possible. Turner speaks of how the frontier created democrats; he writes that the rigors of the frontier instilled (and I would argue
selected for) what Turner called a "competency"—a capacity to get done
what needed doing—which translated into a truly democratic confidence.
Hard country breeds capable people—capable, among other things, of genuine democracy.

But let's take a little closer look at this competence. It is, has always   14
been, and must necessarily be the competence, not simply of individuals,
but of a *demos,* of a people. To have this kind of competence, a people must
be bound together in ways that enable them to work together. What the project of inhabiting hard country does, above all, is to create these bonds. And
when I speak of bonds here, I do not mean to evoke anything particularly
soft or mushy. These are practical bonds, although they do often lead to
a kind of affection among those so bonded. But they are in the first instance practical. They are the kinds of bonds that made of barn-building and
similar acts of cooperation something that must be understood as a culture.

It is a culture bred of hard places, nurtured by the practice of inhabiting those places.

I want to draw attention to two words I have just used. The first is "prac- 15 tice" (and its derivative "practical"). The second is "inhabitation." These words are rooted—quite literally rooted—in the same quite literal soil. Inhabitation depends upon habits; to inhabit is to dwell in a place in an habituated way. To do this requires practice. This practice revolves around certain practical necessities of living in hard country, necessities like a good barn. But to say a "good barn" is not to speak lightly, for not just any barn will do, and this is true of [a] great range of such practical necessities. What was done must be done well or it would not survive—it would not enable survival. Thus, the practices that lie at the root of all true inhabitation— especially of the inhabitation of hard country—are always practices that carry within themselves demanding standards of excellence.

It is these standards of excellence, arising out of the soil itself, bodied 16 forth in certain habituated and deeply shared patterns of behavior—it is these lived standards of excellence that alone give meaning to the concept of "value." Over the past decade or so, more and more people have en- gaged in a vague recognition of the fact that "values" are somehow an im- portant political factor. This has been a rather astonishing realization for liberals, instructed as we all have been in the liberal dogma that values are private concerns, and no business of the state. But as politics has increas- ingly become a game of "values, values, who's got the values?" even liber- als have had to pay lip service to this new political icon.

But we have not yet understood that values are not something that sim- 17 ply come out of a black box in the individual soul, as the liberal dogma would have it, or from a deep voice on a mountaintop, as the fundamental- ists think. What makes values shared and what makes them politically pow- erful is that they arise out of the challenge of living well together in hard country. When people do that long enough to develop a pattern of shared values, those values acquire a political potency.

It is here that the West has the capacity to contribute something deep 18 and important and lasting to the history of politics and civilization. Simply because we have for so many generations worked on the project of living together in hard country, we have, although we don't recognize it, devel- oped among ourselves certain patterns of behavior, which amount to shared values. The question is whether we will recognize this Western fact of life. The question is whether those of us who call ourselves liberals and those of us who call ourselves conservatives, all of whom are inhabitants of the West, can begin to turn to each other and begin to recognize what it is we have built together in terms of shared patterns of inhabitation and there- fore of shared values. That is the challenge of the West. If we can begin to understand how we have been shaped by this country, shaped in similar ways, not so that we think alike all the time, not so that we believe alike, but so that we in fact have developed some shared values that give us the capacity to do difficult and important work together, then on this basis we can begin to contribute to democracy and to the history of civilization.

I say this as a politician who is willing to bet his career on the fact that this is a possibility. I am absolutely convinced that people will respond to being appealed to as inhabitants of a common place. They are willing to respond to anyone who will speak to their weariness with the kind of deadlock that our politics all too often creates. They will respond to a politics that speaks directly to their deep desire to be respected and to be treated as people—people who are capable of treating other people with respect. They will respond to a politics that speaks to their commonly shaped patterns of doing good work, to a politics that says to people on the right and on the left, "You are one people; you understand each other better than you think you do and you are capable of treating each other as if you do understand each other." And finally, they will respond to a politics that addresses their sense of what a good city or a good community might be, and how we would have to treat each other if we were going to go about the task of creating it.   19

It is said of Athens that in spite of its deep social divisions, it sustained its experiment in democracy and developed an outstanding culture because, in the end, each of the contestants in each divisive issue cared more about Athens than they cared about winning. I am convinced that in communities across the West, a majority of the people care more about their communities than they care about winning. But they have not been given a politics that encourages them to behave in that way. They have been given a politics that only encourages them to care about winning.   20

Are we capable of real politics in the West? I believe we are if we are willing to face ourselves and our neighbors in a way that we have never done. We need to be willing in the first instance to face the implications of our historical unwillingness to face ourselves. Jefferson, democrat that he was, believer that he was in the idea that democracy could only exist when it was practiced on a small scale, was yet willing through the Louisiana Purchase to engage in the building of an empire. He did that because in the long run he believed that democracy could only survive if it was rooted on the farm and that it could be rooted on the farm only if agriculture could expand endlessly. So he bought into an empire, and our ancestors bought into an empire, and we, by inheritance, bought into an empire. Part of the reason for this is because we, like Jefferson, have been unwilling to image the possibility of a good city. Jefferson could not image a city being good. All too of-   21 ten, I think, we are guilty of the same way of thinking. Robinson Jeffers, in his poem "Shine Perishing Republic," talks about the republic "heavily thickening into empire," and he ends the poem by writing:

But for the children, I would have them keep their distance
    from the thickening center; corruption
Never has been compulsory, when the cities lie at the
    monster's feet, there are left the mountains.

That has been too much the Western attitude. We believed—we still believe—that we can somehow escape ourselves by slipping into the mountains, avoiding the hard task of facing up to ourselves in cities. Our mistake has always been that we have let empire shape our cities, rather than letting cities shape themselves and, above all, demanding of people that they shape their cities. 22

But the complicity goes beyond that. Once Thomas Jefferson bought the Louisiana Purchase, we had no choice but to buy both the military and the bureaucratic superstructure that went with it. We can take the attitude of saying all of that has been forced on the West. Or we can say that we have been complicit in it and that we have the capacity to do something about it. The way we will do something about it is to claim our homeland—to say this is our home, and to be able to say "our" and mean it, not only of the people that think and dress and behave like us, but of the other inhabitants of the region who are equally rooted here. When the West is ready to do that, then it will be ready for a real politics of inhabitation. 23

I will make one final prediction: that when that time comes, we will understand that, like every other region of the country, we are going to have to be in control of our homeland. That means that 90 percent of it can't be owned someplace else. The imperial presence would have to be removed from the ownership of Western lands. The West will not be ready for its own politics until it is ready to claim its own land. The real test of that will be whether we ever understand that the U.S. Senate was created in order that land-dominated regions like the West might assert their own land-based ways of life. When the time comes, when we are ready to develop a history and politics of the West, we will begin to elect a cadre of U.S. senators who will go to Washington to assert sovereignty over this country that we inhabit. Will we do it? Are we serious? Or are we just playing games? 24

In 1636 John Winthrop, soon to become governor of the Massachusetts Bay Colony, sailed with a shipload of Pilgrims from England toward the land to the west. As they sailed, he prepared for his shipmates a sermon on how they should expect to go about the task of inhabiting the fiercely inhospitable land that they hoped to make their home. He knew how hard it 25 would be. And he knew how, out of that hardship, they might create what he called "the city on a hill." This is what he said to them: "We must delight in each other. We must labor together, suffer together, rejoice and mourn together, keeping always before our eyes our condition as members of one body."

In our time, Wendell Berry, in a poem called "Work Song," sought to capture once again the essence of the enterprise of winning a good living from a hard piece of land. "This is no paradisal dream," he wrote. But in a land-rooted voice of hope that is the true voice of the West, he concluded, "Its hardship is its possibility."   26

Working with the Text

1. The essay claims that hard country breeds democracy, both by fostering certain kinds of individuals and by forcing them to collaborate. Explain in detail how both processes work. What does Kemmis mean by "hard country," and why is this landscape peculiarly Western? Why have Kemmis's constituents failed to perceive the political legacy of their environment?

2. What is the "something deep and important and lasting" that the American West can contribute to "the history of politics and civilization"? Why is Hegel a better guide to this contribution than Jefferson? What must change before the contribution can be made?

3. Think about Kemmis's essay in relation to some of the images in the Image Portfolio, in particular John Gast's *American Progress.* How does this image speak to a perspective about limits in the United States? How does this perspective compare to that of the essay?

4. Because the essay began as a speech, it retains many of the features of prose written for a specific occasion. Identify some of these features and discuss how they contribute to the overall tone of the essay. How does Kemmis's colloquialism inflect his argument? Are we more or less receptive to his "predictions" when they bear the imprint of oral delivery?

5. Propose another type of "hard country," a place you believe might produce a people with unusual capacities. Describe this landscape, and speculate about its influence upon individuals and upon groups. Alternatively, consider Kemmis's claim that "places select people" in the light of a particular place. It's probably best to choose a town or region you know but not one you currently occupy, as overfamiliarity can compromise perspective. What kinds of people does the place select?

Georgia Charismatics

RANDALL BALMER

Randall Balmer teaches at Barnard College, Columbia University. The New York Times News Service distributes his weekly commentaries on American religion. He is the author of *A Perfect Babel of Confusion* (1989), *Mine Eyes Have Seen the Glory: Journey into the Evangelical Subculture in America* (1991), *The Presbyterians* (with John Fitzmer) (1993), and *Grant Us Courage: Travels Along the Mainline of American Protestantism* (1996). Balmer adapted *Mine Eyes* for television and hosted the PBS series based on the book in 1993. *Mine Eyes*—part "personal odyssey," part "travelogue"—explores the evangelical subculture of America "in all its variation and diversity." In the following chapter, Balmer profiles the encounter between a Pentecostal congregation in rural Georgia and the much more orthodox Episcopal Church, a Protestant denomination traditionally associated with establishment wealth and power. Balmer documents the anomalous effort of the Charismatics, those who "generally look askance at Episcopalians" because "Episcopalians have frequently looked askance at them," to "make history" by officially identifying themselves with a mainline church.

In Valdosta, Georgia, a large billboard looms over North Valdosta Road, a winding, four-lane divided highway on the outskirts of town. On a white background next to a bejeweled crown, tall, bold letters spell out: CHURCH OF THE KING. Beneath that, a smaller sign reads: 1

> **Sunday 10:30 AM & 7:00 PM Thursday 7:00 PM**
> **Stan J. White, Pastor**

The sign is tasteful and artistic, but it is also quite conspicuous, even from a distance, part of the Mail Pouch Tobacco genre of American roadside advertising that grabs you by the lapels and demands your attention. 2

145

Less than a hundred feet away, in front of a parking lot and a gray   3
cinder-block warehouse, the same people responsible for the billboard have
planted another, much smaller sign, perhaps three feet wide and four feet
high. You have to walk close to see the fine print at the bottom, but it also
reads "Church of the King." Above that, a familiar shield on a light blue and
white background:

> THE
>
> EPISCOPAL CHURCH
>
> WELCOMES YOU

Therein lies a story.   4

The name emblazoned on the billboard belongs to a man in his late twen-   5
ties with chiseled features and a slight frame. Stan White has dark hair and
deep eyes that are brooding but not unfriendly. He carries a gentle and un-
prepossessing mien of seriousness about him; he's the fellow who asked too
many questions in your high school algebra class. He comes to the office
during the week dressed casually; on Good Friday, 1990, for instance, he
wore a meticulously starched button-down shirt, designer denims, and boat
shoes with white sweatsocks.

The prep-school attire, however, is misleading. Stan White has impecca-   6
ble pentecostal credentials and boasts that he is a fourth-generation pentecostal preacher. "I'm very proud of my pentecostal heritage," he insists.
White's great-great uncle, a Missionary Baptist preacher, had a pentecostal
experience about 1908 and was promptly kicked out of the Missionary
Baptist denomination. He then joined the Assemblies of God when it was
organized at Hot Springs, Arkansas, in 1914. White's grandfather and grandmother were also ordained in the Assemblies of God, as was his father,
James White, a native of Columbus, Georgia, who served churches in southern California and Florida before returning to Georgia twenty-five years ago
to take over a struggling Assembly of God in Valdosta. James White, a handsome, white-haired gentleman known affectionately to his many devoted
followers as "Brother Jimmy," guided Evangel Assembly of God from a
handful of people in 1968 into one of Valdosta's largest congregations, with
two weekly television broadcasts, a fifteen-hundred-seat auditorium, and
approximately three million dollars in assets.

In the early 1980s, Stan White, after two years at Valdosta State College   7
and a job in data processing at an oil company in Houston, felt a call to the
ministry. He joined the pastoral staff of his father's church as minister of mu-

sic in 1982. In the ensuing years the elder White, edging toward retirement, asked his son to take on more and more of the pastoral duties at Evangel. About this time, in the mid-eighties, some extraordinary changes began to take place in Stan's life and, by extension, in the life of the congregation at Evangel Assembly of God.

"Evangel had always been a teaching church," White explained, and beginning in 1984 or thereabouts the church started to talk about what it meant to worship God. "I began to understand the importance of worship," he said, "as more than just preaching followed by an altar call." White still believed then, as he does now, in the "present reality of the Holy Spirit. That doesn't mean that we speak in tongues in our worship services. Rather, we believe in tongues as a personal devotional experience." The "present reality of the Holy Spirit" manifested itself at Evangel Assembly of God in lively and spontaneous services marked by outstretched arms, dancing, clapping, and shouting. 8

Despite the spirited worship, however, White sensed that something was missing from the services, and he grew increasingly uneasy with the altar calls week after week that seemed to be directed toward winning new converts rather than nurturing those already within the fold. White turned to church history. Growing up pentecostal, he explained, he had little understanding of anything that had happened before the Azusa Street pentecostal revivals in Los Angeles just after the turn of the century. While reading Irenaeus and other church fathers, White became convinced that the early church had been both liturgical and sacramental, and that seemed to suggest that pentecostalism, despite its insistence upon the gifts of the Spirit as described in the Book of Acts, hadn't fully appropriated the richness of worship in the early church. 9

In pentecostalism, White explained, the sacraments are called "ordinances," and Evangel Assembly of God in Valdosta observed the Lord's Supper once a month at most and sometimes as infrequently as once a year. "We didn't treat them with any respect or dignity," he said. In the midst of rethinking evangelical worship, White became seized with what he calls an "ecumenical spirit." He studied Roman Catholicism as well as Anglicanism, Lutheranism, and other high-church traditions. A friend gave him a copy of the Episcopal *Book of Common Prayer,* which White began using in his private devotions. Most important, he attended a liturgical church and, much to his surprise, felt a spiritual quickening. "I experienced God there," White said, his voice still registering astonishment several years after the event. "That wasn't supposed to happen. It shocked me." 10

Gradually, and somewhat tentatively, White shared some of his thinking with his family and with his Assembly of God congregation. He began to teach about church history, the creeds, and the sacraments. "We started 11 incorporating some of those elements into our worship," he said, including a weekly celebration of the Lord's Supper. By 1987 Evangel Assembly of God in Valdosta, Georgia, was very likely the only pentecostal church in the nation to open its services with a processional.

A large segment of the congregation greeted these changes with enthu- 12 siasm, others with curiosity, even bemusement. Still others weren't so sure. On Thursday, August 11, 1988, the deacons called an emergency board meeting to remove Stan White as pastor. His father, James, who was semi-retired by then and who had built the church from virtually nothing, tendered his resignation as well.

"I thought at the time, 'Well, it's over,'" Stan White recalled. If he still 13 sounded a trifle defensive about the incident, he seemed not at all bitter. "They said my theology was newfangled," he said. "They didn't realize that my theology was old."

At ten minutes of seven o'clock on Good Friday, 1990, a half dozen auto- 14 mobiles and pickup trucks gathered in the parking lot of Church of the King, the warehouse on North Valdosta Road that once served as a boat show-room. A small group of people, ranging in age from mid-teens to mid-sixties, congregated outside the door. Each new arrival set off another round of greeting and hugging. Nearly everyone carried two books: a Bible and a red leather deluxe edition of the *Book of Common Prayer*. Whereas the Bibles were worn and well-thumbed, the prayer books quite obviously were new, the gilded edges barely disturbed. These were celebratory, commem-orative editions, for in two days, on Easter Sunday evening, the people gath-ered here, together with about two hundred of their fellow congregants from Church of the King, would be confirmed in the Episcopal Church.

Although the conversation occasionally touched on other matters, it 15 quickly veered back to the events coming on Sunday night. "We're so ex-cited, we can hardly stand it," one woman remarked before breaking into giddy laughter. "This is all still pretty new to us," a man explained, "but I think we're ready."

Ready or not, they had not come this far on impulse alone. After Stan 16 White's ouster from Evangel Assembly of God, a number of people from that congregation urged him to start his own church and to continue com-bining pentecostal worship with liturgical forms. White claims that begin-ning another church was the farthest thing from his mind; he had no intention of dividing Evangel Assembly of God even more than it already was. "We're not rebellious people," he insisted. "We're not fighting people." The entreaties mounted nevertheless, and after consulting with his family and with other members of his former congregation he decided to relinquish his Assemblies of God credentials and to announce a meeting for those who might be interested in forming a new church. Two-hundred-and-fifty showed for what became the first gathering of Church of the King. Starting a church from scratch, however, proved to be no easy task. "We didn't have so much as a paper clip," White said. The fledgling congregation met at two other locations—a furniture warehouse and the city auditorium—before moving to the warehouse on North Valdosta Road.

Intellectually, White kept moving as well. He maintains that he was scrupulous about not violating Assemblies of God theology while at Evangel, but the lack of denominational constraints at Church of the King afforded him considerable freedom to experiment. The clergy started wearing vestments, the congregation repeated several creeds, and Church of the King celebrated the Lord's Supper every Sunday. [17]

As the congregation approached its first anniversary in August 1989, White observed forty days of fasting and prayer in order to seek guidance and direction for the church. It had been a good year, on balance, with strong and growing attendance, a number of outreach programs, and general satisfaction with the attempt to combine historic forms with charismatic fervor. Church of the King was also interracial, with African-Americans accounting for about 30 percent of its membership. "One of our real missions," White said, "has been to break down the walls of prejudice."[1] White himself, however, was growing restless. I wanted not merely to implement these historic creeds and practices, but also to identify with the historic church," he explained. "I suddenly had the sense that I was just bootlegging all this." [18]

White initially resisted those sentiments, and the sentiment that followed was even more preposterous. "I felt my spirit drawn to the Episcopal Church, almost like a call," he said. "I'm not spooky spiritual or anything like that, but I felt drawn to the Episcopal Church." White demurred at first, sure that his family, his pastoral staff, and certainly his congregation wouldn't abide such a dramatic move. "I just didn't think they'd go for it," he said, "and even if they did, I was *sure* the Episcopalians wouldn't go for it." [19]

Finally, after a protracted inner struggle, White said, "Okay, God, I'll make some inquiries." White remembered that he felt at the time a bit like Abraham preparing to sacrifice Isaac, his beloved son, because he was certain that everything he had worked for would crumble in ashes once he declared his intentions to seek affiliation with the Episcopal Church. White first floated the idea with an acquaintance, Jacoba Hurst, rector of St. Anne's Episcopal Church in Tifton, Georgia, who later told me he was so astonished by White's overture "that I thought he had been under some stress." Hurst and White talked for five hours the next day, at the conclusion of which Hurst telephoned Harry W. Shipps, Episcopal bishop of Georgia. "There was [20] a long silence at the other end of the phone," Hurst recalled, but he succeeded in setting up a discreet meeting. The bishop was a trifle skeptical at first, but White's earnestness and sincerity persuaded him to accede.

White then had to confront his congregation. His voice timid and anxious, he asked permission to pursue affiliation with the Episcopal Church, careful to point out that it was a long process and that their efforts might be derailed at any one of several junctures. "The words were barely out of my mouth," White recounted, "before the entire congregation rose from its chairs in a standing ovation." 21

Church of the King is by no means the Episcopal Church's first encounter with the charismatic movement. In the fall of 1959 the Reverend Dennis J. Bennett, rector of St. Mark's Episcopal Church in Van Nuys, California, began to speak in tongues. "It was an entirely rational experience, without hysteria or frenzy," he explained later. "One expresses without understanding. But you know it's love and devotion toward God. The exact meaning seems to come later, when you have developed the gift."[2] Bennett, himself born and reared in London, shared this discovery with his pastoral staff at St. Mark's, and soon other members of the suburban, upper-middle-class parish also began speaking in tongues. 22

Other parishioners looked askance at this new phenomenon. For Episcopalians, known to some wags as "God's frozen people," this was new and alien territory. With the endorsement of the bishop of Los Angeles, the vestry of St. Mark's secured Father Bennett's resignation. "It's a good thing this is all cleared up," one older parishioner remarked. "We're Episcopalians, not a bunch of wild-eyed hillbillies!"[3] 23

Bishop Francis Eric Bloy of Los Angeles assigned a new priest to Van Nuys and expressly forbade speaking in tongues under Episcopal auspices in his diocese. Bennett accepted a call to St. Luke's, a mission parish in Seattle. His ministry there, marked once again by emotive outpourings of the Holy Spirit, transformed a dying church into one of the largest, most vibrant parishes in the nation. 24

In the three decades since the outbreak of glossolalia in Van Nuys, the charismatic renewal movement has taken hold within the Episcopal Church, although it has by no means met with universal approbation. Some of the most salubrious parishes in the nation—St. Luke's in Seattle, Church of the Redeemer in Houston, St. Paul's in Darien, Connecticut—count themselves part of the charismatic renewal. In Darien, two parishes vie for the allegiance of the town's Episcopalians: St. Luke's, a traditional, highbrow parish, what some Britons might revile as "Tories on their knees," and St. Paul's, the charismatic parish. 25

The charismatic movement has caught on in other liturgical traditions as 26
well, most notably in the Roman Catholic Church. In the winter of 1967 four
members of the Duquesne University faculty, all of them Roman Catholics,
attended a Protestant charismatic prayer meeting in Pittsburgh. There they
received "spiritual blessings." Soon, similar stirrings occurred among Roman
Catholics on other campuses, and by June 1967 Catholic charismatics organized a conference at the University of Notre Dame. The conference has
taken place annually since then, growing each year, a reflection of the vitality of the charismatic movement within American Catholicism.

There is a general pattern to the growth of the charismatic movement. A 27
group of people within a liturgical or high-church tradition seeks some kind
of spiritual presence, a sense of immediacy or even of emotional fulfillment,
so they turn to pentecostal or charismatic forms. These spiritual expressions,
nevertheless, are rooted within their liturgical traditions. What makes the go-
ings on in Valdosta so extraordinary is that, in the case of Church of the
King, the pattern was reversed. Here, a group of charismatics sought to
ground their evangelical and spiritual vitality within the historic church.

That is not to say that individual evangelicals have not been drawn to 28
liturgical traditions. Indeed, in recent years a large number of evangelicals
have become enamored of high-church liturgy, especially that of the Episcopalians. The "evangelicals on the Canterbury trail" phenomenon has been
well documented.[4] The Episcopal Church has attracted many young, educated evangelicals, in part because of the popularity of C. S. Lewis, an Anglican churchman, and also because it appeals to their sense of history,
tradition, and aesthetics. Other evangelicals have gravitated to the sacramentalism of the liturgical church. Martin Luther's assault on the Roman
Catholic doctrine of transubstantiation—that the bread and wine *actually
become* Christ's body and blood in the course of the Mass, even though they
retain the outward appearance of bread and wine—prompted a rethinking
of the sacraments and opened the door for other reformulations of sacramental theology. Although Luther (and Lutherans, his spiritual heirs) maintained a "high" view of the Lord's Supper, the theology of other Reformers
reduced the bread and wine to mere symbols of the body and blood of
Christ. Indeed, most American evangelicals have adopted Ulrich Zwingli's
memorialist view of Holy Communion—the Lord's Supper merely *reminds*
us of the death of Christ—rather than Luther's understanding that the com-
municant actually partakes of the grace of God.

A more exalted view of the sacraments also signals a subtle shift in the- 29
ology. Traditionally, American evangelicals have defined conversion as an
instantaneous, datable experience of grace akin to St. Paul's conversion on
the road to Damascus and consonant with evangelicals' generally dualistic

view of the world—good versus evil, righteousness versus unrighteousness. A fuller sacramental theology implies that God *continually* imparts grace to the believer in ways we cannot fully comprehend. The Christian life, in this view, is less a radical redirection than a spiritual pilgrimage.

The aesthetic deprivation so characteristic of evangelical worship should not be dismissed, either, as a factor in evangelicals' attraction to liturgical traditions. Many evangelicals, having grown weary of the relentless quest for novelty and innovation in evangelical worship, have opted instead for the ancient traditions of creed and liturgy that often come packaged with the strains of Bach, Mozart, and Haydn.

Most evangelicals, however, generally look askance at Episcopalians because—well, because Episcopalians have frequently looked askance at them. The United States has no established religion in the sense of a state church, but no denomination in America is more identified with the establishment—those who control wealth and power—than the Episcopalians.[5] Of the nation's forty-one presidents, twelve have been Episcopalians; twenty out of one hundred U.S. Senators—one-fifth—identify themselves as Episcopalians, a representation far greater than their proportion in the American population. For much of this century, on the other hand, evangelicals have felt themselves cut off from the corridors of wealth and power and influence. They feel awkward with the formalism and ceremony of high-church liturgy. "I'm always uncomfortable in an Episcopal church," a Methodist told me once. "I feel like I'm at a fancy dinner party, and I'm never sure which fork to use."

Despite the growth of the charismatic movement, then, and the gravitation of some evangelicals to liturgical traditions, Church of the King, an entire charismatic congregation seeking affiliation with the Episcopal Church, remains something of an anomaly. This is not a congregation consisting overwhelmingly of educated, professional, upwardly mobile evangelicals. South Central Georgia has much to recommend it, with pine trees alternating with grassy fields and peach trees in neat, carefully calibrated rows. This is Baptist country (I tried to tally the number of Baptist churches between Albany and Valdosta, but I quickly lost count). Many of the restaurants in Valdosta will take a dollar off the price of your Sunday dinner if you can produce a bulletin as proof that you attended church that morning. Despite its undeniable charms, however, Valdosta, Georgia, hardly strikes a casual observer as the crossroads of culture, and that makes Church of the King's pilgrimage from pentecostalism to Episcopalianism all the more extraordinary.

"I envision a church that is fully charismatic, fully evangelical, but also fully liturgical and sacramental," Stan White told me. "We want to see all those elements alive and working simultaneously."

* * *

Carolyn Dinkins, an affable, attractive woman in her late thirties, sets a 34
bountiful table at her lakefront home outside of Valdosta. She absented herself early from the Sunday morning service on Easter to complete prepara-
tions for the noon meal. Robert, her husband, stayed longer in order to
socialize after the service and also, it seemed, to augment the guest list. Carolyn Dinkins took it in stride, and when it was time to sit down to macaroni
and cheese, string beans, squash, creamed corn, roast venison, country
stuffed sausages, apple cobbler, and buttermilk biscuits with Georgia cane
syrup, more than a dozen people had gathered, a congenial mixture of visitors and old friends. Ed and Jane Black had driven down from the Atlanta
area to witness the day's events. Gordon and Blake Weisser, retirees from
Houston, put Valdosta on their itinerary when they read about Church of the
King in an Episcopal newsletter.

For the Dinkinses, Ken and Rachel Reeves fall into the category of old 35
friends. The Reeveses lived in Valdosta until recently; now they manage a
trailer park in Dade City, Florida, but they hope to move back to Georgia
soon. Patricia and Bennett Thagard are farmers outside of Valdosta. Bennett,
a rugged, burly man, possesses a ready smile and a bone-crushing hand-
shake, both of which have assumed the status of legend among the congregants at Church of the King. "When people found out a few years ago that
Bennett Thagard had become a Christian," Ann White, Stan's mother, had
told me on Friday evening, "they just couldn't believe it. 'Bennett Thagard?'
they said. But let me tell you, the Lord just got a-hold of him!"

The Sunday table was abuzz with the historical significance of the con- 36
firmations that would take place that evening. The Prayers of the People at
Church of the King that morning had included the petition that God would
"do his thing tonight." Before dinner at the Dinkins home, the guests had
gathered in the spacious kitchen and held hands in a large circle while
Robert Dinkins prayed. He had acknowledged before God "the momentous
occasion" ahead and asked that "the Holy Spirit will be there in all its power
tonight." The excitement was building, even among the visitors. "When Gordon and I went to Canterbury," Blake Weisser, the voluble guest from Houston, said, "I felt like a pilgrim. Today I feel like a pilgrim in Valdosta." Robert
Dinkins recounted his own pilgrimage. "I started attending Evangel Assembly of God in 1961," he said. "I used to be a segregationist till God turned
me around." Dinkins recalled his initial misgivings about Stan White and his
movement toward the high church. "He made me so mad sometimes," he
said, shaking his head, but the more Dinkins studied the Bible for himself,
the more persuaded he became that White was on to something. "The Lord
began to lead the congregation into uncharted areas as far as the pentecostal
movement is concerned."

Ken Reeves recalled his dismay when he learned that the deacons at   37
Evangel Assembly of God had dismissed White. He and Dinkins tried to
fight it at first. "We made it clear to the deacons that they weren't speaking
for us," Reeves said. Several days later, however, a sense of peace descended upon Dinkins as he was driving home. "The Lord told me, 'I have
done this thing. I have confused the deacons' minds.' By the time I got
home," Dinkins said, "I had peace about it."

When I asked those gathered around the table what their emotions   38
might be at their confirmation that evening, Carolyn Dinkins responded first.
"It's a blessing that we're about to receive," she said. "We anticipate that
something supernatural will happen to us." Rachel Reeves said, "I believe a
divine impartation is going to take place tonight." Robert Dinkins went even
further. "We really anticipate that the power will be so great that the priests
won't be able to stand because of the presence of the Holy Spirit."

As part of the congregation's preparation for confirmation, the bishop   39
had imposed a sacramental fast from mid-January, when he accepted them
into the Episcopal Church as baptized members, until their confirmation on
Easter Sunday evening. When I asked if there was a sense that they felt hungry for the bread and wine of Holy Communion, everyone around the table
nodded. Carolyn Dinkins dredged up her best southern accent: "We are
ready for the sacrament, honey!"

The interior of Church of the King, the former boat showroom, has been   40
tastefully decorated in cool colors. The steel beams supporting the roof are
white, with long rows of fluorescent lights suspended from them. The
cinder-block walls sport a fresh coat of paint the color of eggshells tinted
ever so slightly with a lavender hue. The carpet is plush and purple, and the
congregation sits on comfortable chairs upholstered in a gray tweed fabric.

The decor may be cool, but the service is anything but cold. At six-forty-   41
five the music started, loud and lively and celebratory. The congregation
rose spontaneously to its feet:

He's alive again.
The stone's been rolled away.
He's alive again.
He's no longer where He lay.
He's alive again,
I can hear the angels say,
"Let all the world rejoice, He's alive."[6]

Gregg Kennard, the church's minister of music, directed the fifty-voice choir   42
and the orchestra—three trumpets, a violin, a flute, two clarinets, an electric

bass guitar, and a percussion section, including timpani—from behind the keyboard of a synthesizer.

By the time the orchestra segued into the next song, "Celebrate Jesus, Celebrate!" some hands were clapping, while others flailed the air. "Let's bless the Lord," Kennard shouted into his microphone. The congregation obliged with arms beating the air in ecstasy. Each song dissolved seamlessly into the next; the congregation appeared to know—through intuition or practice, I couldn't be sure which—how to respond to each one. When the tempo picked up for "Sing unto the Lord a New Song," the congregation quickened its pace and began dancing, a kind of quick, rhythmic hopping from one foot to the other, with arms swinging up and back in a bouncy military swagger. Midway through "Sing unto the Lord a New Song," Church of the King looked more like Tuesday night aerobics class than Easter Sunday in an Episcopal parish.   43

Outside the sanctuary, crucifer, acolytes, dancers, thurifer, clergy, and bishops fell into line during "How Magnificent is Your Name, O Lord," a loud and stately march. The acolytes in their new red cassocks looked a bit unsteady, their eyes shifting furtively as they processed around the back of the auditorium and up the center aisle, leaving the pungent, sweet smell of incense in their wake. The visiting clergy, Episcopal priests from all over the diocese and from other dioceses as well, numbered two dozen. They processed just behind the pastoral staff of Church of the King and sat in a special section to the right of the altar. Four bishops wearing miters and dressed in their liturgical finery brought up the rear, followed by Bishop Shipps, a tall, bearded man walking with his crozier, the symbol of his office.   44

There had been an almost palpable air of excitement in the auditorium since five o'clock that afternoon. The processional itself symbolized the extraordinary character of the evening's events—the venerable pageantry juxtaposed with loud and lively celebration—even as the music swelled toward a crescendo. With the cross and the banners in their stands, the clergy at their chairs, the dancers in repose, and the bishops at their stations, the singing finally reached a climax, whereupon the congregation, bishops and clergy included, broke into sustained and spontaneous applause.   45

Stan White, wearing a white surplice over a black cassock, stepped to the podium and savored the moment before leading the congregation in another song of praise. One of the bishops and several of the visiting clergy had their arms outstretched, the traditional pentecostal posture of praise to God and openness to the Holy Spirit. Only at the reading of the Psalm, well into the service, did the congregation sit down. "Happy are they who have not walked in the counsel of the wicked," the congregation   46 said in unison, "nor lingered in the way of sinners, nor sat in the seats of the scornful."

My eyes wandered to the contingent of clergy seated in the section ad-   47
jacent to me. When Jacoba Hurst brought Stan White, this erstwhile Assemblies of God pastor, before the commission on ministry for the diocese of Georgia, Hurst feared that he had ushered White into the seat of the scornful. "Some of these guys are rather hostile, dour clerics who don't suffer fools gladly," Hurst told me. "They were reserved and cautious at first," he said, but then something extraordinary happened. "There was the presence of God in that room," Hurst said. "I couldn't speak. It was like some kind of revival." The committee interrogated White at some length and then asked him to withdraw so they could deliberate. Hurst noticed to his surprise that several members of the committee, these "hostile, dour clerics," were weeping. "I had a tremendous sense of destiny," he said about White's candidacy for ordination. "We felt that he was there by appointment from God. I really feel that he's been sent to the Episcopal Church."

John Howe, the bishop of Orlando, seemed to agree. When he strode to   48
the podium to deliver the homily, he asked, "Are we having fun yet?" Judging by the congregation's enthusiastic response, the answer was Yes. "This is a very exciting evening," he said. "This is something, I think, of historic proportions." Howe's sermon referred both to the archbishop of Canterbury, the spiritual head of the worldwide Anglican communion, and Charles Parham, a pentecostal preacher from Topeka, Kansas, generally regarded as the progenitor of pentecostalism in America. Quoting a nineteenth-century Anglican churchman, Howe compared the Episcopal Church to a great carved marble fireplace and the spiritual ardor of nineteenth-century Methodists and twentieth-century pentecostals to a fire. The fire, Howe declared, belongs in the fireplace! "We welcome this congregation of charismatic Christians into our church," Howe said, whereupon the bishops, the priests, and the congregation responded with an ovation. "Let the fire loose in the fireplace," he bellowed in conclusion. "Amen!"

After yet another song, this one punctuated with rhythmic clapping,   49
White stepped to the podium and echoed the refrain. Presenting his congregation as candidates for confirmation in the Episcopal Church, White addressed Bishop Shipps and said, "It's our desire to put the fire in the fireplace."

The five bishops in all their high-church splendor spread out in front of the   50
altar. Then the members of Church of the King, numbering well over two hundred, formed a single queue in the center aisle, each one waiting for the next available bishop. Each bishop dabbed oil on the candidate's forehead, laid his hands on the candidate, and recited the formula for confirmation

from the *Book of Common Prayer:* "Strengthen, O Lord, your servant Rachel [or James or Nancy] with your Holy Spirit; empower her for your service; and sustain her all the days of her life. Amen." Each bishop, veteran of thousands of confirmations over the years, had his own style; the bishop nearest to me concluded each recitation with a smile and a light, playful slap on the cheek.

Many received their confirmations with outstretched arms. Not a few 51 eyes were filled with tears, including those in the ranks of the clergy. The choir sang the Doxology in the background:

Praise God, from whom all blessings flow.
Praise him, all creatures here below.
Praise him above, ye heavenly hosts.
Praise Father, Son, and Holy Ghost.

Bennett and Patricia Thagard came forward, as did Ken and Rachel Reeves. Rachel's eyes were full when she turned away from the bishop; she sobbed after she returned to her seat. Robert Dinkins, the former segregationist, walked up the center aisle with Carolyn. As the queue began to thin out, Stan White announced, "If we've missed you, come on down."

After the congregation exchanged the peace, White stepped to the 52 podium and introduced Bishop Shipps to a standing ovation. "I'm really not used to that kind of welcome," the bishop remarked, genuinely embarrassed. Then, recovering quickly: "I hope the clergy on my left will take note of it." Shipps said that the evening was "a very, very happy occasion for me" and added that it was "an Easter day that I will remember more clearly than any other in my life."

When White took the podium again, he ruminated a bit. He said that 53 Church of the King sought "orthodox, creedal Christianity married and blended with the fire and vigor of the pentecostal experience." He recounted his own pentecostal roots: his great-great-uncle and his grandfather, both pentecostal preachers. His grandmother was also an Assemblies of God minister. White asked her to stand, one of the newest confirmands in the Episcopal Church. White then introduced his father, "Brother Jimmy," and his mother, Ann, also new Episcopalians.

Before the celebration of the Eucharist, Bishop Shipps consecrated the 54 altar, a simple table of white marble that had been the object of considerable interest to members of the Friday evening prayer group. ("That's not at all what I expected," someone had remarked at the time.) During the Sunday morning service Stan White had explained that the altar would be consecrated after the confirmations and before the celebration of the Eucharist that evening. "That doesn't mean you can't touch it or anything like that," he said. "It means only that the altar should be treated with reverence and respect." During that same service, at the conclusion of his extemporaneous homily, White had given an altar call, the script of which came straight from a Billy Graham crusade. He asked for all heads bowed and every eye closed. "You don't want to leave this place this morning," he implored, "without knowing that everything is right between you and God." White acknowledged each hand with a simple "yes" and then, as the synthesizer played softly in the background, offered a formula prayer for those seeking salvation. "Dear Jesus, I ask you to forgive me today," White intoned. "Cleanse me . . . wash me in your blood . . . make me righteous in your eyes."

With the consecration Sunday evening, Church of the King had a real altar, rather than the spiritualized altar most evangelicals refer to when they talk about "altar calls" or "laying all on the altar." "Sanctify this Table dedicated to you," the bishop prayed. "Let it be to us a sign of the heavenly Altar where your saints and angels praise you forever. Accept here the continual recalling of the sacrifice of your Son."

When it came time to receive Holy Communion—"the memorial of our redemption," in the words of the *Book of Common Prayer*—the celebrant held up the bread and the wine from the newly consecrated altar and announced "the gifts of God for the people of God." He invited the congregation to "take them in remembrance that Christ died for you, and feed on him in your heart by faith, with thanksgiving." The congregation queued up once more to receive the sacrament. A few genuflected, some dipped the wafer into the cup, a way of receiving known as intinction. Many turned away with tears in their eyes.

By the end of the recessional (a reprise of "How Magnificent Is Your Name"), it was nine-thirty. The memorable service of "Confirmation, Consecration of an Altar, and a Celebration of the Holy Eucharist" had lasted more than two and a half hours. Euphoria had gradually given way to exhaustion. The congregation heaved a kind of collective sigh, and the reception afterwards in the rear portion of the warehouse provided occasion to exchange congratulations and to evaluate the day's events. "If that don't move you, you got to be dead," one parishioner said breathlessly to another. "That's all I got to say."

Visitors were equally impressed. The Reverend Robert South had driven over six hundred miles from Belhaven, North Carolina, to witness the event. "This was so exciting, I had to come down," he said. "This is history in the making." Is this the wave of the future in the Episcopal Church? "I hope we don't stifle these people. I hope we'll adopt a lot of these things. This is what we should be doing." The Reverend Nan Peete, a black woman from the diocese of Atlanta, also cited the event as "historic" and noted with satisfaction that Church of the King was "a truly integrated congregation." Peete's mother, who described herself as a high-church Episcopalian from Chicago, said, "It was just so different. It was wonderful, energizing, exciting!"

Bobby Ingram, another visitor, commended Stan White for his foresight. Ingram, headed for seminary in the fall, described himself as part of the "carnage" from a charismatic community in the Washington, D.C., area. There, he said, the leaders of the community became intoxicated with their own charisma and the power it afforded them. Ingram admired Stan White because he elected to "connect with some wisdom" by affiliating with a tradition that would hold him accountable lest he get carried away. 59

I asked the Reverend W. Birt Sams, a retired priest in the diocese, if he ever thought he would see anything like this evening. "Never, never," he said emphatically. "We have quite a lot of charismatic influence in this diocese," he added, "but this outdoes everything and anything we've ever had." 60

Many other Episcopalians concurred. Louise Shipps, the bishop's wife, said she was "overwhelmed" by the service. "We are really rejoicing in this," she said. "We are going to learn so much. We are being offered so much by these people." Brother Albert, an Episcopal monk dressed in a tunic and sandals, said simply, "This was quite an experience." 61

"I loved it," John King, an Episcopal layman from Waycross, Georgia, declared. "I think in about five years this church will be one of the largest in the diocese. It has an emotional appeal that a lot of the mainline churches don't have." Between bites of cookies, King tried to illustrate his point. "I defy you to either hum or whistle a song from the Episcopal hymnal" he said. The music at Church of the King, on the other hand, was lively and rhythmic. "People like that," he said. 62

Bishop Harry Shipps agreed. "I don't think this would go over big in Massachusetts," he acknowledged, but in the South, with its predominant evangelical ethos, Episcopalians are more attuned to evangelical sympathies. Judging from the overwhelmingly positive response he's had from other bishops, Shipps predicted broad acceptance of Church of the King within Episcopal circles. "Everybody," he said, "is just so excited about this." Although he anticipated that the "problem will be with liberals," he cited what he called the "remarkable unanimity" within the diocese. "I hope this is not an isolated phenomenon," he said. "I believe it's going to happen elsewhere. I'm convinced that the church catholic is going to include both Roman Catholics and pentecostals—and they're going to be a happy family." 63

Indeed, the Roman Catholics of Valdosta, at least, had weighed in with a large floral bouquet of "prayerful congratulations" to Church of the King. "If anyone had told me years ago that St. John's Catholic Church would be sending us flowers," Stan White remarked in the morning service, "I never would have believed them." The pentecostals in town were less 64 forthcoming. When I asked James White, Stan's father, how his erstwhile colleagues in the Assemblies of God would react to the day's events, he shook his head. "I don't know if the Assemblies of God will pay any attention," he said sadly, "but they would probably dismiss it as a lapse into dead orthodoxy." Ann White was characteristically more direct. "I don't think they understand it at all," she said.

The din of the fellowship hall began slowly to abate. The congregation,   65
many of them newly rooted within historic Christianity, emerged from the sanctuary of Church of the King into the bracing air of a spring night in Georgia.

Throughout the evening Stan White wore a proud, fixed smile, the ex-   66
pression of a father having just announced the birth of his first child. His congregation's pilgrimage from the pentecostalism of Evangel Assembly of God to the charismatic fervor of Church of the King, rooted in the sacramentalism of the historic church, may have been long and gradual, but it had also been joyous, and it had culminated in sweet and unabashed celebration. No one, least of all Stan White, had second thoughts about the journey. "I see God's hand now," White said. "I'm almost thankful that the deacons released me. I can look back and see the providence of God."

NOTES

1. Quoted in Barbara White, "Pastor, Congregation Find their Roots," *Florida Times-Union,* 14 April 1990, Religion section, p. 4.

2. Quoted in "Rector and a Rumpus," *Newsweek,* 4 July 1960, p. 77.

3. Quoted in ibid. See also "Speaking in Tongues," *Time,* 15 August 1960, pp. 55, 57.

4. See Mark A. Noll, "Evangelicals on the Canterbury Trail," *Eternity* 29 (March 1978): 14–19ff. Robert E. Webber (also of Wheaton College) appropriated Noll's title for his own book, *Evangelicals on the Canterbury Trail* (Wilton, Conn.: Morehouse, 1989).

5. For a treatment of Episcopalians' outsized influence in American culture, see Kit and Frederica Konolige, *The Power of their Glory: American's Ruling Class: The Episcopalians* (New York: Wyden Books, 1978).

6. Lyrics by Phil Driscoll and Lari Gass, Mighty Horn Music.

Working with the Text

1. The merger of the Church of the King with the Episcopal Church erased a series of long-standing cultural differences—and, according to several of Balmer's interview subjects, will continue to do so. Identify the ways in which the assimilation affected theological, aesthetic, and social borders, both in Valdosta and in the larger Christian community. Where did the breaching of traditional borders create new boundaries?

2. Why does Balmer focus so intently on Stan White's family and on the noon meal at the Dinkins's home? On the physical setting of the Church of the King? Given that California and Pennsylvania hosted the birth of Pentecostalism within the Episcopal and Roman Catholic churches, respectively, why does Bishop Shipps claim that the South is more receptive to a reconciliation of liturgical and Pentecostal forms than is the rest of the United States? Do you think Balmer agrees? Why or why not?

3. What is the role of the charismatic leader in the events Balmer describes? How much of the historic merger can be credited to Stan White and how much to other people or forces? Does the essay take a position on this question, take multiple positions, or withhold judgment? Why?

4. Balmer's subjects use vibrant metaphors for the merger, for example, marriage, pilgrimage, and fire in a marble fireplace. How do these function in their immediate contexts and in the essay as a whole? Do they offer additional information and/or insight? The essay also makes occasional use of symbols, which have both literal and figurative meaning. What are the major symbols in the essay, and how do they function?

5. Visit a religious service in a tradition not your own. Try to attend with a member of the congregation, both to guide your conduct in the service and to explain unfamiliar features and terms, so that you may better understand what you see and hear. Afterward, write an account of the service, using the final several pages of Balmer's essay as a model. Strive to capture the tone of the service, as well as its sequence, and something of the personality of major participants. Do not analyze what you see; simply record it as accurately and as vividly as possible.

How the Other Half Lives

JACOB RIIS

Journalist and social reformer Jacob Riis was born in Denmark in 1849. After immigrating to the United States in 1870, he worked for several different New York City newspapers, often reporting on the living conditions within slums and on the exploitation of the lower classes. Later in life, he was a major force in the movement to improve housing and education for the poor and to create public parks and other amenities to improve urban life. He died in 1914. His most famous book, *How the Other Half Lives* (1890), was among the first publications to bring to light the squalor of tenement dwellings, which housed New York City's poorest and least powerful residents. In the following excerpt from that book, Riis looks unsparingly at tenement life and urges reform.

Enough of them [tenements] everywhere. Suppose we look into one? 1
No.—Cherry Street. Be a little careful, please! The hall is dark and you might stumble over the children pitching pennies back there. Not that it would hurt them; kicks and cuffs are their daily diet. They have little else. Here where the hall turns and dives into utter darkness is a step, and another, another. A flight of stairs. You can feel your way, if you cannot see it. Close? Yes! What would you have? All the fresh air that ever enters these stairs comes from the hall door that is forever slamming, and from the windows of dark bedrooms that in turn receive from the stairs their sole supply of the elements God meant to be free, but man deals out with such niggardly hand. That was a woman filling her pail by the hydrant you just bumped against. The sinks are in the hallway, that all the tenants may have access—and all be poisoned alike by their summer stenches. Hear the pump squeak! It is the lullaby of tenement house babes. In summer, when a thousand thirsty throats pant for a cooling drink in this block, it is worked in vain. But the saloon, whose open door you passed in the hall, is always there. The smell of it has followed you up. Here is a door. Listen! That short hacking cough, that tiny, helpless wail—what do they mean? They mean that the soiled bow of white you saw on the door downstairs will have another story to tell—Oh! a sadly familiar story—before the day is at an end. The child is dying with measles. With half a chance it might have lived; but it had none. That dark bedroom killed it.

162

"It was took all of a suddint," says the mother, smoothing the throbbing   2
little body with trembling hands. There is no unkindness in the rough voice
of the man in the jumper, who sits by the window grimly smoking a clay
pipe, with the little life ebbing out in his sight, bitter as his words sound:
"Hush, Mary! If we cannot keep the baby, need we complain—such as we?"

Such as we! What if the words ring in your ears as we grope our way up   3
the stairs and down from floor to floor, listening to the sounds behind the
closed doors—some of quarrelling, some of coarse songs, more of profanity. They are true. When the summer heats come with their suffering they
have meaning more terrible than words can tell. Come over here. Step carefully over this baby—it is a baby, [in] spite of its rags and dirt—under these
iron bridges called fire escapes, but loaded down, despite the incessant
watchfulness of the firemen, with broken household goods, with washtubs
and barrels, over which no man could climb from a fire. This gap between
dingy brick walls is the yard. That strip of smoke-colored sky up there is the
heaven of these people. Do you wonder the name does not attract them to
the churches? That baby's parents live in the rear tenement here. She is at
least as clean as the steps we are now climbing. There are plenty of houses
with half a hundred such in. The tenement is much like the one in front we
just left, only fouler, closer, darker—we will not say more cheerless. The
word is a mockery. A hundred thousand people lived in rear tenements in
New York last year. Here is a room neater than the rest. The woman, a stout
matron with hard lines of care in her face, is at the washtub. "I try to keep
the childer clean," she says, apologetically, but with a hopeless glance
around. The spice of hot soapsuds is added to the air already tainted with
the smell of boiling cabbage, of rags and uncleanliness all about. It makes
an overpowering compound. It is Thursday, but patched linen is hung upon
the pulley line from the window. There is no Monday cleaning in the tenements. It is washday all the week round, for a change of clothing is scarce
among the poor. They are poverty's honest badge, these perennial lines of
rags hung out to dry, those that are not the washerwoman's professional
shingle. The true line to be drawn between pauperism and honest poverty
is the clothesline. With it begins the effort to be clean that is the first and the
best evidence of a desire to be honest.

What sort of an answer, think you, would come from these tenements to   4
the question "Is life worth living?" were they heard at all in the discussion?
It may be that this, cut from the last report but one of the Association for the
Improvement of the Condition of the Poor, a long name for a weary task,
has a suggestion of it: "In the depth of winter the attention of the Association was called to a Protestant family living in a garret in a miserable tenement in Cherry Street. The family's condition was most deplorable. The man,
his wife, and three small children shivering in one room through the roof of

which the pitiless winds of winter whistled. The room was almost barren of furniture; the parents slept on the floor, the elder children in boxes, and the baby was swung in an old shawl attached to the rafters by cords by way of a hammock. The father, a seaman, had been obliged to give up that calling because he was in consumption, and was unable to provide either bread or fire for his little ones."[1]

Perhaps this may be put down as an exceptional case, but one that came to my notice some months ago in a Seventh Ward tenement was typical enough to escape that reproach. There were nine in the family: husband, wife, an aged grandmother, and six children; honest, hard-working Germans, scrupulously neat, but poor. All nine lived in two rooms, one about ten feet square that served as parlor, bedroom, and eating room, the other, a small half room made into a kitchen. The rent was seven dollars and a half a month, more than a week's wages for the husband and father, who was the only breadwinner in the family. That day the mother had thrown herself out of the window, and was carried up from the street dead. She was "discouraged," said some of the other women from the tenement, who had come in to look after the children while a messenger carried the news to the father at the shop. They went stolidly about their task, although they were evidently not without feeling for the dead woman. No doubt she was wrong in not taking life philosophically, as did the four families a city missionary found housekeeping in the four corners of one room. They got along well enough together until one of the families took a boarder and made trouble. Philosophy, according to my optimistic friend, naturally inhabits the tenements. The people who live there come to look upon death in a different way from the rest of us—do not take it as hard. He has never found time to explain how the fact fits into his general theory that life is not unbearable in the tenements. Unhappily for the philosophy of the slums, it is too apt to be of the kind that readily recognizes the saloon, always handy, as the refuge from every trouble, and shapes its practice according to the discovery. . . .

Today, what is a tenement? The law defines it as a house "occupied by three or more families, living independently and doing their cooking on the premises; or by more than two families on a floor, so living and cooking and

5

6

---

1. Riis trimmed this quotation and slightly altered its ending thereby omitting some interesting material on the resources of New York's poor. After the word "consumption" the original text continues "and was earning a precarious living by gathering roots and flowers in the woods and selling them on the streets. But the inclement weather had kept him from going out, and a sick child claimed the mother's attention, so that these parents though willing were unable to provide either bread or fire for their little ones." The report goes on to say that the family was aided by the society, moved to better quarters, and that the father was better now owing to the help and care of his friends. The Board of Health was notified, and steps were taken to repair the tenement. N.Y.A.I.C.P., *Forty-fifth Annual Report, 1888* (New York, 1888), pp. 56–57.

having a common right in the halls, stairways, yards, etc." That is the legal meaning, and includes flats and apartment houses, with which we have nothing to do.[2] In its narrower sense the typical tenement was thus described when last arraigned before the bar of public justice: "It is generally a brick building from four to six stories high on the street, frequently with a store on the first floor which, when used for the sale of liquor, has a side opening for the benefit of the inmates and to evade the Sunday law; four families occupy each floor, and a set of rooms consists of one or two dark closets, used as bedrooms, with a living room twelve feet by ten. The staircase is too often a dark well in the center of the house, and no direct through ventilation is possible, each family being separated from the other by partitions. Frequently the rear of the lot is occupied by another building of three stories high with two families on a floor." The picture is nearly as true today as ten years ago, and will be for a long time to come. The dim light admitted by the air shaft shines upon greater crowds than ever. Tenements are still "good property," and the poverty of the poor man his destruction. A barrack downtown where he *has to live* because he is poor brings in a third more rent than a decent flat house in Harlem. The statement once made a sensation that between seventy and eighty children had been found in one tenement. It no longer excites even passing attention, when the sanitary police report counting 101 adults and 91 children in a Crosby Street house, one of twins, built together. The children in the other, if I am not mistaken, numbered 89, a total of 180 for two tenements! Or when a midnight inspection in Mulberry Street unearths a hundred and fifty "lodgers" sleeping on filthy floors in two buildings. Spite of brownstone trimmings, plate glass and mosaic vestibule floors, the water does not rise in summer to the second story, while the beer flows unchecked to the all-night picnics on the roof. The saloon with the side door and the landlord divide the prosperity of the place between them, and the tenant, in sullen submission, foots the bills.

Where are the tenements of today? Say rather: where are they not? In fifty years they have crept up from the Fourth Ward slums and the Five Points the whole length of the island, and have polluted the Annexed District to the Westchester line. Crowding all the lower wards, wherever business leaves a foot of ground unclaimed; strung along both rivers, like ball and chain tied to the foot of every street, and filling up Harlem with their restless, pent-up multitudes, they hold within their clutch the wealth and business of New York, hold them at their mercy in the day of mob rule and wrath. The bulletproof shutters, the stacks of hand grenades, and the Gatling

7

---

2. This definition of a tenement was the one established by the 1867 New York statute.

guns of the Subtreasury are tacit admissions of the fact and of the quality of the mercy expected. The tenements today are New York, harboring three-fourths of its population. When another generation shall have doubled the census of our city, and to that vast army of workers, held captive by poverty, the very name of home shall be as a bitter mockery, what will the harvest be?

Working with the Text

1. Jacob Riis, a 19th-century journalist and social reformer, took it upon himself to expose the wretched conditions in which some three-fourths of the citizens of New York City lived in the 1880s. He notes elsewhere of tenement dwellers, or the "other half," that "the evil they breed" is "but as a just punishment upon the community that gave it no other choice. . . ." What is "the evil they breed"? He also says the fact that "we have to own [these evils] the child of our own doing does not excuse [them]." Who is the "we" he is referring to? Does Riis convince you that "we" are to blame for the "evils" of the "other half"?

2. In what ways does Riis seem ambivalent in his feelings toward the "other half"? When does he seem most sympathetic? What fears does he express about the "restless, pent-up multitudes" in tenement housing? What alarm does he sound about "another generation [doubling] the census of our city"? What, ultimately, do you think motivated him to write about the living conditions of the poor?

3. Riis notes of tenements that "[t]he saloon with the side door and the landlord divide the prosperity of the place between them, and the tenant, in sullen submission, foots the bills." Do you see this as exploitation or as legitimate business practice?

4. Riis quotes a friend as saying that people who live in tenements "come to look upon death in a different way from the rest of us—do not take it as hard." Why might this be true?

5. How would you compare the situation Riis describes more than a hundred years ago with issues revolving around poverty and substandard living conditions today? Note, for example, that Riis suggests tenement dwellers "touch the family file with deadly moral contagion," which is their "worst crime." How is this related to today's debates over "family values"?

6. Choose a location outside the United States where people live in poverty. As in question 5, compare the situation Riis describes from more than a hundred years ago with issues revolving around poverty and substandard living conditions today.

Helping and Hating the Homeless

PETER MARIN

Freelance writer Peter Marin studied literature at Swarthmore College and received his master's degree from Columbia University in 1958. Awarded fellowships by both the Guggenheim Foundation and the National Endowment for the Arts, Marin has published fiction and poetry, as well as several works of nonfiction, including *The World of the Homeless* (1986) and *Freedom and Its Discontents: Reflections on Four Decades of American Moral Experience* (1995). He has written for a variety of publications and has been a contributing editor to *Harper's* magazine since 1982. In the following 1987 essay for *Harper's,* Marin looks at mainstream America's often contradictory and irrational response to the homeless, arguing that "the homeless embody all that bourgeois culture has for centuries tried to eradicate and destroy."

When I was a child, I had a recurring vision of how I would end as an old man: alone, in a sparsely furnished second-story room I could picture quite precisely, in a walk-up on Fourth Avenue in New York, where the second-hand bookstores then were. It was not a picture which frightened me. I liked it. The idea of anonymity and solitude and marginality must have seemed to me, back then, for reasons I do not care to remember, both inviting and inevitable. Later, out of college, I took to the road, hitchhiking and traveling on freights, doing odd jobs here and there, crisscrossing the country. I liked that too: the anonymity and the absence of constraint and the rough community I sometimes found. I felt at home on the road, perhaps because I felt at home nowhere else, and periodically, for years, I would return to that world, always with a sense of relief and release.

I have been thinking a lot about that these days, now that transience and homelessness have made their way into the national consciousness, and especially since the town I live in, Santa Barbara, has become well known because of the recent successful campaign to do away with the meanest aspects of its "sleeping ordinances"—a set of foolish laws making it illegal for the homeless to sleep at night in public places. During that campaign I got to know many of the homeless men and women in Santa Barbara, who tend to gather, night and day, in a small park at the lower end of town, not far from the tracks and the harbor, under the rooflike, overarching branches of a gigantic fig tree, said to be the oldest on the continent. There one enters much the same world I thought, as a child, I would die in, and the one in which I traveled as a young man: a "marginal" world inhabited by all those unable to find a place in "our" world. Sometimes, standing on the tracks close to the park, you can sense in the wind, or in the smell of tar and ties, the presence and age of that marginal world: the way it stretches backward and inevitably forward in time, parallel to our own world, always present, always close, and yet separated from us—at least in the mind—by a gulf few of us are interested in crossing.

Late last summer, at a city council meeting here in Santa Barbara, I saw, close up, the consequences of that strange combination of proximity and distance. The council was meeting to vote on the repeal of the sleeping ordinances, though not out of any sudden sense of compassion or justice. Council members had been pressured into it by the threat of massive demonstrations—"The Selma of the Eighties" was the slogan one heard among the homeless. But this threat that frightened the council enraged the town's citizens. Hundreds of them turned out for the meeting. One by one they filed to the microphone to curse the council and castigate the homeless. Drinking, doping, loitering, panhandling, defecating, urinating, molesting, stealing—the litany went on and on, was repeated over and over, accompanied by fantasies of disaster: the barbarian hordes at the gates, civilization ended. 3

What astonished me about the meeting was not what was said; one could have predicted that. It was the power and depth of the emotion revealed: the mindlessness of the fear, the vengefulness of the fury. Also, almost none of what was said had anything to do with the homeless people I know—not the ones I once traveled with, not the ones in town. They, the actual homeless men and women, might not have existed at all. 4

If I write about Santa Barbara, it is not because I think the attitudes at work here are unique. They are not. You find them everywhere in America. In the last few months I have visited several cities around the country, and in each of them I have found the same thing: more and more people in the streets, more and more suffering. (There are at least 350,000 homeless people in the country, perhaps as many as 3 million.) And, in talking to the good citizens of these cities, I found, almost always, the same thing: confusion and ignorance, or simple indifference, but anger too, and fear. 5

What follows here is an attempt to explain at least some of that anger and fear, to clear up some of the confusion, to chip away at the indifference. It is not meant to be definitive; how could it be? The point is to try to illuminate some of the darker corners of homelessness, those we ordinarily 6 ignore, and those in which the keys to much that is now going on may be hidden.

The trouble begins with the word "homeless." It has become such an abstraction, and is applied to so many different kinds of people, with so many different histories and problems, that it is almost meaningless.

Homelessness, in itself, is nothing more than a condition visited upon men and women (and, increasingly, children) as the final stage of a variety of problems about which the word "homelessness" tells us almost nothing. Or, to put it another way, it is a catch basin into which pour all of the people disenfranchised or marginalized or scared off by processes beyond their control, those which lie close to the heart of American life. Here are the groups packed into the single category of "the homeless":

- Veterans, mainly from the war in Vietnam. In many American cities, vets make up close to 50 percent of all homeless males.
- The mentally ill. In some parts of the country, roughly a quarter of the homeless would, a couple of decades ago, have been institutionalized.
- The physically disabled or chronically ill, who do not receive any benefits or whose benefits do not enable them to afford permanent shelter.
- The elderly on fixed incomes whose funds are no longer sufficient for their needs.
- Men, women, and whole families pauperized by the loss of a job.
- Single parents, usually women, without the resources or skills to establish new lives.
- Runaway children, many of whom have been abused.
- Alcoholics and those in trouble with drugs (whose troubles often begin with one of the other conditions listed here).
- Immigrants, both legal and illegal, who often are not counted among the homeless because they constitute a "problem" in their own right.
- Traditional tramps, hobos, and transients, who have taken to the road or the streets for a variety of reasons and who prefer to be there.

You can quickly learn two things about the homeless from this list. First, you can learn that many of the homeless, before they were homeless, were people more or less like ourselves: members of the working or middle class. And you can learn that the world of the homeless has its roots in various policies, events, and ways of life for which some of us are responsible and from which some of us actually prosper.

We decide, as a people, to go to war, we ask our children to kill and to   10
die, and the result, years later, is grown men homeless on the street.

We change, with the best intentions, the laws pertaining to the mentally   11
ill, and then, without intention, neglect to provide them with services; and
the result, in our streets, drives some of us crazy with rage.

We cut taxes and prune budgets, we modernize industry and shift the   12
balance of trade, and the result of all these actions and errors can be read,
sleeping form by sleeping form, on our city streets.

The liberals cannot blame the conservatives. The conservatives cannot   13
blame the liberals. Homelessness is the *sum total* of our dreams, policies, intentions, errors, omissions, cruelties, kindnesses, all of it recorded, in flesh,
in the life of the streets.

You can also learn from this list one of the most important things there   14
is to know about the homeless—that they can be roughly divided into two
groups: those who have had homelessness forced upon them and want
nothing more than to escape it; and those who have at least in part *chosen*
it for themselves, and now accept, or in some cases, embrace it.

I understand how dangerous it is to introduce the idea of choice into a   15
discussion of homelessness. It can all too easily be used to justify indifference or brutality toward the homeless, or to argue that they are only getting
what they "deserve." And yet it seems to me that it is only by taking choice
into account, in all of the intricacies of its various forms and expressions,
that one can really understand certain kinds of homelessness.

The fact is, many of the homeless are not only hapless victims but vol-   16
untary exiles, "domestic refugees," people who have turned not against life
itself but against *us,* our life, American life. Look for a moment at the vets.
The price of returning to America was to forget what they had seen or
learned in Vietnam, to "put it behind them." But some could not do that, and
the stress of trying showed up as alcoholism, broken marriages, drug addic-
tion, crime. And it showed up too as life on the street, which was for some
vets a desperate choice made in the name of life—the best they could manage. It was a way of avoiding what might have occurred had they stayed
where they were: suicide, or violence done to others.

We must learn to accept that there may indeed be people, and not only   17
vets, who have seen so much of our world, or seen it so clearly, that to live
in it becomes impossible. Here, for example, is the story of Alice, a homeless middle-aged woman in Los Angeles, where there are, perhaps, 50,000
homeless people. It was set down a few months ago by one of my students
at the University of California, Santa Barbara, where I taught for a semester.
I had encouraged them to go find the homeless and listen to their stories.
And so, one day, when this student saw Alice foraging in a dumpster outside a McDonald's, he stopped and talked to her:

She told me she had led a pretty normal life as she grew up and eventually went to college. From there she went on to Chicago to teach school. She was single and lived in a small apartment.

One night, after she got off the train after school, a man began to follow her to her apartment building. When she got to her door she saw a knife and the man hovering behind her. She had no choice but to let him in. The man raped her.

After that, things got steadily worse. She had a nervous breakdown. She went to a mental institution for three months, and when she went back to her apartment she found her belongings gone. The landlord had sold them to cover the rent she hadn't paid.

She had no place to go and no job because the school had terminated her employment. She slipped into depression. She lived with friends until she could muster enough money for a ticket to Los Angeles. She said she no longer wanted to burden her friends, and that if she had to live outside, at least Los Angeles was warmer than Chicago.

It is as if she began back then to take on the mentality of a street person. She resolved herself to homelessness. She's been out West since 1980, without a home or job. She seems happy, with her best friend being her cat. But the scars of memories still haunt her, and she is running from them, or should I say *him*.

18 This is, in essence, the same story one hears over and over again on the street. You begin with an ordinary life; then an event occurs—traumatic, catastrophic; smaller events follow, each one deepening the original wound; finally, homelessness becomes inevitable, or begins to *seem* inevitable to the person involved—the only way out of an intolerable situation. You are struck continually, hearing these stories, by something seemingly unique in American life, the absolute isolation involved. In what other culture would there be such an absence or failure of support from familial, social, or institutional sources? Even more disturbing is the fact that it is often our supposed sources of support—family, friends, government organizations—that have caused the problem in the first place.

19 Everything that happened to Alice—the rape, the loss of job and apartment, the breakdown—was part and parcel of a world gone radically wrong, a world, for Alice, no longer to be counted on, no longer worth living in. Her homelessness can be seen as flight, as failure of will or nerve, even, perhaps, as *disease*. But it can also be seen as a mute, furious refusal, a self-imposed exile far less appealing to the rest of us than ordinary life, but *better*, in Alice's terms.

20 We like to think, in America, that everything is redeemable, that everything broken can be magically made whole again, and that what has been "dirtied" can be cleansed. Recently I saw on television that one of the soaps had introduced the character of a homeless old woman. A woman in her

thirties discovers that her long-lost mother has appeared in town, on the streets. After much searching the mother is located and identified and embraced; and then she is scrubbed and dressed in style, restored in a matter of days to her former upper-class habits and role.

A triumph—but one more likely to occur on television than in real life. Yes, many of those on the streets could be transformed, rehabilitated. But there are others whose lives have been irrevocably changed, damaged beyond repair, and who no longer want help, who no longer recognize the *need* for help, and whose experience in our world has made them want only to be left alone. How, for instance, would one restore Alice's life, or reshape it in a way that would satisfy *our* notion of what a life should be? What would it take to return her to the fold? How to erase the four years of homelessness, which have become as familiar to her, and as much a home, as her "normal" life once was? Whatever we think of the way in which she has resolved her difficulties, it constitutes a sad peace made with the world. Intruding ourselves upon it in the name of redemption is by no means as simple a task—or as justifiable a task—as one might think. 21

It is important to understand too that however disorderly and dirty and unmanageable the world of homeless men and women like Alice appears to us, it is not without its significance, and its rules and rituals. The homeless in our cities mark out for themselves particular neighborhoods, blocks, buildings, doorways. They impose on themselves often obsessively strict routines. They reduce their world to a small area, and thereby protect themselves from a world that might otherwise be too much to bear. 22

Daily the city eddies around the homeless. The crowds flowing past leave a few feet, a gap. We do not touch the homeless world. Perhaps we cannot touch it. It remains separate even as the city surrounds it. 23

The homeless, simply because they are homeless, are strangers, alien—and therefore a threat. Their presence, in itself, comes to constitute a kind of violence; it deprives us of our sense of safety. Let me use myself as an example. I know, and respect, many of those now homeless on the streets of Santa Barbara. Twenty years ago, some of them would have been my companions and friends. And yet, these days, if I walk through the park near my home and see strangers bedding down for the night, my first reaction, if not fear, is a sense of annoyance and intrusion, of worry and alarm. I think of my teenage daughter, who often walks through the park, and then of my house, a hundred yards away, and I am tempted—only tempted, but tempted, still—to call the "proper" authorities to have the strangers moved on. Out of sight, out of mind. 24

Notice: I do not bring them food. I do not offer them shelter or a shower in the morning. I do not even stop to talk. Instead, I think: my daughter, my 25 house, my privacy. What moves me is not the threat of *danger*—nothing as animal as that. Instead there pops up inside of me, neatly in a row, a set of anxieties, ones you might arrange in a dollhouse living room and label: Family of bourgeois fears. The point is this: Our response to the homeless is fed by a complex set of cultural attitudes, habits of thought, and fantasies and fears so familiar to us, so common, that they have become a *second* nature and might as well be instinctive, for all the control we have over them. And it is by no means easy to untangle this snarl of responses. What does seem clear is that the homeless embody all that bourgeois culture has for centuries tried to eradicate and destroy.

If you look to the history of Europe you find that homelessness first appeared (or is first acknowledged) at the very same moment that bourgeois culture begins to appear. The same processes produced them both: the breakup of feudalism, the rise of commerce and cities, the combined triumphs of capitalism, industrialism, and individualism. The historian Fernand Braudel, in *The Wheels of Commerce,* describes, for instance, the armies of impoverished men and women who began to haunt Europe as far back as the eleventh century. And the makeup of these masses? Essentially the same then as it is now: the unfortunates, the throwaways, the misfits, the deviants.   26

> In the eighteenth century, all sorts and conditions were to be found in this human dross . . . widows, orphans, cripples, . . . journeymen who had broken their contracts, out-of-work labourers, homeless priests with no living, old men, fire victims, . . . war victims, deserters, discharged soldiers, would-be vendors of useless articles, vagrant preachers with or without licenses, "pregnant servant-girls and unmarried mothers driven from home," children sent out "to find bread or to maraud."

Then, as now, distinctions were made between the "homeless" and the supposedly "deserving" poor, those who knew their place and willingly sustained, with their labors, the emergent bourgeois world.   27

> The good paupers were accepted, lined up and registered on the official list; they had a right to public charity and were sometimes allowed to solicit it outside churches in prosperous districts, when the congregation came out, or in market places. . . .
>
>   When it comes to beggars and vagrants, it is a very different story, and different pictures meet the eye: crowds, mobs, processions, sometimes mass emigrations, "along the country highways or the streets of the Towns and Villages," by beggars "whom hunger and nakedness has driven from home." . . . The towns dreaded these alarming visitors and drove them out as soon as they appeared on the horizon.

And just as the distinctions made about these masses were the same then as they are now, so too was the way society saw them. They seemed   28 to bourgeois eyes (as they still do) the one segment of society that remained resistant to progress, unassimilable and incorrigible, inimical to all order.

It is in the nineteenth century, in the Victorian era, that you can find the beginnings of our modern strategies for dealing with the homeless: the notion that they should be controlled and perhaps eliminated through "help." With the Victorians we begin to see the entangling of self-protection with social obligation, the strategy of masking self-interest and the urge to control as *moral duty*. Michel Foucault has spelled this out in his books on madness and punishment: the zeal with which the overseers of early bourgeois culture tried to purge, improve, and purify all of urban civilization—whether through schools and prisons, or, quite literally, with public baths and massive new water and sewage systems. Order, ordure—this is, in essence, the tension at the heart of bourgeois culture, and it was the singular genius of the Victorians to make it the main component of their medical, aesthetic, *and* moral systems. It was not a sense of justice or even empathy which called for charity or new attitudes toward the poor; it was *hygiene*. The very same attitudes appear in nineteenth-century America. Charles Loring Brace, in an essay on homeless and vagrant children written in 1876, described the treatment of delinquents in this way: "Many of their vices drop from them like the old and verminous clothing they left behind. . . . The entire change of circumstances seems to cleanse them of bad habits." Here you have it all: *vices, verminous clothing, cleansing them of bad habits*—the triple association of poverty with vice with dirt, an equation in which each term comes to stand for all of them.

These attitudes are with us still; that is the point. In our own century the person who has written most revealingly about such things is George Orwell, who tried to analyze his own middle-class attitudes toward the poor. In 1933, in *Down and Out in Paris and London,* he wrote about tramps:

> In childhood we are taught that tramps are blackguards, . . . a repulsive, rather dangerous creature, who would rather die than work or wash, and wants nothing but to beg, drink or rob hen-houses. The tramp monster is no truer to life than the sinister Chinaman of the magazines, but he is very hard to get rid of. The very word "tramp" evokes his image.

All of this is still true in America, though now it is not the word "tramp" but the word "homeless" that evokes the images we fear. It is the homeless who smell. Here, for instance, is part of a paper a student of mine wrote about her first visit to a Rescue Mission on skid row.

> The sermon began. The room was stuffy and smelly. The mixture of body odors and cooking was nauseating. I remember thinking: How can these people share

this facility? They must be repulsed by each other. They had strange habits and dispositions. They were a group of dirty, dishonored, weird people to me.

When it was over I ran to my car, went home, and took a shower. I felt extremely dirty. Through the day I would get flashes of that disgusting smell.

To put it as bluntly as I can, for many of us the homeless are *shit*. And our policies toward them, our spontaneous sense of disgust and horror, our wish to be rid of them—all of this has hidden in it, close to its heart, our feelings about excrement. Even Marx, that most bourgeois of revolutionaries, described the deviant *lumpen* in *The Eighteenth Brumaire of Louis Bonaparte* as "scum, offal, refuse of all classes." These days, in puritanical Marxist nations, they are called "parasites"—a word, perhaps not incidentally, one also associates with human waste. 32

What I am getting at here is the *nature* of the desire to help the homeless—what is hidden behind it and why it so often does harm. Every government program, almost every private project, is geared as much to the needs of those giving help as it is to the needs of the homeless. Go to any government agency, or, for that matter, to most private charities, and you will find yourself enmeshed, at once, in a bureaucracy so tangled and oppressive, or confronted with so much moral arrogance and contempt, that you will be driven back out into the streets for relief. 33

Santa Barbara, where I live, is as good an example as any. There are three main shelters in the city—all of them private. Between them they provide fewer than a hundred beds a night for the homeless. Two of the three shelters are religious in nature: the Rescue Mission and the Salvation Army. In the mission, as in most places in the country, there are elaborate and stringent rules. Beds go first to those who have not been there for two months, and you can stay for only two nights in any two-month period. No shelter is given to those who are not sober. Even if you go to the mission only for a meal, you are required to listen to sermons and participate in prayer, and you are regularly proselytized—sometimes overtly, sometimes subtly. There are obligatory, regimented showers. You go to bed precisely at ten: lights out, no reading, no talking. After the lights go out you will find fifteen men in a room with double-decker bunks. As the night progresses the room grows stuffier and hotter. Men toss, turn, cough, and moan. In the morning you are awakened precisely at five forty-five. Then breakfast. At seven-thirty you are back on the street. 34

The town's newest shelter was opened almost a year ago by a consortium of local churches. Families and those who are employed have first call on the beds—a policy which excludes the congenitally homeless. Alcohol is not simply forbidden *in* the shelter; those with a history of alcoholism must sign a "contract" pledging to remain sober and chemical-free. Finally, in a 35 paroxysm of therapeutic bullying, the shelter has added a new wrinkle: If you stay more than two days you are required to fill out and then discuss with a social worker a complex form listing what you perceive as your personal failings, goals, and strategies—all of this for men and women who simply want a place to lie down out of the rain!

It is these attitudes, in various forms and permutations, that you find re- 36 peated endlessly in America. We are moved either to "redeem" the homeless or to punish them. Perhaps there is nothing consciously hostile about it. Perhaps it is simply that as the machinery of bureaucracy cranks itself up to deal with these problems, attitudes assert themselves automatically. But whatever the case, the fact remains that almost every one of our strategies for helping the homeless is simply an attempt to rearrange the world *cosmetically,* in terms of how it looks and smells to *us.* Compassion is little more than the passion for control.

The central question emerging from all this is, What does a society owe 37 to its members in trouble, and *how* is that debt to be paid? It is a question which must be answered in two parts: first, in relation to the men and women who have been marginalized against their will, and then, in a slightly different way, in relation to those who have chosen (or accept or even prize) their marginality.

As for those who have been marginalized against their wills, I think the 38 general answer is obvious: A society owes its members whatever it takes for them to regain their places in the social order. And when it comes to specific remedies, one need only read backward the various processes which have created homelessness and then figure out where help is likely to do the most good. But the real point here is not the specific remedies required—affordable housing, say—but the basis upon which they must be offered, the necessary underlying ethical notion we seem in this nation unable to grasp: that those who are the inevitable casualties of modern industrial capitalism and the free-market system are entitled, *by right,* and by the simple virtue of their participation in that system, to whatever help they need. They are entitled to help to find and hold their places in the society whose social contract they have, in effect, signed and observed.

Look at that for just a moment: the notion of a contract. The majority of 39 homeless Americans have kept, insofar as they could, to the terms of that contract. In any shelter these days you can find men and women who have worked ten, twenty, forty years, and whose lives have nonetheless come to nothing. These are people who cannot afford a place in the world they helped create. And in return? Is it life on the street they have earned? Or the cruel charity we so grudgingly grant them?

But those marginalized against their will are only half the problem. 40
There remains, still, the question of whether we owe anything to those who
are voluntarily marginal. What about them: the street people, the rebels, and
the recalcitrants, those who have torn up their social contracts or returned
them unsigned?

I was in Las Vegas last fall, and I went out to the Rescue Mission at the 41
lower end of town, on the edge of the black ghetto, where I first stayed
years ago on my way west. It was twilight, still hot; in the vacant lot next-
door to the mission 200 men were lining up for supper. A warm wind blew
along the street lined with small houses and salvage yards, and in the distance I could see the desert's edge and the smudge of low hills in the fad-
ing light. There were elderly alcoholics in line, and derelicts, but mainly the
men were the same sort I had seen here years ago: youngish, out of work,
restless and talkative, the drifters and wanderers for whom the word "wan-
derlust" was invented.

At supper—long communal tables, thin gruel, stale sweet rolls, ice wa- 42
ter—a huge black man in his twenties, fierce and muscular, sat across from
me. "I'm from the Coast, man," he said. "Never been away from home before. Ain't sure I like it. Sure don't like *this* place. But I lost my job back
home a couple of weeks ago and figured, why wait around for another. I
thought I'd come out here, see me something of the world."

After supper, a squat Portuguese man in his mid-thirties, hunkered down 43
against the mission wall, offered me a smoke and told me: "Been sleeping in
my car, up the street, for a week. Had my own business back in Omaha. But
I got bored, man. Sold everything, got a little dough, came out here. Thought
I'd work construction. Let me tell you, this is one tough town."

In a world better than ours, I suppose, men (or women) like this might 44
not exist. Conservatives seem to have no trouble imagining a society so well
disciplined and moral that deviance of this kind would disappear. And leftists envision a world so just, so generous, that deviance would vanish along
with inequity. But I suspect that there will always be something at work in
some men and women to make them restless with the systems others devise
for them, and to move them outward toward the edges of the world, where
life is always riskier, less organized, and easier going.

Do we owe anything to these men and women, who reject our com- 45
pany and what we offer and yet nonetheless seem to demand *something*
from us?

We owe them, I think, at least a place to exist, a way to exist. That 46
may not be a *moral* obligation, in the sense that our obligation to the
involuntarily marginal is clearly a moral one, but it is an obligation nevertheless, one you might call an existential obligation.

Of course, it may be that I think we owe these men something because   47
I have liked men like them, and because I want their world to be there always, as a place to hide or rest. But there is more to it than that. I think we
as a society need men like these. A society needs its margins as much as it
needs art and literature. It needs holes and gaps, *breathing spaces,* let us
say, into which men and women can escape and live, when necessary, in
ways otherwise denied them. Margins guarantee to society a flexibility, an
elasticity, and allow it to accommodate itself to the natures and needs of its
members. When margins vanish, society becomes too rigid, too oppressive
by far, and therefore inimical to life.

It is for such reasons that, in cultures like our own, marginal men and   48
women take on a special significance. They are all we have left to remind
us of the narrowness of the received truths we take for granted. "Beyond the
pale," they somehow redefine the pale, or remind us, at least, that *something* is still out there, beyond the pale. They preserve, perhaps unconsciously, a dream that would otherwise cease to exist, the dream of having
a place in the world, and of being *left alone.*

Quixotic? Infantile? Perhaps. But remember. . . . [w]hat we are talking   49
about here is *freedom,* and with it, perhaps, an echo of the dream men
brought, long ago, to wilderness America. I use the word "freedom" gingerly, in relation to lives like these: skewed, crippled, emptied of everything
we associate with a full, or realized, freedom. But perhaps this is the condition into which freedom has fallen among us. Art has been "appreciated" out
of existence; literature has become an extension of the university, replete
with tenure and pensions; and as for politics, the ideologies which ring us
round seem too silly or shrill by far to speak for life. What is left, then, is this
mute and intransigent independence, this "waste" of life which refuses even
interpretation, and which cannot be assimilated to any ideology, and which
therefore can be put to no one's use. In its crippled innocence and the perfection of its superfluity it amounts, almost, to a rebellion against history,
and that is no small thing.

Let me put it as simply as I can: What we see on the streets of our cities   50
are two dramas, both of which cut to the troubled heart of the culture and
demand from us a response we may not be able to make. There is the drama
of those struggling to survive by regaining their place in the social order.
And there is the drama of those struggling to survive outside of it.

The resolution of both struggles depends on a third drama occurring at   51
the heart of the culture: the tension and contention between the magna-
nimity we owe to life and the darker tendings of the human psyche: our fear
of strangeness, our hatred of deviance, our love of order and control. How
we mediate by default or design between those contrary forces will deter-

mine not only the destinies of the homeless, but also something crucial about the nation, and perhaps—let me say it—about our own souls.

Working with the Text

1. In paragraph 3 Marin records the litany of complaints leveled at the homeless during a Santa Barbara town meeting: "Drinking, doping, loitering, panhandling, defecating, urinating, molesting, stealing." He goes on to suggest that "almost none of what was said had anything to do with the homeless people I know." How does he account for these images? How do you?

2. When Marin suggests that some people are homeless by choice, why does he go on to note "how dangerous it is to introduce the idea of choice into a discussion of homelessness"? What is he suggesting about feelings of difference when he says of these "voluntary exiles" that they "have turned not against life itself but against *us,* our life, American life"? What is your response to such an attitude toward "American life"?

3. In what sense does Marin suggest that the world of the homeless is a community?

4. Analyze what Marin considers society's obligation to those who have been "marginalized against their wills." Why does he believe society bears this obligation? Do you agree with his assessment?

 5. In arguing that we owe those who are marginalized by choice "a place to exist, a way to exist" (paragraph 46), Marin makes a complex point about the need for margins in a society. In an essay describe what he is getting at here. Do you agree with him?

Feelings About Difference

DAVID SIBLEY

David Sibley is a British sociologist and currently senior lecturer at the University of Hull in England. His first major work was *Outsiders of Urban Societies* (1981), which looked at the economic and social situation of transient populations in established capitalist countries—"gypsies" and other "traveling people" who move about nomadically with no fixed address or home. He is also the author of *Geographies of Exclusion: Society and Difference in the West* (revised 1995) and co-author of *Adolescent Drinking and Family Life* (1993). His teaching and research focus on human geography and issues of how communities develop in terms of the physical space they occupy. In the following essay Sibley considers some ways in which notions of difference (or deviation from the "norm") are created through images of cleanliness and dirt, "white" and "black."

The senior partner of a well-known professional firm around here put his home on the market with us and said: "You sent me a Mr. Shah and you sent me a Mr. Patel and you sent me a Mr. Whatever-it-was." He said: "I recognize that a lot of the big money comes from several thousand miles east of Dover nowadays, and I don't want you to think that I've got any prejudice at all, but would you be able to send me an Englishman one day?" (Suburban London estate agent)[1]

There are several possible routes into the problem of social and spatial exclusion. I want to start by considering people's feelings about others because of the importance of feelings in their effect on social interaction, particularly in instances of racism and related forms of oppression. If, for example, we consider the question of residential segregation, which is one of the most widely investigated issues in urban geography, it could be argued that the resistance to a different sort of person moving into a neighbourhood stems from feelings of anxiety, nervousness or fear. Who is felt to belong and not to belong contributes in an important way to the shaping of social space. It is often the case that this kind of hostility to others is articulated as a concern about property values but certain kinds of difference, as they are culturally constructed, trigger anxieties and a wish on the part of those who feel threatened to distance themselves from others. This may, of course, have economic consequences.

Feelings about others, people marked as different, may also be associ- 2
ated with places. Nervousness about walking down a street in a district
which has been labelled as dangerous, nauseousness associated with particular smells or, conversely, excitement, exhilaration or a feeling of calm
may be the kinds of sensations engendered by other environments. Repulsion and desire, fear and attraction, attach both to people and to places in
complex ways. Central to this question is the construction of the self, the
way in which individual identity relates to social, cultural and spatial contexts. In this chapter, I will suggest some of the connections between the self
and material and social worlds, moving towards a conception of the "ecological self."[2]

Alternative Perspectives on the Self

Central to early visions of the self was the idea of human individuality.[3] Ra- 3
tionalist philosophers recognized that only human beings were consciously
aware of their own life, which gave them the capacity to act autonomously.
Nineteenth-century romanticism similarly encouraged a view of the free
spirit, and this notion of the self was reinforced by capitalist forms of social
organization according to which people are highly individuated and assumed to have control of their own destinies. The subject was thus detached
from his or her social milieu.

A shift in conceptions of the self was signalled by Freudian psycho- 4
analysis. Freud situated the self in society and argued for connections between the developing self and the material world. Central to his thesis was
the unconscious, that "aspect of psychoanalysis that directly challenges the
emphasis in Western thought on the power of reason and rationality, of reflective and conscious control over the self." Although Freud suggested that
on one level the unconscious was detached from reality, on another level "it
is deeply entwined with the needs of the human body, the nature of external reality, and actual social relations."[4] The importance of external reality
for the psyche was outlined in *Civilization and its Discontents,* published in
1929. In this book, Freud wrote about the repression of libidinal desires
specifically in relation to the materialism of capitalist societies. He claimed
that one form of repression was an excessive concern with cleanliness and
order.[5] Personal hygiene, for example, is widely accepted as desirable on
medical and social grounds, but it removes bodily smell as a source of sexual stimulation. Washing and deodorizing the body has assumed a ritual
quality and in some people can become obsessive and compulsive. This
kind of observation raises issues about the role of dominant social and political structures in the sublimation of desire and the shaping of the self.

What are the sanctions against a group or an individual represented as dirty or disorderly? In *Civilization and its Discontents* Freud brackets cleanliness and order, both distancing the subject from the uncertainties and fears of the urban-industrial environment. However, as Smith observes, "order is a part of the tragedy of modern urban culture: it brings frustration but it cannot be done without."[6] . . .

The Generalized Other

The concept of "the generalized other" provides a means of spatializing the   5
problem and producing what we might describe as an ecological account of the self, one which situates the self in a full social and cultural context. The term "generalized other" was first used by George Herbert Mead, who noted the elision of people and objects to whom the child relates in developing a sense of self. He argued that:

> It is possible for inanimate objects, no less than for other human organisms, to form parts of the generalized and organized—the completely socialized—other for any given individual . . . Any thing—any object or set of objects, whether animate or inanimate, human or animal, or merely physical—towards which he acts, or to which he responds socially, is an element in what for him is the generalized other.[7]

Mead's interpretation of the relationship between self and other has funda-   6
mental implications for geographical studies of social interaction because it locates the individual in the social and material world. Ian Burkitt gives prominence to Mead's object relations theory for similar reasons.[8] He argues that:

> Mead's conception of the self and the psychical apparatus is more useful than Derrida's or Freud's in studying *the body in action.* That is because Mead recognized the practical nature of the psyche, *that it is always connected to social practice* and does not exist in some separate textual or mental domain. Whereas Derrida and Freud struggled with the metaphor of the mystic writing pad [for Derrida, a cultural and historical text written into the unconscious, positioning the subject in a textual world], Mead conceptualized that which remains open to new experiences and information as the active person *in their various social locations and settings* (the "I"). It is the embeddedness in social contexts that allows the individual to be constantly receptive to new stimuli, while at the same time the body carries the forms of history in terms of the cultural image of the self and the disciplines involved in social interaction (the "me"). So the "I" and the "me" are not just psychical but also bodily [my italics].

The social positioning of the self means that the boundary between self   7
and other is formed through a series of cultural representations of people and things which frequently elide so that the non-human world also pro-

vides a context for selfhood. To give one example of this kind of cultural representation, in racist discourse animals represented as transgressive and therefore threatening unsullied categories of things and social groups, like rats which come out of the sewers and spread disease, have in turn been used to represent threatening minority groups, like Jews and Gypsies, who are thus constructed as bad objects to which the self relates. To animalize or de-humanize a minority group in this way, of course, legitimates persecution. Interestingly from a geographical perspective, one of the few applications of Mead's generalized other has been in studies of the organization of domestic space by Csikszentmihalyi and Rochberg-Halton,[9] where things in the home which are both positively valued and rejected are seen to have a defining role in relation to the self. They note, in particular, that

> the impact of inanimate objects in this self-awareness process is much more important than one would infer from its neglect. Things tell us who we are, not in words but by embodying our intentions. In our everyday traffic of existence, we can also learn about ourselves from objects, almost as much as from people.[10]

People and things come to stand for each other, Csikszentmihalyi and Rochberg-Halton suggest, so that object relations can include relating to others through the material environment. Thus, for one woman,

> her home environment reflects an expanded boundary of the self, one that includes a number of past and present relationships. The meanings of the objects she is surrounded by are signs of her ties to this larger system of which she is a part.[11]

This seemed to me to be a promising but little-developed direction for research, one in which the signing of spaces could be examined specifically in relation to the social self. It had considerable implications for studies of inclusion and exclusion in other spaces.

Conclusion

. . . In subsequent chapters, the geographies of exclusion, the literal mappings of power relations and rejection, are informed by the generalized other. Apart from the collapse of categories like the public and the private which I see as a necessary feature of these geographies, the generalized other of object relations theory gives an invitation to open up debates about otherness, to examine the interconnections of people and things as they constitute and are constituted by places, what I take to be the ecological self (and the ecological other). This has to be taken one step at a time, however. I first look at social boundaries, filling in some details about the people who erect the boundaries and those who are excluded by them, and I then consider the issue of exclusionary landscapes as they have developed in different times and places.

NOTES

1. Daniel Meadows, *Nattering in Paradise: A word from the suburbs,* Simon and Schuster, London, 1988, p. 40.

2. This term comes from Ulric Neisser, "Five kinds of self-knowledge," *Philosophical Psychology,* 1 (1), 1988, 35–59. Neisser makes a number of interesting points about the ways in which the self relates to the environment, although he does not say what the environment is. He suggests (1) that we perceive ourselves as embedded within the environment, and acting with respect to it; (2) that the self and the environment exist objectively; information about the self allows us to perceive not only the location of the ecological self but also the nature of its interaction with the environment; (3) that much of the relevant information is kinetic, i.e., relating to movement. Optical structure is particularly important, but self-specifying information is often available to several perceptual modalities at once; and (4) the ecological self is veridically perceived from earliest infancy, but self perception develops with increasing age and skill. I use the term "ecological self" in a more inclusive sense, to refer to the self defined in relation to people, things and places, as they relate to each other.

3. Ian Burkitt provides an excellent account of the western self in an historical context in I. Burkitt, "The shifting concept of the self," *History of the Human Sciences,* 7 (2), 1994, 7–28.

4. Anthony Elliott, *Social Theory and Psychoanalysis in Transition,* Basil Blackwell, Oxford, 1992, pp. 16–17.

5. Michael Smith, *The City and Social Theory,* Basil Blackwell, Oxford, 1980, pp. 57–58.

6. ibid., p. 58.

7. George Herbert Mead, *Mind, Self and Society,* Chicago University Press, Chicago, 1934.

8. Burkitt, op. cit., p. 23.

9. Mihalyi Csikszentmihalyi and Eugene Rochberg-Halton, *The Meaning of Things: Domestic symbols and the self,* Cambridge University Press, Cambridge, 1981.

10. ibid., p. 91.

11. ibid., p. 104. In a later essay, Eugene Rochberg-Halton suggested that "the meaning of things one values is not limited just to the individual object itself but also includes the spatial context in which the object is placed, forming a domain of personal territoriality. In other words, the background context or gestalt of the thing also reveals something and results show how different rooms reveal different conceptions of the self" (Eugene Rochberg-Halton, "Object relations, role models and the cultivation of the self," *Environment and Behavior,* 16 (3), 1984, 335–368).

Images of Difference

The determination of a border between the inside and the outside according to "the simple logic of excluding filth," as Kristeva puts it, or the imperative of "distancing from disgust" (Constance Perin) translates into several   9

different corporeal or social images which signal imperfection or a low ranking in a hierarchy of being. Exclusionary discourse draws particularly on
colour, disease, animals, sexuality and nature, but they all come back to the
idea of dirt as a signifier of imperfection and inferiority, the reference point
being the white, often male, physically and mentally able person. In this
chapter, I will discuss ways in which psychoanalytical theory has been used
in the deconstruction of stereotypes, those "others" from which the subject
is distanced, and I will then examine some of the particular cultural sources
of stereotyping in western societies. Stereotypes play an important part in
the configuration of social space because of the importance of distanciation
in the behaviour of social groups, that is, distancing from others who are
represented negatively, and because of the way in which group images and
place images combine to create landscapes of exclusion. The issues I examine concern oppression and denial. I try to show how difference is harnessed in the exercise of power and the subordination of minorities.[1]

Stereotypes

The reception and acceptance of stereotypes, "images of things we fear and   10
glorify," as Sander Gilman puts it,[2] is a necessary part of coming to terms
with the world. In the following passage from his psychoanalytical account
of the deep structure of stereotypes, Gilman assigns a central role to stereotyping in the structuring or bounding of the self:

> The child's sense of self splits into a "good" self which, as the self mirroring the
> earlier stage of the complete control of the world [the stage of pre-Oedipal unity
> with the mother] is free from anxiety, and the "bad" self which is unable to
> control the environment and is thus exposed to anxieties. The split is but a
> single stage in the development of the normal personality. In it lies, however,
> the root of all stereotypical perceptions. For, in the normal course of develop-
> ment, the child's understanding of the world becomes seemingly ever more
> sophisticated. The child is able to distinguish even finer gradations of "good-
> ness" and "badness" so that by the later Oedipal stage an illusion of verisimili-
> tude is cast over the inherent (and irrational) distinction between the "good"
> and "bad" world and self, between control and loss of control, between acqui-
> escence and denial.[3]

Both the self and the world are split into good and bad objects, and the   11
bad self, the self associated with fear and anxiety over the loss of control, is
projected onto bad objects. Fear precedes the construction of the bad object,
the negative stereotype, but the stereotype—simplified, distorted and at a
distance—perpetuates that fear. Most personalities draw on a range of
stereotypes, not necessarily wholly good, not necessarily wholly bad, as a
means of coping with the instabilities which arise in our perceptions of the

world. They make the world seem secure and stable. While both good and bad stereotypes serve to maintain the boundaries of the self, to protect the self from transgressions when it appears to be threatened, most people have a large and sophisticated array of objects to draw on. As Gilman reminds us:

> Our Manichean perception of the world as "good" and "bad" is triggered by the recurrence of the type of insecurity which induced our initial division of the world into "good" and "bad." For the pathological individual, every confrontation sets up this echo . . . for the non-pathological individual, the stereotype is a momentary coping mechanism, one that can be used and then discarded once anxiety is overcome.[4]

It is evident that good and bad both resonate in stereotypical representations of others. As Zygmunt Bauman commented on taboos, which is what many stereotypes are, "the human attitude is an intricate mixture of interest and fear, reverence and abhorrence, impulsion and repulsion."[5] Thus, the stereotype may capture something that has been lost, an emotional lack, a desire, at the same time that it represents fear or anxiety. The good stereotype may represent an unattainable fantasy whereas the bad stereotype may be perceived as a real, malign presence from which people want to distance themselves. A common good stereotype of Gypsies, for example, locates them in the past or in a distant country where they are seen through a romantic mist. This is convenient because the good stereotype does not then contradict the bad stereotype. The Gypsy as a "good object," an association of Gypsies with desire, is conveyed nicely in Hermann Hesse's poem *Glorious World*:

> Sultry wind in the tree at night, dark Gypsy woman
> World full of foolish yearning and the poet's breath.

Compare this with a characterization of Gypsies by Gina Ferrero, the daughter of the racist anthropologist Cesare Lombroso, in a commentary on her father's writing:[6]

> an entire race of criminals, with all the passions and vices common to delinquent types: idleness, ignorance, impetuous fury, vanity, love of orgies and ferocity.

Both a fear for the boundaries of the self and a desire to merge are intimated in these representations, but in fact both dehumanize and contribute to a deviant image because both are, by definition, distortions. As Homi Bhabha suggests,[7] the stereotype is a simplification because it is an arrested, fixated form of representation which denies the play of difference. "Others" disturb the observer's world-view, but the stereotype removes them from the scene in the sense that they are distinct from the world of everyday ex-

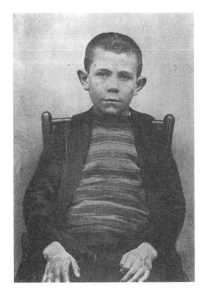

Boy Morally Insane

Boy Morally Insane

Head of Criminal

Head of Criminal

"Criminal types" from Cesare Lombroso's collection. Lombroso's use of photographic portraits in his work on criminality and madness demonstrates the historical importance of physical categorization in the cultural construction of normality and deviance (source: Ferrero 1911).

perience. Because there is little or no interaction with "others," the stereotyped image, whether "good" or "bad," is not challenged.

Obviously, it is negative stereotypes which are of greatest consequence   14
in understanding instances of social and spatial exclusion. Here, Julia Kristeva's conception of abjection, that unattainable desire to expel those things
which threaten the boundary, and the abject, that list of threatening things
and threatening others, seems to me to be fundamental. The earliest experience of abjection in the child is a reaction to excrement as the infant is so-
cialized into adult categorizations of the pure and the defiled, and this then
becomes a metaphor for other sources of defilement which are embodied in
stereotypes. The sources of bodily defilement are projected onto others,
whose world is *epidermalized*. As Iris Young argues:

> When the dominant culture defines some groups as different, as the Other, the
> members of these groups are imprisoned in their bodies. Dominant discourse
> defines them in terms of bodily characteristics and constructs those bodies as
> ugly, dirty, defiled, impure, contaminated or sick.[8]

Or, as Stallybrass and White put it succinctly: "Differentiation depends upon
disgust."[9] Verbal and visual images which have their source in the idea of
defilement shade into those which represent the body as less than perfect.
Thus, the photographs [on page 187], which come from Cesare Lombroso's
catalogue of the other,[10] point to a connection between visual images of
physical imperfection, according to his scale of being which differentiates the
normal and the deviant, and mental illness or disability, conditions which
threaten the boundaries of the self. An obsession with scaling and mea-
surement of physical characteristics in order to determine moral boundaries
and marginalize the other was particularly characteristic of nineteenth-century
and early twentieth-century science, but the association of appearances and
moral characteristics is an enduring one.

I suggested in the last chapter that the social self could also be seen as   15
a place-related self, and this applies also to stereotypes of the other which
assume negative or positive qualities according to whether the stereotyped
individual or group is "in place" or "out of place." The cases that I discuss
later in the book demonstrate how this condition of being discrepant or,
conversely, of belonging, is identified. The issue concerns the extension of
the "generalized other" to things, material objects and places. Thus, a place
stereotype might be a romantic representation of a landscape to which a social group are seen to belong or not, depending on the consistency or in-
congruity of the group and place stereotypes. For the moment, I will focus
on some of the main signifiers of otherness in western cultures as a prelude
to an integration of the social and spatial dimensions of the problem. The
key areas that I examine are those of colour, disease and nature.

Black and White

The use of colour to signify positive/negative, life/death, superior/inferior, safe/dangerous, and so on, is evident in all cultures. Here, I will refer only to the use of colour in white European cultures, and then only black and white, because a cross-cultural account of the use of a wide palette of colours would be long-winded and not particularly relevant. The justification for considering these two colours is, first, that European nations are implicated in most accounts of racism and colonialism and rules expressed in terms of black and white have been important in the process of regulating and dominating the colonized and, second, that they are readily associated with defilement and purity. [16]

Black is used routinely to describe dirt which, in turn, is associated with shame and disease. In other words, it has both practical and moral associations, which make it a potent marker of social difference. In the common usage of white Europeans, it is a negative signifier of class, race, ethnicity. The way in which black has been used to indicate class difference is suggested by the illustrations [on pages 190 and 191], which come from a teachers' guide to health and cleanliness (published by the Health and Cleanliness Council in London in the 1920s and written by two Ph.D.s, one of whom was also the author of *Psychoanalysis in the Classroom*!). Black is also the colour of death, a source of defilement, a state which threatens life, and of the corpse, which signifies decay and contagion: "If dung signifies the other side of the border, the place where I am not and permits me to be, the corpse, the most sickening of all wastes, is a border that has encroached upon everything."[11] It is notable that organizations that have been devoted in a big way to death, the extreme rejection of difference, like the Nazis and other fascists, have adopted black for their collective identity. [17]

Black, then, has been used in white societies to signal fear. A clear example of the use of black and associated images to convey a threatening otherness appears in Emily Brontë's *Wuthering Heights,* in which, as Rosemary Jackson notes, [18]

> The family excludes everything foreign to itself as being unnatural. It guarantees ontological stability through limitation and closure. By the end of *Wuthering Heights,* the threat represented by Cathy and Heathcliff has been exorcised by confining it to their own vampiric relationship: they are merely restless spirits drifting around the abandoned closure of the Heights.[12]

The fear instilled in the family by Heathcliff depended on his portrayal from the beginning as other, as an outsider. Thus, as he came into the family (chapter 4):

Dirt and blackness as signifiers in a white society. Moral instruction by the Health and Cleanliness Council, London (probably 1920s).

Children Know Well Their Teacher's Attitude Towards Dirt.

> We crowded round, and over Miss Cathy's head I had a peep at the dirty, ragged, black haired child . . . I was frightened, and Mrs. Earnshaw was ready to fling it out of doors. She did fly up, asking how he could fashion to bring that gipsy brat into the house, when they had their own bairns to feed and fend for?

Black-haired, dirty, Gypsy combine to suggest a threatening difference, drawing on an ethnic stereotype well established in British culture.

Black and white as racial signifiers have deep significance. In white, former colonial societies, as Dyer observes,

> there are inevitable associations of white with light, and therefore safety, and black with dark and therefore danger, and . . . this explains racism (whereas one might well argue about the safety of the cover of darkness and the danger of exposure to light).[13]

In a colonial context, black and white represent a whole set of social characteristics and power relations. Dyer's conclusion about three films portraying the white presence in colonial Africa—*Jezebel* (USA, 1938), *Simba* (Britain, 1955) and *Night of the Living Dead* (USA, 1969)—is that "they all associate whiteness with order, rationality, rigidity, qualities brought out by contrast with black disorder, irrationality and looseness."

This use of white and black is clearly intended to make white social behaviour virtuous and to legitimate white rule. However, white people should consider the question also from a black perspective. bell hooks argues that whites have a deep emotional investment in the myth of "sameness" even as their actions reflect the primacy of whiteness as "the sign informing who they are and how they think."[14] In other words, whites do not think about themselves as white but only about others as not-white and other, which was the point of Dyer's examination of whiteness in films about colonialism. It is useful then to compare the dominant white view of blackness with black experience, like bell hooks's observations on the meaning of whiteness in her own childhood:

> Returning to memories of growing up in the social circumstances created by racial apartheid, to all black spaces on the edge of town, I reinhabit a location where black folks associated whiteness with the terrible, the terrifying, the terrorizing. White people were regarded as terrorists, especially those who dared to enter the segregated space of blackness.[15]

An-other voice? White has been normalized in Europe, North America and Australasia and, in order to recognize that what seems normal is also a symbol of domination, it is important to listen to and to appreciate black perspectives rather than, as bell hooks suggests white people do, "[travel] around the world in pursuit of the other and otherness"—a sobering comment on academic enthusiasm for difference.

Returning to the wider associations of blackness in white societies, the association between black and dirt, between dirt and disease, emphasizes the threatening quality of blackness. Removing blackness, injecting light, removes fear, but this fear may be a fear of others as much as a fear of darkness. Thus, Corbin maintained that Haussmann's plans for Paris in the mid-nineteenth century were designed to make the city *less dark:* "His town-planning was partly aimed at eliminating the darkness at the centre of the city, where darkness stood for the foul-smelling environment of the poor, the smell of the poor"—and the poor themselves.[16] However, despite the common use of black to signify obscurity, shade, shadows, fear, misfortune, death and evil, it has not always been so. Thus, in mediaeval Europe, black knights were courageous; numerous black madonnas, as in Tarragona cathedral, Spain, and Czestochowa, Poland, were objects of reverence. The positive associations of blackness were lost with colonialism, however, and with industrialization and the development of the class system under capitalism black assumed wider significance through its association with dirt, disorder and the threat to the bourgeoisie posed by the working class.

In the same system of values, whiteness is a symbol of purity, virtue and goodness and a colour which is easily polluted. Since whiteness is often not quite white, it is something to be achieved—an ideal state of pure, untainted whiteness. Thus, white may be connected with a heightened consciousness of the boundary between white and not-white, with an urge to clean, to expel dirt and resist pollution, whether whiteness is attributed to people or to material objects. As Sassoon remarks, white "has a highly accentuated hygienic symbolism," although, in consumer culture, there has been to some extent an "emancipation from white [which] has come about after several decades of emblematic monochromatism [*sic*]."[17] As a marker of the boundary between purified interior spaces—the home, the nation, and so on—and exterior threats posed by dirt, disorderly minorities or immigrants, white is still a potent symbol.

NOTES

1. Some recent post-modern writing, for example, Iain Chambers's *Migrancy, Culture and Identity,* Routledge, London, 1994, celebrates difference with some enthusiasm. The theme of Chambers's book is that there are fusions, hybrids and new forms of difference that follow from increasing global movement and interconnectedness. I think that it is important not to be carried away by this. Problems defined by the firm contours of territorially based conflict, associated with race, ethnicity, sexuality and disability, are persistent features of socio-spatial relations. Many people live in one place for a long time and some have difficulty getting along with those who are different from themselves. Unfortunately, the African musicians whom Chambers admires and who have certainly enriched British culture are still

subject to racism outside the sympathetic environment of the club or the music festival.

2. Sander Gilman, *Difference and Pathology: Stereotypes of sexuality, race and madness,* Cornell University Press, Ithaca, N.Y., 1985. This book, with its emphasis on visual representation, develops object relations theory to incorporate the world as it is perceived.

3. ibid., p. 17.

4. ibid., p. 18.

5. Zygmunt Bauman, "Semiotics and the function of culture," in Julia Kristeva *et al.* (eds), *Essays in Semiotics,* Mouton, The Hague, 1971, pp. 279–295.

6. Gina Ferrero, *Criminal Man,* The Knickerbocker Press, New York, 1911, p. 140.

7. Homi Bhabha, *The Location of Culture,* Routledge, London, 1994. Bhabha presents a deep analysis of the "colonial other," but his arguments have much wider relevance.

8. Iris Young, *Justice and the Politics of Difference,* Princeton University Press, Princeton, N.J., 1990, p. 126. Young bases her argument on Julia Kristeva's *Powers of Horror.*

9. Peter Stallybrass and Allon White, *The Politics and Poetics of Transgression,* Methuen, London, 1986, p. 191.

10. The subjects of Lombroso's moralizing discourse were primarily people with learning disabilities. The importance of photography as an aid to classifying mentally ill and disabled others is discussed in some detail by Sander Gilman, *Disease and Representation,* Cornell University Press, Ithaca, N.Y., 1988, pp. 39–43. Lombroso's photographs are reproduced in Ferrero, op. cit.

11. Julia Kristeva, *Powers of Horror,* Columbia University Press, New York, 1982, p. 3.

12. Rosemary Jackson, *Fantasy: The literature of subversion,* Methuen, London, 1981, p. 129.

13. Richard Dyer, *The Matter of Images: Essays on representation,* Routledge, London, 1993, pp. 142–145.

14. bell hooks, *Black Looks: Race and representation,* Turnaround, London, 1992.

15. ibid., p. 170. Later in this chapter (p. 174), she remarks:

> Reminded of another time when I was strip searched by French officials, who were stopping black people to make sure we were not illegal immigrants and/ or terrorists, I think that one fantasy of whiteness is that the threatening Other is always a terrorist. This projection enables many white people to imagine there is no representation of whiteness as terror, as terrorizing. Yet it is this representation of whiteness in the black imagination, first learned in the confines of [a] poor black community, that is sustained by my travels to many different locations.

16. Alain Corbin, *The Fragrant and the Foul: Odor and the French social imagination,* Harvard University Press, Cambridge, Mass., 1986, pp. 134–135.

17. Joseph Sassoon, "Colors, artefacts, and ideologies," in P. Gagliardi (ed.), *Symbols and Artefacts: Views of the corporate landscape,* de Gruyter, Berlin, 1990, p. 172.

Working with the Text

1. In his second paragraph, Sibley writes, "Repulsion and desire, fear and attraction, attach both to people and to places in complex ways. Central to this question is the construction of the self, . . ." How does he go on to develop this point? How is the self constructed in relation to "the generalized other"? To "good" and "bad" stereotypes?

2. Sibley is writing about exclusion, about "the people who erect the boundaries and the people who are excluded by them." Who is he talking about here? Do you see yourself more among those who erect boundaries or among those who are excluded? Why? Are the categories mutually exclusive? Or do boundaries differ according to different social situations?

3. Sibley points to "the idea of dirt as a signifier of imperfection and inferiority," implying that cleanliness and dirtiness become a determination of "the inside and the outside." How does this tie into his discussion of images of white and black? Do you find his argument here convincing? Sibley quotes Sander Gilman to the effect that goodness becomes associated with control and badness with loss of control. What relation does this idea bear to the idea of exclusion?

4. What does Sibley suggest is the relationship between "others" and stereotypes? How do stereotypes remove disturbing "others" from the scene? Do stereotypes in effect replace "others"? Can you think of examples where this happens globally, either to people outside the U.S. or international identities inside the U.S.?

5. Quoting bell hooks, Sibley suggests that whites "do not think about themselves as white but only about others as not-white and other." Use your own experience, both as a member of a dominant group and as a member of a marginal group, to evaluate this statement in an essay. If you can imagine no marginal group of which you are a member (the group need not reflect a class, ethnicity, or sexual orientation), you may borrow from the experience of your peers. If you can imagine no dominant group, recognize that your reading of these words places you in one: the literate.

In the Waiting Room

ELIZABETH BISHOP

Born in Worcester, Massachusetts, in 1911, Elizabeth Bishop (who died in 1979) is among the most widely admired of American poets. She published her first volume of poetry in 1946 and won the Pulitzer Prize in 1955 for *North and South*. She lived for a number of years in Brazil, later returning to Massachusetts where she taught at Harvard. Her *Complete Poems* was published in 1979. Bishop's work often focuses on seemingly unremarkable incidents and objects through which she communicates a special insight. A unique clarity and precision characterize her language. In the following poem, a young girl's mundane visit to a doctor's waiting room is transformed by a revelation, a moment in which "nothing stranger / had ever happened."

In Worcester, Massachusetts,
I went with Aunt Consuelo
to keep her dentist's appointment
and sat and waited for her
in the dentist's waiting room.   5
It was winter. It got dark
early. The waiting room
was full of grown-up people,
arctics and overcoats,
lamps and magazines.   10
My aunt was inside
what seemed like a long time
and while I waited I read
the *National Geographic*
(I could read) and carefully   15
studied the photographs:
the inside of a volcano,
black, and full of ashes;
then it was spilling over
in rivulets of fire.   20
Osa and Martin Johnson
dressed in riding breeches,

laced boots, and pith helmets.
A dead man slung on a pole
—"Long Pig," the caption said. 25
Babies with pointed heads
wound round and round with string;
black, naked women with necks
wound round and round with wire
like the necks of light bulbs. 30
Their breasts were horrifying.
I read it right straight through.
I was too shy to stop.
And then I looked at the cover:
the yellow margins, the date. 35

Suddenly, from inside,
came an *oh!* of pain
—Aunt Consuelo's voice—
not very loud or long.
I wasn't at all surprised; 40
even then I knew she was
a foolish, timid woman.
I might have been embarrassed,
but wasn't. What took me
completely by surprise 45
was that it was *me:*
my voice, in my mouth.
Without thinking at all
I was my foolish aunt,
I—we—were falling, falling, 50
our eyes glued to the cover
of the *National Geographic,*
February, 1918.

I said to myself: three days
and you'll be seven years old. 55
I was saying it to stop
the sensation of falling off
the round, turning world
into cold, blue-black space.
But I felt: you are an *I,* 60
you are an *Elizabeth,*
you are one of *them.*

Why should you be one, too?
I scarcely dared to look
to see what it was I was.   65
I gave a sidelong glance
—I couldn't look any higher—
at shadowy gray knees,
trousers and skirts and boots
and different pairs of hands   70
lying under the lamps.
I knew that nothing stranger
had ever happened, that nothing
stranger could ever happen.
Why should I be my aunt,   75
or me, or anyone?
What similarities—
boots, hands, the family voice
I felt in my throat, or even
the *National Geographic*   80
and those awful hanging breasts—
held us all together
or made us all just one?
How—I didn't know any
word for it—how "unlikely" . . .   85
How had I come to be here,
like them, and overhear
a cry of pain that could have
got loud and worse but hadn't?

The waiting room was bright   90
and too hot. It was sliding
beneath a big black wave,
another, and another.

Then I was back in it.
The War was on. Outside,   95
in Worcester, Massachusetts,
were night and slush and cold,
and it was still the fifth
of February, 1918.

Working with the Text

1. This poem describes a sudden revelation or insight, the epiphany of a child who suddenly sees herself as "an *I*," "an *Elizabeth,*" and "one of *them*." What, specifically, leads the speaker to this realization? What role did the *National Geographic* play? Why was the speaker "too shy to stop" reading?

2. What exactly did the speaker realize? Why did it produce physical sensations of disorientation? What does she mean when she says, "I scarcely dared to look / to see what it was I was"? Where could she have looked, and what would she have seen? Why does she insist that nothing stranger had ever happened or could ever happen? How does the series of questions beginning at line 75 function? How and why does the revelation end?

3. How do dates and places function in the poem? Why is February 1918 important in world history? Why does it matter that the date of the *National Geographic* and the date of the speaker's revelation are the same? What is the importance of Worcester, Massachusetts? Of the dentist's office? Why does Bishop not reveal where the *National Geographic* photographs were taken?

4. The clarity of Bishop's language and the flexibility of her prosody places "In the Waiting Room" closer to prose than many poems. How is the poem's meaning served by this proximity? In other words, what does it gain from the conventions of prose, and what does it gain from those of poetry?

5. Bishop uses figurative language very sparingly in this poem. Consider the simile of the light bulb in line 30 and the metaphor of the wave in line 92; write a brief essay on their meanings and effects. Which figure do you consider more startling? How does that judgment affect your reading of the poem?

Vested Interests

MARGORIE GARBER

Marjorie Garber is Professor of English and Director of the Humanities Center at Harvard University. She is the author of three books on Shakespeare as well as numerous books of cultural criticism on such topics as the moral and ethical aspects of animal rights, the erotics of home-ownership, and the study and teaching of humanities. In her 1991 book, *Vested Interests: Cross-Dressing and Cultural Anxiety,* Garber investigates the ways in which clothing constructs (and deconstructs) gender and gender differences, examining the nature and significance of cross-dressing in popular culture, high fashion, religion, and the arts. Garber is particularly interested in the ways that culture "creates transvestites"—not as the exception but rather as the ground of culture itself. The following selection, drawn from Chapter 9, "Religious Habits," explores the problem of classifying items of "religious dress" along conventional gender lines.

As the French say, there are three sexes—men, women, and clergymen.
SYDNEY SMITH, *Lady Holland's Memoir* (1855)[1]

In early 1980 a retired American Bishop sent four ecclesiastical vestments— an alb, cincture, stole, and amice—out to be cleaned. When they were returned to him, according to the publication *Christian Century,* the cleaner's slip indicated that the Rev. John Baumgartner had been charged for "one dress, long; one scarf; one rope; and one apron."[2] This difficulty of classifying items of religious dress, not only according to their ecclesiastical names and functions, but also in accordance with the conventions of sartorial *gender,* is emblematic of a kind of crossover in vested interests that has over the years taken on a complex significance.

The deliberate cultural misreading of priests' garments as women's clothing was perhaps most memorably, if irreverently, expressed by Tallulah Bankhead, when she encountered a robed thurifer swinging his incense vessel in an Anglican church: "Love the drag, darling," Tallulah is said to have remarked, "but your purse is on fire." Boy George, the pop icon of male-to-female cross-dressing, who once referred to himself as a drag queen, offered a different perspective on his attire when interviewed by the authors of *Men in Frocks,* an oral history of female impersonators on the London club scene: "I dress in a similar way to a priest or an archbishop," George wrote in answer to their inquiries. "I wear robes, not dresses, and to be a transvestite you must wear women's undergarments. I don't."[3]

Boy George's first real professional success—a harbinger of things to come—took place when he appeared onstage in the late 1970's dressed in a nun's habit. Yet some of his most startling outfits—smocks covered with Hebrew lettering, worn with a wide-brimmed black hat and braided artificial earlocks—were designed to echo and parody another kind of religious "cross-dressing," the costume of the observant Hasidic Jew.[4] Since, as we will shortly see, the feminization of the Jewish male was a common pejorative trope of nineteenth-century social theory, the appearance of Boy George, the most defiantly transvestic figure of the seventies and eighties, *both* in women's clothes *and* in mock-Hasidic garb made the associative link between Jews and women—a staple of anti-Semitic pseudoscience—all too clear. In the context of George's pop group, Culture Club, this was apparently intended as a send-up, a parody of prejudice as well as of belief. But the use of Western religious costume as part of a lexicon of gender-bending, whether intended as serious social commentary or as a pop throwaway, is a striking manifestation of cultural anxiety.

Madonna, the pop figure who perhaps more than any other has read the temper of the times, artfully manipulates these categories in many of her music videos, whose conflation of religious and erotic themes has sometimes scandalized her critics. The resonances of her given name (in full, Madonna Louise Veronica Ciccone) and reminiscences of her own Catholic upbringing inflect the tone of songs like "Papa Don't Preach" and "Like a Prayer."[5] In a restaging of the latter for her "Blond Ambition" tour Madonna, like Boy George, uncannily evoked Hasidic as well as Catholic images when she and her back-up singers, dressed in long black caftans, waved their hands above their heads as they danced in a "church" lit with votive candles.

Jews and Catholics—especially Jewish men and Catholic nuns—have borne the main brunt of this gender critique. But even Protestants have been targets of transvestic mimicry, in the persistent portrayal of "mannish" or "unfeminine" women as old maids or "church hens" who channel their sexual frustration into crushes on the rector or repressive social morality. Consider the success of male comedian Dana Carvey's character, "the Church Lady," for years a featured comic turn on the television show "Saturday Night Live." The Church Lady, her stockings drooping around her ankles above her sensible shoes, her mouth pursed in sanctimonious certainty, deplores, with relentless good cheer, those who, like "your Gary Harts" and "your Jimmy Swaggarts," have their "bulbous knotty parts" caught between Beelzebub and a hard place. Carvey's Church Lady dispenses "Church Chat"

3

4

5

to sinners in a parody of repressive prurience: the spinster as both male- and female-manquée. The persistent popularity of this character (portrayed by a comic who also does a respectfully swishy George Bush imitation and a character called "Lyle, the effeminate heterosexual") suggests something of urban America's unease with religious fundamentalism—and also something of its abiding suspicion that religion itself is somehow "unmanly." We might recall as well the popular distrust, in the sixties, of long-haired and sandaled "Jesus freaks"—young men who were often, against much evidence to the contrary, described as "effeminate" or as "looking like girls." Things have changed since the time of muscular Christianity, both in the U.S. and in Britain.

As the example of Bishop Baumgartner's cleaning bill suggests, one   6
thing that has certainly changed over time is the way in which religious costume is *read*. Western ecclesiastical dress today shares with the academic robe and the military uniform the distinction of representing one of the few remaining "legible" dress codes. Where once sumptuary laws tried to ensure that class, rank, occupation, and (to a certain extent) gender were immediately readable in and through details of costume, by the close of the twentieth century only the likes of cardinals, monks, nuns (in habits), uniformed police officers and lieutenant colonels can be decoded with certainty, by rank and hierarchy, according to established items of signifying dress: collars, stoles, surplices, soutanes, birettas, liturgical or academic colors, stripes, medals, and epaulets.

This is not to say that signifying styles do not exist in other social realms: 7
a punk teenager today may wear a Mohawk haircut dyed pink, as well as a black leather jacket and multiple earrings, as a sign of the group to which he (or she) belongs; a gay man might signify his specific sexual interests by the placement of a ring of keys at his hip; a bride in the U.S. or Western Europe is still identifiable by her long white gown and veil. But religious costume, like military uniform, aims at making the appearance of the wearer literally "uniform" in *professional* terms: an archbishop, a Carmelite nun, or a Hasidic rabbi—like a Green Beret, or (on commencement day) a professor with a degree in Forestry from Yale—can be identified, at least in context, by those who know the vestimentary signifying code. Individual style is supposedly screened out as professional uniformity takes over: hence the army haircut, the wimple, the mortarboards for academic women as well as men.

But the case of ecclesiastical or religious dress is particularly fascinating   8
because of the ways in which particular items of clothing have tended to cross *over* gender lines, not through uniformity *per se*—although, as we will see, there have been attempts to make women's and men's costumes the same within specific orders or denominations—but rather by the migra-

tion of styles over time from one gender to another. In eighteenth-century England, for example, parasols were popular for ladies, but umbrellas became items of daily use for clergymen who officiated at burial services—at least fifty years before fashionable gentlemen began to carry them (Mayo, 83).

Terms like "defrocking" or "unfrocking," to describe the dismissal of priests, seem quaint and slightly precious today, but the word "frock" began as a term for a monk's garment, and has only fairly recently become a word for female as opposed to male attire; the frock was the monk's, friar's, and then the clergyman's identifying costume, and a man's "frock coat" had skirts like a "frock"; so too, with "gown," which in its original Latin form meant a furred garment for elderly or infirm monks. Trousers were viewed by the ancient Romans as the costume of barbarians, and were thus eschewed by churches and monasteries in favor of the gown (Mayo, 22). 9

Wigs, an extravagant French court style for men, were, perhaps surprisingly, taken over with enthusiasm by the English clergy as well as by lawyers from the time of Charles II. At first the clergy spoke out against them, since the Fathers of the early Church had denounced the wearing of wigs *by women* as vanity, and, indeed, as mortal sin, the instrument of the devil. For *men,* however, wigs became and remained fashionable, despite the traditional Pauline belief that "if a man have long hair it is a shame to him" (I Cor. 11:14–15). Soon "the clergy were all to be found in wigs,"[6] which were regarded as a badge of respectability. 10

"It was observed that a periwig procured many persons a respect, and even veneration, which they were strangers to before, and to which they had not the least claim from their personal merit. The judges and physicians, who thoroughly understood this magic of the wig, gave it all the advantage of length as well as size."[7] Gentlemen, including clergy, who wore wigs were invariably clean-shaven; the wig thus not only augmented the phallus but replaced the beard. Puritans, however, protested against the fashion, and by 1770 the wig had again gone out of style. Five years previously periwig makers had petitioned the King, reporting with dismay "that men will wear their own hair."[8] Anglican clergy and some Non-conformists, however, continued to wear wigs for another fifty years, and the legal profession in the U.K., still apparently relying on the "magic of the wig," retains it to this day, although among laypersons the wig now counts as an item of female rather than male adornment—becoming in some quarters the very sign of female impersonation. 11

The role of religion in Western culture as itself an oppositional structure that depends upon discriminating between insiders and outsiders and upon sharply delineated male and female spheres leads to a construction of both Christianity and Judaism that almost inevitably invites both gender parody 12 and gender crossover. The male nun, the female monk, the feminized Jewish man are recurrent figures of fantasy as well as of history and propaganda.

Transvestite Saints

The transvestite female saints of the Middle Ages were legion as well as legend, despite the Deuteronomic prohibition against wearing the clothes of the opposite sex. Pelagia, the archetype of the transvestite saint, is said to have been a dancing girl and prostitute; when she changed her ways, and converted to Christianity, she also changed her name and her clothes, wearing a hair shirt beneath her male outer garments, and taking the name of Pelagius. Only after her death was she revealed to have been a woman. St Eugenia, who cross-dressed in order to join an all-male religious community and shortly became an abbot, was accused of rape by a rich lady who desired her; to disprove this charge she disrobed to prove that she was a woman. Thecla, a wealthy and beautiful virgin, became a follower of St. Paul and cut her hair, assuming for a while the garments of a man.

Saint Anna entered a monastery dressed as a man and was thought to be a eunuch; a monk who had been told that "brother Euphemius" might really be a woman pushed her down a cliff. The list of these female transvestites is long, and their stories follow a familiar pattern: Saints Perpetua, Anthanasia, Apollinaris or Dorotheus, Euphroysne, Anastasia Patricia, and others all don male clothing at a time of personal crisis—marking a break with a former existence—and in doing so fulfill the words of St. Jerome, that a woman who "wishes to serve Christ more than the world . . . will cease to be a woman and will be called man."[9]

Perhaps the most striking attribute of some of these female transvestite saints was that they are said to have been *bearded*. St. Wilgefortis, also known as Uncumber, wanted to remain a virgin and devote herself to the contemplative life, but her father insisted on marrying her off to the King of Sicily. Wilgefortis prayed for deliverance, and was answered by the sudden growth of a long moustache and a curling beard. When the King glimpsed this feature of his bride through her veil (which she had artfully contrived to push aside), he rejected her; her father then had her crucified. The names by which Wilgefortis is known in various languages—based on roots meaning "deliverer" or "(un)trouble"[10]—suggest the extremity of her plight and the irony of her father's "solution." In England Uncumber became the patron of married women who wanted to get rid of their husbands. (St. Galla and St. Paula were other bearded female saints who also attempted to avoid marriage through this miraculous stratagem.)[11]

13

14

15

Stories of pious women dressed as men to avoid becoming the source   16
of sexual temptation are over and over again conjoined with tales of their
"fathering" children. John Anson provides a persuasive psychoanalytic reading, noting that the chroniclers of these tales were male celibate clerics, and
that therefore the question for interpreters of the saints' legends is not one
of female psychology (why would a woman dress as a man in this situation?) but rather of "monastic fantasy":

> what finally comes into view with these lives is the guilty desire that underlies
> the whole dreamwork; for instead of an overture rejected, a sexual act is com-
> mitted and laid to the blame of the saint, who undergoes the punishment as a
> kind of surrogate. Thus, quite simply, the secret longing for a woman in a
> monastery is brilliantly concealed by disguising the woman as a man and mak-
> ing her appear guilty of the very temptation to which the monks are most sub-
> ject; finally, after she has been punished for their desires, their guilt is
> compensated by turning her into a saint with universal remorse and sanctimo-
> nious worship.[12]

But this fantasy of the cross-dressed woman fathering a child has impli-   17
cations for the religious culture as well as for the individual. Here psychoanalysis crosses with social and political tensions in a time of institutional
change. The transvestite effect, the overdetermined appearance of the transvestite, reflects what might in this case be called a genealogical anxiety—an
anxiety about the question of *paternity* which, in the case of the Catholic
Church, is in fact a foundational mystery. For twelfth-century monasticism
the story of the cross-dressed "father" might well, as Anson suggests, bear
the brunt of a celibate clerisy's repressed and conflicted desires, but it also
points toward other kinds of conflict, social and theological as well as sexual. The identity of the Father was the mystery—and the certainty—on
which the faith was based. These "local" stories of other mysterious paterni-
ties, with their transvestite under- and overtones, reanimate the conundrum
of divine fatherhood in the context of a world-turned-upside-down. A crisis
of belief is here displaced onto the axis of gender.

The social dissymmetry we have noticed again and again—that to wish   18
to be a man is regarded as somehow "natural" or of higher status, whereas
to wish to be a woman is perverse—presumably influences the fact that,
whereas there are many female transvestite saints, there are no male transvestites who are similarly revered. (As the authors of *Men in Frocks* point
out, succinctly, "she cross-dresses because she wants to be taken seriously;
he generally cross-dresses because he doesn't" [Kirk and Heath, 9].) There
was even a female transvestite pope, the legendary Pope Joan, in the ninth
century, who was said to have fallen in love with a monk who was her
teacher and cross-dressed to join him in a life of scholarship; after his death,

she was chosen as pope, only to be undone by her own sexuality: she be-came pregnant by a Benedictine monk who resembled her dead lover, and her gender was supposedly revealed when, in the middle of a papal pro-cession, she went into labor and gave birth to a child. Throughout the thir-teenth, fourteenth, and fifteenth centuries the truth of this story was largely accepted; a statue of Pope Joan was installed in the Cathedral of Siena, and at the Council of Constance in 1415 John Hus denounced the delegates for permitting a woman to be pope. Only later did Joan's story become reas-signed to legend rather than to fact. (We might note that in this account, whether legendary or factual, "female" failings are what get Pope Joan into trouble, quite literally; but her heterosexuality is confirmed by the story of both her initial love affair and her pregnancy, so that even in this particular she is finally unthreatening to established norms and hierarchies.)

The most famous of all cross-dressed saints, of course, was St. Joan, [19] whose transvestism was viewed as itself a mark of abomination. The trans-vestite female saints of the Christian monastic tradition were among Joan's models. Like them she broke with her parents, refused to marry the husband they had chosen for her, and rejected male domination even as she assumed male privilege. Yet unlike these women she did not choose the costume, or the life, of a monk; instead, crossing class as well as gender lines, she main-tained herself as a knight.

It was in fact for transvestism, not for heresy, that Joan was put on trial [20] by the Inquisition. No less than five charges against her detailed her trans-vestism as emblematic of her presumption: she was unwomanly and im-modest, ran the charges, she wore sumptuous clothing to which she was not entitled by rank, and she carried arms.

> The said Jeanne put off and entirely abandoned woman's clothes, with her hair cropped short and round in the fashion of young men, she wore shirt, breeches, doublet, with hose joined together. . . .
>
> And in general, having cast aside all womanly decency not only to the scorn of feminine modesty, but also of well instructed men, she had worn the apparel and garments of most dissolute men, and, in addition, had some weapons of defence.[13]

Her questioners at the trial repeatedly asked why she had assumed male [21] garb, and repeatedly she insisted that she had done so at the command of God and his angels—not for convenience in the field. "The dress is a small, nay the least thing," she is famously reported to have said at the fourth pub-lic session (Barrett, 70), but nonetheless she would not exchange her men's clothes for women's, even when bribed with the promise of the right to hear Mass.

The final draft of the charges against her makes clear her determined [22] obstinacy: "The said Catherine and Mary [Joan's 'voices'] instituted this woman in the name of God, to take and wear a man's clothes; and she had worn them and still wears them, stubbornly obeying the said command, to such an extent that this woman had declared she would rather die than relinquish these clothes" (Barrett, 227–28). Marina Warner points out that Joan throughout the trial identified herself as a woman in man's clothes, that she never tried to pass as a man—that, in fact, the paradox or singularity of her transvestism, her identity as, precisely, a woman who chose—or was directed—to dress as a man, was a source of her subversive strength. "She was usurping a man's function but shaking off the trammels of his sex altogether to occupy a different, third order, neither male nor female, like the angels."[14]

Her defenders were deeply concerned about the transvestite issue, and before her capture learned arguments were propounded, claiming that the victory at Orléans proved the rightness of her condition and her cause, and arguing as well that the Deuteronomic prohibition had been overturned by the new dispensation of which she was a sign. Warner effectively posits Joan's transvestism as itself a structure of *language:* "a figure of speech to lay claim to greatness beyond the expected potential of her sex"; for the virgin martyrs "transvestism becomes the transitive verb in a sentence of self-obliteration" (Warner 149, 157). Yet the clothing she chose, and the trial itself, declare not invisibility or annihilation but rather a special and unmistakable visibility or legibility.   23

The French analyst Catherine Clément notes the case of an anorexic girl who wanted not to have periods so as "to be neither boy nor girl." As Clément comments, she wanted "to play the disorder of androgyny against the order of the female cycle [called *règles,* or rules, in French], to be neither one thing nor the other, *neuter.*"[15] Many accounts of Joan suggest that she was amenorrheic, and that because she did not menstruate she occupied a physiological position that was neither male nor female.[16] This desire to see Joan as somehow beyond gender—"neither boy nor girl"—reflects not only a contemporary religious fantasy, but also a peculiar modern anxiety about the entrapment of gender and gender roles.   24

Thus, for example, feminist Andrea Dworkin reads Joan's case as one of the triumphant avoidance of heterosexual intercourse; when, after her recantation, she was returned to her prison cell dressed in women's clothes, she became vulnerable, in Dworkin's view, to rape or attempted rape by her captors.[17] Dworkin, who regards heterosexual intercourse as an instrument for the enslavement of women, needs her Joan to be a woman, *not* a transvestite. For her, Joan's male clothing must be a polemical and rhetorical signifier *against* men, rather than a signifier of maleness. She therefore makes short work of those who would romanticize and aestheticize Joan's cross-dressing, the "scholars and artists" by whom she is "[e]ssentially seen as a   25 transvestite."[18] Joan, according to Dworkin, became "an exile from gender with a male vocation and male clothes" (Dworkin, 100).

By contrast actresses cast as Joan in G.B. Shaw's play have interpreted her transvestism as a reflection of "normative" culture. Jane Alexander, for example, offers a classic version of the progress narrative. "It's very much like Calamity Jane," she explains: 26

> Calamity simply dressed in men's clothes because she had to do men's work. Riding a horse was the primary mode of transportation for Joan and for Calamity, and it doesn't make a lot of sense if you want to get somewhere fast to be doing it with a skirt and sidesaddle. That was all. It was utilitarian.[19]

Alexander's emphatic dismissal of homosexuality as a factor ("I didn't see her at all butch or dyke") retains the notion of a Joan who is both transcendent and "normal": "I don't think that she had a crush on anybody except maybe the saints, and so everything was projected out. It was just a young sexuality that was substituting for what might have grown up later with the love of a good man." Two other recent Joans, Sarah Miles and Lee Grant, both draw an analogy with Peter Pan (Hill, 103, 144), while Janet Suzman offers a provocative argument about the transformative agency of clothing: "what happens when you wear pants or chain mail is that you naturally change . . . when you wear that sort of clothes it just happens. They dictate what you do" (Hill, 157). Suzman's intuition—very much that of an actress—unwittingly echoes the fears of the Puritan antitheatricalists who objected to cross-dressing on the Renaissance stage: that wearing the clothing of the other gender might change the wearer, that a disquieting power—a power at once sexual and political—did somehow inhere in clothes.   27

NOTES

1. Sydney Smith, *Lady Holland's Memoir* (London, 1855), 1: 9.

2. *Christian Century;* quoted in the *Church Times,* February 15, 1980. Cited in Janet Mayo, *A History of Ecclesiastical Dress* (London: B.T. Bamford, 1984), 9.

3. Boy George, in Kris Kirk and Ed Heath, *Men in Frocks* (London: Gay Men's Press, 1984), 112.

4. Mablen Jones, *Getting it On: The Clothing of Rock 'n' Roll* (New York; Abbeville Press, 1987), 144.

5. In "Like a Prayer," as Susan McClary points out, Madonna is drawing upon "two very different semiotic codes associated with two very different forms of Christianity: Catholicism and the black Gospel church." Susan McClary, "Living to Tell: Madonna's Resurrection of the Fleshly" *Genders* 7 (March 1990), 14.

6. Mayo, *History of Ecclesiastical Dress,* 80.

7. F.W. Fairholt, *Costume in England,* enlarged and revised by H.A. Dillon (London: G. Bell and Sow, 1885), 1: 319.

8. Letter from Horace Walpole to Lord Hertford, 12 February 1765; *Letters,* 6: 188. Mayo, *History of Ecclessiastical Dress,* 82.

9. Vern L. Bullough, *Sexual Variance in Society and History* (Chicago: University of Chicago Press, 1976), 367. Jerome, *Commentarius in Epistolam ad Ephesios,* 3:5 (658), in J.P. Migne, *Patrologiae Latinae* (Paris: Garnier Bros, 1884) 26: 567.

10. In Spain she was known as Librada, in northern France Livrade, in southern France Debarras, all from *Liberata;* in Germany she was Onhkummer, in Flanders Ontcommer, in England Uncumber, from German *kummer,* trouble. Bullough, *Sexual Variance,* 368.

11. *Butler's Lives of the Saints,* ed. Herbert Thurston and Donald Attwater (New York, P.J. Kennedy & Sons, 1956), 3:151-52; 4:36–37.

12. John Anson, "The Female Transvestite in Early Monasticism: The Origin and Development of a Motif," *Viator: Medieval and Renaissance Studies* 5 (1974), 30.

13. W.P. Barrett, trans. *The Trial of Jeanne d'Arc* (London: G. Routledge, 1931), 152–54.

14. Marina Warner, *Joan of Arc: The Image of Female Heroism* (New York: Vintage Books, 1982), 146.

15. Catherine Clément, *Miroirs du sujet* (Paris: C. Bourgeois, 1978), 83–84. Warner, *Joan of Arc,* 158.

16. So said her squire, Jean d'Aulon: "I've heard it said by many women, who saw the Maid undressed many times and knew her secrets, that she never suffered from the secret illness of women and that no one could ever notice or learn anything of it from her clothes or in any other way." Jean Baptiste Joseph Ayroles, *La Vraie Vie de Jeanne d'Arc* (Paris: Gaume, 1890–1902), 4:215. Warner, *Joan of Arc,* 19. The same claim was later made in the *Almanach de Gotha* (Gotha, Germany: Justus Perthes, 1822), 63 and by Jules Michelet (*Histoire de France* [Paris, 1844], 5:53).

17. See, for example, Régine Pernoud, *Joan of Arc,* trans. Edward Hyams (New York: Stein & Day, 1966), 220.

18. Andrea Dworkin, *Intercourse* (New York: The Free Press, 1987), 100.

19. Holy Hill, ed., *Playing Joan: Actresses on the Challenge of Shaw's Saint Joan* (New York: Theater communication group, 1987) 135.

Working with the Text

1. One of the most important aspects of cross-dressing, suggests Garber, is the way in which it challenges easy notions of either/or thinking, putting into question the categories of "female" and "male." How is male/female (an apparent ground of distinction between "this" and "that"), itself put in question, overturned, or erased by figures such as Boy George or Joan of Arc?

2. Garber suggests that cross-dressing allows for a borderline to become permeable, so that it permits border crossings from one (apparently distinct) category to another: male/female, black/white, Jew/Christian, noble/bourgeois, master/servant. How does dress enable border crossing, both in terms of identity and globally?

3. Whereas in the eighteenth century aristocrats, members of the clergy, and other professional men wore fashionable wigs to procure respect, today, notes Garber, for a man to wear a stylish wig is to adopt the very sign of female impersonation. What does this suggest about the markers or signs of gender difference?

4. In her discussion of transvestite saints, Garber refers to several instances of female transvestite saints (women crosss-dressing as men), noting that throughout history male transvestism (men cross-dressing as women) has been relatively rare in the religious world. How do we account for this? What does it imply about the relationship between the sociopolitical world and gender? About religion and gender?

The Baseball Game

JOHN HARTIGAN

John Hartigan attended the University of Michigan and later received his Ph.D. from the University of California, Santa Cruz. An anthropologist and historian, his work has appeared in *Visual Anthropology Review, Cultural Studies,* and *White Trash: Studies in Race and Class.* A recipient of a Guggenheim grant and a former fellow at the National Museum of American History at the Smithsonian Institute, Hartigan is currently Assistant Professor in Sociology and Anthropology at Knox College. His book *Racial Situations: Class Predicaments of Whiteness in Detroit* studies the white urban underclass of Detroit, "perhaps this country's 'blackest' city," in order to better understand the ways "people actually construct meaningful lives in relation to race." In the following excerpt, Hartigan explores the ways in which class background influences the experience and understanding of racial identity and difference.

The family's summer Sunday ritual was to play baseball at a field up at Trumbull Avenue, close to the apartment building where they all grew up. They invited Rebecca and me along, incorporating us into the overlarge teams. By the time we had finished breakfast one Sunday, a large crowd of family members was forming. Leroy and his wife Grace were there, with one of their daughters, Erika, and their son, little Leroy. Then Jerry's sister Mabel arrived with two of her boys. While we were all sitting out on the porch,

Library Resource Center
Renton Technical College
3000 N.E. 4th St.
Renton, WA 98056

Jessie Rae explained to those who had missed the previous game that today we were playing for a case of beer. Last week, with fewer people, they played as a team against some black men who were also at the field. By the game's end, several people from both teams decided to have a "real game" next week—hence, the wagered case. Jessie Rae also said that, on account of this arrangement, Jerry's brother David would not be playing this week. She explained that when he heard the racial arrangement, he announced that "no way am I playing with niggers." Jessie Rae added, "And I just told him, well screw you. Who wants you anyways?" Mabel laughed and Erika said he was stupid. Leroy wanted to know what his problem was with "colored people," and "what's he afraid of?" Jessie and Mabel took turns telling stories about how "weird" David is; they centered around how "he thinks he's better than the rest of us," rather than examining his racial opinions. The two women stressed how he never "hangs out" or drinks with any of them; that "he never works a day in his life" (especially not on cars); and his very unconventional choice of going to school to be a hair stylist. David teased his brothers about how, once he had his degree, he would never have to do any work on his car. Leroy summed the matter up by saying that "he's a faggot."

Jessie Rae later called a friend in the downriver suburb of Taylor, where David had gone to play baseball with some of their extended family members. By the time he had arrived in Taylor, no one was around who wanted to play. Jessie Rae told us that while she was on the phone to her friend, David had walked into her place. She explained, "I was on the phone with her and I heard a door slam. I said, 'What was that'? And she said, 'Oh that's just David storming out all mad.' I said, I bet he's gonna go crying to momma. 'Momma, they won't let me play.'"   2

Everybody laughed, while Erika and Mabel repeated the sentiment, "who needs him," adding that he was "being a baby." They responded to his refusal to play with blacks by characterizing him as "childish," infantilizing his behavior, and questioning his masculinity. When another relation, Tommy, showed up from Taylor, Leroy filled him in. Tommy was also disgusted to hear about David, and also decided that "he's a faggot." But they did not consider his disposition in racial terms; rather, his actions were a reflection of his inability to socialize in this place.   3

One of the last arrivals was little Jerry and his fiancée Becky. By this time, the group was breaking up into gendered orders: The women stayed on the porch talking, while Sam and Tommy tossed the ball in the street, and Leroy went to look at little Leroy's carburetor. Becky stood by the porch, noticeably uncomfortable about hanging out. She did not want to actually sit on the frayed particle board covering the rotting steps. Earline had "warned" us about her in our first conversation, describing her as "pretty   4 different. Everybody tries to be nice to her and all. We try to tolerate her 'cause little Jerry likes her so much. But she doesn't fit in. And you can tell that she don't want to. You'll see what I mean when you meet her. She's really different." She is from Trenton, a largely white and wealthy suburb. Jessie Rae braced herself for Becky's arrival that morning with a few choice comments about her being "spoiled." "She's always had everything handed to her. And she's making little Jerry take care of her the same way." She claimed that Becky was also spoiling Jerry, pointing out, "Like the other day, he was saying something about wanting a new glove. And she just went out and got him one. Just like that! You can't be doing that all the time. She's just trying to make him as spoiled as she is."

Little Jerry works at a steady job as a meat packer and spends as little   5
time as possible in the old neighborhood, unlike his sister Jean. Part of his attraction to Becky seems to be her insistence on maintaining distance from his family, too. He was the first man I met who made noticeable use of deodorant and after-shave; his face was clean and his hair trim. Although his efforts at hygiene inscribed a clear sense of remove from the others, he quickly fell into sync with the men's teasing, rough play, and conversations about cars.

Several runs were made to the store for cigarettes and beer, while   6
people scrambled to find bats, mitts, and plausible bases. Mabel went to several houses over a range of a few miles to gather these. After an hour and a half of waiting, we got under way. Marvin and Charlotte were playing, too. He drove a carload that included Earline, Paula, and Louise over to the field. Jessie Rae gleefully noted how low the rear of his car was riding. "There some fat women in that backseat," she laughed. Her daughter Jean pulled up with her boyfriend in a big, rusted-out, burnt-red Cadillac. Erika and Jessie Rae were making fun of the car before it was even parked, calling it "a yacht" and commenting, over its loud exhaust, what a good muffler it had. Jean leaped out yelling at them, her big pregnant belly only somewhat slowing her. "Don't none of you make fun of my car." Jessie Rae kept laughing, until Jean got right up in her face. "Say something now! I'll slap you! I'll slap you bitch." Jessie faced her down with an icy stare, glaring until Jean backed off. But they continued to ride each other verbally, in the animated, vicious public mocking they relied upon to break down people's pretensions. Jean went on to pick on Erika. Later, Jessie Rae made a point of assuring Rebecca and me that "You'll get used to us all in a while and find out that this is just normal."

The field was across the Lodge freeway, just the other side of the nearby   7
housing projects, and in front of Jefferson High, the school the adults had all attended—it has long since closed. Sam talked a lot about the school and the building where they grew up. "We all lived in the same building on Cass

and Canfield. You'll never have another building like that. 'Cause everybody watched out for everybody else. If somebody lost their job, their rent was paid and their groceries was bought. Then, when somebody else lost their job, their rent was paid. Nobody went without there, ain't that right Jessie Rae?" She confirmed this, as did Tommy, saying, "You'll never have another place like that again. People took care of each other there." He and Jerry, Tommy, and all of Jessie Rae's siblings grew up in that building; it was where Jessie Rae and Jimmy met as teenagers and fell in love. Before that, they had lived across the Lodge in another building. Sam recalled, "It cost me a nickel to get across that bridge. The black kids would make you pay to cross it." About the high school, he only noted, "Man, there was a lot of greasy fights in that place. There was a lot of fights there."

We parked by the field and slowly unpacked the supplies and equip- 8 ment. The place was empty and Jessie wondered aloud where the other team was. Since they were not around, we chose up teams, with Leroy and Sam picking sides. Jerry was made the pitcher because of his bad leg—he could barely walk now. Twenty people were formed into two teams, and the small kids or those not interested in the game settled in the bleachers around the cases of beer, pop, and assorted bags of food.

Teasing and heckling were constant for the batter, the outfield, and any- 9 body in the general vicinity of the game, often between members of the same team. The men were subjected to teasing about their guts or about stupid plays in last week's game. The women were heckled about batting stances and other technical aspects of the game, but they dished out most of the verbal abuse. Men carried beers along when it was their turn in the outfield, and batters threatened to hit the array of big and small bottles with a grounder.

The background was impressive. Behind us was the abandoned hulk of 10 their old high school, surrounded by the devastation of old, empty apartment buildings, their interiors exposed by collapsing outer walls or missing window frames, stripped by salvagers. This site was even more desolate than parts of Briggs. A fire started during the first game, somewhere to the north. People casually noticed, watching the large black column of smoke steadily rising, but not commenting until about ten minutes later as the cloud grew enormous and the first fire engines were heard. Then, several people remarked on how slow the fire department was, and wasn't that "just pathetic." When Erika said something to her mom about how it was still burning, her mom said, "Don't you worry about it, you just let it burn."

Several young black men were playing basketball on the court adjacent 11 to the field. At least eight or nine ragged men, mostly black, drifted by through the course of the game, checking the dumpsters or looking for bottles along the fence. One black man came by and asked Jerry if we were

keeping the growing pile of cans. Jerry said we were. He asked for a cigarette; Jerry gave him one and they talked for a bit. Before the end of the first
game, two black men left the nearby basketball court and sat watching in
the bleachers. Jerry asked if they wanted to play, and Leroy and Sam each
chose one for their team. By the time the first game wrapped up, two more
black men stopped by. They were the ones who had made the arrangement
for the game this week. Jerry told them to decide who wanted to bat first
and who would field first. That left the teams at twelve a side, but Jerry encouraged them to get into the game anyway. After a couple of innings, Sam
said to me while we were waiting our turns at bat, "Now this is family—
black people and white people playing together. This is what it's all about.
This is family." Since one of his brothers had chosen not to play because of
the racial mix, his repeated reference to "family" was quite striking.

But there was a problem, and neither Sam nor I noticed it developing.   12
During the break between games, while the sides were being increased, little Jerry and Becky went to the store. We were just starting and their team
was already out in the field when they returned. She noticed right away that
one of the black men was using her glove. She asked loudly and repeatedly,
"Has anybody seen my glove?" She posed this question while looking right
at the black man nearest where she had been playing. He gave her the glove
and the game resumed, while somebody from the sidelines offered him an
unused glove. I did not pay much attention to the matter, until I noticed her
complaining to little Jerry about something. He seemed to be trying to ignore her. I found out later that she was upset because the same black man
was playing "too close" to her. It was a crowded outfield, and little Jerry told
her not to worry about it. She remained visibly bothered by the presence of
the two black men in the outfield, but the game ended rather quickly, due
to the preponderance of outfielders.

As it wrapped up, a few people thought about leaving, but most wanted   13
to stay and start a third game. Little Jerry and Becky, though, were through
for the day and started packing up their things. Jerry asked his son to leave
their gloves, but little Jerry said they needed them both. Jerry got mad.
"What, don't you trust me? You think I'm just gonna leave it here?" Little Jerry
said they played baseball every day and they would need them tomorrow.
Becky was already walking to the car with their equipment, but Jerry just
kept asking out loud, "Don't you trust me? Don't you trust me?" Jerry followed them to the car, and it was unclear what was being said. Jessie Rae
hollered to Jerry that they did not need the gloves, there were plenty. Then
Jerry exploded and really began shouting, "Just take your shit and get out of
here. I don't need you and I don't want to see you no more. Don't be coming back here. I don't need your cheap ass shit."

His face went bright red and the veins bulged in his throat as he 14
screamed at them. Jessie Rae tried to calm him down, thinking it was just
about the gloves. "She said they use it everyday Jerry, let it drop." "Naw, that
ain't it," he snarled, storming back from the car. "That ain't it at all! Y'know
what she said to me? You know what she said!? She said, 'I don't want no
nigger using my glove. Can you believe that bitch? How could she act that
way? She had the nerve to say, 'I don't want no nigger using my glove.'"
Jerry stomped the sidelines in a rage, dragging his bad leg and kicking
empty cans with his good one. "Fuck her! That does it! I don't want to see
her sorry ass no more. We don't need her." As Jerry raged, the gathering
slowly dissolved. Two of the black men went over to play basketball. The
other two waited to see if another game would start. Marvin asked aloud as
he watched their car roar out of the lot, "Who's she calling a nigger?"

The momentum for another game dwindled as Jerry's fury continued 15
unabated and his curses toward Becky and his son were fired with
undimmed passion. Leroy and Grace went off with their kids, and those of
us who lived in the three houses ended up back there shortly. Sam got a
barbecue going and we ate well after dark in the unlit yard. While we ate,
Jessie Rae elaborated on the incident in the field, saying that Becky had tried
to provoke little Jerry into a fight with the black men, trying to get him to
say something to the man nearest her. Jessie Rae noted that even though the
man could hear her prodding little Jerry, "He had the respect enough to just
let it drop. He could have started something but he had the respect enough
to just drop it."

Not much more attention was given to the incident, but it was reexam- 16
ined that next Friday, when Marvin, Jerry, and Sam were sitting out in the
yard. Talk eventually turned toward the baseball game. Jerry told us that his
son called and said he was working long hours for the next few weeks and
would not be coming out for any more games. Jerry reiterated how sick he
was of Becky, and that he wished little Jerry would "come to his senses" and
leave her. Marvin said she was lucky she didn't get hit for her bout of "nigger talk," stressing, "They'll hit you for shit like that down here." While Marvin reflected on the incident in the field and Becky's discomfort at being too
close to a black man, Jerry brought up the glove. "She said, 'I ain't gonna let
no nigger use my glove.' Well she can just keep her ass out in Trenton. You
can't come down here talking like that. That's like calling me a honky." He
noted that the name was not illicit but had to be used only in certain circumstances. He illustrated this point by recalling a black friend of his who
lived across the street. "We were always talking like that to each other. He'd
be calling me honky and I'd be calling him nigger. If you know somebody,
you might joke around like that. Like Jingo, when he lived across the street.

It was always nigger this and honky that, some people don't mind it. Marvin, here, does. He don't like to ever be called that. And I don't ever use that word with him." Marvin nodded and pointed out, "She was the only one using that language. She's lucky that Charlotte [Marvin's wife] didn't hear her. She'd a really been hurting then."

The two men shifted to the topic of women fighting, bragging on Jessie   17
Rae's and Charlotte's past exploits, and said nothing more about the game. The only time in the next year that little Jerry stopped by was when Jean had her baby.

This racial situation was clearly shaped by the play of class distinctions   18
among these whites. This scene of interracial mixing brought into sharp relief the class rifts within this extended family, and also makes clear the discontinuities in whites' racial thinking. David and Becky, the two whites who made an issue out of race by expressing their disdain for or discomfort over socializing with blacks, both also strove to distinguish or distance themselves from the poverty that characterized this family. Their striving for upward mobility and higher class standing was articulated through an assertion of the need for careful racial boundary maintenance by avoiding interracial situations. Although the contours were easily blurred—David, after all, was living off of government loans while he was going to school, and it was unclear what occupational status Becky held—the classed inflections of their unwillingness to socialize were sharply read by Jerry and Jessie Rae. This is underscored by the fact that neither David or Becky was challenged for being racist. Rather, they both were regarded as being pretentious.

This spatial setting highlights the contrasting racial sensibilities between   19
Becky and these other whites. She attempted to follow a racial decorum that did not apply. Becky found a couple of outlets to signify her discomfort; first over her glove, then over her proximity to the black man in the outfield, and finally her quiet use of "nigger" with Jerry. These ranged in degrees of subtlety, but they were all cues that it appears she felt other whites should be able to read, responding to her discomfort supportively. To the extent that they noticed the cues, these whites let them pass in favor of maintaining a scene that Sam considered as "family," despite his own brother's loud absence. In turn, she was criticized for not being able to "read" or maneuver in this context without creating a disruption. Marvin criticized Becky because her comments were inappropriate in that setting: "She was the only one using that language." He implied that there are contexts, largely reciprocal situations, where that "language" would not be out of line. Becky's comments effectively disrupted their place, the site where they played baseball regularly; as a result of her outburst, they did not return to the field for over a month after this incident. The space where such interracial socializing is possible is very precarious.

The role of "nigger" in this . . . situation . . . underscores the ambiguity   20
and context-dependent nature of white racialness in this zone. Even when
the term is not "spoken"—Paula did not say it, and Becky tactfully whispered it to Jerry—"nigger" sounds potentially in white speech as something
that might be said; that is, the weight of white racism, traditionally and in the
national context, reverberates with white racialness. Perhaps this echo effect
is intensified in the inner city, where the fallout of the investment in whiteness is palpable in the environment of material and social devastation. Jerry
and Jessie Rae are located in an area where face-to-face confrontations are
frequent. This class predicament shapes the significance of their white
racialness in a matter that will appear in sharp relief against the background
of the second half of this book.

The use of "nigger" in this context demonstrates an aspect of how class   21
shapes racial meanings in this setting. Neither Jerry or Jessie Rae rejected usage of the term out of hand; it fit with the abusive mocking they used on
each other. Jean tried hard to insult her mom, and Jessie Rae just ignored
her. It was part of how they played with language—very roughly. They did
not preclude the use of "nigger" for the sake of refinement. But the further
point is that the term was manipulated in the classed inflection of this situation. Jerry insisted on broadcasting Becky's use of the word "nigger" to the
whole gathering. Considering how angry he was, maybe he could not have
kept it to himself. Jerry was no master of discretion, and no one in the family seemed surprised that he announced so loudly what Becky had said. But
judging by the effects his comments had and the certain way they played to
an already polarizing situation in which he and Jessie Rae were interested in
severing little Jerry's relationship with Becky, it is fair to speculate on
whether or not his actions strictly addressed the breach of racial decorum. If
he intentionally relayed her comments with a desire to bring out their utmost divisive effects, then it is possible to see Jerry's desire to drive Becky
off as more important than his wish to maintain racial harmony. If he had
treasured the interracial connections that were enacted by the game more
highly, he might have kept Becky's words to himself. What he achieved by
publicizing his anger was to keep her from coming back again for quite a
long time. Maybe he hoped to split the couple up. All this is speculation. But
whether he emphasized Becky's impropriety in order to highlight the obvious class differences or whether he acted purely out of frustration and disgust, there was no sense of racial solidarity for which he would have
shielded her rupture of decorum from all those present. Even though it
meant repelling his son, Jerry was compelled to objectify her lack of tact and
her inability to negotiate in this heterogeneous racial zone. The point I want
to stress is that the evaluation of the significance of race did not occur in
an abstract manner. On the one hand, it melded seamlessly with the vola-

tile conditions of their everyday lives; on the other, the role of "race" was evaluated in terms of whether or how class matters. The racial reading was a function of how Jerry prioritized the importance of the animated class distinctions between himself, his son, and Becky.

This situation conveys a great deal about the local dynamics that shape the significance of race, unpredictable, involving sudden and surprising outbursts that racially polarized the social interactions. It also undercuts whites' interest in assertions of or associations with a larger racial collective—whiteness. It's not the ideological conditioning by whiteness that is most significant, but the multiple ways their words, actions, and interests—as whites—can be objectified and interpreted. What matters is how they prioritize, mobilize, or manipulate "race" in relation to others' concerns, such as class distinctions and family matters. "Race" is read through these other frames, not as an abstraction and not from a unified core of beliefs.

Working with the Text

1. Describe the social status of the white family in Hartigan's essay. What possessions, habits, and language are most revealing of class? Do we know as much about the class of the African-Americans in the story? Why or why not?

2. What is the role of aggressive teasing among Hartigan's characters? How does it differ from genuine conflict? Explain how epithets such as "faggot" and "nigger" draw and redraw borders between individuals and groups.

3. Hartigan argues that "local dynamics," in this case class and family tensions, always affect the significance of race: " 'Race' is read through these other frames, not as an abstraction and not as a unified core of beliefs." Are additional "frames" visible in the story he tells? Could you, for example, analyze the conflict between David, Becky, and the rest of the family in terms of gender?

4. Sounding very much like Kai Erikson's subjects in "Collective Trauma: Loss of Communality," Sam recalls the family's old apartment building as a place where "everybody watched out for everybody else." What role does this memory play in Hartigan's narrative? How has the dispersal of the apartment's residents reconfigured the geography of race and class?

5. "The space where . . . interracial socializing is possible is very precarious," writes Hartigan. From your own experience, write a brief narrative that illustrates this precariousness. You need not describe outright conflict, but you should choose an incident in which the participants' actions (rather than your commentary upon those actions)

clearly signal potential disruption. Using Hartigan's story as a model, be sure to make your narrative as vivid as possible, using concrete detail to create sensory and affective texture.

The White Man's Indian

ROBERT BERKHOFER JR.

A professor of history at Western Michigan University, Robert Berkhofer has focused much of his research and writing on how our concept of the past is shaped by historians as they interpret documents and events within the framework of popular imagery. His most recent book is *Beyond the Great Story: History as Text and Discourse* (1995). In his earlier work, *The White Man's Indian* (1979), Berkhofer accounts for the ways in which early European settlers in America perceived the native peoples—not in terms of their reality but through a variety of stereotypes, many of which continue to persist today. Scholars have since extended, developed, and challenged the rather absolute terms of Berkhofer's argument; nevertheless, the following selection offers one of the first and most influential reconsiderations of colonial contact.

From the very beginning of White penetration of the Western Hemisphere, Europeans realized that it was inhabited by peoples divided among themselves. Even Columbus on his first voyage distinguished between peaceful and hostile Indians on the basis of cannibalism and military ardor. Subsequent Spanish explorers, conquerors, and writers noted the differences among the many Indian societies of the New World, especially between the Aztec and Inca civilizations and other peoples. Both French and English explorers remarked the contrasts between the Eskimos and other peoples to the south of them. Early English adventurers into Virginia spoke of *Indians, savages,* and *infidels* in one breath at the same time as they carefully studied the various alliances and specific characteristics of the tribes around Jamestown. The ability to differentiate one tribe from another only increased as White knowledge accumulated over time, but the general term *Indian* or a synonym continued to coexist with—and in spite of—such information. If Whites understood the many differences among Native American peoples, why did they persist in using the general designations, which required the lumping together of all Native Americans as a collective entity? The answer to this question reveals much about later as well as early White images of Native Americans.

Increased knowledge of the fundamental differences among peoples of the world also seemed to promote Europeans' recognition of the similarities among themselves. In other words, exploration and expansion overseas resulted from and reinforced nationalism at the same time that it promoted an overall collective vision of a Europe in contradistinction to the rest of the world. The transition in thinking can perhaps be seen best in the increasing use of "Europe" for self-reference during the fifteenth and sixteenth centuries in preference to the older "Christendom." Another indication would be the new word *continent* to characterize the emerging geographical notions of collective physical self-definition of Europeanness in contrast to other peoples broadly conceived. Humanist scholars endowed the old image of mythical Europa with new secular characteristics in tune with their times and what they considered her place in history. The basic attributes ascribed to continents showed most vividly in the symbolic pictures applied to title pages and to maps, but the same meaning lay behind the more prosaic written descriptions and discourses on the peoples of the world. Europeans portrayed their own continent in terms of intellectual, cultural, military, and political superiority, for Europa was usually pictured wearing a crown, armed with guns, holding orb and scepter, and handling or surrounded by scientific instruments, pallets, books, and Christian symbols. While Asia was richly dressed, rarely did she possess superior signs of power, learning, or religion. America and Africa appeared naked, and the former usually wore a feathered headdress and carried a bow and arrow. Europe, in brief, represented civilization and Christianity and learning confronting nature in America.

The general terms *heathen, barbarian, pagan, savage,* and even *Indian* revealed these criteria of judgment at the same time that they validated the use of collective terms for the peoples of other continents. The European takeover of the New World proved to Europeans, at least, their own superiority and confirmed the reliability of the classification of peoples by continents. Common concepts combined with successful conquest reinforced the general impression of the deficiency of primitives everywhere and validated the continuation of the general conception and the glossing over of the growing knowledge of specific social and cultural differences among New World peoples. Even among themselves and the peoples they had long known well, Europeans correlated whole nationalities with uniform moral and intellectual attributes; it should be no surprise that they should stereotype the new peoples they met elsewhere. If Shakespeare had his Caliban to symbolize New World savagery, he also had his Shylock, his Othello, as well as his Irishmen, Turks, Italians, and others to appeal to his audiences' preconceptions.

Part of this stereotyping of national as well as continental characteristics   4
must be ascribed to the confusion among the realms of culture and biology,
nation and race prevalent then and until recently in Western thought.
Lifestyles, bloodlines, and national boundaries were all mixed together in
White analysis of humankind. Until social heritage and biological heredity
were separated in the twentieth century, national character, racialism, and
culture were confused and therefore blended together, whether of nations
or of continents. Although as time passed the relations among environment,
biology, and culture might be seen as dynamic, with each being the cause
as well as the effect of the others, their confusion due to imprecise delin-
eation and misunderstanding of the mechanism of transmission meant that
race and national character studies were the same thing until very recent
times. Nations, races, and cultures were all basically seen as one interchangeable category for the understanding of peoples, and individuals were
usually judged as members of their collectivity rather than as different,
separate humans. Therefore, general terms embracing stereotyped characteristics made sense to Whites and could exist alongside knowledge of
specific societies with individual characteristics or of individuals with varying qualities.

One important consequence of this style of thought was the continu-   5
ance of the general term *Indian*. The use of the general term demanded a
definition, and this definition was provided by moral qualities as well as by
description of customs. In short, character and culture were united into one
summary judgment. The definition and characterization of *Indian* as a general term constitutes the subject proper of this book as opposed to the history of the evolution of images and conceptions of specific tribes. The basic
question to be asked of such overall White Indian imagery and conception
is not, therefore, why its invention in the first place but why its continuance,
or perpetuation, for so many succeeding centuries? To what extent do these
old approaches to the *Indian* still constitute the chief White views of Native
Americans even today?

Persisting Fundamental Images and Themes

The centuries-long confusion and melding of what seem to us funda-   6
mentally different, even incorrect, ways of understanding human societies
account for several persistent practices found throughout the history of
White interpretation of Native Americans as Indians: (1) generalizing from
one tribe's society and culture to all Indians, (2) conceiving of Indians
in terms of their deficiencies according to White ideals rather than in terms
of their own various cultures, and (3) using moral evaluation as description
of Indians.

Not only does the general term *Indian* continue from Columbus to the   7
present day, but so also does the tendency to speak of one tribe as exemplary of all Indians and conversely to comprehend a specific tribe according
to the characteristics ascribed to all Indians. That almost no account in the
sixteenth century portrays systematically or completely the customs and beliefs of any one tribe probably results from the newness of the encounter
and the feeling that all Indians possessed the same basic qualities. Although
eyewitness accounts and discourses by those who had lived among Native
Americans in the seventeenth and eighteenth centuries often describe in detail the lives of a specific tribe or tribes, they also in the end generalize from
this knowledge to all Indians. The famous reporters on Native American cultures in the colonial period of the United States, for example, invariably
treated their tribe(s) as similar enough to all other Indians in customs and
beliefs to serve as illustrations of that race in thought and deed. Even in the
century that saw the rise of professional anthropology, most social scientists
as well as their White countrymen continued to speak and write as if a specific tribe and all Indians were interchangeable for the purposes of description and understanding of fundamental cultural dynamics and social
organization. Today, most Whites who use the word *Indian* have little idea
of specific tribal peoples or individual Native Americans to render their usage much more than an abstraction, if not a stereotype. Even White writers
on the history of White images of the Indian tend to treat all Native American cultures as a single Indian one for the purposes of analyzing the validity of White stereotypes.

Another persistent theme in White imagery is the tendency to describe   8
Indian life in terms of its lack of White ways rather than being described
positively from within the framework of the specific culture under consideration. Therefore, tribal Americans were usually described not as they were
in their own eyes but from the viewpoint of outsiders, who often failed to
understand their ideas or customs. Images of the Indian, accordingly, were
(and are) usually what he was not or had not in White terms, rather than in
terms of individual tribal cultures and social systems as modern anthropologists aim to do. This negative prototype of the deficient Indian began with
Columbus but continues into the present as any history of the White education of Native Americans reveals. To this day such education is still too often treated as philanthropy to the "culturally deprived" Indian.

Description by deficiency all too readily led to characterization by eval-   9
uation, and so most of the White studies of Indian culture(s) were (and are)
also examinations of Indian moral character. Later White understanding of
the Indian, like that of earlier explorers and settlers, expressed moral judgments upon lifestyles as well as presented their description, or mixed ideology with ethnography, to use modern terms. Ethnographic description

according to modern standards could not truly be separated from ideology and moral judgment until *both* cultural pluralism and moral relativism were accepted as ideals. Not until well into the twentieth century did such acceptance become general among intellectuals, and even then only a few Whites truly practiced the two ideals in their outlook on Native Americans. Thus eyewitness description prior to this century and so much still in our time combines moral evaluation with ethnographic detail, and moral judgments all too frequently passed for science in the past according to present-day understanding. If ideology was fused with ethnography in firsthand sources, then those images held by Whites who never had experience with Native Americans were usually little more than stereotype and moral judgment.

Whether describing physical appearance or character, manners or 10 morality, economy or dress, housing or sexual habits, government or religion, Whites overwhelmingly measured the Indian as a general category against those beliefs, values, or institutions they most cherished in themselves at the time. For this reason, many commentators on the history of White Indian imagery see Europeans and Americans as using counterimages of themselves to describe Indians and the counterimages of Indians to describe themselves. Such a negative reference group could be used to define White identity or to prove White superiority over the worst fears of their own depravity. If the Puritans, for example, could project their own sins upon people they called savages, then the extermination of the Indian became a cleansing of those sins from their own midst as well as the destruction of a feared enemy.

Since White views of Indians are inextricably bound up with the evalu- 11 ation of their own society and culture, then ambivalence of Europeans and Americans over the worth of their own customs and civilization would show up in their appraisal of Indian life. Even with the image of the Indian as a reverse or negative model of White life, two different conclusions about the quality of Indian existence can be drawn. That Indians lacked certain or all aspects of White civilization could be viewed as bad or good depending upon the observer's feelings about his own society and the use to which he wanted to put the image. In line with this possibility, commentators upon the history of White imagery of the Indian have found two fundamental but contradictory conceptions of Indian culture.

In general and at the risk of oversimplifying some four centuries of im- 12 agery, the good Indian appears friendly, courteous, and hospitable to the initial invaders of his lands and to all Whites so long as the latter honored the obligations presumed to be mutually entered into with the tribe. Along with handsomeness of physique and physiognomy went great stamina and endurance. Modest in attitude if not always in dress, the noble Indian exhibited great calm and dignity in bearing, conversation, and even under torture. Brave in combat, he was tender in love for family and children. Pride in himself and independence of other persons combined with a plain existence and wholesome enjoyment of nature's gifts. According to this version, the Indian, in short, lived a life of liberty, simplicity, and innocence.

On the other side, a list of almost contradictory traits emerged of the bad Indian in White eyes. Nakedness and lechery, passion and vanity led to lives of polygamy and sexual promiscuity among themselves and constant warfare and fiendish revenge against their enemies. When habits and customs were not brutal they appeared loathsome to Whites. Cannibalism and human sacrifice were the worst sins, but cruelty to captives and incessant warfare ranked not far behind in the estimation of Whites. Filthy surroundings, inadequate cooking, and certain items of diet repulsive to White taste tended to confirm a low opinion of Indian life. Indolence rather than industry, improvidence in the face of scarcity, thievery and treachery added to the list of traits on this side. Concluding the bad version of the Indian were the power of superstition represented by the "conjurers" and "medicine men," the hard slavery of women and the laziness of men, and even timidity or defeat in the face of White advances and weaponry. Thus this list substituted license for liberty, a harsh lot for simplicity, and dissimulation and deceit for innocence. 13

Along with the persistence of the dual image of good and bad but general deficiency overall went a curious timelessness in defining the Indian proper. In spite of centuries of contact and the changed conditions of Native American lives, Whites picture the "real" Indian as the one before contact or during the early period of that contact. That Whites of earlier centuries should see the Indian as without history makes sense given their lack of knowledge about the past of Native American peoples and the shortness of their encounter. That later Whites should harbor the same assumption seems surprising given the discoveries of archeology and the changed condition of the tribes as the result of White contact and policy. Yet most Whites still conceive of the "real" Indian as the aborigine he once was, or as they imagine he once was, rather than as he is now. White Europeans and Americans expect even at present to see an Indian out of the forest or a Wild West show rather than on farm or in city, and far too many anthropologists still present this image by describing aboriginal cultures in what they call the "ethnographic present," or as if tribes live today as they once did. Present-day historians of the United States, likewise, omit the Indian entirely after the colonial period or the last battles on the Plains for the same reason. If Whites do not conceive of themselves still living as Anglo-Saxons, Gauls, or Teutons, then why should they expect Indians to be unchanged from aboriginal times, Native Americans ask of their White peers? 14

If Whites of the early period of contact invented the Indian as a con-   15
ception and provided its fundamental meaning through imagery, why did
later generations perpetuate that conception and imagery without basic alteration although Native Americans changed? The answer to this question
must be sought partially in the very contrast presumed between Red and
White society that gave rise to the idea of the Indian in the first place. Since
Whites primarily understood the Indian as an antithesis to themselves, then
civilization and Indianness as they defined them would forever be opposites. Only civilization had history and dynamics in this view, so therefore
Indianness must be conceived of as ahistorical and static. If the Indian
changed through the adoption of civilization as defined by Whites, then he
was no longer truly Indian according to the image, because the Indian was
judged by what Whites were not. Change toward what Whites were made
him ipso facto less Indian.

The history of White-Indian contact increasingly proved to Whites, par-   16
ticularly in the late eighteenth and nineteenth centuries, that civilization and
Indianness were inherently incompatible and verified the initial conception
that gave rise to the imagery. Death through disease and warfare decimated
the aboriginal population in the face of White advance and gave rise by the
time of the American Revolution to the idea of the vanishing race. If Whites
regarded the Indian as a threat to life and morals when alive, they regarded
him with nostalgia upon his demise—or when that threat was safely past.

Indians who remained alive and who resisted adoption of civilization   17
appeared to accept White vices instead of virtues and so became those imperfect creatures, the degraded or reservation Indian. If there is a third major White image of the Indian, then this degraded, often drunken, Indian
constitutes the essence of that understanding. Living neither as an assimilated White nor an Indian of the classic image, and therefore neither noble
nor wildly savage but always scorned, the degraded Indian exhibited the
vices of both societies in the opinion of White observers. Degenerate and
poverty-stricken, these unfortunates were presumed to be outcasts from
their own race, who exhibited the worse qualities of Indian character with
none of its redeeming features. Since White commentators pitied when they
did not scorn this degenerate Indian, the image carried the same unfavorable evaluation overall as the bad or ignoble Indian.

Complete assimilation would have meant the total disappearance of In-   18
dianness. If one adds to these images the conceptions of progress and evolution, then one arrives at the fundamental premises behind much of White
understanding of the Indian from about the middle of the eighteenth century to very recent times. Under these conceptions civilization was destined
to triumph over savagery, and so the Indian was to disappear either through

death or through assimilation into the larger, more progressive White society. For White Americans during this long period of time, the only good Indian was indeed a dead Indian—whether through warfare or through assimilation. Nineteenth-century frontiersmen acted upon this premise; missionaries and philanthropists tried to cope with the fact. In the twentieth century anthropologists rushed to salvage ethnography from the last living members left over from the ethnographic present, and historians treated Indians as "dead" after early contact with Whites. In these ways modern Native Americans and their contemporary lifestyles have largely disappeared from the White imagination—unless modern Indian activism reverses this historic trend for longer than the recurring but transitory White enthusiasm for things Indian.

That the White image of the Indian is doubly timeless in its assumption   19
of the atemporality of Indian life and its enduring judgment of deficiency does not mean that the imagery as a whole does not have its own history. The problem is how to show both the continuity and the changes in the imagery. Ideally such a history would embody both (1) what changed, what persisted, and why, and (2) what images were held by whom, when, where, and why. On the whole, scholars of the topic attempt only one or the other of these approaches and adopt quite different strategies in doing so. One group traces the imagery in the cultural context and intellectual history of a nation or of Western civilization. The other group examines the socioeconomic forces and vested interests of White individuals and groups. To oversimplify somewhat, the first group of scholars sees the imagery as a reflection of White cultures and as the primary explanation of White behavior vis-à-vis Native Americans, while the second group understands the imagery to be dependent upon the political and economic relationships prevailing in White societies at various times. Usually the former concentrates upon imagery and ideas, and the latter emphasizes policy and actual behavior toward Native Americans. As a result of these differences in attention and explanation, nowhere does one find a comprehensive history of White imagery.

If the remarkable thing about the idea of the Indian is not its invention   20
but its persistence and perpetuation, then the task of this book becomes one of delineating that continuity in spite of seeming changes in intellectual and political currents and alterations in social and economic institutions. Accordingly, Part Two searches beneath the "scientific" conception of the Indian as it moves from premises in Christian cosmogony to modern anthropology for the familiar imagery. Part Three examines the persistence of the dual imagery of the Indian in imaginative and ideological literature and art despite changing intellectual and political climates. The last part turns to the continuing use of the basic Indian imagery to justify White public and private poli-

cies and actual dealings with Native Americans as political regimes altered and economic institutions changed.

Working with the Text

1. Berkhofer says that early European settlers recognized differences among the different Native American peoples, but that they persisted nonetheless in forming a monolithic concept of the "Indian." What motivated the use of this collective term? Can you think of contemporary examples of the same conceptualization?

2. "Indians" were defined according to moral qualities as well as customs, character as well as culture, according to Berkhofer. Which of these two aspects of the definition do you think would lead to greater accuracy?

3. What does Berkhofer mean when he refers to "the tendency to describe Indian life in terms of its lack of White ways rather than being described positively from within the framework of the specific culture under consideration"? How did "Europeans and Americans [use] counterimages of themselves to describe Indians and the counterimages of Indians to describe themselves"? Does contemporary popular culture continue to have a tendency to do this? Respond to these points in an essay.

4. Why, according to Berkhofer, have these stereotyped, often ill-informed images of Native Americans persisted? Why was "Indianness" conceived of as "ahistorical and static"?

5. If you have read David Sibley's "Feelings about Difference," recall his points about exclusion, otherness, and the idea that whites do not think of themselves as white but of others as not-white. How might this phenomenon influence the persistence of the "idea of the Indian" (as Berkhofer puts it) and what you know about Native American life today?

Ethnicity: Identity and Difference

STUART HALL

Jamaican-born sociologist Stuart Hall immigrated to England in the 1950s. He is Professor of Sociology at the Open University, London. He is the author of *Reproducing Ideologies* (1984) and *The Hard Road to Renewal* (1988). He has co-edited numerous volumes, including *The Idea of the Modern State* (1984), *Politics and Ideology* (1986), and *Visual Culture* (1999). In the following essay, first delivered as a speech in 1989, Hall considers the extent to which we must "reconceptualize what identities might mean in [the] more diverse and pluralized situation" of our current multicultural society.

The Return of Identity

I'm concerned with what is sometimes called the "return of the question of identity"—not that the question of identity ever went away, but it has come back with a particular kind of force. That return has something to do with the fact that the question of identity focuses on that point where a whole series of different developments in society and a set of related discourses intersect. Identity emerges as a kind of unsettled space, or an unresolved question in that space, between a number of intersecting discourses. My purpose is to mark some of those points of intersection, especially around questions of cultural identity, and to explore them in relation to the subject of ethnicity in politics.

Let me start by saying something about what seems to have been the logic of the way in which we have thought and talked about questions of identity until recently. The logic of the discourse of identity assumes a stable subject, i.e., we've assumed that there is something which we can call our identity which, in a rapidly shifting world, has the great advantage of staying still. Identities are a kind of guarantee that the world isn't falling apart quite as rapidly as it sometimes seems to be. It's a kind of fixed point of thought and being, a ground of action, a still point in the turning world. That's the kind of ultimate guarantee that identity seems to provide us with.

The logic of identity is the logic of something like a "true self." And the language of identity has often been related to the search for a kind of authenticity to one's experience, something that tells me where I come from. The logic and language of identity is the logic of depth—in here, deep inside me, is my Self which I can reflect upon. It is an element of continuity. I think most of us do recognize that our identities have changed over time, but we have the hope or nostalgia that they change at the rate of a glacier. So, while we're not the fledglings that we were when we were one year old, we are the same sort of person.

Disruption of Identity

So where does the recent disruption of identity come from? What is displacing this depth—the autonomous origin, point of reference, and guaranteed continuity that has been so long associated with the language of identity? What is it about the turbulence of the world we live in that is increasingly mirrored in the vicissitudes of identity?

While, historically, many things have displaced or decentered the stable sense of identity that I just described, I want to focus on four great decenterings in intellectual life and in Western thought that have helped to destabilize the question of identity. I'll attach particular names to three of them, just for convenience sake. I don't want to say they alone did it, but it is quite useful to summarize by hooking the ideas to a particular name. The fourth cannot be attached to a single name, but is just as important.

Marx begins the de-centering of that stable sense of identity by reminding us that there are always *conditions* to identity which the subject cannot construct. *Men and women make history but not under conditions of their own making.* They are partly made by the histories that they make. We are always constructed in part by the practices and discourses that make us, such that we cannot find within ourselves as individual selves or subjects or identities the point of origin from which discourse or history or practice originates. History has to be understood as a continuous dialectic or dialogic relationship between that which is already made and that which is making the future. While Marx's argument deconstructed a lot of games, I'm particularly interested in his impact on the identity/language game. Marx interrupted that notion of the sovereign subject who opens his or her mouth and speaks, for the first time, the truth. Marx reminds us that we are always lodged and implicated in the practices and structures of everybody else's life.

Secondly, there is the very profound displacement which begins with Freud's discovery of the unconscious. If Marx displaced us from the past, Freud displaced us from below. Identity is itself grounded on the huge unknowns of our psychic lives, and we are unable, in any simple way, to reach through the barrier of the unconscious into the psychic life. We can't read the psychic *directly* into the social and the cultural. Nevertheless, social, cultural and political life cannot be understood except in relationship to the formations of the unconscious life. This in itself destabilizes the notion of the self, of identity, as a fully self-reflective entity. It is not possible for the self to reflect and know completely its own identity since it is formed not only in the line of the practice of other structures and discourses, but also in a complex relationship with unconscious life.

Thirdly, we must consider Saussure and his model of language and linguistics which has so transformed theoretical work. Saussurian linguistics suggests that speech—discourse, enunciation itself—is always placed within the relationships of language. In order to speak, in order to say anything new, we must first place ourselves within the existing relations of language. There is no utterance so novel and so creative that it does not already bear on it the traces of how that language has been spoken before we opened our mouths. Thus we are always within language. To say something new is first of all to reaffirm the traces of the past that are inscribed in the words we use. In part, to say something new is first of all to displace all the old things that the words mean—to fight an entire system of meanings. For example, think of how profound it has been in our world to say the word "Black" in a new way. In order to say "Black" in a new way, we have to fight off everything else that Black has always meant—all its connotations, all its negative and positive figurations, the entire metaphorical structure of Christian thought, for example. The whole history of Western imperial thought is condensed in the struggle to dislocate what Black used to mean in order to make it mean something new, in order to say "Black is Beautiful." I'm not talking about Saussure's specific theories of language only. I'm talking about what happens to one's conception of identity when one suddenly understands that one is always inside a system of languages that partly speak us, which we are always positioned within and against.

These are the great figures of modernism. We might say that if modernity unleashes the logic of identity I was talking about earlier, modernism is modernity experienced as trouble. In the face of modernity's promise of the great future: "I am, I am Western man, therefore I know everything. Everything begins with me," modernism says, "Hold on. What about the past? What about the languages you speak? What about the unconscious life you don't know about? What about all those other things that are speaking you?"

However, there's a fourth force of destabilization. This could be given a variety of names. If you wanted to stay within the episteme of Western knowledge, you could say Nietzsche. But I want to say something else. I want to talk about the de-centering of identity that arises as a consequence of the end of the notion of truth as having something directly to do with Western discourses of rationality. This is the great de-centering of identity

8

9

10

that is a consequence of the relativization of the Western world—of the discovery of other worlds, other peoples, other cultures, and other languages. Western rational thought, despite its imperializing claim to be *the* form of universal knowledge, suddenly appears as just another episteme. To use Foucault's words, just another regime of truth. Or Nietzsche's, not absolute Knowledge, not total Truth, just another *particular* form of knowledge harnessed to particular forms of historical power. The linkage between knowledge and power is what made that regime True, what enabled that regime to claim to speak the truth about identity for everyone else across the globe.

When that installation of Western rationality begins to go and to be seen not as absolute, disinterested, objective, neutral, scientific, nonpowerful truth, but dirty truth—truth implicated in the hard game of power—that is the fourth game that destabilizes the old logic of identity. 11

Collective Identities

I've been talking so far about intellectual, theoretical, conceptual displacements of the notion of identity, but I want to talk about some of the displacements of identity that come from social and cultural life rather than from conceptual and theoretical thought. The great social collectivities which used to stabilize our identities—the great stable collectivities of class, race, gender and nation—have been, in our times, deeply undermined by social and political developments. 12

The whole adventure of the modern world was, for a long time, blocked out in terms of these great collective identities. As one knew one's class, one knew one's place in the social universe. As one knew one's race, one knew one's racial position within the great races of the world in their hierarchical relationship to one another. As one knew one's gender, one was able to locate oneself in the huge social divisions between men and women. As one knew one's national identity, one certainly knew about the pecking order of the universe. These collective identities stabilized and staged our sense of ourselves. That logic of identity that seemed so confident at the beginning of my talk, was in part held in place by these great collective social identities. 13

Now, it is not the best kept secret in the world that all sorts of things have rocked and shaken those great collective, stable, social identities of the past. I don't want to talk about any of those developments in detail, but if you think, for instance, of class, it certainly is not true that, in societies like yours and mine, questions of class—of social structure and of social inequality that are raised by the notion of class—have gone away. But, nevertheless, the way in which class identities were understood and experienced, the way in which people located themselves in relation to class identities, 14 the way in which we understood those identities as organized politically—those stable forms of class identity are much more difficult to find at this point in the twentieth century than they were 100 years ago. In fact, looking backwards, we're not sure whether the great stable identities of class were ever quite as stable as we told ourselves they were. There's a kind of narrative of class that always makes the past look simpler than it probably was. If you go back into English nineteenth century life, you will find that class was a pretty complex formation even then. I think there is, nevertheless, some relative sense in which the nation-state, the great class formations of industrial capitalism, certainly the way in which gender was conceptualized, and, toward the end of the nineteenth century, the way in which the entire population of the world could be thought of in terms of the great family of races—I do think there is a way in which these great structuring principles did tie down the question of our social and cultural identities and that they have been very considerably fractured, fragmented, undermined, dispersed in the course of the last fifty years.

The Universe is Coming

Now, this fragmentation of social identity is very much a part of the modern and, indeed, if you believe in it, the postmodern experience. That sense of fragmentation has a peculiar and particular shape to it. Specifically, if I may say this metaphorically, the fragmentation goes local and global at one and the same time, while the great stable identities in the middle do not seem to hold.   15

Take "the nation." The nation-state is increasingly besieged from on top by the interdependence of the planet—by the interdependency of our ecological life, by the enormous interpenetration of capital as a global force, by the complex ways in which world markets link the economies of backward, developed, and overdeveloped nations. These enormous systems are increasingly undermining the stability of any national formation. Nation-states are in trouble, though I am not going to prophesy that the nation-state, that has dominated the history of the world for so long, is going to bow out gracefully.   16

So on the one hand, the nation and all the identities that go with it appear to have gone upwards—reabsorbed into larger communities that overreach and interconnect national identities. But at the same time there is also movement down below. Peoples and groups and tribes who were previously harnessed together in the entities called the nation-states begin to rediscover identities that they had forgotten. So for example if you come to England and hope to see some great stable cultural identity called "the English"—who represent everybody else—what you will find instead is that the   17

Scots, for example, are about to fly off somewhere. They say "We are Scottish and we are European, but we certainly aren't British." And the Welsh say "We're not British either because you've forgotten us and we might as well go somewhere else." And at the same time the Northwest and the Northeast of England, that were left to rot by Mrs. Thatcher, are not truly British any longer either—they're sort of marginal to everybody else. Then the old trade unionists and all Blacks are somebody else, too. You're left with the English as a tight little island somewhere around London with about 25 souls and the Thatcher government hovering over it. And they are continually asking the question—not only about the rest of the world but about most of the people in their own society—"are you one of us?"

So at one and the same time people feel part of the world and part of their village. They have neighborhood identities and they are citizens of the world. Their bodies are endangered by Chernobyl, which didn't knock on the door and say "Can I float radiation over your sovereign territory?" Or another example, we had the warmest winter I've ever experienced in England, last year—the consequence in part of the destruction of rain forests thousands of miles away. An ecological understanding of the world is one that challenges the notion that the nation-state and the boundaries of sovereignty will keep things stable because they won't. The universe is coming! 18

So on the one hand, we have global identities because we have a stake in something global and, on the other hand, we can only know ourselves because we are part of some face-to-face communities. This brings me back to the question of the fate of cultural identity in this maelstrom. Given this theoretical and conceptual de-centering that I've just spoken about, given the relativization of the great stable identities that have allowed us to know who we are—how can we think about the question of cultural identity? 19

Post-Identity?: Cover Stories

There is some language for the notion of doing without identity all together. That is my somewhat unfavorable reference to the extreme version of postmodernism. The argument is that the Self is simply a kind of *perpetual signifier* ever wandering the earth in search of a *transcendental signified* that it can never find—a sort of endless nomadic existence with utterly atomized individuals wandering in an endlessly pluralistic void. Yet, while there are certain conceptual and theoretical ways in which you can try to do without identity, I'm not yet convinced that you can. I think we have to try to re-conceptualize what identities might mean in this more diverse and pluralized situation. 20

This takes us back to some of the very profound things that people have said about identity within recent forms of theorizing. First of all, we are 21 reminded of the structure of "identification" itself. Identity, far from the simple thing that we think it is (ourselves always in the same place), understood properly is always a structure that is split; it always has ambivalence within it. The story of identity is a cover story. A cover story for making you think you stayed in the same place, though with another bit of your mind you do know that you've moved on. What we've learned about the structure of the way in which we identify suggests that identification is not one thing, one moment. We have now to reconceptualize identity as a *process of identification,* and that is a different matter. It is something that happens over time, that is never absolutely stable, that is subject to the play of history and the play of difference.

I don't want to bore you autobiographically, but I could tell you some- 22
thing about the process of my own identification. If I think about who I am, I have been—in my own much too long experience—several identities. And most of the identities that I have been I've only known about *not* because of something deep inside me—the real self—but because of how other people have recognized me.

So, I went to England in the 1950s, before the great wave of migration 23
from the Caribbean and from the Asian subcontinent. I came from a highly respectable, lower middle class Jamaican family. When I went back home at the end of the 50s, my mother, who was very classically of that class and culture, said to me "I hope they don't think you're an immigrant over there!" I had never thought of myself as an immigrant! And now I thought, well actually, I guess that's what I am. I migrated just at that moment. When she hailed me, when she said "Hello immigrant," she asked me to refuse it and in the moment of refusal—like almost everything my mother ever asked me to do—I said "That's who I am! I'm an immigrant." And I thought at last, I've come into my *real* self.

And then, at the end of the 60s and the early 70s, somebody said to me 24
"These things are going on in the political world—I suppose you're really Black." Well, I'd never thought of myself as Black, either! And I'll tell you something, nobody in Jamaica ever did. Until the 1970s, that entire population experienced themselves as all sorts of other things, but they never called themselves Black. And in that sense, Black has a history as an identity that is partly *politically* formed. It's not the color of your skin. It's not given in nature.

Another example: at that very moment I said to my son, who is the re- 25
sult of a mixed marriage, "You're Black." "No," he said, "I'm brown." "You don't understand what I'm saying! You're looking to the wrong signifier! I'm not talking about what color you are. People are all sorts of colors. The question is whether you are *culturally, historically, politically* Black. *That's* who you are."

The Other

So experience belies the notion that identification happens once and for   26
all—life is not like that. It goes on changing and part of what is changing is
not the nucleus of the "real you" inside, it is history that's changing. History
changes your conception of yourself. Thus, another critical thing about identity is that it is partly the relationship between you and the Other. Only
when there is an Other can you know who you are. To discover that fact is
to discover and unlock the whole enormous history of nationalism and of
racism. Racism is a structure of discourse and representation that tries to expel the Other symbolically—blot it out, put it over there in the Third World,
at the margin.

The English are racist not because they hate the Blacks but because they   27
don't know who they are without the Blacks. They have to know who they
are *not* in order to know who they are. And the English language is absolutely replete with things that the English are not. They are not Black, they
are not Indian or Asian, but they are not Europeans and they are not Frogs
either and on and on. The Other. It is a fantastic moment in Fanon's *Black
Skin, White Masks* when he talks of how the gaze of the Other fixes him in
an identity. He knows what it is to be Black when the white child pulls the
hand of her mother and says "Look momma, a Black man." And he says "I
was fixed in that gaze." That is the gaze of Otherness. And there is no identity that is without the dialogic relationship to the Other. The Other is not
outside, but also inside the Self, the identity. So identity is a process, identity is split. Identity is not a fixed point but an ambivalent point. Identity is
also the relationship of the Other to oneself.

Difference(s)

You could tell that story also in terms of a psychic conception of identity.   28
Some of the most important work that modern psychoanalysts have
done—Lacan and so forth—and that feminists have done in terms of sexual
identity is to show the importance of the relationship of the Other. The *construction of difference* as a process, as something that goes on over time, is
something that feminism has been showing us is never finished. The notion
that identity is complete at some point—the notion that masculinity and
femininity can view each other as a perfectly replicating mirror image of
each another—is untenable after the slightest reading of any feminist text or
after reading Freud's *Three Essays on Sexuality.*

So the notion that identity is outside representation—that there are our   29
selves and then the language in which we describe ourselves—is untenable.
Identity is within discourse, within representation. It is constituted in part by

representation. Identity is a narrative of the self; it's the story we tell about the self in order to know who we are. We impose a structure on it. The most important effect of this reconceptualization of identity is the surreptitious return of difference. Identity is a game that ought to be played against difference. But now we have to think about identity *in relation to* difference. There are differences between the ways in which genders are socially and psychically constructed. But there is no fixity to those oppositions. It is a relational opposition, it is a relation of difference. So we're then in the difficult conceptual area of trying to think identity *and* difference.

There are two *different* notions of difference operating. There are the great differences of the discourse of racism—Black and white, civilized and primitive, them and us. But this new conception of difference is a conception much closer to that notion of difference one finds in Derrida. In Derrida you find a notion of *differance* that recognizes the endless, ongoing nature of the construction of meaning but that recognizes also that there is always the play of identity and difference and always the play of difference *across* identity. You can't think of them without each other.

You see, there has been in our lifetime—not in yours, but in mine—a *politics* of identity. There was a *politics* of identity in 1968 in which the various social movements tried to organize themselves politically within one identity. So the identity of being a woman was the subject of the feminist movement. The identity of being a Black person was the identity of the Black movement. And in that rather simpler universe, there was one identity to each movement. While you were in it, you had one identity. Of course, even then, all of us moved between these so-called stable identities. We were sampling these different identities, but we maintained the notion, the myth, the narrative that we were really all the same. That notion of essential forms of identity is no longer tenable.

The Thatcher Project

So, how can one think about identity in this new context? I want to say just a word about the way this has emerged politically in the United Kingdom in the last ten years. I referred a few moments ago to a very narrow and exclusive conception of Englishness that lies at the absolute center of the political project of Thatcherism. When I first started to write about Thatcherism in the early 70s, I thought it was largely an economic and political project. It is only more recently that I understood how profoundly it is rooted in a certain exclusive and essentialist conception of Englishness. Thatcherism is *in defense* of a certain definition of Englishness. England didn't go to the Falklands War inadvertently. It went because there was something there about the connection of the great imperial past, of the empire, of the lion whose tail cannot be tweaked, of the little country that stood up to the great dictator. It's a way of mythically living all the great moments of the English past again. Well, it happens that this time it had to be in the South Atlantic, miles away from anything—in a little corner of the globe that most English people can't identify on the map. This is Marx's famous phrase "The first time is history, the second time is farce." And the third time is an extremely long trip to the South Atlantic. This is the moment of decline that is always a moment of danger in national cultures.

The Return of the Repressed

So it's a very profound part of the Thatcher project to try to restore the iden-   33
tity that in their view *belongs* to Great Britain—Great Britain, Inc., Ltd.—a great firm, Great Britain restored to a world power. But in this very moment of the attempted symbolic restoration of the great English identities that have mastered and dominated the world over three or four centuries, there has come home to roost in English society some *other* British folks. They come from Jamaica, Pakistan, Bangladesh, India—all that part of the colonial world that the English, just in the 1950s, decided they could do without. Just in the very moment when they decided they could do without us, we all took the banana boat and came right back home. We turned up saying "You said this was the mother country. Well, I just came home." We now stand as a permanent reminder of that forgotten, suppressed, hidden history. Every time they walk out on the street, some of us—some of the Other—are there. There we are, *inside* the culture, going to their schools, speaking their language, playing their music, walking down their streets, looking like we own a part of the turf, looking like we belong. Some third generation Blacks are starting to say "We are the Black British." After all, who are we? We're not Jamaicans any more. We have a relationship to that past, but we can't be that entirely any more. You can see that debates around questions of identity are at the center of political life in England today.

Ethnicities: Old and New

What does all that I've been saying have to do with ethnicity? I've left the   34
question of ethnicity to the last because ethnicity is the way in which I want to rethink the relationships between identity and difference. I want to argue that ethnicity is what we all require in order to think [about] the relationship between identity and difference. What do I mean by that? There is no way, it seems to me, in which people of the world can act, can speak, can create, can come in from the margins and talk, can begin to reflect on their own experience unless they come from some *place,* they come from some history,

they inherit certain cultural traditions. What we've learned about the theory of enunciation is that there's no enunciation without positionality. You have to position yourself *somewhere* in order to say anything at all. Thus, we cannot do without that sense of our own positioning that is connoted by the term ethnicity. And the relation that peoples of the world now have to their own past is, of course, part of the discovery of their own ethnicity. They need to honor the hidden histories from which they come. They need to understand the languages which they've been not taught to speak. They need to understand and revalue the traditions and inheritances of cultural expression and creativity. And in that sense, the past is not only a position from which to speak, but it is also an absolutely necessary resource in what one has to say. There is no way, in my view, in which those elements of ethnicity that depend on understanding the past, understanding one's roots, can be done without.

But, on the other hand, there comes the play of difference. This is the   35
recognition that our relationship to that past is quite a complex one, we can't pluck it up out of where it was and simply restore it to ourselves. If you ask my son, who is seventeen and who was born in London, where he comes from, he cannot tell you he comes from Jamaica. Part of his identity is there, but he has to *discover* that identity. He can't just take it out of a suitcase and plop it on the table and say "That's mine." It's not an essence like that. He has to learn to tell himself the story of his past. He has to interrogate his own history, he has to relearn that part of him that has an investment in that culture. For example, he's learning wood sculpture, and in order to do that he has had to discover the traditions of sculpturing of a society in which he has never lived.

So the relationship of the kind of ethnicity I'm talking about to the past   36
is not a simple, essential one—it is a constructed one. It is constructed in history, it is constructed politically in part. It is part of narrative. We tell ourselves the stories of the parts of our roots in order to come into contact, creatively, with it. So this new kind of ethnicity—the emergent ethnicities—has a relationship to the past, but it is a relationship that is partly through memory, partly through narrative, one that has to be recovered. It is an act of cultural recovery.

Yet it is also an ethnicity that has to recognize its position in relation to   37
the importance of difference. It is an ethnicity that cannot deny the role of difference in discovering itself. And I'll tell you a simple, quick story to show you what I mean. About two years ago I was involved in a photographic exhibition that was organized by the Commonwealth Institute in England, and the idea behind it was very simple. Photography is one of the languages in which people speak about their own past and their own experience and construct their own identity. Large numbers of people in the marginal soci-

eties of the British Commonwealth have been the *objects* of someone else's representation, not the *subject* of their own representations. The purpose of this exhibition was to enable some people in those regions to use the creative medium of photography to speak and address their own experience—to empower their ethnicities.

When we came to look at the exhibition, one saw two things at one and the same time. First of all, we saw the enormous excitement of people who are able for the first time to speak about what they have always known—to speak about their culture, their languages, their people, their childhood, about the topography in which they grew up. The arts in our society are being transformed hourly by the new discourses of subjects who have been marginalized coming into representation for the first time. But we also saw something else that we were not prepared for. From those local ethnic enclaves, what they want to speak about as well is the entire world. They want to tell you how they went from the village to Manhattan. They are not prepared to be ethnic archivists for the rest of their lives. They are not prepared only to have something to say of marginalization forever. They have a stake in the whole dominant history of the world, they want to rewrite the history of the world, not just tell my little story. So they use photography to tell us about the enormous migrations of the world and how people now move—of how all our identities are constructed out of a variety of different discourses. We need a place to speak from, but we no longer speak about ethnicity in a narrow and essentialist way.

That is the new ethnicity. It is a new conception of our identities because it has not lost hold of the place and the ground from which we can speak, yet it is no longer contained within that place as an essence. It wants to address a much wider variety of experience. It is part of the enormous cultural relativization of the entire globe that is the historical accomplishment—horrendous as it has been in part—of the twentieth century. Those are the new ethnicities, the new voices. They are neither locked into the past nor able to forget the past. Neither all the same nor entirely different. Identity *and* difference. It is a new settlement between identity and difference.

Of course, alongside the new ethnicities are the *old* ethnicities and the coupling of the old, essentialist identities to power. The old ethnicities still have dominance, they still govern. Indeed, as I tried to suggest when I referred to Thatcherism, as they are relativized their propensity to eat everything else increases. They can only be sure that they really exist at all if they consume everyone else. The notion of an identity that knows where it came from, where home is, but also lives in the symbolic—in the Lacanian sense—knows you can't really go home again. You can't be something else than who you are. You've got to find out who you are in the flux of the past

38

39

40

and the present. That new conception of ethnicity is now struggling in different ways across the globe against the present danger and the threat of the dangerous old ethnicity. That's the stake of the game.

Working with the Text

1. Hall offers two lists of reasons why identity no longer seems stable, the first a list of conceptual or theoretical pressures on identity and the second a list of political pressures. Where do the two lists seem most closely aligned? In other words, as you move into the final third of the essay, which theoretician seems most relevant to Hall's political argument? Whose ideas does the essay finally draw most heavily upon? Why?

2. After reading the essay, can you define identity? Why or why not?

3. The essay ends by sketching an ongoing power struggle between "new" and "old" ethnicities, with the old still dominant and predatory. In the decade since Hall published his remarks, the Thatcher government that furnished his negative examples fell from power; to what degree does this historical change qualify the essay's claims? Which features of the essay now seem dated, and which remain compelling?

4. This essay started out as a speech and retains many features of oral presentation, both at the level of phrasing ("I've chosen to talk about questions of identity . . .") and at the level of structure. Describe one such relic of oral delivery and discuss how it serves the essay's argument about identity.

5. When Hall talks about his own identity, he tends to shift into a narrative mode, suggesting that stories best convey the idea of identity-as-process. Narrate an episode from your own life in which *difference* helped to change your sense of who you were, then analyze the episode using the language of Freud and Derrida, as Hall has explained it.

We Real Cool

GWENDOLYN BROOKS

Gwendolyn Brooks, among the most influential black poets of the century, was born in Topeka, Kansas in 1917, but made Chicago her home, graduating from the city's Wilson Junior College in 1936. Author of more than 20 books, including novels, an autobiography, and an anthology, she is admired for her elegant, biting satires of urban black life, using traditional forms such as the sonnet, ballad, and monologue to dramatize and protest against social and race problems. Her second book, *Annie Allen* (1949), won the Pulitzer Prize. Her many works have been collected in *Selected Poems* and *Blacks*. In 1971 she was appointed Distinguished Professor in the Arts at City College in New York, and served as Poetry Consultant to the Library of Congress in 1985–86. She died in 2000. At first look, the following poem seems as if it were overheard in a pool hall, a kind of anthem from contemporary street life.

The Pool Players.
Seven at the Golden Shovel.

We real cool. We
Left school. We

Lurk late. We   5
Strike straight. We

Sing sin. We
Thin gin. We

Jazz June. We
Die soon.   10

Working with the Text

1. The brevity and simple language of this poem make it seem a fairly "straightforward" song of boasts and despair—at first. But a closer look

may open up more meanings and resonances. What do the subtitles tell us? Describe the speakers, where they are, what they are doing, what their day is like. Who else might say this poem beside the pool players? How would they say it?

2. A small poem may cover as much ground as a long epic—this poem, for instance, may seem to span a lifetime. Trace the change of tone in the poem—how does the speaker sound in the first stanzas, how does he (or she or they) sound at the end? Certainly the boast of being "cool" and dying "soon" carries some complexity or contradiction of feeling—can you depict the shifts of voice?

3. Find the words of a recent, popular song you know that addresses a similar topic to Brooks's poem; compare how each song "tells its tale." Describe the tactics and "plot line" of each poem. Could the song you found be anthologized as a poem, would it make an interesting story 40 years later? Why or why not? How can a song outlive its time?

4. There are several patterns of repetition in this poem: the end sounds of words, the beginning sounds of words, and even the same words are repeated in the poem. With a pencil, mark out these different patterns. What do you learn of the craft of the poet here? How has Brooks hidden her craft to make the poem seem simple?

5. "We Real Cool" helps us understand how certain works of art can seem very close to "real experience," even when the form of the art obeys very strict aesthetic patterns. Try out this poem on a couple of friends and, if possible, on people of very different ages and backgrounds: ask each to read it once, then record them reading it out loud. Play back this "medley" of voices. How has each person interpreted it differently? What different "message" does the poem carry in each voice?

6. This poem has been included in the U.S. Library of Congress's archive of "Americans' Favorite Poems," a project by former U.S. Poet Laureate Robert Pinsky. You can learn more about what poems people chose as their favorites, and get information about a video of a young man from Boston reading this poem, at www.favoritepoem.org.

Critical Questions Revisited: From Reading to Writing

Essay Topic 1: Can you have a community that has significant internal differences?

YOUR PAPER: Explore the question of whether a community can have significant internal differences, or whether there must be some kind of fundamental internal sameness or quality to make it communal. Do communities have hierarchies or classes? Under what conditions can a community stay coherent even if there are hierarchies or divisions? Are there ways that communities find an equilibrium where what people have in common outweighs what differences exist among them?

SUGGESTED STRATEGIES

- What are some of the meaningful examples of community in the readings in this chapter, even in the readings where there is no explicit definition of community?
- How do these writers explore a sense of ambivalence—or even repulsion—that members of a community feel about others who live in that community?
- Are there examples where communities succeed by mutual agreement (however unspoken) to live *with* their differences? Do some differences make more of a difference than others?

Essay Topic 2: Do communities have to be defined against something? Or can they be defined in and of themselves?

YOUR PAPER: Based on the readings in this chapter, and from your own experience, argue whether communities have to be defined against something, or that they can exist on their own terms. You might think about a community that you know well, and consider what makes it a community—its shared values, background, goals, physical place? Or you might think about the various definitions and examples of "community" in the readings in this chapter. If a community is defined or held together by difference defined against something else, then how does that get expressed? Are all communities based to some degree on people's sense of being insiders or outsiders?

SUGGESTED STRATEGIES

- Think about a community you know well. What makes it a community from your perspective? Why do its members feel a part of it?
- Find one or more definitions of community in the readings. Do these definitions depend on sense of sameness or otherness? Or both?
- Thinking about the chapter examples or your own example, how do people *express* their sense of community? Can you express a sense of commonality and difference at the same time?

- Can you form any conclusions about the relationship between community and difference based on these examples?

Essay Topic 3: How do language or labels express and enforce otherness?

YOUR PAPER: Based on evidence from the readings, and your own examples drawn from other sources (such as the newspaper), analyze the ways that "names" and "labels" express and enforce otherness. Consider, for example, the ways that language and images are used to erase differences among groups or within groups, in order to replace those differences with a simplified image. What is the larger purpose of these simplified images? How do these labels or images make it difficult to ever get beyond basic differences? How does this erasing or simplification serve larger cultural purposes? How would you explore at least one of these larger purposes or cultural values?

SUGGESTED STRATEGIES

- Locate in the readings (here, or in examples that you might find on your own) at least a couple of key places where the writers characterize the differences of other groups. (Be sure to distinguish between a writer like Jacob Riis, who himself uses a lot of labeling language, and writers such as Sibley, Marin, and Berkhofer, who analyze the way others use labeling language.)
- What are these labels and categories associated with? What values are attached to these labels? What is at stake for the people who use them?
- Based on at least one extended example that you analyze, can you draw any conclusions about how seemingly simple labels or images signal more complex cultural meaning?

Essay Topic 4: How are representations of what is "normal" related to definitions of "otherness" in a community?

YOUR PAPER: Analyze the relationship between a community or culture's implicit sense of what is "normal" and its representation of otherness. How do definitions of normalcy function, both explicitly and implicitly? You might consider this question at a social level (e.g., gender, class) or at a cultural level (e.g., national, racial). Think about the ways that "normal" behavior or identity gets represented. Where do these representations come from? Does their being represented *as* normal hide some underlying tension? How might you characterize, in a specific analyzed example, the relationship between "normalcy" and "otherness"?

SUGGESTED STRATEGIES

- Based on one rich example from the readings, or of your own, make a list of the values or norms that are implied in the expression of otherness: e.g., cleanliness, morality, success, civilization (or their opposites).

- How are values, characteristics, or behavior particular to a culture represented as normal? Can you identify ways that beliefs about what is normal operate in implicit or unspoken ways?

- Do the invisible and unarticulated codes of "normalcy" do the most damage to those who don't "fit"?

CHAPTER 3

NEGOTIATING BORDERS:
The Dynamics of Difference

Mary Louise Pratt: *Arts of the Contact Zone* [essay]
Richard White: *The Middle Ground* [essay]
Roger Williams: *A Key into the Language of America* [phrasebook]
Wong Sam and Assistants: *An English-Chinese Phrase Book* [phrasebook]
Bob Blauner: *Talking Past Each Other: Black and White Languages of Race* [essay]
Rita Dove: *Arrow* [poem]
Martin Luther King, Jr.: *Letter from Birmingham Jail* [essay]
Tim O'Brien: *Sweetheart of the Song Tra Bong* [essay]
Luis Alberto Urrea: *Across the Wire* [essay]
Mary Gaitskill: *On Not Being a Victim* [essay]
Lester Bangs: *The White Noise Supremacists* [essay]
Sherry Turkle: *TinySex and Gender Trouble* [essay]
Frantz Fanon: *The Fact of Blackness* [essay]
Art Spiegelman: *MAUS: A Survivor's Tale* [graphic story]
Andrea Lowenstein: *Confronting Stereotypes: MAUS in Crown Heights* [essay]

Critical Questions

Before reading: What happens when "different" groups meet and regard each other as alien, as other?

Taking it further: Can "culture" be understood as arising between two contentious groups? Can any one group have a single, separate, and distinct culture? What roles do opposition and resistance to "assigned" categories of identity play in self-formation, and group formation? How can groups adjust their differences to accommodate each other?

DOES DIFFERENCE MAKE A DIFFERENCE?

The writings of the previous chapter look at how we construct difference, mapping the exclusions that underlie notions of "we" and "them." This chapter builds upon such explorations of otherness and difference to consider what happens when people on either side of cultural differences interact. The selections display a range of means and contexts for negotiating differences: communication through fear and withdrawal; strategies of persuasion and appeals to common values; the construction of sympathy or mutual self-interests; provocation and improvisation. Some selections proceed from the premise of a shared humanity that provides a bond within cultures and potentially across them. Others do not accept the notion of a universal nature and believe that their identity derives, to some degree, from cultural difference. Some selections depict culture as an ongoing "war of position" in which a dominant culture occupies one side of a border dictating the terms of behavior to a subordinated group on the other—a view that often assumes that opposition and resistance to be primary markers of identity for both "sides." Other texts propose a less fixed model of borders, culture, and identity based on the dynamics of accommodation and reciprocal impact on one another. At the most basic level, the selections of this chapter explore what it might mean to take responsibility for creating the other.

CAN A CONTACT ZONE BE A COMMUNITY?

All of these questions bear on the nature of exchange that takes place when diverse people come into contact with one another. What many of the essays in this chapter imply is that for communication and understanding to take place across differences, we have to become more conscious of the nature of those differences as defining the social sphere in which we live. That is, we can only speak *across* difference, if we speak with a consciousness *of* difference. A key feature of communicating across difference is the acknowledgment that two sides may simply have fundamentally different ways of *perceiving* a situation. Language depends on perception and perceptions are rooted in social position. Often one of the challenges of even talking about differences is to understand that certain words or concepts might have conflicting meanings for people in different positions. For example, the selections by Frantz Fanon and Art Spiegelman imply that the ways those in power see us to a large degree determine who we are. Roger Williams and Wong Sam suggest that the language of a native culture is not only attainable but also crucial to a new immigrant's survival. Rita Dove's poem reflects upon both the problems and possibilities of language according to whose words get quoted and whose speech becomes public.

Mary Louise Pratt sees sites of intercultural encounter as "contact zones," "social spaces where cultures meet, clash, and grapple with each other, often in contexts of highly asymmetrical relations of power." Martin Luther King focuses our attention on how writers communicate in a context of inequality, strategically using the reasoning, values, and intellectual sources of the dominant culture to argue against their objections to his "marginal" tactics. Richard White warns against the assumption that cultural contact always results in either conquest or resistance, proposing a "middle ground" where worlds can overlap, giving rise to new, shared systems of meanings and exchange sometimes as the result of happy misunderstanding, an optimistic point of view to some degree shared by Andrea Freud Lowenstein, who turns her gaze to the power relations and identity politics of the classroom between teacher and student. Other selections, such as the essay by Bob Blauner, explicitly reject the notion of a socially or politically productive cultural misunderstanding, tracing the underlying causes of miscommunications between races. Similarly, Lester Bangs begins with the premise that difference is a given and an important determinant of the dynamics of interaction. Detecting an undiscerning smugness in rock and roll's seeming liberalism, Bangs savagely denounces its indiscriminate efforts to loosen the ethnocentric grip of racial difference by simply "ignoring" it.

Other essays are themselves models or strategies of communication for negotiating difference and power imbalances. Luis Urrea's stories of being among the poor while not being poor moves us from issues of communication across differences back to questions of identity, adaptation, and survival. In portraying a woman "playing soldier" in the Vietnam War, Tim O'Brien offers a vision of gender that is more flexible, deceptive, and vulnerable than we may like to admit. Mary Gaitskill, too, examines gender dynamics, analyzing incidents of rape, acts she proposes are as much a violation of a man's masculine identity as they are of the woman who is raped. Sherry Turkle extends the focus of gender and sexuality issues into cyberspace. In particular, Turkle describes contexts of "virtual cross-dressing" where men and women pose as different genders and have different constructed identities. The implications that we interact through *constructed* identities rather than fixed, natural, or "essential" identities bears not only on the nature of cyberspace, but echoes back through the whole chapter about communication and interaction in any "contact zone."

Arts of the Contact Zone

MARY LOUISE PRATT

A native of Canada, Mary Louise Pratt attended the University of Toronto and later received her doctorate from Stanford University. She now teaches comparative literature, as well as Spanish and Portuguese, at Stanford. The subjects of her research and writing have ranged widely and include literature, linguistics, political and cultural studies, and history. Among her books are *Toward a Speech Act Theory of Literary Discourse* (1977), *Women, Culture, and Politics in Latin America* (co-authored, 1990), *Imperial Eyes: Studies in Travel Writing and Transculturation* (1992), and, most recently, *Critical Passions* (1999), an edition of essays by Jean Franco. In the following essay Pratt considers the ways early European travelers to Africa and the Americas, in writing about these new worlds for a European audience, essentially "invented" them along Eurocentric lines. Rather than describing these lands and their peoples in terms of their positive reality, these travelers wrote of their "inferiority" to Europe and Europeans. For Pratt, communication is within "contact zones, . . . social spaces where cultures meet, clash, and grapple with each other, often in contexts of highly asymmetrical relations of power." She finds such zones particularly applicable to the contemporary United States.

Whenever the subject of literacy comes up, what often pops first into my mind is a conversation I overheard eight years ago between my son Sam and his best friend, Willie, aged six and seven, respectively: "Why don't you trade me Many Trails for Carl Yats . . . Yesits . . . Ya-strum-scrum." "That's not how you say it, dummy, it's Carl Yes . . . Yes . . . oh, I don't know." Sam and Willie had just discovered baseball cards. Many Trails was their decoding, with the help of first-grade English phonics, of the name Manny Trillo. The name they were quite rightly stumped on was Carl Yastrzemski. That was the first time I remembered seeing them put their incipient literacy to their own use, and I was of course thrilled.

Sam and Willie learned a lot about phonics that year by trying to decipher surnames on baseball cards, and a lot about cities, states, heights, weights, places of birth, stages of life. In the years that followed, I watched Sam apply his arithmetic skills to working out batting averages and subtracting retirement years from rookie years; I watched him develop senses of patterning and order by arranging and rearranging his cards for hours on end, and aesthetic judgment by comparing different photos, different series, layouts, and color schemes. American geography and history took shape in his mind through baseball cards. Much of his social life revolved around trading them, and he learned about exchange, fairness, trust, the importance of processes as opposed to results, what it means to get cheated, taken advantage of, even robbed. Baseball cards were the medium of his economic life too. Nowhere better to learn the power and arbitrariness of money, the absolute divorce between use value and exchange value, notions of long- and short-term investment, the possibility of personal values that are independent of market values.

Baseball cards meant baseball card shows, where there was much to be learned about adult worlds as well. And baseball cards opened the door to baseball books, shelves and shelves of encyclopedias, magazines, histories, biographies, novels, books of jokes, anecdotes, cartoons, even poems. Sam learned the history of American racism and the struggle against it through baseball; he saw the depression and two world wars from behind home plate. He learned the meaning of commodified labor, what it means for one's body and talents to be owned and dispensed by another. He knows something about Japan, Taiwan, Cuba, and Central America and how men and boys do things there. Through the history and experience of baseball stadiums he thought about architecture, light, wind, topography, meteorology, the dynamics of public space. He learned the meaning of expertise, of knowing about something well enough that you can start a conversation with a stranger and feel sure of holding your own. Even with an adult—especially with an adult. Throughout his preadolescent years, baseball history was Sam's luminous point of contact with grown-ups, his lifeline to caring. And, of course, all this time he was also playing baseball, struggling his way through the stages of the local Little League system, lucky enough to be a pretty good player, loving the game and coming to know deeply his strengths and weaknesses.

Literacy began for Sam with the newly pronounceable names on the picture cards and brought him what has been easily the broadest, most varied, most enduring, and most integrated experience of his thirteen-year life. Like many parents, I was delighted to see schooling give Sam the tools with which to find and open all these doors. At the same time I found it unforgivable that schooling itself gave him nothing remotely as meaningful to do, let alone anything that would actually take him beyond the referential, masculinist ethos of baseball and its lore.

However, I was not invited here to speak as a parent, nor as an expert on literacy. I was asked to speak as an MLA [Modern Language Association] member working in the elite academy. In that capacity my contribution is undoubtedly supposed to be abstract, irrelevant, and anchored outside the real world. I wouldn't dream of disappointing anyone. I propose immediately to head back several centuries to a text that has a few points in common with baseball cards and raises thoughts about what Tony Sarmiento, in his comments to the conference, called new visions of literacy. In 1908 a Peruvianist named Richard Pietschmann was exploring in the Danish Royal Archive in Copenhagen and came across a manuscript. It was dated in the city of Cuzco in Peru, in the year 1613, some forty years after the final fall of the Inca empire to the Spanish and signed with an unmistakably Andean indigenous name: Felipe Guaman Poma de Ayala. Written in a mixture of Quechua and ungrammatical, expressive Spanish, the manuscript was a letter addressed by an unknown but apparently literate Andean to King Philip III of Spain. What stunned Pietschmann was that the letter was twelve hundred pages long. There were almost eight hundred pages of written text and four hundred of captioned line drawings. It was titled *The First New Chronicle and Good Government*. No one knew (or knows) how the manuscript got to the library in Copenhagen or how long it had been there. No one, it appeared, had ever bothered to read it or figured out how. Quechua was not thought of as a written language in 1908, nor Andean culture as a literate culture.

Pietschmann prepared a paper on his find, which he presented in London in 1912, a year after the rediscovery of Machu Picchu by Hiram Bingham. Reception, by an international congress of Americanists, was apparently confused. It took twenty-five years for a facsimile edition of the work to appear in Paris. It was not till the late 1970s, as positivist reading habits gave way to interpretive studies and colonial elitisms to postcolonial pluralisms, that Western scholars found ways of reading Guaman Poma's *New Chronicle and Good Government* as the extraordinary intercultural tour de force that it was. The letter got there, only 350 years too late, a miracle and a terrible tragedy.

I propose to say a few more words about this erstwhile unreadable text, in order to lay out some thoughts about writing and literacy in what I like to call the *contact zones*. I use this term to refer to social spaces where cultures meet, clash, and grapple with each other, often in contexts of highly asymmetrical relations of power, such as colonialism, slavery, or their aftermaths as they are lived out in many parts of the world today. Eventually I will use the term to reconsider the models of community that many of us rely on in teaching and theorizing and that are under challenge today. But first a little more about Guaman Poma's giant letter to Philip III.

Insofar as anything is known about him at all, Guaman Poma exemplified the sociocultural complexities produced by conquest and empire. He was an indigenous Andean who claimed noble Inca descent and who had adopted (at least in some sense) Christianity. He may have worked in the Spanish colonial administration as an interpreter, scribe, or assistant to a Spanish tax collector—as a mediator, in short. He says he learned to write from his half brother, a mestizo whose Spanish father had given him access to religious education.

Guaman Poma's letter to the king is written in two languages (Spanish and Quechua) and two parts. The first is called the *Nueva corónica,* "New Chronicle." The title is important. The chronicle of course was the main writing apparatus through which the Spanish presented their American conquests to themselves. It constituted one of the main official discourses. In writing a "new chronicle," Guaman Poma took over the official Spanish genre for his own ends. Those ends were, roughly, to construct a new picture of the world, a picture of a Christian world with Andean rather than European peoples at the center of it—Cuzco, not Jerusalem. In the *New Chronicle* Guaman Poma begins by rewriting the Christian history of the world from Adam and Eve, incorporating the Amerindians into it as offspring of one of the sons of Noah. He identifies five ages of Christian history that he links in parallel with the five ages of canonical Andean history—separate but equal trajectories that diverge with Noah and reintersect not with Columbus but with Saint Bartholomew, claimed to have preceded Columbus in the Americas. In a couple of hundred pages, Guaman Poma constructs a veritable encyclopedia of Inca and pre-Inca history, customs, laws, social forms, public offices, and dynastic leaders. The depictions resemble European manners and customs description, but also reproduce the meticulous detail with which knowledge in Inca society was stored on *quipus* and in the oral memories of elders.

Guaman Poma's *New Chronicle* is an instance of what I have proposed to call an *autoethnographic* text, by which I mean a text in which people undertake to describe themselves in ways that engage with representations others have made of them. Thus if ethnographic texts are those in which European metropolitan subjects represent to themselves their others (usually their conquered others), autoethnographic texts are representations that the so-defined others construct *in response* to or in dialogue with those texts. Autoethnographic texts are not, then, what are usually thought of as autochthonous forms of expression or self-representation (as the Andean *quipus* were). Rather they involve a selective collaboration with and appropriation of idioms of the metropolis or the conqueror. These are merged or infiltrated to varying degrees with indigenous idioms to create self-representations intended to intervene in metropolitan modes of understanding. Autoethnographic works are often addressed to both metropolitan audiences and the speaker's own community. Their reception is thus highly indeterminate. Such texts often constitute a marginalized group's point of entry into the dominant circuits of print culture. It is interesting to think, for example, of American slave autobiography in its autoethnographic dimensions, which in some respects distinguish it from Euramerican autobiographical tradition. The concept might help explain why some of the earliest published writing by Chicanas took the form of folkloric manners and customs sketches written in English and published in English-language newspapers or folklore magazines (see Treviño). Autoethnographic representation often involves concrete collaborations between people, as between literate ex-slaves and abolitionist intellectuals, or between Guaman Poma and the Inca elders who were his informants. Often, as in Guaman Poma, it involves more than one language. In recent decades autoethnography, critique, and resistance have reconnected with writing in a contemporary creation of the contact zone, the *testimonio*.

Guaman Poma's *New Chronicle* ends with a revisionist account of the 11
Spanish conquest, which, he argues, should have been a peaceful encounter of equals with the potential for benefiting both, but for the mindless greed of the Spanish. He parodies Spanish history. Following contact with the Incas, he writes, "In all Castille, there was a great commotion. All day and at night in their dreams the Spaniards were saying, 'Yndias, yndias, oro, plata, oro, plata del Piru'" ("Indies, Indies, gold, silver, gold, silver from Peru"). The Spanish, he writes, brought nothing of value to share with the Andeans, nothing "but armor and guns con la codicia de oro, plata oro y plata, yndias, a las Yndias, Piru" ("with the lust for gold, silver, gold and silver, Indies, the Indies, Peru") (372). I quote these words as an example of a conquered subject using the conqueror's language to construct a parodic, oppositional representation of the conqueror's own speech. Guaman Poma mirrors back to the Spanish (in their language, which is alien to him) an image of themselves that they often suppress and will therefore surely recognize. Such are the dynamics of language, writing, and representation in contact zones.

The second half of the epistle continues the critique. It is titled *Buen go-* 12
bierno y justicia, "Good Government and Justice," and combines a description of colonial society in the Andean region with a passionate denunciation of Spanish exploitation and abuse. (These, at the time he was writing, were decimating the population of the Andes at a genocidal rate. In fact, the

potential loss of the labor force became a main cause for reform of the system.) Guaman Poma's most implacable hostility is invoked by the clergy, followed by the dreaded *corregidores,* or colonial overseers. He also praises good works, Christian habits, and just men where he finds them, and offers at length his views as to what constitutes "good government and justice." The Indies, he argues, should be administered through a collaboration of Inca and Spanish elites. The epistle ends with an imaginary question-and-answer session in which, in a reversal of hierarchy, the king is depicted asking Guaman Poma questions about how to reform the empire—a dialogue imagined across the many lines that divide the Andean scribe from the imperial monarch, and in which the subordinated subject single-handedly gives himself authority in the colonizer's language and verbal repertoire. In a way, it worked—this extraordinary text did get written—but in a way it did not, for the letter never reached its addressee.

To grasp the import of Guaman Poma's project, one needs to keep in   13
mind that the Incas had no system of writing. Their huge empire is said to be the only known instance of a full-blown bureaucratic state society built and administered without writing. Guaman Poma constructs his text by appropriating and adapting pieces of the representational repertoire of the invaders. He does not simply imitate or reproduce it; he selects and adapts it along Andean lines to express (bilingually, mind you) Andean interests and aspirations. Ethnographers have used the term *transculturation* to describe processes whereby members of subordinated or marginal groups select and invent from materials transmitted by a dominant or metropolitan culture. The term, originally coined by Cuban sociologist Fernando Ortiz in the 1940s, aimed to replace overly reductive concepts of acculturation and assimilation used to characterize culture under conquest. While subordinate peoples do not usually control what emanates from the dominant culture, they do determine to varying extents what gets absorbed into their own and what it gets used for. Transculturation, like autoethnography, is a phenomenon of the contact zone.

As scholars have realized only relatively recently, the transcultural char-   14
acter of Guaman Poma's text is intricately apparent in its visual as well as its written component. The genre of the four hundred line drawings is European—there seems to have been no tradition of representational drawing among the Incas—but in their execution they deploy specifically Andean systems of spatial symbolism that express Andean values and aspirations.[1] . . .

In sum, Guaman Poma's text is truly a product of the contact zone. If   15
one thinks of cultures, or literatures, as discrete, coherently structured, monolingual edifices, Guaman Poma's text, and indeed any autoethnographic work, appears anomalous or chaotic—as it apparently did to the European scholars Pietschmann spoke to in 1912. If one does not think of

cultures this way, then Guaman Poma's text is simply heterogeneous, as the Andean region was itself and remains today. Such a text is heterogeneous on the reception end as well as the production end: it will read very differently to people in different positions in the contact zone. Because it deploys European and Andean systems of meaning making, the letter necessarily means differently to bilingual Spanish-Quechua speakers and to monolingual speakers in either language; the drawings mean differently to monocultural readers, Spanish or Andean, and to bicultural readers responding to the Andean symbolic structures embodied in European genres.

In the Andes in the early 1600s there existed a literate public with considerable intercultural competence and degrees of bilingualism. Unfortunately, such a community did not exist in the Spanish court with which Guaman Poma was trying to make contact. It is interesting to note that in the same year Guaman Poma sent off his letter, a text by another Peruvian was adopted in official circles in Spain as the canonical Christian mediation between the Spanish conquest and Inca history. It was another huge encyclopedic work, titled the *Royal Commentaries of the Incas,* written, tellingly, by a mestizo, Inca Garcilaso de la Vega. Like the mestizo half brother who taught Guaman Poma to read and write, Inca Garcilaso was the son of an Inca princess and a Spanish official, and had lived in Spain since he was seventeen. Though he too spoke Quechua, his book is written in eloquent, standard Spanish, without illustrations. While Guaman Poma's life's work sat somewhere unread, the *Royal Commentaries* was edited and reedited in Spain and the New World, a mediation that coded the Andean past and present in ways thought unthreatening to colonial hierarchy.[2] The textual hierarchy persists; the *Royal Commentaries* today remains a staple item on Ph.D. reading lists in Spanish, while the *New Chronicle and Good Government,* despite the ready availability of several fine editions, is not. However, though Guaman Poma's text did not reach its destination, the transcultural currents of expression it exemplifies continued to evolve in the Andes, as they still do, less in writing than in storytelling, ritual, song, dance-drama, painting and sculpture, dress, textile art, forms of governance, religious belief, and many other vernacular art forms. All express the effects of long-term contact and intractable, unequal conflict.

Autoethnography, transculturation, critique, collaboration, bilingualism, mediation, parody, denunciation, imaginary dialogue, vernacular expression—these are some of the literate arts of the contact zone. Miscomprehension, incomprehension, dead letters, unread masterpieces, absolute heterogeneity of meaning—these are some of the perils of writing in the contact zone. They all live among us today in the transnationalized metropolis of the United States and are becoming more widely visible, more pressing, and, like Guaman Poma's text, more decipherable to those who once would have ignored them in defense of a stable, centered sense of knowledge and reality.

Contact and Community

The idea of the contact zone is intended in part to contrast with ideas of community that underlie much of the thinking about language, communication, and culture that gets done in the academy. A couple of years ago, thinking about the linguistic theories I knew, I tried to make sense of a utopian quality that often seemed to characterize social analyses of language by the academy. Languages were seen as living in "speech communities," and these tended to be theorized as discrete, self-defined, coherent entities, held together by a homogeneous competence or grammar shared identically and equally among all the members. This abstract idea of the speech community seemed to reflect, among other things, the utopian way modern nations conceive of themselves as what Benedict Anderson calls "imagined communities."[3] In a book of that title, Anderson observes that with the possible exception of what he calls "primordial villages," human communities exist as *imagined* entities in which people "will never know most of their fellow-members, meet them or even hear of them, yet in the minds of each lives the image of their communion." "Communities are distinguished," he goes on to say, "not by their falsity/genuineness, but by *the style in which they are imagined*" (15; emphasis mine). Anderson proposes three features that characterize the style in which the modern nation is imagined. First, it is imagined as *limited,* by "finite, if elastic, boundaries"; second, it is imagined as *sovereign;* and, third, it is imagined as *fraternal,* "a deep, horizontal comradeship" for which millions of people are prepared "not so much to kill as willingly to die" (15). As the image suggests, the nation-community is embodied metonymically in the finite, sovereign, fraternal figure of the citizen-soldier.

Anderson argues that European bourgeoisies were distinguished by their ability to "achieve solidarity on an essentially imagined basis" (74) on a scale far greater than that of elites of other times and places. Writing and literacy play a central role in this argument. Anderson maintains, as have others, that the main instrument that made bourgeois nation-building projects possible was print capitalism. The commercial circulation of books in the various European vernaculars, he argues, was what first created the invisible networks that would eventually constitute the literate elites and those they ruled as nations. (Estimates are that 180 million books were put into circulation in Europe between the years 1500 and 1600 alone.)

Now obviously this style of imagining of modern nations, as Anderson describes it, is strongly utopian, embodying values like equality, fraternity, liberty, which the societies often profess but systematically fail to realize. The prototype of the modern nation as imagined community was, it seemed to me, mirrored in ways people thought about language and the speech community. Many commentators have pointed out how modern views of language as code and competence assume a unified and homogeneous social world in which language exists as a shared patrimony—as a device, precisely, for imagining community. An image of a universally shared literacy is also part of the picture. The prototypical manifestation of language is generally taken to be the speech of individual adult native speakers face-to-face (as in Saussure's famous diagram) in monolingual, even monodialectal situations—in short, the most homogeneous case linguistically and socially. The same goes for written communication. Now one could certainly imagine a theory that assumed different things—that argued, for instance, that the most revealing speech situation for understanding language was one involving a gathering of people each of whom spoke two languages and understood a third and held only one language in common with any of the others. It depends on what workings of language you want to see or want to see first, on what you choose to define as normative.

In keeping with autonomous, fraternal models of community, analyses of language use commonly assume that principles of cooperation and shared understanding are normally in effect. Descriptions of interactions between people in conversation, classrooms, medical and bureaucratic settings, readily take it for granted that the situation is governed by a single set of rules or norms shared by all participants. The analysis focuses then on how those rules produce or fail to produce an orderly, coherent exchange. Models involving games and moves are often used to describe interactions. Despite whatever conflicts or systematic social differences might be in play, it is assumed that all participants are engaged in the same game and that the game is the same for all players. Often it is. But of course it often is not, as, for example, when speakers are from different classes or cultures, or one party is exercising authority and another is submitting to it or questioning it. Last year one of my children moved to a new elementary school that had more open classrooms and more flexible curricula than the conventional school he started out in. A few days into the term, we asked him what it was like at the new school. "Well," he said, "they're a lot nicer, and they have a lot less rules. But know *why* they're nicer?" "Why?" I asked. "So you'll obey all the rules they don't have," he replied. This is a very coherent analysis with considerable elegance and explanatory power, but probably not the one his teacher would have given. 21

When linguistic (or literate) interaction is described in terms of orderliness, games, moves, or scripts, usually only legitimate moves are actually 22 named as part of the system, where legitimacy is defined from the point of view of the party in authority—regardless of what other parties might see themselves as doing. Teacher-pupil language, for example, tends to be described almost entirely from the point of view of the teacher and teaching, not from the point of view of pupils and pupiling (the word doesn't even exist, though the thing certainly does). If a classroom is analyzed as a social world unified and homogenized with respect to the teacher, whatever students do other than what the teacher specifies is invisible or anomalous to the analysis. This can be true in practice as well. On several occasions my fourth grader, the one busy obeying all the rules they didn't have, was given writing assignments that took the form of answering a series of questions to build up a paragraph. These questions often asked him to identify with the interests of those in power over him—parents, teachers, doctors, public authorities. He invariably sought ways to resist or subvert these assignments. One assignment, for instance, called for imagining "a helpful invention." The students were asked to write single-sentence responses to the following questions:

> What kind of invention would help you?
> How would it help you?
> Why would you need it?
> What would it look like?
> Would other people be able to use it also?
> What would be an invention to help your teacher?
> What would be an invention to help your parents?

Manuel's reply read as follows:

A grate adventchin

> Some inventchins are GRATE!!!!!!!!!!! My inventchin would be a shot that would put every thing you learn at school in your brain. It would help me by letting me graduate right now!! I would need it because it would let me play with my friends, go on vacachin and, do fun a lot more. It would look like a regular shot. Ather peaple would use to. This inventchin would help my teacher parents get away from a lot of work. I think a shot like this would be GRATE!

Despite the spelling, the assignment received the usual star to indicate the task had been fulfilled in an acceptable way. No recognition was available, however, of the humor, the attempt to be critical or contestatory, to parody the structures of authority. On that score, Manuel's luck was only slightly better than Guaman Poma's. What is the place of unsolicited oppositional discourse, parody, resistance, critique in the imagined classroom community? Are teachers supposed to feel that their teaching has been most successful when they have eliminated such things and unified the social world, probably in their own image? Who wins when we do that? Who loses?

Such questions may be hypothetical, because in the United States in the 1990s, many teachers find themselves less and less able to do that even if they want to. The composition of the national collectivity is changing and so are the styles, as Anderson put it, in which it is being imagined. In the 1980s in many nation-states, imagined national syntheses that had retained hegemonic force began to dissolve. Internal social groups with histories and lifeways different from the official ones began insisting on those histories and lifeways *as part of their citizenship,* as the very mode of their membership in the national collectivity. In their dialogues with dominant institutions, many groups began asserting a rhetoric of belonging that made demands beyond those of representation and basic rights granted from above. In universities we started to hear, "I don't just want you to let me be here, I want to belong here; this institution should belong to me as much as it does to anyone else." Institutions have responded with, among other things, rhetorics of diversity and multiculturalism whose import at this moment is up for grabs across the ideological spectrum.

These shifts are being lived out by everyone working in education today, and everyone is challenged by them in one way or another. Those of us committed to educational democracy are particularly challenged as that notion finds itself besieged on the public agenda. Many of those who govern us display, openly, their interest in a quiescent, ignorant, manipulable electorate. Even as an ideal, the concept of an enlightened citizenry seems to have disappeared from the national imagination. A couple of years ago the university where I work went through an intense and wrenching debate over a narrowly defined Western-culture requirement that had been instituted there in 1980. It kept boiling down to a debate over the ideas of national patrimony, cultural citizenship, and imagined community. In the end, the requirement was transformed into a much more broadly defined course called Cultures, Ideas, Values.[4] In the context of the change, a new course was designed that centered on the Americas and the multiple cultural histories (including European ones) that have intersected here. As you can imagine, the course attracted a very diverse student body. The classroom functioned not like a homogeneous community or a horizontal alliance but like a contact zone. Every single text we read stood in specific historical relationships to the students in the class, but the range and variety of historical relationships in play were enormous. Everybody had a stake in nearly everything we read, but the range and kind of stakes varied widely.

It was the most exciting teaching we had ever done, and also the hardest. We were struck, for example, at how anomalous the formal lecture became in a contact zone (who can forget Atahuallpa throwing down the Bible because it would not speak to him?). The lecturer's traditional (imagined) task—unifying the world in the class's eyes by means of a monologue that

23

24

25

rings equally coherent, revealing, and true for all, forging an ad hoc community, homogeneous with respect to one's own words—this task became not only impossible but anomalous and unimaginable. Instead, one had to work in the knowledge that whatever one said was going to be systematically received in radically heterogeneous ways that we were neither able nor entitled to prescribe.

The very nature of the course put ideas and identities on the line. All the students in the class had the experience, for example, of hearing their culture discussed and objectified in ways that horrified them; all the students saw their roots traced back to legacies of both glory and shame; all the students experienced face-to-face the ignorance and incomprehension, and occasionally the hostility, of others. In the absence of community values and the hope of synthesis, it was easy to forget the positives; the fact, for instance, that kinds of marginalization once taken for granted were gone. Virtually every student was having the experience of seeing the world described with him or her in it. Along with rage, incomprehension, and pain, there were exhilarating moments of wonder and revelation, mutual understanding, and new wisdom—the joys of the contact zone. The sufferings and revelations were, at different moments to be sure, experienced by every student. No one was excluded, and no one was safe.

The fact that no one was safe made all of us involved in the course appreciate the importance of what we came to call "safe houses." We used the term to refer to social and intellectual spaces where groups can constitute themselves as horizontal, homogeneous, sovereign communities with high degrees of trust, shared understandings, temporary protection from legacies of oppression. This is why, as we realized, multicultural curricula should not seek to replace ethnic or women's studies, for example. Where there are legacies of subordination, groups need places for healing and mutual recognition, safe houses in which to construct shared understandings, knowledges, claims on the world that they can then bring into the contact zone.

Meanwhile, our job in the Americas course remains to figure out how to make that crossroads the best site for learning that it can be. We are looking for the pedagogical arts of the contact zone. These will include, we are sure, exercises in storytelling and in identifying with the ideas, interests, histories, and attitudes of others; experiments in transculturation and collaborative work and in the arts of critique, parody, and comparison (including unseemly comparisons between elite and vernacular cultural forms); the redemption of the oral; ways for people to engage with suppressed aspects of history (including their own histories), ways to move *into and out of* rhetorics of authenticity; ground rules for communication across lines of difference and hierarchy that go beyond politeness but maintain mutual respect; a systematic approach to the all-important concept of *cultural mediation.*

26

27

28

These arts were in play in every room at the extraordinary Pittsburgh conference on literacy. I learned a lot about them there, and I am thankful.

WORKS CITED

Adorno, Rolena. *Guaman Poma de Ayala: Writing and Resistance in Colonial Peru*. Austin: U of Texas P, 1986.

Anderson, Benedict. *Imagined Communities: Reflections on the Origins and Spread of Nationalism*. London: Verso, 1984.

Garcilaso de la Vega, El Inca. *Royal Commentaries of the Incas*. 1613. Austin: U of Texas P, 1966.

Guaman Poma de Ayala, Felipe. *El primer nueva corónica y buen gobierno*. Manuscript. Ed. John Murra and Rolena Adorno. Mexico: Siglo XXI, 1980.

Pratt, Mary Louise. "Linguistic Utopias." *The Linguistics of Writing*. Ed. Nigel Fabb et al. Manchester: Manchester UP, 1987. 48–66.

Treviño, Gloria. "Cultural Ambivalence in Early Chicano Prose Fiction." Diss. Stanford U, 1985.

NOTES

1. For an introduction in English to these and other aspects of Guaman Poma's work, see Rolena Adorno. Adorno and Mercedes Lopez-Baralt pioneered the study of Andean symbolic systems in Guaman Poma.

2. It is far from clear that the *Royal Commentaries* was as benign as the Spanish seemed to assume. The book certainly played a role in maintaining the identity and aspirations of indigenous elites in the Andes. In the mid–eighteenth century, a new edition of the *Royal Commentaries* was suppressed by Spanish authorities because its preface included a prophecy by Sir Walter Raleigh that the English would invade Peru and restore the Inca monarchy.

3. The discussion of community here is summarized from my essay "Linguistic Utopias."

4. For information about this program and the contents of courses taught in it, write Program in Cultures, Ideas, Values (CIV), Stanford Univ., Stanford, CA 94305.

Working with the Text

1. Pratt uses the example of her son's education through baseball cards to suggest how we learn to "read" texts—to decode their various intricacies and to make meaning of the whole through understanding the many different parts. How does this idea of learning to "read" relate to Guaman Poma's *The First New Chronicle and Good Government*? What does Pratt mean when she says the "letter got there, only 350 years too late, a miracle and a terrible tragedy"?

2. What is a "contact zone," in Pratt's terminology? In your opinion, does the internet enhance or inhibit the emergence of contact zones? What kinds of zones have you seen emerge on the Web or Usenet, and what features of Pratt's model do they express, abandon, or adapt? For

example, what happens in cyberspace to Pratt's "contexts of highly asymmetrical relations of power"?

3. What kinds of writing do contact zones encourage? Pratt describes two in detail: ethnographic and autoethnographic. How do these differ from one another in style, purpose, and audience? Why are autoethnographic texts harder to interpret? Can you think of contemporary examples of contact zone expression? What about global media, especially television? When political and religiously-based interests communicate through global media, is that a kind of contact zone expression, by Pratt's definition?

4. Describe the relationship between Pratt's argument and her rhetorical strategy, between *what* she says and *how* she says it. Do you find a gap between what her essay claims to value and the values implicit in her stylistic choices? If so, what is the purpose of the gap? Is it possible to theorize about the contact zone in the language of the contact zone?

5. Choose an essay you read earlier in the semester that seems to be the product of a contact zone. Using terms and ideas from "Arts of the Contact Zone," analyze how your essay expresses the encounter of two incommensurate cultures. Then, briefly assess the usefulness of Pratt's model as an interpretive tool. For example, does it help you to understand your essay more deeply? Or is its primary value in giving more precise expression to an understanding you already hold?

The Middle Ground

RICHARD WHITE

Historian Richard White is a leading scholar in the American West, Native American history, and environmental history. A graduate of the University of California, Santa Cruz, White earned his doctorate at the University of Washington where he taught for eight years before joining the faculty at Stanford University. A recipient of a MacArthur Fellowship, White has written five books including *The Middle Ground: Indians, Empires and Republics in the Great Lakes Region, 1650–1815* (1992), a history of the early contact and relations among the Amerindians of the Great Lakes region and the newly arrived Europeans, which was a finalist for the Pulitzer Prize. In the excerpt from this book that follows, White proposes a "middle ground" approach to ethnohistory that he describes as "the area between the historical foreground of European invasion and occupation and the background of Indian defeat and retreat." Rejecting the idea that any group can "have" a culture all by itself, White suggests that cultures are literally created at the moment of contact.

Introduction

Stories of cultural contact and change have been structured by a pervasive dichotomy: absorption by the other or resistance to the other. A fear of lost identity, a Puritan taboo on mixing beliefs and bodies, hangs over the process. Yet what if identity is conceived not as [a] boundary to be maintained but as a nexus of relations and transactions actively engaging a subject? The story or stories of interaction must then be more complex, less linear and teleological.

JAMES CLIFFORD, *The Predicament of Culture*

The history of Indian-white relations has not usually produced complex stories. Indians are the rock, European peoples are the sea, and history seems a constant storm. There have been but two outcomes: The sea wears down and dissolves the rock; or the sea erodes the rock but cannot finally absorb its battered remnant, which endures. The first outcome produces stories of conquest and assimilation; the second produces stories of cultural persistence. The tellers of such stories do not lie. Some Indian groups did disappear; others did persist. But the tellers of such stories miss a larger process and a larger truth. The meeting of sea and continent, like the meeting of whites and Indians, creates as well as destroys. Contact was not a battle of primal forces in which only one could survive. Something new could appear.

As many scholars have noted, American myth, in a sense, retained the wider possibilities that historians have denied American history. Myths have depicted contact as a process of creation and invention. With Daniel Boone and his successors, a "new man" appeared, created by the meeting of whites and Indians, a product of the violent absorption of the Indians by the whites. Myth, however, only partially transcended the stories of conquest and resistance. Only whites changed. Indians disappeared. Whites conquered Indians and made them a sacrifice in what Richard Slotkin called a "regeneration through violence."

The story told in this book steps outside these simpler stories and   3
incorporates them in a more complex and less linear narrative. The book
is about a search for accommodation and common meaning. It is almost
circular in form. It tells how Europeans and Indians met and regarded each
other as alien, as other, as virtually nonhuman. It tells how, over the next
two centuries, they constructed a common, mutually comprehensible world
in the region around the Great Lakes the French called the *pays d'en haut.*
This world was not an Eden, and it should not be romanticized. Indeed, it
could be a violent and sometimes horrifying place. But in this world the
older worlds of the Algonquians and of various Europeans overlapped, and
their mixture created new systems of meaning and of exchange. But finally,
the narrative tells of the breakdown of accommodation and common meanings and the re-creation of the Indians as alien, as exotic, as other.

In this story, the accommodation I speak of is not acculturation under a   4
new name. As commonly used, *acculturation* describes a process in which
one group becomes more like another by borrowing discrete cultural traits.
Acculturation proceeds under conditions in which a dominant group is
largely able to dictate correct behavior to a subordinate group. The process
of accommodation described in this book certainly involves cultural change,
but it takes place on what I call the middle ground. The middle ground is
the place in between: in between cultures, peoples, and in between empires
and the nonstate world of villages. It is a place where many of the North
American subjects and allies of empires lived. It is the area between the historical foreground of European invasion and occupation and the background of Indian defeat and retreat.

On the middle ground diverse peoples adjust their differences through   5
what amounts to a process of creative, and often expedient, misunderstandings. People try to persuade others who are different from themselves by appealing to what they perceive to be the values and practices of those others.
They often misinterpret and distort both the values and the practices of
those they deal with, but from these misunderstandings arise new meanings
and through them new practices—the shared meanings and practices of the
middle ground.

This accommodation took place because for long periods of time in   6
large parts of the colonial world whites could neither dictate to Indians nor
ignore them. Whites needed Indians as allies, as partners in exchange, as
sexual partners, as friendly neighbors. The processes of the middle ground
were not confined to the groups under discussion here. Indeed, a middle
ground undoubtedly began among the Iroquois and the Hurons during a
period earlier than the one this book examines. The middle ground was not
simply a phenomenon of the *pays d'en haut,* but this mutual accommodation had a long and full existence there. The *pays d'en haut,* or upper coun-

try, was the land upriver from Montreal, but strictly speaking it did not begin until the point where voyageurs passed beyond Huronia on the eastern
shore of Lake Huron. The *pays d'en haut* included the lands around Lake
Erie but not those near southern Lake Ontario, which fell within Iroquoia. It
took in all the Great Lakes and stretched beyond them to the Mississippi. In
the seventeenth century, the *pays d'en haut* included the lands bordering
the rivers flowing into the northern Great Lakes and the lands south of the
lakes to the Ohio. As the French fur trade expanded, the *pays d'en haut* expanded with it, but in the frame of this book, the *pays d'en haut* retains its
original boundaries.

I have, with some reluctance, referred to the people living within
the *pays d'en haut* as Algonquians. The term is admittedly problematic. *Algonquian* refers to a language group the domain of whose speakers
stretched far beyond the *pays d'en haut*. And not all the peoples of the
pays d'en haut were Algonquian speakers. The Huron-Petuns were Iro-
quoian as, later, were the offshoots of the Iroquois—the Mingos. The Win-
nebagos were Siouan. I have, however, taken the term as a collective name
for the inhabitants of the *pays d'en haut* because Algonquian speakers were
the dominant group, and because with the onslaught of the Iroquois, the Algonquians forged a collective sense of themselves as people distinct from,
and opposed to, the Five Nations, or the Iroquois proper. Most, and often
all, of these villagers of the *pays d'en haut* were also enemies of the Sioux
and of the peoples south of the Ohio. A collection of individually weak
groups—originally refugees—these villagers created a common identity as
children of Onontio, that is, of the French governor. I have imposed the
name "Algonquian" on them to distinguish them from Onontio's other children, with whom they often had little contact. 7

In writing this history of the *pays d'en haut,* I am practicing the "new Indian history." But as new histories age, they become, in part, new ortho-
doxies while surreptitiously taking on elements of the older history they
sought to displace. This book is "new Indian history" because it places Indian peoples at the center of the scene and seeks to understand the reasons
for their actions. It is only incidentally a study of the staple of the "old history"—white policy toward Indians. But this book is also, and indeed primarily, a study of Indian-white relations, for I found that no sharp
distinctions between Indian and white worlds could be drawn. Different
peoples, to be sure, remained identifiable, but they shaded into each other. 8

For the purposes of this book, many of the conventions of both the new
history and the old are of dubious utility for understanding the world I seek
to explain. I am, for example, describing imperialism, and I am describing
aspects of a world system. But this is an imperialism that weakens at its periphery. At the center are hands on the levers of power, but the cables have, 9

in a sense, been badly frayed or even cut. It is a world system in which minor agents, allies, and even subjects at the periphery often guide the course of empires. This is an odd imperialism and a complicated world system. Similarly, the European writings of the period on Indians—the endless dissertations on the *sauvage* (savage)—become of marginal utility for understanding a world where Europeans living alongside Indians of necessity developed a far more intimate and sophisticated knowledge of Indian peoples than did European savants. What Rousseau thought about Indians matters, but to understand the *pays d'en haut,* it does not matter as much as what the habitants of Vincennes or Kaskaskia thought, or what Onontio, the French governor at Quebec, thought.

The usual conventions of writing about Indians were as unhelpful as unmodified ideas about imperialism, world systems, or savagery. Ethnohistorians have increasingly come to distrust the tribe as a meaningful historical unit, and the *pays d'en haut* was certainly not a place where tribal loyalties controlled human actions. I have used tribal designations throughout this book, but they should be understood largely as ethnic rather than political or even cultural designations. The meaningful political unit in this study is the village, and Indian villages usually contained members of several tribes, just as Anglo-American villages in the backcountry usually contained members of several different ethnic groups.   10

I have also tried to avoid the ethnohistorical technique of upstreaming, although diligent readers will, I am sure, find places where I have indulged in it. Upstreaming is a technique of using ethnologies of present-day or nineteenth-century Indian groups to interpret Indian societies of the past. If assimilationist studies have a built-in bias toward the disappearance of earlier culture, then upstreaming has a bias toward continuity.   11

I have similarly tried to avoid using the term *traditional* to convey any meaning but old. The Indian people I describe in this book have no essential Indianness. They are people who for a long time resolutely fought the European tendency to create them as the other. They asserted a separate identity, but they also claimed a common humanity in a shared world. They lost the fight to establish that claim, and this book is in part the story of that loss. Just as anthropologists and ethnologists have come to recognize how they, through their research, create the other as object, it is time for historians and ethnohistorians to pay more attention to such creations in the past and their own roles in perpetuating and adding to them.   12

The world of the *pays d'en haut,* then, is not a traditional world either seeking to maintain itself unchanged or eroding under the pressure of whites. It is a joint Indian-white creation. Within it well-known European and Anglo-American names appear: the Comte de Frontenac, Sir Jeffrey Amherst, William Johnson, Daniel Boone, George Washington, Benjamin Franklin, and   13

Thomas Jefferson. So, too, do well-known Indian names such as Pontiac and Tecumseh. That so many names significant in the larger American history occur in this story without dominating it indicates that the parameters of American history need readjusting. Colonial and early-American historians have made Indians marginal to the periods they describe. They have treated them as curiosities in a world that Indians also helped create.

This was a world created in the midst of great and far-reaching changes. To readers it may seem a world in perpetual crisis, but this is partially an artifact of the way I tell the story and of the nature of the records. I open with the onslaught of the Iroquois, who may appear initially as a deus ex machina. The wars of the Iroquois proper, or the Five (later Six) Nations, were, however, a result of changes as complicated as any I present here. The reader should not mistake their warfare for "normal" Indian warfare in North America. It, too, was a complex product of European expansion. By devoting a key part of the first portion of the book to the Fox, and by focusing a middle portion of the book on the confrontation along the Ohio, I emphasize the major crises of the alliance. This tactic is necessary because in crises the relations among these people emerged most clearly and also because the crises generated the most records. It should be remembered, however, that during most of the time between 1680 and 1763, the vast majority of Algonquians remained Onontio's loyal children.

The real crisis and the final dissolution of this world came when Indians asked to have the power to force whites onto the middle ground. Then the desire of whites to dictate the terms of accommodation could be given its head. As a consequence, the middle ground eroded. The American Republic succeeded in doing what the French and English empires could not do. Americans invented Indians and forced Indians to live with the consequences of this invention. It is the Americans' success that gives the book its circularity. Europeans met the other, invented a long-lasting and significant common world, but in the end reinvented the Indian as other. Ever since, we have seen the history of the colonial and early republican period through that prism of otherness.

Refugees: a world made of fragments

Human populations construct their cultures in interaction with one another, and not in isolation.

ERIC WOLF, *Europe and the People Without History*

The Frenchmen who traveled into the *pays d'en haut,* as they called the lands beyond Huronia, thought they were discovering new worlds. They were, however, doing something more interesting. They were becoming cocreators of a world in the making. The world that had existed before they arrived was no more. It had been shattered. Only fragments remained. Like a knife scoring a pane of glass, warfare apparently far more brutal than any known previously among these peoples had etched the first fine dangerous lines across the region in the 1640s. Broad cracks had appeared, as epidemics of diseases unknown before in these lands carried off tens of thousands of people. And then, between 1649 and the mid-1660s, Iroquois attacks had fallen like hammer blows across the length and breadth of the lands bordering the Great Lakes and descended down into the Ohio Valley.

The Iroquois desired beaver and the hunting lands that yielded them, and they wanted captives to replace their dead or to atone at the torture stake for their loss. The coupling of the demands of the fur trade with Iroquois cultural imperatives for prisoners and victims created an engine of destruction that broke up the region's peoples. Never again in North America would Indians fight each other on this scale or with this ferocity. Amid the slaughter people fled west. The largely Algonquian-speaking world west of Iroquoia broke up, and the Iroquois pushed the fragments west.[1]

Pierre Esprit Radisson and his brother-in-law Médard Chouart, better known as Des Groseilliers, were the bravest and most experienced of the French who followed the refugees west. In the late 1650s and early 1660s when Iroquois war parties haunted the rivers and portages, they made several voyages, going as far as the Mississippi in search of furs. Sometimes they traveled with Jesuits in search of souls; always they traveled with Huron-Petuns, Ottawas, and other refugees who had come to Montreal for guns and other goods. Their travels took them into a world of horrors. They recorded events that they could not fully decipher.

In 1658 Radisson and Des Groseilliers departed on the voyage which eventually took them to the Mississippi. Their own party contained twenty-nine Frenchmen, who desired "but to do well" for themselves, and six Indians, all or mostly Hurons. As was customary, they formed a convoy, with others going west. Of the French, only Radisson and Des Groseilliers had experience in the western woods. The novice voyageurs advanced carelessly upriver, laughing at the caution of Radisson and Des Groseilliers and calling them women. After three days' travel, a single Iroquois appeared on shore with a hatchet in his hand, signaling the French to land. Even after the

———

1. For recent accounts of the Iroquois wars, see Francis Jennings, *The Ambiguous Iroquois Empire* (New York: W. W. Norton, 1984), 84–113; Daniel Richter, "War and Culture: The Iroquois Experience," *William and Mary Quarterly* 40 (1983): 528–89; and Bruce Trigger, *The Children of Aataentsic: A History of the Huron People to 1660,* 2 vols. (Montreal: McGill-Queens University Press, 1972), 2:767–97, 820–21.

Habit of an Ottawa Indian

Iroquois threw his hatchet away and sat on the ground, the novices feared to approach him. The Iroquois finally rose, advanced into the water, and said (in the fractured English of the Radisson manuscript): "I might have escaped your sight, but that I would have saved you. I fear not death." When the canoes finally closed on him, and their occupants, binding him, took him on board, he began to sing his death song.

When he had finished singing, he made a speech. "Brethren," he began, 20 "the day the sun is favorable to me [it] appointed me to tell you that you are witless, before I die." The enemy, he told them, was all around. The enemy watched the French; it listened to them. It regarded them as easy prey.

"Therefore I was willing to die to give you notice. . . . I would put myself in death's hands to save your lives." He instructed them on how to proceed if they were to save themselves. The "poor wretch," wrote Radisson, "spoke the truth and gave good instructions." The next day, the party met Iroquois warriors on the river. After initial panic, the French and Hurons forted up. They then brought in the prisoner "who soon was dispatched, burned and roasted, and eaten. The Iroquois had so served them." Why the Iroquois warrior had surrendered to save the French, the French never knew. In the end, all the French but Radisson and Des Groseilliers decided to return to the French settlements. The two brothers-in-law, endangered and saved by events they did not understand, continued in company with the Indians. They could explain cruelty; they could not make sense of kindness, if that is what the Iroquois by the river had intended.[2]

The refugee villages in the West welcomed Radisson and Des Groseilliers 21 and those who followed. Those who had no traders eagerly sought them. In the 1660s, the Miami and Mascouten refugees who had settled inland from Green Bay invited Nicolas Perrot and a companion to visit them. When the French landed at the Mascouten village, an old man carrying a red stone calumet—a long-stemmed pipe decorated with feathers—and a woman with a bag containing a pot of cornmeal met them. Behind the old man and the woman came two hundred young men with "headresses of various sort, and their bodies . . . covered with tattooing in black, representing many kinds of figures." The young men carried weapons. The old man first presented the calumet to the French on the side next to the sun. He then presented the calumet to the sun, the earth, and all the directions. He rubbed Perrot's head, back, legs, and feet.

The old man spread a painted buffalo skin and sat Perrot and his com- 22 panion upon it, but when he tried to kindle a fire with flint, he failed. Perrot drew forth his fire steel and immediately made fire. "The old man uttered long exclamations about the iron, which seemed to him a spirit." He lighted the calumet and they smoked. They ate porridge and dried meat and sucked the juice of green corn. They refilled the calumet, and the Mascouten blew smoke into Perrot's face. Perrot felt himself being smoked like drying meat, but he uttered no complaint. When the Mascoutens tried to carry the Frenchmen into the village, however, Perrot stopped them. Men who could shape iron, Perrot said, had the strength to walk.

At the village the ceremonies were renewed. The Miami chiefs, entirely 23 naked except for embroidered moccasins, met them at its edge. They came

---

2. Arthur Adams (ed.), *The Explorations of Pierre Esprit Radisson* (Minneapolis: Ross & Haines, 1967), 80–84; also see Introduction.

singing and holding their calumets. A war chief raised Perrot to his shoulders and carried him into the village where he was housed and feasted.

The next day the French gave a gun and a kettle as presents, and Perrot told the Miamis and Mascoutens that acquaintance with the French would transform their lives. "I am the dawn of that light, which is beginning to appear in your lands, as it were, that which precedes the sun, who will soon shine brightly and will cause you to be born again, as if in another land, where you will find more easily and in greater abundance, all that can be necessary to man." The gun, he said, was for the young men, the kettle was for the old; and he tossed a dozen awls and knives to the women, adding some cloth for their children. The French expected gifts of beaver in return, but it turned out that the Miamis singed their beaver in the fire, burning off their fur, before eating them. They had no beaver skins.   24

A week later a leading chief of the Miamis gave a feast to thank the sun for having brought Perrot to them. He made the feast in honor of a medicine bundle which contained "all that inspires their dreams." Perrot did not approve of the altar. He told the chief that he adored a God who would not let him eat food sacrificed to evil spirits or the skins of animals. The Miamis were greatly surprised. They asked Perrot if he would eat if they closed the bundles. He agreed. The chief then asked to be consecrated to Perrot's spirit "whom he would . . . prefer to his own who had not taught them to make hatchets, kettles, and all else that men needed." Perrot departed leaving the Miamis and Mascoutens to make sense of him while he tried to make sense of them. Neither Perrot nor the Indians were sure of the intentions of the other. Both sides, however, knew what they wanted from each other.[3]   25

Refugees were never quite sure what to make of Catholic priests. On August 8, 1665, Father Claude-Jean Allouez embarked from Three Rivers with six other Frenchmen and four hundred Indians who had come to Three Rivers to trade. The Indians objected to taking Allouez. They thought he was a witch. They thought the baptism that he administered caused children to die. A headman threatened to abandon the Jesuit on an island if he persisted in following them. When Allouez's canoe broke, the Hurons reluctantly agreed to carry him. They changed their minds the next day, however, and Allouez and his companions had to repair the broken canoe and follow as best they could.   26

Eventually the Indians relented again and agreed to take all the French except for Allouez. He, they said, did not have the skill to paddle nor the strength to carry loads on a portage. Only after Allouez prayed for divine   27

---

3. Claude Charles Le Roy, Sieur de Bacqueville de La Potherie, *History of the Savage Peoples Who Are the Allies of New France,* in Blair (ed.), *Indian Tribes,* 1:322–32. Hereafter cited as La Potherie, *History.*

assistance did the Indians consent to take him, but he became the butt of their jokes, and they stole every item of his wardrobe that they could lay hands on.

Allouez endured the usual hardships of the dangerous passage to the lakes, and he created other hardships for himself. The Indians ate lichen soup; they once ate a rancid deer that had been dead for five days. When the Indians were careless with the powder they were transporting, it blew up and badly burned four warriors. Allouez interfered with the shaman's attempt to cure a burned man. Furious, the shaman smashed the canoe that carried Allouez. 28

In September Allouez reached the mission of Saint Espirit at Chequamegon. He discovered that the Indians there had abandoned their belief that baptism brought death. They now thought the rite essential for a long life. Not all Indians proved to be so taken with Christian ceremonies. Allouez preached to more than ten visiting nations only to be often greeted with contempt, mockery, scorn, and importunity.[4] 29

Allouez only tasted the hardships the northern Great Lakes offered; Radisson and Des Groseilliers drank more deeply of them. In 1661–62 they wintered with a band of Huron-Petuns, a farming people driven to the inhospitable shores of Lake Superior. The Huron-Petun men were not as skilled hunters as the surrounding Crees, Ojibwas, or even the Ottawas. They had few food reserves. Snow usually aided hunters, but this winter the snow fell in such quantities and was of such a lightness that the hunters could not go forth. Even though they made snowshoes six feet long and a foot and a half wide, the snow would not support them. Those who did struggle out made such noise floundering in the snow that the animals heard them at a distance and fled. Famine overtook the Huron-Petuns. 30

Apparently (the broken English of Radisson's manuscript is unclear), the already hungry Huron-Petuns were joined by 150 Ottawa families who had even less food than the Hurons. They, too, had to have their share, although Radisson regarded them as the "cursedest, unablest, the unfamous, and cowardliest people I have ever seen amongst four score nations." The Indians ate their dogs. They retraced their steps to earlier kills to eat the bones and entrails that they had discarded. The men ate their bowstrings, lacking strength to draw the bow. Starving, the women became barren. The famished died with a noise that made the survivors' hair stand on end. The living scraped bark from trees, dried it over fires, and made it into a meal. They ate skins; they boiled and ate skin clothing. They ate the beaver skins their children had used as diapers, although the children had "beshit them above a hundred times." Five hundred died before the weather changed. Then the 31

---

4. *JR*, 1666–67, 50:249–99.

snow crusted, and the deer, breaking through the crust, became trapped. Hunters could walk up to them and cut their throats with knives.[5]

Four years after his difficult passage into the *pays d'en haut,* the Fox greeted Father Allouez as a manitou, or an other-than-human person. The previous winter, Senecas had attacked a Fox village while the warriors were away hunting. The Senecas had slaughtered seventy women and children and the few men in the village. They had led thirty more women into captivity. Allouez gave the Fox presents to dry the tears caused by the Iroquois attack. He then explained to them "the principal Articles of our Faith, and made known the Law and the Commandments of God." [32]

Later, in private, a Fox told Allouez that his ancestor had come from heaven, and that "he had preached the unity and Sovereignty of a God who had made all the other Gods; that he had assured them that he would go to Heaven after his death, where he should die no more; and that his body would not be found in the place where it had been buried." And this, indeed, the Fox said, had happened. The man informed Allouez that he was dismissing all his wives but one and was resolved to pray and obey God. [33]

As for the other Fox, Allouez wrote his superior, "Oh, my God! What ideas and ways contrary to the Gospel these poor people have, and how much need there is of very powerful grace to conquer their hearts." They accepted the unity and sovereignty of God, but "for the rest, they have not a word to say." Allouez credited their resistance to an earlier visit by "two traders in Beaver-skins." If these French "had behaved as they ought, I would have had less trouble giving these poor people other ideas of the whole French nation." The Fox asked Allouez to stay near them, to teach them to pray to "the great Manitou." Allouez could protect them from their enemies and intercede with the Iroquois to restore their relatives. Allouez postponed his answer, telling them in the meantime to obey the true God, "who alone could procure them what they asked for and more." That evening four Miami warriors brought more immediate consolation. They gave three Iroquois scalps and a half-smoked arm to the relatives of the dead.[6] [34]

A few days later, entering the village of the Mascoutens, Allouez received the same treatment earlier accorded Perrot. They summarized in their requests to him the horrors of the period: [35]

> This is well, black Gown, that thou comest to visit us. Take pity on us; thou art a Manitou; we give thee tobacco to smoke. The Nadouessious and the Iroquois are eating us; take pity on us. We are often ill, our children are dying, we are

---

5. Adams (ed.), *Radisson,* 131–33.
6. *JR* 54:219–27.

hungry. Hear me, Manitou; I give thee tobacco to smoke. Let the earth give us corn, and the rivers yield us fish; let not disease kill us any more, or famine treat us any longer so harshly!

Toward evening, Allouez gathered the Mascoutens together. He was not, he told them, the manitou who was master of their lives. He was the manitou's creature. The Mascoutens, he reported, only "half understood" him, but they "showed themselves well satisfied to have a knowledge of the true God."[7]   36

On his way to the Illinois country in the late winter of 1677, Father Allouez passed near the Potawatomi villages around Green Bay. He learned that a young man whom he had baptized had been killed by a bear in a particularly gruesome manner. The bear had "torn off his scalp, disembowled him, and dismembered his entire body." The bear had, in short, treated the young man as a warrior treated the body of an enemy. Allouez, being acquainted with the hunter's parents, detoured to console them. He prayed with the parents, comforting the distressed mother as best he could.   37

Afterward, "by way of avenging . . . this death," the relatives and friends of the dead man declared war on the bears. They killed more than five hundred of them, giving the Jesuits a share of the meat and skins because, they said, "God delivered the bears into their hands as satisfaction for the death of the Young man who had been so cruelly treated by one of their nation."[8]   38

Working with the Text

1. What does Richard White mean by the term "middle ground"? Who creates the middle ground? Under what circumstances? To what ends? What kinds of issues are dealt with on the middle ground? Why are more formal issues easier for us to perceive?

2. Describe the process through which the middle ground emerges. Why is the first stage of the process "at once the most noticed and the least interesting"? Is there a covert critique of other models of cultural contact in this observation? In the overall dynamism of White's model?

3. To illustrate his scheme, White recounts an episode in which a Huron chief devises a prophecy with both Christian and Indian elements, in the hope of securing a complicated peace with the French and the Iroquois. The chief, known as the Baron, failed to achieve his ends, however, as Christian culture denied him the authority to communicate

---

7. *Ibid.,* 229–31.
8. *JR* 60:151–53.

revealed truth. Why does White offer the Baron's *unsuccessful* hybrid as a prominent example of the "middle ground"?

4. White's model finds considerable value in the products of cultural misprision, in the mistakes people make when seeking to understand an unfamiliar culture. Think back to a time when you misunderstood a feature of an alien culture (a new country, a new region, a new clique in school). Describe your mistake, then try to discover its hidden value, the "crazy wisdom" it may have hidden within.

5. Choose an essay you read earlier in the semester that seems interested in the middle ground, as White has described it. (Those who worked with the previous selection, "Arts of the Contact Zone" may wish to return to the essay they chose in response to the fifth question.) Using White's terms and ideas, analyze how your essay expresses—or conspicuously fails to express—the middle ground. Then, briefly assess the usefulness of White's model as an interpretive tool. For example, does it help you to understand your essay more deeply? Or is its primary value in giving more precise expression to an understanding you already hold? How does it compare to Pratt's model as an analytical tool?

A Key into the Language of America

ROGER WILLIAMS

Puritan Roger Williams (1603–83) helped found the colony of Providence on the principles of religious toleration and the strict separation of church and state, principles that animated his position that European claims on native land were morally unfounded because all men—heathen and Christian—had the same secular rights. Williams's regard for native languages and cultures is exceptional among Puritans. Throughout his life he advocated for Indian rights and religious principles. He wrote several polemical tracts; the most famous, *The Bloody Tenant of Persecution,* is a plea for liberty of human conscience as a human right. The following selection from his first work, *A Key into the Language of America,* is notable for its effort to understand the native point of view. A promotional tract by design, it asserts that colonization should proceed through land purchases and treaties. The following excerpt introduces the treatise by comparing the names the

English give the Native Americans with the names they give themselves. Williams depicts the encounter of European and native as an ironic meeting of degenerate civilization and barbaric virtue.

To my Deare and Welbeloved *Friends* and *Countreymen, in* old and new *England*

I present you with a *Key;* I have not heard of the like, yet framed, since it   1
pleased God to bring that mighty *Continent of America* to light: Others of
my Countrey-men have often, and excellently, and lately written of the *Countrey* (and none that I know beyond the goodnesse and worth of it.) This *Key,*
respects the *Native Language* of it, and happily may unlocke some *Rarities*
concerning the *Natives* themselves, not yet discovered.

I drew the *Materialls* in a rude lumpe at Sea, as a private *helpe* to my   2
owne memory, that I might not by my present absence *lightly lose* what I
had so *dearely bought* in some few years *hardship,* and *charges* among the
Barbarians; yet being reminded by some, what pitie it were to bury those
Materialls in my *Grave* at land or Sea; and withall, remembring how oft I
have been importun'd by *worthy friends,* of all sorts, to afford them some
helps this way.

I resolved (by the assistance of the *most High*) to cast those *Materialls*   3
into this *Key, pleasant* and *profitable* for *All,* but speally for my *friends* residing in those parts:

A little *Key* may open a *Box,* where lies a *bunch* of *Keyes.*   4

With this I have entred into the secrets of those *Countries,* where ever   5
English dwel about two hundred miles, betweene the *French* and *Dutch*
Plantations; for want of this, I know what grosse *mis-takes* my selfe and others have run into.

There is a mixture of this *Language North* and *South,* from the place of   6
my abode, about six hundred miles; yet within the two hundred miles
(aforementioned) their *Dialects* doe exceedingly differ; yet not so, but
(within that compasse) a man may, by this *helpe,* converse with *thousands*
of *Natives* all over the *Countrey:* and by such converse it may please the *Father of Mercies* to spread *civilitie,* (and in his owne most holy season) *Christianitie;* for *one Candle* will light *ten thousand,* and it may please *God*
to blesse a *little Leaven* to season the *mightie Lump* of those *Peoples* and
Territories.

It is expected, that having had so much converse with these *natives,* I   7
should write some litle of them.

Concerning them (a little to gratifie expectation) I shall touch upon   8
foure Heads:

First, by what *Names* they are distinguished.   9

Secondly, Their *Originall* and *Descent.*   10

Thirdly, their *Religion, Manners, Customes,* &c.   11

Fourthly, That great *Point* of their *Conversion.*   12

To the first, their *Names* are of two sorts: 13

First, those of the *English giving:* as *Natives, Salvages Indians, Wild-*   14
men, (so the *Dutch* call them *Wilden*) *Abergeny men, Pagans, Barbarians,*
Heathen.

Secondly, their *Names,* which they give themselves.   15

I cannot observe, that they ever had (before the comming of the *Eng-*   16
lish, French or *Dutch* amongst them) any *Names* to difference *themselves*
from strangers, for they knew none; but two sorts of *names* they had, and
have amongst *themselves.*

First, *generall,* belonging to all *Natives,* as *Ninnuock, Ninnimissinnû-*   17
wock, Eniskeetompaûwog, which signifies *Men, Folke,* or *People.*

Secondly, particular *names,* peculiar to severall *Nations,* of them amongst   18
themselves, as, *Nanhigganĕuck, Massachusêuck, Cawasumsêuck, Cowwesĕuck,*
Quintikóock, Quinnipiĕuck, Pequttóog, &c.

They have often asked mee, why we call them *Indians Natives,* &c. And   19
understanding the reason, they will call themselves *Indians,* in opposition
to *English,* &c.

For the second Head proposed, their *Originall* and *Descent.*   20

From *Adam* and *Noah* that they spring, it is granted on all hands.   21

But for their later *Descent,* and whence they came into those parts, it   22
seemes as hard to finde, as to finde the *Wellhead* of some fresh *Streame,*
which running many miles out of the *Countrey* to the salt *Ocean,* hath
met with many mixing *Streames* by the way. They say themselves, that they
have *sprung* and *growne* up in that very place, like the very *trees* of the
Wildernesse.

They say that their *Great God Cawtantowwit* created those parts, as I ob-   23
served in the Chapter of their *Religion.* They have no *Clothes, Bookes,* nor
Letters, and conceive their *Fathers* never had; and therefore they are easily
perswaded that the *God* that made *English* men is a greater *God,* because
Hee hath so richly endowed the *English* above *themselves:* But when they
heare that about sixteen hundred yeeres agoe, *England* and the *Inhabitants*
thereof were like unto *themselves,* and since have received from *God,*
Clothes, Bookes, &c. they are greatly affected with a secret hope concerning
themselves.

Wise and *Judicious* men, with whom I have discoursed, maintaine their   24
Originall to be *Northward* from *Tartaria:* and at my now taking ship, at the
Dutch Plantation, it pleased the *Dutch* Governour, (in some discourse with
mee about the *Natives*), to draw their *Line* from *Iceland,* because the name

Sackmakan (the name for an *Indian* Prince, about the *Dutch*) is the name for a *Prince* in *Iceland.*

Other opinions I could number up: under favour I shall present (not   25
mine opinion, but) my *Observations* to the judgement of the Wise.

First, others (and my selfe) have conceived some of their words to hold   26
affinitie with the *Hebrew.*

Secondly, they constantly *annoint* their *heads* as the *Jewes* did.   27

Thirdly, they give *Dowries* for their wives, as the *Jewes* did.   28

Fourthly (and which I have not so observed amongst other *Nations* as   29
amongst the *Jewes,* and *these:*) they constantly separate their Women (during the time of their monthly sicknesse) in a little house along by themselves foure or five dayes, and hold it an *Irreligious thing* for either *Father* or *Husband* or any *Male* to come neere them.

They have often asked me if it bee so with *women* of other *Nations,* and   30
whether they are so *separated:* and for their practice they plead *Nature* and *Tradition.* Yet againe I have found a greater *Affinity* of their Language with the *Greek* Tongue.

2. As the *Greekes* and other *Nations,* and our selves call the seven *Star-*   31
res (or Charles Waine the *Beare,*) so doe they *Mosk* or *Paukunnawaw* the Beare.

3. They have many strange Relations of one *Wétucks,* a man that wrought   32
great *Miracles* amongst them, and *walking upon the waters,* &c. with some kind of broken Resemblance to the *Sonne of God.*

Lastly, it is famous that the *Sowwest* (*Sowaniu*) is the great Subject of   33
their discourse. From thence their *Traditions.* There they say (at the *South-west*) is the Court of their *great God Cautántouwit:* At the *South-west* are their *Forefathers* soules; *to the South-west* they goe themselves when they dye; From the *South-west* came their *Corne,* and Beanes out of their Great *God Cautántowwits* field: and indeed the further *Northward* and *Westward* from us their Corne will not grow, but to the *South-ward* better and better. I dare not conjecture in these *Uncertainties,* I believe they are *lost,* and yet hope (in the Lords holy season) some of the wildest of them shall be found to share in the blood of the Son of God. To the third *Head,* concerning their *Religion, Customes, Manners* &c. I shall here say nothing, because in those 32. Chapters of the whole Book, I have briefly touched those of all sorts, from their *Birth* to their *Burialls,* and have endeavored (as the Nature of the worke would give way) to bring some short *Observations* and *Applications* home to *Europe* from *America.*

Therefore fourthly, to that great Point of their *Conversion* so much to bee   34
longed for, and by all *New-English* so much pretended, and I hope in Truth.

For my selfe I have uprightly laboured to suite my endeavours to my   35
pretences; and of later times (out of desire to attaine their Language) I have

run through varieties of *Intercourses* with them Day and Night, Summer and Winter, by Land and Sea, particular passages tending to this, I have related divers, in the Chapter of their Religion.

Many solemne discourses I have had with all *sorts of Nations* of them,   36
from one end of the Countrey to another (so farre as opportunity, and the little Language I have could reach.)

I know there is no small *preparation* in the hearts of Multitudes of them.   37
I know their many solemne *Confessions* to my self, and one to another of their lost *wandring Conditions.*

I know strong *Convictions* upon the *Consciences* of many of them, and   38
their desires uttred that way.

I know not with how little *Knowledge* and *Grace* of Christ the Lord may   39
save, and therefore neither will *despaire,* nor *report* much.

But since it hath pleased some of my Worthy *Country-men* to mention   40
(of late in print) *V Vequash,* the *Pequt Captaine,* I shall be bold so farre to second their *Relations,* as to relate mine owne Hopes of Him (though I dare not be so confident as others.

Two dayes before his Death, as I past up to *Qunnihticut* River, it   41
pleased my worthy friend Mr. *Fenwick* whom I visited at his house in *Say-Brook* Fort at the mouth of that River) to tell me that my old friend *V Vequash* lay very sick: I desired to see him, and Himselfe was pleased to be my Guide two mile where *V Vequash* lay.

Amongst other discourse concerning his *sicknesse* and *Death* (in which   42
hee freely bequeathed his son to Mr. *Fenwick*) I closed with him concerning his *Soule:* Hee told me that some two or three yeare before he had lodged at my House, where I acquainted him with the *Condition* of *all mankind,* & his *Own* in particular, how *God* created *Man* and *All things:* how *Man* fell from *God,* and of his present *Enmity* against *God,* and the *wrath of God* against *Him* untill *Repentance:* said he *your words were never out of my heart to this present;* and said hee *me much pray to Jesus Christ:* I told him so did many *English, French,* and *Dutch,* who had never turned to *God,* nor loved Him: He replyed in broken English: *me so big naughty Heart, me heart all one stone! Savory expressions* using to breath *from compunct and broken Hearts,* and a sence of *inward hardnesse* and *unbrokennesse.* I had many discourses with him in his Life, but this was the summe of our last parting untill our generall meeting.

Now because this is the great Inquiry of all men what *Indians* have   43
been converted? what have the *English* done in those parts? what hopes of the *Indians* receiving the Knowledge of Christ!

And because to this Question, some put an edge from the boast of the   44
Jesuits in *Canada* and *Maryland,* and especially from the wonderfull conversions made by the Spaniards and Portugalls in the *West-Indies,* besides

what I have here written, as also, beside what I have observed in the Chapter of their Religion! I shall further present you with a briefe Additionall discourse concerning this Great Point, being comfortably perswaded that that Father of Spirits, who was graciously pleased to perswade *Japhet* (the Gentiles) to dwell in the Tents of *Shem* (the Jewes) will in his holy season (I hope approaching) perswade, these Gentiles of *America* to partake of the mercies of *Europe,* and then shall bee fulfilled what is written, by the Prophet *Malachi,* from the rising of the Sunne in (*Europe*) to the going down of the same (in *America*) my Name shall be great among the Gentiles.) So I desire to hope and pray,

Your unworthy Country-man
Roger Williams

DIRECTIONS FOR THE USE OF THE LANGUAGE

1. A Dictionary *or* Grammer *way* I *had consideration of but purposely avoided, as not so accommodate to the Benefit of all, as* I *hope this Forme is.*

2. A Dialogue *also I had thoughts of, but avoided for brevities sake, and yet (with no small paines) I have so framed every Chapter and the matter of it, as I may call it an Implicite Dialogue.*

3. *It is framed chiefly after the* Narrogánset *Dialect, because most spoken in the Countrey, and yet (with attending to the variation of peoples and Dialects) it will be of great use in all parts of the Countrey.*

4. *Whatever your occasion bee either of Travell, Discourse, Trading & c. turne to the Table which will direct you to the Proper Chapter.*

5. *Because the Life of all Language is in the Pronuntiation, I have been at the painies and charges to Cause the Accents, Tones, or sounds to be affixed, (which some understand, according to the* Grecke *Language, Acutes, Graves, Circumflexes) for example, in the second leafe*[17] *in the word* Ewò *He: the sound or Tone must not be put on* E, *but* wò *where the grave Accent is.*

   In the same leafe, in the word Ascowequássin, *the sound must not be on any of the Syllables, but on* quáss, *where the Acute or sharp sound is.*

   In the same leafe in the word Anspaumpmaûntam, *the sound must not be on any other syllable but* Maûn, *where the* Circumflex *or long sounding Accent is.*

6. *The* English *for every* Indian *word or phrase stands in a straight line directly against the* Indian: *yet sometimes there are two words for the same thing (for their Language is exceeding copious, and they have five*

or six words sometimes for one thing) and then the English *stands against them both: for example in the second leafe,*

Cowáunckamish & Cuckquénamish.   *I pray your Favour.*

Chapter XX

OF THEIR NAKEDNESSE *AND* CLOTHING

Paûskesu.	*Naked.*
Pauskesítchick	*Naked men and women.*
Nippóskiss.	*I am naked.*

They have a two-fold nakednesse: 45

First ordinary and constant, when although they have a Beasts skin, or   46
an English mantle on, yet that covers ordinarily but their hinder parts and all
the foreparts from top to toe, (except their secret parts, covered with a little
Apron, after the patterne of their and our first Parents) I say all else open
and naked.

Their male children goe starke naked, and have no Apron untill they   47
come to ten or twelve yeeres of age; their Female they, in a modest blush
cover with a little Apron of an hand breadth from their very birth.

Their second nakednesse is when their men often abroad and both men   48
and women within doòres, leave off their beasts skin, or English cloth, and
so (excepting their little Apron) are wholly naked; yet but few of the women
but will keepe their skin or cloth (though loose) or neare to them ready to
gather it up about them.

Costume hath used their minds and bodies to it, and in such a freedom   49
from any wantonnesse, that I have never seen that wantonnesse amongst
them, as, (with griefe) I have heard of in *Europe.*

Nippóskenitch	*I am rob'd of my coat.*
Nippóskenick ewò.	*He takes away my Coat.*
Acòh.	*Their Deere skin.*
Tummóckquashunck.	*A Beavers coat.*
Nkéquashunck.	*An Otters coat.*
Mohéwonck.	*A Rakoone-skin coat.*
Natóquashunck.	*A Wolves-skin coat.*
Mishannéquashunck.	*A Squirrill-skin coat.*

Obs. Our English clothes are so strange unto them, and their bodies in-   50
ured so to indure the weather, that when (upon gift &c.) some of them have
had *English* cloathes, yet in a showre of raine, I have seen them rather expose their skins to the wet then their cloaths, and therefore pull them off,
and keep them drie.

Obs. While they are amongst the *English* they keep on the *English* ap-   51
parell, but pull of all as soone as they come againe into their owne Houses,
and Company.

GENERALL *OBSERVATIONS* OF THEIR GARMENTS

How deep are the purposes and Councells, of God? what should bee the rea-   52
son of this mighty difference of One mans children that all the Sones of men
on this side the way (in *Europe, Asia* and *Africa,* should have such plenteous
clothing for Body, for Soule! and the rest of *Adams* sonnes and Daughters on
the other side, or *America* (some thinke as big as the other three,) should
neither have nor desire clothing for their naked Soules, or Bodies.

More particular:

O what a Tyrant's Custome long
　　How doe men make a tush,
At what's in use, though ne're so fowle:
　　Without once shame or blush?

Many thousand proper Men and Women,
　　I have seen met in one place:
Almost all naked, yet not one,
　　Thought want of clothes disgrace.

Israell was naked, wearing cloathes!
　　The best clad *English-man,*
Not cloth'd with Christ, more naked is:
　　Then naked *Indian.*

from Chapter XXI

OF RELIGION, THE SOULE, &C.

Manìt-manittó-wock.   *God, Gods.*

Obs. He that questions whether God made the World, the *Indians* will   53
teach him. I must acknowledge I have received in my converse with them
many Confirmations of those two great points, *Heb.* 11. 6. *viz:*

1. That God is.

2. That hee is a rewarder of all them that diligently seek him.

They will generally confesse that God made all: but then in speciall, al-   54
though they deny not that *English-mans* God made *English* Men, and the
Heavens and Earth there! yet their Gods made them and the Heaven, and
Earth where they dwell.

Nummusquaunamúckqun manìt.   *God is angry with me?*

Obs. I have heard a Poore *Indian* lamenting the losse of a child at break   55
of day, call up his Wife and children, and all about him to Lamentation, and
with abundance of teares cry out! O God thou host taken away my child!
thou art angry with me: O turne thine anger from me, and spare the rest of
my children.

If they receive any good in hunting, fishing, Harvest &c. they acknowl-   56
edge God in it.

Yea, if it be but an ordinary accident, a fall, &c. they will say God was an-   57
gry and did it, *musquántum manit* God is angry. But herein is their Misery.

First they branch their God-head into many Gods.   58

Secondly, attribute it to Creatures.   59

First, many Gods: they have given me the Names of thirty seven, which   60
I have, all which in their solemne Worships they invocate: as

Kautántowwit the great *South-West* God, to whose

House all soules goe, and from whom came their Corne, Beanes, as   61
they say.

Wompanànd.	*The Easterne God.*
Chekesuwànd.	*The Westerne God.*
Wunnanaméanit.	*The Northerne God.*
Sowwanànd.	*The Southerne God.*
Wetuómanit.	*The house God.*

Even as the Papists have their He and Shee Saint Protectors as *St. George,*   62
St. Patrick, St. Denis, Virgin *Mary,* &c.

Squáuanit.	*The Womans God.*
Muckquachuckquànd.	*The Childrens God.*

Obs. I was once with a *Native* dying of a wound, given him by some   63
murtherous *English* (who rob'd him and run him through with a Rapier,
from whom in the heat of his wound, he at present escaped from them,
but dying of his wound, they suffered Death at new *Plymouth,* in *New-*
England, this *Native* dying call'd much upon *Muckquachuckquànd,* which
of other *Natives* I understood (as they believed) had appeared to the dying
young man, many yeares before, and bid him when ever he was in distresse
call upon him.

Secondly, as they have many of these famed Deities: so worship they   64
the Creatures in whom they conceive doth rest some Deitie:

Keesuckquànd.	*The Sun God.*
Nanepaûshat.	*The Moone God.*
Pawnpágussit.	*The Sea.*
Yotáanit.	*The Fire God.*

Supposing that Deities be in these, &c.   65

When I have argued with them about their Fire-God: can it say they be,   66
but this fire must be a God, or Divine power, that out of a stone will arise in
a Sparke, and when a Poore naked *Indian* is ready to starve with cold in the
House, and especially in the Woods, often saves his life, doth dresse all our
Food for us, and if it be angry will burne the House about us, yea if a spark
fall into the drie wood, burnes up the Country, (though this burning of the
Wood to them they count a Benefit both for destroying of vermin, and keeping downe the Weeds and thickets?)

Præsentem narrat quælibet herba Deum,

Every little Grasse doth tell,
  The sons of Men, there God doth dwell.

Besides there is a generall Custume amongst them, at the apprehension   67
of any Excellency in Men, Women, Birds, Beasts, Fish, &c. to cry out *Manittóo,* that is, it is a God, as thus if they see one man excell others in Wisdome,
Valour, strength, Activity &c. they cry out *Manittóo* A God: and therefore
when they talke amongst themselves of the *English* ships, and great buildings, of the plowing of their Fields, and especially of Bookes and Letters,
they will end thus: *Manittôwock* They are Gods: *Cummanittôo,* you are a
God, &c. A strong Conviction naturall in the soule of man, that God is; filling all things, and places, and that all Excellencies dwell in God, and proceed from him, and that they only are blessed who have that Jehovah their
portion.

Nickómmo.   *A Feast or Dance.*

Of this Feast they have publike, and private and that of two sorts.   68
First in sicknesse, or Drouth, or Waste, or Famine.   69
Secondly, after Harvest, after hunting, when they enjoy a caulme of   70
Peace, Health, Plenty, Prosperity, then *Nickómo* a Feast, especially in Win-
ter, for then (as the Turke saith of the Christian, rather the Antichristian,)
they run mad once a yeare) in their kind of Christmas feasting.

Powwáw.   *A Priest.*
Powwaûog.   *Priests.*

Obs. These doe begin and order their service, and Invocation of their   71
Gods, and all the people follow, and joyne interchangeably in a laborious
bodily service, unto sweating, especially of the Priest, who spends himselfe
in strange Antick Gestures, and Actions even unto fainting.

In sicknesse the Priest comes close to the sick person, and performes   72
many strange Actions about him, and threaten and conjures out the sick-

nesse. They conceive that there are many Gods or divine Powers within the body of a man: In his pulse, his heart, his Lungs, &c.

I confesse to have most of these their customes by their owne Relation, for after once being in their Houses and beholding what their Worship was, I durst never bee an eye witnesse, Spectatour, or looker on, least I should have been partaker of Sathans Inventions and Worships, contrary to *Ephes.* 5. 14.

| Nanouwétea. | *An over-Seer and Orderer of their Worship.* |
| Neen nanowwúnnemun. | *I will order or oversee.* |

They have an exact forme of King, Priest, and Prophet, as was in Israel typicall of old in that holy Land of *Canaan,* and as the Lord Jesus ordained in his spirituall Land of *Canaan* his Church throughout the whole World: their Kings or Governours called *Sachimaüog,* Kings, and *Atauskowaüg* Rulers doe govern: Their Priests, performe and manage their Worship: Their wise men and old men of which number the Priests are also,) whom they call *Taupowaüog* they make solemne speeches and Orations, or Lectures to them, concerning Religion, Peace, or Warre and all things.

| Nowemaúsitteem. | *I give away at the Worship.* |

He or she that makes this *Nickòmmo* Feast or Dance, besides the Feasting of sometimes twenty, fifty, an hundreth, yea I have seene neere a thousand persons at one of these Feasts) they give I say a great quantity of money, and all sort of their goods (according to and sometimes beyond their Estate) in severall small parcells of goods, or money, to the value of eighteen pence, two Shillings, or thereabouts to one person: and that person that receives this Gift, upon the receiving of it goes out, and hollowes thrice for the health and prosperity of the Party that gave it, the Mr. or Mistris of the Feast.

Nowemacaûnash.	*Ile give these things.*
Nitteaûguash.	*My money.*
Nummaumachíuwash.	*My goods.*

Obs. By this Feasting and Gifts, the Divell drives on their worships pleasantly (as he doth all false worships, by such plausible Earthly Arguments of uniformities, universalities, Antiquities, Immunities, Dignities, Rewards, unto submitters, and the contrary to Refusers) so that they run farre and neere and aske

Awaun. Nákommit?	*Who makes a Feast?*
Nkekinneawaûmen.	*I goe to the Feast.*
Kekineawaûi.	*He is gone to the Feast.*

They have a modest Religious perswasion not to disturb any man, either   77
themselves *English, Dutch,* or any in their Conscience, and worship, and
therefore say:

Aquiewopwaŭwash.	*Peace, hold your peace.*
Aquiewopwaŭwock.	
Peeyaúntam.	*He is at Prayer.*
Peeyaúntamwock.	*They are praying.*
Cowwéwonck.	*The Soule,*

Derived from *Cowwene* to sleep, because say they, it workes and operates   78
when the body sleepes. *Míchachunck* the soule, in a higher notion, which
is of affinity, with a word signifying a looking glasse, or cleere resemblance,
so that it hath its name from a cleere sight or discerning, which indeed
seemes very well to suit with the nature of it.

Wuhóck	*The Body.*
Nohòck: cohòck.	*My body, your body.*
Awaunkeesitteoúwincohòck:	*Who made you?*
Tunna-awwa com-	*Whether goes your soule*
mítchichunck-kitonck-quèan?	*when you die?*
An. Sowánakitaŭwaw.	*It goes to the South-West.*

Obs. They beleive that the soules of Men and Women goe to the Sou-   79
west, their great and good men and Women to *Cautàntouwit* his House,
where they have hopes (as the Turkes have of carnall Joyes): Murtherers
thieves and Lyers, their Soules (say they) wander restlesse abroad.

Now because this Book (by Gods good providence) may come into the   80
hand of many fearing God, who may also have many an opportunity of oc-
casionall discourse with some of these their wild brethren and Sisters, and
may speake a word for their and our glorious Maker, which may also prove
some preparatory Mercy to their Soules: I shall propose some proper expressions concerning the Creation of the World, and mans Estate, and in
particular theirs also, which from my selfe many hundreths of times, great
numbers of them have heard with great delight, and great convictions: which
who knowes (in Gods holy season) may rise to the exalting of the Lord Jesus
Christ in their conversion, and salvation?

Nétop Kunnatótemous.	*Friend, I will aske you a Question.*
Natótema:	*Speake on.*
Tocketunnántum?	*What thinke you?*
Awaun Keesiteoûwin Kéesuck?	*Who made the Heavens?*
Aûke Wechêkom?	*The Earth, the Sea?*
Mittauke.	*The World.*

Some will answer *Tattá* I cannot tell, some will answer *Manittôwock* the 81
Gods.

Tasuóg, Maníttowock.	*How many Gods bee there?*
Maunaûog Mishaúnawock.	*Many, great many.*
Nétop machàge.	*Friend, not so.*
Pausuck naúnt manìt.	*There is onely one God.*
Cuppíssittone.	*You are mistaken.*
Cowauwaúnemun.	*You are out of the way.*

A phrase which much pleaseth them, being proper for their wandring in 82
the woods, and similitudes greatly please them.

Kukkakótemous, wâchit-quáshouwe.   *I will tell you, presently.*

Obs. After I had (as farre as my language would reach) discoursed (upon 83
a time) before the chiefe *Sachim* or *Prince* of the Countrey, with his *Arch-priests,* and many other in a full Assembly; and being night, wearied with
travell and discourse, I lay downe to rest; and before I slept, I heard this pas-
sage:

A *Qunnihticut* Indian (who had heard our discourse) told the *Sachim* 84
Miantunnómu, that soules went [not] up to Heaven, or downe to Hell; For,
saith he, Our fathers have told us, that our soules goe to the *Southwest.*

The *Sachim* answered, But how doe you know your selfe, that your 85
soules goe to the *Southwest,* did you ever see a soule goe thither?

The Native replyed; when did he (naming my selfe) see a soule goe to 86
Heaven or Hell?

The *Sachim* againe replied: He hath books and writings, and one which 87
God himselfe made, concerning mens soules, and therefore may well know
more than wee that have none, but take all upon trust from our forefathers.

The said *Sachim,* and the chiefe of his people, discoursed by them- 88
selves, of keeping the Englishmans day of worship, which I could easily
have brought the Countrey to, but that I was perswaded, and am, that Gods
way is first to turne a soule from it's Idolls, both of heart, worship, and conversation, before it is capable of worship, to the true and living God, according to I *Thes.* 1. 9. You turned to God from Idolls to serve or worship
the living and true God. As also, that the two first Principles and Foundations of true Religion or Worship of the true God in Christ, are Repentance
from dead workes, and Faith towards God before the Doctrine of Baptisme
or washing and the laying on of hands, which containe the Ordinances and
Practises of worship; the want of which, I conceive, is the bane of million of
soules in England, and all other Nations professing to be Christian Nations
who are brought by publique authority to Baptisme and fellowship with

God in Ordinances of worship, before the saving worke of Repentance, and a true turning to God, *Heb.* 6. 2.

Nétop, kitonckquêan kunnúp-pamin michéme.	*Friend, when you die you perish everlastingly.*
Michéme cuppauqua neímmin.	*You are everlastingly undone.*
Cummusquaunamúckqun manìt.	*God is angry with you.*
Cuppauquanúckqun	*He will destroy you.*
Wuchè cummanittówock manâuog.	*For your many Gods.*
Wáme pìtch chíckauta mit-taùke.	*The whole world shall ere long be burnt.*

Obs. Upon the relating that God hath once destroyed the world by water; and that He will visit it the second time with consuming fire: I have been asked this profitable question of some of them, What then will become of us? Where then shall we be?   89

Obs. This mocking (between their great ones) is a great kindling of Warres amongst them: yet I have known some of their chiefest say, what should I hazard the lives of my precious Subjects, them and theirs to kindle a Fire, which no man knowes how farre, and how long it will burne, for the barking of a Dog?   90

Sékineam.	*I have no mind to it.*
Nisékineug.	*He likes not me.*
Nummánneug.	*He hates me.*
Sekinneauhettùock.	
Maninnewauhettùock.	*They hate each other.*
Nowetompátimmin	*We are Friends.*
Wetompáchick.	*Friends.*
Nowepinnátimin.	*We joyne together.*
Nowepinnâchick.	*My Companions in War or Associats.*
Nowechusettimmin.	*We are Confederates.*
Néchuse ewò	*This is my Associate.*
Wechusittûock.	*They joyne together.*
Nwéche kokkêwem.	*I will be mad with him.*
Chickaûta wêtu.	*An house fired.*

Once lodging in an Indian house full of people, the whole Company (Women especially) cryed out in apprehension that the Enemy had fired the House, being about midnight: The house was fired but not by an Enemy: the men ran up on the house top, and with their naked hands beat out the Fire: One scorcht his leg, and suddenly after they came into the house againe, undauntedly cut his leg with a knife to let out the burnt blood.   91

Yo ánawhone	*There I am wounded.*
Missínnege	*A Captive.*
Nummissinnàm ewo.	*This is my Captive.*
Waskeiûhettimmitch.	*At beginning of the fight.*
Nickqueintónckquock	*They come against us.*
Nickqueintouôog.	*I will make Warre upon them.*
Nippauquanaûog.	*I will destroy them.*
Queintauatíttea.	*Let us goe against them.*
Kunnauntatáuchuckqun.	*He comes to kill you.*
Paúquana.	*There is slaughter.*
Pequttôog paúquanan.	*The Pequts are slaine.*
Awaun Wuttúnnene?	*Who have the Victory?*
Tashittáwho?	*How many are slaine?*
Neestáwho.	*Two are slaine.*
Piuckqunneánna.	*Ten are slaine.*

Obs. Their Warres are farre lesse bloudy, and devouring then the cruell 92
Warres of *Europe;* and seldome twenty slaine in a pitcht field: partly because
when they fight in a wood every Tree is a Bucklar.

When they fight in a plaine, they fight with leaping and dancing, that 93
seldome an Arrow hits, and when a man is wounded, unless he that shot fol-
lowes upon the wounded, they soone retire and save the wounded; and yet
having no Swords, nor Guns, all that are slaine are commonly slain with
great Valour and Courage: for the Conquerour ventures into the thickest,
and brings away the Head of his Enemy.

Niss-nissoke.	*Kill kill.*
Kúnnish	*I will kill you.*
Kunnìshickqun ewò.	*He will kill you.*
Kunníshickquock.	*They will kill you.*
Siuckissûog.	*They are stout men.*
Nickummissuog.	*They are Weake.*
Nnickummaunamaûog.	*I shall easily vanquish them.*
Neene núppamen.	*I am dying?*
Cowaúnckamish.	*Quarter, quarter.*
Kunnanaumpasúmmish.	*Mercy, Mercy.*
Kekuttokaûnta,	*Let us parley.*
Aquétuck.	*Let us cease Armes.*
Wunnishaûnta.	*Let us agree.*
Cowammáunsh.	*I love you.*
Wunnêtu ntá.	*My heart is true.*
Tuppaûntash.	*Consider what I say.*
Tuppaúntamoke.	*Doe you all consider.*

Cummequaùnum cummit-tamussusuck ká cummuck iaûg.	*Remember your Wives, and Children.*
Eatch kèen anawâyean.	*Let all be as you say.*
Cowawwunnaûwem.	*You speake truly.*
Cowauôntam.	*You are a wise man.*
Wetompátitea.	*Let us make Friends.*

Working with the Text

1. In his introduction, Williams expresses the hope that, by providing insight into indigenous American language, his *Key* "happily may unlocke some Rarities concerning the Natives themselves, not yet discovered." What assumptions about the nature and powers of language underlie Williams's statement? Do these assumptions differ from our own?

2. Williams reports that his informants readily call themselves "Indians," once Europeans reveal the reason for the name. Given that "Indians" represents a geographical mistake of some magnitude, is it ironic that Native Americans seem satisfied with this explanation? Or is there a better way to think about the role of mistakes in bridging cultural difference? For those who have read Richard White's essay, does White's idea of the "middle ground" offer a useful model for thinking about this and other perceptual errors?

3. Though the excerpt above is only a sample of the phrasebook, even a single table reveals social preoccupations: topics, methods of approach (informative, interrogative, evaluative), forms of interpersonal address, and rhetorical goals, to name just a few. What inferences about seventeenth-century American life can you draw from Williams's *Key*? Do you find it more revealing of Native American culture or of European culture? How do you make such a determination?

4. Using the reference room of your library or Internet resources, do some research into the life of Roger Williams and the founding of Rhode Island. Then write a brief essay about how the *Key* relates to Williams's political or religious thought. Limit your topic by focusing on a single idea or cluster of ideas. And do not be alarmed if you find contradiction, as well as congruence, between the *Key* and Williams's well-attested beliefs.

5. Regardless of whether you have read *The English-Chinese Phrase Book* of Wong Sam and his assistants, turn to the questions at the end of that essay and look, specifically, at questions 4 and 5, which propose projects having to do with contemporary phrasebooks, published and student-produced. Undertake—or continue—one of the projects. If you

have done one already, write an essay about what you discovered when you investigated your own culture's habitual phrases.

An English–Chinese Phrase Book

WONG SAM AND ASSISTANTS

The following appeared in *The Big Aiiieeee: An Anthology of Chinese-American and Japanese-American Literature*, edited by Jeffrey Paul Chan, Frank Chin, Lawson Fusao Inada, and Shawn Wang. As the introductory note suggests, the phrasebook was developed in the 1870s as an aide for Chinese immigrants' interactions with English-speaking Americans and American culture at large. The translations it includes reveal a great deal about the life of Chinese immigrants of the day and their interactions with English-speaking Americans.

Who was Wong Sam? Who were his assistants? We don't know. We don't 1 know how they convinced Wells, Fargo to print and distribute the bilingual *An English-Chinese Phrase Book* in its 130 offices throughout the West in towns where Chinamen lived and worked. We do know that whoever he was, Wong Sam revised the 1875 edition two years later, and Wells, Fargo published and distributed this larger version of the *Phrase Book* in more than two hundred towns with Chinese American populations.

This is not the kind of phrase book used alphabetically by subject. The 2 Chinese learn writing, painting, philosophy, [and] martial arts through a process of memorization, recitation, and internalization of specific "sets." In the *Phrase Book,* the sets contain strategy and tactics for business and criminal law, and for dealing with white people in general. These sets are "fast," unlike those of *The Analects* of Confucius, which take years—a lifetime—to internalize. No, these sets are meant to be memorized quickly, fun to recite, and internalized by the time a Chinaman has his first experience with a white man.

Try these phrases out loud with a different voice for every other line, 3 and it will be instantly apparent that Wong Sam and Assistants' tactics and strategy for dealing with the white man's application of the law do not include submission, acculturation, and assimilation. The Christian prayers found at the back of the *Phrase Book* are themselves a strategy for raising money to publish the book.

Eighteen seventy-five.   4

Rye Patch, Nevada. Salem, Oregon. Sierra City, California. You have to do   5
business. Get from one place to another, buy clothes, secure licenses. Have
an answer for the cops when they ask why your friend is dead on your
doorstep. Read these sets. Memorize them. Recite them. Free-associate with
them, riff with them and discover how they work. Internalize them until all
the phrases are instinct. Wong Sam and his assistants compiled a book of
phrases that prepared the Chinese for any situation, anywhere in the American West. The *Phrase Book* is that set. Free! At any Wells, Fargo office.

你有乜貨物出賣
What goods have you for sale?

樣樣都有
I have all kinds.

我想買條好褲
I want to get a pair of your best pants.

你愛點樣價銀
What do you ask for them?

你舷減少些
Can you take less for them?

先生　不舷
I cannot, sir.

沒還有好過沒樣麼
Have you any other kind better than these?

沒肯賣賒款麼
Will you sell on credit?

我賣現銀　先生
No sir, I sell for cash.

倘沒俾好貨過我　我時時與沒交易
I will come to deal with you always if you give me the best kinds (quality).

為何咁貴
How is it that it is so dear?

煩沒與我交易
Please give me your custom.

好貨稅餉太重　另值我本銀十元
Well, sir, it costs us $10, and besides we have to pay very heavy duty on our best goods.

好生意
Is business good?

甚好　多謝
Very well, I thank you.

買客甚少
The buyers are very few.

生意焉舷興旺
How can the business be prosperous!

有人缺本
Some men lose capital.

有人賺銀
Some men get profits.

價銀太高
The price is too high.

我唔舷俾淂咁多
I am not able to pay.

我賣甚公平
I sell very justly.

孩子我都不騙
I don't cheat, even a boy.

自然係真
Certainly, it is true.

賣客甚多
The sellers are too many.

價錢憑貨物
The price depends on the goods.

佢應當對面講
He ought to speak face to face.

倘若我愛物我再回來
If I want anything I will call on you again.

吩咐攔阻
In order to prevent.

貨物頂好
The goods are first-class.

乜價錢嗎
What is the price?

價錢係眞
And the price is fixed.

四元銀一叫順
Four dollars per dozen.

先驗明貨正買
Examine the goods before you buy.

我必先說沒知
I must tell you before.

我有時買來平
Sometimes I bought them cheap.

有時我平賣
Sometimes I sold them cheap.

我如今照市價賣
Now I sell them at market prices.

自然係眞實
Certainly, it is true.

因謂稅餉太重
Because the duty is too heavy.

買賣甚艱難
To buy and sell is very difficult.

有時我買得貴
Sometimes I buy them dear.

因此我賣亦貴
Of course I must sell them dear.

我一樣價錢賣
I sell them at one price.

中意咁多就買咁多
Buy as many as you like.

你要價錢高
You ask too high a price.

唔係價高　先生
It is not dear, sir.

不防我騙沒
Don't fear I am cheating you.

我有鞋帽衣服
I also have clothes, shoes and caps.

你肯俾我看麼
Can you let me see them?

倘你如意看就看　此物不
是好得
If you like to see, you might see, they are not very good.

你肯賣平些
Can you sell it cheaper?

你愛幾多
How much do you want?

我如今無
I have none now.

俾貨我看過
Show me some goods.

沒愛幾多銀
What do you charge for it?

乜誰命沒來
Who sent you here for it?

我唔相信沒
I cannot trust you.

我下禮拜俾汝
I shall pay you next week.

我望汝相信我
I hope you will trust me.

我防汝走去
I fear you will run away.

為何汝唔買
Why don't you buy them?

我明日來取
I will come for them to-morrow.

信道理捱欺
Christians bear great trials.

佢強搶我物
He took it from me by violence.

我無意打佢
I struck him accidentally.

我認唔該佢還想來打我
I have made an apology, but still he wants to strike me.

佢無事打我
He assaulted me without provocation.

我賃汝樓要汝包水
I will rent the house if you include the water.

你肯去我包汝回
I guarantee to bring him back, if he will go.

此人欲播工銀
The men are striking for wages.

我身分足用
I am content with my situation.

你同佢鬭款
You contend with him about the account.

裝滿箱蘋果
The box contains apples.

佢詐病
He feigned to be sick.

女人暈倒在會堂
The lady fainted in church.

佢誓了願
He ended what he said with an oath.

此樓無意燒了
The house was burned by accident.

此樓有意燒了
The house was set on fire by an incendiary.

佢想白認我行李
He tried to obtain my baggage by false pretenses.

佢強搶我泥口
He claimed my mine.

佢強霸我地
He squatted on my lot.

倘佢唔走我定然逐佢出去
I will expel him if he don't leave the place.

幾時滿期
When will the lease expire?

你幾時滿號
When is the expiration of your lease?

我下禮拜四滿號
Next Thursday my month will have expired.

昨日我工滿號一月
Yesterday was the expiration of one month of labor.

我下禮拜四滿號
My month will have expired on Thursday next.

佢簽名于紙上
He endorsed the note.

佢做我認頭
He went my security.

你肯誓願麼
Can you swear to that.

佢誓了願
He has sworn already.

佢誓願幾次
He swore several times.

我保佢前後
I guarantee him back and fore.

我包個樓係好個
I warranted the house to be a good one.

佢在審事堂誓假願
He perjured himself in Court.

佢在衙門誓願官府廳
He gave his oath to the judge in Court.

佢誓假願
He was fined for perjury.

佢託名捉拿
He was arrested for forgery.

倘有材料我可做工之于汝
If you find the materials I will furnish laborers.

倘汝唔賠我定劫汝家物
I will attach his furniture if you idemnify me.

倘若滿號汝無俾我定然封汝舖之契
I will close the mortgage on your store if you don't pay me when the time has expired.

我定封汝舖之契若滿號無俾
I will close the mortgage on your store if you don't pay me when the time has expired.

佢逼勒我可銀
He tries to extort money from me.

汝去假託逼勒佢照（招）
They are going to extort a confession from him by false pretensions.

逼佢招出
The confession was extorted from him by force.

唬怕勒逼佢招認罪
The confessions were extorted from them by threats

我保佢出監
I bailed him out of jail.

我摘水上船
I bailed the water out of the boat.

佢一仟五佰銀保單
He gave bonds for $1,500.

佢案情昨日十點鐘開審
His case was tried yesterday at 10 A. M.

官府定然定罪于過
The judge will certainly convict him.

佢受大頭人定佢罪
He was convicted by the jury.

佢如今定罪
He is now a convict.

佢取人來見証係眞
He brought a man to prove the fact.

人曰我講所見之事
The man said: "I will testify what I saw."

佢口供已經信了
His testimony was believed.

佢搾冶汝工艮
He will retain your wages.

佢騙了我之工艮
He cheated me out of my wages.

佢誆騙東家
He swindled his employer.

佢騙了我斯文銀
He defrauded me out of my salary.

案情昨日罷了
The case was ended yesterday.

後回審定了罪
He was found guilty, by the last trial.

決命佢去做十年苦工
He will be sent to the penitentiary for 10 years.

佢已經命去省監
He has been sent to the State Prison.

佢誣告我偷鏢
He falsely accused me of stealing his watch.

汝犯了國法
You have violated the Constitution of this State.

他眠埋伏之地
They were lying in ambush.

佢被誤殺
He came to his death by homicide.

佢被夜盜謀殺
He was murdered by a thief.

佢犯罪自儘
He committed suicide.

佢受賊人用繩索索死
He was choked to death with a lasso, by a robber.

佢受人縊死
He was strangled to death by a man.

佢飢死在監
He was starved to death in prison.

佢在霜冷死
He was frozen to death in the snow.

佢在灣投水死
He was going to drown himself in the bay.

後尋數日捉治兇手
After searching for several days they caught the murderer.

汝明得係真實
Did they find anything in his possession.

也有
They did.

佢受人陰殺
He was killed by an assassin.

佢想陰害我
He tried to assassinate me.

佢想陰殺我
He tried to kill me by assassination.

佢係功打之人
He is an assaulter.

佢在房淹死
He was smothered in his room.

佢搌死在房裡
He was suffocated in his room.

佢受仇人用炮打死
He was shot dead by his enemy.

佢受朋友用藥道死
He was poisoned to death by his friend.

佢想用藥道死
He tries to kill him by poisoning.

佢加刑死在監
He tries to inflict death by poison.

立意攻擊禍害肉身
Assault with the intention to do bodily injury.

佢手拈規例
He took the law in his own hand.

佢想奪去我位
He tried to deprive me of my situation.

佢不義搶去我工銀
He wrongfully deprived me of my wages.

我夜間回家
I go home at night.

我也回家
I have gone home.

我去歸
I went home.

我 在 家 住
I abide at home.

我 在 大 埠 住
I abode at San Francisco.

我 也 曾 在 屋 崙 住
I have lived in Oakland.

我 日 出 起 身
I arise at sunrise.

我 今 早 四 點 鐘 起 身
I arose this morning at 4 o'clock.

我 有 時 上 晝 三 點 起 身
I have arisen at 3 A. M. some mornings.

我 四 點 鐘 醒
I awake at 4 o'clock.

我 今 早 五 點 鐘 醒
I awoke this morning at 5 o'clock.

我 有 時 七 點 鐘 醒
I awaken at 7 A. M. sometimes.

我 七 點 鐘 開 工
I begin work at 7 A. M.

我 上 晝 八 點 鐘 開 工
You began work at 8 A. M.

我 六 點 鐘 開 工
We have begun work at 6 A. M.

我 綁 起 此 麥
We bind the wheat up.

我 綁 治 個 瘡
We bound up the wound.

我 用 鐵 鍊 綁 治 個 孩 子
We have bound that boy with a chain.

汝 毀 了 窗 門
You break windows.

我 毀 了 刀
I broke my knife.

他 毀 了 國 法
They have broken the laws of the State.

丟 佢 下 水
Cast him into the water.

我 捉 個 人 入 監 今 日
We cast a man into prison to-day.

人 他 放 出 去
They have cast the man out.

斬 柴 過 個 人
You cut wood for the man.

佢 無 意 斬 了 隻 手
He cut a man's hand off by an accident.

我 斬 倒 此 樹
We have cut the tree down.

乃 日 汝 得 順 便 到 來
What day is the most convenient for you to come?

汝 幾 時 順 便 到 此 處
What day is the most convenient for you to be here?

汝 乃 日 便 到 位
What day is the most convenient for you to be present?

乜 日 汝 到 來
What day can you come?

乃 日 汝 如 意 來 拜 見
What day is the best time for you to call?

幾 時 汝 有 好 機 會 到 此
What day is the best chance for you to get here?

汝 定 乜 日 到 來
What certain day can you arrive?

乃 日 汝 可 舩 起 程
On what day is it possible for you to depart?

乃 日 汝 著 便 起 程
What will be the most suitable day for you to start?

乃 日 汝 可 肷 放 落 工 夫
At what day can you leave the work?

乃 日 汝 可 肷 離 開 事 業
At what day can you get away from your avocation?

乃 日 汝 肷 淂 去
What day can you get away?

我 唔 估 到 汝 來 此 處
I did not think that you would come here.

我 唔 曾 望 汝 到 此
I did not expect that you would be here.

我 唔 估 汝 肯 來
I did not suppose that you would come.

我 唔 知 汝 願 來
I did not know that you would come.

我 唔 估 汝 想 來
I never thought that you would come.

我 唔 估 汝 到 來
I have not been expecting you.

我 唔 估 係 汝
I could not think it were you.

你 驚 揚 於 我
You have taken me by surprise.

我 並 無 等 候 見 汝
Well! I never expected to see you.

汝 可 肷 來 淂
Is it possible that you have come?

順 便 來 見
Call in when convenient.

不 過 係 順 便 來 拜 見
I call in because it is convenient.

我 因 為 淂 閒 到 來
I came because I had an opportunity.

我 因 為 順 便 到 來
I came because it was convenient.

一 有 便 處 我 就 到 來
I came at the first opportunity.

我 因 方 便 到 來
My convenience caused me to come.

我 中 意 來
It suits me to come.

因 合 宜 我 來
There is an appropriateness in my coming.

我 合 宜 到 來
There is a fitness in my coming.

我 因 朋 友 唔 來 我 就 來
I came because my friend did not come.

我 咁 樣 做 因 為 我 中 意
I do so because I love to.

我 來 因 我 有 個 好 機 會
I came for I had a splendid chance.

我 來 因 我 有 好 機 會
I came for I had a good chance.

我 估 我 過 時 就 入 來
Well! I thought I would drop in while passing.

我 估 我 行 過 之 時 順 便 入
來 見
Well! I thought I would make a visit while passing.

我 估 庭 昔 過 此 地
Well! I thought I would step in while passing by here.

我 估 我 會 庭 一 時 之 久
Well! I thought I would step in for a moment.

我 來 因 我 有 淂 閒
Oh! I came because my time was not occupied.

我 來 因 我 在 家 無 工 夫 做
Oh! I came because I had nothing to do at home.

我方便因此我來
The commodiousness of the cars enabled me to come conveniently.

你要乜野呀先生
Well, sir! what will you have?

好呀先生我幫沒做乜野
Well, sir! what can I do for you?

你想愛乜野先生
Well, sir! what do you wish?

尊駕沒要乜呀
Well, sir! what do you want?

你想買乜野先生
Well, sir! what do you want to buy?

一擔貨過崙屋每日來回
沒要幾多艮一個月
What will be the charges per month for a vegetable dealer and his two baskets to Oakland and return, daily?

我買沒貨我要沒送到我
處
I buy goods from you, I want you to deliver them to my place.

連箱借與我明日送回沒
Lend to me, with the box too, I will return it to you to-morrow.

我要沒包我出入費用
I want you to pay all my fare of coming and going.

你嫌我貨價錢貴因此沒
唔買
You dislike my goods because it is so dear. and you don't buy.

等幾日然後講沒知
Wait for a few days, then I will tell you.

沒幾時齊備
When will you be ready?

沒肯相信我
Will you trust me?

佢係拐帶之人
He is a kidnapper.

佢係我書管學生頭
He is a monitor in our school.

放牛乳油入碗櫃
Put the butter in the cupboard.

倒白糖出來牛乳盤
Empty the sugar into the milk-pan.

沒愛我幫沒
You want me to help you?

佢內外病症
He is sick in mind and body.

佢心算度即如他手做工
咁辛苦
He is performing hard mental as well as physical labor.

留住他一禮拜工艮等佢
在此長做
I keep back a week's wages in order to secure his stay.

多煩沒俾回我沒所留住
之工艮
Please give me now that portion of my wages which you have withheld from me.

耶穌係我中保
Christ is our mediator.

我高過佢
I am taller than he.

每間店鋪有一個出番之
人敢說英話
There is not a store which has not an interpreter -- one who can speak the English language.

Working with the Text

1. According to the introductory note, the *Phrase Book* contains strategies for dealing with "any situation, anywhere in the American West." What does this selection of phrases tell you about the life of Chinese immigrants to the United States in the 1870s?

2. Why would a company such as Wells, Fargo—a transportation and banking company—distribute the *Phrase Book* for free?

3. The phrases in Wong Sam's *Book* are grouped together by various means, presumably to aid both location and memorization. Are they primarily conceptual, topical, verbal, grammatical, or other? Is there a comprehensive system of classification at work—or more than one? Or do categories seem more *ad hoc*? How many tiers or levels of classification do you detect? What beliefs or social attitudes are represented (directly or indirectly) in the grouping of phrases?

4. Who is currently producing phrasebooks and for whom? Browse your local bookstore or the Internet; do you find more of Wong Sam's heirs translating from English to a foreign language or from one English idiom to another? What does your answer reveal about contemporary culture? Finally, examine one example of a modern phrasebook, as you examined the work of Wong Sam and his assistants. What phrases are most important, and what do these phrases reveal about the culture that produced them?

5. Imagine that you have just arrived in your house, apartment, or dormitory with no knowledge of the English language. What 25 phrases would you most need to know to survive in your domain? List them in random order; then try to arrange them in an order based on the *Phrase Book*. Finally, bring your list to class, and collate them with your classmates' lists. What features of undergraduate domestic life do your collected lists emphasize?

Talking Past Each Other: Black and White Languages of Race

BOB BLAUNER

Born in Chicago to Jewish lower middle class parents, Bob Blauner studied at the University of Chicago and received his Ph.D. at the University of California at Berkeley, where he has been a professor of sociology since 1963. His first major scholarly work was *Alienation and Freedom: The Factory Worker and His Industry* (1964). His later works, include *Racial Oppression in America* (1972) and *Black Lives, White Lives: Three Decades of Race Relations in America* (1989). In the following essay, Blauner reflects on some of the borders to be negotiated if black and white Americans are to achieve a permanent understanding.

For many African-Americans who came of age in the 1960s, the assassination of Martin Luther King, Jr. in 1968 was a defining moment in the development of their personal racial consciousness. For a slightly older group, the 1955 lynching of the fourteen-year-old Chicagoan Emmett Till in Mississippi had been a similar awakening. Now we have the protest and violence in Los Angeles and other cities in late April and early May of 1992, spurred by the jury acquittal of four policemen who beat motorist Rodney King.

The aftermath of the Rodney King verdict, unlike any other recent racial violence, will be seared into the memories of Americans of *all* colors, changing the way they see each other and their society. Spring 1992 marked the first time since the 1960s that incidents of racial injustice against an African-American—and by extension the black community—have seized the entire nation's imagination. Even highly publicized racial murders, such as those of African-American men in two New York City neighborhoods—Howard Beach (1986) and Bensonhurst (1989)—stirred the consciences of only a minority of whites. The response to the Rodney King verdict is thus a long-overdue reminder that whites still have the capacity to feel deeply about white racism—when they can see it in unambiguous terms.

The videotaped beating by four Los Angeles police officers provided this concreteness. To be sure, many whites focused their response on the subsequent black rioting, while the anger of blacks tended to remain fixed on the verdict itself. However, whites initially were almost as upset as blacks:

An early poll reported that 86 percent of European-Americans disagreed with the jury's decision. The absence of any black from the jury and the trial's venue, Simi Valley, a lily-white suburban community, enabled mainstream whites to see the parallels with the Jim Crow justice of the old South. When we add to this mixture the widespread disaffection, especially of young people, with the nation's political and economic conditions, it is easier to explain the scale of white emotional involvement, unprecedented in a matter of racial protest since the 1960s.

In thirty years of teaching, I have never seen my students so overwrought, 4 needing to talk, eager to do something. This response at the University of California at Berkeley cut across the usual fault lines of intergroup tension, as it did at high schools in Northern California. Assemblies, marches, and class discussions took place all over the nation in predominantly white as well as nonwhite and integrated high schools. Considering that there were also incidents where blacks assaulted white people, the scale of white involvement is even more impressive.

While many whites saw the precipitating events as expressions of racist 5 conduct, they were much less likely than blacks to see them as part of some larger pattern of racism. Thus two separate polls found that only half as many whites as blacks believe that the legal system treats whites better than blacks. (In each poll, 43 percent of whites saw such a generalized double standard, in contrast to 84 percent of blacks in one survey, 89 percent in the other.)

This gap is not surprising. For twenty years European-Americans have 6 tended to feel that systematic racial inequities marked an earlier era, not our own. Psychological denial and a kind of post-1960s exhaustion may both be factors in producing the sense among mainstream whites that civil rights laws and other changes resolved blacks' racial grievances, if not the economic basis of urban problems. But the gap in perceptions of racism also reflects a deeper difference. Whites and blacks see racial issues through different lenses and use different scales to weigh and assess injustice.

I am not saying that blacks and whites have totally disparate value systems and worldviews. I think we were more polarized in the late 1960s. It was then that I began a twenty-year interview study of racial consciousness published in 1989 as *Black Lives, White Lives*. By 1979 blacks and whites had come closer together on many issues than they had been in 1968. In the late 1970s and again in the mid-to-late 1980s, both groups were feeling quite pessimistic about the nation's direction. They agreed that America had become a more violent nation and that people were more individualistic and less bound by such traditional values as hard work, personal responsibility, and respect for age and authority. But with this and other convergences, there remained a striking gap in the way European-Americans and African-

Americans evaluated *racial* change. Whites were impressed by the scale of integration, the size of the black middle class, and the extent of demonstrable progress. Blacks were disillusioned with integration, concerned about the people who had been left behind, and much more negative in their overall assessment of change.

In the 1990s this difference in general outlook led to different reactions   8
to specific racial issues. That is what makes the shared revulsion over the Rodney King verdict a significant turning point, perhaps even an opportunity to begin bridging the gap between black and white definitions of the racial situation.

I want to advance the proposition that there are two languages of race in   9
America. I am not talking about black English and standard English, which refer to different structures of grammar and dialect. "Language" here signifies a system of implicit understandings about social reality, and a racial language encompasses a worldview.

Blacks and whites differ on their interpretations of social change from   10
the 1960s through the 1990s because their racial languages define the central terms, especially "racism," differently. Their racial languages incorporate different views of American society itself, especially the question of how central race and racism are to America's very existence, past and present. Blacks believe in this centrality, while most whites, except for the more race-conscious extremists, see race as a peripheral reality. Even successful, middle-class black professionals experience slights and humiliations—incidents when they are stopped by police, regarded suspiciously by clerks while shopping, or mistaken for messengers, drivers, or aides at work—that remind them they have not escaped racism's reach. For whites, race becomes central on exceptional occasions: collective, public moments such as the recent events, when the veil is lifted, and private ones, such as a family's decision to escape urban problems with a move to the suburbs. But most of the time European-Americans are able to view racial issues as aberrations in American life, much as Los Angeles Police Chief Daryl Gates used the term "aberration" to explain his officers' beating of Rodney King in March 1991.

Because of these differences in language and worldview, blacks and   11
whites often talk past one another, just as men and women sometimes do. I first noticed this in my classes, particularly during discussions of racism. Whites locate racism in color consciousness and its absence in color blindness. They regard it as a kind of racism when students of color insistently underscore their sense of difference, their affirmation of ethnic and racial membership, which minority students have increasingly asserted. Many black, and increasingly also Latino and Asian, students cannot understand

this reaction. It seems to them misinformed, even ignorant. They in turn sense a kind of racism in the whites' assumption that minorities must assimilate to mainstream values and styles. Then African-Americans will posit an idea that many whites find preposterous: Black people, they argue, cannot be racist, because racism is a system of power, and black people as a group do not have power.

In this and many other arenas, a contest rages over the meaning of   12
racism. Racism has become the central term in the language of race. From the 1940s through the 1980s new and multiple meanings of racism have been added to the social science lexicon and public discourse. The 1960s were especially critical for what the English sociologist Robert Miles has called the "inflation" of the term "racism." Blacks tended to embrace the enlarged definitions, whites to resist them. This conflict, in my view, has been at the very center of the racial struggle during the past decade.

The Widening Conception of Racism

The term "racism" was not commonly used in social science or American pub-   13
lic life until the 1960s. "Racism" does not appear, for example, in the Swedish economist Gunnar Myrdal's classic 1944 study of American race relations, *An American Dilemma*. But even when the term was not directly used, it is still possible to determine the prevailing understandings of racial oppression.

In the 1940s racism referred to an ideology, an explicit system of beliefs   14
postulating the superiority of whites based on the inherent, biological inferiority of the colored races. Ideological racism was particularly associated with the belief systems of the Deep South and was originally devised as a rationale for slavery. Theories of white supremacy, particularly in their biological versions, lost much of their legitimacy after the Second World War due to their association with Nazism. In recent years cultural explanations of "inferiority" are heard more commonly than biological ones, which today are associated with such extremist "hate groups" as the Ku Klux Klan and the White Aryan Brotherhood.

By the 1950s and early 1960s, with ideological racism discredited, the focus   15
shifted to a more discrete approach to racially invidious attitudes and behavior, expressed in the model of prejudice and discrimination. "Prejudice" referred (and still does) to hostile feelings and beliefs about racial minorities and the web of stereotypes justifying such negative attitudes. "Discrimination" referred to actions meant to harm the members of a racial minority group. The logic of this model was that racism implied a double standard, that is, treating a person of color differently—in mind or action—than one would a member of the majority group.

By the mid-1960s the terms "prejudice" and "discrimination" and the im-   16
plicit model of racial causation implied by them were seen as too weak to
explain the sweep of racial conflict and change, too limited in their analytical power, and for some critics too individualistic in their assumptions. Their
original meanings tended to be absorbed by a new, more encompassing
idea of racism. During the 1960s the referents of racial oppression moved
from individual actions and beliefs to group and institutional processes,
from subjective ideas to "objective" structures or results. Instead of intent,
there was now an emphasis on process: those more objective social processes
of exclusion, exploitation, and discrimination that led to a racially stratified
society.

The most notable of these new definitions was "institutional racism."   17
In their 1967 book *Black Power,* Stokely Carmichael and Charles Hamilton
stressed how institutional racism was different and more fundamental than
individual racism. Racism, in this view, was built into society and scarcely
required prejudicial attitudes to maintain racial oppression.

This understanding of racism as pervasive and institutionalized spread   18
from relatively narrow "movement" and academic circles to the larger public with the appearance in 1968 of the report of the commission on the urban riots appointed by President Lyndon Johnson and chaired by Illinois
Governor Otto Kerner. The Kerner Commission identified "white racism" as
a prime reality of American society and the major underlying cause of ghetto
unrest. America, in this view, was moving toward two societies, one white
and one black (it is not clear where other racial minorities fit in). Although
its recommendations were never acted upon politically, the report legiti-
mated the term "white racism" among politicians and opinion leaders as a
key to analyzing racial inequality in America.

Another definition of racism, which I would call "racism as atmosphere,"   19
also emerged in the 1960s and 1970s. This is the idea that an organization or
an environment might be racist because its implicit, unconscious structures
were devised for the use and comfort of white people, with the result that
people of other races will not feel at home in such settings. Acting on this understanding of racism, many schools and universities, corporations, and other
institutions have changed their teaching practices or work environments to
encourage a greater diversity in their clientele, students, or work force.

Perhaps the most radical definition of all was the concept of "racism as   20
result." In this sense, an institution or an occupation is racist simply because
racial minorities are underrepresented in numbers or in positions of prestige
and authority.

Seizing on different conceptions of racism, the blacks and whites I talked to   21
in the late 1970s had come to different conclusions about how far America

had moved toward racial justice. Whites tended to adhere to earlier, more limited notions of racism. Blacks for the most part saw the newer meanings as more basic. Thus African-Americans did not think racism had been put to rest by civil rights laws, even by the dramatic changes in the South. They felt that it still pervaded American life, indeed, had become more insidious because the subtle forms were harder to combat than old-fashioned exclusion and persecution.

Whites saw racism largely as a thing of the past. They defined it in terms   22
of segregation and lynching, explicit white supremacist beliefs, or double standards in hiring, promotion, and admissions to colleges or other institutions. Except for affirmative action, which seemed the most blatant expression of such double standards, they were positively impressed by racial change. Many saw the relaxed and comfortable relations between whites and blacks as the heart of the matter. More crucial to blacks, on the other hand, were the underlying structures of power and position that continued to provide them with unequal portions of economic opportunity and other possibilities for the good life.

The newer, expanded definitions of racism just do not make much sense   23
to most whites. I have experienced their frustrations directly when I try to explain the concept of institutional racism to white students and popular audiences. The idea of racism as an "impersonal force" loses all but the most theoretically inclined. Whites are more likely than blacks to view racism as a personal issue. Both sensitive to their own possible culpability (if only unconsciously) and angry at the use of the concept of racism by angry minorities, they do not differentiate well between the racism of social structures and the accusation that they as participants in that structure are personally racist.

The new meanings make sense to blacks, who live such experiences in   24
their bones. But by 1979 many of the African-Americans in my study, particularly the older activists, were critical of the use of racism as a blanket explanation for all manifestations of racial inequality. Long before similar ideas were voiced by the black conservatives, many blacks sensed that too heavy an emphasis on racism led to the false conclusion that blacks could only progress through a conventional civil rights strategy of fighting prejudice and discrimination. (This strategy, while necessary, had proved very limited.) Overemphasizing racism, they feared, was interfering with the black community's ability to achieve greater self-determination through the politics of self-help. In addition, they told me that the prevailing rhetoric of the 1960s had affected many young blacks. Rather than taking responsibility for their own difficulties, they were now using racism as a "cop-out."

In public life today this analysis is seen as part of the conservative dis-   25
course on race. Yet I believe that this position originally was a progressive one, developed out of self-critical reflections on the relative failure of 1960s

movements. But perhaps because it did not seem to be "politically correct," the left-liberal community, black as well as white, academic as well as political, has been afraid of embracing such a critique. As a result, the neoconservatives had a clear field to pick up this grass-roots sentiment and to use it to further their view that racism is no longer significant in American life. This is the last thing that my informants and other savvy African-Americans close to the pulse of their communities believe.

By the late 1970s the main usage of racism in the mind of the white public had undoubtedly become that of "reverse racism." The primacy of "reverse racism" as "the really important racism" suggests that the conservatives and the liberal-center have, in effect, won the battle over the meaning of racism.   26

Perhaps this was inevitable because of the long period of backlash against all the progressive movements of the 1960s. But part of the problem may have been the inflation of the idea of racism. While institutional racism exists, such a concept loses practical utility if every thing and every place is racist. In that case, there is effectively nothing to be done about it. And without conceptual tools to distinguish what is important from what is not, we are lost in the confusion of multiple meanings.   27

Back to Basics

While public discourse was discounting white racism as exaggerated or a thing of the past, the more traditional forms of bigotry, harassment, and violence were unfortunately making a comeback. (This upsurge actually began in the early 1980s but was not well noticed, due to some combination of media inattention and national mood.) What was striking about the Bernhard Goetz subway shootings in New York, the white-on-black racial violence in Howard Beach, the rise of organized hate groups, campus racism, and skinhead violence is that these are all examples of old-fashioned racism. They illustrate the power and persistence of racial prejudices and hate crimes in the tradition of classical lynchings. They are precisely the kind of phenomena that many social analysts expected to diminish, as I did.   28

If there was one positive effect of this upsurge, it was to alert many whites to the destructive power of racial hatred and division in American life. At the same time, these events also repolarized racial attitudes in America. They have contributed to the anger and alienation of the black middle class and the rapid rise of Afrocentrism, particularly among college students.   29

As the gap in understanding has widened, several social scientists have proposed restricting the concept of racism to its original, more narrow meaning. However, the efforts of African-Americans to enlarge the meaning of racism is part of that group's project to make its view of the world and of American society competitive with the dominant white perspective. In addi-   30 tion, the "inflated" meanings of racism are already too rooted in common speech to be overturned by the advice of experts. And certainly some way is needed to convey the pervasive and systematic character of racial oppression. No other term does this as well as racism.

The question then becomes what to do about these multiple and confusing meanings of racism and their extraordinary personal and political charge. I would begin by honoring both the black and white readings of the term. Such an attitude might help facilitate the interracial dialogue so badly needed and yet so rare today. 31

Communication can only start from the understandings that people have. While the black understanding of racism is, in some sense, the deeper one, the white views of racism (ideology, double standard) refer to more specific and recognizable beliefs and practices. Since there is also a cross-racial consensus on the immorality of racist ideology and racial discrimination, it makes sense whenever possible to use such a concrete referent as discrimination, rather than the more global concept of racism. And reemphasizing discrimination may help remind the public that racial discrimination is not just a legacy of the past. 32

The intellectual power of the African-American understanding lies in its more critical and encompassing perspective. In the Rodney King events, we have an unparalleled opportunity to bridge the racial gap by pointing out that racism and racial division remain essential features of American life and that incidents such as police beatings of minority people and stacked juries are not aberrations but part of a larger pattern of racial abuse and harassment. Without resorting to the overheated rhetoric that proved counterproductive in the 1960s, it now may be possible to persuade white Americans that the most important patterns of discrimination and disadvantage are not to be found in the "reverse racism" of affirmative action but sadly still in the white racism of the dominant social system. And, when feasible, we need to try to bridge the gap by shifting from the language of race to that of ethnicity and class. 33

Race or Ethnicity?

In the American consciousness the imagery of race—especially along the black-white dimension—tends to be more powerful than that of class or ethnicity. As a result, legitimate ethnic affiliations are often misunderstood to be racial and illegitimate. 34

Race itself is a confusing concept because of the variance between scientific and common sense definitions of the term. Physical anthropologists who study the distribution of those characteristics we use to classify "races" teach us that race is a fiction because all peoples are mixed to various de- 35 grees. Sociologists counter that this biological fiction unfortunately remains a sociological reality. People define one anther racially, and thus divide society into racial groups. The "fiction" of race affects every aspect of people's lives, from living standards to landing in jail.

The consciousness of color differences, and the invidious distinctions   36
based on them, have existed since antiquity and are not limited to any one corner of the world. And yet the peculiarly modern division of the world into a discrete number of hierarchically ranked races is a historic product of Western colonialism. In precolonial Africa the relevant group identities were national, tribal, or linguistic. There was no concept of an African or black people until this category was created by the combined effects of slavery, imperialism, and the anticolonial and Pan-African movements. The legal definitions of blackness and whiteness, which varied from one society to another in the Western hemisphere, were also crucial for the construction of modern-day races. Thus race is an essentially political construct, one that translates our tendency to see people in terms of their color or other physical attributes into structures that make it likely that people will act for or against them on such a basis.

The dynamic of ethnicity is different, even though the results at times   37
may be similar. An ethnic group is a group that shares a belief in its common past. Members of an ethnic group hold a set of common memories that make them feel that their customs, culture, and outlook are distinctive. In short, they have a sense of peoplehood. Sharing critical experiences and sometimes a belief in their common fate, they feel an affinity for one another, a "comfort zone" that leads to congregating together, even when this is not forced by exclusionary barriers. Thus if race is associated with biology and nature, ethnicity is associated with culture. Like races, ethnic groups arise historically, transform themselves, and sometimes die out.

Much of the popular discourse about race in America today goes awry   38
because ethnic realities get lost under the racial umbrella. The positive meanings and potential of ethnicity are overlooked, even overrun, by the more inflammatory meanings of race. Thus white students, disturbed when blacks associate with each other, justify their objections through their commitment to *racial* integration. They do not appreciate the ethnic affinities that bring this about, or see the parallels to Jewish students meeting at the campus Hillel Foundation or Italian-Americans eating lunch at the Italian house on the Berkeley campus.

When blacks are "being ethnic," whites see them as "being racial." Thus   39
they view the identity politics of students who want to celebrate their blackness, their *chicanoismo,* their Asian heritages, and their American Indian roots as racially offensive. Part of this reaction comes from a sincere desire, almost a yearning, of white students for a color-blind society. But because

the ethnicity of darker people so often gets lost in our overracialized perceptions, the white students misread the situation. When I point out to my class that whites are talking about race and its dynamics and the students of color are talking about ethnicity and its differing meaning, they can begin to appreciate each other's agendas.

Confounding race and ethnicity is not just limited to the young. The 40
general public, including journalists and other opinion makers, does this regularly, with serious consequences for the clarity of public dialogue and sociological analysis. A clear example comes from the Chicago mayoral election of 1983. The establishment press, including leading liberal columnists, regularly chastised the black electorate for giving virtually all its votes to Harold Washington. Such racial voting was as "racist" as whites voting for the other candidate because they did not want a black mayor. Yet African-Americans were voting for ethnic representation just as Irish-Americans, Jews, and Italians have always done. Such ethnic politics is considered the American way. What is discriminatory is the double standard that does not confer the same rights on blacks, who were not voting primarily out of fear or hatred as were many whites.

Such confusions between race and ethnicity are exacerbated by the am- 41
biguous sociological status of African-Americans. Black Americans are *both* a race and an ethnic group. Unfortunately, part of our heritage of racism has been to deny the ethnicity, the cultural heritage of black Americans. Liberal-minded whites have wanted to see blacks as essentially white people with black skins. Until the 1960s few believed that black culture was a real ethnic culture.

Because our racial language is so deep-seated, the terminology of black 42
and white just seems more "natural" and commonsensical than more ethnic labels like African-American or European-American. But the shift to the term African-American has been a conscious attempt to move the discourse from a language of race to a language of ethnicity. "African-American," as Jesse Jackson and others have pointed out, connects the group to its history and culture in a way that the racial designation, black, does not. The new usage parallels terms for other ethnic groups. Many whites tend to dismiss this concern about language as mere sloganeering. But "African-American" fits better into the emerging multicultural view of American ethnic and racial arrangements, one more appropriate to our growing diversity. The old race relations model was essentially a view that generalized (often inappropriately) from black-white relations. It can no longer capture—if it ever could—the complexity of a multiracial and multicultural society.

The issue is further complicated by the fact that African-Americans are 43
not a homogeneous group. They comprise a variety of distinct ethnicities. There are the West Indians with their long histories in the U.S., the darker

Library Resource Center
Renton Technical College
3000 N.E. 4th St.
Renton, WA 98056

Puerto Ricans (some of whom identify themselves as black), the more recently arrived Dominicans, Haitians, and immigrants from various African countries, as well as the native-born African-Americans, among whom regional distinctions can also take on a quasi-ethnic flavor.

Blacks from the Caribbean are especially likely to identify with their   44
homeland rather than taking on a generic black or even African-American identity. While they may resist the dynamic of "racialization" and even feel superior to native blacks, the dynamic is relentless. Their children are likely to see themselves as part of the larger African-American population. And yet many native-born Americans of African descent also resist the term "African-American," feeling very little connection to the original homeland. Given the diversity in origin and outlook of America's largest minority, it is inevitable that no single concept can capture its full complexity or satisfy all who fall within its bounds.

For white Americans, race does not overwhelm ethnicity. Whites see the   45
ethnicity of other whites; it is their own whiteness they tend to overlook. But even when race is recognized, it is not conflated with ethnicity. Jews, for example, clearly distinguish their Jewishness from their whiteness. Yet the long-term dynamic still favors the development of a dominant white racial identity. Except for recent immigrants, the various European ethnic identities have been rapidly weakening. Vital ethnic communities persist in some cities, particularly on the East Coast. But many whites, especially the young, have such diverse ethnic heritages that they have no meaningful ethnic affiliation. In my classes only the Jews among European-Americans retain a strong sense of communal origin.

Instead of dampening the ethnic enthusiasms of the racial minorities,   46
perhaps it would [be] better to encourage the revitalization of whites' European heritages. But a problem with this approach is that the relationship between race and ethnicity is more ambiguous for whites than for people of color. Although for many white groups ethnicity has been a stigma, it also has been used to gain advantages that have marginalized blacks and other racial minorities. Particularly for working-class whites today, ethnic community loyalties are often the prism through which they view their whiteness, their superiority.

Thus the line between ethnocentrism and racism is a thin one, easily   47
crossed—as it was by Irish-Americans who resisted the integration of South Boston's schools in the 1970s and by many of the Jews and Italians that sociologist Jonathan Rieder describes in his 1985 book *Canarsie*.

White students today complain of a double standard. Many feel that   48
their college administrations sanction organization and identification for people of color, but not for them. If there can be an Asian business organi-

zation and a black student union, why can't there be a white business club or a white student alliance? I'd like to explain to them that students of color are organized ethnically, not racially, that whites have Hillel and the Italian theme house. But this makes little practical sense when such loyalties are just not that salient for the vast majority.

Out of this vacuum the emerging identity of "European-American" has come   49
into vogue. I interpret the European-American idea as part of a yearning for a usable past. Europe is associated with history and culture. "America" and "American" can no longer be used to connote white people. "White" itself is a racial term and thereby inevitably associated with our nation's legacy of social injustice.

At various California colleges and high schools, European-American   50
clubs have begun to form, provoking debate about whether it is inherently racist for whites to organize as whites—or as European-Americans. Opponents invoke the racial analogy and see such organizations as akin to exclusive white supremacist groups. Their defenders argue from an ethnic model, saying that they are simply looking for a place where they can feel at home and discuss their distinctive personal and career problems. The jury is still out on this new and, I suspect, burgeoning phenomenon. It will take time to discover its actual social impact.

If the European-Americans forming their clubs are truly organizing on   51
an ethnic or panethnic rather than a racial model, I would have to support these efforts. Despite all the ambiguities, it seems to me a gain in social awareness when a specific group comes to be seen in ethnic rather than racial terms. During the period of the mass immigration of the late nineteenth century and continuing through the 1920s, Jews, Italians, and other white ethnics were viewed racially. We no longer hear of the "Hebrew race," and it is rare for Jewish distinctiveness to be attributed to biological rather than cultural roots. Of course, the shift from racial to ethnic thinking did not put an end to anti-Semitism in the United States—or to genocide in Germany, where racial imagery was obviously intensified.

It is unrealistic to expect that the racial groupings of American society   52
can be totally "deconstructed," as a number of scholars now are advocating. After all, African-Americans and native Americans, who were not immigrants, can never be exactly like other ethnic groups. Yet a shift in this direction would begin to move our society from a divisive biracialism to a more inclusive multiculturalism.

To return to the events of spring 1992, I ask what was different about these   53
civil disturbances. Considering the malign neglect of twelve Reagan-Bush years, the almost two decades of economic stagnation, and the retreat of the

public from issues of race and poverty, the violent intensity should hardly be astonishing.

More striking was the multiracial character of the response. In the San Francisco Bay area, rioters were as likely to be white as nonwhite. In Los Angeles, Latinos were prominent among both the protesters and the victims. South Central Los Angeles is now more Hispanic than black, and this group suffered perhaps 60 percent of the property damage. The media have focused on the specific grievances of African-Americans toward Koreans. But I would guess that those who trashed Korean stores were protesting something larger than even the murder of a fifteen-year-old black girl. Koreans, along with other immigrants, continue to enter the country and in a relatively short time surpass the economic and social position of the black poor. The immigrant advantage is real and deeply resented by African-Americans, who see that the two most downtrodden minorities are those that did not enter the country voluntarily.

During the 1960s the police were able to contain riots within the African-American community. This time Los Angeles police were unable to do so. Even though the South Central district suffered most, there was also much destruction in other areas including Hollywood, downtown, and the San Fernando Valley. In the San Francisco Bay area the violence occurred primarily in the white business sections, not the black neighborhoods of Oakland, San Francisco, or Berkeley. The violence that has spilled out of the inner city is a distillation of all the human misery that a white middle-class society has been trying to contain—albeit unsuccessfully (consider the homeless). As in the case of an untreated infection, the toxic substances finally break out, threatening to contaminate the entire organism.

Will this widened conflict finally lead Americans toward a recognition of our common stake in the health of the inner cities and their citizens, or toward increased fear and division? The Emmett Till lynching in 1955 set the stage for the first mass mobilization of the civil rights movement, the Montgomery bus boycott later that year. Martin Luther King's assassination provided the impetus for the institution of affirmative action and other social programs. The Rodney King verdict and its aftermath must also become not just a psychologically defining moment but an impetus to a new mobilization of political resolve.

Working with the Text

1. Blauner states that in his experience, most whites find it difficult to make sense of the concept of institutional racism, in part because they "do not differentiate well between the racism of social structures and the accusation that they as participants in that structure are personally

racist." The concept makes sense to blacks, however, because they "live such experiences in their bones." How do you respond to this conclusion?

2. Blauner's white students often regard the desire of blacks or Hispanics or Asian-Americans to create racially exclusive groups as "reverse racism." In what ways does Blauner feel that considering such groups in the context of ethnicity can help his white students get beyond this view? Do you agree?

3. Blauner advocates the term *African-American* and also sometimes uses the term *European-American* instead of *white*? Why? Do you agree with his reasoning?

4. In discussing the disadvantages of encouraging "the revitalization of whites' European heritages" Blauner suggests that "the line between ethnocentricism and racism is a thin one." Why, then, does Blauner tentatively support the emergence of European-American clubs on college campuses?

5. Blauner suggests that the "shared revulsion over the Rodney King verdict" in 1992 was a "significant turning point, perhaps even an opportunity to begin bridging the gap between black and white definitions of the racial situation." Considering black and white attitudes about the "racial situation" today, what do you think of Blauner's prediction?

6. Choose an event more recent than the Rodney King verdict that changed black and white definitions of the racial situation. Working collaboratively with a group of your classmates, research the event by reading old periodical accounts. (If you have not yet done so, this would be a good time to learn how to find and read newspapers on microfilm.) Make a brief presentation of your research to the class, dividing the task among the researchers so that each is responsible for a segment related to—but not reiterating—the others.

Arrow

RITA DOVE

Poet Rita Dove is the author of ten books of poems, including the Pulitzer Prize–winning *Thomas and Beulah* and, most recently, *On the Bus with Rosa Parks* (1999), nominated for the National Book Critics Circle Award. She has also written a book of short stories, *Fifth Sunday* (1985), the novel *Through the Ivory Gate* (1992), and the verse drama *The Darker Face of the Earth* (1996). She writes a weekly column, "Poet's Choice," for *The Washington Post*, and she is the editor of *Best American Poetry 2000*. From 1993–1995 she served as Poet Laureate of the United States and Consultant to the Library of Congress, the youngest women and first African-American to receive the honor. She is presently the Commonwealth Professor of English at the University of Virginia. The following poem, *Arrow*, neatly satirizes an "eminent scholar"'s presentation of a classical Greek satire (*Thesmophoriazusae*, produced in 411 BC), and dramatizes the power imbalances between speaker and audience, men and women, white privilege and black subordination.

The eminent scholar "took the bull by the horns,"
substituting urban black speech for the voice
of an illiterate cop in Aristophanes' *Thesmophoriazusae.*
And we sat there.
Dana's purple eyes deepened, Becky   5
twitched to her hairtips
and Janice in her red shoes
scribbled *he's an arschloch; do you want
to leave? He's a model product of his
education,* I scribbled back; *we can learn from this.*   10

So we sat through the applause
and my chest flashed hot, a void
sucking at my guts until I was all
flamed surface. I would have to speak up.
Then the scholar progressed   15

to his prize-winning translations of
the Italian Nobel Laureate. He explained the poet
to us: immense difficulty
with human relationships; sensitive;
women were a scrim through which he could see   20
heaven.
We sat through it. Quite lovely, these poems.
We could learn from them although they were saying
you women are nothing, nothing at all.

When the moment came I raised my hand,   25
phrased my question as I had to: sardonic,
eminently civil my condemnation
phrased in the language of fathers—
felt the room freeze behind me.
And the answer came as it had to: 30
humanity—celebrate our differences—
the virility of ethnicity. My students
sat there already devising

their different ways of coping:
Dana knowing it best to have   35
the migraine at once, get the poison out quickly
Becky holding it back for five hours   and Janice
making it to the evening reading and
party afterwards

in black pants and tunic with silver mirrors   40
her shoes pointed and studded, wicked witch shoes:
Janice who will wear red for three days or
yellow brighter
than her hair so she can't be
seen   at all   45

Working with the Text

1. Some notes to the poem may help us understand how these power
   relations are confronted: Aristophanes's satire pokes fun at the eminent
   Greek tragedian Euripedes, who is to be punished for his misogynist
   dramas at an all-woman festival of Thesmophoria. Evidently, the
   scholar believes himself a "humanist" who can "celebrate our
   differences" through his translations using "black speech" and later,
   Italian poems (possibly by Eugenio Montale) that claim "you women
   are nothing." How does Dove concede a measure of humanity to this

scholar? How is her critique aided by detailing his power and self-justifications? Does his ready-made answer suggest that no real conversation is taking place?

2. The poem may show a battle between texts: the scholar's translations and talk, and the women in the audience answering. Whose words get quoted, whose speech becomes public? How do the women react to bigotry in the artistic language they hear? How do their physical responses take on the vocabulary of color? The women's witty responses—using the German word for "asshole," wearing a (Greek?) tunic full of mirrors—are still "phrased in the language of fathers." Have they conceded their own language to patriarchy? What other verbal means are available?

3. All the women—the students or the speaker we take to be Dove—devise "ways of coping" by the end of the poem. What are they? How are these methods particular to women? In what ways might they succeed with women? With men? Does the poem's final image of invisibility seem a defeat or ironic victory?

 4. The poem shows how the literary "canon," the collection of literary texts and interpretations that schools present, is being confronted by new generations of students. In what way do the "counter-languages" by women in the poem offer the beginnings of a "counter-canon"? How could this new canon make use of the play and the poems? What wider set of conversations about art and representation does the poem demand? Is the poem itself a form of "counter-canon"?

Letter from Birmingham Jail

MARTIN LUTHER KING, JR.

The great civil rights leader Martin Luther King, Jr., was born in Atlanta and graduated from Morehouse College and the Crozer Theological Seminary, later receiving a doctorate in theology from Boston University. A pastor in Montgomery, Alabama, he was instrumental in organizing a boycott that led to the desegregation of Montgomery's buses in 1956, and advocated a theory of nonviolent protest as a means to rectify racist laws and practices. He was awarded the Nobel Peace Prize in 1964. In 1968, at the age of thirty-nine, King was assassinated in Memphis, Tennessee. In the early 1960s, King led a large contingent of nonviolent protesters in demonstrations to end segregation and legalized racial discrimination in Birmingham, Alabama. Jailed for his activities in Birmingham and criticized by white moderates who considered the protests too "extreme," King wrote the following famous letter to some of his critics, in an attempt to explain and justify his beliefs and actions.

April 16, 1963
Birmingham, Alabama

MY DEAR FELLOW CLERGYMEN:

While confined here in the Birmingham city jail, I came across your recent statement calling my present activities "unwise and untimely." Seldom do I pause to answer criticism of my work and ideas. If I sought to answer all the criticisms that cross my desk, my secretaries would have little time for anything other than such correspondence in the course of the day, and I would have no time for constructive work. But since I feel that you are men of genuine good will and that your criticisms are sincerely set forth, I want to try to answer your statement in what I hope will be patient and reasonable terms.

I think I should indicate why I am here in Birmingham, since you have been influenced by the view which argues against "outsiders coming in." I have the honor of serving as president of the Southern Christian Leadership Conference, an organization operating in every southern state, with headquarters in Atlanta, Georgia. We have some eighty-five affiliated organizations across the South, and one of them is the Alabama Christian Movement for Human Rights. Frequently we share staff, educational, and financial resources with our affiliates. Several months ago the affiliate here in Birmingham asked us to be on call to engage in a nonviolent direct-action program if such were deemed necessary. We readily consented, and when the hour came we lived up to our promise. So I, along with several members of my staff, am here because I was invited here. I am here because I have organizational ties here.

But more basically, I am in Birmingham because injustice is here. Just as the prophets of the eighth century B.C. left their villages and carried their "thus saith the Lord" far beyond the boundaries of their home towns, and just as the Apostle Paul left his village of Tarsus and carried the gospel of Jesus Christ to the far corners of the Greco-Roman world, so am I compelled to carry the gospel of freedom beyond my own home town. Like Paul, I must constantly respond to the Macedonian call for aid.

Moreover, I am cognizant of the interrelatedness of all communities and   4
states. I cannot sit idly by in Atlanta and not be concerned about what happens in Birmingham. Injustice anywhere is a threat to justice everywhere.
We are caught in an inescapable network of mutuality, tied in a single garment of destiny. Whatever affects one directly, affects all indirectly. Never
again can we afford to live with the narrow, provincial "outside agitator"
idea. Anyone who lives inside the United States can never be considered an
outsider anywhere within its bounds.

You deplore the demonstrations taking place in Birmingham. But your   5
statement, I am sorry to say, fails to express a similar concern for the conditions that brought about the demonstrations. I am sure that none of you
would want to rest content with the superficial kind of social analysis that
deals merely with effects and does not grapple with underlying causes. It is
unfortunate that demonstrations are taking place in Birmingham, but it is
even more unfortunate that the city's white power structure left the Negro
community with no alternative.

In any nonviolent campaign there are four basic steps: collection of the   6
facts to determine whether injustices exist; negotiation; self-purification; and
direct action. We have gone through all these steps in Birmingham. There
can be no gainsaying the fact that racial injustice engulfs this community.
Birmingham is probably the most thoroughly segregated city in the United
States. Its ugly record of brutality is widely known. Negroes have experienced grossly unjust treatment in the courts. There have been more
unsolved bombings of Negro homes and churches in Birmingham than
in any other city in the nation. These are the hard, brutal facts of the case.
On the basis of these conditions, Negro leaders sought to negotiate with
the city fathers. But the latter consistently refused to engage in good-faith
negotiation.

Then, last September, came the opportunity to talk with leaders of Bir-   7
mingham's economic community. In the course of the negotiations, certain
promises were made by the merchants—for example, to remove the stores'
humiliating racial signs. On the basis of these promises, the Reverend Fred
Shuttlesworth and the leaders of the Alabama Christian Movement for Human Rights agreed to a moratorium on all demonstrations. As the weeks and
months went by, we realized that we were the victims of a broken promise.
A few signs, briefly removed, returned; the others remained.

As in so many past experiences, our hopes had been blasted, and the   8
shadow of deep disappointment settled upon us. We had no alternative except to prepare for direct action, whereby we would present our very bodies as a means of laying our case before the conscience of the local and the
national community. Mindful of the difficulties involved, we decided to undertake a process of self-purification. We began a series of workshops on

nonviolence, and we repeatedly asked ourselves: "Are you able to accept blows without retaliation?" "Are you able to endure the ordeal of jail?" We decided to schedule our direct-action program for the Easter season, realizing that except for Christmas, this is the main shopping period of the year. Knowing that a strong economic-withdrawal program would be the by-product of direct action, we felt that this would be the best time to bring pressure to bear on the merchants for the needed change.

Then it occurred to us that Birmingham's mayoral election was coming up in March, and we speedily decided to postpone action until after election day. When we discovered that the Commissioner of Public Safety, Eugene "Bull" Connor, had piled up enough votes to be in the run-off, we decided again to postpone action until the day after the run-off so that the demonstrations could not be used to cloud the issues. Like many others, we waited to see Mr. Connor defeated, and to this end we endured postponement after postponement. Having aided in this community need, we felt that our direct-action program could be delayed no longer. 9

You may well ask, "Why direct action? Why sit-ins, marches, and so forth? Isn't negotiation a better path?" You are quite right in calling for negotiation. Indeed, this is the very purpose of direct action. Nonviolent direct action seeks to create such a crisis and foster such a tension that a community which has constantly refused to negotiate is forced to confront the issue. It seeks so to dramatize the issue that it can no longer be ignored. My citing the creation of tension as part of the work of the nonviolent-resister may sound rather shocking. But I must confess that I am not afraid of the word "tension." I have earnestly opposed violent tension, but there is a type of constructive, nonviolent tension which is necessary for growth. Just as Socrates felt that it was necessary to create a tension in the mind so that individuals could rise from the bondage of myths and half-truths to the unfettered realm of creative analysis and objective appraisal, so must we see the need for nonviolent gadflies to create the kind of tension in society that will help men rise from the dark depths of prejudice and racism to the majestic heights of understanding and brotherhood. 10

The purpose of our direct-action program is to create a situation so crisis packed that it will inevitably open the door to negotiation. I therefore concur with you in your call for negotiation. Too long has our beloved Southland been bogged down in a tragic effort to live in monologue rather than dialogue. 11

One of the basic points in your statement is that the action that I and my associates have taken in Birmingham is untimely. Some have asked: "Why didn't you give the new city administration time to act?" The only answer that I can give to this query is that the new Birmingham administration must be prodded about as much as the outgoing one, before it will act. We are 12 sadly mistaken if we feel that the election of Albert Boutwell as mayor will bring the millennium to Birmingham. While Mr. Boutwell is a much more gentle person than Mr. Connor, they are both segregationists, dedicated to maintenance of the status quo. I have hoped that Mr. Boutwell will be reasonable enough to see the futility of massive resistance to desegregation. But he will not see this without pressure from devotees of civil rights. My friends, I must say to you that we have not made a single gain in civil rights without determined legal and nonviolent pressure. Lamentably, it is an historical fact that privileged groups seldom give up their privileges voluntarily. Individuals may see the moral light and voluntarily give up their unjust posture; but, as Reinhold Niebuhr has reminded us, groups tend to be more immoral than individuals.

We know through painful experience that freedom is never voluntarily   13
given by the oppressor; it must be demanded by the oppressed. Frankly, I have yet to engage in a direct-action campaign that was "well timed" in view of those who have not suffered unduly from the disease of segregation. For years now I have heard the word "Wait!" It rings in the ear of every Negro with piercing familiarity. This "Wait" has almost always meant "Never." We must come to see, with one of our distinguished jurists, that "justice too long delayed is justice denied."

We have waited for more than 340 years for our constitutional and God-   14
given rights. The nations of Asia and Africa are moving with jetlike speed toward gaining political independence, but we still creep at horse-and-buggy pace toward gaining a cup of coffee at a lunch counter. Perhaps it is easy for those who have never felt the stinging darts of segregation to say, "Wait." But when you have seen vicious mobs lynch your mothers and fathers at will and drown your sisters and brothers at whim; when you have seen hate-filled policemen curse, kick, and even kill your black brothers and sisters; when you see the vast majority of your twenty million Negro brothers smothering in an airtight cage of poverty in the midst of an affluent society; when you suddenly find your tongue twisted and your speech stammering as you seek to explain to your six-year-old daughter why she can't go to the public amusement park that has just been advertised on television, and see tears welling up in her eyes when she is told that Funtown is closed to colored children, and see ominous clouds of inferiority beginning to form in her little mental sky, and see her beginning to distort her personality by developing an unconscious bitterness toward white people; when you have to concoct an answer for a five-year-old son who is asking, "Daddy, why do white people treat colored people so mean?"; when you take a cross-country drive and find it necessary to sleep night after night in the uncomfortable corners of your automobile because no motel will accept you; when you are humiliated day in and day out by nagging signs reading "white" and

"colored"; when your first name becomes "nigger," your middle name becomes "boy" (however old you are) and your last name becomes "John," and your wife and mother are never given the respected title "Mrs."; when you are harried by day and haunted by night by the fact that you are a Negro, living constantly at tiptoe stance, never quite knowing what to expect next, and are plagued with inner fears and outer resentments; when you are forever fighting a degenerating sense of "nobodiness"—then you will understand why we find it difficult to wait. There comes a time when the cup of endurance runs over, and men are no longer willing to be plunged into the abyss of despair. I hope, sirs, you can understand our legitimate and unavoidable impatience.

You express a great deal of anxiety over our willingness to break laws.   15
This is certainly a legitimate concern. Since we so diligently urge people to obey the Supreme Court's decision of 1954 outlawing segregation in the public schools, at first glance it may seem rather paradoxical for us consciously to break laws. One may well ask: "How can you advocate breaking some laws and obeying others?" The answer lies in the fact that there are two types of laws: just and unjust. I would be the first to advocate obeying just laws. One has not only a legal but a moral responsibility to obey just laws. Conversely, one has a moral responsibility to disobey unjust laws. I would agree with St. Augustine that "an unjust law is no law at all."

Now, what is the difference between the two? How does one determine   16
whether a law is just or unjust? A just law is a man-made code that squares with the moral law or the law of God. An unjust law is a code that is out of harmony with the moral law. To put it in the terms of St. Thomas Aquinas: An unjust law is a human law that is not rooted in eternal law and natural law. Any law that uplifts human personality is just. Any law that degrades human personality is unjust. All segregation statutes are unjust because segregation distorts the soul and damages the personality. It gives the segregator a false sense of superiority and the segregated a false sense of inferiority. Segregation, to use the terminology of the Jewish philosopher Martin Buber, substitutes an "I-it" relationship for an "I-thou" relationship and ends up relegating persons to the status of things. Hence segregation is not only politically, economically, and sociologically unsound, it is morally wrong and sinful. Paul Tillich has said that sin is separation. Is not segregation an existential expression of man's tragic separation, his awful estrangement, his terrible sinfulness? Thus it is that I can urge men to obey the 1954 decision of the Supreme Court, for it is morally right; and I can urge them to disobey segregation ordinances, for they are morally wrong.

Let us consider a more concrete example of just and unjust laws. An un-   17
just law is a code that a numerical or power majority group compels a minority group to obey but does not make binding on itself. This is *difference*

made legal. By the same token, a just law is a code that a majority compels a minority to follow and that it is willing to follow itself. This is *sameness* made legal.

Let me give another explanation. A law is unjust if it is inflicted on a minority that, as a result of being denied the right to vote, had no part in enacting or devising the law. Who can say that the legislature of Alabama which set up that state's segregation laws was democratically elected? Throughout Alabama all sorts of devious methods are used to prevent Negroes from becoming registered voters, and there are some counties in which, even though Negroes constitute a majority of the population, not a single Negro is registered. Can any law enacted under such circumstances be considered democratically structured?   18

Sometimes a law is just on its face and unjust in its application. For instance, I have been arrested on a charge of parading without a permit. Now, there is nothing wrong in having an ordinance which requires a permit for a parade. But such an ordinance becomes unjust when it is used to maintain segregation and to deny citizens the First-Amendment privilege of peaceful assembly and protest.   19

I hope you are able to see the distinction I am trying to point out. In no sense do I advocate evading or defying the law, as would the rabid segregationist. That would lead to anarchy. One who breaks an unjust law must do so openly, lovingly, and with a willingness to accept the penalty. I submit that an individual who breaks a law that conscience tells him is unjust, and who willingly accepts the penalty of imprisonment in order to arouse the conscience of the community over its injustice, is in reality expressing the highest respect for law.   20

Of course, there is nothing new about this kind of civil disobedience. It was evidenced sublimely in the refusal of Shadrach, Meshach, and Abednego to obey the laws of Nebuchadnezzar, on the ground that a higher moral law was at stake. It was practiced superbly by the early Christians, who were willing to face hungry lions and the excruciating pain of chopping blocks rather than submit to certain unjust laws of the Roman Empire. To a degree, academic freedom is a reality today because Socrates practiced civil disobedience. In our own nation, the Boston Tea Party represented a massive act of civil disobedience.   21

We should never forget that everything Adolf Hitler did in Germany was "legal" and everything the Hungarian freedom fighters did in Hungary was "illegal." It was "illegal" to aid and comfort a Jew in Hitler's Germany. Even so, I am sure that, had I lived in Germany at the time, I would have aided and comforted my Jewish brothers. If today I lived in a Communist country where certain principles dear to the Christian faith are suppressed, I would openly advocate disobeying that country's anti-religious laws.   22

I must make two honest confessions to you, my Christian and Jewish   23
brothers. First, I must confess that over the past few years I have been
gravely disappointed with the white moderate. I have almost reached the regrettable conclusion that the Negro's great stumbling block in his stride
toward freedom is not the White Citizen's Counciler or the Ku Klux Klanner,
but the white moderate, who is more devoted to "order" than to justice; who
prefers a negative peace which is the absence of tension to a positive peace
which is the presence of justice; who constantly says, "I agree with you in
the goal you seek, but I cannot agree with your methods of direct action";
who paternalistically believes he can set the timetable for another man's freedom; who lives by a mythical concept of time and who constantly advises the
Negro to wait for a "more convenient season." Shallow understanding from
people of good will is more frustrating than absolute misunderstanding from
people of ill will. Lukewarm acceptance is much more bewildering than outright rejection.

I had hoped that the white moderate would understand that law and or-   24
der exist for the purpose of establishing justice and that when they fail in
this purpose they become the dangerously structured dams that block the
flow of social progress. I had hoped that the white moderate would understand that the present tension in the South is a necessary phase of the transition from an obnoxious negative peace, in which the Negro passively
accepted his unjust plight, to a substantive and positive peace, in which all
men will respect the dignity and worth of human personality. Actually, we
who engage in nonviolent direct action are not the creators of tension. We
merely bring to the surface the hidden tension that is already alive. We bring
it out in the open, where it can be seen and dealt with. Like a boil that can
never be cured so long as it is covered up but must be opened with all its
ugliness to the natural medicines of air and light, injustice must be exposed,
with all the tension its exposure creates, to the light of human conscience
and the air of national opinion, before it can be cured.

In your statement you assert that our actions, even though peaceful,   25
must be condemned because they precipitate violence. But is this a logical
assertion? Isn't this like condemning a robbed man because his possession
of money precipitated the evil act of robbery? Isn't this like condemning
Socrates because his unswerving commitment to truth and his philosophical
inquiries precipitated the act by the misguided populace in which they
made him drink hemlock? Isn't this like condemning Jesus because his
unique God-consciousness and never-ceasing devotion to God's will precipitated the evil act of crucifixion? We must come to see that, as the federal
courts have consistently affirmed, it is wrong to urge an individual to cease
his efforts to gain his basic constitutional rights because the quest may precipitate violence. Society must protect the robbed and punish the robber.

I had also hoped that the white moderate would reject the myth con-   26
cerning time in relation to the struggle for freedom. I have just received a
letter from a white brother in Texas. He writes: "All Christians know that the
colored people will receive equal rights eventually, but it is possible that
you are in too great a religious hurry. It has taken Christianity almost two
thousand years to accomplish what it has. The teachings of Christ take time
to come to earth." Such an attitude stems from a tragic misconception of
time, from the strangely irrational notion that there is something in the very
flow of time that will inevitably cure all ills. Actually, time itself is neutral; it
can be used either destructively or constructively. More and more I feel that
the people of ill will have used time much more effectively than have the
people of good will. We will have to repent in this generation not merely for
the hateful words and actions of the bad people, but for the appalling silence
of the good people. Human progress never rolls in on wheels of inevitability; it comes through the tireless efforts of men willing to be co-workers with
God, and without this hard work, time itself becomes an ally of the forces of
stagnation. We must use time creatively, in the knowledge that the time is
always ripe to do right. Now is the time to make real the promise of democracy and transform our pending national elegy into a creative psalm of brotherhood. Now is the time to lift our national policy from the quicksand of
racial injustice to the solid rock of human dignity.

You speak of our activity in Birmingham as extreme. At first I was rather   27
disappointed that fellow clergymen would see my nonviolent efforts as
those of an extremist. I began thinking about the fact that I stand in the middle of two opposing forces in the Negro community. One is a force of complacency, made up in part of Negroes who, as a result of long years of
oppression, are so drained of self-respect and a sense of "somebodiness"
that they have adjusted to segregation; and in part of a few middle-class Negroes who, because of a degree of academic and economic security and because in some ways they profit by segregation, have become insensitive to
the problems of the masses. The other force is one of bitterness and hatred,
and it comes perilously close to advocating violence. It is expressed in the
various black nationalist groups that are springing up across the nation, the
largest and best-known being Elijah Muhammad's Muslim movement. Nour-
ished by the Negro's frustration over the continued existence of racial discrimination, this movement is made up of people who have lost faith in
America, who have absolutely repudiated Christianity, and who have concluded that the white man is an incorrigible "devil."

I have tried to stand between these two forces, saying that we need   28
emulate neither the "do-nothingism" of the complacent nor the hatred and
despair of the black nationalist. For there is the more excellent way of love and

nonviolent protest. I am grateful to God that, through the influence of the Negro church, the way of nonviolence became an integral part of our struggle.

If this philosophy had not emerged, by now many streets of the South 29 would, I am convinced, be flowing with blood. And I am further convinced that if our white brothers dismiss as "rabble-rousers" and "outside agitators" those of us who employ nonviolent direct action, and if they refuse to support our nonviolent efforts, millions of Negroes will, out of frustration and despair, seek solace and security in black-nationalist ideologies—a development that would inevitably lead to a frightening racial nightmare.

Oppressed people cannot remain oppressed forever. The yearning for 30 freedom eventually manifests itself, and that is what has happened to the American Negro. Something within has reminded him of his birthright of freedom, and something without has reminded him that it can be gained. Consciously or unconsciously, he has been caught up by the *Zeitgeist,* and with his black brothers of Africa and his brown and yellow brothers of Asia, South America, and the Caribbean, the United States Negro is moving with a sense of great urgency toward the promised land of racial justice. If one recognizes this vital urge that has engulfed the Negro community, one should readily understand why public demonstrations are taking place. The Negro has many pent-up resentments and latent frustrations, and he must release them. So let him march; let him make prayer pilgrimages to the city hall; let him go on freedom rides—and try to understand why he must do so. If his repressed emotions are not released in nonviolent ways, they will seek expression through violence; this is not a threat but a fact of history. So I have not said to my people, "Get rid of your discontent." Rather, I have tried to say that this normal and healthy discontent can be channeled into the creative outlet of nonviolent direct action. And now this approach is being termed extremist.

But though I was initially disappointed at being categorized as an ex- 31 tremist, as I continued to think about the matter I gradually gained a measure of satisfaction from the label. Was not Jesus an extremist for love: "Love your enemies, bless them that curse you, do good to them that hate you, and pray for them which despitefully use you, and persecute you." Was not Amos an extremist for justice: "Let justice roll down like waters and righteousness like an ever-flowing stream." Was not Paul an extremist for the Christian gospel: "I bear in my body the marks of the Lord Jesus." Was not Martin Luther an extremist: "Here I stand; I cannot do otherwise, so help me God." And John Bunyan: "I will stay in jail to the end of my days before I make a butchery of my conscience." And Abraham Lincoln: "This nation cannot survive half slave and half free." And Thomas Jefferson: "We hold these truths to be self-evident, that all men are created equal. . . ." So the question is not whether we will be extremists, but what kind of extremists we will be. Will we be extremists for hate or for love? Will we be extremists for the preservation of injustice or for the extension of justice? In that dramatic scene on Calvary's hill three men were crucified. We must never forget that all three were crucified for the same crime—the crime of extremism. Two were extremists for immorality, and thus fell below their environment. The other, Jesus Christ, was an extremist for love, truth, and goodness, and thereby rose above his environment. Perhaps the South, the nation, and the world are in dire need of creative extremists.

I had hoped that the white moderate would see this need. Perhaps I was too optimistic; perhaps I expected too much. I suppose I should have realized that few members of the oppressor race can understand the deep groans and passionate yearnings of the oppressed race, and still fewer have the vision to see that injustice must be rooted out by strong, persistent, and determined action. I am thankful, however, that some of our white brothers in the South have grasped the meaning of this social revolution and committed themselves to it. They are still all too few in quantity, but they are big in quality. Some—such as Ralph McGill, Lillian Smith, Harry Golden, James McBride Dabbs, Ann Braden, and Sarah Patton Boyle—have written about our struggle in eloquent and prophetic terms. Others have marched with us down nameless streets of the South. They have languished in filthy, roach-infested jails, suffering the abuse and brutality of policemen who view them as "dirty nigger-lovers." Unlike so many of their moderate brothers and sisters, they have recognized the urgency of the moment and sensed the need for powerful "action" antidotes to combat the disease of segregation.

Let me take note of my other major disappointment. I have been so greatly disappointed with the white church and its leadership. Of course, there are some notable exceptions. I am not unmindful of the fact that each of you has taken some significant stands on this issue. I commend you, Reverend Stallings, for your Christian stand on this past Sunday, in welcoming Negroes to your worship service on a nonsegregated basis. I commend the Catholic leaders of this state for integrating Spring Hill College several years ago.

But despite these notable exceptions, I must honestly reiterate that I have been disappointed with the church. I do not say this as one of those negative critics who can always find something wrong with the church. I say this as a minister of the gospel, who loves the church; who was nurtured in its bosom; who has been sustained by its spiritual blessings and who will remain true to it as long as the cord of life shall lengthen.

When I was suddenly catapulted into the leadership of the bus protest in Montgomery, Alabama, a few years ago, I felt we would be supported by the white church. I felt that the white ministers, priests, and rabbis of the

South would be among our strongest allies. Instead, some have been outright opponents, refusing to understand the freedom movement and misrepresenting its leaders; all too many others have been more cautious than courageous and have remained silent behind the anesthetizing security of stained-glass windows.

In spite of my shattered dreams, I came to Birmingham with the hope   36
that the white religious leadership of this community would see the justice of our cause and, with deep moral concern, would serve as the channel through which our just grievances could reach the power structure. I had hoped that each of you would understand. But again I have been disappointed.

I have heard numerous southern religious leaders admonish their wor-   37
shipers to comply with a desegregation decision because it is the law, but I have longed to hear white ministers declare: "Follow this decree because integration is morally right and because the Negro is your brother." In the midst of blatant injustices inflicted upon the Negro, I have watched white churchmen stand on the sideline and mouth pious irrelevancies and sanctimonious trivialities. In the midst of a mighty struggle to rid our nation of racial and economic injustice, I have heard many ministers say: "Those are social issues, with which the gospel has no real concern." And I have watched many churches commit themselves to a completely otherworldly religion which makes a strange, un-Biblical distinction between body and soul, between the sacred and the secular.

I have traveled the length and breadth of Alabama, Mississippi, and all   38
the other southern states. On sweltering summer days and crisp autumn mornings I have looked at the South's beautiful churches with their lofty spires pointing heavenward. I have beheld the impressive outlines of her massive religious-education buildings. Over and over I have found myself asking: "What kind of people worship here? Who is their God? Where were their voices when the lips of Governor Barnett dripped with words of interposition and nullification? Where were they when Governor Wallace gave a clarion call for defiance and hatred? Where were their voices of support when bruised and weary Negro men and women decided to rise from the dark dungeons of complacency to the bright hills of creative protest?"

Yes, these questions are still in my mind. In deep disappointment I have   39
wept over the laxity of the church. But be assured that my tears have been tears of love. Yes, I love the church. How could I do otherwise? I am in the rather unique position of being the son, the grandson, and the great-grandson of preachers. Yes, I see the church as the body of Christ. But, oh! How we have blemished and scarred that body through social neglect and through fear of being nonconformists.

There was a time when the church was very powerful—in the time   40
when the early Christians rejoiced at being deemed worthy to suffer for

what they believed. In those days the church was not merely a thermome-
ter that recorded the ideas and principles of popular opinion; it was a ther-
mostat that transformed the mores of society. Whenever the early Christians
entered a town, the people in power became disturbed and immediately
sought to convict the Christians for being "disturbers of the peace" and "outside agitators." But the Christians pressed on, in the conviction that they
were "a colony of heaven," called to obey God rather than man. Small in
number, they were big in commitment. They were too God-intoxicated to be
"astronomically intimidated." By their effort and example they brought an
end to such ancient evils as infanticide and gladiatorial contests.

Things are different now. So often the contemporary church is a weak, 41
ineffectual voice with an uncertain sound. So often it is an archdefender of
the status quo. Far from being disturbed by the presence of the church, the
power structure of the average community is consoled by the church's
silent—and often even vocal—sanction of things as they are.

But the judgment of God is upon the church as never before. If today's 42
church does not recapture the sacrificial spirit of the early church, it will lose
its authenticity, forfeit the loyalty of millions, and be dismissed as an irrelevant social club with no meaning for the twentieth century. Every day I meet
young people whose disappointment with the church has turned into outright disgust.

Perhaps I have once again been too optimistic. Is organized religion too 43
inextricably bound to the status quo to save our nation and the world? Perhaps I must turn my faith to the inner spiritual church, the church within the
church, as the true *ekklesia* and the hope of the world. But again I am thankful to God that some noble souls from the ranks of organized religion have
broken loose from the paralyzing chains of conformity and joined us as active partners in the struggle for freedom. They have left their secure congregations and walked the streets of Albany, Georgia, with us. They have
gone down the highways of the South on tortuous rides for freedom. Yes,
they have gone to jail with us. Some have been dismissed from their
churches, have lost the support of their bishops and fellow ministers. But
they have acted in the faith that right defeated is stronger than evil triumphant. Their witness has been the spiritual salt that has preserved the
true meaning of the gospel in these troubled times. They have carved a tunnel of hope through the dark mountain of disappointment.

I hope the church as a whole will meet the challenge of this decisive 44
hour. But even if the church does not come to the aid of justice, I have no
despair about the future. I have no fear about the outcome of our struggle in
Birmingham, even if our motives are at present misunderstood. We will reach
the goal of freedom in Birmingham and all over the nation, because the goal
of America is freedom. Abused and scorned though we may be, our destiny

is tied up with America's destiny. Before the pilgrims landed at Plymouth, we were here. For more than two centuries our forebears labored in this country without wages; they made cotton king; they built the homes of their masters while suffering gross injustice and shameful humiliation—and yet out of a bottomless vitality they continued to thrive and develop. If the inexpressible cruelties of slavery could not stop us, the opposition we now face will surely fail. We will win our freedom because the sacred heritage of our nation and the eternal will of God are embodied in our echoing demands.

Before closing I feel impelled to mention one other point in your statement that has troubled me profoundly. You warmly commended the Birmingham police force for keeping "order" and "preventing violence." I doubt that you would have so warmly commended the police force if you had seen its dogs sinking their teeth into unarmed, nonviolent Negroes. I doubt that you would so quickly commend the policemen if you were to observe their ugly and inhumane treatment of Negroes here in the city jail; if you were to watch them push and curse old Negro women and young Negro girls; if you were to see them slap and kick old Negro men and young boys; if you were to observe them, as they did on two occasions, refuse to give us food because we wanted to sing our grace together. I cannot join you in your praise of the Birmingham police department. 45

It is true that the police have exercised a degree of discipline in handling the demonstrators. In this sense they have conducted themselves rather "nonviolently" in public. But for what purpose? To preserve the evil system of segregation. Over the past few years I have consistently preached that nonviolence demands that the means we use must be as pure as the ends we seek. I have tried to make clear that it is wrong to use immoral means to attain moral ends. But now I must affirm that it is just as wrong, or perhaps even more so, to use moral means to preserve immoral ends. Perhaps Mr. Connor and his policemen have been rather nonviolent in public, as was Chief Pritchett in Albany, Georgia, but they have used the moral means of nonviolence to maintain the immoral end of racial injustice. As T. S. Eliot has said, "The last temptation is the greatest treason: To do the right deed for the wrong reason." 46

I wish you had commended the Negro sit-inners and demonstrators of Birmingham for their sublime courage, their willingness to suffer, and their amazing discipline in the midst of great provocation. One day the South will recognize its real heroes. They will be the James Merediths, with the noble sense of purpose that enables them to face jeering and hostile mobs, and with the agonizing loneliness that characterizes the life of the pioneer. They will be old, oppressed, battered Negro women, symbolized in a seventy-two-year-old woman in Montgomery, Alabama, who rose up with a sense of dignity and with her people decided not to ride segregated buses, and who responded with ungrammatical profundity to one who inquired about her 47 weariness: "My feets is tired, but my soul is at rest." They will be the young high school and college students, the young ministers of the gospel and a host of their elders, courageously and nonviolently sitting in at lunch counters and willingly going to jail for conscience' sake. One day the South will know that when these disinherited children of God sat down at lunch counters, they were in reality standing up for what is best in the American dream and for the most sacred values in our Judaeo-Christian heritage, thereby bringing our nation back to those great wells of democracy which were dug deep by the founding fathers in their formulation of the Constitution and the Declaration of Independence.

Never before have I written so long a letter. I'm afraid it is much too long to take your precious time. I can assure you that it would have been much shorter if I had been writing from a comfortable desk, but what else can one do when he is alone in a narrow jail cell, other than write long letters, think long thoughts, and pray long prayers? 48

If I have said anything in this letter that overstates the truth and indicates an unreasonable impatience, I beg you to forgive me. If I have said anything that understates the truth and indicates my having a patience that allows me to settle for anything less than brotherhood, I beg God to forgive me. 49

I hope this letter finds you strong in the faith. I also hope that circumstances will soon make it possible for me to meet each of you, not as an integrationist or a civil-rights leader but as a fellow clergyman and a Christian brother. Let us all hope that the dark clouds of racial prejudice will soon pass away and the deep fog of misunderstanding will be lifted from our fear-drenched communities, and in some not too distant tomorrow the radiant stars of love and brotherhood will shine over our great nation with all their scintillating beauty. 50

YOURS FOR THE CAUSE OF PEACE AND BROTHERHOOD,
MARTIN LUTHER KING, JR.

Working with the Text

1. King's letter was written in response to a statement issued by a group of white religious leaders criticizing him for his activism on behalf of civil rights; it makes its argument by refuting theirs, point by point. Choose one point, and analyze exactly how King refutes it, paying particular attention to the interplay of *logos* (logic) and *pathos* (appeal to values or emotions).

2. Describe the tone of the essay, and, citing specific words and phrases, demonstrate how that tone is achieved. Locate specific tropes and/or rhetorical figures, then consider both their local and their cumulative

effects. Why, if King's essay is a "letter," does it often sound so much like a sermon?

3. According to King, who or what is the greatest threat to civil rights? Why? Forty years later, does a similar threat confront those who continue to battle racism in American culture?

4. Choose a published argument, and refute it point by point. Where you can, point out errors of fact or interpretation; elsewhere, concede what you can't refute but demonstrate (i.e., don't simply claim) its relative insignificance next to the higher mandate of your position.

5. Imagine yourself jailed for your convictions. If such an eventuality seems impossible to you, put yourself in the position of someone in history—Galileo, for example—who was so imprisoned. Imagine the charges against you, and compose a short "letter" in defense of your beliefs and your actions.

Sweetheart of the Song Tra Bong

TIM O'BRIEN

Originally from small-town Minnesota, Tim O'Brien graduated from Macalaster College in 1968 and was immediately drafted into the army. Though against the war, O'Brien served in Vietnam from 1969–70 with what has been called the "unlucky" American division due to its involvement in the My Lai massacre in 1968, an event that figures prominently in his latest novel *In the Lake of the Woods* (1994). After Vietnam he became a graduate student at Harvard, leaving to become a newspaper reporter at *The Washington Post*. O'Brien's career as a reporter gave way to his fiction writing after publication of his memoir *If I Die in a Combat Zone, Box Me Up and Send Me Home* (1973). In *The Things They Carried* (1990), which was a finalist for both the Pulitzer Prize and the National Book Critics Circle Award, O'Brien imaginatively retells the interconnected stories of the men of Alpha Company, an infantry platoon in Vietnam. The book is preoccupied with the process of storytelling itself, the way imagination and language and memory can blur fact, and the difference between "truth" and "reality." The following chapter tells a seemingly apocryphal story of a young woman who in impersonating a combat soldier uncovers the "mystery of herself."

Vietnam was full of strange stories, some improbable, some well beyond   1
that, but the stories that will last forever are those that swirl back and forth
across the border between trivia and bedlam, the mad and the mundane.
This one keeps returning to me. I heard it from Rat Kiley, who swore up and
down to its truth, although in the end, I'll admit, that doesn't amount to
much of a warranty. Among the men in Alpha Company, Rat had a reputation for exaggeration and overstatement, a compulsion to rev up the facts,
and for most of us it was normal procedure to discount sixty or seventy percent of anything he had to say. If Rat told you, for example, that he'd slept
with four girls one night, you could figure it was about a girl and a half. It
wasn't a question of deceit. Just the opposite: he wanted to heat up the
truth, to make it burn so hot that you would feel exactly what he felt. For
Rat Kiley, I think, facts were formed by sensation, not the other way around,
and when you listened to one of his stories, you'd find yourself performing
rapid calculations in your head, subtracting superlatives, figuring the square
root of an absolute and then multiplying by maybe.

Still, with this particular story, Rat never backed down. He claimed   2
to have witnessed the incident with his own eyes, and I remember how upset he became one morning when Mitchell Sanders challenged him on its
basic premise.

"It can't happen," Sanders said. "Nobody ships his honey over to Nam. It   3
don't ring true. I mean, you just can't import your own personal poontang."

Rat shook his head. "I *saw* it, man. I was right there. This guy did it."   4

"His girlfriend?"   5

"Straight on. It's a fact." Rat's voice squeaked a little. He paused and   6
looked at his hands. "Listen, the guy sends her the money. Flies her over.
This cute blonde—just a kid, just barely out of high school—she shows up
with a suitcase and one of those plastic cosmetic bags. Comes right out to
the boonies. I swear to God, man, she's got on culottes. White culottes and
this sexy pink sweater. There she *is*."

I remember Mitchell Sanders folding his arms. He looked over at me for   7
a second, not quite grinning, not saying a word, but I could read the amusement in his eyes.

Rat saw it, too.   8

"No lie," he muttered. "Culottes."   9

When he first arrived in-country, before joining Alpha Company, Rat   10
had been assigned to a small medical detachment up in the mountains west
of Chu Lai, near the village of Tra Bong, where along with eight other
enlisted men he ran an aid station that provided basic emergency and
trauma care. Casualties were flown in by helicopter, stabilized, then shipped
out to hospitals in Chu Lai or Danang. It was gory work, Rat said, but pre-

dictable. Amputations, mostly—legs and feet. The area was heavily mined, thick with Bouncing Betties and homemade booby traps. For a medic, though, it was ideal duty, and Rat counted himself lucky. There was plenty of cold beer, three hot meals a day, a tin roof over his head. No humping at all. No officers, either. You could let your hair grow, he said, and you didn't have to polish your boots or snap off salutes or put up with the usual rear-echelon nonsense. The highest ranking NCO was an E-6 named Eddie Diamond, whose pleasures ran from dope to Darvon, and except for a rare field inspection there was no such thing as military discipline.

As Rat described it, the compound was situated at the top of a flat-crested hill along the northern outskirts of Tra Bong. At one end was a small dirt helipad; at the other end, in a rough semicircle, the mess hall and medical hootches overlooked a river called the Song Tra Bong. Surrounding the place were tangled rolls of concertina wire, with bunkers and reinforced firing positions at staggered intervals, and base security was provided by a mixed unit of RFs, PFs, and ARVN infantry. Which is to say virtually no security at all. As soldiers, the ARVNs were useless; the Ruff-and-Puffs were outright dangerous. And yet even with decent troops the place was clearly indefensible. To the north and west the country rose up in thick walls of wilderness, triple-canopied jungle, mountains unfolding into higher mountains, ravines and gorges and fast-moving rivers and waterfalls and exotic butterflies and steep cliffs and smoky little hamlets and great valleys of bamboo and elephant grass. Originally, in the early 1960s, the place had been set up as a Special Forces outpost, and when Rat Kiley arrived nearly a decade later, a squad of six Green Berets still used the compound as a base of operations. The Greenies were not social animals. Animals, Rat said, but far from social. They had their own hootch at the edge of the perimeter, fortified with sandbags and a metal fence, and except for the bare essentials they avoided contact with the medical detachment. Secretive and suspicious, loners by nature, the six Greenies would sometimes vanish for days at a time, or even weeks, then late in the night they would just as magically reappear, moving like shadows through the moonlight, filing in silently from the dense rain forest off to the west. Among the medics there were jokes about this, but no one asked questions.

While the outpost was isolated and vulnerable, Rat said, he always felt a curious sense of safety there. Nothing much ever happened. The place was never mortared, never taken under fire, and the war seemed to be somewhere far away. On occasion, when casualties came in, there were quick spurts of activity, but otherwise the days flowed by without incident, a smooth and peaceful time. Most mornings were spent on the volleyball court. In the heat of midday the men would head for the shade, lazing away the long afternoons, and after sundown there were movies and card games and sometimes all-night drinking sessions.

It was during one of those late nights that Eddie Diamond first brought up the tantalizing possibility. It was an offhand comment. A joke, really. What they should do, Eddie said, was pool some bucks and bring in a few mama-sans from Saigon, spice things up, and after a moment one of the men laughed and said, "Our own little EM club," and somebody else said, "Hey, yeah, we pay our fuckin' dues, don't we?" It was nothing serious. Just passing time, playing with the possibilities, and so for a while they tossed the idea around, how you could actually get away with it, no officers or anything, nobody to clamp down, then they dropped the subject and moved on to cars and baseball. 13

Later in the night, though, a young medic named Mark Fossie kept coming back to the subject. 14

"Look, if you think about it," he said, "it's not that crazy. You could actually do it." 15

"Do what?" Rat said. 16

"You know. Bring in a girl. I mean, what's the problem?" 17

Rat shrugged. "Nothing. A war." 18

"Well, see, that's the thing," Mark Fossie said. "No war *here*. You could really do it. A pair of solid brass balls, that's all you'd need." 19

There was some laughter, and Eddie Diamond told him he'd best strap down his dick, but Fossie just frowned and looked at the ceiling for a while and then went off to write a letter. 20

Six weeks later his girlfriend showed up. 21

The way Rat told it, she came in by helicopter along with the daily resupply shipment out of Chu Lai. A tall, big-boned blonde. At best, Rat said, she was seventeen years old, fresh out of Cleveland Heights Senior High. She had long white legs and blue eyes and a complexion like strawberry ice cream. Very friendly, too.

At the helipad that morning, Mark Fossie grinned and put his arm around her and said, "Guys, this is Mary Anne." 22

The girl seemed tired and somewhat lost, but she smiled. 23

There was a heavy silence. Eddie Diamond, the ranking NCO, made a small motion with his hand, and some of the others murmured a word or two, then they watched Mark Fossie pick up her suitcase and lead her by the arm down to the hootches. For a long while the men were quiet. 24

"That fucker," somebody finally said. 25

At evening chow Mark Fossie explained how he'd set it up. It was expensive, he admitted, and the logistics were complicated, but it wasn't like going to the moon. Cleveland to Los Angeles, LA to Bangkok, Bangkok to 26

Saigon. She'd hopped a C-130 up to Chu Lai and stayed overnight at the USO and the next morning hooked a ride west with the resupply chopper.

"A cinch," Fossie said, and gazed down at his pretty girlfriend. "Thing is, 27 you just got to *want* it enough."

Mary Anne Bell and Mark Fossie had been sweethearts since grammar 28 school. From the sixth grade on they had known for a fact that someday they would be married, and live in a fine gingerbread house near Lake Erie, and have three healthy yellow-haired children, and grow old together, and no doubt die in each other's arms and be buried in the same walnut casket. That was the plan. They were very much in love, full of dreams, and in the ordinary flow of their lives the whole scenario might well have come true.

On the first night they set up house in one of the bunkers along the 29 perimeter, near the Special Forces hootch, and over the next two weeks they stuck together like a pair of high school steadies. It was almost disgusting, Rat said, the way they mooned over each other. Always holding hands, always laughing over some private joke. All they needed, he said, were a couple of matching sweaters. But among the medics there was some envy. It was Vietnam, after all, and Mary Anne Bell was an attractive girl. Too wide in the shoulders, maybe, but she had terrific legs, a bubbly personality, a happy smile. The men genuinely liked her. Out on the volleyball court she wore cut-off blue jeans and a black swimsuit top, which the guys appreciated, and in the evenings she liked to dance to music from Rat's portable tape deck. There was a novelty to it; she was good for morale. At times she gave off a kind of come-get-me energy, coy and flirtatious, but apparently it never bothered Mark Fossie. In fact he seemed to enjoy it, just grinning at her, because he was so much in love, and because it was the sort of show that a girl will sometimes put on for her boyfriend's entertainment and education.

Though she was young, Rat said, Mary Anne Bell was no timid child. 30 She was curious about things. During her first days in-country she liked to roam around the compound asking questions: What exactly was a trip flare? How did a Claymore work? What was behind those scary green mountains to the west? Then she'd squint and listen quietly while somebody filled her in. She had a good quick mind. She paid attention. Often, especially during the hot afternoons, she would spend time with the ARVNs out along the perimeter, picking up little phrases of Vietnamese, learning how to cook rice over a can of Sterno, how to eat with her hands. The guys sometimes liked to kid her about it—our own little native, they'd say—but Mary Anne would just smile and stick out her tongue. "I'm here," she'd say, "I might as well learn something."

The war intrigued her. The land, too, and the mystery. At the beginning 31 of her second week she began pestering Mark Fossie to take her down to the village at the foot of the hill. In a quiet voice, very patiently, he tried to tell her that it was a bad idea, way too dangerous, but Mary Anne kept after him. She wanted to get a feel for how people lived, what the smells and customs were. It did not impress her that the VC owned the place.

"Listen, it can't be that bad," she said. "They're human beings, aren't they? Like everybody else?"   32

Fossie nodded. He loved her.   33

And so in the morning Rat Kiley and two other medics tagged along as security while Mark and Mary Anne strolled through the ville like a pair of tourists. If the girl was nervous, she didn't show it. She seemed comfortable. and entirely at home; the hostile atmosphere did not seem to register. All morning Mary Anne chattered away about how quaint the place was, how she loved the thatched roofs and naked children, the wonderful simplicity of village life. A strange thing to watch, Rat said. This seventeen-year-old doll in her goddamn culottes, perky and fresh-faced, like a cheerleader visiting the opposing team's locker room. Her pretty blue eyes seemed to glow. She couldn't get enough of it. On their way back up to the compound she stopped for a swim in the Song Tra Bong, stripping down to her underwear, showing off her legs while Fossie tried to explain to her about things like ambushes and snipers and the stopping power of an AK-47.   34

The guys, though, were impressed.   35

"A real tiger," said Eddie Diamond. "D-cup guts, trainer-bra brains."   36

"She'll learn," somebody said.   37

Eddie Diamond gave a solemn nod. "There's the scary part. I promise you, this girl will most definitely learn."   38

In parts, at least, it was a funny story, and yet to hear Rat Kiley tell it you'd almost think it was intended as straight tragedy. He never smiled. Not even at the crazy stuff. There was always a dark, far-off look in his eyes, a kind of sadness, as if he were troubled by something sliding beneath the story's surface. Whenever we laughed, I remember, he'd sigh and wait it out, but the one thing he could not tolerate was disbelief. He'd get edgy if someone questioned one of the details. "She *wasn't* dumb," he'd snap. "I never said that. Young, that's all I said. Like you and me. A *girl,* that's the only difference, and I'll tell you something: it didn't amount to jack. I mean, when we first got here—all of us—we were real young and innocent, full of romantic bullshit, but we learned pretty damn quick. And so did Mary Anne."   39

Rat would peer down at his hands, silent and thoughtful. After a moment his voice would flatten out.   40

"You don't believe it?" he'd say. "Fine with me. But you don't know human nature. You don't know Nam."   41

Then he'd tell us to listen up.   42

* * *

A good sharp mind, Rat said. True, she could be silly sometimes, but she   43
picked up on things fast. At the end of the second week, when four casualties came in, Mary Anne wasn't afraid to get her hands bloody. At times, in
fact, she seemed fascinated by it. Not the gore so much, but the adrenaline
buzz that went with the job, that quick hot rush in your veins when the
choppers settled down and you had to do things fast and right. No time for
sorting through options, no thinking at all; you just stuck your hands in and
started plugging up holes. She was quiet and steady. She didn't back off
from the ugly cases. Over the next day or two, as more casualties trickled in,
she learned how to clip an artery and pump up a plastic splint and shoot in
morphine. In times of action her face took on a sudden new composure, almost serene, the fuzzy blue eyes narrowing into a tight, intelligent focus.
Mark Fossie would grin at this. He was proud, yes, but also amazed. A different person, it seemed, and he wasn't sure what to make of it.

Other things, too. The way she quickly fell into the habits of the bush.   44
No cosmetics, no fingernail filing. She stopped wearing jewelry, cut her hair
short and wrapped it in a dark green bandanna. Hygiene became a matter
of small consequence. In her second week Eddie Diamond taught her how
to disassemble an M-16, how the various parts worked, and from there it
was a natural progression to learning how to use the weapon. For hours at
a time she plunked away at C-ration cans, a bit unsure of herself, but as it
turned out she had a real knack for it. There was a new confidence in her
voice, a new authority in the way she carried herself. In many ways she remained naive and immature, still a kid, but Cleveland Heights now seemed
very far away.

Once or twice, gently, Mark Fossie suggested that it might be time to   45
think about heading home, but Mary Anne laughed and told him to forget
it. "Everything I want," she said, "is right here."

She stroked his arm, and then kissed him.   46

On one level things remained the same between them. They slept to-   47
gether. They held hands and made plans for after the war. But now there
was a new imprecision in the way Mary Anne expressed her thoughts on
certain subjects. Not necessarily three kids, she'd say. Not necessarily a
house on Lake Erie. "Naturally we'll still get married," she'd tell him, "but it
doesn't have to be right away. Maybe travel first. Maybe live together. Just
test it out, you know?"

Mark Fossie would nod at this, even smile and agree, but it made him   48
uncomfortable. He couldn't pin it down. Her body seemed foreign somehow—too stiff in places, too firm where the softness used to be. The bub-
bliness was gone. The nervous giggling, too. When she laughed now, which
was rare, it was only when something struck her as truly funny. Her voice

seemed to reorganize itself at a lower pitch. In the evenings, while the men played cards, she would sometimes fall into long elastic silences, her eyes fixed on the dark, her arms folded, her foot tapping out a coded message against the floor. When Fossie asked about it one evening, Mary Anne looked at him for a long moment and then shrugged. "It's nothing," she said. "Really nothing. To tell the truth, I've never been happier in my whole life. Never."

Twice, though, she came in late at night. Very late. And then finally she did not come in at all.   49

Rat Kiley heard about it from Fossie himself. Before dawn one morning, the kid shook him awake. He was in bad shape. His voice seemed hollow and stuffed up, nasal-sounding, as if he had a bad cold. He held a flashlight in his hand, clicking it on and off.   50

"Mary Anne," he whispered, "I can't *find* her."   51

Rat sat up and rubbed his face. Even in the dim light it was clear that the boy was in trouble. There were dark smudges under his eyes, the frayed edges of somebody who hadn't slept in a while.   52

"Gone," Fossie said. "Rat, listen, she's sleeping with somebody. Last night, she didn't even . . . I don't know what to *do*."   53

Abruptly then, Fossie seemed to collapse. He squatted down, rocking on his heels, still clutching the flashlight. Just a boy—eighteen years old. Tall and blond. A gifted athlete. A nice kid, too, polite and good-hearted, although for the moment none of it seemed to be serving him well.   54

He kept clicking the flashlight on and off.   55

"All right, start at the start," Rat said. "Nice and slow. Sleeping with who?"   56

"I don't know who. Eddie Diamond."   57

"Eddie?"   58

"Has to be. The guy's always there, always hanging on her."   59

Rat shook his head. "Man, I don't know. Can't say it strikes a right note, not with Eddie."   60

"Yes, but he's—"   61

"Easy does it," Rat said. He reached out and tapped the boy's shoulder. "Why not just check some bunks? We got nine guys. You and me, that's two, so there's seven possibles. Do a quick body count."   62

Fossie hesitated. "But I can't . . . If she's there, I mean, if she's with somebody—"   63

"Oh, Christ."   64

Rat pushed himself up. He took the flashlight, muttered something, and moved down to the far end of the hootch. For privacy, the men had rigged up curtained walls around their cots, small makeshift bedrooms, and in the dark Rat went quickly from room to room, using the flashlight to pluck out the faces. Eddie Diamond slept a hard deep sleep—the others, too. To be sure, though, Rat checked once more, very carefully, then he reported back to Fossie.

"All accounted for. No extras."   66

"Eddie?"   67

"Darvon dreams." Rat switched off the flashlight and tried to think it out.   68
"Maybe she just—I don't know—maybe she camped out tonight. Under the stars or something. You search the compound?"

"Sure I did."   69

"Well, come on," Rat said. "One more time."   70

Outside, a soft violet light was spreading out across the eastern hillsides.   71
Two or three ARVN soldiers had built their breakfast fires, but the place was mostly quiet and unmoving. They tried the helipad first, then the mess hall and supply hootches, then they walked the entire six hundred meters of perimeter.

"Okay," Rat finally said. "We got a problem."   72

When he first told the story, Rat stopped there and looked at Mitchell   73
Sanders for a time.

"So what's your vote? Where was she?"   74

"The Greenies," Sanders said.   75

"Yeah?"   76

Sanders smiled. "No other option. That stuff about the Special Forces—   77
how they used the place as a base of operations, how they'd glide in and out—all that had to be there for a *reason*. That's how stories work, man."

Rat thought about it, then shrugged.   78

"All right, sure, the Greenies. But it's not what Fossie thought. She   79
wasn't sleeping with any of them. At least not exactly. I mean, in a way she was sleeping with *all* of them, more or less, except it wasn't sex or anything. They was just lying together, so to speak, Mary Anne and these six grungy weirded-out Green Berets."

"Lying down?" Sanders said.   80

"You got it."   81

"Lying down how?"   82

Rat smiled. "Ambush. All night long, man, Mary Anne's out on fuckin'   83
ambush."

Just after sunrise, Rat said, she came trooping in through the wire, tired-   84
looking but cheerful as she dropped her gear and gave Mark Fossie a brisk hug. The six Green Berets did not speak. One of them nodded at her, and the others gave Fossie a long stare, then they filed off to their hootch at the edge of the compound.

"Please," she said. "Not a word."   85

Fossie took a half step forward and hesitated. It was as though he had 86
trouble recognizing her. She wore a bush hat and filthy green fatigues; she
carried the standard M-16 automatic assault rifle; her face was black with
charcoal.

Mary Anne handed him the weapon. "I'm exhausted, she said. "We'll 87
talk later."

She glanced over at the Special Forces area, then turned and walked 88
quickly across the compound toward her own bunker. Fossie stood still for
a few seconds. A little dazed, it seemed. After a moment, though, he set his
jaw and whispered something and went after her with a hard, fast stride.

"Not later!" he yelled. "Now!" 89

What happened between them, Rat said, nobody ever knew for sure. 90
But in the mess hall that evening it was clear that an accommodation had
been reached. Or more likely, he said, it was a case of setting down some
new rules. Mary Anne's hair was freshly shampooed. She wore a white
blouse, a navy blue skirt, a pair of plain black flats. Over dinner she kept
her eyes down, poking at her food, subdued to the point of silence. Eddie
Diamond and some of the others tried to nudge her into talking about the
ambush—What was the feeling out there? What exactly did she see and
hear?—but the questions seemed to give her trouble. Nervously, she'd look
across the table at Fossie. She'd wait a moment, as if to receive some sort of
clearance, then she'd bow her head and mumble out a vague word or two.
There were no real answers.

Mark Fossie, too, had little to say. 91

"Nobody's business," he told Rat that night. Then he offered a brief 92
smile. "One thing for sure, though, there won't be any more ambushes. No
more late nights."

"You laid down the law?" 93

"Compromise," Fossie said. "I'll put it this way—we're officially engaged." 94

Rat nodded cautiously. 95

"Well hey, she'll make a sweet bride," he said. "Combat ready." 96

Over the next several days there was a strained, tightly wound quality to 97
the way they treated each other, a rigid correctness that was enforced by
repetitive acts of willpower. To look at them from a distance, Rat said, you
would think they were the happiest two people on the planet. They spent
the long afternoons sunbathing together, stretched out side by side on top
of their bunker, or playing backgammon in the shade of a giant palm tree,
or just sitting quietly. A model of togetherness, it seemed. And yet at close
range their faces showed the tension. Too polite, too thoughtful. Mark Fossie tried hard to keep up a self-assured pose, as if nothing had ever come
between them, or ever could, but there was a fragility to it, something ten-

tative and false. If Mary Anne happened to move a few steps away from him, even briefly, he'd tighten up and force himself not to watch her. But then a moment later he'd be watching.

In the presence of others, at least, they kept on their masks. Over meals they talked about plans for a huge wedding in Cleveland Heights—a two-day bash, lots of flowers. And yet even then their smiles seemed too intense. They were too quick with their banter; they held hands as if afraid to let go. 98

It had to end, and eventually it did. 99

Near the end of the third week Fossie began making arrangements to send her home. At first, Rat said, Mary Anne seemed to accept it, but then after a day or two she fell into a restless gloom, sitting off by herself at the edge of the perimeter. She would not speak. Shoulders hunched, her blue eyes opaque, she seemed to disappear inside herself. A couple of times Fossie approached her and tried to talk it out, but Mary Anne just stared out at the dark green mountains to the west. The wilderness seemed to draw her in. A haunted look, Rat said—partly terror, partly rapture. It was as if she had come up on the edge of something, as if she were caught in that no-man's-land between Cleveland Heights and deep jungle. Seventeen years old. Just a child, blond and innocent, but then weren't they all? 100

The next morning she was gone. The six Greenies were gone, too. 101

In a way, Rat said, poor Fossie expected it, or something like it, but that did not help much with the pain. The kid couldn't function. The grief took him by the throat and squeezed and would not let go. 102

"Lost," he kept whispering. 103

It was nearly three weeks before she returned. But in a sense she never returned. Not entirely, not all of her. 104

By chance, Rat said, he was awake to see it. A damp misty night, he couldn't sleep, so he'd gone outside for a quick smoke. He was just standing there, he said, watching the moon, and then off to the west a column of silhouettes appeared as if by magic at the edge of the jungle. At first he didn't recognize her—a small, soft shadow among six other shadows. There was no sound. No real substance either. The seven silhouettes seemed to float across the surface of the earth, like spirits, vaporous and unreal. As he watched, Rat said, it made him think of some weird opium dream. The silhouettes moved without moving. Silently, one by one they came up the hill, passed through the wire, and drifted in a loose file across the compound. It was then, Rat said, that he picked out Mary Anne's face. Her eyes seemed to shine in the dark—not blue, though, but a bright glowing jungle green. She did not pause at Fossie's bunker. She cradled her weapon and moved swiftly to the Special Forces hootch and followed the others inside. 105

Briefly, a light came on, and someone laughed, then the place went   106
dark again.

Whenever he told the story, Rat had a tendency to stop now and then,   107
interrupting the flow, inserting little clarifications or bits of analysis and personal opinion. It was a bad habit, Mitchell Sanders said, because all that matters is the raw material, the stuff itself, and you can't clutter it up with your
own half-baked commentary. That just breaks the spell. It destroys the magic.
What you have to do, Sanders said, is trust your own story. Get the hell out
of the way and let it tell itself.

But Rat Kiley couldn't help it. He wanted to bracket the full range of   108
meaning.

"I know it sounds far-out," he'd tell us, "but it's not like *impossible* or   109
anything. We all heard plenty of wackier stories. Some guy comes back from
the bush, tells you he saw the Virgin Mary out there, she was riding a goddamn goose or something. Everybody buys it. Everybody smiles and asks
how fast was they going, did she have spurs on. Well, it's not like that. This
Mary Anne wasn't no virgin but at least she was real. I saw it. When she
came in through the wire that night, I was right there, I saw those eyes of
hers, I saw how she wasn't even the same person no more. What's so impossible about that? She was a girl, that's all. I mean, if it was a guy,
everybody'd say, Hey, no big deal, he got caught up in the Nam shit, he got
seduced by the Greenies. See what I mean? You got these blinders on about
women. How gentle and peaceful they are. All that crap about how if we
had a pussy for president there wouldn't be no more wars. Pure garbage.
You got to get rid of that sexist attitude."

Rat would go on like that until Mitchell Sanders couldn't tolerate it any   110
longer. It offended his inner ear.

"The story," Sanders would say. "The whole tone, man, you're wreck-   111
ing it."

"The *sound*. You need to get a consistent sound, like slow or fast, funny   112
or sad. All these digressions, they just screw up your story's *sound*. Stick to
what happened."

Frowning, Rat would close his eyes.   113

"Tone?" he'd say. "I didn't know it was all that complicated. The girl   114
joined the zoo. One more animal—end of story."

"Yeah, fine. But tell it right."   115

At daybreak the next morning, when Mark Fossie heard she was back,   116
he stationed himself outside the fenced-off Special Forces area. All morning
he waited for her, and all afternoon. Around dusk Rat brought him something to eat.

"She has to come out," Fossie said. "Sooner or later, she has to."   117

"Or else what?" Rat said.   118

"I go get her. I bring her out."   119

Rat shook his head. "Your decision. I was you, though, no way I'd mess   120
around with any Greenie types, not for nothing."

"It's Mary Anne in there."   121

"Sure, I know that. All the same, I'd knock real extra super polite."   122

Even with the cooling night air Fossie's face was slick with sweat. He   123
looked sick. His eyes were bloodshot; his skin had a whitish, almost colorless cast. For a few minutes Rat waited with him, quietly watching the
hootch, then he patted the kid's shoulder and left him alone.

It was after midnight when Rat and Eddie Diamond went out to check   124
on him. The night had gone cold and steamy, a low fog sliding down from
the mountains, and somewhere out in the dark they heard music playing.
Not loud but not soft either. It had a chaotic, almost unmusical sound, without rhythm or form or progression, like the noise of nature. A synthesizer, it
seemed, or maybe an electric organ. In the background, just audible, a
woman's voice was half singing, half chanting, but the lyrics seemed to be
in a foreign tongue.

They found Fossie squatting near the gate in front of the Special Forces   125
area. Head bowed, he was swaying to the music, his face wet and shiny. As
Eddie bent down beside him, the kid looked up with dull eyes, ashen and
powdery, not quite in register.

"Hear that?" he whispered. "You *hear?* It's Mary Anne."   126

Eddie Diamond took his arm. "Let's get you inside. Somebody's radio,   127
that's all it is. Move it now."

"Mary Anne. Just listen."   128

"Sure, but—"   129

"Listen!"   130

Fossie suddenly pulled away, twisting sideways, and fell back against   131
the gate. He lay there with his eyes closed. The music—the noise, whatever
it was—came from the hootch beyond the fence. The place was dark except
for a small glowing window, which stood partly open, the panes dancing in
bright reds and yellows as though the glass were on fire. The chanting
seemed louder now. Fiercer, too, and higher pitched.

Fossie pushed himself up. He wavered for a moment then forced the   132
gate open.

"That voice," he said. "Mary Anne."   133

Rat took a step forward, reaching out for him, but Fossie was already   134
moving fast toward the hootch. He stumbled once, caught himself, and hit
the door hard with both arms. There was a noise—a short screeching sound,
like a cat—and the door swung in and Fossie was framed there for an in-

stant, his arms stretched out, then he slipped inside. After a moment Rat and
Eddie followed quietly. Just inside the door they found Fossie bent down on
one knee. He wasn't moving.

Across the room a dozen candles were burning on the floor near the   135
open window. The place seemed to echo with a weird deep-wilderness
sound—tribal music—bamboo flutes and drums and chimes. But what hit
you first, Rat said, was the smell. Two kinds of smells. There was a topmost
scent of joss sticks and incense, like the fumes of some exotic smokehouse,
but beneath the smoke lay a deeper and much more powerful stench. Impossible to describe, Rat said. It paralyzed your lungs. Thick and numbing,
like an animal's den, a mix of blood and scorched hair and excrement and
the sweet-sour odor of moldering flesh—the stink of the kill. But that wasn't
all. On a post at the rear of the hootch was the decayed head of a large black
leopard; strips of yellow-brown skin dangled from the overhead rafters. And
bones. Stacks of bones—all kinds. To one side, propped up against a wall,
stood a poster in neat black lettering: ASSEMBLE YOUR OWN GOOK!! FREE SAMPLE
KIT!! The images came in a swirl, Rat said, and there was no way you could
process it all. Off in the gloom a few dim figures lounged in hammocks, or on
cots, but none of them moved or spoke. The background music came from a
tape deck near the circle of candles, but the high voice was Mary Anne's.

After a second Mark Fossie made a soft moaning sound. He started to   136
get up but then stiffened.

"Mary Anne?" he said.   137

Quietly then, she stepped out of the shadows. At least for a moment she   138
seemed to be the same pretty young girl who had arrived a few weeks earlier. She was barefoot. She wore her pink sweater and a white blouse and a
simple cotton skirt.

For a long while the girl gazed down at Fossie, almost blankly, and in   139
the candlelight her face had the composure of someone perfectly at peace
with herself. It took a few seconds, Rat said, to appreciate the full change.
In part it was her eyes: utterly flat and indifferent. There was no emotion
in her stare, no sense of the person behind it. But the grotesque part, he
said, was her jewelry. At the girl's throat was a necklace of human tongues.
Elongated and narrow, like pieces of blackened leather, the tongues were
threaded along a length of copper wire, one overlapping the next, the tips
curled upward as if caught in a final shrill syllable.

Briefly, it seemed, the girl smiled at Mark Fossie.   140

"There's no sense talking," she said. "I know what you think, but it's   141
not . . . it's not *bad*."

"Bad?" Fossie murmured.   142

"It's not."   143

In the shadows there was laughter. 144

One of the Greenies sat up and lighted a cigar. The others lay silent. 145

"You're in a place," Mary Anne said softly, "where you don't belong." 146

She moved her hand in a gesture that encompassed not just the hootch 147
but everything around it, the entire war, the mountains, the mean little villages, the trails and trees and rivers and deep misted-over valleys.

"You just don't *know*," she said. "You hide in this little fortress, behind 148
wire and sandbags, and you don't know what it's all about. Sometimes I want
to *eat* this place. Vietnam. I want to swallow the whole country—the dirt, the
death—I just want to eat it and have it there inside me. That's how I feel. It's
like . . . this appetite. I get scared sometimes—lots of times—but it's not *bad*.
You know? I feel close to myself. When I'm out there at night, I feel close to
my own body, I can feel my blood moving, my skin and my fingernails,
everything, it's like I'm full of electricity and I'm glowing in the dark—I'm on
fire almost—I'm burning away into nothing—but it doesn't matter because I
know exactly who I am. You can't feel like that anywhere else."

All this was said softly, as if to herself, her voice slow and impassive. She 149
was not trying to persuade. For a few moments she looked at Mark Fossie,
who seemed to shrink away, then she turned and moved back into the gloom.

There was nothing to be done. 150

Rat took Fossie's arm, helped him up, and led him outside. In the dark- 151
ness there was that weird tribal music, which seemed to come from the
earth itself, from the deep rain forest, and a woman's voice rising up in a
language beyond translation.

Mark Fossie stood rigid. 152

"Do something, he whispered. "I can't just let her go like that." 153

Rat listened for a time, then shook his head. 154

"Man, you must be deaf. She's already gone." 155

Rat Kiley stopped there, almost in midsentence, which drove Mitchell 156
Sanders crazy.

"What next?" he said. 157

"Next?" 158

"The girl. What happened to her?" 159

Rat made a small, tired motion with his shoulders. "Hard to tell for sure. 160
Maybe three, four days later I got orders to report here to Alpha Company.
Jumped the first chopper out, that's the last I ever seen of the place. Mary
Anne, too."

Mitchell Sanders stared at him. 161

"You can't do that." 162

"Do what?" 163

"Jesus Christ, it's against the *rules*," Sanders said. |164

"Against human *nature*. This elaborate story, you can't say, Hey, by the |165
way, I don't know the *ending*. I mean, you got certain obligations."

Rat gave a quick smile. "Patience, man. Up to now, everything I told you |166
is from personal experience, the exact truth, but there's a few other things I
heard secondhand. Thirdhand, actually. From here on it gets to be . . . I
don't know what the word is."

"Speculation." |167

"Yeah, right." Rat looked off to the west, scanning the mountains, as if |168
expecting something to appear on one of the high ridgelines. After a second
he shrugged. "Anyhow, maybe two months later I ran into Eddie Diamond
over in Bangkok—I was on R&R, just this fluke thing—and he told me some
stuff I can't vouch for with my own eyes. Even Eddie didn't really see it. He
heard it from one of the Greenies, so you got to take this with a whole shak-
erful of salt."

Once more, Rat searched the mountains, then he sat back and closed |169
his eyes.

"You know," he said abruptly, "I loved her." |170

"Say again?" |171

"A lot. We all did, I guess. The way she looked, Mary Anne made you |172
think about those girls back home, how clean and innocent they all are,
how they'll never understand any of this, not in a billion years. Try to tell them
about it, they'll just stare at you with those big round candy eyes. They won't
understand zip. It's like trying to tell somebody what chocolate tastes like."

Mitchell Sanders nodded. "Or shit." |173

"There it is, you got to taste it, and that's the thing with Mary Anne. She |174
was *there*. She was up to her eyeballs in it. After the war, man, I promise
you, you won't find nobody like her."

Suddenly, Rat pushed up to his feet, moved a few steps away from us, |175
then stopped and stood with his back turned. He was an emotional guy.

"Got hooked, I guess," he said. "I loved her. So when I heard from Eddie |176
about what happened, it almost made me . . . Like you say, it's pure
speculation."

"Go on," Mitchell Sanders said. "Finish up." |177

What happened to her, Rat said, was what happened to all of them. You |178
come over clean and you get dirty and then afterward it's never the same. A
question of degree. Some make it intact, some don't make it at all. For Mary
Anne Bell, it seemed, Vietnam had the effect of a powerful drug: that mix of
unnamed terror and unnamed pleasure that comes as the needle slips in and
you know you're risking something. The endorphins start to flow, and the
adrenaline, and you hold your breath and creep quietly through the moon-

lit nightscapes; you become intimate with danger; you're in touch with the far side of yourself, as though it's another hemisphere, and you want to string it out and go wherever the trip takes you and be host to all the possibilities inside yourself. Not *bad,* she'd said. Vietnam made her glow in the dark. She wanted more, she wanted to penetrate deeper into the mystery of herself, and after a time the wanting became needing, which turned then to craving.

According to Eddie Diamond, who heard it from one of the Greenies, she took a greedy pleasure in night patrols. She was good at it; she had the moves. All camouflaged up, her face smooth and vacant, she seemed to flow like water through the dark, like oil, without sound or center. She went barefoot. She stopped carrying a weapon. There were times, apparently, when she took crazy, death-wish chances—things that even the Greenies balked at. It was as if she were taunting some wild creature out in the bush, or in her head, inviting it to show itself, a curious game of hide-and-go-seek that was played out in the dense terrain of a nightmare. She was lost inside herself. On occasion, when they were taken under fire, Mary Anne would stand quietly and watch the tracer rounds snap by, a little smile at her lips, intent on some private transaction with the war. Other times she would simply vanish altogether—for hours, for days. | 179

And then one morning, all alone, Mary Anne walked off into the mountains and did not come back. | 180

No body was ever found. No equipment, no clothing. For all he knew, Rat said, the girl was still alive. Maybe up in one of the high mountain villes, maybe with the Montagnard tribes. But that was guesswork. | 181

There was an inquiry, of course, and a week-long air search, and for a time the Tra Bong compound went crazy with MP and CID types. In the end, however, nothing came of it. It was a war and the war went on. Mark Fossie was busted to PFC, shipped back to a hospital in the States, and two months later received a medical discharge. Mary Anne Bell joined the missing. | 182

But the story did not end there. If you believed the Greenies, Rat said, Mary Anne was still somewhere out there in the dark. Odd movements, odd shapes. Late at night, when the Greenies were out on ambush, the whole rain forest seemed to stare in at them—a watched feeling—and a couple of times they almost saw her sliding through the shadows. Not quite, but almost. She had crossed to the other side. She was part of the land. She was wearing her culottes, her pink sweater, and a necklace of human tongues. She was dangerous. She was ready for the kill. | 183

Working with the Text

1. Stories that last, writes O'Brien, are "those that swirl back and forth across the border between trivia and bedlam, the mad and the

mundane." How is "Sweetheart" such a story? What in the story is trivia and what is bedlam, what mad and what mundane? What kind of a border lies between these domains, which are not true opposites and therefore not natural adversaries? What other borders does O'Brien's story explore?

2. Near the beginning, the narrator reflects on truth, noting that he heard the story he was about to tell from Rat Kiley, an unreliable source. Is this a disclaimer? If so, what are its purposes? Why is the story of Mary Anne a twice told tale, in the first place? O'Brien goes on to insist that Kiley typically exaggerated, not to deceive but to "heat up the truth." Does this line function as a guide to interpretation? What "truth" might O'Brien's story be "heating up"?

3. When Mary Anne returns from three weeks on patrol, according to Kiley, her eyes have turned from blue to "a bright glowing jungle green." What is the significance of this transformation? Of her later claim to be "glowing in the dark"?

 4. What is the significance of the setting of "Sweetheart"? How much does it matter that the war Mary Anne encounters is in Vietnam, rather than, say, Normandy or Kuwait?

 5. Narrate a story about a conventional character "type" who undergoes a frightening, possibly surreal transformation. Try to write as though telling the tale orally, though you need not furnish prefatory material or interruptions, as O'Brien has done.

Across the Wire

LUIS ALBERTO URREA

Born in Tijuana, Mexico, to an American mother and a Mexican father, Luis Alberto Urrea graduated from the University of California at San Diego in 1977. After working for several years as a film extra, Urrea began a career as a teacher. He has taught expository writing at Harvard and elsewhere. In addition to a novel, Urrea has also published *The Fever of Being* (1994), a collection of poems that won the Western States Book Award for poetry. He currently edits the literary magazine *Many Mountains Moving*. In the 1980s he joined a crew of relief workers helping poor people on the Mexican side of the U.S.–Mexican border, and he has written two books based on these experiences: *Across the Wire: Life and Hard Times on the Mexican Border* (1993) and *By the Lake of Sleeping Children: The Secret Life of the Mexican Border* (1996). The following chapter from *Across the Wire* describes the harrowing living conditions experienced by the poor on Mexico's border and what it feels like to bring these people the little relief that is possible.

Border Story

When I was younger, I went to war. The Mexican border was the battlefield. 1
There are many Mexicos; there are also many Mexican borders, any one of which could fill its own book. I, and the people with me, fought on a specific front. We sustained injuries and witnessed deaths. There were machine guns pointed at us, knives, pistols, clubs, even skyrockets. I caught a street-gang member trying to stuff a lit cherry bomb into our gas tank. On the same night, a drunk mariachi opened fire on the missionaries through the wall of his house.

We drove five beat-up vans. We were armed with water, medicine, sham- 2
poo, food, clothes, milk, and doughnuts. At the end of a day, like returning veterans from other battles, we carried secrets in our hearts that kept some of us awake at night, gave others dreams and fits of crying. Our faith sustained us—if not in God or "good," then in our work.

Others of us had no room for or interest in such drama, and came away 3
unscathed—and unmoved. Some of us sank into the mindless joy of fundamentalism, some of us drank, some of us married impoverished Mexicans. Most of us took it personally. Poverty *is* personal: it smells and it shocks and it invades your space. You come home dirty when you get too close to the poor. Sometimes you bring back vermin: they hide in your hair, in your underpants, in your intestines. These unpleasant possibilities are a given. They are the price you occasionally have to pay.

In Tijuana and environs, we met the many ambassadors of poverty: lice, 4
scabies, tapeworm, pinworm, ringworm, fleas, crab lice. We met diphtheria, meningitis, typhoid, polio, *turista* (diarrhea), tuberculosis, hepatitis, VD, impetigo, measles, chronic hernia, malaria, whooping cough. We met madness and "demon possession."

These were the products of dirt and disregard—bad things afflicting 5
good people. Their world was far from our world. Still, it would take you only about twenty minutes to get there from the center of San Diego.

For me, the worst part was the lack of a specific enemy. We were fight- 6
ing a nebulous, all-pervasive *It*. Call it hunger. Call it despair. Call it the

Devil, the System, Capitalism, the Cycle of Poverty, the Fruits of the Mexican Malaise. It was a seemingly endless circle of disasters. Long after I'd left, the wheel kept on grinding.

At night, the Border Patrol helicopters swoop and churn in the air all along the line. You can sit in the Mexican hills and watch them herd humans on the dusty slopes across the valley. They look like science fiction crafts, their hard-focused lights raking the ground as they fly.   7

Borderlands locals are so jaded by the sight of nightly people-hunting that it doesn't even register in their minds. But take a stranger to the border, and she will see the spectacle: monstrous Dodge trucks speeding into and out of the landscape; uniformed men patrolling with flashlights, guns, and dogs; spotlights; running figures; lines of people hurried onto buses by armed guards; and the endless clatter of the helicopters with their harsh white beams. A Dutch woman once told me it seemed altogether "un-American."   8

But the Mexicans keep on coming—and the Guatemalans, the Salvadorans, the Panamanians, the Colombians. The seven-mile stretch of Interstate 5 nearest the Mexican border is, at times, so congested with Latin American pedestrians that it resembles a town square.   9

They stick to the center island. Running down the length of the island is a cement wall. If the "illegals" (currently, "undocumented workers"; formerly, "wetbacks") are walking north and a Border Patrol vehicle happens along, they simply hop over the wall and trot south. The officer will have to drive up to the 805 interchange, or Dairy Mart Road, swing over the overpasses, then drive south. Depending on where this pursuit begins, his detour could entail five to ten miles of driving. When the officer finally reaches the group, they hop over the wall and trot north. Furthermore, because freeway arrests would endanger traffic, the Border Patrol has effectively thrown up its hands in surrender.   10

It seems jolly on the page. But imagine poverty, violence, natural disasters, or political fear driving you away from everything you know. Imagine how bad things get to make you leave behind your family, your friends, your lovers; your home, as humble as it might be; your church, say. Let's take it further—you've said good-bye to the graveyard, the dog, the goat, the mountains where you first hunted, your grade school, your state, your favorite spot on the river where you fished and took time to think.   11

Then you come hundreds—or thousands—of miles across territory utterly unknown to you. (Chances are, you have never traveled farther than a hundred miles in your life.) You have walked, run, hidden in the backs of trucks, spent part of your precious money on bus fare. There is no AAA or Travelers Aid Society available to you. Various features of your journey north might include police corruption; violence in the forms of beatings, rape, murder, tor-   12 ture, road accidents; theft; incarceration. Additionally, you might experience loneliness, fear, exhaustion, sorrow, cold, heat, diarrhea, thirst, hunger. There is no medical attention available to you. There isn't even Kotex.

Weeks or months later, you arrive in Tijuana. Along with other immigrants, you gravitate to the bad parts of town because there is nowhere for you to go in the glittery sections where the *gringos* flock. You stay in a run-down little hotel in the red-light district, or behind the bus terminal. Or you find your way to the garbage dumps, where you throw together a small cardboard nest and claim a few feet of dirt for yourself. The garbage-pickers working this dump might allow you to squat, or they might come and rob you or burn you out for breaking some local rule you cannot possibly know beforehand. Sometimes the dump is controlled by a syndicate, and goon squads might come to you within a day. They want money, and if you can't pay, you must leave or suffer the consequences.

In town, you face endless victimization if you aren't streetwise. The police come after you, street thugs come after you, petty criminals come after you; strangers try your door at night as you sleep. Many shady men offer to guide you across the border, and each one wants all your money now, and promises to meet you at a prearranged spot. Some of your fellow travelers end their journeys right here—relieved of their savings and left to wait on a dark corner until they realize they are going nowhere.

If you are not Mexican, and can't pass as *tijuanense,* a local, the tough guys find you out. Salvadorans and Guatemalans are routinely beaten up and robbed. Sometimes they are disfigured. Indians—Chinantecas, Mixtecas, Guasaves, Zapotecas, Mayas—are insulted and pushed around; often they are lucky—they are merely ignored. They use this to their advantage. Often they don't dream of crossing into the United States: a Mexican tribal person would never be able to blend in, and they know it. To them, the garbage dumps and street vending and begging in Tijuana are a vast improvement over their former lives. As Doña Paula, a Chinanteca friend of mine who lives at the Tijuana garbage dump, told me, "This is the garbage dump. Take all you need. There's plenty here for *everyone!*"

If you are a woman, the men come after you. You lock yourself in your room, and when you must leave it to use the pestilential public bathroom at the end of your floor, you hurry, and you check every corner. Sometimes the lights are out in the toilet room. Sometimes men listen at the door. They call you "good-looking" and "bitch" and *"mamacita,"* and they make kissing sounds at you when you pass.

You're in the worst part of town, but you can comfort yourself—at least there are no death squads here. There are no torturers here, or bandit land barons riding into your house. This is the last barrier, you think, between you and the United States—*los Yunaites Estaites.*

You still face police corruption, violence, jail. You now also have a wide   18
variety of new options available to you: drugs, prostitution, white slavery,
crime. Tijuana is not easy on newcomers. It is a city that has always thrived
on taking advantage of a sucker. And the innocent are the ultimate suckers
in the Borderlands.

If you have saved up enough money, you go to one of the *coyotes*   19
(people-smugglers), who guide travelers through the violent canyons immediately north of the border. Lately, these men are also called *polleros,* or
"chicken-wranglers." Some of them are straight, some are land pirates. Negotiations are tense and strange: *polleros* speak a Spanish you don't quite
understand—like the word *polleros.* Linguists call the new border-speak
"Spanglish," but in Tijuana, Spanglish is mixed with slang and *pochismos*
(the polyglot hip talk of Mexicans infected with *gringoismo;* the *cholos* in
Mexico, or Chicanos on the American side).

Suddenly, the word for "yes," *sí,* can be *simón* or *siról.* "No" is *chale.*   20
"Bike" *(bicicleta)* is *baica.* "Wife" *(esposa)* is *waifa.* "The police" *(la policía)*
are *la chota.* "Women" are *rucas* or *morras.* You don't know what they're talking about.

You pay them all your money—sometimes it's your family's lifelong sav-   21
ings. Five hundred dollars should do it. *"Orale,"* the dude tells you, which
means "right on." You must wait in Colonia Libertad, the most notorious
barrio in town, ironically named "Liberty."

The scene here is baffling. Music blares from radios. Jolly women at   22
smoky taco stands cook food for the journeys, sell jugs of water. You can
see the Border Patrol agents cruising the other side of the fence; they trade
insults with the locals.

When the appointed hour comes, you join a group of *pollos* (chickens)   23
who scuttle along behind the *coyote.* You crawl under the wires, or, if you
go a mile east, you might be amazed to find that the famous American Border Fence simply stops. To enter the United States, you merely step around
the end of it. And you follow your guide into the canyons. You might be
startled to find groups of individuals crossing the line without *coyotes* leading them at all. You might wonder how they have mastered the canyons,
and you might begin to regret the loss of your money.

If you have your daughters or mothers or wives with you—or if you are   24
a woman—you become watchful and tense, because rape and gang rape are
so common in this darkness as to be utterly unremarkable. If you have any
valuables left after your various negotiations, you try to find a sly place to hide
them in case you meet *pandilleros* (gang members) or *rateros* (thieves—
ratmen). But, really, where can you put anything? Thousands have come be-

fore you, and the hiding places are pathetically obvious to robbers: in shoulder bags or clothing rolls, pinned inside clothes, hidden in underwear, inserted in body orifices.

If the *coyote* does not turn on you suddenly with a gun and take everything from you himself, you might still be attacked by the *rateros*. If the *rateros* don't get you, there are roving zombies that you can smell from fifty yards downwind—these are the junkies who hunt in shambling packs. If the junkies somehow miss you, there are the *pandilleros*—gang-bangers from either side of the border who are looking for some bloody fun. They adore "taking off" illegals because it's the perfect crime: there is no way they can ever be caught. They are Tijuana *cholos,* or Chicano *vatos,* or Anglo head-bangers. 25

Their sense of fun relies heavily on violence. Gang beatings are their preferred sport, though rape in all its forms is common, as always. Often the *coyote* will turn tail and run at the first sight of *pandilleros*. What's another load of desperate chickens to him? He's just making a living, taking care of business. 26

If he doesn't run, there is a good chance he will be the first to be assaulted. The most basic punishment these young toughs mete out is a good beating, but they might kill him in front of the *pollos* if they feel the immigrants need a lesson in obedience. For good measure, these boys—they are mostly *boys,* aged twelve to nineteen, bored with Super Nintendo and MTV—beat people and slash people and thrash the women they have just finished raping. 27

Their most memorable tactic is to hamstring the *coyote* or anyone who dares speak out against them. This entails slicing the muscles in the victim's legs and leaving him to flop around in the dirt, crippled. If you are in a group of *pollos* that happens to be visited by these furies, you are learning border etiquette. 28

Now, say you are lucky enough to evade all these dangers on your journey. Hazards still await you and your family. You might meet white racists, complimenting themselves with the tag "Aryans"; they "patrol" the scrub in combat gear, carrying radios, high-powered flashlights, rifles, and bats. Rattlesnakes hide in bushes—you didn't count on that complication. Scorpions, tarantulas, black widows. And, of course, there is the Border Patrol *(la migra)*. 29

They come over the hills on motorcycles, on horses, in huge Dodge Ramcharger four-wheel drives. They yell, wear frightening goggles, have guns. Sometimes they are surprisingly decent; sometimes they are too tired or too bored to put much effort into dealing with you. They collect you in a large group of fellow *pollos,* and a guard (a Mexican Border Patrol agent!) jokes with your group in Spanish. Some cry, some sulk, most laugh. Mexicans hate 30 to be rude. You don't know what to think—some of your fellow travelers take their arrest with aplomb. Sometimes the officers know their names. But you have been told repeatedly that the Border Patrol sometimes beats or kills people. Everyone talks about the Mexican girl molested inside its building.

The Border Patrol puts you into trucks that take you to buses that take   31
you to compounds that load you onto other buses that transport you back to Tijuana and put you out. Your *coyote* isn't bothered in the least. Some of the regulars who were with you go across and get brought back a couple of times a night. But for you, things are different. You have been brought back with no place to sleep. You have already spent all your money. You might have been robbed, so you have only your clothes—maybe not all of them. The robbers may have taken your shoes. You might be bloodied from a beating by *pandilleros,* or an "accident" in the Immigration and Naturalization Service compound. You can't get proper medical attention. You can't eat, or afford to feed your family. Some of your compatriots have been separated from their wives or their children. Now their loved ones are in the hands of strangers, in the vast and unknown United States. The Salvadorans are put on planes and flown back to the waiting arms of the military. As you walk through the cyclone fence, back into Tijuana, the locals taunt you and laugh at your misfortune.

If you were killed, you have nothing to worry about.   32

Now what?   33

Perhaps you'll join one of the other groups that break through the Tor-   34
tilla Curtain every night. The road-runners. They amass at dusk along the cement canal that separates the United States from Mexico. This wide alley is supposedly the Tijuana River, but it's usually dry, or running with sewage that Tijuana pumps toward the U.S. with great gusto.

As soon as everybody feels like it—there are no *coyotes* needed   35
here—you join the groups passing through the gaping holes in the fence. Houses and alleys and cantinas back up against it, and in some spots, people have driven stolen cars into the poles to provide a wider passage. You rush across the canal and up the opposite slope, timing your dash between passing *migra* trucks and the overflights of helicopters. Following the others, you begin your jog toward the freeway. Here, there are mostly just Border Patrol officers to outrun—not that hard if you're in good shape. There are still some white-supremacist types bobbling around, but the cops will get them if they do anything serious. No, here the problem is the many lanes of I-5.

You stand at the edge of the road and wonder how you're going to cut   36
across five lanes of traffic going sixty miles an hour. Then, there is the problem of the next five lanes. The freeway itself is constructed to run parallel to

the border, then swing north. Its underpasses and storm-drain pipes offer another subterranean world, but you don't know about them. All you know is you have to get across at some point, and get far from the hunters who would take you back.

If you hang around the shoulder of I–5 long enough, you will find that   37 many of your companions don't make it. So many have been killed and injured that the *gringos* have put up warning signs to motorists to watch for running people. The orange signs show a man, a woman, and a child charging across. Some *gringos* are so crazy with hate for you that they speed up, or aim for you as you run.

The vague blood of over a hundred slain runners shadows the concrete.   38

On either side of the border, clustered near the gates, there are dapper-   39 looking men, dressed in nice cowboy clothes, and they speak without looking anyone in the eye. They are saying, "Los Angeles. San Bernardino. San Francisco."

They have a going concern: business is good.   40

Once you've gotten across the line, there will always be the question of   41 *Where do I go now?* "Illegal aliens" have to eat, sleep, find work. Once across, you must begin another journey.

Not everyone has the energy to go on. Even faith—in Jesus, the Virgin   42 Mary, or the Streets of Gold—breaks down sooner or later. Many of these immigrants founder at the border. There is a sad swirl of humanity in Tijuana. Outsiders eddy there who have simply run out of strength. If North America does not want them, Tijuana wants them even less. They become the outcasts of an outcast region. We could all see them if we looked hard enough: they sell chewing gum. Their children sing in traffic. In bars downtown, the women will show us a breast for a quarter. They wash our windshields at every stoplight. But mostly, they are invisible. To see them, we have to climb up the little canyons all around the city, where the cardboard shacks and mud and smoke look like a lost triptych by Hieronymus Bosch. We have to wade into the garbage dumps and the orphanages, sit in the little churches and the hospitals, or go out into the back country, where they raise their goats and bake red bricks and try to live decent lives.

They are not welcome in Tijuana. And, for the most part, Tijuana itself   43 is not welcome in the Motherland. Tijuana is Mexico's cast-off child. She brings in money and *gringos,* but nobody would dare claim her. As a Mexican diplomat once confided to me, "We both know Tijuana is not Mexico. The border is nowhere. It's a no-man's-land."

I was born there.   44

My Story

I was born in Tijuana, to a Mexican father and an American mother. I was   45
registered with the U.S. government as an American Citizen, Born Abroad.
Raised in San Diego, I crossed the border all through my boyhood with abandon, utterly bilingual and bicultural. In 1977, my father died on the border,
violently. (The story is told in detail in a chapter entitled "Father's Day.")

In the Borderlands, anything can happen. And if you're in Tijuana long   46
enough, anything *will* happen. Whole neighborhoods appear and disappear
seemingly overnight. For example, when I was a boy, you got into Tijuana
by driving through the Tijuana River itself. It was a muddy floodplain
bustling with animals and belching old cars. A slum that spread across
the riverbed was known as "Cartolandia." In border-speak, this meant "Land
of Cardboard."

Suddenly, it was time for Tijuana to spruce up its image to attract more   47
American dollars, and Cartolandia was swept away by a flash flood of trac-
tors. The big machines swept down the length of the river, crushing shacks
and toppling fences. It was like magic. One week, there were choked multitudes of sheds; the next, a clear, flat space awaiting the blank concrete of
a flood channel. Town—no town.

The inhabitants of Cartolandia fled to the outskirts, where they were bet-   48
ter suited to Tijuana's new image as Shopping Mecca. They had effectively
vanished. Many of them homesteaded the Tijuana municipal garbage dump.
The city's varied orphanages consumed many of their children.

Tijuana's characteristic buzz can be traced directly to a mixture of dread   49
and expectation: there's always something coming.

I never intended to be a missionary. I didn't go to church, and I had no   50
reason to believe I'd be involved with a bunch of Baptists. But in 1978, I had
occasion to meet a remarkable preacher known as Pastor Von (Erhardt
George von Trutzschler III, no less): as well as being a minister, he was a
veteran of the Korean War, a graphic artist, a puppeteer, a German baron,
an adventurer, and a practical joker. Von got me involved in the hardships
and discipline he calls "Christian Boot Camp."

After working as a youth pastor in San Diego for many years, he had dis-   51
covered Mexico in the late sixties. His work there began with the typical
church do-good activities that everyone has experienced at least once: a bag
of blankets for the orphans, a few Christmas toys, alms for the poor. As
Protestantism spread in Mexico, however, interest in Von's preaching grew.
Small churches and Protestant orphanages and Protestant *barrios,* lacking
ministers of their own, began asking Von to teach. Preaching and pastoring
led to more work; work led to more needs; more needs pulled in more

workers. On it went until Von had put in thirty or so years slogging through the Borderlands mud, and his little team of die-hard renegades and border rats had grown to a nonprofit corporation (Spectrum Ministries, Inc.), where you'll find him today.

Von's religious ethic is similar in scope to Teresa of Calcutta's. Von favors actual works over heavy evangelism. Spectrum is based on a belief Christians call "living the gospel." This doctrine is increasingly rare in America, since it involves little lip service, hard work, and no glory.   52

Von often reminds his workers that they are "ambassadors of Christ" and should comport themselves accordingly. Visitors are indelicately stripped of their misconceptions and prejudices when they discover that the crust on Von and his crew is a mile thick: the sight of teenybopper Bible School girls enduring Von's lurid pretrip briefing is priceless. Insouciantly, he offers up his litany: lice, worms, pus, blood; diarrhea, rattletrap outhouses, no toilet paper; dangerous water and food; diseased animals that will leave you with scabies; rats, maggots, flies; *odor*. Then he confuses them by demanding love and respect for the poor. He caps his talk with: "Remember—you are not going to the zoo. These are people. Don't run around snapping pictures of them like they're animals. Don't rush into their shacks saying, 'Ooh, gross!' They live there. Those are their homes."   53

Because border guards often "confiscate" chocolate milk, the cartons must be smuggled into Mexico under bags of clothes. Because the floors of the vans get so hot, the milk will curdle, so the crew must first freeze it. The endless variations of challenge in the Borderlands keep Von constantly alert—problems come three at a time and must be solved on the run.   54

Like the time a shipment of tennis shoes was donated to Spectrum. They were new, white, handsome shoes. The only problem was that no two shoes in the entire shipment matched. Von knew there was no way the Mexican kids could use *one* shoe, and they—like teens everywhere—were fashion-conscious and wouldn't be caught dead in unmatching sneakers.   55

Von's solution was practical and witty. He donned unmatched shoes and made his crew members wear unmatched shoes. Then he announced that it was the latest California surfer rage; kids in California weren't considered hip unless they wore unmatched shoes. The shipment was distributed, and shoeless boys were shod in the faux fashion craze begun by Chez Von.   56

Von has suffered for his beliefs. In the ever more conservative atmosphere of American Christianity (read: Protestantism), the efforts of Spectrum have come under fire on several occasions. He was once denounced because he refused to use the King James Bible in his sermons—clearly the sign of a heretic.   57

Von's terse reply to criticism: "It's hard to 'save' people when they're dead."   58

* * *

Von has a Monday night ministerial run into Tijuana, and in his heyday,   59
he was hitting three or four orphanages a night. I was curious, unaware of
the severity of the poverty in Tijuana. I knew it was there, but it didn't really
mean anything to me. One night, in late October 1978, my curiosity got the
better of me. I didn't believe Von could show me anything about my home-
town that I didn't know. I was wrong. I quickly began to learn just how little I really knew.

He managed to get me involved on the first night. Actually, it was Von   60
and a little girl named América. América lived in one of the orphanages
barely five miles from my grandmother's house in the hills above Tijuana.

She had light hair and blue eyes like mine—she could have been my   61
cousin. When she realized I spoke Spanish, she clutched my fingers and
chattered for an hour without a break. She hung on harder when Von announced it was time to go. She begged me not to leave. América resorted to
a tactic many orphanage children master to keep visitors from leaving—she
wrapped her legs around my calf and sat on my foot. As I peeled her off, I
promised to return on Von's next trip.

He was waiting for me in the alley behind the orphanage.   62

"What did you say to that girl?" he asked.   63

"I told her I'd come back next week."   64

He glared at me. "Don't *ever* tell one of my kids you're coming back,"   65
he snapped. "Don't you know she'll wait all week for you? Then she'll wait
for months. Don't say it if you don't mean it."

"I mean it!" I said.   66

I went back the next time to see her. Then again. And, of course, there   67
were other places to go before we got to América's orphanage, and there
were other people to talk to after we left. Each location had people waiting
with messages and questions to translate. It didn't take long for Von to approach me with a proposition. It seemed he had managed the impressive
feat of spending a lifetime in Mexico without picking up any Spanish at all.
Within two months, I was Von's personal translator.

It is important to note that translation is often more delicate an art than   68
people assume. For example, Mexicans are regularly amused to read *TV
Guide* listings for Spanish-language TV stations. If one were to leave the
tilde (~) off the word *años,* or "years," the word becomes the plural for
"anus." Many cheap laughs are had when "The Lost Years" becomes "The
Lost Butt Holes."

It was clear that Von needed reliable translating. Once, when he had   69
arranged a summer camping trip for *barrio* children, he'd written a list of
items the children needed to take. A well-meaning woman on the team
translated the list for Von, and they Xeroxed fifty or sixty copies.

The word for "comb" in Spanish is *peine,* but leave out a letter, and the   70
word takes on a whole new meaning. Von's note, distributed to every child
and all their families, read:

You must bring CLEAN CLOTHES

TOOTH PASTE

SOAP

TOOTHBRUSH

SLEEPING BAG

and BOYS—You Must Remember

to BRING YOUR PENIS!

Von estimates that in a ten-year period his crew drove several *million*   71
miles in Mexico without serious incident. Over five hundred people came
and went as crew members. They transported more than sixty thousand visitors across the border.

In my time with him, I saw floods and three hundred-mile-wide prairie   72
fires, car wrecks and gang fights, monkeys and blood and shit. I saw human
intestines and burned flesh. I saw human fat through deep red cuts. I saw
people copulating. I saw animals tortured. I saw birthday parties in the sad-
dest sagging shacks. I looked down throats and up wombs with flashlights.
I saw lice, rats, dying dogs, rivers black with pollywogs, and a mound of
maggots three feet wide and two feet high. One little boy in the back country cooked himself with an overturned pot of boiling *frijoles;* when I asked
him if it hurt, he sneered like Pancho Villa and said, "Nah." A maddened
Pentecostal tried to heal our broken-down van by laying hands on the engine block. One girl who lived in a brickyard accidentally soaked her dress
in diesel fuel and lit herself on fire. When I went in the shed, she was standing there, naked, her entire front burned dark brown and red. The only part
of her not burned was her vulva; it was a startling cleft, a triangular island
of white in a sea of burns.

I saw miracles, too. A boy named Chispi, deep in a coma induced by   73
spinal meningitis, suffered a complete shutdown of one lobe of his brain.
The doctors in the intensive care unit, looking down at his naked little body
hard-wired to banks of machinery and pumps, just shook their heads. He
was doomed to be a vegetable, at best. His mother, fished out of the cantinas in Tijuana's red-light district, spent several nights sitting in the hospital
cafeteria sipping vending-machine coffee and telling me she hoped there
were miracles left for people like her.

Chispi woke up. The machines were blipping and pinging, and he sat   74
up and asked for Von. His brain had regenerated itself. They unhitched him,
pulled out the catheters, and pulled the steel shunt out of his skull. He went

home. There was no way anybody could explain it. Sometimes there were happy endings, and you spent as much time wondering about them as grieving over the tragedies.

God help me—it was fun. It was exciting and nasty. I strode, fearless, 75 through the Tijuana garbage dumps and the Barrio of Shallow Graves. I was doing good deeds, and the goodness thrilled me. But the squalor, too, thrilled me. Each stinking gray *barrio* gave me a wicked charge. I was arrested one night by Tijuana cops; I was so terrified that my knees wobbled like Jell-O. After they let me go, I was happy for a week. Mexican soldiers pointed machine guns at my testicles. I thought I was going to die. Later, I was so relieved, I laughed about it for days. Over the years, I was cut, punctured, sliced: I love my scars. I had girlfriends in every village, in every orphanage, at each garbage dump. For a time, I was a hero. And at night, when we returned, caked in dried mud, smelly, exhausted, and the good Baptists of Von's church looked askance at us, we felt dangerous. The housewives, grandmothers, fundamentalists, rock singers, bikers, former drug dealers, schoolgirls, leftists, republicans, jarheads, and I were all transformed into *The Wild Bunch*.

It added a certain flair to my dating life as well. It was not uncommon 76 for a Mexican crisis to track me down in the most unlikely places. I am reminded of the night I was sitting down to a fancy supper at a woman's apartment when the phone rang. A busload of kids from one of our orphanages had flipped over, killing the American daughter of the youth minister in charge of the trip. All the *gringos* had been arrested. The next hour was spent calling Tijuana cops, Mexican lawyers, cousins in Tijuana, and Von. I had to leave early to get across the border.

Incredibly, in the wake of this tragedy, the orphanage kids were taken 77 to the beach by yet another *gringo* church group, and one of the boys was hit by a car and killed.

My date was fascinated by all this, no doubt. 78

Slowly, it became obvious that nobody outside the experience under- 79 stood it. Only among ourselves was hunting for lice in each other's hair considered a nice thing. Nobody but us found humor in the appalling things we saw. No one else wanted to discuss the particulars of our bowel movements. By firsthand experience, we had become diagnosticians in the area of gastrointestinal affliction. Color and content spoke volumes to us: pale, mucus-heavy ropes of diarrhea suggested amoebas. Etc.

One of Von's pep talks revolved around the unconscionable wealth in 80 the United States. "Well," he'd say to some unsuspecting *gringo*, "you're probably not rich. You probably don't even have a television. Oh, you *do?* You have three televisions? One in each room? Wow. But surely you don't have furniture? You do? Living room furniture and beds in the bedroom? Imagine that!

"But you don't have a floor, do you? Do you have carpets? Four walls? A roof! What do you use for light—candles? *Lamps!* No way. Lamps.   81

"How about your kitchen—do you have a stove?"   82

He'd pick his way through the kitchen: the food, the plates and pots and   83
pans, the refrigerator, the ice. Ice cream. Soda. Booze. The closets, the clothes in the closets. Then to the bathroom and the miracle of indoor plumbing. Whoever lived in that house suddenly felt obscenely rich.

I was never able to reach Von's level of commitment. The time he   84
caught scabies, he allowed it to flourish in order to grasp the suffering of those from whom it originated. He slept on the floor because the majority of the world's population could not afford a bed.

Working with the Text

1. Urrea begins with a description of what it is like to be a poor Mexican in Tijuana who is trying to get across the border. How does this lead into the section headed "My Story"?

2. Near the end of this essay, Urrea writes, "God help me—it was fun. It was exciting and nasty. I strode, fearless, through the Tijuana garbage dumps and the Barrio of Shallow Graves. I was doing good deeds, and the goodness thrilled me. But the squalor, too, thrilled me. Each stinking gray *barrio* gave me a wicked charge." In what sense can you see facing these most appalling of human circumstances as thrilling?

3. How does Urrea use language and writing strategies to help convey his meaning? What is the effect of using a phrase like "ambassadors of poverty" when referring to lice, fleas, and other vermin? What about his use of pronouns, such as *we/us* and *you?* How does he rhetorically move between references to himself as an individual and his recollections of his co-workers as a collective group? How do these techniques point to his overall strategies of crossing borders? What are the different borders being crossed in this essay?

4. Urrea describes Pastor Von's warning the "teenybopper Bible School girls" working with the ministry not to treat the poor like animals and demand that the girls treat them with "love and respect." What does this suggest about the way volunteers sometimes approach the beneficiaries of their charity?

5. Could you work with a group like Spectrum Ministries? What would it take to get you involved?

On Not Being a Victim

MARY GAITSKILL

Born in Lexington, Kentucky, fiction writer Mary Gaitskill has said that she suffered a troubled adolescence, her rebelliousness leading her strict parents to institutionalize her several times. She ran away from home at sixteen and spent a number of years on the fringes of society, often supporting herself as a stripper. She eventually resumed her education and received a B.A. from the University of Michigan in 1981. She began publishing stories soon after, and her first collection, *Bad Behavior*, appeared in 1988. Since then she has published *Two Girls, Fat and Thin* (1991), a novel, and *Because They Wanted To* (1997), another collection of short stories. In the following essay, which originally appeared in the *Atlantic Monthly*, Gaitskill considers the subject of rape—what it means to be the female "victim" of male violation and how human subjectivity in interpreting "rules" can lead to disastrous consequences.

In the early 1970s, I had an experience that could be described as acquaintance rape. Actually, I have had two or three such experiences, but this one most dramatically fits the profile. I was sixteen and staying in the apartment of a slightly older girl I'd just met in a seedy community center in Detroit. I'd been in her apartment for a few days when an older guy she knew came over and asked us if we wanted to drop some acid. In those years, doing acid with complete strangers was consistent with my idea of a possible good time, so I said yes. When I started peaking, my hostess decided she had to go see her boyfriend, and there I was, alone with this guy, who, suddenly, was in my face.

He seemed to be coming on to me, but I wasn't sure. My perception was quite loopy, and on top of that he was black and urban-poor, which meant that I, being very inexperienced and suburban-white, did not know how to read him the way I might have read another white kid. I tried to distract him with conversation, but it was hard, considering that I was having trouble with logical sentences, let alone repartee. During one long silence, I asked him what he was thinking. Avoiding my eyes, he answered, "That if I wasn't such a nice guy you could really be getting screwed." The remark sounded

364

to me like a threat, albeit a low-key one. But instead of asking him to explain himself or to leave, I changed the subject. Some moments later, when he put his hand on my leg, I let myself be drawn into sex because I could not face the idea that if I said no, things might get ugly. I don't think he had any idea how unwilling I was—the cultural unfamiliarity cut both ways—and I suppose he may have thought that all white girls just kind of lie there and don't do or say much. My bad time was made worse by his extreme gentleness; he was obviously trying very hard to please me, which, for reasons I didn't understand, broke my heart. Even as inexperienced as I was, I sensed that in his own way he intended a romantic encounter.

For some time afterward I described this event as "the time I was raped." 3 I knew when I said it that the statement wasn't quite accurate, that I hadn't, after all, said no. Yet it *felt* accurate to me. In spite of my ambiguous, even empathic feelings for my unchosen partner, unwanted sex on acid is a nightmare, and I did feel violated by the experience. At times I even flat-out lied about what had happened, grossly exaggerating the violence and the threat—not out of shame or guilt, but because the pumped-up version was more congruent with my feelings of violation than the confusing facts. Every now and then, in the middle of telling an exaggerated version of the story, I would remember the actual man and internally pause, uncertain of how the memory squared with what I was saying or where my sense of violation was coming from—and then I would continue with my story. I am ashamed to admit this, both because it is embarrassing to me and because I am afraid the admission could be taken as evidence that women lie "to get revenge." I want to stress that I would not have lied that way in court or in any other context that might have had practical consequences; it didn't even occur to me to take my case to court. My lies were told not for revenge but in service of what I felt to be the metaphorical truth.

I remember my experience in Detroit, including its aftermath, every time 4 I hear or read yet another discussion of what constitutes "date rape." I remember it when yet another critic castigates "victimism" and complains that everyone imagines himself or herself to be a victim and that no one accepts responsibility anymore. I could imagine telling my story as a verification that rape occurs by subtle threat as well as by overt force. I could also imagine telling it as if I were one of those crybabies who want to feel like victims. Both stories would be true and not true. The complete truth is more complicated than most of the intellectuals who have written scolding essays on victimism seem willing to accept. I didn't understand my own story fully until I described it to an older woman many years later, as a proof of the unreliability of feelings. "Oh, I think your feelings were reliable," she returned.

"It sounds like you were raped. It sounds like you raped yourself." I immediately knew that what she said was true, that in failing even to try to speak up for myself, I had, in a sense, raped myself.

I don't say this in a tone of self-recrimination. I was in a difficult situation: I was very young, and he was aggressive. But my inability to speak for myself—to *stand up* for myself—had little to do with those facts. I was unable to stand up for myself because I had never been taught how.

When I was growing up in the 1960s, I was taught by the adult world that good girls never had sex and bad girls did. This rule had clarity going for it but little else; as it was presented to me, it allowed no room for what I actually might feel, what I might want or not want. Within the confines of this rule, I didn't count for much, and I quite vigorously rejected it. Then came the less clear "rules" of cultural trend and peer example that said that if you were cool you wanted to have sex as much as possible with as many people as possible. This message was never stated as a rule, but, considering how absolutely it was woven into the social etiquette of the day (at least in the circles I cared about), it may as well have been. It suited me better than the adults' rule—it allowed me my sexuality, at least—but again it didn't take into account what I might actually want or not want.

The encounter in Detroit, however, had nothing to do with being good or bad, cool or uncool. It was about someone wanting something I didn't want. Since I had been taught only how to follow rules that were somehow more important than I was, I didn't know what to do in a situation where no rules obtained and that required me to speak up on my own behalf. I had never been taught that my behalf mattered. And so I felt helpless, even victimized, without really knowing why.

My parents and my teachers believed that social rules existed to protect me and that adhering to these rules constituted social responsibility. Ironically, my parents did exactly what many commentators recommend as a remedy for victimism. They told me they loved me and that I mattered a lot, but this was not the message I got from the way they conducted themselves in relation to authority and social convention—which was not only that I didn't matter but that *they* didn't matter. In this, they were typical of other adults I knew as well as of the culture around them. When I began to have trouble in school, both socially and academically, a counselor exhorted me to "just play the game"—meaning to go along with everything from school policy to the adolescent pecking order—regardless of what I thought of "the game." My aunt, with whom I lived for a short while, actually burned my jeans and T-shirts because they violated what she understood to be the standards of decorum. A close friend of mine lived in a state of war with her father because of her hippie clothes and hair—which were, of course, de rigueur among her peers. Upon discovering that she was smoking pot, he had her institutionalized.

Many middle-class people—both men and women—were brought up, like I was, to equate responsibility with obeying external rules. And when the rules no longer work, they don't know what to do—much like the enraged, gun-wielding protagonist of the movie *Falling Down,* played by Michael Douglas, who ends his ridiculous trajectory by helplessly declaring, "I did everything they told me to." If I had been brought up to reach my own conclusions about which rules were congruent with my internal experience of the world, those rules would have had more meaning for me. Instead, I was usually given a series of static pronouncements. For example, when I was thirteen, I was told by my mother that I couldn't wear a short skirt because "nice girls don't wear skirts above the knee." I countered, of course, by saying that my friend Patty wore skirts above the knee. "Patty is not a nice girl," returned my mother. But Patty *was* nice. My mother is a very intelligent and sensitive person, but it didn't occur to her to define for me what she meant by "nice," what "nice" had to do with skirt length, and how the two definitions might relate to what I had observed to be nice or not nice—and then let me decide for myself. It's true that most thirteen-year-olds aren't interested in, or much capable of, philosophical discourse, but that doesn't mean that adults can't explain themselves more completely to children. Part of becoming responsible is learning how to make a choice about where you stand in respect to the social code and then holding yourself accountable for your choice. In contrast, many children who grew up in my milieu were given abstract absolutes that were placed before us as if our thoughts, feelings, and observations were irrelevant.

Recently I heard a panel of feminists on talk radio advocating that laws be passed prohibiting men from touching or making sexual comments to women on the street. Listeners called in to express reactions both pro and con, but the one I remember was a woman who said, "If a man touches me and I don't want it, I don't need a law. I'm gonna beat the hell out of him." The panelists were silent. Then one of them responded in an uncertain voice, "I guess I just never learned how to do that." I understood that the feminist might not want to get into a fistfight with a man likely to be a lot bigger than she, but if her self-respect was so easily shaken by an obscene comment made by some slob on the street, I wondered, how did she expect to get through life? She was exactly the kind of woman whom the cultural critics Camille Paglia and Katie Roiphe have derided as a "rape-crisis feminist"— puritans, sissies, closet-Victorian ladies who want to legislate the ambiguity out of sex. It was very easy for me to feel self-righteous, and

I muttered sarcastically at my radio as the panel yammered about self-esteem.

I was conflicted, however. If there had been a time in my own life when   11
I couldn't stand up for myself, how could I expect other people to do it? It could be argued that the grown women on the panel should be more capable than a sixteen-year-old girl whacked out on acid. But such a notion presupposes that people develop at a predictable rate or react to circumstances by coming to universally agreed-upon conclusions. This is the crucial unspoken presumption at the center of the date-rape debate as well as of the larger discourse on victimism. It is a presumption that in a broad but potent sense reminds me of a rule.

Feminists who postulate that boys must obtain a spelled-out "yes" be-   12
fore having sex are trying to establish rules, cut in stone, that will apply to any and every encounter and that every responsible person must obey. The new rule resembles the old good girl/bad girl rule not only because of its implicit suggestion that girls have to be protected but also because of its absolute nature, its iron-fisted denial of complexity and ambiguity. I bristle at such a rule and so do a lot of other people. But should we really be so puzzled and indignant that another rule has been presented? If people have been brought up believing that to be responsible is to obey certain rules, what are they going to do with a can of worms like "date rape" except try to make new rules that they see as more fair or useful than the old ones?

But the "rape-crisis feminists" are not the only absolutists here; their crit-   13
ics play the same game. Camille Paglia, author of *Sexual Personae,* has stated repeatedly that any girl who goes alone into a frat house and proceeds to tank up is cruising for a gang bang, and if she doesn't know that, well, then she's "an idiot." The remark is most striking not for its crude unkindness but for its reductive solipsism. It assumes that all college girls have had the same life experiences as Paglia, and have come to the same conclusions about them. By the time I got to college, I'd been living away from home for years and had been around the block several times. I never went to a frat house, but I got involved with men who lived in rowdy "boy houses" reeking of dirty socks and rock and roll. I would go over, drink, and spend the night with my lover of the moment; it never occurred to me that I was in danger of being gang-raped, and if I had been, I would have been shocked and badly hurt. My experience, though some of it had been bad, hadn't led me to conclude that boys plus alcohol equals gang bang, and I was not naive or idiotic. Katie Roiphe, author of *The Morning After: Fear, Sex, and Feminism on Campus,* criticizes girls who, in her view, create a myth of false innocence: "But did these twentieth-century girls, raised on Madonna videos and the six o'clock news, really trust that people were good until they themselves were raped? Maybe. Were these girls, raised on horror movies and

glossy Hollywood sex scenes, really as innocent as all that?" I am sympathetic to Roiphe's annoyance, but I'm surprised that a smart chick like her apparently doesn't know that people process information and imagery (like Madonna videos and the news) with a complex subjectivity that doesn't in any predictable way alter their ideas about what they can expect from life.

Roiphe and Paglia are not exactly invoking rules, but their comments 14 seem to derive from a belief that everyone except idiots interprets information and experience in the same way. In that sense, they are not so different in attitude from those ladies dedicated to establishing feminist-based rules and regulations for sex. Such rules, just like the old rules, assume a certain psychological uniformity of experience, a right way.

The accusatory and sometimes painfully emotional rhetoric conceals an 15 attempt not only to make new rules but also to codify experience. The "rape-crisis feminists" obviously speak for many women and girls who have been raped or have *felt* raped in a wide variety of circumstances. They would not get so much play if they were not addressing a widespread and real experience of violation and hurt. By asking, "Were they really so innocent?" Roiphe doubts the veracity of the experience she presumes to address because it doesn't square with hers or with that of her friends. Having not felt violated herself—even though she says she has had an experience that many would now call date rape—she cannot understand, or even quite believe, that anyone else would feel violated in similar circumstances. She therefore believes all the fuss to be a political ploy or, worse, a retrograde desire to return to crippling ideals of helpless femininity. In turn, Roiphe's detractors, who have not had her more sanguine "morning after" experience, believe her to be ignorant and callous, or a secret rape victim in deep denial. Both camps, believing their own experience to be the truth, seem unwilling to acknowledge the emotional truth on the other side.

It is at this point that the "date-rape debate" resembles the bigger debate 16 about how and why Americans seem so eager to identify themselves and be identified by others as victims. Book after article has appeared, written in baffled yet hectoring language, deriding the P.C. goody-goodies who want to play victim and the spoiled, self-centered fools who attend twelve-step programs, meditate on their inner child, and study pious self-help books. The revisionist critics have all had a lot of fun with the recovery movement, getting into high dudgeon over those materially well-off people who describe their childhoods as "holocausts" and winding up with a fierce exhortation to return to rationality. Rarely do such critics make any but the most superficial attempt to understand why the population might behave thus.

In a fussing, fuming essay in these pages ("Victims, All?" October 1991) 17 that has almost become a prototype of the genre, David Rieff expressed his outrage and bewilderment that affluent people would feel hurt and disappointed by life. He angrily contrasted rich Americans obsessed with their inner children to Third World parents concerned with feeding their actual children. On the most obvious level, the contrast is one that needs to be made, but I question Rieff's idea that suffering is one definable thing, that he knows what it is, and that since certain kinds of emotional pain don't fit this definition they can't really exist. This idea doesn't allow him to have much respect for other people's experience—or even to see it. It may be ridiculous and perversely self-aggrandizing for most people to describe whatever was bad about their childhood as a "holocaust," but I suspect that when - people talk like that they are saying that as children they were not given enough of what they would later need in order to know who they are or to live truly responsible lives. Thus they find themselves in a state of bewildering loss that they can't articulate, except by wild exaggeration—much like I defined my inexplicable feelings after my Detroit episode. "Holocaust" may be a grossly inappropriate exaggeration. But to speak in exaggerated metaphors about psychic injury is not so much the act of a crybaby as it is a distorted attempt to explain one's own experience. I think the distortion comes from a desperate desire to make one's experience have consequence in the eyes of others, and that such desperation comes from a crushing doubt that one's own experience counts at all.

In her book *I'm Dysfunctional, You're Dysfunctional,* Wendy Kaminer   18
speaks harshly of women in some twelve-step programs who talk about being metaphorically raped. "It is an article of faith here that suffering is relative; no one says she'd rather be raped metaphorically than in fact," she writes, as if not even a crazy person would prefer a literal rape to a metaphorical one. But actually, I might. About two years after my "rape" in Detroit, I was raped for real. The experience was terrifying: my attacker repeatedly said he was going to kill me, and I thought he might. The terror was acute, but after it was over it actually affected me less than many other mundane instances of emotional brutality I've suffered or seen other people suffer. Frankly, I've been scarred more by experiences I had on the playground in elementary school. I realize that the observation may seem bizarre, but for me the rape was a clearly defined act, perpetrated upon me by a crazy asshole whom I didn't know or trust; it had nothing to do with me or who I was, and so, when it was over, it was relatively easy to dismiss. Emotional cruelty is more complicated. Its motives are often impossible to understand, and it is sometimes committed by people who say they like or even love you. Nearly always it's hard to know whether you played a role in what happened, and, if so, what the role was. The experience *sticks* to you. By the time I was raped I had seen enough emotional cruelty to feel that the rape, although bad, was not especially traumatic.

My response may seem strange to some, but my point is that pain can be 19 an experience that defies codification. If thousands of Americans say that they are in psychic pain, I would not be so quick to write them off as self-indulgent fools. A metaphor like "the inner child" may be silly and schematic, but it has a fluid subjectivity, especially when projected out into the world by such a populist notion as "recovery." Ubiquitous recovery-movement phrases like "We're all victims" and "We're all co-dependent" may not seem to leave a lot of room for interpretation, but they are actually so vague that they beg for interpretation and projection. Such phrases may be fair game for ridicule, but it is shallow to judge them on their face value, as if they hold the same meaning for everyone. What is meant by an "inner child" depends on the person speaking, and not everyone will see it as a metaphor for helplessness. I suspect that most inner-child enthusiasts use the image of themselves as children not so that they can *avoid* being responsible but to learn responsibility by going back to the point in time when they *should* have been taught responsibility—the ability to think, choose, and stand up for themselves—and were not. As I understand it, the point of identifying an "inner child" is to locate the part of yourself that didn't develop into adulthood and then to develop it yourself. Whether or not this works is an open question, but it is an attempt to accept responsibility, not to flee it.

When I was in my late teens and early twenties, I could not bear to 20 watch movies or read books that I considered demeaning to women in any way; I evaluated everything I saw or read in terms of whether it expressed a "positive image" of women. I was a very P.C. feminist before the term existed, and, by the measure of my current understanding, my critical rigidity followed from my inability to be responsible for my own feelings. In this context, being responsible would have meant that I let myself feel whatever discomfort, indignation, or disgust I experienced without allowing those feelings to determine my entire reaction to a given piece of work. In other words, it would have meant dealing with my feelings and what had caused them, rather than expecting the outside world to assuage them. I could have chosen not to see the world through the lens of my personal unhappiness and yet maintained a kind of respect for my unhappiness. For example, I could have decided to avoid certain films or books because of my feelings without blaming the film or book for making me feel the way I did.

My emotional irresponsibility did not spring from a need to feel victim- 21 ized, although it may have looked that way to somebody else. I essentially was doing what I had seen most mainstream cultural critics do—it was from them that I learned to view works of art in terms of the message they imparted and, further, that the message could be judged on the basis of consensual ideas about what life is, and how it can and should be seen. My ideas, like most P.C. ideas, were extreme, but they were consistent with more mainstream thought—they just shifted the parameters of acceptability a bit.

Things haven't changed much: at least half the book and film reviews   22 that I read praise or condemn a work on the basis of the likability of the characters (as if there is a standard idea of what is likable) or because the author's point of view is or is not "life-affirming"—or whatever the critic believes the correct attitude toward life to be. The lengthy and rather hysterical debate about the film *Thelma and Louise,* in which two ordinary women become outlaws after one of them shoots the other's rapist, was predicated on the idea that stories are supposed to function as instruction manuals, and that whether the film was good or bad depended on whether the instructions were correct. Such criticism assumes that viewers or readers need to see a certain type of moral universe reflected back at them or, empty vessels that they are, they might get confused or depressed or something. A respected mainstream essayist writing for *Time* faulted my novel *Two Girls, Fat and Thin* for its nasty male characters, which he took to be a moral statement about males generally. He ended his piece with the fervent wish that fiction not "diminish" men or women but rather seek to "raise our vision of" both—in other words, that it should present the "right" way to the reader, who is apparently not responsible enough to figure it out alone.

I have changed a lot from the P.C. teenager who walked out of movies   23 that portrayed women in a demeaning light. As I've grown older, I've become more confident of myself and my ability to determine what happens to me, and, as a result, those images no longer have such a strong emotional charge. I don't believe they will affect my life in any practical sense unless I allow them to do so. I no longer feel that misogynistic stories are about me or even about women (whether they purport to be or not) but rather are about the kinds of experience the authors wish to render—and therefore are not my problem. I consider my current view more balanced, but that doesn't mean my earlier feelings were wrong. The reason I couldn't watch "disrespect to women" at that time was that such depictions were too close to my own experience (most of which was not unusual), and I found them painful. I was displaying a simplistic self-respect by not subjecting myself to something I was not ready to face. Being unable to separate my personal experience from what I saw on the screen, I was not dealing with my own particular experience—I think, paradoxically, because I hadn't yet learned to value it. It's hard to be responsible for something that isn't valuable. Someone criticizing me as dogmatic and narrow-minded would have had a point, but the point would have ignored the truth of my unacknowledged experience, and thus ignored me.

Many critics of the self-help culture argue against treating emotional or   24 metaphoric reality as if it were equivalent to objective reality. I agree that they are not the same. But emotional truth is often bound up with truth of a more objective kind and must be taken into account. This is especially true of conundrums such as date rape and victimism, both of which often are discussed in terms of unspoken assumptions about emotional truth anyway. Sarah Crichton, in a cover story for *Newsweek* on "Sexual Correctness," described the "strange detour" taken by some feminists and suggested that "we're not creating a society of Angry Young Women. These are Scared Little Girls." The comment is both contemptuous and superficial; it shows no interest in *why* girls might be scared. By such logic, anger implicitly is deemed to be the more desirable emotional state because it appears more potent, and "scared" is used as a pejorative. It's possible to shame a person into hiding his or her fear, but if you don't address the cause of the fear, it won't go away. Crichton ends her piece by saying, "Those who are growing up in environments where they don't have to figure out what the rules should be, but need only follow what's been prescribed, are being robbed of the most important lesson there is to learn. And that's how to live." I couldn't agree more. But unless you've been taught how to think for yourself, you'll have a hard time figuring out your own rules, and you'll feel scared—especially when there is real danger of sexual assault.

One reason I had sex with strangers when I didn't really want to was   25
that part of me wanted the adventure, and that tougher part ran roughshod over the part of me that was scared and uncertain. I'll bet the same thing happened to many of the boys with whom I had these experiences. All people have their tough, aggressive selves as well as their more delicate selves. If you haven't developed these characteristics in ways that are respectful of yourself and others, you will find it hard to be responsible for them. I don't think it's possible to develop yourself in such ways if you are attuned to following rules and codes that don't give your inner world enough importance. I was a strong-willed child with a lot of aggressive impulses, which, for various reasons, I was actively discouraged from developing. They stayed hidden under a surface of extreme passivity, and when they did appear it was often in a wildly irresponsible, almost crazy way. My early attraction to aggressive boys and men was in part a need to see *somebody* act out the distorted feelings I didn't know what to do with, whether it was destructive or not. I suspect that boys who treat girls with disrespectful aggression have failed to develop their more tender, sensitive side and futilely try to regain it by "possessing" a woman. Lists of instructions about what's nice and what isn't will not help people in such a muddled state, and it's my observation that many people are in such a state to a greater or lesser degree.

I am not idealistic enough to hope that we will ever live in a world with-   26
out rape and other forms of sexual cruelty; I think men and women will always have to struggle to behave responsibly. But I think we could make the

struggle less difficult by changing the way we teach responsibility and social conduct. To teach a boy that rape is "bad" is not as effective as making him see that rape is a violation of his own masculine dignity as well as a violation of the raped woman. It's true that children don't know big words and that teenage boys aren't all that interested in their own dignity. But these are things that children learn more easily by example than by words, and learning by example runs deep.

A few years ago I invited to dinner at my home a man I'd known casually for two years. We'd had dinner and comradely drinks a few times. I didn't have any intention of becoming sexual with him, but after dinner we slowly got drunk and were soon floundering on the couch. I was ambivalent not only because I was drunk but because I realized that although part of me was up for it, the rest of me was not. So I began to say no. He parried each "no" with charming banter and became more aggressive. I went along with it for a time because I was amused and even somewhat seduced by the sweet, junior-high spirit of his manner. But at some point I began to be alarmed, and then he did and said some things that turned my alarm into fright. I don't remember the exact sequence of words or events, but I do remember taking one of his hands in both of mine, looking him in the eyes, and saying, "If this comes to a fight you would win, but it would be very ugly for both of us. Is that really what you want?" 27

His expression changed and he dropped his eyes; shortly afterward he left. 28

I consider that small decision to have been a responsible one because it was made by taking both my vulnerable feelings and my carnal impulses into account. When I spoke, my words came from my feeling of delicacy as well as from my capacity for aggression. And I respected my friend as well by addressing both sides of his nature. It is not hard for me to make such decisions now, but it took me a long time to get to this point. I only regret that it took so long, both for my young self and for the boys I was with, under circumstances that I now consider disrespectful to all concerned. 29

Working with the Text

1. "The exception proves the rule," says the old saw, but most people don't know that the word "proves," in this case, means "tests" or "challenges," rather than "confirms." What "rules" does Gaitskill's experience test? Do they survive? Why or why not?

2. An argument based on experience stands or falls on *ethos,* the character of the author as it emerges in writing. Describe the *ethos* of this essay. Citing specific words and phrases, demonstrate how it is crafted. Do

elements of it conflict, and, if so, how does Gaitskill manage the conflicts? How does it serve—or detract from—the essay's purposes?

3. Gaitskill defends the use of provocative language—"holocaust," for example—to communicate extreme emotional pain. Is such exaggeration legitimate? If so, do we implicitly accept the equality of individual injury and mass atrocity? If not, do we deny people their subjective truth?

4. Gaitskill uses her experience to challenge the conclusions of a range of social critics, singling out Camille Paglia, Katie Roiphe, David Rieff, Wendy Kaminer, and Sarah Crichton for particular attention. Using a periodical index, find a contemporary essay or book excerpt by one of these authors, and assess the legitimacy of Gaitskill's critique. Has Gaitskill quoted the author judiciously and represented his or her position fairly? Does she succeed in refuting the author's argument? If so, how? If not, why not?

5. Choose an episode from your own experience that has the potential to offer evidence in a larger cultural debate. In a first draft, concentrate on narrating the episode as concretely as possible; then, reflect briefly upon the significance of the episode in the light of contemporary argument.

The White Noise Supremacists

LESTER BANGS

Rock critic Lester Bangs (1948–1982) worked as a dishwasher and a salesman before beginning to write feature articles and music reviews in the late 1960s for *creem, Rolling Stone, The Village Voice,* and numerous other publications until his death by an accidental prescription-drug overdose at the age of 33. Bangs's friend Greil Marcus compiled a posthumous edition of selected essays and reviews, *Psychotic Reactions and Carburetor Dung* (1987). A biography of Bangs entitled "Let It Blurt: The Life and Times of Lester Bangs, America's Greatest Rock Critic" by Jim DeRogatis was published in 2000. The acerbic Bangs is considered by many to have been the most provocative and iconoclastic rock critic of the 1970s. Many of his ideas—such as the trash aesthetic and the related debunking of technique as a criterion of judgment—remain current. Bangs was the first to popularize the term "heavy metal" (which he pulled from the confluence of a

William Burroughs novel and a Steppenwolf song). In the following essay, Bangs denounces the "Racist Chic and Racist Cool" New Wave scene, while scrutinizing his own complicity in racial bigotry and liberal guilt.

The other day I was talking on the phone with a friend who hangs out on the CBGB's scene a lot. She was regaling me with examples of the delights available to females in the New York subway system. "So the train came to a sudden halt and I fell on my ass in the middle of the car, and not only did nobody offer to help me up but all these boons just sat there laughing at me." 1

"Boons?" I said. "What's boons?" 2

"You know," she said. "Black guys." 3

"Why do you call them that?" 4

"I dunno. From 'baboons,' I guess." 5

I didn't say anything. 6

"Look, I know it's not cool," she finally said. "But neither is being a woman in this city. Every fucking place you go you get these cats hassling you, and sometimes they try to pimp you. And a lot of the times when they hassle you they're black, and when they try to pimp me they're always black. Eventually you can't help it, you just end up reacting." 7

Sometimes I think nothing is simple but the feeling of pain. 8

When I was first asked to write this article, I said sure, because the racism (not to mention the sexism, which is even more pervasive and a whole other piece) on the American New Wave scene had been something that I'd been bothered by for a long time. When I told the guys in my own band that I was doing this, they just laughed. "Well, I guess the money's good," said one. "What makes you think the racism in punk has anything special about it that separates it from the rest of the society?" asked another. 9

"Because the rest of society doesn't go around acting like racism is real hip and cool," I answered heatedly. 10

"Oh yeah," he sneered. "Just walk into a factory sometime. Or jail." 11

All right. Power is what we're talking about, or the feeling that you don't have any, or how much ostensible power you can rip outta some other poor sucker's hide. It works the same everywhere, of course, but one of the things that makes the punk stance unique is how it seems to assume substance or at least style by the *abdication* of power: *Look at me! I'm a cretinous little wretch! And proud of it!* So many of the people around the CBGB's and Max's scene have always seemed emotionally if not outright physically crippled—you see speech impediments, hunchbacks, limps, but most of all an overwhelming spiritual flatness. You take parental indifference, a crappy educational system, lots of drugs, media overload, a society with no values left except the hysterical emphasis on physical perfection, 12 and you end up with these little nubbins: the only rebellion around, as *Life* magazine once labeled the Beats. Richard Hell gave us the catchphrase "Blank Generation," although he insists that he didn't mean a crowd with all the dynamism of a static-furry TV screen but rather a bunch of people finally freed by the collapse of all values to reinvent themselves, to make art statements of their whole lives. Unfortunately, such a great utopian dream, which certainly is not on its first go-round here, remains just that, because most people would rather follow. What you're left with, aside from the argument that it beats singles bars, is compassion. When the Ramones bring that sign onstage that says "GABBA GABBA HEY," what it really stands for is "We accept you." Once you get past the armor of dog collars, black leather, and S&M affectations, you've got some of the gentlest or at least most harmless people in the world: Sid Vicious legends aside, almost all their violence is self-directed.

So if they're all such a bunch of little white lambs, why do some of them   13 have it in for little black lambs? Richard Pinkston, a black friend I've known since my Detroit days, tells me, "When I go to CBGB's I feel like I'm in East Berlin. It's like, I don't mind liberal guilt if it gets me in the restaurant, even if I know the guy still hates me in his mind. But it's like down there they're *striving* to be offensive however they can, so it's more vocal and they're freer. It's semi–mob thinking."

Richard Hell and the Voidoids are one of the few integrated bands on   14 the scene ("integrated"—what a stupid word). I heard that when he first formed the band, Richard got flak from certain quarters about Ivan Julian, a black rhythm guitarist from Washington, D.C., who once played with the Foundations of "Build Me Up Buttercup" fame. I think it says something about what sort of person Richard is that he told all those people to get fucked then and doesn't much want to talk about it now. "I don't remember anything special. I just think that most people that say stuff like what you're talking about are so far beneath contempt that it has no effect that's really powerful. Among musicians there's more professional jealousy than any kind of racial thing; there's so much backbiting in any scene, it's like girls talking about shoes. All musicians are such scum anyway that it couldn't possibly make any difference because you expect 'em to say the worst shit in the world about you."

I called up Ivan, who was the guy having trouble at the pinhead lunch   15 counter in the first place. "Well, I was first drawn to this scene by the simple fact of a lot of people with musical and social attitudes more or less in common. No one's ever said anything to my face, but I overheard shit. A lot of people are just ignorant assholes. I don't think there's any more racism at CBGB's, where I went every night for about the first year I lived here, than anywhere else in New York City. Maybe a little bit less, because I find New

York City a million times more racist than D.C., or Maryland and Virginia where I grew up. There's racism there, outright killings around where I lived, but here it's a lot more insidious. You get four or five different extremes, so many cultures that can't stand each other. It's like, when we toured Europe I was amazed at the bigotry between people from two parts of the same country. They'd accept me, but to each other they were niggers, man. And at CBGB's it's sorta the same way, sometimes. Mutants can learn to hate each other and have prejudices too. Like Mingus said in *Beneath the Underdog:* forty or fifty years ago, in the ghetto, the lighter you were the better you were. Then you'd turn another corner and if you were somewhat light, like Mingus, there'd be a buncha guys saying 'Shit-colored mutha' ready to trash your ass. My point is, regardless of how much people might have in common they still draw away. There are certain people on the scene, like say this girl in one band who's nothing but a loudmouthed racist bitch—it's obvious we want nothing to do with each other, so I stay away from her and vice versa.

"I'll tell you one thing: the entrepreneurs, record company people and shit are a hell of a lot worse. People like Richard Gottehrer, who produced our album, and Seymour Stein and a lot of the other people up at Sire Records. They were *totally* condescending, they'd talk to you differently, like you were a child or something. I heard a lot of clichés on the level of being invited over to somebody's house for fried chicken." | 16

I was reminded instantly of the day I was in the office of a white woman of some intelligence, education, and influence in the music business, and the subject of race came up "Oh," she said, "I liked them so much better when they were just *Negroes*. When they became *blacks* . . ." She wrinkled her nose irritably. | 17

"Race hate?" says Voidoids lead guitarist Bob Quine. "Sure, it gives me 'n' Ivan something to do onstage: *The Defiant Ones*." | 18

But the ease and insight of the Voidoids are somewhat anomalous on the New York scene. This scene and the punk stance in general are riddled with self-hate, which is always reflexive, and anytime you conclude that life stinks and the human race mostly amounts to a pile of shit, you've got the perfect breeding ground for fascism. A lot of outsiders, in fact, think punk *is* fascist, but that's only because they can't see beyond certain buzzwords, symbols, and pieces of regalia that (I *think*) really aren't that significant: Ron Asheton of the Stooges used to wear swastikas, Iron Crosses, and jackboots onstage, but I don't remember any right-wing rants ever popping up in the music he did with Iggy or his own later band, which many people were not exactly thrilled to hear was called the New Order. | 19

In the past three years Ron's sartorial legacy has given us an international subculture whose members might easily be mistaken at first glance for | 20 little brownshirts. They aren't, for the most part. Only someone as dumb as the Ramones are always accused of being could be offended when they sing "I'm a Nazi schatze," or tell us that the first rule is to obey the laws of Germany and then follow it with "Eat kosher salami." I've hung out with the Ramones, and they treat everybody of any race or sex the same—who *they* hate isn't Jews or blacks or gays or anybody but certain spike-conk assholes who just last week graduated from *The Rocky Horror Picture Show* lines to skag-dabblings and now stumble around Max's busting their nuts trying to be decadent.

Whereas you don't have to try at all to be a racist. It's a little coiled clot   21
of venom lurking there in all of us, white and black, goy and Jew, ready to strike out when we feel embattled, belittled, brutalized. Which is why it has to be monitored, made taboo and restrained, by society and the individual. But there's a difference between hate and a little of the old *épater* gob at authority: swastikas in punk are basically another way for kids to get a rise out of their parents and maybe the press, both of whom deserve the irritation. To the extent that most of these spikedomes ever had a clue on what that stuff originally meant, it only went so far as their intent to shock. "It's like a stance," as Ivan says. "A real immature way of being dangerous."

Maybe. Except that after a while this casual, even ironic embrace of the   22
totems of bigotry crosses over into the real poison. Around 1970 there was a carbuncle named Wayne McGuire who kept contributing installments of something he called "An Aquarian Journal" to *Fusion* magazine, wherein he suggested between burblings of regurgitated Nietzsche and bad Céline ellipses that the Velvet Underground represented some kind of mystical milestone in the destiny of the Aryan race, and even tried to link their music with the ideas of Mel Lyman, who was one of the prototypes for the current crop of mindnapping cult-daddies.

On a less systematic level, we had little outcroppings like Iggy hollering,   23
"Our next selection tonight for all you Hebrew ladies in the audience is entitled 'Rich Bitch'!" on the 1974 recorded-live bootleg *Metallic K.O.,* and my old home turf *creem* magazine, where around the same time I was actually rather proud of myself for writing things like (in an article on David Bowie's "soul" phase): "Now, as we all know, white hippies and beatniks before them would never have existed had there not been a whole generational subculture with a gnawing yearning to be nothing less than the downest baddest *niggers*. . . . Everybody has been walking around for the last year or so acting like faggots ruled the world, when in actuality it's the *niggers* who control and direct everything just as it always has been and properly should be."

I figured all this was in the Lenny Bruce spirit of let's-defuse-them-   24
epithets-by-slinging-'em-out—in Detroit I thought absolutely nothing of going to parties with people like David Ruffin and Bobby Womack where I'd

get drunk, maul the women, and improvise blues songs along the lines of "Sho' wish ah wuz a nigger / Then mah dick'd be bigger," and of course they all laughed. It took years before I realized what an asshole I'd been, not to mention how lucky I was to get out of there with my white hide intact.

I'm sure a lot of those guys were very happy to see this white kid drunk   25
on his ass making a complete fool if not a human TV set out of himself, but to this day I wonder how many of them hated my guts right then. Because Lenny Bruce was wrong—maybe in a better world than this such parlor games would amount to cleansing jet offtakes, and between friends, where a certain bond of mutual trust has been firmly established, good natured racial tradeoffs can be part of the vocabulary of understood affections. But beyond that trouble begins—when you fail to realize that no matter how harmless your intentions are, there is no reason to think that any shit that comes out of your mouth is going to be understood or happily received. Took me a long time to find it out, but those words are *lethal,* man, and you shouldn't just go slinging them around for effect. This seems almost too simple and obvious to say, but maybe it's good to have something simple and obvious stated once in a while, especially in this citadel of journalistic overthink. If you're black or Jewish or Latin or gay those little vernacular epithets are bullets that riddle your guts and then fester and burn there, like torture-flak hailing on you wherever you go. Ivan Julian told me that whenever he hears the word "nigger," no matter who says it, black or white, he wants to kill. Once when I was drunk I told Hell that the only reason hippies ever existed in the first place was because of niggers, and when I mentioned it to Ivan while doing this article I said, "You probably don't even remember—" "Oh yeah, I remember," he cut me off. And that was two years ago, one ostensibly harmless little slip. You take a lifetime of that, and you've got grounds for trying in any way possible, even if it's only by convincing one individual at a time, to remove those words from the face of the earth. Just like Hitler and Idi Amin and all other enemies of the human race.

Another reason for getting rid of all those little verbal barbs is that no   26
matter how *you* intend them, you can't say them without risking misinterpretation by some other bigoted asshole; your irony just might be his cup of hate. Things like the *creem* articles and partydown exhibitionism represented a reaction against the hippie counterculture and what a lot of us regarded as its pious pussyfooting around questions of racial and sexual identity, questions we were quite prepared to drive over with bulldozers. We believed nothing could be worse, more pretentious and hypocritical, than the hippies and the liberal masochism in whose sidecar they toked along, so we embraced an indiscriminate, half-joking and half-hostile mindlessness which seemed to represent, as Mark Jacobson pointed out in his *Voice* piece on Legs McNeil, a new kind of cool. "I don't discriminate," I

used to laugh, "I'm prejudiced against *everybody!*" I thought it made for a nicely charismatic mix of Lenny Bruce freespleen and W. C. Fields misanthropy, conveniently ignoring Lenny's delirious, nigh-psychopathic inability to resolve the contradictions between his idealism and his infantile, scatological exhibitionism, as well as the fact that W. C. Fields's racism was as real and vile as—or more real and vile than—anybody else's. But when I got to New York in 1976 I discovered that some kind of bridge had been crossed by a lot of the people I thought were my peers in this emergent Cretins' Lib generation.

This was stuff even I had to recognize as utterly repellent. I first noticed it the first time I threw a party. The staff of *Punk* magazine came, as well as members of several of the hottest CBGB's bands, and when I did what we always used to do at parties in Detroit—put on soul records so everybody could dance—I began to hear this: "What're you playing all that nigger disco shit for, Lester?"

"That's not nigger disco shit," I snarled, "that's *Otis Redding,* you assholes!" But they didn't want to hear about it, and now I wonder if in any way I hadn't dug my own grave, or at least helped contribute to their ugliness and the new schism between us. The music editor of this paper has theorized that one of the most important things about New Wave is how much of it is almost purely white music, and what a massive departure that represents from the almost universally blues-derived rock of the past. I don't necessarily agree with that—it ignores the reggae influence running through music as diverse as that of the Clash, Pere Ubu, Public Image Ltd., and the Police, not to mention the Chuck Berry licks at the core of Steve Jones's attack. But there is at least a grain of truth there—the Contortions' James Brown/Albert Ayler spasms aside, most of the SoHo bands are as white as John Cage, and there's an evolution of sound, rhythm, and stance running from the Velvets through the Stooges to the Ramones and their children that takes us farther and farther from the black-stud postures of Mick Jagger that Lou Reed and Iggy partake in but that Joey Ramone certainly doesn't. I respect Joey for that, for having the courage to be himself, especially at the sacrifice of a whole passel of macho defenses. Joey is a white American kid from Forest Hills, and as such his cultural inputs have been white, from "The Jetsons" through Alice Cooper. But none of this cancels out the fact that most of the greatest, deepest music America has produced has been, when not entirely black, the product of miscegenation. "You can't appreciate rock 'n' roll without appreciating where it comes from," as Pinkston put it.

Musical questions, however, can be passed off as matters of taste. Something harder to pass off entered the air in 1977, when I started encountering little zaps like this: I opened up a copy of a Florida punk fanzine called *New*

Order and read an article by Miriam Linna of the Cramps, Nervus Rex, and now Zantees: "I love the Ramones [because] this is the celebration of everything American—everything teenaged and wonderful and white and urban. . . ." You could say the "white" jumping out of that sentence was just like Ornette Coleman declaring *This Is Our Music,* except that the same issue featured a full-page shot of Miriam and one of her little friends posing proudly with their leathers and shades and a pistol in front of the headquarters of the United White People's Party, under a sign bearing three flags: "GOD" (cross), "COUNTRY" (stars and stripes), "RACE" (swastika).

Sorry, Miriam, I can go just so far with affectations of kneejerk cretinism 30 before I puke. I remember the guy in the American Nazi Party being asked, "What about the six million?" in PBS's *California Reich,* and answering, "Well, the way I heard it it was only really four-and-a-half million, but I wish it was six," and I imagine you'd find that pretty hilarious too. I probably would have at one time. If that makes me a wimp now, good, that means you and anybody else who wants to get their random vicarious kicks off White Power can stay the fuck away from me.

More recently, I've heard occasional stories like the one about one of 31 the members of Teenage Jesus and the Jerks yelling "Hey, you bunch of fucking niggers" at a crowd of black kids in front of Hurrah one night and I am not sorry to report getting the shit kicked out of him for it. When I told this to Richard Hell, he dismissed it: "He thinks he's being part of something by doing that—joining a club that'll welcome him with open arms, trying to get accepted. It's not real. Maybe I'm naive, but I think that's what all racism is— not really directed at the target but designed to impress some other moron."

He may be right, but so what? James Chance of the Contortions used to 32 come up to Bob Quine pleading for Bob to play him his Charlie Parker records. Now, in a *New York Rocker* interview, James dismisses the magical qualities of black music as "just a bunch of nigger bullshit." Why? Because James wants to be famous, and ripping off Albert Ayler isn't enough. My, isn't he *outrageous?* ("He's got the shtick down," said Danny Fields, stifling a yawn, when they put James on the cover of *Soho Weekly News.*) And congrats to Andy Shernoff of the Dictators, who did so well they're now called the Rhythm Dukes, for winning the *Punk* magazine Drunk as a Skunk contest by describing "Camp Runamuck" as "where Puerto Ricans are kept until they learn to be human."

Mind you, I like a cheap laugh at somebody else's expense as well as 33 the next person. So I got mine off Nico, who did "Deutschland Über Alles" at CBGB's last month and was just naive enough to explain to Mary Harron, in a recent interview in *New Wave Rock,* why she was dropped by Island Records: "I made a mistake. I said in *Melody Maker* to some interviewer that I didn't like negroes. That's all. They took it so *personally* . . . although it's a whole different race. I mean, Bob Marley doesn't resemble a *negro,* does he? . . . He's an archetype of Jamaican . . . but with the features like white people. I don't like the features. They're so much like animals. . . . it's cannibals, no?"

Haw haw haw, doncha just love them dumb kraut cunts? And speaking   34
of dumbness and krauts, my old pal Legs McNeil has this band called Shrapnel, who are busy refighting World War II onstage in dogtags, army surplus clothes, and helmets that fall over their eyes like cowlicks, while they sing songs with titles like "Combat Love." Personally I think it's not offensive (well, about as offensive as "Hogan's Heroes") that they're too young to remember Vietnam—it's funny. The whole show is a cartoon (it's no accident that they open their set with the "Underdog" theme) and a damn good one. Musically they're up there too—tight dragstrip guitar wranglings that could put them on a par with the MC$_5$ someday, combined with a stage act that could make them as popular as Kiss. The only problem, which has left me with such mixed feelings I hardly know what to say to them, is that the lyrics of some of the songs are nothing but racist swill. The other night I sat in the front row at CBGB's and watched them deliver one of the hottest sets I've seen from any band this year while a kid in the seat right next to me kept yelling out requests for "'Hey Little Gook!' 'Hey Little Gook!'" the whole time. Christgau, who considers them "proto-fascist" and hates them, told me they also had lyrics on the order of "Send all the spics back to Cuba." I mentioned this to Legs and he seemed genuinely upset: "No," he swore, "it's 'Send all the *spies* back to Cuba.'"

"Okay," I said (Christgau still doesn't believe him), "what about 'Hey Lit-   35
tle Gook'?"

"Aw c'mon," he said, "that's just like in a World War II movie where they   36
say 'kraut' and 'slants' and stuff like that!"

I told him I thought there was a difference between using words in dra-   37
matic context and just to draw a cheap laugh in a song. But the truth is that by now I was becoming more confused than ever. All I knew was that when you added all this sort of stuff up, you realized a line had been crossed by certain people we thought we knew, even believed in, while we weren't looking. Either that or they were always across that line and we never bothered to look until we tripped over it. And sometimes you even find that you yourself have drifted across that line. I was in Bleecker Bob's the other night, drunk and stoned, when a black couple walked in. They asked for some disco record, Bob didn't have it of course, a few minutes went by, and reverting in the haze to my Detroit days I said something about such and such band or music having to do with "niggers." A couple more minutes went by. Then Bob said, "You know what, Lester? When you said that, those two people were standing right behind you."

I looked around and they were out on the sidewalk, looking at the dis-   38
play in his front window. Stricken, I rushed out and began to burble: "Listen . . . somebody just told me what I said in there . . . and I know it doesn't
mean anything to you, I'm not asking for some kind of absolution, but I just
want you to know that . . . I have some idea . . . how utterly, utterly *awful*
it was. . . ."

I stared at them helplessly. The guy just smiled, dripping contempt. "Oh,   39
that's okay, man . . . it's just your head. . . ." I've run up against a *million ass-*
holes like you before, and I'll meet a million after you—so fucking what?

I stumbled back into the store, feeling like total garbage, like the com-   40
pleat hypocrite, like I had suddenly glimpsed myself as everything I claimed
to despise. Bob said, "Look, Lester, don't worry about it, forget it, it happens
to everybody," and, the final irony, sold me a reggae album I wondered how
I was going to listen to.

If there's nothing more poisonous than bigotry, there's nothing more pa-   41
thetic than liberal guilt. I feel like an asshole even retelling the story here, as
if I expected some sort of expiation for what cannot be undone, or as if such
a tale would be news to anybody. In a way Bob was right: I put a dollop
more pain in the world, and that was that. There is certainly something almost emetically self-serving about the unreeling of such confessions in the
pages of papers like the *Voice*—it's the sort of thing that contributed to the
punk reaction in the first place. But it illustrates one primal fact: how easily
and suddenly you may find yourself imprisoned and suffocated by the very
liberation from cant, dogma, and hypocrisy you thought you'd achieved.
That sometimes—usually?—you'll find that you don't know where to draw
the line until you're miles across it in a field of land mines. Like wanting the
celebration of violent disorder that was the Sex Pistols, ending up with Sid
and Nancy instead, yet realizing the next day that you still want to hear Sid
sing "Somethin' Else" and see *The Great Rock 'n' Roll Swindle,* and not just
because you want to understand this whole episode better but to get your
kicks. These are contradictions that refuse to be resolved, which maybe is
what most of life eventually amounts to.

But that's begging the question again. Most people, I guess, don't even   42
think about drawing the lines: they just seem to go through life reacting at
random, like the cabdriver who told me that the report we were listening to
on the radio about Three Mile Island was just a bunch of bullshit dreamed
up by the press to sell papers or keep us tuned in. And maybe if you go on
like that (assuming, of course, that we all *don't* melt), nothing will blow up
in your face. But you may end up imploding instead. A lot of people around
CBGB's are already mad at me about this article, and the arguments seem
mostly to run along the lines of Why don't you can it because there's not
really that much racism down here and all you're gonna do is create more

problems for our scene just when this Sid Vicious thing had blown over. I mentioned Pinkston's experience and was told he was paranoid. Like the people at Harrisburg who didn't wanna leave their jobs and actually believed it would be safe to stick around after the pregnant women and children were evacuated, these kids are not gonna believe this stuff exists until it happens to them. Hell, a lot of them are Jewish and still don't believe it even though they know about the neighborhoods their parents can't get into.

When I started writing this, I was worried I might trigger incidents of punk-bashing by black gangs. Now I realize that nobody cares. Most white people think the whole subject of racism is boring, and anybody looking for somebody to stomp is gonna find them irrespective of magazine articles. Because nothing could make the rage of the underclass greater than it is already, and nothing short of a hydrogen bomb on their own heads or a sudden brutal bigoted slap in the face will make almost anybody think about anybody else's problems but their own. And that's where you cross over the line. At least when you allow the poison in you to erupt, that can be dealt with; maybe the greater evil occurs when you refuse to recognize that the poison even exists. In other words, when you assent by passivity or indifference. Hell, most people *live* on the other side of that line.

There is something called Rock Against Racism (and now Rock Against Sexism) in England, an attempt at simple decency by a lot of people whom one would think too young and naive to begin to appreciate the contradictions. Yippie bullshit aside, it could never happen in New York, which is deeply saddening, not because you want to think that rock 'n' roll can save the world but because since rock 'n' roll is bound to stay in your life you would hope to see it reach some point where it might not add to the cruelty and exploitation already in the world. In a place where people are as walled off from one another as we are in America now, all you can do is try to make some sort of simple, humble, and finally private beginning. You feel like things like this should not need to be said, articles like this should perhaps not even be written. You may think, as I do of the sexism in the Stranglers' and Dead Boys' lyrics, that the people and things I've talked about here are so stupid as to be beneath serious consideration. But would you say the same thing to the black disco artist who was refused admittance to Studio 54 even though he had a Top Ten crossover hit which they were probably playing inside the damn place at the time, the doorman/bouncer explaining to a white friend of the artist, "I'm not letting this guy in—he just looks like another street nigger to me"? Or would you rather argue the difference between Racist Chic and Racist Cool? If you would, just make sure you do it in the nearest factory. Or jail.

—Village Voice, 30 April 1979

Working with the Text

1. Bangs has much to say about punk rock and collective identity, *circa* 1979. What are some of the features of that identity? To what extent does it depend on distinctions between "self" and "other"? Who are the typical "others," and how do they serve the collective identity? Why, for Bangs, is racism an unacceptable form of "othering"?

2. Why does the author find racism in punk rock more offensive than racism in other subcultures? Why is it more difficult to discern? To combat? Why, despite repeated reference to the existence of a "line" between liberation and racism, does Bangs never tell us where the line is?

3. Describe Bangs's argumentative strategy. What, precisely, is his position? Why does he use so much narration to make his points? Why does so much of the narration focus on him—and portray him so negatively?

4. Now describe Bangs's prose style. Find five sentences that exemplify his unconventional diction and syntax; then explain how they work and what effects they create. Finally, relate Bangs's style to the argument he is making. What polemical goals does it serve? Aesthetic goals? Are these related?

5. After studying Bangs's style carefully, try your hand at writing in an experimental mode. You may wish to begin as Bangs did: by writing a brief music review. Select an album that is itself unconventional, whether rock or jazz or symphonic; listen carefully, and try to respond to the music in its own idiom, however you perceive that. Don't worry too much about polish; instead, try primarily to create a different sound than you normally produce.

TinySex and Gender Trouble

SHERRY TURKLE

With degrees in sociology and psychology from Harvard University, clinical psychologist Sherry Turkle has been a professor of the sociology of science at the Massachusetts Institute of Technology since 1976. The recipient of both a Rockefeller and a Guggenheim fellowship, Turkle has taken a cross-disciplinary approach in much of her research and writing. Among her scholarly works are *Psychoanalysis, Creativity, and Literature* (1978) and *Psychoanalytic Politics: Jacques Lacan and Freud's French Revolution* (1994). Her work has increasingly focused on the role of computers as cultural objects. In the following chapter from her book, *Life on the Screen: Identity in the Age of the Internet* (1995), Turkle considers the potential of electronic communication (and the anonymity and role-playing it allows) for transforming our conceptions of gender and sexuality and for creating new modes of communication across—and beyond—gender lines.

1   From my earliest effort to construct an online persona, it occurred to me that being a virtual man might be more comfortable than being a virtual woman.

2   When I first logged on to a MUD (Multi-User Dungeon or Multi-User Domain), I named and described a character but forgot to give it a gender. I was struggling with the technical aspects of the MUD universe—the difference between various MUD commands such as "saying" and "emoting," "paging" and "whispering." Gender was the last thing on my mind. This rapidly changed when a male-presenting character named Jiffy asked me if I was "really an it." At his question, I experienced an unpleasurable sense of disorientation which immediately gave way to an unfamiliar sense of freedom.

3   When Jiffy's question appeared on my screen, I was standing in a room of LambdaMOO filled with characters engaged in sexual banter in the style of the movie *Animal House*. The innuendos, double entendres, and leering invitations were scrolling by at a fast clip; I felt awkward, as though at a party to which I had been invited by mistake. I was reminded of junior high school dances when I wanted to go home or hide behind the punch bowl. I was reminded of kissing games in which it was awful to be chosen and awful not to be chosen. Now, on the MUD, I had a new option. I wondered if playing a male might allow me to feel less out of place. I could stand on the sidelines

and people would expect *me* to make the first move. And I could choose not to. I could choose simply to "lurk," to stand by and observe the action. Boys, after all, were not called prudes if they were too cool to play kissing games. They were not categorized as wallflowers if they held back and didn't ask girls to dance. They could simply be shy in a manly way—aloof, above it all.

Two days later I was back in the MUD. After I typed the command that joined me, in Boston, to the computer in California where the MUD resided, I discovered that I had lost the paper on which I had written my MUD password. This meant that I could not play my own character but had to log on as a guest. As such, I was assigned a color: Magenta. As "Magenta_guest" I was again without gender. While I was struggling with basic MUD commands, other players were typing messages for all to see such as "Magenta_guest gazes hot and enraptured at the approach of Fire_Eater." Again I was tempted to hide from the frat party atmosphere by trying to pass as a man. When much later I did try playing a male character, I finally experienced that permission to move freely I had always imagined to be the birthright of men. Not only was I approached less frequently, but I found it easier to respond to an unwanted overture with aplomb, saying something like, "That's flattering, Ribald_Temptress, but I'm otherwise engaged." My sense of freedom didn't just involve a different attitude about sexual advances, which now seemed less threatening. As a woman I have a hard time deflecting a request for conversation by asserting my own agenda. As a MUD male, doing so (nicely) seemed more natural; it never struck me as dismissive or rude. Of course, my reaction said as much about the construction of gender in my own mind as it did about the social construction of gender in the MUD.

Playing in MUDs, whether as a man, a woman, or a neuter character, I quickly fell into the habit of orienting myself to new cyberspace acquaintances by checking out their gender. This was a strange exercise, especially because a significant proportion of the female-presenting characters were RL men, and a good number of the male-presenting characters were RL women. I was not alone in this curiously irrational preoccupation. For many players, guessing the true gender of players behind MUD characters has become something of an art form. Pavel Curtis, the founder of LambdaMOO, has observed that when a female-presenting character is called something like FabulousHotBabe, one can be almost sure there is a man behind the mask. Another experienced MUDder shares the folklore that "if a female-presenting character's description of her beauty goes on for more than two paragraphs, 'she' [the player behind the character] is sure to be an ugly woman."

The preoccupation in MUDs with getting a "fix" on people through "fixing" their gender reminds us of the extent to which we use gender to shape our relationships. Corey, a twenty-two-year-old dental technician, says that her name often causes people to assume that she is male—that is, until she

4

5

6

meets them. Corey has long blonde hair, piled high, and admits to "going for the Barbie look."

> I'm not sure how it started, but I know that when I was a kid the more people said, "Oh, you have such a cute boy's name," the more I laid on the hairbows. [With my name] they always expected a boy—or at least a tomboy.

Corey says that, for her, part of the fun of being online is that she gets   7
to see "a lot of people having the [same] experience [with their online names that] I've had with my name." She tells me that her girlfriend logged on as Joel instead of Joely, "and she saw people's expectations change real fast." Corey continues:

> I also think the neuter characters [in MUDs] are good. When I play one, I realize how hard it is not to be either a man or a woman. I always find myself trying to be one or the other even when I'm trying to be neither. And all the time I'm talking to a neuter character [she reverses roles here] . . . I'm thinking "So who's behind it?"

In MUDs, the existence of characters other than male or female is disturbing, evocative. Like transgressive gender practices in real life, by breaking the conventions, it dramatizes our attachment to them.

Gender-swapping on MUDs is not a small part of the game action. By   8
some estimates, Habitat, a Japanese MUD, has 1.5 million users. Habitat is a MUD operated for profit. Among the registered members of Habitat, there is a ratio of four real-life men to each real-life woman. But inside the MUD the ratio is only three male characters to one female character. In other words, a significant number of players, many tens of thousands of them, are virtually cross-dressing.

Gender Trouble

What is virtual gender-swapping all about? Some of those who do it claim   9
that it is not particularly significant. "When I play a woman I don't really take it too seriously," said twenty-year-old Andrei. "I do it to improve the ratio of women to men. It's just a game." On one level, virtual gender-swapping is easier than doing it in real life. For a man to present himself as female in a chat room, on an IRC channel, or in a MUD, only requires writing a description. For a man to play a woman on the streets of an American city, he would have to shave various parts of his body; wear makeup, perhaps a wig, a dress, and high heels; perhaps change his voice, walk, and mannerisms. He would have some anxiety about passing, and there might be even more anxiety about not passing, which would pose a risk of violence and possibly arrest. So more men are willing to give virtual cross-dressing a try. But once they are online as female, they soon find that

maintaining this fiction is difficult. To pass as a woman for any length of time requires understanding how gender inflects speech, manner, the inter- pretation of experience. Women attempting to pass as men face the same kind of challenge. One woman said that she "worked hard" to pass in a room on a commercial network service that was advertised as a meeting place for gay men.

> I have always been so curious about what men do with each other. I could never even imagine how they talk to each other. I can't exactly go to a gay bar and eavesdrop inconspicuously. [When online] I don't actually have [virtual] sex with anyone. I get out of that by telling the men there that I'm shy and still un- sure. But I like hanging out; it makes gays seem less strange to me. But it is not so easy. You have to think about it, to make up a life, a job, a set of reactions.

Virtual cross-dressing is not as simple as Andrei suggests. Not only can   10 it be technically challenging, it can be psychologically complicated. Taking a virtual role may involve you in ongoing relationships. In this process, you may discover things about yourself that you never knew before. You may discover things about other people's response to you. You are not in danger of being arrested, but you are embarked on an enterprise that is not without some gravity and emotional risk.

In fact, one strong motivation to gender-swap in virtual space is to have   11 TinySex as a creature of another gender, something that suggests more than an emotionally neutral activity. Gender-swapping is an opportunity to explore conflicts raised by one's biological gender. Also, as Corey noted, by enabling people to experience what it "feels" like to be the opposite gender or to have no gender at all, the practice encourages reflection on the way ideas about gender shape our expectations. MUDs and the virtual personae one adopts within them are objects-to-think-with for reflecting on the social construction of gender.

Case, a thirty-four-year-old industrial designer who is happily married to   12 a coworker, is currently MUDding as a female character. In response to my question, "Has MUDding ever caused you any emotional pain?" he says, "Yes, but also the kind of learning that comes from hard times."

> I'm having pain in my playing now. The woman I'm playing in MedievalMUSH [Mairead] is having an interesting relationship with a fellow. Mairead is a lawyer. It costs so much to go to law school that it has to be paid for by a corporation or a noble house. A man she met and fell in love with was a nobleman. He paid for her law school. He bought my [Case slips into referring to Mairead in the first person] contract. Now he wants to marry me although I'm a commoner. I finally said yes. I try to talk to him about the fact that I'm essentially his property. I'm a commoner, I'm basically property and to a certain extent that doesn't bother me. I've grown up with it, that's the way life is. He wants to deny the situation.

He says, "Oh no, no, no. . . . We'll pick you up, set you on your feet, the whole world is open to you."

But everytime I behave like I'm now going to be a countess some day, you know, assert myself—as in, "And I never liked this wallpaper anyway"—I get pushed down. The relationship is pull up, push down. It's an incredibly psychologically damaging thing to do to a person. And the very thing that he liked about her—that she was independent, strong, said what was on her mind—it is all being bled out of her.

Case looks at me with a wry smile and sighs, "A woman's life." He continues:

I see her [Mairead] heading for a major psychological problem. What we have is a dysfunctional relationship. But even though it's very painful and stressful, it's very interesting to watch myself cope with this problem. How am I going to dig my persona's self out of this mess? Because I don't want to go on like this. I want to get out of it. . . . You can see that playing this woman lets me see what I have in my psychological repertoire, what is hard and what is easy for me. And I can also see how some of the things that work when you're a man just backfire when you're a woman.

Case has played Mairead for nearly a year, but even a brief experience   13
playing a character of another gender can be evocative. William James said, "Philosophy is the art of imagining alternatives." MUDs are proving grounds for an action-based philosophical practice that can serve as a form of consciousness-raising about gender issues. For example, on many MUDs, offering technical assistance has become a common way in which male characters "purchase" female attention, analogous to picking up the check at an RL dinner. In real life, our expectations about sex roles (who offers help, who buys dinner, who brews the coffee) can become so ingrained that we no longer notice them. On MUDs, however, expectations are expressed in visible textual actions, widely witnessed and openly discussed. When men playing females are plied with unrequested offers of help on MUDs, they often remark that such chivalries communicate a belief in female incompetence. When women play males on MUDs and realize that they are no longer being offered help, some reflect that those offers of help may well have led them to believe they needed it. As a woman, "First you ask for help because you think it will be expedient," says a college sophomore, "then you realize that you aren't developing the skills to figure things out for yourself."

All the World's a Stage

Any account of the evocative nature of gender-swapping might well defer to   14
Shakespeare, who used it as a plot device for reframing personal and political choices. *As You Like It* is a classic example, a comedy that uses gender-

swapping to reveal new aspects of identity and to permit greater complexity of relationships. In the play, Rosalind, the Duke's daughter, is exiled from the court of her uncle Frederick, who has usurped her father's throne. Frederick's daughter, Rosalind's cousin Celia, escapes with her. Together they flee to the magical forest of Arden. When the two women first discuss their plan to flee, Rosalind remarks that they might be in danger because "beauty provoketh thieves sooner than gold." In response, Celia suggests that they would travel more easily if they rubbed dirt on their faces and wore drab clothing, thus pointing to a tactic that frequently provides women greater social ease in the world—becoming unattractive. Rosalind then comes up with a second idea—becoming a man: "Were it not better, /Because that I am more than common tall, / That I did suit me all points like a man?"

In the end, Rosalind and Celia both disguise themselves as boys, Ganymede and Aliena. In suggesting this ploy, Rosalind proposes a disguise that will be both physical ("A gallant curtle-axe on my thigh, / A boar-spear in my hand") and emotional ("and—in my heart, / Lie there what hidden woman's fear there will"). She goes on, "We'll have a swashbuckling and martial outside, / as many other mannish cowards have / That do outface it with their semblances." 15

In these lines, Rosalind does not endorse an essential difference between men and women; rather, she suggests that men routinely adopt the same kind of pose she is now choosing. Biological men have to construct male gender just as biological women have to construct female gender. If Rosalind and Celia make themselves unattractive, they will end up less feminine. Their female gender will end up deconstructed. Both strategies—posing as men and deconstructing their femininity—are games that female MUDders play. One player, a woman currently in treatment for anorexia, described her virtual body this way: 16

> In real life, the control is the thing. I know that it is very scary for me to be a woman. I like making my body disappear. In real life that is. On MUDs, too. On the MUD, I'm sort of a woman, but I'm not someone you would want to see sexually. My MUD description is a combination of smoke and angles. I like that phrase "sort of a woman." I guess that's what I want to be in real life too.

In addition to virtual cross-dressing and creating character descriptions that deconstruct gender, MUDders gender-swap as double agents. That is, in MUDs, men play women pretending to be men, and women play men pretending to be women. Shakespeare's characters play these games as well. In *As You Like It,* when Rosalind flees Frederick's court she is in love with Orlando. In the forest of Arden, disguised as the boy Ganymede, she encounters Orlando, himself lovesick for Rosalind. As Ganymede, Rosalind says she 17 will try to cure Orlando of his love by playing Rosalind, pointing out the flaws of femininity in the process. In current stagings, Rosalind is usually played by a woman who at this point in the play pretends to be a man who pretends to be a woman. In Shakespeare's time, there was yet another turn because all women's parts were played by boys. So the character of Rosalind was played by a boy playing a girl playing a boy who plays a girl so she can have a flirtatious conversation with a boy. Another twist occurs when Rosalind playing Ganymede playing Rosalind meets Phebe, a shepherdess who falls passionately in love with "him."

As You Like It, with its famous soliloquy that begins "All the world's a [18] stage," is a play that dramatizes the power of the theater as a metaphor for life. The visual pun of Rosalind's role underscores the fact that each of us is an actor playing one part or many parts. But the play has another message that speaks to the power of MUDs as new stages for working on the politics of gender. When Rosalind and Orlando meet "man to man" as Ganymede and Orlando, they are able to speak freely. They are able to have conversations about love quite different from those that would be possible if they followed the courtly conventions that constrain communications between men and women. In this way, the play suggests that donning a mask, adopting a persona, is a step toward reaching a deeper truth about the real, a position many MUDders take regarding their experiences as virtual selves.

Garrett is a twenty-eight-year-old male computer programmer who [19] played a female character on a MUD for nearly a year. The character was a frog named Ribbit. When Ribbit sensed that a new player was floundering, a small sign would materialize in her hand that said, "If you are lost in the MUD, this frog can be a friend."

When talking about why he chose to play Ribbit, Garrett says: [20]

> I wanted to know more about women's experiences, and not just from reading about them. . . . I wanted to see what the difference felt like. I wanted to experiment with the other side. . . . I wanted to be collaborative and helpful, and I thought it would be easier as a female. . . . As a man I was brought up to be territorial and competitive. I wanted to try something new. . . . In some way I really felt that the canonically female way of communicating was more productive than the male—in that all this competition got in the way.

And indeed, Garrett says that as a female frog, he did feel freer to express the helpful side of his nature than he ever had as a man. "My competitive side takes a back seat when I am Ribbit."

Garrett's motivations for his experiment in gender-swapping run deep. [21] Growing up, competition was thrust upon him and he didn't much like it. Garrett, whose parents divorced when he was an infant, rarely saw his father. His mother offered little protection from his brother's bullying. An older cousin regularly beat him up until Garrett turned fourteen and could inflict some damage of his own. Garrett got the clear idea that male aggression could only be controlled by male force.

In his father's absence, Garrett took on significant family responsibility.   22
His mother ran an office, and Garrett checked in with her every day after school to see if she had any errands for him to run. If so, he would forgo the playground. Garrett recalls these days with great warmth. He felt helpful and close to his mother. When at ten, he won a scholarship to a prestigious private boarding school for boys, a school he describes as being "straight out of Dickens," there were no more opportunities for this kind of collaboration. To Garrett, life now seemed to be one long competition. Of boarding school he says:

> It's competitive from the moment you get up in the morning and you all got to take a shower together and everyone's checking each other out to see who's got pubic hair. It's competitive when you're in class. It's competitive when you're on the sports field. It's competitive when you're in other extracurricular activities such as speeches. It's competitive all day long, every day.

At school, the older boys had administrative authority over the younger   23
ones. Garrett was not only the youngest student, he was also from the poorest family and the only newcomer to a group that had attended school together for many years. "I was pretty much at the bottom of the food chain," he says. In this hierarchical environment, Garrett learned to detest hierarchy, and the bullies at school reinforced his negative feelings about masculine aggression.

Once out of high school, Garrett committed himself to finding ways to   24
"get back to being the kind of person I was with my mother." But he found it difficult to develop collaborative relationships, particularly at work. When he encouraged a female coworker to take credit for some work they had done together—"something," he says "that women have always done for men"—she accepted his offer, but their friendship and ability to work together were damaged. Garrett sums up the experience by saying that women are free to help men and both can accept the woman's self-sacrifice, "but when a man lets a woman take the credit, the relationship feels too close, too seductive [to the woman]."

From Garrett's point of view, most computer bulletin boards and dis-   25
cussion groups are not collaborative but hostile environments, characterized by "flaming." This is the practice of trading angry and often *ad hominem* remarks on any given topic.

> There was a premium on saying something new, which is typically something that disagrees to some extent with what somebody else has said. And that in itself provides an atmosphere that's ripe for conflict. Another aspect, I think, is

the fact that it takes a certain degree of courage to risk really annoying someone. But that's not necessarily true on an electronic medium, because they can't get to you. It's sort of like hiding behind a wall and throwing stones. You can keep throwing them as long as you want and you're safe.

Garrett found MUDs different and a lot more comfortable. "On MUDs," 26 he says, "people were making a world together. You got no prestige from being abusive."

Garrett's gender-swapping on MUDs gave him an experience-to-think- 27 with for thinking about gender. From his point of view, all he had to do was to replace male with female in a character's description to change how people saw him and what he felt comfortable expressing. Garrett's MUD experience, where as a female he could be collaborative without being stigmatized, left him committed to bringing the helpful frog persona into his life as a male, both on and off the MUD. When I met him, he had a new girlfriend who was lending him books about the differences in men's and women's communication styles. He found they reinforced the lessons he learned in the MUD.

By the time I met Garrett, he was coming to feel that his gender- 28 swapping experiment had reached its logical endpoint. Indeed, between the time of our first and second meeting, Garrett decided to blow his cover on the MUD and tell people that in RL he was really male. He said that our discussions of his gender-swapping had made him realize that it had achieved its purpose.

For anthropologists, the experience of *dépaysement* (literally, "decoun- 29 trifying" oneself) is one of the most powerful elements of fieldwork. One leaves one's own culture to face something unfamiliar, and upon returning home it has become strange—and can be seen with fresh eyes. Garrett described his decision to end his gender-swapping in the language of *dépaysement*. He had been playing a woman for so long that it no longer seemed strange. "I'd gotten used to it to the extent that I was sort of ignoring it. OK, so I log in and now I'm a woman. And it really didn't seem odd anymore." But returning to the MUD as a male persona *did* feel strange. He struggled for an analogy and came up with this one:

> It would be like going to an interview for a job and acting like I do at a party or a volleyball game. Which is not the way you behave at an interview. And so it is sort of the same thing. [As a male on the MUD] I'm behaving in a way that doesn't feel right for the context, although it is still as much me as it ever was.

When Garrett stopped playing the female Ribbit and started playing a 30 helpful male frog named Ron, many of Garrett's MUDding companions interpreted his actions as those of a woman who now wanted to try playing a man. Indeed, a year after his switch, Garrett says that at least one of his MUD friends, Dredlock, remains unconvinced that the same person has actually played both Ribbit and Ron. Dredlock insists that while Ribbit was erratic (he says, "She would sometimes walk out in the middle of a conversation"), Ron is more dependable. Has Garrett's behavior changed? Is Garrett's behavior the same but viewed differently through the filter of gender? Garrett believes that both are probably true. "People on the MUD have . . . seen the change and it hasn't necessarily convinced them that I'm male, but they're also not sure that I'm female. And so, I've sort of gotten into this state where my gender is unknown and people are pretty much resigned to not knowing it." Garrett says that when he helped others as a female frog, it was taken as welcome, natural, and kind. When he now helps as a male frog, people find it unexpected and suspect that it is a seduction ploy. The analogy with his real life is striking. There, too, he found that playing the helping role as a man led to trouble because it was easily misinterpreted as an attempt to create an expectation of intimacy.

Case, the industrial designer who played the female Mairead in   31
MedievalMUSH, further illustrates the complexity of gender-swapping as a vehicle for self-reflection. Case describes his RL persona as a nice guy, a "Jimmy Stewart–type like my father." He says that in general he likes his father and he likes himself, but he feels he pays a price for his low-key ways. In particular, he feels at a loss when it comes to confrontation, both at home and in business dealings. While Garrett finds that MUDding as a female makes it easier to be collaborative and helpful, Case likes MUDding as a female because it makes it easier for him to be aggressive and confrontational. Case plays several online "Katharine Hepburn–types," strong, dynamic, "out there" women who remind him of his mother, "who says exactly what's on her mind and is a take-no-prisoners sort." He says:

> For virtual reality to be interesting it has to emulate the real. But you have to be able to do something in the virtual that you couldn't in the real. For me, my female characters are interesting because I can say and do the sorts of things that I mentally want to do, but if I did them as a man, they would be obnoxious. I see a strong woman as admirable. I see a strong man as a problem. Potentially a bully.

In other words, for Case, if you are assertive as a man, it is coded as "being a bastard." If you are assertive as a woman, it is coded as "modern and together."

> My wife and I both design logos for small businesses. But do this thought experiment. If I say "I will design this logo for $3,000, take it or leave it," I'm just a typical pushy businessman. If she says it, I think it sounds like she's a "together" woman. There is too much male power-wielding in society, and so if you use power as a man, that turns you into a stereotypical man. Women can do it more easily.

Case's gender-swapping has given him permission to be more assertive 32 within the MUD, and more assertive outside of it as well:

> There are aspects of my personality—the more assertive, administrative, bureaucratic ones—that I am able to work on in the MUDs. I've never been good at bureaucratic things, but I'm much better from practicing on MUDs and playing a woman in charge. I am able to do things—in the real, that is—that I couldn't have before because I have played Katharine Hepburn characters.

Case says his Katharine Hepburn personae are "externalizations of a 33 part of myself." In one interview with him, I use the expression "aspects of the self," and he picks it up eagerly, for MUDding reminds him of how Hindu gods could have different aspects or subpersonalities, all the while having a whole self.

> You may, for example, have an aspect who is a ruthless business person who can negotiate contracts very, very well, and you may call upon that part of yourself while you are in tense negotiation, to do the negotiation, to actually go through and negotiate a really good contract. But you would have to trust this aspect to say something like, "Of course, I will need my lawyers to look over this," when in fact among your "lawyers" is the integrated self who is going to do an ethics vet over the contract, because you don't want to violate your own ethical standards and this [ruthless] aspect of yourself might do something that you wouldn't feel comfortable with later.

Case's gender-swapping has enabled his inner world of hard-bitten 34 negotiators to find self-expression, but without compromising the values he associates with his "whole person." Role playing has given the negotiators practice; Case says he has come to trust them more. In response to my question, "Do you feel that you call upon your personae in real life?" Case responds:

> Yes, an aspect sort of clears its throat and says, "I can do this. You are being so amazingly conflicted over this and I know exactly what to do. Why don't you just let me do it?" MUDs give me balance. In real life, I tend to be extremely diplomatic, nonconfrontational. I don't like to ram my ideas down anyone's throat. On the MUD, I can be, "Take it or leave it." All of my Hepburn characters are that way. That's probably why I play them. Because they are smart-mouthed, they will not sugarcoat their words.

In some ways, Case's description of his inner world of actors who ad- 35 dress him and are capable of taking over negotiations is reminiscent of the language of people with multiple personality. In most cases of multiple personality, it is believed that repeated trauma provokes a massive defense: An "alter" is split off who can handle the trauma and protect the core personality from emotional as well as physical pain. In contrast, Case's inner actors are not split off from his sense of himself. He calls upon their strengths with increasing ease and fluidity. Case experiences himself very much as a collective self, not feeling that he must goad or repress this or that aspect of himself into conformity. To use Marvin Minsky's language, Case feels at ease in his society of mind.

Garrett and Case play female MUD characters for very different reasons. 36 There is a similar diversity in women's motivations for playing male characters. Some share my initial motivation, a desire for invisibility or permission to be more outspoken or aggressive. "I was born in the South and I was taught that girls didn't speak up to disagree with men," says Zoe, a thirty-four-year-old woman who plays male and female characters on four MUDs.

> We would sit at dinner and my father would talk and my mother would agree. I thought my father was a god. Once or twice I did disagree with him. I remember one time in particular when I was ten, and he looked at me and said, "Well, well, well, if this little flower grows too many more thorns, she will never catch a man."

Zoe credits MUDs with enabling her to reach a state of mind where she 37 is better able to speak up for herself in her marriage ("to say what's on my mind before things get all blown out of proportion") and to handle her job as the financial officer for a small biotechnology firm.

> I played a MUD man for two years. First I did it because I wanted the feeling of an equal playing field in terms of authority, and the only way I could think of to get it was to play a man. But after a while, I got very absorbed by MUDding. I became a wizard on a pretty simple MUD—I called myself Ulysses—and got involved in the system and realized that as a man I could be firm and people would think I was a great wizard. As a woman, drawing the line and standing firm has always made me feel like a bitch and, actually, I feel that people saw me as one, too. As a man I was liberated from all that. I learned from my mistakes. I got better at being firm but not rigid. I practiced, safe from criticism.

Zoe's perceptions of her gender trouble are almost the opposite of Case's. 38 Case sees aggressiveness as acceptable only for women; Zoe sees it as acceptable only for men. Comparison with Garrett is also instructive. Like Case, Garrett associated feminine strength with positive feelings about his mother; Zoe associated feminine strength with loss of her father's love. What these stories have in common is that in all three cases, a virtual gender swap gave people greater emotional range in the real. Zoe says:

> I got really good at playing a man, so good that whoever was on the system would accept me as a man and talk to me as a man. So, other guys talked to Ulysses "guy to guy." It was very validating. All those years I was paranoid about how men talked about women. Or I thought I was paranoid. And then, I got a chance to be a guy and I saw that I wasn't paranoid at all.

Zoe talked to me about her experiences in a face-to-face interview, but   39
there is a great deal of spontaneous discussion of these issues on Internet
bulletin boards and discussion groups. In her paper "Gender Swapping on
the Internet," Amy Bruckman tracks an ongoing discussion of gender issues
on the electronic discussion group rec.games.mud. Individuals may post to
it, that is, send a communication to all subscribers. Postings on specific topics frequently start identifiable discussion "threads," which may continue for
many months.

On one of these threads, several male participants described how play-   40
ing female characters had given them newfound empathy with women.
One contributor, David, described the trials and tribulations of playing a female character:

> Other players start showering you with money to help you get started, and I had
> never once gotten a handout when playing a male player. And then they feel
> they should be allowed to tag along forever, and feel hurt when you leave them
> to go off and explore by yourself. Then when you give them the knee after they
> grope you, they wonder what your problem is, reciting that famous saying,
> "What's your problem? It's only a game."

Carol, an experienced player with much technical expertise about   41
MUDs, concurred. She complained about male players' misconception that
"women can't play MUDs, can't work out puzzles, can't even type 'kill monster' without help." Carol noted that men offered help as a way to be in-
gratiating, but in her case this seduction strategy was ineffectual: "People
offering me help to solve puzzles *I* wrote are not going to get very far."

Ellen, another contributor to the rec.games.mud discussion, tried   42
gender-bending on an adventure-style MUD, thinking she would find out:

> if it was true that people would be nasty and kill me on sight and other stuff I'd
> heard about on r.g.m. [an abbreviation of rec.games.mud]. But, no, everyone
> was helpful (I was truly clueless and needed the assistance); someone gave me
> enough money to buy a weapon and armor and someone else showed me
> where the easy-to-kill newbie [a new player] monsters were. They definitely
> went out of their way to be nice to a male-presenting newbie. . . . (These were
> all male-presenting players, btw [by the way].)
>
> One theory is that my male character [named Argyle and described as "a
> short squat fellow who is looking for his socks"] was pretty innocuous. Maybe
> people are only nasty if you are "a broad-shouldered perfect specimen of a
> man" or something of that nature, which can be taken as vaguely attacking.

Ellen concluded that harassment relates most directly to self-presentation: 43
"People are nice if they don't view you as a threat." Short, squat, a bit lost,
in search of socks, and thus connoting limpness—Argyle was clearly not
a threat to the dominant status of other "men" on the MUD. In the MUD culture Ellen played in, men tended to be competitive and aggressive toward

each other; Argyle's nonthreatening self-presentation earned him kind treatment.

For some men and women, gender-bending can be an attempt to under-   44
stand better or to experiment safely with sexual orientation. But for everyone who tries it, there is the chance to discover, as Rosalind and Orlando did in the Forest of Arden, that for both sexes, gender is constructed.

Virtual Sex

Virtual sex, whether in MUDs or in a private room on a commercial online   45
service, consists of two or more players typing descriptions of physical actions, verbal statements, and emotional reactions for their characters. In cyberspace, this activity is not only common but, for many people, it is the centerpiece of their online experience.

On MUDs, some people have sex as characters of their own gender.   46
Others have sex as characters of the other gender. Some men play female personae to have netsex with men. And in the "fake-lesbian syndrome," men adopt online female personae in order to have netsex with women. Although it does not seem to be as widespread, I have met several women who say they present as male characters in order to have netsex with men. Some people have sex as nonhuman characters, for example, as animals on FurryMUDs. Some enjoy sex with one partner. Some use virtual reality as a place to experiment with group situations. In real life such behavior (where possible) can create enormous practical and emotional confusion. Virtual adventures may be easier to undertake, but they can also result in significant complications. Different people and different couples deal with them in very different ways.

Martin and Beth, both forty-one, have been married for nineteen years   47
and have four children. Early in their marriage, Martin regretted not having had more time for sexual experimentation and had an extramarital affair. The affair hurt Beth deeply, and Martin decided he never wanted to do it again. When Martin discovered MUDs he was thrilled. "I really am monogamous. I'm really not interested in something outside my marriage. But being able to have, you know, a Tiny romance is kind of cool." Martin decided to tell Beth about his MUD sex life and she decided to tell him that she does not mind. Beth has made a conscious decision to consider Martin's sexual relationships on MUDs as more like his reading an erotic novel than like his having a rendezvous in a motel room. For Martin, his online affairs are a way to fill the gaps of his youth, to broaden his sexual experience without endangering his marriage.

Other partners of virtual adulterers do not share Beth's accepting atti-   48
tude. Janet, twenty-four, a secretary at a New York law firm, is very upset by

her husband Tim's sex life in cyberspace. After Tim's first online affair, he confessed his virtual infidelity. When Janet objected, Tim told her that he would stop "seeing" his online mistress. Janet says that she is not sure that he actually did stop.

> Look, I've got to say the thing that bothers me most is that he wants to do it in the first place. In some ways, I'd have an easier time understanding why he would want to have an affair in real life. At least there, I could say to myself, "Well, it is for someone with a better body, or just for the novelty." It's like the first kiss is always the best kiss. But in MUDding, he is saying that he wants that feeling of intimacy with someone else, the "just talk" part of an encounter with a woman, and to me that comes closer to what is most important about sex.
>
> First I told him he couldn't do it anymore. Then, I panicked and figured that he might do it anyway, because unlike in real life I could never find out. All these thousands of people all over the world with their stupid fake names . . . no way I would ever find out. So, I pulled back and said that talking about it was strictly off limits. But now I don't know if that was the right decision. I feel paranoid whenever he is on the computer. I can't get it off my mind, that he is cheating, and he probably is tabulating data for his thesis. It must be clear that this sex thing has really hurt our marriage.

This distressed wife struggles to decide whether her husband is unfaithful   49
when his persona collaborates on writing real-time erotica with another persona in cyberspace. And beyond this, should it make a difference if unbeknownst to the husband his cyberspace mistress turns out to be a nineteen-year-old male college freshman? What if "she" is an infirm eighty-year-old man in a nursing home? And even more disturbing, what if she is a twelve-year-old girl? Or a twelve-year-old boy?

TinySex poses the question of what is at the heart of sex and fidelity. Is   50
it the physical action? Is it the feeling of emotional intimacy with someone other than one's primary partner? Is infidelity in the head or in the body? Is it in the desire or in the action? What constitutes the violation of trust? And to what extent and in what ways should it matter who the virtual sexual partner is in the real world? The fact that the physical body has been factored out of the situation makes these issues both subtler and harder to resolve than before.

Janet feels her trust has been violated by Tim's "talk intimacy" with an-   51
other woman. Beth, the wife who gave her husband Martin permission to have TinySex, feels that he violated her trust when he chose to play a female character having a sexual encounter with a "man." When Beth read the log of one of these sessions, she became angry that Martin had drawn on his knowledge of her sexual responses to play his female character.

For Rudy, thirty-six, what was most threatening about his girlfriend's   52
TinySex was the very fact that she wanted to play a character of the oppo-

site sex at all. He discovered that she habitually plays men and has sex with female characters in chat rooms on America Online (like MUDs in that people can choose their identities). This discovery led him to break off the relationship. Rudy struggles to express what bothers him about his ex-girlfriend's gender-bending in cyberspace. He is not sure of himself, he is unhappy, hesitant, and confused. He says, "We are not ready for the psychological confusion this technology can bring." He explains:

> It's not the infidelity. It's the gnawing feeling that my girlfriend—I mean, I was thinking of marrying her—is a dyke. I know that everyone is bisexual, I know, I know . . . but that is one of those things that I knew but it never had anything to do with me. . . . It was just intellectual.
>
> What I hate about the rooms on America Online is that it makes it so easy for this sort of thing to become real. Well, in the sense that the rooms are real. I mean, the rooms, real or not, make it too easy for people to explore these things. If she explored it in real life, well, it would be hard on me, but it would have been hard for her. If she really wanted to do it, she would do it, but it would have meant her going out and doing it. It seems like more of a statement. And if she had really done it, I would know what to make of it. Now, I hate her for what she does online, but I don't know if I'm being crazy to break up with her about something that, after all, is only words.

Rudy complained that virtual reality made it too easy for his girlfriend to explore what it might be like to have a sexual relationship with another woman, too easy for her to experience herself as a man, too easy to avoid the social consequences of her actions. MUDs provide a situation in which we can play out scenarios that otherwise might have remained pure fantasy. Yet the status of these fantasies-in-action in cyberspace is unclear. Although they involve other people and are no longer pure fantasy, they are not "in the world." Their boundary status offers new possibilities. TinySex and virtual gender-bending are part of the larger story of people using virtual spaces to construct identity.

Working with the Text

1. Turkle says that her sense of freedom in playing a MUD male "said as much about the construction of gender in my own mind as it did about the social construction of gender in the MUD." To what extent do you think gender is "constructed" rather than biological?

2. Turkle notes that it is difficult for a male to pass as female or for a female to pass as male online. How would you go about "passing" in this context? Do you think you could succeed? What would make you suspect that a persona you encountered online was trying to "pass"?

3. Turkle also says that passing involves "gravity and emotional risk." How do her examples of people who pass as a different gender online support her point? Do you think that these people actually "reach a deeper truth about what is real"?

4. In discussing Garrett, who played both a female and a male frog, Turkle mentions that many other players didn't believe that the same person played both characters. "Has Garrett's behavior changed?" she asks, or "[i]s Garrett's behavior the same but viewed differently through the filter of gender?" What do you think is the likely answer to this question?

5. Ellen, who played a male character named Argyle, found other male players helpful, which Turkle suggests was because Argyle was described as innocuous, even ineffectual. Does this suggest something about communication between males that conforms to your own experience?

6. What do you think about TinySex, particularly when it goes beyond a marriage as the concluding examples describe? Would you consider a partner who participated in such online activity unfaithful to you?

The Fact of Blackness

FRANTZ FANON

Frantz Fanon (1925–1961) was born in the French colony of Martinque. He emigrated to France and joined the resistance movement during the second world war. After the war he remained in France to study. His book *Black Skin, White Masks* (1952), quickly became one of the most influential statements of anti-colonial revolutionary thought. In 1953 Fanon was appointed the Head of the Psychiatry Department at the Blida-Joinville Hospital in Algeria. When the war for Algerian independence broke out, he resigned his post with the French government and began working for the Algerian independence movement. He completed his final indictment of the colonial condition in *The Wretched of the Earth* (1961), which was published by Jean-Paul Sartre following Fanon's death from leukemia. The following selection from *Black Skin* explores the racialized relation between the "seer" and the "seen." Fanon invites us to consider how he, as a black man, functions as a visual, and in turn ideological, "sign." He suggests that as a cultural practice, how we look and see is always constructed in the field of race. The differences we see—such as skin color and other markers of race—appear to ground their "truth" beyond history, in nature.

"Dirty nigger!" Or simply, "Look, a Negro!"   1

I came into the world imbued with the will to find a meaning in things,   2
my spirit filled with the desire to attain to the source of the world, and then I found that I was an object in the midst of other objects.

Sealed into that crushing objecthood, I turned beseechingly to others.   3
Their attention was a liberation, running over my body suddenly abraded into nonbeing, endowing me once more with an agility that I had thought lost, and by taking me out of the world, restoring me to it. But just as I reached the other side, I stumbled, the movements, the attitudes, the glances of the other fixed me there, in the sense in which a chemical solution is fixed by a dye. I was indignant; I demanded an explanation. Nothing happened. I burst apart. Now the fragments have been put together again by another self.

As long as the black man is among his own, he will have no occasion,   4
except in minor internal conflicts, to experience his being through others. There is of course the moment of "being for others," of which Hegel speaks, but every ontology is made unattainable in a colonized and civilized society. It would seem that this fact has not been given sufficient attention by those who have discussed the question. In the *Weltanschauung* of a colonized people there is an impurity, a flaw that outlaws any ontological explanation. Someone may object that this is the case with every individual, but such an objection merely conceals a basic problem. Ontology—once it is finally admitted as leaving existence by the wayside—does not permit us to understand the being of the black man. For not only must the black man be black; he must be black in relation to the white man. Some critics will take it on themselves to remind us that this proposition has a converse. I say that this is false. The black man has no ontological resistance in the eyes of the white man. Overnight the Negro has been given two frames of reference within which he has had to place himself. His metaphysics, or, less pretentiously, his customs and the sources on which they were based, were wiped out because they were in conflict with a civilization that he did not know and that imposed itself on him.

The black man among his own in the twentieth century does not know   5
at what moment his inferiority comes into being through the other. Of course I have talked about the black problem with friends, or, more rarely, with American Negroes. Together we protested, we asserted the equality of all men in the world. In the Antilles there was also that little gulf that exists among the almost-white, the mulatto, and the nigger. But I was satisfied

with an intellectual understanding of these differences. It was not really dramatic. And then. . . .

And then the occasion arose when I had to meet the white man's eyes. 6
An unfamiliar weight burdened me. The real world challenged my claims. In the white world the man of color encounters difficulties in the development of his bodily schema. Consciousness of the body is solely a negating activity. It is a third-person consciousness. The body is surrounded by an atmosphere of certain uncertainty. I know that if I want to smoke, I shall have to reach out my right arm and take the pack of cigarettes lying at the other end of the table. The matches, however, are in the drawer on the left, and I shall have to lean back slightly. And all these movements are made not out of habit but out of implicit knowledge. A slow composition of my *self* as a body in the middle of a spatial and temporal world—such seems to be the schema. It does not impose itself on me; it is, rather, a definitive structuring of the self and of the world—definitive because it creates a real dialectic between my body and the world.

For several years certain laboratories have been trying to produce a 7
serum for "denegrification"; with all the earnestness in the world, laboratories have sterilized their test tubes, checked their scales, and embarked on researches that might make it possible for the miserable Negro to whiten himself and thus to throw off the burden of that corporeal malediction. Below the corporeal schema I had sketched a historico-racial schema. The elements that I used had been provided for me not by "residual sensations and perceptions primarily of a tactile, vestibular, kinesthetic, and visual character,"[1] but by the other, the white man, who had woven me out of a thousand details, anecdotes, stories. I thought that what I had in hand was to construct a physiological self, to balance space, to localize sensations, and here I was called on for more.

"Look, a Negro!" It was an external stimulus that flicked over me as I 8
passed by. I made a tight smile.

"Look, a Negro!" It was true. It amused me. 9

"Look, a Negro!" The circle was drawing a bit tighter. I made no secret 10
of my amusement.

"Mama, see the Negro! I'm frightened!" Frightened! Frightened! Now 11
they were beginning to be afraid of me. I made up my mind to laugh myself to tears, but laughter had become impossible.

I could no longer laugh, because I already knew that there were legends, 12
stories, history, and above all *historicity*, which I had learned about from Jaspers [presumably philosopher Karl Jaspers (1883–1969)]. Then, assailed at various points, the corporeal schema crumbled, its place taken by a racial

---

1. Jean Lhermitte, *L'Image de noire corps* (Paris, Nouvelle Revue critique, 1939), p. 17.

epidermal schema. In the train it was no longer a question of being aware of my body in the third person but in a triple person. In the train I was given not one but two, three places. I had already stopped being amused. It was not that I was finding febrile coordinates in the world. I existed triply: I occupied space. I moved toward the other . . . and the evanescent other, hostile but not opaque, transparent, not there, disappeared. Nausea. . . .

I was responsible at the same time for my body, for my race, for my ancestors. I subjected myself to an objective examination, I discovered my blackness, my ethnic characteristics; and I was battered down by tom-toms, cannibalism, intellectual deficiency, fetishism, racial defects, slave-ships, and above all else, above all: "Sho' good eatin'." 13

On that day, completely dislocated, unable to be abroad with the other, the white man, who unmercifully imprisoned me, I took myself far off from my own presence, far indeed, and made myself an object. What else could it be for me but an amputation, an excision, a hemorrhage that spattered my whole body with black blood? But I did not want this revision, this thematization. All I wanted was to be a man among other men. I wanted to come lithe and young into a world that was ours and to help to build it together. 14

But I rejected all immunization of the emotions. I wanted to be a man, nothing but a man. Some identified me with ancestors of mine who had been enslaved or lynched: I decided to accept this. It was on the universal level of the intellect that I understood this inner kinship—I was the grandson of slaves in exactly the same way in which President Lebrun was the grandson of tax-paying, hard-working peasants. In the main, the panic soon vanished. 15

In America, Negroes are segregated. In South America, Negroes are whipped in the streets, and Negro strikers are cut down by machine-guns. In West Africa, the Negro is an animal. And there beside me, my neighbor in the university, who was born in Algeria, told me: "As long as the Arab is treated like a man, no solution is possible." 16

"Understand, my dear boy, color prejudice is something I find utterly foreign. . . . But of course, come in, sir, there is no color prejudice among us. . . . Quite, the Negro is a man like ourselves. . . . It is not because he is black that he is less intelligent than we are. . . . I had a Senegalese buddy in the army who was really clever. . . ." Where am I to be classified? Or, if you prefer, tucked away? 17

"A Martinican, a native of 'our' old colonies." 18

Where shall I hide? 19

"Look at the nigger! . . . Mama, a Negro! . . . Hell, he's getting mad. . . . Take no notice, sir, he does not know that you are as civilized as we. . . ." 20

My body was given back to me sprawled out, distorted, recolored, clad in mourning in that white winter day. The Negro is an animal, the Negro is 21 bad, the Negro is mean, the Negro is ugly; look, a nigger, it's cold, the nigger is shivering, the nigger is shivering because he is cold, the little boy is trembling because he is afraid of the nigger, the nigger is shivering with cold, that cold that goes through your bones, the handsome little boy is trembling because he thinks that the nigger is quivering with rage, the little white boy throws himself into his mother's arms: Mama, the nigger's going to eat me up.

All round me the white man, above the sky tears at its navel, the earth rasps under my feet, and there is a white song, a white song. All this whiteness that burns me. . . .   22

I sit down at the fire and I become aware of my uniform. I had not seen it. It is indeed ugly. I stop there, for who can tell me what beauty is?   23

Where shall I find shelter from now on? I felt an easily identifiable flood mounting out of the countless facets of my being. I was about to be angry. The fire was long since out, and once more the nigger was trembling.   24

"Look how handsome that Negro is! . . ."   25

"Kiss the handsome Negro's ass, madame!"   26

Shame flooded her face. At last I was set free from my rumination. At the same time I accomplished two things: I identified my enemies and I made a scene. A grand slam. Now one would be able to laugh.   27

The field of battle having been marked out, I entered the lists.   28

What? While I was forgetting, forgiving, and wanting only to love, my message was flung back in my face like a slap. The white world, the only honorable one, barred me from all participation. A man was expected to behave like a man. I was expected to behave like a black man—or at least like a nigger. I shouted a greeting to the world and the world slashed away my joy. I was told to stay within bounds, to go back where I belonged.   29

They would see, then! I had warned them, anyway. Slavery? It was no longer even mentioned, that unpleasant memory. My supposed inferiority? A hoax that it was better to laugh at. I forgot it all, but only on condition that the world not protect itself against me any longer. I had incisors to test. I was sure they were strong. And besides. . . .   30

What! When it was I who had every reason to hate, to despise, I was rejected? When I should have been begged, implored, I was denied the slightest recognition? I resolved, since it was impossible for me to get away from an *inborn complex,* to assert myself as a BLACK MAN. Since the other hesitated to recognize me, there remained only one solution: to make myself known.   31

In *Anti-Semite and Jew* (p. 95), Sartre says: "They [the Jews] have allowed themselves to be poisoned by the stereotype that others have of them, and they live in fear that their acts will correspond to this stereotype. . . . We may say that their conduct is perpetually overdetermined from the inside."   32

All the same, the Jew can be unknown in his Jewishness. He is not   33
wholly what he is. One hopes, one waits. His actions, his behavior are the
final determinant. He is a white man, and, apart from some rather debatable
characteristics, he can sometimes go unnoticed. He belongs to the race of
those who since the beginning of time have never known cannibalism.
What an idea, to eat one's father! Simple enough, one has only not to be a
nigger. Granted, the Jews are harassed—what am I thinking of? They are
hunted down, exterminated, cremated. But these are little family quarrels.
The Jew is disliked from the moment he is tracked down. But in my case
everything takes on a *new* guise. I am given no chance. I am overdetermined from without. I am the slave not of the "idea" that others have of me
but of my own appearance.

I move slowly in the world, accustomed now to seek no longer for up-   34
heaval. I progress by crawling. And already I am being dissected under
white eyes, the only real eyes. I am *fixed*. Having adjusted their microtomes,
they objectively cut away slices of my reality. I am laid bare. I feel, I see in
those white faces that it is not a new man who has come in, but a new kind
of man, a new genus. Why, it's a Negro!

I slip into corners, and my long antennae pick up the catch-phrases   35
strewn over the surface of things—nigger underwear smells of nigger—
nigger teeth are white—nigger feet are big—the nigger's barrel chest—I slip
into corners, I remain silent, I strive for anonymity, for invisibility. Look, I
will accept the lot, as long as no one notices me!

"Oh, I want you to meet my black friend. . . . Aimé Césaire, a black man   36
and a university graduate. . . . Marian Anderson, the finest of Negro
singers. . . . Dr. Cobb, who invented white blood, is a Negro. . . . Here, say
hello to my friend from Martinique (be careful, he's extremely sensitive). . . ."

Shame. Shame and self-contempt. Nausea. When people like me, they   37
tell me it is in spite of my color. When they dislike me, they point out that it
is not because of my color. Either way, I am locked into the infernal circle.

I turn away from these inspectors of the Ark before the Flood and I at-   38
tach myself to my brothers, Negroes like myself. To my horror, they too reject me. They are almost white. And besides they are about to marry white
women. They will have children faintly tinged with brown. Who knows,
perhaps little by little. . . .

I had been dreaming.   39

"I want you to understand, sir, I am one of the best friends the Negro   40
has in Lyon."

The evidence was there, unalterable. My blackness was there, dark and   41
unarguable. And it tormented me, pursued me, disturbed me, angered me.

Negroes are savages, brutes, illiterates. But in my own case I knew that   42
these statements were false. There was a myth of the Negro that had to be

destroyed at all costs. The time had long since passed when a Negro priest
was an occasion for wonder. We had physicians, professors, statesmen. Yes,
but something out of the ordinary still clung to such cases. "We have a Senegalese history teacher. He is quite bright. . . . Our doctor is colored. He is
very gentle."

It was always the Negro teacher, the Negro doctor; brittle as I was be-   43
coming, I shivered at the slightest pretext. I knew, for instance, that if the
physician made a mistake it would be the end of him and of all those who
came after him. What could one expect, after all, from a Negro physician? As
long as everything went well, he was praised to the skies, but look out, no
nonsense, under any conditions! The black physician can never be sure how
close he is to disgrace. I tell you, I was walled in: No exception was made
for my refined manners, or my knowledge of literature, or my understanding of the quantum theory.

I requested, I demanded explanations. Gently, in the tone that one uses   44
with a child, they introduced me to the existence of a certain view that was
held by certain people, but, I was always told, "We must hope that it will
very soon disappear." What was it? Color prejudice.

> It [colour prejudice] is nothing more than the unreasoning hatred of one race for
> another, the contempt of the stronger and richer peoples for those whom they
> consider inferior to themselves and the bitter resentment of those who are kept
> in subjection and are so frequently insulted. As colour is the most obvious out-
> ward manifestation of race it has been made the criterion by which men are
> judged, irrespective of their social or educational attainments. The light-skinned
> races have come to despise all those of a darker colour, and the dark-skinned
> peoples will no longer accept without protest the inferior position to which they
> have been relegated.[2]

I had read it rightly. It was hate; I was hated, despised, detested, not by   45
the neighbor across the street or my cousin on my mother's side, but by an
entire race. I was up against something unreasoned. The psychoanalysts say
that nothing is more traumatizing for the young child than his encounters
with what is rational. I would personally say that for a man whose only
weapon is reason there is nothing more neurotic than contact with unreason.

I felt knife blades open within me. I resolved to defend myself. As a   46
good tactician, I intended to rationalize the world and to show the white
man that he was mistaken.

In the Jew, Jean-Paul Sartre says, there is   47

> a sort of impassioned imperialism of reason: for he wishes not only to convince
> others that he is right; his goal is to persuade them that there is an absolute and
> unconditioned value to rationalism. He feels himself to be a missionary of the

---

2. Sir Alan Burns, *Colour Prejudice* (London, Allen and Unwin, 1948), p. 16.

universal; against the universality of the Catholic religion, from which he is excluded, he asserts the "catholicity" of the rational, an instrument by which to attain to the truth and establish a spiritual bond among men.[3]

And the author adds, though there may be Jews who have made intuition the basic category of their philosophy, their intuition   48

> has no resemblance to the Pascalian subtlety of spirit, and it is this latter—based on a thousand imperceptible perceptions—which to the Jew seems his worst enemy. As for Bergson, his philosophy offers the curious appearance of an anti-intellectualist doctrine constructed entirely by the most rational and most critical of intelligences. It is through argument that he establishes the existence of pure duration, of philosophic intuition; and that very intuition which discovers duration or life, is itself universal, since anyone may practice it, and it leads toward the universal, since its objects can be named and conceived.[4]

With enthusiasm I set to cataloguing and probing my surroundings. As   49
times changed, one had seen the Catholic religion at first justify and then condemn slavery and prejudices. But by referring everything to the idea of the dignity of man, one had ripped prejudice to shreds. After much reluctance, the scientists had conceded that the Negro was a human being; *in vivo* and *in vitro* the Nergo had been proved analogous to the white man: the same morphology, the same histology. Reason was confident of victory on every level. I put all the parts back together. But I had to change my tune.

That victory played cat and mouse; it made a fool of me. As the other   50
put it, when I was present, it was not; when it was there, I was no longer. In the abstract there was agreement: The Negro is a human being. That is to say, amended the less firmly convinced, that like us he has his heart on the left side. But on certain points the white man remained intractable. Under no conditions did he wish any intimacy between the races, for it is a truism that "crossings between widely different races can lower the physical and mental level. . . . Until we have a more definite knowledge of the effect of race-crossings we shall certainly do best to avoid crossings between widely different races."[5]

For my own part, I would certainly know how to react. And in one   51
sense, if I were asked for a definition of myself, I would say that I am one who waits; I investigate my surroundings, I interpret everything in terms of what I discover, I become sensitive.

---

3. *Anti-Semite and Jew* (New York, Grove Press, 1960), pp. 112–13.
4. *Ibid.*, p. 115.
5. Jon Alfred Mjoen, "Harmonic and Disharmonic Race-crossings," The Second International Congress of Eugenics (1921), *Eugenics in Race and State,* vol. II, p. 60, quoted in Sir Alan Burns, *op. cit.,* p. 120.

Library Resource Center
Renton Technical College
3000 N.E. 4th St.
Renton, WA 98056

In the first chapter of the history that the others have compiled for me,   52
the foundation of cannibalism has been made eminently plain in order that
I may not lose sight of it. My chromosomes were supposed to have a few
thicker or thinner genes representing cannibalism. In addition to the *sex-linked,* the scholars had now discovered the *racial-linked.*[6] What a shameful science!

But I understand this "psychological mechanism." For it is a matter of   53
common knowledge that the mechanism is only psychological. Two centuries ago I was lost to humanity, I was a slave forever. And then came men
who said that it all had gone on far too long. My tenaciousness did the rest;
I was saved from the civilizing deluge. I have gone forward.

Too late. Everything is anticipated, thought out, demonstrated, made the   54
most of. My trembling hands take hold of nothing; the vein has been mined
out. Too late! But once again I want to understand.

Since the time when someone first mourned the fact that he had arrived   55
too late and everything had been said, a nostalgia for the past has seemed
to persist. Is this that lost original paradise of which Otto Rank speaks? How
many such men, apparently rooted to the womb of the world, have devoted
their lives to studying the Delphic circles or exhausted themselves in attempts to plot the wanderings of Ulysses! The pan-spiritualists seek to prove
the existence of a soul in animals by using this argument: A dog lies down
on the grave of his master and starves to death there. We had to wait for
Janet to demonstrate that the aforesaid dog, in contrast to man, simply
lacked the capacity to liquidate the past. We speak of the glory of Greece,
Artaud says; but, he adds, if modern man can no longer understand the
Choephoroi of Aeschylus, it is Aeschylus who is to blame. It is tradition to
which the anti-Semites turn in order to ground the validity of their "point of
view." It is tradition, it is that long historical past, it is that blood relation between Pascal and Descartes, that is invoked when the Jew is told, "There is
no possibility of your finding a place in society." Not long ago, one of those
good Frenchmen said in a train where I was sitting: "Just let the real French
virtues keep going and the race is safe. Now more than ever, national union
must be made a reality. Let's have an end of internal strife! Let's face up to
the foreigners (here he turned toward my corner) no matter who they are."

It must be said in his defense that he stank of cheap wine; if he had   56
been capable of it, he would have told me that my emancipated-slave blood
could not possibly be stirred by the name of Villon or Taine.

An outrage!   57

The Jew and I: Since I was not satisfied to be racialized, by a lucky turn   58
of fate I was humanized. I joined the Jew, my brother in misery.

---

6. In English in the original. (Translator's note.)

An outrage!   59

At first thought it may seem strange that the anti-Semite's outlook should   60
be related to that of the Negrophobe. It was my philosophy professor, a native of the Antilles, who recalled the fact to me one day: "Whenever you
hear anyone abuse the Jews, pay attention, because he is talking about you."
And I found that he was universally right—by which I meant that I was answerable in my body and in my heart for what was done to my brother. Later
I realized that he meant, quite simply, an anti-Semite is inevitably anti-Negro.

You come too late, much too late. There will always be a world—a   61
white world—between you and us. . . . The other's total inability to liquidate
the past once and for all. In the face of this affective ankylosis of the white
man, it is understandable that I could have made up my mind to utter my
Negro cry. Little by little, putting out pseudopodia here and there, I secreted
a race. And that race staggered under the burden of a basic element. What
was it? *Rhythm!* Listen to our singer, Léopold Senghor:

> It is the thing that is most perceptible and least material. It is the archetype
> of the vital element. It is the first condition and the hallmark of Art, as breath is
> of life: breath, which accelerates or slows, which becomes even or agitated
> according to the tension in the individual, the degree and the nature of his
> emotion. This is rhythm in its primordial purity, this is rhythm in the master-
> pieces of Negro art, especially sculpture. It is composed of a theme—sculptural
> form—which is set in opposition to a sister theme, as inhalation is to exhalation,
> and that is repeated. It is not the kind of symmetry that gives rise to monotony;
> rhythm is alive, it is free. . . . This is how rhythm affects what is least intellectual
> in us, tyrannically, to make us penetrate to the spirituality of the object; and that
> character of abandon which is ours is itself rhythmic.[7]

Had I read that right? I read it again with redoubled attention. From the   62
opposite end of the white world a magical Negro culture was hailing me.
Negro sculpture! I began to flush with pride. Was this our salvation?

I had rationalized the world and the world had rejected me on the basis   63
of color prejudice. Since no agreement was possible on the level of reason,
I threw myself back toward unreason. It was up to the white man to be
more irrational than I. Out of the necessities of my struggle I had chosen the
method of regression, but the fact remained that it was an unfamiliar
weapon; here I am at home; I am made of the irrational; I wade in the irrational. Up to the neck in the irrational. And now how my voice vibrates!

Those who invented neither gunpowder nor the compass
Those who never learned to conquer steam or electricity
Those who never explored the seas or the skies

---

7. "Ce que l'homme noir apporte," in Claude Nordey. *L'Homme de couleur* (Paris, Plon, 1939), pp.
309–10.

But they know the farthest corners of the land of anguish
Those who never knew any journey save that of abduction
Those who learned to kneel in docility
Those who were domesticated and Christianized
Those who were injected with bastardy. . . .

    Yes, all those are my brothers—a "bitter brotherhood" imprisons all of us   64
alike. Having stated the minor thesis, I went overboard after something else.

. . . . But those without whom the earth would not be the earth
Tumescence all the more fruitful
than
the empty land
still more the land
Storehouse to guard and ripen all
on earth that is most earth
My blackness is no stone, its deafness
hurled against the clamor of the day
My blackness is no drop of lifeless water
on the dead eye of the world
My blackness is neither a tower nor a cathedral
It thrusts into the red flesh of the sun
It thrusts into the burning flesh of the sky
It hollows through the dense dismay of its own pillar of patience.[8]

    Eyah! the tom-tom chatters out the cosmic message. Only the Negro has   65
the capacity to convey it, to decipher its meaning, its import. Astride the
world, my strong heels spurring into the banks of the world, I stare into
the shoulders of the world as the celebrant stares at the midpoint between
the eyes of the sacrificial victim.

    But they abandon themselves, possessed, to the essence
of all things, knowing nothing of externals but possessed by
the movement of all things
    uncaring to subdue but playing the play of the world
    truly the eldest sons of the world
    open to all the breaths of the world
    meeting-place of all the winds of the world
    undrained bed of all the waters of the world
    spark of the sacred fire of the World
    flesh of the flesh of the world, throbbing with the very movement of
      the world![9]

---

8. Aimé Césaire, *Cahier d'un retour au pays natal* (Paris, Présence Africaine, 1956), pp. 77–78.
9. *Ibid.,* p. 78.

Blood! Blood! . . . Birth! Ecstasy of becoming! Three-quarters engulfed in   66
the confusions of the day, I feel myself redden with blood. The arteries of
all the world, convulsed, torn away, uprooted, have turned toward me and
fed me.

"Blood! Blood! All our blood stirred by the male heart of the sun."[10]   67

Sacrifice was a middle point between the creation and myself—now I   68
went back no longer to sources but to The Source. Nevertheless, one had to
distrust rhythm, earth-mother love, this mystic, carnal marriage of the group
and the cosmos.

In *La vie sexuelle en Afrique noire,* a work rich in perceptions, De   69
Pédrals implies that always in Africa, no matter what field is studied, it will
have a certain magico-social structure. He adds:

> All these are the elements that one finds again on a still greater scale in the do-
> main of secret societies. To the extent, moreover, to which persons of either
> sex, subjected to circumcision during adolescence, are bound under penalty of
> death not to reveal to the uninitiated what they have experienced, and to the
> extent to which initiation into a secret society always excites to acts of *sacred
> love,* there is good ground to conclude by viewing both male and female
> circumcision and the rites that they embellish as constitutive of minor secret
> societies.[11]

I walk on white nails. Sheets of water threaten my soul on fire. Face to   70
face with these rites, I am doubly alert. Black magic! Orgies, witches' sab-
baths, heathen ceremonies, amulets. Coitus is an occasion to call on the
gods of the clan. It is a sacred act, pure, absolute, bringing invisible forces
into action. What is one to think of all these manifestations, all these initia-
tions, all these acts? From every direction I am assaulted by the obscenity of
dances and of words. Almost at my ear there is a song:

First our hearts burned hot
Now they are cold
All we think of now is Love
When we return to the village
When we see the great phallus
All how then we will make Love
For our parts will be dry and clean.[12]

The soil, which only a moment ago was still a tamed steed, begins to   71
revel. Are these virgins, these nymphomaniacs? Black Magic, primitive mentality, animism, animal eroticism, it all floods over me. All of it is typical of

---

10. *Ibid.,* p. 79.
11. De Pédrals, *La vie sexuelle en Afrique noire* (Paris, Payot), p. 83.
12. A. M. Vergiat, *Les rites secrets des primitifs de l'Oubangui* (Paris, Payot, 1951), p. 113.

peoples that have not kept pace with the evolution of the human race. Or, if one prefers, this is humanity at its lowest. Having reached this point, I was long reluctant to commit myself. Aggression was in the stars. I had to choose. What do I mean? I had no choice. . . .

Yes, we are—we Negroes—backward, simple, free in our behavior. That is because for us the body is not something opposed to what you call the mind. We are in the world. And long live the couple, Man and Earth! Besides, our men of letters helped me to convince you; your white civilization overlooks subtle riches and sensitivity. Listen:

> Emotive sensitivity. *Emotion is completely Negro as reason is Greek.*[13] Water rippled by every breeze? Unsheltered soul blown by every wind, whose fruit often drops before it is ripe? Yes, in one way, the Negro today is richer *in gifts than in works.*[14] But the tree thrusts its roots into the earth. The river runs deep, carrying precious seeds. And, the Afro-American poet, Langston Hughes, says:

I have known rivers
ancient dark rivers
my soul has grown deep
like the deep rivers.

> The very nature of the Negro's emotion, of his sensitivity, furthermore, explains his attitude toward the object perceived with such basic intensity. It is an abandon that becomes need, an active state of communion, indeed of identification, however negligible the action—I almost said the personality—of the object. A rhythmic attitude: The adjective should be kept in mind.[15]

So here we have the Negro rehabilitated, "standing before the bar," ruling the world with his intuition, the Negro recognized, set on his feet again, sought after, taken up, and he is a Negro—no, he is not a Negro but the Negro, exciting the fecund antennae of the world, placed in the foreground of the world, raining his poetic power on the world, "open to all the breaths of the world." I embrace the world! I am the world! The white man has never understood this magic substitution. The white man wants the world; he wants it for himself alone. He finds himself predestined master of this world. He enslaves it. An acquisitive relation is established between the world and him. But there exist other values that fit only my forms. Like a magician, I robbed the white man of "a certain world," forever after lost to him and his. When that happened, the white man must have been rocked backward by a force that he could not identify, so little used as he is to such reactions. Somewhere beyond the objective world of farms and banana trees and rubber trees, I had subtly brought the real world into being. The essence of the

---

13. My italics—F.F.
14. My italics—F.F.
15. Léopold Senghor, "Ce que l'homme noir apporte," in Nordey, *op. cit.*, p. 205.

world was my fortune. Between the world and me a relation of coexistence was established. I had discovered the primeval One. My "speaking hands" tore at the hysterical throat of the world. The white man had the anguished feeling that I was escaping from him and that I was taking something with me. He went through my pockets. He thrust probes into the least circumvolution of my brain. Everywhere he found only the obvious. So it was obvious that I had a secret. I was interrogated; turning away with an air of mystery, I murmured:

Tokowaly, uncle, do you remember the nights gone by
When my head weighed heavy on the back of your patience or
Holding my hand your hand led me by shadows and signs
The fields are flowers of glowworms, stars hang on the bushes, on
    the trees
Silence is everywhere
Only the scents of the jungle hum, swarms of reddish bees that overwhelm
    the crickets' shrill sounds,
And covered tom-tom, breathing in the distance of the night.
You, Tokowaly, you listen to what cannot be heard, and
you explain to me what the ancestors are saying in the liquid calm of the
    constellations,
The bull, the scorpion, the leopard, the elephant, and the fish we know,
And the white pomp of the Spirits in the heavenly shell that has no end,
But now comes the radiance of the goddess Moon and the veils of the
    shadows fall.
Night of Africa, my black night, mystical and bright, black and shining.[16]

I made myself the poet of the world. The white man had found a poetry   74
in which there was nothing poetic. The soul of the white man was corrupted, and, as I was told by a friend who was a teacher in the United States, "The presence of the Negroes beside the whites is in a way an insurance policy on humanness. When the whites feel that they have become too mechanized, they turn to the men of color and ask them for a little human sustenance." At last I had been recognized, I was no longer a zero.

I had soon to change my tune. Only momentarily at a loss, the white   75
man explained to me that, genetically, I represented a stage of development: "Your properties have been exhausted by us. We have had earth mystics such as you will never approach. Study our history and you will see how far this fusion has gone." Then I had the feeling that I was repeating a cycle. My originality had been torn out of me. I wept a long time, and then I began to

---

16. Léopold Senghor, *Chants d'ombre* (Paris Editions du Seuil, 1945).

live again. But I was haunted by a galaxy of erosive stereotypes: the Negro's *sui generis* odor . . . the Negro's *sui generis* good nature . . . the Negro's *sui generis* gullibility. . . .

I had tried to flee myself through my kind, but the whites had thrown themselves on me and hamstrung me. I tested the limits of my essence; beyond all doubt there was not much of it left. It was here that I made my most remarkable discovery. Properly speaking, this discovery was a rediscovery. 76

I rummaged frenetically through all the antiquity of the black man. What I found there took away my breath. In his book *L'abolition de l'esclavage* Schoelcher presented us with compelling arguments. Since then, Frobenius, Westermann, Delafosse—all of them white—had joined the chorus: Ségou, Djenné, cities of more than a hundred thousand people; accounts of learned blacks (doctors of theology who went to Mecca to interpret the Koran). All of that, exhumed from the past, spread with its insides out, made it possible for me to find a valid historic place. The white man was wrong, I was not a primitive, not even a half-man, I belonged to a race that had already been working in gold and silver two thousand years ago. And too there was something else, something else that the white man could not understand. Listen: 77

> What sort of men were these, then, who had been torn away from their families, their countries, their religions, with a savagery unparalleled in history?
>
> Gentle men, polite, considerate, unquestionably superior to those who tortured them—that collection of adventurers who slashed and violated and spat on Africa to make the stripping of her the easier.
>
> The men they took away knew how to build houses, govern empires, erect cities, cultivate fields, mine for metals, weave cotton, forge steel.
>
> Their religion had its own beauty, based on mystical connections with the founder of the city. Their customs were pleasing, built on unity, kindness, respect for age.
>
> No coercion, only mutual assistance, the joy of living, a free acceptance of discipline.
>
> Order—Earnestness—Poetry and Freedom.
>
> From the untroubled private citizen to the almost fabulous leader there was an unbroken chain of understanding and trust. No science? Indeed yes; but also, to protect them from fear, they possessed great myths in which the most subtle observation and the most daring imagination were balanced and blended. No art? They had their magnificent sculpture, in which human feeling erupted so unrestrained yet always followed the obsessive laws of rhythm in its organization of the major elements of a material called upon to capture, in order to redistribute, the most secret forces of the universe. . . .[17]

---

17. Aimé Césaire, Introduction to Victor Schoelcher, *Esclavage et colonisation* (Paris, Presses Universitaires de France, 1948), p. 7.

Monuments in the very heart of Africa? Schools? Hospitals? Not a single good burgher of the twentieth century, no Durand, no Smith, no Brown even suspects that such things existed in Africa before the Europeans came. . . .

But Schoelcher reminds us of their presence, discovered by Caillé, Mollien, the Cander brothers. And, though he nowhere reminds us that when the Portuguese landed on the banks of the Congo in 1498, they found a rich and flourishing state there and that the courtiers of Ambas were dressed in robes of silk and brocade, at least he knows that Africa had brought itself up to a juridical concept of the state, and he is aware, living in the very flood of imperialism, that European civilization, after all, is only one more civilization among many—and not the most merciful.[18]

I put the white man back into his place; growing bolder, I jostled him and told him point-blank, "Get used to me, I am not getting used to anyone." I shouted my laughter to the stars. The white man, I could see, was resentful. His reaction time lagged interminably. . . . I had won. I was jubilant.   78

"Lay aside your history, your investigations of the past, and try to feel yourself into our rhythm. In a society such as ours, industrialized to the highest degree, dominated by scientism, there is no longer room for your sensitivity. One must be tough if one is to be allowed to live. What matters now is no longer playing the game of the world but subjugating it with integers and atoms. Oh, certainly, I will be told, now and then when we are worn out by our lives in big buildings, we will turn to you as we do to our children—to the innocent, the ingenuous, the spontaneous. We will turn to you as to the childhood of the world. You are so real in your life—so funny, that is. Let us run away for a little while from our ritualized, polite civilization and let us relax, bend to those heads, those adorably expressive faces. In a way, you reconcile us with ourselves."   79

Thus my unreason was countered with reason, my reason with "real reason." Every hand was a losing hand for me. I analyzed my heredity. I made a complete audit of my ailment. I wanted to be typically Negro—it was no longer possible. I wanted to be white—that was a joke. And, when I tried, on the level of ideas and intellectual activity, to reclaim my negritude, it was snatched away from me. Proof was presented that my effort was only a term in the dialectic: 80

But there is something more important: The Negro, as we have said, creates an anti-racist racism for himself. In no sense does he wish to rule the world: He seeks the abolition of all ethnic privileges, wherever they come from; he asserts his solidarity with the oppressed of all colors. At once the subjective, existential, ethnic idea of *negritude* "passes," as Hegel puts it, into the objective,

18. *Ibid.,* p. 8.

positive, exact idea of *proletariat*. "For Césaire," Senghor says, "the white man is the symbol of capital as the Negro is that of labor. . . . Beyond the black-skinned men of his race it is the battle of the world proletariat that is his song."

That is easy to say, but less easy to think out. And undoubtedly it is no coincidence that the most ardent poets of negritude are at the same time militant Marxists.

But that does not prevent the idea of race from mingling with that of class: The first is concrete and particular, the second is universal and abstract; the one stems from what Jaspers calls understanding and the other from intellection; the first is the result of a psychobiological syncretism and the second is a methodical construction based on experience. In fact, negritude appears as the minor term of a dialectical progression: The theoretical and practical assertion of the supremacy of the white man is its thesis; the position of negritude as an antithetical value is the moment of negativity. But this negative moment is insufficient by itself, and the Negroes who employ it know this very well; they know that it is intended to prepare the synthesis or realization of the human in a society without races. Thus negritude is the root of its own destruction, it is a transition and not a conclusion, a means and not an ultimate end.[19]

When I read that page, I felt that I had been robbed of my last chance.   81 I said to my friends, "The generation of the younger black poets has just suffered a blow that can never be forgiven." Help had been sought from a friend of the colored peoples, and that friend had found no better response than to point out the relativity of what they were doing. For once, that born Hegelian had forgotten that consciousness has to lose itself in the night of the absolute, the only condition to attain to consciousness of self. In opposition to rationalism, he summoned up the negative side, but he forgot that this negativity draws its worth from an almost substantive absoluteness. A consciousness committed to experience is ignorant, has to be ignorant, of the essences and the determinations of its being.

Orphée Noir is a date in the intellectualization of the *experience* of being   82 black. And Sartre's mistake was not only to seek the source of the source but in a certain sense to block that source:

> Will the source of Poetry be dried up? Or will the great black flood, in spite of everything, color the sea into which it pours itself? It does not matter: Every age has its own poetry; in every age the circumstances of history choose a nation, a race, a class to take up the torch by creating situations that can be expressed or transcended only through Poetry; sometimes the poetic impulse coincides with the revolutionary impulse, and sometimes they take different courses. Today let us hail the turn of history that will make it possible for the

---

19. Jean-Paul Sartre, *Orphée Noir*, preface to *Anthologie de la nouvelle poésie nègre et malgache* (Paris, Presses Universitaires de France, 1948), pp. xl ff.

black men to utter "the great Negro cry with a force that will shake the pillars of the world" (Césaire).[20]

And so it is not I who make a meaning for myself, but it is the meaning   83
that was already there, pre-existing, waiting for me. It is not out of my bad nigger's misery, my bad nigger's teeth, my bad nigger's hunger that I will shape a torch with which to burn down the world, but it is the torch that was already there, waiting for that turn of history.

In terms of consciousness, the black consciousness is held out as an ab-   84
solute density, as filled with itself, a stage preceding any invasion, any abolition of the ego by desire. Jean-Paul Sartre, in this work, has destroyed black zeal. In opposition to historical becoming, there had always been the unforeseeable. I needed to lose myself completely in negritude. One day, perhaps, in the depths of that unhappy romanticism. . . .

In any case I *needed* not to know. This struggle, this new decline had to   85
take on an aspect of completeness. Nothing is more unwelcome than the commonplace: "You'll change, my boy; I was like that too when I was young . . . you'll see, it will all pass."

The dialectic that brings necessity into the foundation of my freedom   86
drives me out of myself. It shatters my unreflected position. Still in terms of consciousness, black consciousness is immanent in its own eyes. I am not a potentiality of something, I am wholly what I am. I do not have to look for the universal. No probability has any place inside me. My Negro consciousness does not hold itself out as a lack. It *is*. It is its own follower.

But, I will be told, your statements show a misreading of the processes   87
of history. Listen then:

Africa I have kept your memory Africa
you are inside me
Like the splinter in the wound
like a guardian fetish in the center of the village
make me the stone in your sling
make my mouth the lips of your wound
make my knees the broken pillars of your abasement
AND YET
I want to be of your race alone
workers peasants of all lands . . .
. . . white worker in Detroit black peon in Alabama
uncountable nation in capitalist slavery
destiny ranges us shoulder to shoulder
repudiating the ancient maledictions of blood taboos

---

20. *Ibid.,* p. xliv.

we roll away the ruins of our solitudes
If the flood is a frontier
we will strip the gully of its endless
covering flow
If the Sierra is a frontier
we will smash the jaws of the volcanoes
upholding the Cordilleras
and the plain will be the parade ground of the dawn
where we regroup our forces sundered
by the deceits of our masters
As the contradiction among the features
creates the harmony of the face
we proclaim the oneness of the suffering
and the revolt
of all the peoples on all the face of the earth
    and we mix the mortar of the age of brotherhood
    out of the dust of idols.[21]

Exactly, we will reply, Negro experience is not a whole, for there is not   88
merely *one* Negro, there are *Negroes*. What a difference, for instance, in this
other poem:

The white man killed my father
Because my father was proud
The white man raped my mother
Because my mother was beautiful
The white man wore out my brother in the hot sun of the roads
Because my brother was strong
Then the white man came to me
His hands red with blood
Spat his contempt into my black face
Out of his tyrant's voice:
"Hey boy, a basin, a towel, water."[22]

Or this other one: 89

My brother with teeth that glisten at the compliments of hypocrites
My brother with gold-rimmed spectacles
Over eyes that turn blue at the sound of the Master's voice
My poor brother in dinner jacket with its silk lapels

---

21. Jacques Roumain, "Bois-d'Ebène" Prelude, in *Anthologie de la nouvelle poésie nègre et malgache*, p. 113.
22. David Diop, "Le temps du martyre," in *ibid.*, p. 174.

Clucking and whispering and strutting through the drawing rooms of
     Condescension
How pathetic you are
The sun of your native country is nothing more now than a shadow
On your composed civilized face
And your grandmother's hut
Brings blushes into cheeks made white by years of abasement and
     Mea culpa
But when regurgitating the flood of lofty empty words
Like the load that presses on your shoulders
You walk again on the rough red earth of Africa
These words of anguish will state the rhythm of your uneasy gait
I feel so alone, so alone here![23]

From time to time one would like to stop. To state reality is a wearing   90
task. But, when one has taken it into one's head to try to express existence,
one runs the risk of finding only the nonexistent. What is certain is that, at
the very moment when I was trying to grasp my own being, Sartre, who remained The Other, gave me a name and thus shattered my last illusion.
While I was saying to him:

> "My negritude is neither a tower nor a cathedral,
> it thrusts into the red flesh of the sun,
> it thrusts into the burning flesh of the sky,
> it hollows through the dense dismay of its own pillar of patience . . ."

while I was shouting that, in the paroxysm of my being and my fury, he was
reminding me that my blackness was only a minor term. In all truth, in all
truth I tell you, my shoulders slipped out of the framework of the world, my
feet could no longer feel the touch of the ground. Without a Negro past,
without a Negro future, it was impossible for me to live my Negrohood. Not
yet white, no longer wholly black, I was damned. Jean-Paul Sartre had forgotten that the Negro suffers in his body quite differently from the white
man.[24] Between the white man and me the connection was irrevocably one
of transcendence.[25]

But the constancy of my love had been forgotten. I defined myself as an   91
absolute intensity of beginning. So I took up my negritude, and with tears

---

23. David Diop, "Le Renégat."
24. Though Sartre's speculations on the existence of The Other may be correct (to the extent, we
must remember, to which *Being and Nothingness* describes an alienated consciousness), their application to a black consciousness proves fallacious. That is because the white man is not only The
Other but also the master, whether real or imaginary.
25. In the sense in which the word is used by Jean Wahl in *Existence humaine et transcendance*
(Neuchâtel, La Baconnière, 1944).

in my eyes I put its machinery together again. What had been broken to pieces was rebuilt, reconstructed by the intuitive lianas of my hands.

My cry grew more violent: I am a Negro, I am a Negro, I am a Negro. . . .   92

And there was my poor brother—living out his neurosis to the extreme   93
and finding himself paralyzed:

THE NEGRO: I can't ma'am.

LIZZIE: Why not?

THE NEGRO: I can't shoot white folks.

LIZZIE: Really! That would bother them, wouldn't it?

THE NEGRO: They're white folks, ma'am.

LIZZIE: So what? Maybe they got a right to bleed you like a pig just because they're white?

THE NEGRO: But they're white folks.

A feeling of inferiority? No, a feeling of nonexistence. Sin is Negro as   94
virtue is white. All those white men in a group, guns in their hands, cannot be wrong. I am guilty. I do not know of what, but I know that I am no good.

THE NEGRO: That's how it goes, ma'am. That's how it always goes with white folks.

LIZZIE: You too? You feel guilty?

THE NEGRO: Yes, ma'am.[26]

It is Bigger Thomas—he is afraid, he is terribly afraid. He is afraid, but   95
of what is he afraid? Of himself. No one knows yet who he is, but he knows that fear will fill the world when the world finds out. And when the world knows, the world always expects something of the Negro. He is afraid lest the world know, he is afraid of the fear that the world would feel if the world knew. Like that old woman on her knees who begged me to tie her to her bed:

"I just know, Doctor: Any minute that thing will take hold of me."   96

"What thing?"   97

"The wanting to kill myself. Tie me down, I'm afraid."   98

In the end, Bigger Thomas acts. To put an end to his tension, he acts,   99
he responds to the world's anticipation.[27]

---

26. Jean-Paul Sartre, *The Respectful Prostitute,* in *Three Plays* (New York, Knopf, 1949), pp. 189, 191. Originally, *La Putain respectueuse* (Paris, Gallimard, 1947). See also *Home of the Brave,* a film by Mark Robson.

27. Richard Wright, *Native Son* (New York, Harper, 1940).

Working with the Text

1. Fanon's essay begins with a quote concerning how he is received by others: "'Dirty nigger!' Or simply, 'Look, a Negro!'" What is a "nigger" according to Fanon? What is the relationship between "niggers" or "Negroes" and others?

 2. Ontology is a branch of philosophy that is concerned with the nature of being. Fanon suggests that to be a black man is to have no recourse to "ontological resistance in the eyes of the white man" because "not only must the black man be black; he must be black in relation to the white man." What does he mean by this? Why, according to Fanon, isn't the reverse true (i.e., that a white must be white in relation to the black man)? Do you agree? Give your response in an essay.

3. What is the relationship between the contemporary black man's body and history in this essay?

4. Fanon describes himself as having "burst apart"—the "fragments" of his former self "put together again by another self." What produced this burst, and what were its consequences? Why is it linked to experience, rather than to intellectual reflection?

 5. The episodes Fanon recounts feature him in the grip of terrible ambivalence—for example, feeling both fragmented and disempowered *and* coherent and assertive. How does this ambivalence relate to the notion of "being for others" that he claims we all live with? Give your response in an essay.

MAUS: A Survivor's Tale

ART SPIEGELMAN

Cartoonist Art Spiegelman has been drawing professionally since the mid-1960s. For many years an artist for the trading cards in Topps chewing gum (his creations, among others, include the popular Garbage Pail Kids), Spiegelman has also contributed to a number of underground comics magazines such as *Raw,* which he helped found, published several volumes of his own strips, and drawn attention-grabbing covers for *The New Yorker* magazine. The idea for his highly original book *MAUS*—which relates in comic strip form his father's memories of the Jewish Holocaust in Europe—grew out of old cartoons: "this cat and mouse thing," Spiegelman has said, "is just a metaphor for some kind of oppression." Originally, he had planned for the story to focus on slavery, but he soon found that his parents' experiences as Jews in Nazi Poland, being closer to him personally, provided a stronger inspiration, and he created the frame of current-day scenes in which he interviews his father as source material. *MAUS* created a sensation when it was published in 1986, and a second volume, *MAUS II* (1991), was awarded a special Pulitzer Prize. In the following excerpt, Spiegelman, the artist and author/character, grapples with his role in creating an artistic narrative out of the Holocaust.

Time flies...

Working with the Text

1. The story Spiegelman tells is both biographical and autobiographical. Why do you suppose he chose to render his Jewish characters as mice rather than depicting them as human beings? How do you respond personally to the idea of a narrative about the Holocaust rendered in graphic form?

2. There are extensive resources on the World Wide Web dealing with the Holocaust. Many of them are linked and sorted from the *Beyond Borders* Web site. Look at some of the personal narratives online by survivors and children of survivors. Do you see any parallels to Spiegelman's treatment? Are there places in the online narratives (e.g., the personal testimonials) that remind you of the conversations that he has with the psychiatrist/survivor in the selection?

3. What is the effect of the piled bodies in the first few frames?

4. In addition to being a story about Vladek's experience in the Holocaust, *MAUS* is also a complex meditation about communication and expression. What kinds of questions are raised by the selection about telling, silence, and the recovery of experience from a horrible event? Explore some of these issues of "speaking the unspeakable" as they are represented in the selection and in any online Holocaust narratives you have read.

Confronting Stereotypes: MAUS *in Crown Heights*

ANDREA LOWENSTEIN

Andrea Lowenstein, author of two novels (*This Place* and *The Worry Girl*) and a critical study (*Loathsome Jews and Engulfing Women*), is professor of Languages, Literature, and Philosophy at Medgar Evers College, a predominantly black college in Crown Heights, New York City's mixed neighborhood of African-Caribbeans and the Lubavitcher sect of Hasidic Jews. Crown Heights gained notoriety in 1991 when the already tense relations between Caribbeans and Lubavitchers exploded into a race riot following the death of a young African-Caribbean child run over and killed by a Hasidic driver, and the subsequent murder of another Hasidic man. The events gave rise to Anna Deveare Smith's one-woman play, *Fires in the Mirror,* excerpted in Chapter 1 of this collection. In the following article, Lowenstein details her experience "coming out" to her class as Jewish, while teaching Art Spiegelman's *MAUS: A Survivor's Tale,* a comic-strip narrative concerning life in Nazi Poland and Auschwitz. (A selection from *MAUS* precedes this essay.)

Rose stares at me in disbelief. "You no Jew. You can't be." In our discussion   1
of Art Spiegelman's Maus, *we have been reading about Vladek and Anja's experience of the escalating persecution of the Jews in Poland, and I have just referred to my father's experiences as a Jewish student in Hitler's Germany. Audible whispers pass around the circle of seats.*
    "She is, I could've told you all that!"   2
    "She is not, she can't be!"   3
    "Why can't I be a Jew?" I ask Rose, a thirty-nine-year-old woman from   4
Guyana, who feels a special closeness to me after having shared her struggles as a single mother of a special needs child during several office hours.
    "Because you're down to earth," she answers. "Because you—have feel-   5
ings!" A few students giggle with embarrassment, while others rush in, trying to reassure me.
    "Rose is right, you not like them."   6
    "You talk with us. . . . We laugh in here."   7
    "You not all formal."   8
    "That's right. And you don't look like no Jew either."   9
    "I just assumed you knew I was Jewish," I tell them, trying to catch my   10
breath, "because of my last name. That's why I never mentioned it. Anyway," I ask the class, "what does a Jew look like? What does a Jew act like?"

During the four years I have taught at Medgar Evers, a four-year college   11
of the City University of New York, I have often assigned Art Spiegelman's *Maus: A Survivor's Tale.* In this article, I will concentrate specifically on the experience of using this text with one class which met in the spring semester of 1996. For those readers unfamiliar with it, *Maus* is a two-volume, 269-page narrative in comic strip form whose primary subject is the experience of Vladek, Art Spiegelman's father, in Nazi-governed Poland and during the time he spent imprisoned in Auschwitz. All the humans in the text are portrayed in comic-book animal form; that is, Jews are human-like mice, Nazis are cats, Poles are pigs, the French are frogs, Americans are dogs, and so on. The narrative, which unfolds through over 1500 captioned drawings, alternates between two time periods: the more distant past of the Holocaust and

the more recent past. The scenes from the more distant past are taken directly from taped interviews Spiegelman conducted with his father. The scenes from the recent past portray Vladek and Artie's interaction during the process of recording the interview and follow Artie during the course of his own life; they include the author's own thoughts and feelings about making *Maus* and about his father. Each of these two parallel texts inscribes and informs the other.

I habitually use *Maus* in English 150, the second semester of a two-semester freshman composition course which also functions as an introduction to literature. During the semester in question the class had read *Macbeth,* August Wilson's *Fences,* and Tony Morrison's *The Bluest Eye* before *Maus,* the last reading assignment. As Xin Lui Gale puts it, the success or failure of a particular text or curriculum "depends on how the teacher and students are related to this discourse—politically, economically, socially, culturally and how they interact with this discourse" (64). The college's location, within CUNY and in Crown Heights, is certainly a significant factor in my selection of texts.

Medgar Evers College was founded in 1969 with the mission of serving the predominantly Caribbean and African American neighborhoods of South Brooklyn. The college attracts students from all over Brooklyn and some from the other boroughs, the majority either immigrant or first generation African-Caribbeans, the minority African American. Medgar Evers accepts more students who have passed the GED exam rather than completing four years of high school than any other college in CUNY, and most students at this time took English 150 in their third or fourth semester, after completing one or two remedial composition courses. An unusually large percentage of Medgar Evers students are in their thirties and older, and most balance family, full-time work responsibilities, or both, with their college education. Approximately two-thirds of the students are women.

Medgar Evers is located in Crown Heights, a working-class, largely Caribbean neighborhood, which is also the headquarters of the Lubavitcher sect of Hasidic Jews and consequently the home of many Lubavitchers. In contrast to their Caribbean neighbors, many of the Lubavitchers could afford to live in a more affluent neighborhood, remaining in Crown Heights primarily because of their need to be in walking distance of their synagogue. This is only one of the factors that has led to a history of conflict and distrust between the two communities.

In 1991, when a Hasidic man ran over and killed an African-Caribbean child, the already tense relations between the Caribbean and Lubavitcher Jewish community erupted. Although, like all stories, this one varies according to the narrative perspective, it is generally accepted that a largely

Caribbean, largely youthful crowd erupted in Jew-hatred, and a young visiting rabbinical scholar from Australia was stabbed and subsequently died. The events of those days resulted in national notoriety for Crown Heights and engendered many texts, among them Anna Deveare Smith's one-woman production, *Fire in the Mirror: Crown Heights, Brooklyn and Other Identities,* for which Deveare interviewed and recorded members of the two communities. For many, the name Yankel Rosenbaum still invokes black anti-Semitism. For example, in *Race Matters* (1993) Cornel West commented:

> The vicious murder of Yankel Rosenbaum in Crown Heights in the summer of 1991 bore bone chilling testimony to a growing black anti-Semitism in this country. Although this particular form of xenophobia from below does not have the same institutional power of those racisms that afflict their victims from above, it certainly deserves the same moral condemnation. (75)

Similarly, my students and I often heard the name of the child who was 16 killed, Gavin Cato, invoked by poets and speakers at the college as a martyr to racism and a symbol of white, specifically Jewish, indifference to black life. When I began to teach at Medgar Evers in 1992, I knew that my classroom was situated, in both the literal and symbolic sense, at a focal site of black-Jewish conflict in America, and that my own role as a Jewish professor teaching black students could be viewed, again depending on one's perspective, as that of either an interloper or a border crosser.

For me, as for most people in modern society, the question of identity 17 is a complex one. Some of my identities are old, others are new or in transition. Some are visible, others more hidden, although I do not always realize exactly what is hidden from or visible to whom. For example, I have often heard students at Medgar Evers make slurs or stereotypical statements about gays and lesbians. In reaction (until my then chairperson advised me against doing so before I was awarded tenure), I expended a great deal of energy "coming out" as a lesbian to each new class of students. On the other hand, I felt little need to identify myself as a Jew, as I assumed that anyone who heard my last name would know I was Jewish. It was later that I began to notice similar slurs about Jews, and only during the student dialogue with which I begin this essay that I learned that my "Jewish" name was not necessarily identifiable as such to this group of students and realized that another sort of "coming out" was necessary.

Speaking of her own work as an African American woman committed to 18 working against anti-Semitism in the women's movement, Barbara Smith notes that border crossing can be painful and "virtually guarantee[s] our being thrust between 'the rock' of our own people's suspicion and disapproval and the 'hard place' of the other group's antagonism and distrust" (Bulkin, Pratt, and Smith 85). I often have the experience of hearing students whose attitude toward me personally may be warm and accepting make hurtful remarks about central parts of my identity. Students have, for instance, argued that homosexuals should be banned from teaching, as they generally molest children, or that they should not be allowed to adopt (I am an adoptive mother); some have claimed that AIDS is God's punishment for homosexuality; many have shown themselves to be ignorant of the existence of the Holocaust. Such statements set off a destructive cycle in the classroom that interrupts what bell hooks refers to as the quality "of care and even 'love'" (194) I generally bring to the students I teach and threatens the respectful feelings I have for them and the pleasure I take in their company. My first reaction is the sensation of a blow which literally takes my breath away. This is quickly followed by hurt and anger at the student speakers, who, always sensitive to their teacher's feelings toward them, respond in turn to what they experience as my sudden and inexplicable change. My selection of *Maus,* then, represents an effort to bring together two parts of my identity and engage them in dialogue and an attempt to move the students and myself through such periods of alienation and mistrust, instead of leaving us stuck "between a rock and a hard place."

Despite widely varied backgrounds, by the time we read *Maus* the members of the English 150 class had coalesced into a friendly and generally supportive group. Students sometimes referred to the class as a "family" and some at times jokingly addressed me as "Mom."   19

The first reaction of almost all students when they received the syllabus, which included a description of *Maus* as "a serious comic book about the Holocaust," was dismay or anger. Their immediate assumption was that I, an unknown white teacher, must be assigning comic books to my all-black college-level class because I presumed them to be incapable of reading "real books."   20

> When I first saw the word comic book I thought is this teacher dissing (disrespecting) me? (Kenneth; the parenthetical gloss is his)

> When I first realized that the books are written in cartoon form I was somewhat disappointing. My reason is, because I am not a lover of reading comics, I prefer fine literature. (Celia)

> I disagreed because I alway discourage my kids to read comic books and I am Not a Child, I am a College Student. (Kimberly)

Once the students encountered the actual text, however, this initial reaction changed: 21

The book was most interesting and easy to read mostly due to the comic book form. As a matter of fact two co-workers of mine are anxiously awaiting to read the book. (Yvonne)

The use of mice to represent Jews and other animals never trivialized what happened in the war. At the same time the use of these cartoon characters made the book very interesting. (Sonya)

I realized that even thought it is a comic it is for Adults only. It could give a Young child nightmare, especially the parts where the children are killed. Maybe for teenagers. (Kimberly)

I soon learned this teacher (You) were not dissing me, instead you were stretching my knowledge. (Kenneth)

Every student in the class felt that *Maus* had been worth reading, and almost all mentioned its unique genre as part of the reason.   22

Another reaction found in almost every paper was an expression of sympathy for the Jews and of repugnance against what had been done to them: 23

I was shocked by the burning graves described by Vladek. This was a chilling evil performed by Nazi Germany. (Eudora)

I felt sorrow, hatred, anger and revenge for all the agony and suffering the Jews encountered, but joy that Vladek and other survived. I empathize and sympathize with the gruesome ordeal of the Jews. (Martha)

Several students commented on their prior ignorance of the Holocaust: 24

Before reading these books it was hard for me to imagine what the Jewish people had been through. After reading them I got a better understanding of what had happened in the holocaust. It took a lot of courage for the people who came out alive to have survived. (Della)

Previous to reading the books, the word "Holocaust" was just that to me a word. (Anna)

Before, I read the book, my knowledge of the holocaust was limited. I have now gained a full knowledge of all the torture and anguish the Jews experienced during this time, and also learned that terrible racism and hatred exist among the Germans and Jew. (George)

And several students reflected upon the nature of humanity and our infinite capacity to hurt one another: 25

I wondered whether those Germans could be humans at all. How can humans treat their fellow humans with such cruelty? It make me very angry and sad. (Rose)

The thing that struck me most in this story was the cruelty that human beings can impose on one another. It is very frightening to know the extent in which

people can hate one another . . . the scars may be passed on from one generation to the next. (Della)

To me they were not just Jewish people, but people, humans suffering for what
seem to me be for no reason at all. (Kenneth)

It is important to note that the authors of these essays were, in many   26
cases, the same students who assumed a week *after* having written the
above reactions that because I had feelings I could not possibly be a Jew.
These empathic reactions to the suffering of the Jews in the text and their
identification of them, as Kenneth put it, as "not just Jewish people," but
"humans suffering for no reason at all" might contradict but did not erase
their previous assumptions, as became clear in further discussions. Instead
the two feelings continued to exist side by side. In his *Portraits of White
Racism* David T. Wellman notes that the strongly felt racial prejudice of most
of his interview subjects was far from rational or consistent, but was instead
a patchwork of conflicting but simultaneously held beliefs and images.
Those with the most stereotyped and denigrating images of black Southern-
ers were nevertheless able to maintain one or two close relationships (at
least from their perspectives) with members of the despised group by deciding that these were "good niggers" or "white Negroes" who were the exceptions to the rule (35–38). Sander Gilman makes much the same point in
Difference and Pathology, noting that "since all of the images of the Other
derive from the same deep structure, various signs of difference can be
linked without any recognition of inappropriateness, contradictoriness, or
even impossibility" (21). Similarly, some of the students were capable of
simultaneously dismissing Jews as non-people with no feelings, genuinely
liking me although they knew I was a Jew, and feeling real horror and anger
at the persecution and execution of Jews. Only two students' reaction papers betrayed the less-than-positive attitudes toward Jews which they and
others conveyed during the discussion:

> There are some frames in the book that caused me some serious intellectual dis-
> comfort. In many instances Vladek reveals himself as a unreliable narrator and
> display a behavior that could jeopardize the authenticity and relevancy of his
> facts. (Jean)

> I still have to wonder why they were treated in such a terrible manner. These
> questions still remain to be answer. Why were the Jews torture? Were they dif-
> ferent from other people or what did they do to make others feel this way? I
> hope to find the answer someday. But still think there should not be discrimi-
> nation against anyone even Jew. (Sandra)

After some inner debate, I wrote notes on Jean and Sandra's papers de-   27
scribing and attempting to explain my angry reactions. Similarly, after the
conversation in the beginning of this essay, I decided to tell the students

during the next class meeting that what I had heard from them surprised, hurt, and angered me, and to ask them to examine their generalizations about Jews. This decision came out of my determination to use the reading and discussion of *Maus* as a way to explore the personal effects of stereotyping, specifically anti-Semitism. It was also an effort on my part to break out of the cycle of distancing discussed earlier. I wanted to break through these feelings rather than simply dismissing the speaker as a person (in my mother's phrase, "cutting her out of my heart"), as I probably would have done had the conversation occurred during a social, not a teaching situation. In hindsight, I can also see that by airing my own feelings, I was perhaps taking a leaf from Shylock. "Hath not a Jew hands, organs, dimensions, senses, affections, passions?" I asked the students, "If you prick us, do we not bleed?" Some students took this personal response as an invitation to share their own beliefs and experiences:

> "I never met a Jew before coming to New York. Only on Easter morning, at home [Haiti] we used to have a kind of song, kind of a chant we sung on the way to Church. We would ring the bells and sing, 'Christ is born, the Jews are dead, Bless us Christians, all Jews must die.'"

At that point Jean must have looked at me. "You don't need to look like that, Professor," he assured me. "It didn't mean we wanted to kill you, it was just a ritual, like you taught us about." Most of the other students who had been brought up in the Caribbean agreed that before coming to New York they had not actually known anyone they could identify "for sure" as Jewish. They had, however, heard that Jews looked strange, had their own "Jew language," had long beards, stole children, and had killed Christ. As many authors (Edgar Rosenburg, Sand Gilman, Bryan Cheyette, and myself, among others) have noted, images of the Jew as child-stealer, bogey man, Christ-killer, and stranger can be found in identical form in English and other European medieval texts and traditions. Such medieval notions were certainly easier to retain in Crown Heights than they might have been in a more assimilated Jewish community. Although, as I pointed out to her, several of Audrey's teachers at Medgar Evers were Jewish, she had "never thought of them that way." Instead: 28

> "When we pass one with one of them long beards I tell my kids don't look at them. I tell them he could take you away in his big bag. I make them behave by telling them he going to come for them if they act up." (Audrey)

The most visible Jews in Crown Heights are indeed bearded men, some dressed in a black costume that dates back to the eighteenth century, who keep to themselves, can be heard to murmur to themselves and their friends in a mysterious language, and will in no circumstance make eye contact with strangers (especially women). Those students born in America,   29 especially those who had lived in New York for some time, contributed more modern stereotypes, and the two sets of images were combined in the ensuing discussion.

> "Even if you go in their stores they never look at you. They hate black people. They'll talk about you in their Jew language."
>
> "They're cheap, everyone knows that. Once we lived in an apartment and the landlord was a Jew. He wouldn't give us no heat, and it was the middle of winter."
>
> "Jews will always try to cheat you."
>
> "They worship money."
>
> "Jews all stick together."
>
> "They only care about themselves."

Sandra, who habitually worked with Jewish patients in her job as a home   30
health aide, claimed expertise:

> "They will use that one tore-up paper bag over and over. They don't let you throw nothing away. I had ladies that made me bring my own napkins and toi-let paper. They were too cheap to let me use theirs and I was the one cleaning up their nasty dirt. That's what they're like, believe me, I know."

During the course of this conversation, a few students expressed a kind   31
of reluctant admiration for the perceived solidarity and thriftiness of the Jews, but most expressed resentment and dislike, an openness on their part which surprised me, coming as it did right after my unintentional "coming out" as a Jew and my sharing of my feelings about their comments. A few students felt embarrassed and anxious on my behalf, looking at me in con-cern as they named good Jews they had known and blacks who were just as "cheap" or "nasty." They were not, however, successful in trying to quiet the others, who seemed to believe that I would not be offended, as it had already been established that, according to them, I was "a good Jew"—even, as Rose had put it, "no Jew at all."

George, in particular, was becoming visibly uncomfortable during the   32
discussion. "How would you like it if she said blacks were cheap and dirty and all that?" he asked Sandra. "Don't get all upset," she countered. "Profes-sor knows we don't mean her." George's comment (and my own response to Sandra's paper) pushed me to reconsider some learned assumptions. All my reading and political education had told me of the dangers inherent in the liberal tendency to conflate racism and anti-Semitism, slavery and the Holocaust. As Barbara Smith warns, "It is essential for us to reject any ap-proach which flattens oppressions, distorting this historical reality in an at-tempt to argue for their parity in the long run" (Bulkin, Pratt, and Smith 110). Nevertheless I noticed that most of the student papers which I felt showed

a genuine stretching of boundaries and a making of connections were those which did in fact compare slavery and the Holocaust, especially those which succeeded in contrasting rather than simply conflating the two experiences:

> These kinds of cruelty remind me of the days of slavery. Both peoples were treated as less than animals. For this very reason Jews and Blacks should be sympathetic to each other's concerns. (Della)

> Both Alex Haley's *Roots* and *Maus* shows the effects of mass genocide committed against two groups of people (i.e. slavery for blacks and the holocaust for Jews.) Both suffered from genocide and both relied on spirituality . . . (Paul)

Sonya took the comparison a step further: 33

> Traveling down New York Ave, observing all the Jews as they congregate on the intersection of New York and Eastern Parkway near their synagogue, I've always been filled with curiosity as to why do they always keep to themselves so much? Why are they so different? I generalized about them, thinking there was something wrong with them. After reading I've come to the understanding that. . . . we are both oppressed people with horrifying pasts, both thought to be inferior by their white captors. Neither was treated like human beings, rather like objects to use, misuse, abuse, and when became useless discarded by death. We were both packed like sardines and sent away from our homelands, the Jews by trains and the Blacks by boat. . . . Both dug themselves tunnels and secret passages as a way out. Both kissed their oppressors ass, if that meant survival. . . . The difference is the German solution for the Jews was total destruction; the White solution for the Blacks was total utilization. . . . Unlike the Jews, Blacks were considered more useful alive then dead. Now whenever I pass the intersection of New York Ave and Eastern Parkway I can observe the Jews with new insight, comprehension and realization of our common experience. (Sonya)

My positive comments on this paper reflect my pleasure at Sonya's articu-   34
lateness; her ability to make the leap from connecting the text to her day to
day experiences, and to alter her perceptions accordingly.

I felt less uneasy about the conclusions of another classroom discussion   35
which was based on the scene I have mentioned in which Vladek, having
survived Auschwitz and immigrated to New York, reveals his racial prejudice. In this scene Artie and his wife Françoise are staying briefly and disas-
trously with Vladek in the Catskills. The three of them are driving home
from a humiliating shopping trip in which Vladek has insisted on returning
opened packages of food to the supermarket, when Françoise stops to pick
up an African American hitchhiker. (As Spiegelman portrays all non-Jewish
Americans as dogs, this character is a black dog.) Vladek, astonished and furious, remonstrates frantically in Polish, convinced that the "schwartzer" will
steal his bag of groceries.

I said earlier that I welcomed Spiegelman's portrayal of his father as hu-   36
man and flawed rather than as a saintly victim. Nevertheless, before teaching *Maus* at Medgar Evers for the first time, I indulged in a fantasy in which
I cut this particular scene out of each of the students' books. I feared that
after reading it they would completely dismiss both Vladek and his experiences and that this incident, along with Vladek's chronic (and very stereotypical) cheapness, would merely confirm their worst stereotypes. To some
extent, I was right to worry. Every student but one did write about these
pages in their reaction papers. For the most part, they wrote how disappointed and betrayed they felt by Vladek, for whom by this time in the book
they had allowed themselves to feel some of the affection, empathy, and ex-
asperation they might feel for an elderly and at times irritating member of
their own family:

> The most amazing thing is that after all the prejudices he went through, he him-
> self was prejudiced against blacks. Some people never seem to learn. (Eudora)

> The racism of the Germans does not change his racist outlook as he talk about
> "black" just like how the Nazi talk about Jews. He generate all blacks as
> "Thieves." (Kimberly)

> I found his prejudice ways to be quite annoying. He started talking in Polish
> and continued to do so until the black guy got out. I still can't understand how
> he could be so prejudice after what happen to him. (Audrey)

> What seemed strange to me is that Vladek was racist towards blacks. It didn't
> seem like blacks had did anything to him. (Rose)

George, who during the first classroom discussion had hotly criticized   37
Artie for betraying his father's confidence and who identified Artie and his
father with himself and his own father, felt especially betrayed by Vladek:

> Vladek if anybody should've not been so hasty and quick to prejudge anyone.
> He should've walked away from the war with a broader outlook concerning in-
> dividuals of different races, gender, color, and religion. Especially blacks, the
> reason being there was a Black holocaust as well as a Jewish holocaust. So why
> was the equilibrium of his mentality so unbalanced? Why couldn't he weigh the
> two injustices to equal them out? Why couldn't he say to himself, "I don't know
> what its like to be black of course, but I can understand the many stereotypes
> that they must encounter as I have encountered in the past because I was Jew-
> ish?" I'm not saying that Vladek should of embraced every black person he
> came into contact with or have sympathy for every black face he saw. What I
> am saying is he should of seen the error of his ways and be a little more friend-
> lier to the black man in the car and not portray the reactions of a racist bigot
> like that of the Nazis. (George)

Two students commented that Vladek's disappointing response was one   38
which is not restricted to Jews:

This is an example of hate breeding hate! In a lot of cases, people who are abused tend to abuse someone else. Vladek fails to see that by distrusting "shvatsers" he is guilty of being prejudice. However, Vladek is not the only one guilty of this. Today, many African Americans and Jews fail to see the similarity amongst one another . . . perhaps if both took the time to read about one another's suffering it may bridge the gap which exists between the two. (Paul)

Had we, Vladek and I, taken the time to understand and educate ourselves, this matter of stereotyping could have been avoided. (Sonya)

In the class session in which we discussed this incident. I asked the students to identify the particular stereotype to which Vladek had implicitly referred and to write it on the board. They quickly agreed on "Blacks = thieves." I then asked several students to read out loud the paragraphs in their reaction papers in which they responded to the hitchhiker incident, including all the responses above. After the students had aired their feelings, I questioned their surprise at Vladek's prejudice. 39

"Have you ever been oppressed by someone who you know had suffered prejudice themselves?" I asked, and wrote on the board: "Do oppressed people usually learn from their experiences not to oppress others?" The students responded quite passionately to these questions. Several students shared painful incidents in which they had been the victims of stereotyping by people who should have known better, as they themselves belonged to an oppressed group. The other group members listened responsively, punctuating the speaker's statements with "Yes, that's true," "That happened to me," "I know what you mean." George talked about his own experience of being stereotyped at the hands of other Caribbeans because he is Haitian: 40

They should know what it feel like when someone say all of you are stupid and stink, but they act like they already forgot . . . or maybe they think if they get associated with us, the white man going to think they are boat people too.

Paul shared his experience of black-on-black oppression: 41

Women always looking to find someone lighter than them so they can make a lighter baby. I swear I hear them say that. I had a girl tell me she would have liked to be with me but she owed it to her baby to give him a light skin father!

Other students were especially captured by this statement, one woman conceding that Paul was right; she herself would not consider seriously dating a man darker than her, "for the baby sake," while others attempted to persuade her of the wrongheadedness of this conclusion. 42

Eudora talked about how people made assumptions about her because of her weight: 43

It ain't even about race, creed or religion. It's about just assuming because a girl's big they've 'got to be this big jolly happy person that ought to be happy to get a man some other girl cast off.

Several others talked about how often whites had stereotyped them, and how it made them feel and behave: 44

Like when you told us read this cartoon book, *Maus*. I was leaping to the con- clusion that you were trying to diss us because it happened before with white teachers in high school. I was like, Whoa! Don't start on me. I been through this one. I guess I was getting a little paranoid. (Kenneth)

"Hey, that's not paranoid," Tina responded. "That's just how you feel   45 when someone do it and do it and keep on doing it, you grow to expect it. That's common sense. Paranoid is when you *stop* making sense."

"Like the boy who cried Wolf!" Kimberly added." After a while you lose   46 your belief."

"So could you really call it stereotypes when blacks distrust whites   47 then?" Stella asked. "We got every reason to. I mean what's the difference between stereotypes and learning from experience?"

"You could be suspicious of someone from your experience as long as   48 you keep your mind opened up," Anna reasoned. "Like for Ken to think Pro- fessor was gonna diss him, that's all right because he learned it from his ex- perience with his other white teachers in high school. But he didn't keep on holding on to it in his mind when he found out she wasn't the same way."

"That's right, if he had just kept on saying, 'I don't care, she must be   49 dissing us cause she white,' and not look at what was really going on, that would be prejudice."

"Maybe it's not prejudice, but it's still stereotyping," Paul argued.   50

"No, it's prejudice, cause some of the most disrespectful teachers I had   51 were black. You all know what I'm saying."

After some heated discussion of this question, I asked, "Would it be prej-   52 udiced for Vladek to hate Germans? How about the way Artie drew Poles as pigs?" After more discussion of whether or not it was prejudiced to hate members of a group that had hurt you and yours repeatedly, Sandra re- turned again to the habits of the Jews:

"They *are* cheap. And nasty. They stick together. That ain't no stereotype. Or prejudice or nothing like that. I take care of them so I know."

The fact that this time many students challenged Sandra's statements, point-   53 ing out that she was generalizing on the basis of a few examples, made my experience of this comment far less painful. In fact, this class was a cathar- tic one for all of us: I felt some of the hurt and anger I had previously experienced dissolve as I heard the students' stories, and at the end of the class section most of the students lingered, unwilling to let go of the closeness we had created together.

However, I still felt the need for an exercise that might disrupt the tendency to regard the stereotyping of each group as a completely separate and thus possibly justified phenomenon. In the next class, sending one volunteer to the board as recorder, I asked the students to name some identity groups, including both those they belonged to and others. Then I asked them to come up with some commonly held assumptions or stereotypes about these groups, to be listed in another column. After some discussion about whether they could list stereotypes that were really *true,* and much protest and derision at different items, the students came up with this list, which I copied directly from the board:

54

Jews are cheap
Jew only take care of themself
Korean will try to cheat you every time
Koreans hate black people
Black can sing and dance (musical)
All Blacks good at sports
Black people are stupid (lazy)
Black men desert their family
Black women don't support their men
Black women the African Queen
Gays will give you diseases
Faggots and lesbians will hit on you
Whites call blacks niggers when they're on their own
White people nasty in their personal habits
White people smell
White people hair smell like a dog if it get wet
Puerto Ricans girls easy
Puerto Ricans dress loud
Jamaicans dope addicts
Girls from Belize want to fight
Men are dogs
Black men the worst dogs
Women just want men for the money
Black women want to marry light

Next I asked the class to evaluate each stereotype, eliminating those   55
they could refute through their own experience. Those which applied to
blacks in general went first, quickly refuted by the whole class, with the
gender-based stereotypes close behind. Next, although not without argument, the assumptions based on nationality and religion came down.

"It maybe don't apply to every single one, but I know for a fact
Koreans will cheat you cause it happen to me every time."

"Yeah and men behave doggish to me every time. But you got
mad when I said men are dogs!"

"That's cause I am a man that's no dog, so I know."

"How can you say I'm a dog? I'm the one put African Queen up
there! I'm gonna take it down!"

"You notice the ones about Koreans still up there."

"If we had a Korean in our class I bet it be down in a minute."

"That's right, you got to have a representative. If Professor wasn't a
Jew then maybe nobody would have took down the Jew ones."

"Professor ain't no Jew! Don't call her that!"

"See, there you go! She said she was! Why she say that if it
ain't true?"

"One thing I noticed, if you in the group yourself you know it's
bullshit, excuse my language, but if you not, you all ready to believe
it. Or maybe if you got someone in the group. Like Eudora ain't no
Jamaican but her husband is, so she stand up for them. How he never
smoke no reefer . . ."

"And Stella husband white, and she said his hair don't smell like
no dog."

"I did not say he was white. He's Puerto Rican! I said his *hair* is
like white!"

"We still ain't covered the in-between cases. Like what Professor
asked about would it be prejudice if Vladek hate Germans. Cause
what they did to him deserves hate."

"True, and if every time a white woman see George she hold on to
her bag and cross the street, it ain't stereotype cause lots of black men
is criminals, right?"

"I'm sorry, I will cross the street myself if it is dark and I see a man
coming. Color don't matter when he snatch my purse!"

"Yeah, and when Artie made the Poles pigs, we didn't see nothing
wrong about that after what Professor told us the Poles did to Jews.
But if we didn't know that maybe we would."

"That's 'cause ain't no one here no Pole. You bet we would hear about it if we had one in this class."

"I still say blacks that don't trust whites got no prejudice problem. You gotta be that way to survive, man. If you ain't you a fool and soon get mash up!"

In the same class, we went on to discuss Artie's decision to portray his fa-   56
ther as cheap despite his concern that this might feed into non-Jews' stereotypes. This discussion segued into a discussion of the author's responsibility to tell truth as he or she sees it, with many students situating themselves in the authorial position as they talked about the personal essays they were now working on. Is the responsibility to yourself? To your people? "Which people?" Della wanted to know:

> "I'm black, that's one. A woman, two. Haitian from my father and Spanish from my mother, that's four. American cause I was born here, African and Indian from my roots. You're looking at me, you know there's some white in there somewhere. That make eight. So which people I'm not supposed to say nothing bad about?"

Even *Macbeth* came into the discussion: 57

> "OK, when Shakespeare was writing there was a king, right. So what was he supposed to do, make Macbeth not kill anyone, cause it might reflect bad on kings? He had to write what he knew, even if it got him in trouble!" (Tina)

> "Maybe Shakespeare didn't know no one from Scotland. So he made the Scotts these warlike murderers without even thinking about it. Which is a stereotype based on ignorance, right?" (Ken)

During that class period the students mentioned all four of the texts we   58
had read that semester, comparing them in meaningful ways and discussing the authorial role. For the first time none of the authors (not even Shakespeare!) was referred to as "they," and students shared painful and potentially explosive experiences concerning identity and prejudice. All this took place in an atmosphere of non-violence and cooperation. Through reading and discussing *Maus* the students were able to use Spiegelman's text not only to interrogate their own assumptions about Jews, but to think more widely about the origins and effects of stereotypes and prejudice, to see themselves not only as victims of stereotyping and prejudice, but also as perpetrators, and to reflect upon the effect of stereotyping on both the victim and the perpetrator. I, a Jewish teacher in an all-black classroom, was able to take what felt like effective measures to challenge the anti-Semitism I heard from my students, a change from the helplessness I usually felt in the face of such statements, and to help them see their statements as part of a larger picture. Finally, because of Spiegelman's refusal to politely disappear from his own text, several students embarked on their own projects:

writing comic-strip texts, making films, or writing creatively about their own family situations. As George put it, "If old Artie can do it, I so can I."

POSTSCRIPT

As Art Spiegelman would be the first to assert, stories have more than one ending. Last semester, after I had finished this article, a colleague in my department, a more observant Jew than myself, drew me aside, beaming, to show me a paper in which a student had "really made a leap forward in understanding" after reading Anzia Yezierska's *Bread Givers*. There, intact, was the paragraph I have quoted admiringly [earlier] in which Sonya compares and contrasts the Jewish and black experience and shares her new insight about the Jews on Eastern Parkway. Had Sonya, pleased with her own insight, my reaction to it, and her grade of "A" merely decided to recycle it? Or was the initial paper merely a skillful but cynical exercise in giving a teacher what she wanted, one which she saw would work equally well on the next, equally naïve subject? Like any story, this one depends on who tells it. 59

And one more ending. During a break between classes I recently set out to do some errands in Lubavitcher Crown Heights and found myself profoundly irritated by shopkeepers who would not acknowledge my existence by so much as a look or a word. Although I knew that history had made these men my allies against a potentially hostile world, I found myself resisting this enforced kinship. Was the "real" reason I felt so comfortable with *Maus* as a text the fact that Spiegelman is the same kind of Jew I am—intellectual, irreverent, an obsessive and cynical questioner who is offended by all those who believe they are the sole proprietors of the truth? Did my students at times feel some of the same discomfort with an identity politics that allowed the oppressor to define the terms of allegiance? 60

Perhaps the only truly incontestable conclusion is that *Maus* is a text which leaves the reader, student or teacher, with unsettling questions which have multiple, conflicting answers. For this reason, if for no other, I will continue to teach it. 61

Working with the Text

1. During a classroom discussion, Lowenstein briefly mentions her father's experiences as a Jewish student in Hitler's Germany; to her surprise, her students are shocked to discover that she is Jewish and that she failed to identify herself as such. Lowenstein notes that although she routinely "comes out" as a lesbian to her classes, she had always assumed that anyone who knew her last name would understand she was Jewish. Is it relevant to her discussion, or to

Lowenstein's authority, that she make these identifications? In what ways is a teacher's—or a student's—identity crucial to understanding a text? When is it irrelevant?

2. Lowenstein and her students compile a list of identity groups and stereotypes about them. What assumptions are surprising, disturbing? Why? What is the effect of listing such assumptions? What is gained and lost through describing people collectively? How is this also a way of seeing peoples globally, not just locally?

3. In the *Postscript*, Lowenstein describes her irritation with shop-keepers she meets in Lubavitcher Crown Heights; while she seems comfortable with identifying with Jews such as the intelligent, inquisitive Spiegelman, she resents the "enforced kinship" of Jewish identity with others (such as the unmannerly shopkeepers). What do these discriminations teach us about identity politics? Does your own experience with identity politics confirm or counter such claims?

4. If you have already read the selection from *MAUS*, compare your first reactions to those of Medgar Evers College students. How are the stereotypes assigned to people connected to stereotypes we assign to certain texts?

Critical Questions Revisited: From Reading to Writing

Essay Topic 1: How can people communicate across differences

YOUR PAPER: Write a paper exploring strategies for communicating across differences. How do the writers in this chapter show people negotiating their differences? What are their goals for communicating; what kinds of appeals are used (shared values, fear, reason, etc.); how does communication respond to power?

SUGGESTED STRATEGIES

- Analyze an example in which people must communicate across differences. What prompts them to attempt this; what strategies do they employ?
- How do the maneuvers of communication reflect—and further shape—a sense of difference? How do they respond to an imbalance of power between groups?
- We may understand the communication more fully than the participants. What conclusions can you draw about the role of communication in negotiating differences?

Essay Topic 2: Expressions of survival and resistance in "contact zones"

YOUR PAPER: Adapting Mary Louise Pratt's definition of "contact zones," analyze how people survive and resist in "social spaces" of unequal distribution of power. What options do marginalized groups face (e.g., becoming invisible, seeming to fit in, resisting)? How are these options expressed through writing and representation?

SUGGESTED STRATEGIES

- Analyze, according to Pratt's definition, a "contact zone" from one of the chapter readings, or from a space you know well: classroom, a work environment, a social space on the Internet, etc. How are aspects of "culture" transferred, assimilated, inverted?

- What forms of communication or action in this "contact zone" are crucial? What are their aims, means, results, limitations, unintended consequences?

- Based on your example and analysis, how might you modify and complicate Pratt's definitions? How are aspects of "culture" transferred?

Essay Topic 3: How can a culture be both coherent and based on difference?

YOUR PAPER: Using the ideas and examples presented in the readings, offer models and strategies for how a culture could develop a single identity based on difference. How can a culture recognize different groups without ultimately judging them against a single norm or homogenous world view? What would be necessary to accomplish this?

SUGGESTED STRATEGIES

- Analyze a couple of passages that question how representations of difference produce dichotomies.

- Depict some of the values or issues underlying these representations.

- What specific (or "local") strategies would aid us in conceiving of a culture that incorporates difference?

- How could these strategies be used in the culture at large? What circumstances need be in place? What limitations and outcomes would the strategies face?

Essay Topic 4: What role do individuals play in institutional or group responses to difference?

YOUR PAPER: From specific examples, characterize and analyze the contrast between individual responses and group responses to racism and other forms of difference. Are individuals always implicated in group or institutional responses? How can individuals themselves make a "structural" response to institutionalized racism, intolerance, or marginalization?

SUGGESTED STRATEGIES

- Analyze one or more examples from the readings in which individuals grapple with structural responses to difference (such as the use of stereotypes, belief systems based on hate, imperialism, etc.).
- Characterize the actions of the individual: controlling? resistant? evasive? etc. Might there be multiple and/or contradictory responses?
- Draw conclusions about individual response to "institutionalized difference"—and how groups might in turn respond to and prompt more individual action.

BORDER VISIONS
An Image Portfolio

Critical Questions

Before looking How do our ways of "reading" images differ from our ways of reading written texts?

Taking it further Can images present more than one point of view? What is a "visual narrative"? How do focus, selection, and perspective provide a "subjective" quality to a seemingly objective photograph? How are cultural and social "codes of meaning" presented in images? How are power relations expressed in visual texts?

Images

18A, 18B, 18C, and 18D. Catherine Opie: *Chief, Whitey, Chicken, and Oso Bad.* From *Being and Having* (1995).

19. Dana Fineman: *Portrait of Plastic Surgeons and Patient.*

20A and 20B. Boy George Images: "[Boy George and his Waxwork]" and "[Big Boy]".

21A and 21B. Peter Menzel: *The Ukita Family (Japan) and all their material possessions, 1991 and 2001.*

22. Peter Menzel: *The Batsuur Family (Mongolia), 1993 and 2001.*

23. Dang Ngo: *Demonstrators on Child Labor.* Copyright Dang Ngo. http://www.dangngo.com/.

24. Peter Menzel: *Robo-Babies.*

25A and 25B. Benetton ads: *Handcuffs* and *Bosnia Soldier.* Copyright Benetton Group S.p.A.; images from *http://www.benetton.com/press/campaigns/.*

26. Martha Rosler: *Balloons.* From *Bringing the War Home: House Beautiful.* Images appeared in Neumaier, Diane, ed. *Reframings: New American Feminist Photographies.* Philadelphia: Temple, 1995. Rosler teaches at the Mason Gross School of the Arts of Rutgers University.

WHY PUT IMAGES IN A BOOK ABOUT WRITING?

Why put images in a book about reading and writing? There are several reasons. First, one of the really basic ideas behind this book is that all kinds of expression can be "read" as texts, not just pieces of writing. Every time we see an image, whether in an ad or on television or in a book, we're reading that image. And like written texts, we can choose to do a superficial or literal reading of the text/image or a critical and analytical one. As with written texts, some images *want* the viewer to read them literally and others invite a closer look, expressing some ironic or mixed message. A basic idea of this book is that texts are made from a certain perspective, whether they are maps, essays, or photographs. Thinking about the way we "read" images helps us learn to "read" our world better—and we certainly live in a world where we are surrounded more and more each day by images. In many ways, our culture is becoming increasingly a visual culture: through advertising, television, and even the World Wide Web, which is predominantly a visual medium.

THE SEEING "I"

Just as with the written essays, stories, and poems you are reading throughout *Beyond Borders*, the images in the Portfolio are the expression of a particular subjective perspective. Naturally, we understand this when we look at advertising. We know that a magazine ad has been "constructed" by someone to make us think or feel a certain way. Every advertisement has at least one "argument," such as "buy this product." Most advertisements have a second, implicit argument, such as "buy this product and you will be thin and attractive to members of the opposite sex." In terms of images, however, it is not just visual advertisements that are constructed from a particular perspective, but all images. The first two images in the Portfolio are maps: one from the sixteenth century, showing only the outline of North America; the other a playful inversion of the Western Hemisphere for the purpose of demonstrating the effect of putting South America on top of North America. As we saw in Chapter Four in the discussion about maps and murals, although we think of maps as "truthful" representations, they are actually "symbolic" expressions just like any other kind of text. And although their symbolism may have a high degree of "truth value" when you're using them to navigate, they are nonetheless coded by a certain perspective and constructed to deliver their message in a certain way. By reversing the positions of North and South America, Jesse Levine's Turnabout Map (Plate 1) forces the viewer to see an image that is deeply familiar in a completely different way. For a North American, the reversal of the continents is jarring, maybe even disturbing. But the effect might be very different for someone from South America. As is discussed in several sections of the book, maps always have a point of view: They have authors, contexts, perspectives, and biases. It doesn't make them less useful to acknowledge this fact; it just means that we ought not to see them as objective truth.

A similar point can be made about photographs. As you look at the images in the Portfolio, think about how each image creates a relationship between the viewing "subject" and the photographic "subject" (that is, the person, people, and objects viewed in the picture). Whenever you are trying to examine and analyze an image, it is first important to ask yourself some plain descriptive questions:

Who created this image and why? Why this subject?

What are the details that you notice?

What objects are included in and excluded from the image? What clues do they provide?

Why this particular pose, perspective, framing, composition?

Was the image created through a spur-of-the-moment act or a thoughtful deliberate process?

What did the creator wish to inform the viewer of or persuade the viewer to consider?

For example, look at Plate 9, "Street Arabs," by one of the first photojournalists, Jacob Riis. This particular photograph shows three young boys in some kind of alleyway or corner of a building. They are leaning on each other. Their feet are bare and dirty. Their clothes are worn and threadbare. The boy in the foreground has what looks like a pained expression on his face. They appear to be asleep. The arrangement of the boys (two leaning in, all leaning back deeper into the photograph) follows the lines of the building and the corner in which they are sleeping. The boys are in the center of the photograph.

After observing as many of the physical attributes of the photograph as possible, we can move on to the next level of questions related to the perspective and meaning:

> What do you think the photograph is intended to evoke? Pity? Anger? Scorn?
>
> How are the boys represented as the "objects" of our viewing?
>
> How does the photograph construct a position from which you, the viewer, see the boys?

This particular photograph was taken in the 1890s. At the end of the nineteenth century the photographic process was much slower and more cumbersome than it is now. For Jacob Riis to take his photographs he needed to hold the camera and the subject still for several minutes. Given that, it is unlikely that the boys were sleeping and unaware of his presence. And in fact, we know that he took a whole series involving these three boys, in which he posed them in a variety of ways in order to get the shot he wanted. There are, in fact, some photographs from this session where you can see one of the boys cracking a smile as they pretend to be asleep. Yet, the photograph presents the sleeping boys as if the photographer—and thus also as if we, the viewers—had caught the boys spontaneously in a natural moment. The photograph puts the viewer in the position of a "witness" to a pathetic scene (young boys living on the street). The photograph turns out to be a carefully arranged, posed, and framed moment intended to evoke certain emotions from the late-nineteenth-century viewer (who was surely middle or upper class). None of this negates the "truth" of the conditions that Jacob Riis was trying to expose on the Lower East Side of New York, but it does point out that Riis's photograph does not portray an "objective" reality any more than his written text, *How the Other Half Lives* (included in Chapter 2), is free of bias and perspective.

STORIES AND MEANING

Just as we don't look at all written texts in the same way, we don't look at all pictures in the same way, either. Pictures come in many different genres, styles, and contexts, with different strategies for making meaning and different intentions. Many of these different styles are represented in the Image Portfolio. Images tell stories differently from written texts by being *both* more explicit in some ways, and having the freedom to be more ambiguous in others. That is, graphic images *show*, and therefore make their meaning more apparent; on the other hand, images don't have to fill in all the words in order to convey a meaning and therefore leave other things more to the imagination.

As you look at the images throughout the Portfolio think about how each of the images makes its meaning. There is something very powerful about an image that is different from the power of a written text. Images are another way to think beyond borders, the principle concern of this book.

Working with Images: Notes and Questions

PLATE 1: Jesse Levine, *The Turnabout Map of the Western Hemisphere*

Although the Turnabout Map does not make presumptions to be a new kind of map, it does, similarly, reposition the countries in the Western Hemisphere as a way of making an "argument" about the way we project our cultural and nationalistic biases onto maps. The Turnabout Map claims that the convention of putting North America "on top" is just that: a convention and not grounded in any geographic inevitability. Whether or not that is entirely true, the Turnabout Map makes a startling point, and for citizens of the United States and North America it might be an uncomfortable image. In an even more dramatic way than the Peters projection, the Turnabout Map suggests the idea that reality is a matter of perception, and what you see has everything to do with where you stand.

QUESTIONS

1. What are your initial responses to the Turnabout Map? Does it seem uncomfortable to you? Do you think you would feel differently if you were from South America? (Or, if you are from South America, or elsewhere in the world, how do you think your reaction would be different if you were from North America?)

2. Consider Jesse Levine's statement: "Ever since maps were first drawn, certain countries have been located at the top, others below. Since "on top," "over," and "above," are equated with superiority, while "down there," "beneath," and "below" imply the reverse, these wholly arbitrary placements, over the years, have led to misconceptions and misjudgments." Do you agree with this statement? Where else do you see correlations between geography and cultural/nationalist assumptions?

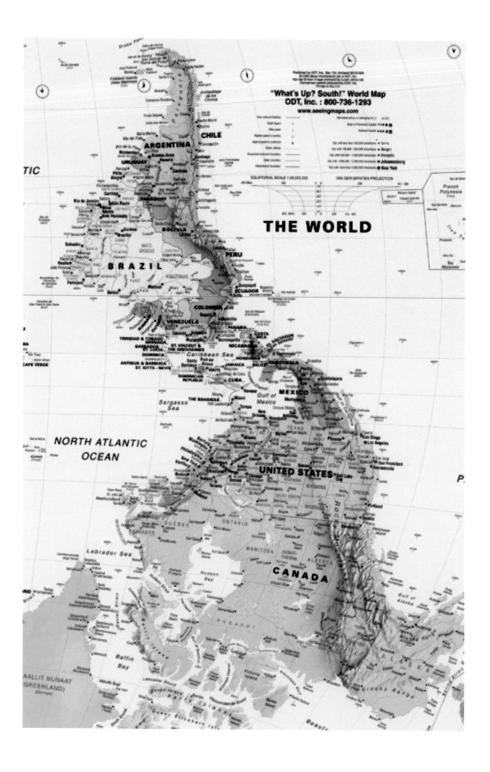

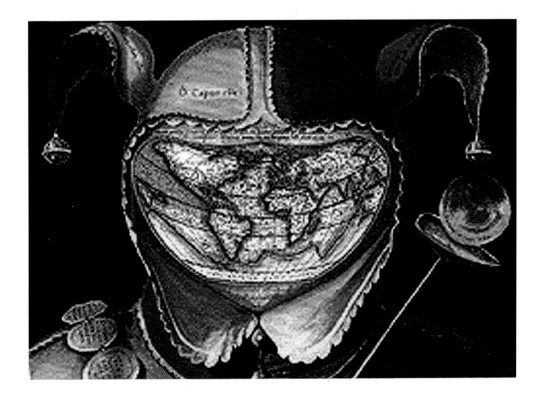

PLATE 2: *Foolscap Map of the World, c. 1590*

This image is one of the earliest known instances in which man's knowledge of the world is used in a visual joke. What is being suggested about the newly discovered world by a map of it within the frame of a foolscap?

QUESTIONS

1. In this era, the sense of the world as round, with many unexplored continents and foreign peoples, became a new concept of "the real." This revision of an older, "flat world" concept may have provided both a feeling of excitement and anxiety. What kind of commentary is provided by the foolscap motif? What combination of forward thinking and past criticism does this map provide?

2. The large blank areas may indicate unexplored regions—look closely at the interior of South America and the present United States, where little of the Amazon basin is detailed, and none of the Great Lakes are drawn. How will the next discoveries change the view of North and South America? What incomplete conceptions of the New World does this map present?

PLATE 3: Patricia Rodriguez: *La Fruta del Diablo* ["The Fruit of the Devil," also known as the Strawberry Mural]

La Fruta del Diablo, ("The Devil's Fruit") was created by Patricia Rodriguez, a teacher and artist at California State University, Monterey Bay, and her students. *La Fruta del Diablo* is based on the Chicano mural tradition in which stories or historical and cultural events, as well as political struggles. This mural was created digitally through the synthesis of computer images. In *La Fruta del Diablo* the images tell the story of the genetic hazards of strawberry harvesting due to dangerous insecticides that are used in production. The composition of the story is circular, which echoes the cyclical process by which the farm workers—particularly the children—are implicated in the agricultural cycles of growth, production, and harvesting.

QUESTIONS

1. How does *La Fruta del Diablo* compare and contrast with other murals you have seen? What do you think are some of the conventions of murals? How do murals make meaning?

2. Does the mural have a point of view? From whose perspective is the mural created?

PLATE 4: Joel Sternfeld: *Studio City*

Joel Sternfeld is a photographer with a very ironic eye. Most of his photographs capture aspects of American life that are both normal and everyday, on the one hand, and slightly bizarre and eccentric, on the other. In this photograph, *Studio City* (which is a city near downtown Los Angeles), a young couple is pictured in a garden or backyard. The picture presents two contradictory impulses. On the one hand, the two young people look relatively nonconformist, with dyed hair and a punk mohawk haircut. Yet, their pose is very traditional. Their posture and framing is reminiscent of traditional portrait photography. As with many Sternfeld photographs, the ironic combination of tendencies forms a single powerful image.

QUESTIONS

1. Do you think that there are "class" dimensions to this photograph? That is, do you think the style or setting implies a certain socioeconomic class?

2. What differences do you observe between the man and the woman? Do they present different attitudes?

3. Does the photograph make a commentary—playful or serious—about youth culture, suburban culture, or American family values?

PLATE 5: Joel Sternfeld: *The Bronx*

The Bronx presents an image that seems somehow off center. At the center of the photograph is a set of sculptures made by the artists Rigoberto Torres and John Ahearn, who have made hundreds of such sculptures throughout the Bronx. They always cast them from the actual faces and bodies (and personalities) of people living in the neighborhoods. This particular set of castings is called "We are family" (1981–82). The castings represent actual residents of the area (whose names are Layman, Victor and Ernest, Kate, Tawana and Staice, Felix and Iris, and Smokey). They are mounted on a building at the intersection of Fox Street and Intervale Avenue, in the Bronx.

QUESTIONS

1. What are the various elements of the photograph? How do they interact with the sculpture at the center?

2. Discuss how the photograph tries to portray the sculpture in the image as being both "in place" and "out of place." How does the photographer's framing and composition contribute to that?

3. What other examples of "public art" can you think of? Choose an example of public art from where you live and explore how it fits into and in part shapes its context.

PLATE 6: Camilo Jose Vergara: *Skeletons on Skid Row*

"The mural was painted by the Mojado Brothers after a design by the early-twentieth-century Mexican artist Guadalupe Posada—but with Los Angeles clothes and Los Angeles humor." The photographs of Camilo Jose Vergara archive the transient landscapes of inner city ghetto life. In detailing the urban environment, his work both publicizes and preserves the memory of aspects of the city that are often left out of the crime scenes, fires, investigative exposés, and politicians' visits that we find in newspapers and newscasts.

QUESTIONS

1. This macabre mural brings a kind of wonder, and also provides a kind of sermon. What message is offered by the question, what social issue is being raised?

2. The skeletons may seem a Los Angeles version of "Day of the Dead" figures. If we look closely, we see that they seem to be holding magic markers. Who might the Mojado Brothers be representing here? What kind of joke is added to the previous senses of the mural's "message"?

PLATE 7: Eugene Richards: *Tom, Manhattan*

Eugene Richards is one of the United States' best known recorders of American life. His subjects range widely from intimate family and personal scenes to public American contexts. The photograph captures a man, Tom, emerging from a sewer grate while passersby move along the street hardly noticing—hardly, that is, except for the woman in the foreground who looks half-watchfully at him.

QUESTIONS

1. What are the different focal points in the picture? Who is looking at whom? How do the various points of focus help create the photograph's effect?

2. How might this photograph express or touch on people's fears, values, or attitudes toward "street people" or symbols of an underclass?

3. Do you think the picture is meant to be playful? Ominous? Both?

PLATE 8: Charlene Williams: *Bird*

The photograph *Bird* is from the collection *Shooting Back: A Photographic View of Life by Homeless Children*. This photograph is a combination of a spontaneous moment and some self-conscious arrangement. Says Charlene Williams, the twelve-year-old photographer: "My favorite picture that I took: that's me and my brother and my sister with a pigeon. My brother had found a pigeon, and the pigeon had been shot in the wing. My brother was trying to fix it, so I just told my brother to look at it, and I just put the timer on, focused it, and ran over there to get into the picture. I want to be a photographer."

QUESTIONS

1. Does the fact that the photograph is posed affect your response to it? Does it matter that the photographer (the twelve-year-old Charlene) is in the picture?

2. What is the focal point of the photograph? How does the focus and composition of the photograph convey a sense of violence or pain? Does it add anything to your reading of the photograph to know that the bird has been shot?

PLATE 9: Jacob Riis: *Street Arabs*

In 1890, Jacob Riis published his pioneering work of investigative journalism, *How the Other Half Lives*, an expose of New York's Lower East Side. *How the Other Half Lives* is a systematic study of New York's tenement neighborhoods and the people who lived there. Riis's urgency arose in response to the increasingly crowded conditions of late-nineteenth-century urban America that were characterized by dense and impoverished housing. There was a strong altruistic side to Riis's crusade as well as a dimension that spoke to and on behalf of middle-class anxieties. Riis was intensely interested in children and urban youth, in part out of sentiment and sympathy, and in part because he felt that every underprivileged child today was a potential criminal tomorrow. Thus we see his interest in what he called "Street Arabs"—not because they were ethnically Arabic, but due to their itinerancy and homeless life on the street.

QUESTIONS

1. What images or feelings does the photograph evoke? What are some of the various elements of the photograph that create its effect?
2. How is the picture framed or composed? Does that add to its argument?

PLATE 10: Santa Fe Railroad Calendar Art: *Land of Pueblos*

Beginning in the late nineteenth century, the Santa Fe Railroad began marketing the American Southwest as a major tourist attraction. Putting together tour packages that combined train and car travel, the railroad, along with the Fred Harvey Company, offered tourists glimpses of the scenic natural landscape and the "exotic" Native American peoples who lived there. The first part of the caption reads: "Taos Pueblo . . . an age-old Indian Pueblo on the Indian-detour trips in Northern New Mexico." It was not more than a decade after the last of the "Indian Wars" that the Sante Fe Railroad began portraying Native cultures as a quaint and intrinsic part of U.S. history.

QUESTIONS

1. How would you describe or paraphrase the assumptions of this ad about Native Americans and their relationship to the land and history? Could you say that the ad has an argument? What elements of this ad help contribute to its "argument"?

2. How is the Santa Fe poster art part of the "invention" of the Southwest? That is, how is it trying to create an image of place for the purposes of making it a commodity? Can you think of other places in the country that could similarly be considered "inventions"?

Santa Fe

*When traveling
to or from California
on the Santa Fe, visit . . .*

Land of Pueblos

"Taos Pueblo" . . . an age-old Indian pueblo on the Indian-detour trips in northern New Mexico.

When you travel to or from California via the Santa Fe, northern New Mexico calls you to visit its unique and colorful Land of Pueblos.

There, at any season of the year, you see Pueblo Indians in one or more age-old ceremonial dances, visit prehistoric cliff dwellings, ranches, adobe missions, and watch the Indians making pottery and silver-and-turquoise jewelry.

Winter is an especially good time of year to schedule a Land of Pueblos trip. Climate is crisp and invigorating. Night-times are memorable, with the air so clear you can almost reach up and "pick a star."

See this Land of Pueblos on a one, two, or three-day *Indian-detour*—the private motor tours that start from Santa Fé, New Mexico.

Convenient, too. Merely arrange to "stop over" at Lamy, New Mexico. A motor coach meets the train. In Santa Fé, Fred Harvey's famous hotel, La Fonda, facing the historic plaza, will be your headquarters.

Let us send you the picture folder giving full details on the colorful Land of Pueblos and the *Indian-detours*. Just mail the coupon.

T. B. Gallaher, General Passenger Traffic Manager
Dept. NW-2, 80 East Jackson Boulevard
Chicago 4, Illinois

Please send me complete information on the Land of Pueblos and tell me how I can explore it on my way to or from California via Santa Fe.

Name_____

Address_____

City_____ State____

SANTA FE SYSTEM LINES . . . Serving the West and Southwest

PLATE 11: John Gast: *American Progress*

John Gast's painting *American Progress* is like a mural intended to be read as a narrative—a story of American movement across the continent. The figure of a woman floating above the scene is meant to symbolize "Progress." The imagery can be read both from right to left (i.e., east to west). In the right foreground you see early settlers, prospectors, and farmers, along with symbols of the westward migration (stagecoach, covered wagon). The Native American Indians are retreating before them, literally being run out of the scene to make way for progress. Moving from foreground to background, more primitive transportation gives way to the railroad and shipping, and the frontier and the farming scenery give way to the city.

QUESTIONS

1. How does the painting portray the "land" of the United States as both a literal, physical space and a metaphorical space? What elements of the painting are symbols and which seem literal?

2. Think about how the painting positions the viewer. What kind of view does the painting create?

PLATE 12: Hulleah Tsinhahjinnie: *Damn! There Goes the Neighborhood!*

Hulleah Tsinhahjinnie is a photographer living in California, with a diverse Native American background. Her mother is of the Seminole and Muskegee nations and her father was of the Dine nation. Her photography is always engaged with Native thought and her interest in the past, present, and future of indigenous communities. This image is from a series where Tsinhahjinnie manipulated well-known historical photographs of Native Americans to give them an ironic twist.

QUESTIONS

1. Does this fit your notion of what a photograph is? What is the source of the humor in the image? How is it ironic?
2. How does the image offer a commentary on U.S. history, and the fate of Native Americans?

PLATE 13: Paul Fusco: *New York City, September, 2001*

This shot was taken by the documentary photographer Paul Fusco, known for his telling portrayals of American life. Fusco took a remarkable series of photos of by-standers to the funeral train carrying Robert F. Kennedy's body (1968). The present image looks quite artificial and posed at first; a longer look provides several narratives and "subplots" at once.

QUESTIONS

1. At what point do you realize that the green "statue" in the foreground is a living person? What expression does she (or he) have? How does her (his) expression and posture combine with that of the embracing couple on the left? What aspects of America are being presented together here?

2. We cannot think of "September 2001" without remembering the images and details of the terrorist attacks in New York and Washington. This photo, accordingly, may be taken as an allegory of America after the attacks. In what ways could this photo serve as an allegory of American pluralism, mixed community, imaginative response? In what ways could it stand as an expression of American vulnerability, confusion, despair? Would ambiguity lend it power?

PLATE 14: Judy Griesedieck: *The border near Chula Vista* (from *A Day in the Life of California*)

Judy Giesedieck is a photographer and journalist who has won numerous awards for her photography. This photograph is part of a series that she took documenting the U.S.-Mexico border. The picture here of the porous fence along the border appeared in the collection *A Day in the Life of California* (1988). The caption that appeared in that collection reads: "East of Chula Vista, the fence that forms the U.S.-Mexican border rapidly disintegrates. Families walk back and forth at will. The U.S. Border Patrol no longer even bothers to fix the gaps. 'Most every family in Tijuana has a barbecue grill made out of that fence,' says Border Patrol supervisory agent Randy Williamson."

QUESTIONS

1. What do you see in the photograph? What are the various elements of the image? What questions does it raise for you? Are the people coming into the U.S. from Mexico or vice versa? Can you tell which side is which?

2. There are three different ways we *see* people in this picture: full face, partial face, faceless. Does that add to the way that the photography might be read or interpreted?

Solutions for a small planet™

This summer, IBM will help people miles from Atlanta follow the excitement of the Olympic Games. With a high-speed network created specifically for the Games, IBM will issue final results in less than a second for distribution to the waiting world. Reaching the people who need them, when they need them. From journalists in Paris to fans on the Olympic home page in Cairo. It's proof IBM can help you get results. Literally.

IBM

Worldwide Olympic Sponsor

PLATE 15: IBM Computer ad: *Pyramids*

This ad is part of a whole series of images produced by IBM with an internationalized theme. The logic of the campaign is to portray the world as becoming a "smaller" place through the international use of technology. Technology itself is depicted as becoming a universal that in some ways bonds people together.

QUESTIONS

1. How does the ad try to humanize high technology?

2. Do you think that the ad tries to bridge the divide between the viewing "subject" (the American readers of the ad) and the exotic "object" or photographic "subject" (the man on the camel)? How so?

3. What are some of the common associations that we receive through the media about the Middle East? How is this ad building on or resisting those images?

PLATE 16: *Live without dead time* **from** *Adbusters* **No. 32 Oct/Nov 2000**

This image is from *Adbusters*, a journal that documents and critiques consumer culture in the United States. The ad spoofs several dimensions of consumer culture, including the ways that advertising is often built on principles of "identification," where the consumer is supposed to see himself or herself in the advertisement. The ad also spoofs the way that some trends or products tend to homogenize people while at the same time linking individuality to the product.

QUESTIONS

1. How is the image a kind of anti-advertisement? Would you call it ironic or a parody? Is there an argument?

2. Does it matter that it is the Gap in the ad?

3. What do you think of the title, "Live without dead time"? What do you think that might mean?

PLATE 17A: Pedro Meyer: *Biblical Times*

PLATE 17B: Pedro Meyer: *Biblical Times* annotated

Pedro Meyer is a photographer who has gradually moved away from the standard documentary mode to more inventive and constructive forms of photography. In recent years he has developed an interest in digital photography and the fusion of different images into a single new composite image. This particular photograph, *Biblical Times, New York City, 1987/93*, is from the book *Truths and Fictions*, in which he experiments with the representation of reality and the question of what constitutes truth and fiction in photography and in life.

QUESTIONS

1. Where are the boundaries of truth in relation to the construction of this photograph? How much manipulation of an image pushes it past a threshold of credibility as a documentary image?

2. Does Meyer's explanation of the photograph change the way you view it? Does it matter that it is two photographs in composite?

was walking around New York, trying to capture some street images, as I often do. And I found this man with hands like an El Greco figure. People were walking by—nobody was paying much attention. I photographed him from one side, then from the other side, but nothing of significance was coming across the viewfinder.

It was impossible to make the background any better, due to the limitations of space and optics. With a long lens I could have thrown the background out of focus, but I would have lost the sensation of the man, his Bible, and those long hands, as well as all the people walking on the street getting in front of him. Unsatisfied as I was, I nevertheless took the picture with a wide-angle lens from close up. In contact sheets of some other pictures I had taken earlier on that same day and on the same street, I found this image with some steam, which was enveloping the people as they walked through. This led me to bring these two scenes together in order to overcome what had eluded me before—that is, to pull in form and content in such a way that the image became more meaningful.

I was actually able to simulate the stream around his hands and around the Bible digitally, at which point the image—as I see it—took on a totally different dimension. His hands become a strong element and the figure walking past conveyed the sense that nobody was paying attention to this Bible salesman, as was the case. The result is actually a much more powerful image of New York. And, though it stretches the conventional journalistic boundaries of today, it is truthful to New York.

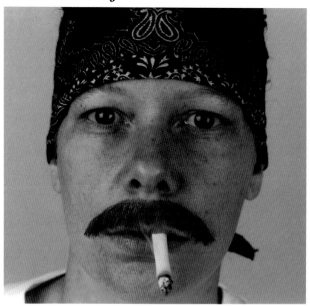

Catherine Opie is a photographer who lives in Los Angeles and is on the staff of the University of California, Irvine. She has a wide range of photographic interests, from urban landscapes to documenting lesbian families and domestic spaces. She is especially interested in documenting the nature of identity, especially self-constructed identity, which is her theme in these four photographs which are titled: "Chief," "Whitey," "Chicken," and "Oso Bad." The pictures present a series of women in "drag" posing as images of male types.

18B: *Whitey*

QUESTIONS

1. What is the effect of shooting the pictures as facial close-ups?

2. What are your impressions looking at the pictures? In what ways are they startling or disruptive? How do the pictures play with the idea of appearance and sexual identity?

18C: *Chicken*

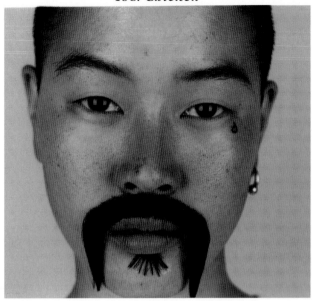

18D: *Oso Bad*

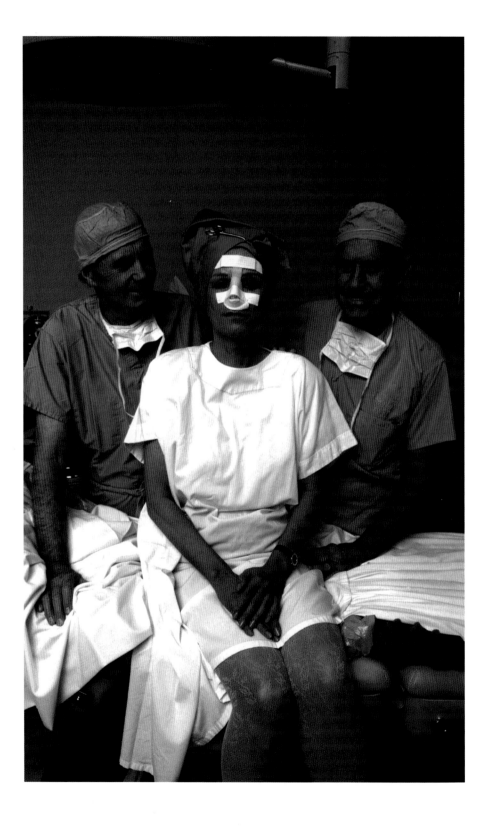

PLATE 19: Dana Fineman: Portrait of Plastic Surgeons and Patient

This photograph, as with Plate 14, is from the 1988 collection, *A Day in the Life of California*. The caption in the collection identifies the photograph this way: "Identical twins James and John Williams are Los Angeles plastic surgeons specializing in liposuction (the removal of fatty tissue from the body through a tube) and rhinoplasty (reshaping the nose by removing bone). The Williamses transform photos into three-dimensional computerized images to show potential patients what the results of the surgery will be. They say no matter how exotic the technique, patients invariably remember the experience simply as a 'nose job.'"

QUESTIONS

1. What do you notice about the features of the photograph? What do you observe about the composition? Do any details jump out at you? What choices did the photographer make about the way she posed and *com*posed the frame?

2. What ideas does the picture evoke for you? In how many different ways can you see that the photograph addresses issues of appearance and a concern about "image"?

PLATE 20A AND 20B: Boy George Images

Boy George (George O'Dowd) is the cross-dressing British lead singer of the 1980s pop band Culture Club.

QUESTIONS

1. In "Boy George and his Waxwork," Boy George poses with his own wax image for Madame Tousaud's wax museum. Why are tourists and museum visitors attacted to these kinds of reproductons of famous people? How is the living Boy George a reproduction of himself? How does Boy George's image (real and wax) raise questions about the construction of identity?

2. How does the "Big Boy" doll contrast with Boy George's persona? Can you think of other icons of boyhood or masculinity that contrast with Boy George's image and performance identity?

PLATE 21A: Peter Menzel: *The Ukita Family* (Japan) *and all their material possessions* **1991.**

First image from the book *Material World: A Global Family Portrait*. Sierra Club, 1994. Second image, *GEO MAGAZINE* (2001).

PLATE 21B: Peter Menzel: *The Ukita Family* (Japan) *and all their material possessions* 2001.

PLATE 22A AND 22B: Peter Menzel: *The Batsuur Family (Mongolia) 1993 and 2001*. Outside their "Ger" with all their possessions 4:00 pm September 28ᵗʰ 1993. Ulaan Baatar, Mongolia.

In his book *Material World: A Global Family Portrait*, photojournalist Peter Menzel records family life in thirty nations around the world. After living with a "statistically average" family in each country, learning about their work, their attitudes toward their possessions, and their hopes for the future, Menzel would take a shot of each family outside their home, surrounded by all their material goods. Menzel revisited the families eight years later and had the families pose for a new family photo with the possessions that were new to them since the last group portrait.

QUESTIONS

1. The Ukita family has prospered in their new home and have added several new material goods. Note the particular items that have been purchased. What is suggested by this evidence?

2. Photographed with the only new possession they have gotten since the first family portrait was taken in 1993—a television set—the Batsuur family currently lives together in the single illuminated room in the apartment behind them in the area called Sector 21 of Ulaan Baatar, Mongolia. Although the

family lost its former home and most of its possessions because of debt and the children must travel over an hour each way to attend school in their old neighborhood, the children say that they are happier in this modern apartment.

In comparing the two photos, what elements, if any, create a sense of the family having achieved a better life?

3. Menzel has noted that magazine photojournalists tend to cover "the extremes" but that "showing only the best and the worst provides just one small part of the world picture." His goal is to "give some insight into the rest of the world: to bring Westerners down from their high-rise tropical vacation towers into the living rooms of the hotel waitstaff; to take a manufacturer into the homes of the people who buy his products or work in his factories abroad; to let military planners see what the victims of the smart bombs look like; and to give my children the opportunity to meet their future neighbors."

What elements of the photos, both in terms of form and content, "give some insight"? What is the nature of the insight that Menzel seeks to offer viewers?

PLATE 23: Dang Ngo: *Demonstrators on Child Labor*

In this photograph, according to the gallery site on the Web, "Young demonstrators demand better working conditions and a free Tibet at the protest against policies of the World Trade Organization. Seattle, Washington." The picture was taken by photographer Dang Ngo, whose themes in his work include globalization and environmental activism, with a particular interest in Southeast Asia. This photograph is part of his series on globalization.

QUESTIONS

1. How does the picture function as a journalistic document? From what perspective or vantage point is the photograph shot (the viewer's perspective)?
2. How do the elements of the protest (in the photograph) form an argument? Can you separate the argument of the protest from the argument of the photograph? Does the photograph enlarge or reduce that argument?

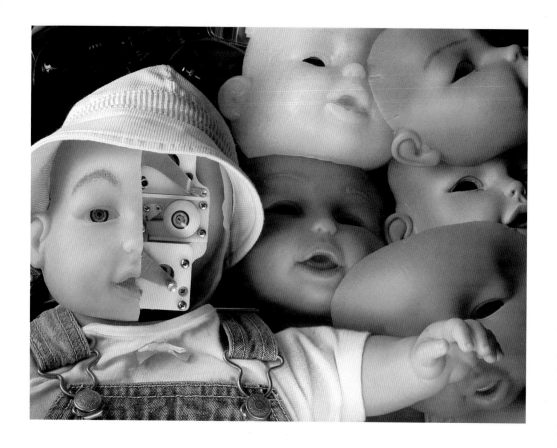

PLATE 24: Peter Menzel: *Robo-Babies*

This photograph was taken by Peter Menzel, the same artist who did the *Material World* photographs in this section. Here, Menzel explores the relationship between human beings and new technologies. The image comes from his collection *Robo-Sapiens*. This image is described this way: "BIT—Baby It—is the prototype for My Real Baby, the most sophisticated robot doll yet made. According to a press release, it is only the "first born" in a series of dolls created from the union of its parent companies, toy giant Hasbro and iRobot, a small Massachusetts robotics firm."

QUESTIONS

1. How has Menzel brought numerous elements together through his composition? How many different kinds of images or objects are in the photograph? From your perspective, do these images work together or against each other?

2. In United States culture, "babies" and "photography" often go together. Does the picture work at all with the conventions of "baby photography" as part of its effect?

PLATE 25A AND 25B: Benetton ads, *Handcuffs* and *Bosnia Soldier*

The photography of Oliviero Toscani, enlisted by the Italian clothing company, Benetton, created controversy from its first appearance in 1989, with the first image of the handcuffed black and white hands. The photographic images that have appeared for more than a dozen years always seek to stimulate and provoke. In addition to the provocative images, the logo and motto of the company are always visible in the ad and important to the overall impact and meaning. In one way or another, most of the images deal with themes of global diversity and harmony, and are reinforced (or made ironic) through the motto "United Colors of Benetton."

QUESTIONS FOR "HANDCUFFS"

1. When it first appeared, people complained that this image invoked stereotypes of a white law enforcement official with a handcuffed black prisoner. Does the photograph bias the viewer toward that interpretation or does the viewer have to bring that bias to it?

2. How do the elements of the image work together to create an interpretation or to resist one?

UNITED COLORS
OF BENETTON.

QUESTIONS FOR "BOSNIA SOLDIER"

1. What are the details of the photographic composition? What details do you notice? What effect is created by having the shirt and pants at an angle?

2. What is the impact of calling the image *Bosnia Soldier* without the body? What might be some differing levels of significance to letting the clothes stand in for the actual person or body? What is the effect of the empty clothes?

PLATE 26: Martha Rosler: *Balloons* from *Bringing the War Home: House Beautiful*

The photograph *Balloons* is part of a collection by Martha Rosler called *Bringing the War Home: House Beautiful*. Her photography in this collection works with "color montage" and focuses thematically on abrupt or startling juxtapositions. The mixed media nature of her art includes writing and video. She lives in Brooklyn and is on the faculty of Rutgers University.

QUESTIONS

1. How has this image been assembled as a montage? How is it composed? What do you observe about the angle from which it has been shot? What is the effect of the montage for you?

2. How would you describe the connection between the viewing subject and the observed subject in the picture? How does the image try to make that connection?

IMAGINED BORDERS:
Frontier and Nation

Critical Questions

Before reading: How is the concept of "nation" constructed imaginatively, in the minds of inhabitants? On what kind of "evidence" is it based (i.e., symbols, unofficial histories, personal anecdote, public events, etc.)?

Taking it further: How do frontiers—the "edges" of nations and other communities—help define communities, both geographically and imaginatively? In particular, how has the concept of the American frontier colored Americans' perceptions of their country, of themselves, and of others? How does the U.S. self-conception as a nation shape its role and place in the world?

A NATION OF BORDERS

The United States was founded on the ideal that peoples of many different backgrounds could come together to make up a single nation and a single society—in short, a place where different people could become "plain Americans." One of the most famous statements of this ideal was set out in the 1770s by a French immigrant to the United States, Hector St. Jean de Crèvecoeur, in answer to the question "What is an American?"

> What is this American, this new man? He is neither an European nor the de-scendent of an European; hence that strange mixture of blood, which you will find in no other country. I could point out to you a family whose grandfather was an Englishman, whose wife was Dutch, whose son married a French woman, and whose present four sons have now four wives of different na-tions. He is an American, who, leaving behind him all his ancient prejudices and manners, receives new ones from the new mode of life he has embraced, the new government he obeys, and the new rank he holds. . . Here individuals of all nations are melted into a new race of men, whose labours and posterity will one day cause great change in the world. . .

The model American set out by Crèvecoeur is continually encountering *borders*. When leaving the borders of the home country, and crossing the borders of this one during this period, immigrants to the United States were asked to relinquish their old nationality and take on a new one. Thus, from the earliest years of the United States as a nation, crossing the *physical* borders of America had important *symbolic* dimensions. America was to be a different kind of country founded not on ancestry or blood-lines, but on an ideal, an ideal that, in theory, applied to all comers. Whether you came from Ireland, or France, or Germany, or Spain, once ar-rived you, too, could *become* "American." Ironically, what was "American" in part had to do with the shaping influence that each immigrant and im-migrant group brought to the new nation.

Crèvecoeur's ideal of diversity melting into unity, as expansive and in-clusive as it may have seemed to him, now looks rather narrow to us. The vision of all Europeans—French, German, Dutch, English—coming together encompassed neither the indigenous people already living within the physical borders of what Europeans called "America," nor the millions of Africans forcibly brought to the United States and the Caribbean. These peoples interpreted the physical and symbolic borders very differently, and they certainly weren't aware of or included in anybody's plans to "melt" with Europeans "into a new race of men."

Finally, Crèvecoeur's vision—and the ideal it expressed—did not include or anticipate the great variety of peoples who would willingly come to America from other places. Not everyone who came to this country was as welcome as the first European groups in Crèvecoeur's era, or eligible for the same opportunities for assimilation and success. Whether Irish or Chinese, Mexican or Filipino, many groups have successfully crossed physical and geographic borders only to encounter cultural, legal, and institutional barriers within America. For more than two hundred years, the nation's complex mixture of races, nationalities, religions, and subcultures has been the basis for a fundamental tension between a nation of diverse peoples and a society of "Americans" who share common space and common ideals. That diversity of people has created not a single unified "new race of men" but a nation often characterized as a "global crossroads," a country defined as much by its differences as by its commonalities. What happens when our differences need as much recognition and public influence as our commonalities? What if we are not a nation of diverse peoples "melted into a new race" but instead a mixed society whose borders and boundaries with the rest of the world have become porous and unstable?

THE AMERICAN FRONTIER AS PLACE AND IDEA

The American *frontier* was more than a physical place; it was an *idea*, one that existed, in many ways, before there was even a geographic frontier. The idea of a *frontier* of civilization implies that there is a *center* of civilization. Imagining a frontier and a center is more that just conceiving positional points; it implies that the people who live at the center represent the center of some cultural ideal; and that those who live at the edge on the frontier live outside that ideal—or at its margins. The Europeans who first encountered native people in the New World and the pioneers who encountered Indians on the Great Plains brought to the "frontier" a whole set of stereotypes and images about normal and abnormal culture and about the center and edge of civilization.

As a place and an idea, the frontier is America's longest-lived cultural border and the most crucial to its cultural identity. In fact, it is the interaction of physical space and cultural identity that gives the frontier its force. As Frederick Jackson Turner says (in the reading in this chapter), the notion of the frontier's openness of opportunity is what gave America its special quality as a land devoted to democracy, equality, and the opportunity for social mobility and individual success. But inside the myth of the frontier is a fairly narrow reading of history. The American frontier moved from east to west, implying civilization's march in a single direction into the wilds and the inevitable conquest of a "savage" people.

The *frontier* is, in the United States, customarily seen as the margin of westward expansion. But, as Patricia Limerick points out in her essay, there is a second usage of *la frontera*, less familiar but much more realistic: the borderlands between Mexico and the United States. The frontier may instead indicate a more complicated meeting between different cultures, not just a line of progress where empty land and primitive people give way to a superior culture. The distinction between frontier and *la frontera* speaks to the importance of understanding the interplay of geography and perception, the physical and the symbolic. Myra Jehlen's essay explores such interplay in an examination of the two radically different forms of maps in use in the age of colonization: *portolani*, or "sailing charts" drawn by sailors during the course of sailing, and *mappae mundi*, world maps philosophically organized, "drawn according to an academic geography that had little to do with observation." Alan Thomas and Ben Crow also examine the "point of view" of supposedly "true" maps, in this case analyzing the cultural distortions inherent in modern map projections.

Jane Tompkins claims that the traditional image of the frontier as a place of adventure and conquest still dominates our culture, precisely because it is not just a place but also an idea. As an idea, it has tended to appeal to some very basic emotional needs in American culture. The tremendous popularity of Buffalo Bill and his traveling Wild West shows (complete with reenactments of Indian fights and buffalo hunts) is evidence that the idea of the frontier and the Wild West have persisted in American culture not as some geographical territory of the past, but as an "inward territory" in the culture's mind and soul. Armond White, likewise, examines the "inward territory" of a more contemporary cultural phenomenon—rap music. Initially seen as an open territory for the taking, the present integration of the rapper "community," according to White, must wrestle with the false borders of race. Agha Shahid Ali's poem offers a surrealistic conversation between a "correspondent" and a speaker whose history is being imagined as documentary film. Whether about bodies, identities, communities, or territories, ultimately what this chapter addresses is *spaces and their boundaries*, understood as both places and ideas.

Papers of Empire

MYRA JEHLEN

Myra Jehlen attended the City University of New York and received her Ph.D. from the University of California, Berkeley. She is currently the Board of Governors' Chair of Literatures at Rutgers University. Her numerous publications deal with American and comparative literature as well as theoretical issues in literary interpretation and history. She has also edited or co-edited a number of volumes: *Ideology and Classic American Literature* (with Sacvan Bercovitch, Cambridge, 1986), *Melville: New Century Views* (Prentice Hall, 1994), and *The English Literatures of America 1500–1800* (with Michael Warner, Routledge, 1996). As a contributor to the *Cambridge History of American Literature* (1994), Jehlen wrote a series of essays entitled "The Literature of Colonization," examining the ways in which America was invented, territorially and figuratively, as a result of both imperial expansion and imaginative appropriation. An excerpt from the first of those essays follows. In examining European concepts of mapping during the age of Columbus, Jehlen discovers an early modern culture "in motion but uncertain about its map."

Literary forms plot their home cultures. The form of the compilation plots a culture of acquisition and expansion but one in which the things acquired and desired are not fully ordered—a culture in motion but uncertain about its map. And, in fact, as the compilations were being assembled, significant changes in the very concept of mapping also emerged. In Columbus's day, there were two radically different kinds of map in use: *mappae mundi,* "world maps," and *portolani,* "sailing charts." World maps were theoretical and drawn according to an academic geography that had little to do with observation. The world this geography projected was philosophically organized, deduced sometimes from scientific law, sometimes from scripture, but only secondarily from actual survey. The portolans were drawn by sailors in the course of navigating; they were carried about and constantly altered on board ship and in the cafés and inns of seaports.

In the Bibliothèque Nationale in Paris, there is a double map called the Christopher Columbus Chart because it is believed, on not entirely reliable evidence, to have been put together in 1492 (see Figure 1). This Christopher

Columbus Chart includes a mappa mundi and a portolan, both showing the Atlantic world extending down the coast of Africa and encompassing the Portuguese discoveries. The right-hand portolan sketches the Atlantic and the Mediterranean, bounded on the north by Norway, on the east by the Black Sea, and on the South by the mouth of the Congo. Besides a number of legendary islands, the portolan also locates major cities and identifies the principal products of each region (ostrich feathers in the Sahara, pepper in Guinea, and so on). The mappa mundi, on the left, shows the world surrounded by nine celestial spheres according to the contemporary, geocentric worldview. Africa—including the Cape of Good Hope (rounded in 1488)—appears along with a suggestive inscription to the effect that "the *mappa mundi,* although drawn on a plane, should be considered to be spherical." Juxtaposed but unintegrated, the right-hand portolan and the left-hand mappa mundi enact an allegory of their era, when historical change was so fundamental that it altered the very concept of *geography,* transforming it from a representation of abiding cosmic relations into a theater of human mobility and mutability.

Columbus, notoriously, denied to the day of his death that the lands he had come upon on his way to the East constituted a continent hitherto unknown to Europe. When it became impossible any longer to maintain that he had arrived in Asia, he produced a new claim that he had found the site of the earthly paradise. We might understand his extraordinary resistance to acknowledging himself a discoverer as a determined effort to retain an original vision of the world: in other words, as a refusal to read a sailing chart as a mappa mundi. Columbus was a sophisticated reader of maps. It is very likely that he used a globe, possibly the one made by Martin Behaim in 1492, which displayed the most current geographical knowledge according

3

FIGURE 1. This combined *mappa mundi* and portolan is commonly referred to as the "Christopher Columbus Chart" because it is believed to have been drawn up in 1492. See discussion in text.

to maps produced in the late 1480s and early 1490s. He was fully adept at deciphering portolans as well as their global equivalents; he just did not accept them as mappae mundi.

One way to describe the philosophical and historical significance of Europe's discovery of America is as a fundamental shift in the meaning and use of maps. In their historical setting, the mappae mundi served their representational purpose without having to conform to the empirical facts depicted on portolans. On the other hand, the way historical change can compel paradigmatic transformations finds its negative example in the sea captain's refusal to abandon his conceptual map of the world for his chart.

The Italian explorer Amerigo Vespucci (1451–1512), in contrast, was not averse to admitting new lands onto his conceptual map. Less sea captain than entrepreneur, he was a well-educated Florentine merchant from a family prominent in the republican aristocracy. He had been selected from among his brothers to direct the family's commercial enterprises. Over the course of either two, three, or four voyages to the New World between 1497 or 1499 and 1504, he approached the impassable land mass we now call South America as a conceptual problem, something to figure out and that might lead to reconfigurations. His *Letter to Soderini* did not yet clearly separate the New World from Asia, but it already abandoned the principle that no large landmass outside those already known could possibly exist. And although he may have invented either one or two voyages to enlarge his role in the exploration of the New World, he did understand it was new. Two events thus epitomize this period of radical change: (1) Vespucci succeeded by proclaiming that the new lands implied a new globe, and (2) Columbus, defining the old globe and unable to fit his new continents onto it, died bitter and unrewarded.

In the sixteenth century, then, the *compilation* and the *sailing chart* were the texts, the representational forms, or an ascendant worldview. Their emergence represents in turn the development of a paradoxical new way of both being in the world and observing it. The paradox has to do with a new relation between being and observing, such that *one's vision is more powerfully objective due to one's newly empowered subjectivity*. Hakluyt's compilations strive above all for documentary validity and practicality. At the same time, however, the sponsors and lieutenants of America's discovery and colonization were also aggressively redefining their concept of the world to suit their notion of how it would be most profitably exploited. *Masters of the portolan, they claimed the right also to redraw the mappa mundi in the image of a world they would remake.*

The expression of this double ambition is an *emerging style of writing* whose dualism, even two-facedness, is veiled. This is the *plain, reportorial, scientific style* associated in its origin especially with the essays of Francis

FIGURE 2. John Ferrar's 1651 "A mapp of Virginia discovered to ye Falls," published in the third edition of Edward William's *Virgo Triumphans: or Virginia
Richly and Truly Valued* (London 1651), shows the Atlantic coast from Cape Cod
to Cape Fear. Ferrar depicts in detail the coastal region and especially the waterways that may be followed inland—the Chesapeake Bay, the two branches of
the Potomac, and the Hudson, which he shows flowing into the Pacific—but
grows a little schematic when he approaches the mountains beyond. Past the
mountains, however, he leaps back all the way to the terms of the mappae
mundi: "The Sea of China and the Indies" is right there, a mere "ten days
march . . . from the head of the Jeames River."

Bacon (1561–1626). These essays were addressed to aspiring young men
much like those Hakluyt imagined colonizing the New World and offered
analyses of concepts (like "riches" and "usury") that might illuminate their
progress. To that end, the essays were written as plainly as possible, es-
chewing linguistic ornamentation as the expression of a wasteful and idle
aristocratic culture. Increasingly the explorers' reports, letters, and narratives
of colonization display the "Baconian" style.

A report on a Virginia voyage sent to Richard Hakluyt by the artist John
White illustrates this style. The following passage is particularly striking because in it White describes a personal disaster, the disappearance and presumed death of his daughter and granddaughter (Virginia Dare, who was
the first English child born in the New World). White, who had headed the

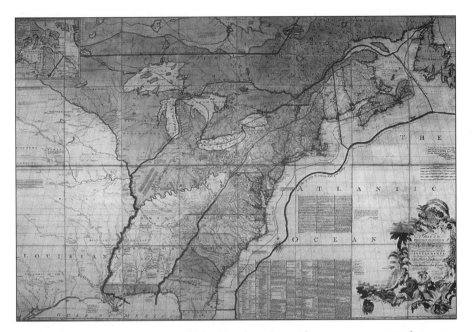

FIGURE 3. John Mitchell's *Map of the British and French Dominions in North America, 1755,* was drawn up for the English Lords of Trade and Plantations to bolster British territorial claims. Three features are especially interesting in our context. The first is the pivoting of the axis of perspective since the Ferrar map drawn a century earlier. Visually, the map of Virginia runs north–south, the eye traveling from the bottom of the page, where European explorers land in America, up through the band of waterways to the mountains and out, back to the "Sea of China" and the route to the Indies. Virginia is a rich find to be sure, a valuable bonus; but the main business remains as Columbus defined it, to find a westward route to the Orient. One looks at the Mitchell map rather from right to left. Moreover, its attention to the left and therefore the west is exaggeratedly and indefinitely drawn out, suggesting the possibility of infinite expansion. The colonial destination is no longer the Indies but America itself.

Empirical and practical, the Mitchell map understands the enterprise of representing the world altogether differently from the philosophical mappae mundi. Still, lest we forget that cartography, ancient or modern, not only depicts but interprets, there are five islands on Mitchell's Lake Superior no one has ever seen. Robert W. Karrow, Jr., a historian of cartography, has shown that Mitchell himself did not invent these islands but that they surfaced on his chart intertextually, from other charts—a caution against drawing too categorical a distinction between the mappae mundi and our modern maps.

One other aspect of Mitchell's map is evocative of the themes of this essay. Near the Great Lakes is the following legend in print too small to read in this reproduction: "The Long and Barbarous Names lately given to Some of these Northern Parts of Canada and the Lakes we have not inserted, as they are of no use, and uncertain Authority." "Lately given" means given by the Indians of the region before the coming of the Europeans.

colonizing expedition, had left them behind at Roanoke to return briefly to England. During his absence, the Roanoke colony met with a catastrophic event, to this day unknown, and when he came back to Virginia, there were no survivors. White's report, titled in Hakluyt's collection *The Fifth Voyage of M. John White into the West Indies and Parts of America called Virgina, in the Year 1590* (1593), appears intent only on establishing its trustworthiness:

> I have sent you (although in a homely style, especially for the contentation of a delicate ear) the true discourse of my last voyage into the West Indies, and parts of America called Virginia, taken in hand about the end of February, in the year of our redemption 1590. And what events happened unto us in this our journey, you shall plainly perceive by the sequel of my discourse.

The report is genuinely "homely," little more than a chronological record-   9
ing of daily activities and findings. Approaching the site of the plantation and finding the letters "CROATOAN" inscribed on a palisade surrounding the shells of houses, White does not pause to express dismay or anxiety. Inside the protective circle, he just continues his survey of "many bars of iron, two pigs of lead, four iron fowlers, iron sacker-shot, and such like heavy things, thrown here and there, almost overgrown with grass and weeds." The plantation has been abandoned. Leaving neither distress signals nor any intelligible indications of their destination, the colonists have disappeared, and White and his companions try to find their trail. "From thence we went along by the water side, towards the point of the creek to see if we could find any of their boats or pinnace, but we could perceive no sign of them, nor any of the last falcons and small ordinance which were left with them, at my departure from them."

Factual writing need not be so laconic or unemotional, however. Proba-   10
bly the best representation of the new functional style in the literature of colonization is Walter Raleigh's (1552?–1618) highly personal narrative of his voyage of Guiana in 1595. Raleigh's title would have pleased Marco Polo: *The Discovery of the Large, Rich and Beautiful Empire of Guiana, with a Relation of the Great and Golden City of Manoa (Which the Spaniards Call El Dorado)* (1596). Envious of the golden conquests of Cortés and Pizarro (over the fabled Aztecs and Incas), Raleigh thought to find deep in the Amazonian wilderness a third great aboriginal empire, the legendary El Dorado. But despite its title and its romantic inspiration, the *Discovery of the Empire of Guiana* is a thoroughly realistic chronicle—realistic, that is, in form and style, not necessarily in content. No doubt influenced by his desires, Raleigh seriously overestimated the wealth of the Indian nation he found; but he always measures it by objective standards. He clearly believes his finding are a colonizer's dream, but he presents them in the voice of sober reason: "I will promise these things that follow which I know to be true. Those that are de-

sirous to discover and to see many nations may be satisfied within this river, . . . above 2000 miles east and west, and 800 miles south and north, and of these, the most either rich in gold, or in other merchandises." He fully means to persuade, not only to inform: "The common soldier shall here fight for gold, and pay himself instead of pence, with plates of half a foot broad, whereas he breaketh his bones in other wars for provender and penury." But the ground on which he argues is solid earth: "There is no country which yieldeth more pleasure to the inhabitants, either for these common delights of hunting, hawking, fishing, fowling, and the rest, than Guiana does."

The *dualism* Columbus announced as the distinguishing feature of the *Diario*—that it would report things as they were while also being an entirely personal narrative—is not specified in Raleigh's *Discovery of the Empire of Guiana;* it is fully implicit. The sentences just cited are unmistakably personal *and they tell a story anyone can tell because it is true.* When this way of telling a story makes use of an image, the image participates in the same dualism. Take this famous passage:

> Guiana is a country that hath yet her maidenhead, never sacked, turned, nor wrought, the face of the earth hath not been torn, not the virtue and salt of the soil spent by manurance, the graves have not been opened for gold, the mines not broken with sledges, nor their images pulled down out of their temples. It hath never been entered by any army of strength, and never conquered or possessed by any Christian prince.

The sexual metaphor is consciously elaborated but it is entirely organic to the argument; it is never ornamental. Nothing appears as a result of associating conquest with rape that is not directly a fact of conquest: soil, graves, mines, and temples are real features of a real Guiana. Raleigh uses almost no adjectives; when he wants to describe the country as healthful or rich or beautiful, he makes a statement: "The soil besides is so excellent and so full of rivers, as it will carry sugar, ginger, and all those other commodities, which the West Indies have." He does not characterize the soil or the geography (as Columbus does in the "excellent soil and the commodious rivers") but describes them: "The soil . . . is . . . excellent and . . . full of rivers." A search is said to reveal "four goodly entrances" to a river, but the adjective "goodly" immediately acquires an objective measure: "whereof the least was as big as the Thames at Woolwich." Raleigh describes everything he sees and does and experiences. But he decidedly rejects conventions or ways of writing that fall into the category of the poetic or even the conventionally literary. He never develops his evocative, vivid descriptions through any of the forms of imaginative writing; the *Discovery of the Empire of Guiana* is a remarkably effective piece of writing that never acknowledges any other purpose but direct communication.

This *avoidance of imaginative and poetic forms* seems particularly significant when we recall that the sixteenth century in literary history is the age of the lyric. There were some lyrical accounts of the conquest certainly. And lyricism does sometimes bathe explorers' reports and shipping logs, recording a thriving commerce between poetry and power. Hakluyt included in his compilations some quite lyrical pieces, such as, for instance, Arthur Barlowe's account of his 1584 reconnoitering mission to the North American coast. Sent by Raleigh as soon as Raleigh received his patent to colonize in the area, Barlowe seems to have understood his task to be to sing the praises of Virginia. He duly evoked a land whose coastal waters "smelt so sweetly . . . as if we had been in the midst of some delicate garden, abounding with all kinds of odoriferous flowers." Landing, they find the soil "the most plentiful, sweet, fruitful, and wholesome of all the world." The people are "most gentle, loving, and faithful, void of all guile, and treason, and such as lived after the manner of the golden age." The conclusion has long been apparent: the earth in Virginia "bringeth forth all things in abundance, as in the first creation, without toil or labour."

More often, however, in the mode of Raleigh's account of El Dorado, even fantastical accounts and fanciful promotions are presented as facts. The explorer John Hawkins (1532–95) or a member of his 1564 expedition to Florida was remarkably matter-of-fact about some rather unlikely discoveries: |13

> [T]he Floridans have pieces of unicorns' horns, which they wear about their necks, whereof the Frenchmen obtained many pieces. Of those unicorns they have many; for that they do affirm it to be a beast with one horn, which coming to the river to drink, putteth the same into the water before he drinketh. Of this unicorn's horn there are of our company, that having gotten the same of the Frenchman, brought home thereof to show.

In such accounts, the New World is *wonderful without being exactly wondrous;* it is marvelous not for its exoticism but for its potential to make the richest resources accessible, even familiar.

Ralph Lane, governor of Roanoke in 1585, extolled the wonders of the island less soberly than Raleigh did those of Guiana: |14

> the goodliest soil under the cope of heaven, so abounding with sweet trees, that bring such sundry rich and most pleasant gums, grapes of such greatness, yet wild . . . the goodliest and most pleasing territory of the world (for the continent is of a huge and unknown greatness, and very well peopled and towned, though savagely) and the climate so wholesome, that we have not had one sick since we touched the land here.

But even though Lane clearly exaggerates, he does not render Roanoke fabulous.

Lane's hyperbolic "goodliest and most pleasing territory of the world" is *not romance, but it is promotion.* And in its intentions, *promotion is never merely factual. It must make readers dream in order to persuade them to act.* Raleigh describes El Dorado in the language of fact and avoids any semblance |15 of romance, but his first purpose in writing the *Discovery of the Empire of Guiana* is to promote colonial voyages. Romance, which calls attention to its imaginary status, as Barlowe calls attention to his use of the myth of Eden, would not serve this purpose. A practical reader might actually be discouraged from hazarding into a country whose best qualities are patently improbable. *The literature of colonial description, insisting on strict realism, conceals the distinction between fancy and fact, fuses the ideal and the real.* Visions appear realistic. The plainer, more functional prose style of imperial writings does carry a new burden of scientific or factual information and also facilitates its gathering. But it is not less ideologically active than its predecessors.

In the fact-focused passages we have been reading, vision and realism 16 confirm one another; *the prose of objectivity masks an appeal to the imagination in a context ostensibly ruled by reason.* The prose of objectivity can also work the other way, just as ideologically, not to evoke but to *block the imagination.* In the following passage, a document from the African slave trade, the sober and plain writing suppresses reader sympathy. "The Voyage Made by Mr. John Hawkins to the Coast of Guinea and the Indies of Nova Hispania, 1564" (this is the same Hawkins who reported earlier on unicorns in Florida and whose writings were published by Hakluyt) describes a raid:

> The captain was advertised by the Portuguese of a town of the Negroes, where was not only great quantity of gold, but also that there were not above forty men, and an hundred women and children in the town, so that he might get an hundred slaves: he determined to stay before the town three or four hours, to see what he could do: and thereupon prepared his men in armour and weapon together, to the number of forty men well appointed, having to their guides certain Portuguese: we landing boat after boat, and diverse of our men scattering themselves, contrary to the captain's will, by one or two in a company, for the hope that they had to find gold in their houses, ransacking the same, in the meantime the Negroes came upon them, and hurt many being thus scattered whereas if five or six had been together, they had been able as their companions did, to give the overthrow to 40 of them. While this was doing the captain who with a dozen men, went through the town, returned, finding 200 Negroes at the water's side, shooting at them in the boats, and cutting them in pieces which were drowned in the water. Thus we returned back somewhat discomforted, although the captain in a singular wise manner carried himself, with countenance very cheerful outwardly: having gotten by our going ten Negroes and lost seven of our best men, and we had 27 of our men hurt.

Nothing has been left out of this account, yet little can be read in it; little, that is, of what must have been—what the account itself tells us was—the terrible devastation of the village and its people. The passage actually *obscures what it describes,* documenting atrocity in a way that makes the reader more or less unable to apprehend it. This opaqueness is oddly unguarded and undefensive, connoting neither denial nor a strong sense of entitlement. On the contrary, rather than the writer's nationalism, callousness, or even racism, what blocks the reader's comprehension is, ironically, the evenness and amplitude of the exposition.

The beginning of the long first sentence seems to propose the "Negroes"   17 as candidates for the reader's sympathy by describing them in traditionally pathetic terms as mostly "women and children," one hundred of them about to become a hundred slaves. At this stage, the focus of the anecdote is on its characters and we seem to be starting a story more than a report. Almost at once, however, the human drama recedes as potential characters flatten into participants, and an incipient plot reduces to a report on strategy. The careful recorder once again provides numbers, now suggesting a balance of forces, forty against forty. But although a confrontation between men is potentially as dramatic as the capture of women, the writer does not concentrate here either but moves on equably; his main point turns out to be that their failure to keep together cost the English more casualties than was necessary. Numbers abound; precision is everywhere: the English advance on the African houses "by one or two in a company"; "if five or six had been together," they could have withstood "40 of them." The captain meets up with "200 Negroes," and finally the sum of it all: ten Africans taken slave, seven Englishmen lost, and twenty-seven injured. End of report.

It has not been all statistics, however; the rest of the story is all here: the   18 raiders meet up with their two hundred victims not just anywhere but at the waterside, where a battle ensues that is full of circumstance and gory detail, the Africans "shooting at them in the boats, and cutting them in pieces which were drowned in the water." Yet these actual bodies are no more real than the numbers, for the major obstacle to understanding has not been abstraction but rather a totality composed indistinguishably of both bodies and numbers that literally mean nothing. *They do not mean or connote; they name, describe, identify.* They tell, and *the very completeness of the account works to inflect all its parts equally; so that the overall clarity with which we see the forest blurs the trees.*

Some considerable portion of a polity's tolerance for violence commit-   19 ted in its name stems from the conviction that the enemy is evil and the victims are unworthy. Hawkins's passage invokes neither judgment. And although its author might assume his readers would bring such views to their reading, one would expect, were ideology to shape their response, some appeal to imperial creeds, such as a reminder of the savagery of the Africans or of their inferior intelligence. Neither is this passage a work of apology and justification, which depend on completeness and equal time, forms one might have thought either politically neutral or, in the exercise of neutrality, possible even subversive. On this passage, ideological content remains latent.

In fact, this story of a slave raid is so unfocused that the author has diffi-   20
culty concluding it. In the penultimate sentence, the captain with his dozen
men confronting two hundred Africans on shore, the Englishmen in the boats,
the bodies (English? African? both?) floating in pieces on the water, are just
there, disparate, unrelated. A *center* is needed to pull the scene together; the
last sentence locates this center where a culture able to conceive of objective
telling logically places it, in the *person of the teller*. In this disinterested world,
a hero emerges, the hitherto sketchy Captain Hawkins, who now assumes
enough agency to be described "carr[ying]" himself "in a singular wise manner." He will interpret the episode for us; it will derive its point from his interpretation. Until now everyone has been described not only externally but
from an indeterminate distance that flattens them into the landscape. Now the
captain is revealed to have not only a face but a being behind that face: the
phrase "with countenance very cheerful *outwardly*" (italics added) implies an
unsuspected interiority that becomes the *episode's theater of meaning*. *Captain
Hawkins's interiority implies England's;* and the slave raid, of which we still
know everything and nothing, achieves meaning as an *episode in the evolution
of an English national character*. The ambition of the objective, empirical narrative reveals itself in this conclusion. The claim to tell all the truth seeks to
take possession of its subject definitively and to encompass it whole. *The
plain factual style colonizes reality;* empirical writing builds empires.

Such was Richard Hakluyt's fervent hope, although in the seventeenth   21
century, it all remained to be done. The New World was a future so far from
being already imagined, it might never come. It had to be invented: conquered, settled, and also enjoined, urged, promoted, written into being.
Hakluyt's "papers of empire," like Mercator's maps, like Columbus's *Diario*
were conceived primarily *as means not for depicting the world or celebrating it or speculating about it but for acting in it*. Thus when one notes that
a plainer, more functionalist prose style became dominant during the period
of colonization, this does not mean any diminution in the status of literature.
A literature emerges in Hakluyt's reports that is more powerful than ever in
its ability to appropriate history on the model of, and in conjunction with,
England's appropriation of foreign lands. *"America" was conceived under
the sign of the printing press*.

Working with the Text

1. Why does Jehlen begin her discussion of the literature of colonization
   by discussing the two kinds of maps: "world maps" and "sailing
   charts"? What distinguishes the two kinds of maps? How does that
   difference set up her argument about writing style and ideas in the
   "literature of colonization"?

2. Can you identify an example that Jehlen gives in the text of where "the plain, reportial, scientific style" carries some dimension of promotion, persuasion, or ideology? Can you locate a similar description from a newspaper or elsewhere, where seemingly factual description reveals an ideological bias? In particular, can you locate an example of writing about global or international activity from a U.S. perspective that reveals this duality?

3. Reread the section about the African slave incident. What is Jehlen's point about the emergence of the "hero" at the end of the passage? How would you describe the connection between her interpretations of that story and her point about writing style related to colonization?

4. Jehlen says at one point: "The literature of colonial description, insisting on strict realism, conceals the distinction between fancy and fact, fuses the ideal and the real." How does her general point about "colonial description" apply specifically to the New World and to "America"? Explore in an essay, Jehlen's conclusion that "America" was conceived under the sign of the printing press.

Maps, Projections, and Ethnocentricity

ALAN THOMAS AND BEN CROW

The following selection from *Third World Atlas* (1994) asks you to consider how the geographic representations of the world we see on maps actually "distort sizes, shapes, relative locations, directions and distances." It also illustrates how the most common representations create a Europe-centered image of the world. The authors have provided a number of different geographic representations to suggest alternative ways of viewing the relation among the world's continents.

The Earth is almost perfectly spherical in shape. (In fact, it is just a little flattened at the poles, so that whereas the distance around the Equator is 40,077 km, the distance along the meridian from South Pole to North Pole and back to South Pole again is only 39,942 km.) The way in which a sphere or globe is represented on a flat surface is called a *projection*. Map projections are bound to be distorted in one way or another—to realize this, think of spreading and stretching out flat the peel of an orange.

Different projections distort sizes, shapes, relative locations, directions   2
and distances in different ways, and are designed for different purposes.
Mercator's projection is probably the most familiar. It was developed in the
sixteenth century as an aid to navigation, but is now commonly used as a
reference base on which to put any kind of geographical information, for
many purposes other than navigation at sea, including cases where other
projections would be better. Mercator's projection has the special property
of maintaining the true direction of any one point relative to another, so that,
for example, a line drawn diagonally on the map at 45° to the equator always points north-east. Shapes are also fairly faithfully reproduced. However, the price paid is that distances and areas are both magnified towards
the poles, so that Greenland, for example, looks much bigger than it really
is, relative to, say, Africa or China. In fact, this distortion becomes mathe-
matically infinite towards the poles and a map on Mercator's projection can
never include the poles themselves. As a result, a false impression is given
of the shortest distance between points around the earth's surface. For example, North America and Russia are in fact quite close to each other across
the polar regions. William-Olsson's projection, on which air routes are
shown on [page 469] is one of several which do show this.

It has been suggested that Mercator's projection promotes a Eurocentric   3
view of the world—Europe is in the centre of the top half of the map and is
disproportionately large. Placing the North Pole at the top (rather than the
bottom or either side) dates back to the Ancient Greeks; measuring longitude from the Greenwich meridian so that London is usually in the middle
of a map derives from British domination of the seas. (There is an early example of a map with a different orientation and a different centre on page
467, left.) Peters' projection was developed recently to "correct the Europe-
centred image of the world as projected by Mercator." It is an "equal-area"
projection; that is, regions on the globe which are equal in land (or sea) area
are represented by equal areas on the map. Peters' projection also conserves
the North–South and East–West directions throughout. However, other directions and, more importantly, distances and shapes, are quite badly distorted, so that near the equator the land surfaces appear to be elongated in
a North–South direction, whereas near the poles they are stretched in an
East–West direction.

Peters' projection still has the North Pole at the top and the Greenwich   4
meridian down the middle! Perhaps, though, the very fact that Peters' projection "looks funny" draws attention to the Third World countries presented
in "their actual central position."

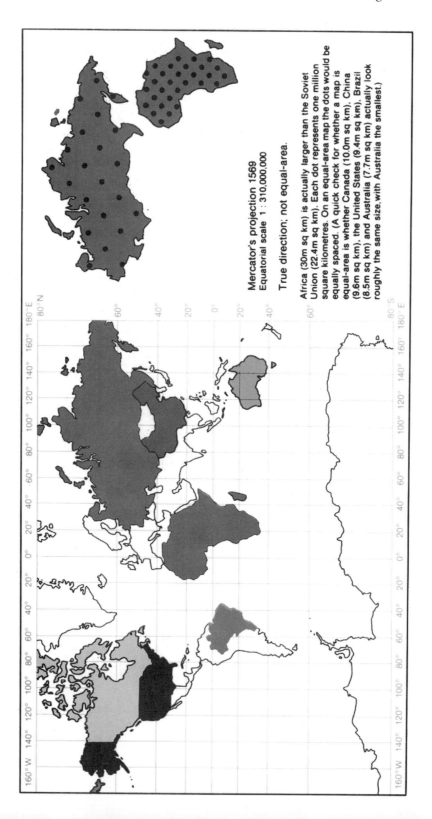

Mercator's projection 1569
Equatorial scale 1 : 310,000,000

True direction; not equal-area.

Africa (30m sq km) is actually larger than the Soviet Union (22.4m sq km). Each dot represents one million square kilometres. On an equal-area map the dots would be equally spaced. (A quick check for whether a map is equal-area is whether Canada (10.0m sq km), China (9.6m sq km), the United States (9.4m sq km), Brazil (8.5m sq km) and Australia (7.7m sq km) actually look roughly the same size with Australia the smallest.)

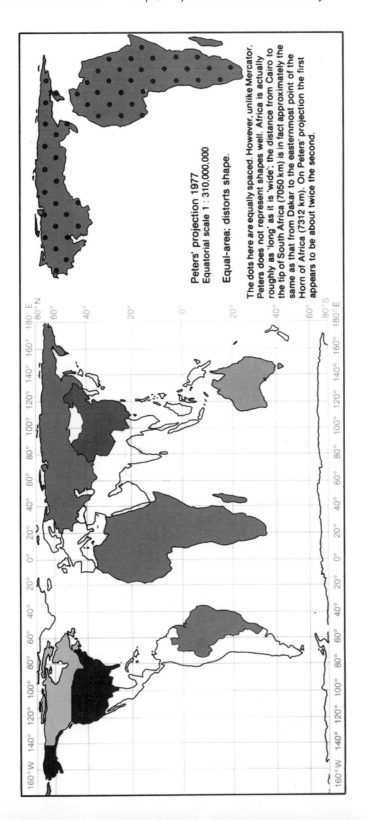

Peters' projection 1977
Equatorial scale 1 : 310,000,000

Equal-area; distorts shape.

The dots here *are* equally spaced. However, unlike Mercator, Peters does not represent shapes well. Africa is actually roughly as 'long' as it is 'wide'; the distance from Cairo to the tip of South Africa (7050 km) is in fact approximately the same as that from Dakar to the easternmost point of the Horn of Africa (7312 km). On Peters' projection the first appears to be about twice the second.

There are numerous other equal-area projections, mostly based on an   5
oval outline and curved lines of longitude and/or latitude. Mollweide's projection, on which the main human races are shown [page 471], is perhaps
the simplest. However, the deformation of shape towards the poles is possibly worse than with Peters' projection, since the surfaces are not simply
elongated but also appear at different angles. . . .

In this Atlas, different projections are used as appropriate, and the vari-   6
ety of centres and types of projection is meant to counter any tendency to
Eurocentrism. The majority of the maps are presented on the equal-area
projection used by the *1980 World Bank Atlas,* namely the Eckert IV projection. This projection does not distort shape as badly as Peters' or Mollweide's. It is drawn here with lines of latitude and longitude to show how it
is constructed. In the main world maps in the Atlas, the land-masses are
shown as large as possible on the page. As a result, New Zealand is slightly
displaced, and Antarctica and most of the Pacific Ocean are omitted.

It is worth pondering how the use of any kind of map affects the way   7
one understands the data presented. Does an equal-area map really present
a good picture of the relative importance of different countries of the world?
The next [few] pages show various types and uses of maps—and ways of
presenting geographical data without maps—that are less straightforward
than simply choosing a different projection.

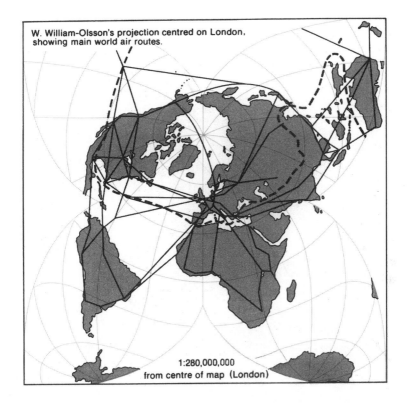

W. William-Olsson's projection centred on London, showing main world air routes.

1:280,000,000
from centre of map (London)

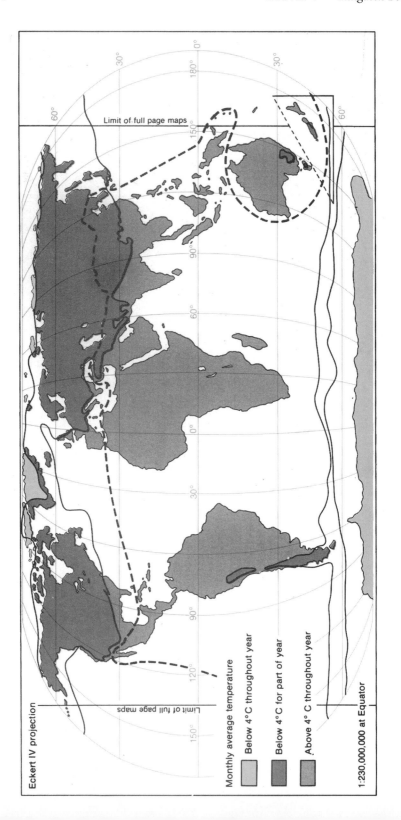

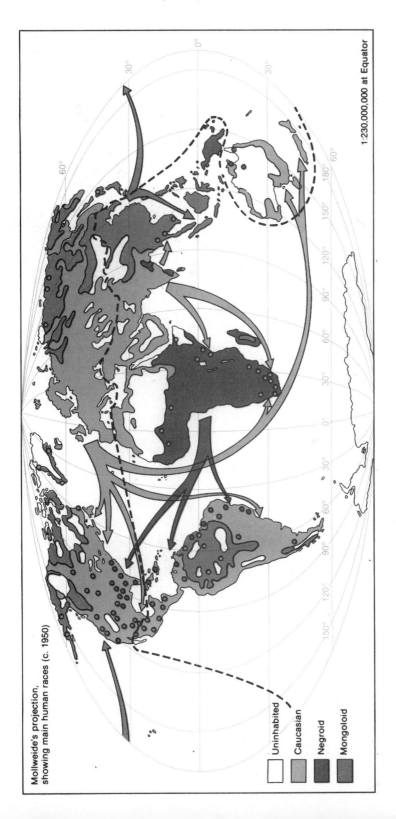

Mollweide's projection, showing main human races (c. 1950)

1:230,000,000 at Equator

Uninhabited
Caucasian
Negroid
Mongoloid

Maps have two rather different types of uses. Some use conventions to   8
present geographical information to a level of detail required for a particular purpose, such as navigation or town planning. Other maps are graphic
illustrations of how certain factors or variables are related spatially. Most of
the maps in this Atlas are of this second type. For example, the maps (and
diagram) [on pages 476–477] all illustrate in different ways how income, as
measured by Gross National Product (GNP), is related to population on a
world basis.

There can never be total lack of bias on any map, but one can differen-   9
tiate between (i) an attempt at objectivity, where the form of graphic representation is chosen to match the information on display; and (ii) a map
putting over a specific message. The left-hand map [on page 474] seems in-
accurate because of the incomplete geographical knowledge of the time,
whereas the [one on the right] is a simple but accurate map on an "equidistant" projection. The [map on page 475] is clearly designed to put over a message, though in its way it is as "accurate" as the [right-hand map on page 480].

[Pages 476–479] show graphic techniques that will crop up throughout   10
this Atlas. One is the "proportional base" where the size of a region on the
page is proportional to its population [page 476] or Gross National Product
(GNP) [page 478], and the "map" does not represent the shape and position
of territory at all closely. Think about exactly what the role of the *spatial* dimension is in such cases. Is it just to locate a country you are interested in?
Or are you referring in your mind to some "normal" map for comparison?
You may be saying to yourself something like: "India is larger than I expected in terms of population." Are you using geographical area as an implicit variable and relating what the map shows to it? If so, this underlines
the importance of the "equal-area" question. If your mind's map is on Mercator's projection, you will be misjudging these comparisons.

Another important question is the level of *aggregation,* or what *units*   11
are used for presenting data. Examples shown [on pages 474–477] are countries, regions and equal population cells. Some data only make sense with
respect to a *country* as the unit: for example, the independence date of a
country, or the way its representatives voted at the United Nations. Other
items are derived from statistics which are collected on a country basis,
whereas some ethnographic or biological data really do not fit into country
units at all. Country data may hide or average out regional or other variations to a misleading extent, particularly when comparing countries having
great regional, social and even climatic variations (like Brazil) with much
smaller and/or more homogenous countries.

Scatter-graphs are used throughout this Atlas in addition to maps where   12
the question is: "Does variable A correlate with variable B?" . . . Does GNP
correlate with the size of a country's population? In such cases, look first to

see how far the two variables do correspond. Thus, on the scatter-graph [page 477], lines have been drawn to represent the average GNP per capita for each region. Note how closely the points of each [shade] bunch around the corresponding line. Then look carefully at any points that fall outside the general pattern, and consider what might account for the anomalies. In the case of sub-Saharan Africa the bunching is quite tight, indicating a close relationship between GNP and population. North Africa/West Asia show a much less clear pattern.

Hereford World Map AD 1285 (simplified)

Note that East (the 'orient') is at the top – a practice common in the Middle Ages in Europe, from which the term 'to orient a map' derives.

An equidistant projection centred on Jerusalem. 'Equidistant' means equal distances on the globe are represented by equal distances on the map

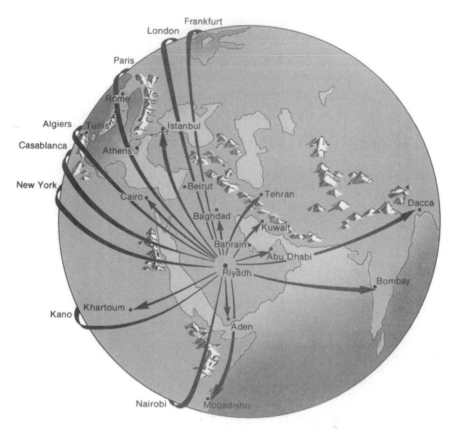

Adapted from a Saudi Arabian Airlines advertisement

These figures show different ways of relating Gross National Product 13
(GNP) to population. Take care that when you study a particular diagram
you notice whether it shows total GNP or per-capita GNP. . .

□ one million inhabitants

A comparison:
the world's countries in proportion to (above) population,
and (below) GNP (mid-1979 figures).

□ $25,000 million
  $1,000 million

The scatter-graph [below] plots countries' GNP against their population (1979 data). The lines show average GNP per capita for each region; those far off the lines have unusually high (or low) average per-capita incomes for the region. Countries with high per-capita income are bottom right, while those with low per-capita income are top left. Note the logarithmic scale on each axis, which is used to accommodate great variations in data. (A linear scale would need to be about two metres long to show the same detail.) It is important to realize that equal intervals in the data are not represented by equal distances along the scale. Thus, the distance along the vertical axis between 2 and 4 is greater than that between 4 and 6. Similarly, the distance on the axis between 2 and 4 is the same as that between 20 and 40, although the intervals are 2 and 20 respectively. Values can still be read off in the normal way.

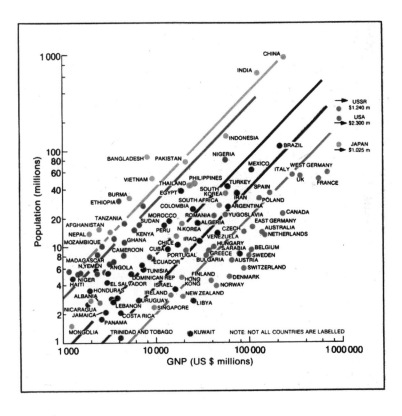

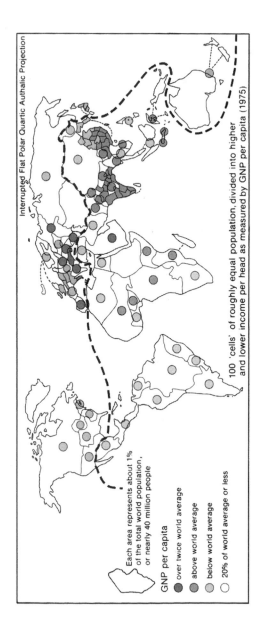

Interrupted Flat Polar Quartic Authalic Projection

100 'cells' of roughly equal population, divided into higher and lower income per head as measured by GNP per capita (1975)

Each area represents about 1% of the total world population, or nearly 40 million people

GNP per capita
- over twice world average
- above world average
- below world average
- 20% of world average or less

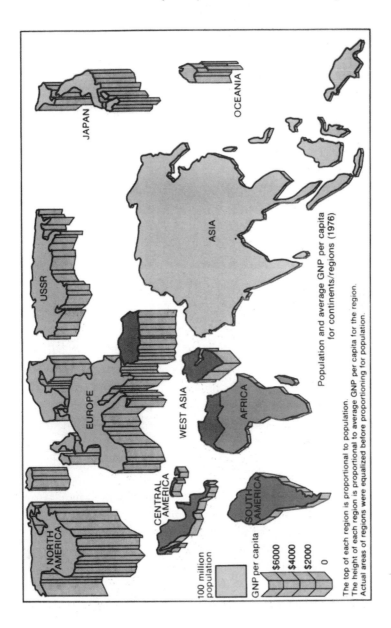

JAPAN

OCEANIA

ASIA

USSR

EUROPE

WEST ASIA

AFRICA

NORTH AMERICA

CENTRAL AMERICA

SOUTH AMERICA

Population and average GNP per capita
for continents/regions (1976)

100 million
population

GNP per capita

$6000
$4000
$2000
0

The top of each region is proportional to population.
The height of each region is proportional to average GNP per capita for the region.
Actual areas of regions were equalized before proportioning for population.

Working with the Text

1. One of the points that this short introductory section makes is that no map, in an absolute sense, can be "true." As the authors write, "Map projections are bound to be distorted in one way or another." To illustrate this point they compare the Mercator projection—which preserves shapes but distorts size, to the Peters projection—which distorts shapes but preserves size (or area). The result of the Mercator projection is that countries north of the equator appear larger than they actually are. Does Mercator's projection promote a "Eurocentric" worldview? What ought to be the primary considerations in representing the world on a flat surface? How should custom or tradition influence this?

2. Denis Wood, a geographer, has written about the Peters projection:

   > "Peters did more than insist that whatever its appearance an equal-area projection was the only fair way to show most things worth showing about the world. He implied—no, he pointed out—that the use of most other projections had a powerful built-in bias. . . . the selection of any map projection is always to choose among competing interests, is inescapably to take—that is, to *promote*, to *embody in the map*—a point of view."

   Do you agree that all maps have a "point of view"? Do you usually think of maps as having authors and audiences, like works of writing or painting?

3. Do you believe that maps can reinforce and reflect cultural biases? For example, in the United States, we are accustomed to seeing world maps with the center line being the "Greenwich meridian." How different would it be if the Western Hemisphere were always off to the far left? Do you assume that all countries simply put themselves in the center of their own maps? Can you locate maps (in the library or on the World Wide Web) that are used in other countries or cultures? How are they different?

4. Look at the map in this book called the "Turnabout Map" by Jesse Levine. As he himself states, his map is "geographically correct." What is the effect of looking at the Western Hemisphere this way? Does it seem disturbing or disorienting? Compose your responses in an informal paper.

The Concept of "Nation": A Definition

BENEDICT ANDERSON

A professor of international studies at Cornell University, Benedict Anderson has written extensively about Indonesian culture and history. Among his books on the subject are *Mythology and the Tolerance of the Javanese, In the Mirror: Literature and Politics in Siam in the American Era, Java in a Time of Revolution: Occupation and Resistance 1944–1946,* and *Language and Power: Exploring Political Era Cultures in Indonesia.* His 1983 *Imagined Communities,* from which the following is excerpted, is something of a departure. Here, Anderson offers "some tentative suggestions for a more satisfactory interpretation of the 'anomaly' of nationalism." In these paragraphs from his introduction, Anderson explains his definition of a nation as "an imagined political community—and imagined as both inherently limited and sovereign."

Theorists of nationalism have often been perplexed, not to say irritated, by these three paradoxes: (1) The objective modernity of nations to the historian's eye vs. their subjective antiquity in the eyes of nationalists. (2) The formal universality of nationality as a socio-cultural concept—in the modern world everyone can, should, will "have" a nationality, as he or she "has" a gender—vs. the irremediable particularity of its concrete manifestations, such that, by definition, "Greek" nationality is sui generis. (3) The "political" power of nationalisms vs. their philosophical poverty and even incoherence. In other words, unlike most other isms, nationalism has never produced its own grand thinkers: no Hobbeses, Tocquevilles, Marxes, or Webers. This "emptiness" easily gives rise, among cosmopolitan and polylingual intellectuals, to a certain condescension. Like Gertrude Stein in the face of Oakland, one can rather quickly conclude that there is "no there there." It is characteristic that even so sympathetic a student of nationalism as Tom Nairn can nonetheless write that: "'Nationalism' is the pathology of modern developmental history, as inescapable as 'neurosis' in the individual, with much the same essential ambiguity attaching to it, a similar built-in capacity for descent into dementia, rooted in the dilemmas of helplessness thrust upon most of the world (the equivalent of infantilism for societies) and largely incurable."[1]

---

1. *The Break-up of Britain,* p. 359.

Part of the difficulty is that one tends unconsciously to hypostasize the   2
existence of Nationalism-with-a-big-N (rather as one might Age-with-a-
capital-A) and then classify "it" as *an* ideology. (Note that if everyone has an
age, Age is merely an analytical expression.) It would, I think, make things
easier if one treated it as if it belonged with "kinship" and "religion," rather
than with "liberalism" or "fascism."

In an anthropological spirit, then, I propose the following definition of   3
the nation: it is an imagined political community—and imagined as both inherently limited and sovereign.

It is *imagined* because the members of even the smallest nation will   4
never know most of their fellow-members, meet them, or even hear of
them, yet in the minds of each lives the image of their communion.[2] Renan
referred to this imagining in his suavely back-handed way when he wrote
that "Or l'essence d'une nation est que tous les individus aient beaucoup de
choses en commun, et aussi que tous aient oublié bien des choses."[3] With a
certain ferocity Gellner makes a comparable point when he rules that "Nationalism is not the awakening of nations to self-consciousness: it *invents*
nations where they do not exist."[4] The drawback to this formulation, however, is that Gellner is so anxious to show that nationalism masquerades
under false pretences that he assimilates "invention" to "fabrication" and
"falsity," rather than to "imagining" and "creation." In this way he implies
that "true" communities exist which can be advantageously juxtaposed to
nations. In fact, all communities larger than primordial villages of face-to-
face contact (and perhaps even these) are imagined. Communities are to be
distinguished, not by their falsity/genuineness, but by the style in which
they are imagined. Javanese villagers have always known that they are connected to people they have never seen, but these ties were once imagined
particularistically—as indefinitely stretchable nets of kinship and clientship.
Until quite recently, the Javanese language had no word meaning the abstraction "society." We may today think of the French aristocracy of the *ancien régime* as a class; but surely it was imagined this way only very late.[5]
To the question "Who is the Comte de X?" the normal answer would have

---

2. Cf. Seton-Watson, *Nations and States,* p. 5: "All that I can find to say is that a nation exists when
a significant number of people in a community consider themselves to form a nation, or behave as
if they formed one." We may translate "consider themselves" as "imagine themselves."
3. Ernest Renan, "Qu'est-ce qu'une nation?" in *Œuvres Complètes,* 1, p. 892. He adds: "tout citoyen
français doit avoir oublié la Saint-Barthélemy, les massacres du Midi au XIIIe siècle. Il n'y a pas en
France dix familles qui puissent fournir la preuve d'une origine franque . . ."
4. Ernest Gellner, *Thought and Change,* p. 169. Emphasis added.
5. Hobsbawm, for example, "fixes" it by saying that in 1789 it numbered about 400,000 in a population of 23,000,000. (See his *The Age of Revolution,* p. 78). But would this statistical picture of the
noblesse have been imaginable under the *ancien régime?*

been, not "a member of the aristocracy," but "the lord of X," "the uncle of the Baronne de Y," or "a client of the Duc de Z."

The nation is imagined as *limited* because even the largest of them, encompassing perhaps a billion living human beings, has finite, if elastic, boundaries, beyond which lie other nations. No nation imagines itself coterminous with mankind. The most messianic nationalists do not dream of a day when all the members of the human race will join their nation in the way that it was possible, in certain epochs, for, say, Christians to dream of a wholly Christian planet. 5

It is imagined as *sovereign* because the concept was born in an age in which Enlightenment and Revolution were destroying the legitimacy of the divinely-ordained, hierarchical dynastic realm. Coming to maturity at a stage of human history when even the most devout adherents of any universal religion were inescapably confronted with the living *pluralism* of such religions, and the allomorphism between each faith's ontological claims and territorial stretch, nations dream of being free, and, if under God, directly so. The gage and emblem of this freedom is the sovereign state. 6

Finally, it is imagined as a *community*, because, regardless of the actual inequality and exploitation that may prevail in each, the nation is always conceived as a deep, horizontal comradeship. Ultimately it is this fraternity that makes it possible, over the past two centuries, for so many millions of people, not so much to kill, as willingly to die for such limited imaginings. 7

These deaths bring us abruptly face to face with the central problem posed by nationalism: what makes the shrunken imaginings of recent history (scarcely more than two centuries) generate such colossal sacrifices? I believe that the beginnings of an answer lie in the cultural roots of nationalism. 8

Working with the Text

1. In this excerpt from a much longer exploration of the concept of "nation," Anderson offers the following definition of a nation: "it is an imagined political community—and imagined as both inherently limited and sovereign." He then explains each of the four key words in that definition: *imagined, limited, sovereign*, and *community*. Try to apply these terms to articles you read in the "national" news section of a newspaper. Find an example of some national coverage that supports one or more of those four criteria for the definition of a nation.

2. Do you agree with Anderson that the essence of being an American is mostly a matter of imagining your relationship to other Americans? (Or, if you are not a U.S. citizen, to whomever your fellow citizens are?) How does this idea relate to immigrants? Could you imagine yourself

as not being a member of a nation? Do you feel a bond with someone simply because he or she is of the same country? If you met your "countryman" in a foreign country, would the bond seem stronger?

3. Anderson writes, "all communities larger than primordial villages of face-to-face contact (and perhaps even these) are imagined. Communities are to be distinguished, not by their falsity/genuineness, but by the style in which they are imagined." Think about two different kinds of communities that you have read about in this book so far and discuss how the "style[s] in which they are imagined" differ. In an essay, consider how a "nation" is a different kind of imagined community than, say, one's neighborhood, one's group of friends, sports team, religious group, etc. Which communities have the strongest imagined ties to you? Are any of these ties conflicting?

The Significance of the Frontier in American History

FREDERICK JACKSON TURNER

Frederick Jackson Turner (1861–1932) was one of the most renowned American historians of his day, and his work continues to exert a significant influence on the study of American history. A native of Wisconsin, Turner taught at the University of Wisconsin and later at Harvard. He published his most famous work, *The Frontier in American History*, in 1920. His other works include *The Rise of the New West* (1906) and, with Edward Channing and Albert Bushnell Hart, *Guide to the Study and Reading of American History* (1912). Central to *The Frontier in American History* is the following essay, which Turner originally delivered as an address to the World's Fair in Chicago in 1893. In this essay Turner notes that the development of America has involved the expansion of frontiers. He then posits that this advance "has meant a steady movement away from the influence of Europe, a steady growth of independence on American lines." He maintains that "to the frontier the American intellect owes its striking characteristics."

In a recent bulletin of the Superintendent of the Census for 1890 appear   1
these significant words: "Up to and including 1880 the country had a frontier of settlement, but at present the unsettled area has been so broken into
by isolated bodies of settlement that there can hardly be said to be a frontier line. In the discussion of its extent, its westward movement, etc., it can
not, therefore, any longer have a place in the census reports." This brief official statement marks the closing of a great historic movement. Up to our
own day American history has been in a large degree the history of the colonization of the Great West. The existence of an area of free land, its continuous recession, and the advance of American settlement westward, explain
American development.

Behind institutions, behind constitutional forms and modifications, lie   2
the vital forces that call these organs into life and shape them to meet changing conditions. The peculiarity of American institutions is the fact that they
have been compelled to adapt themselves to the changes of an expanding
people—to the changes involved in crossing a continent, in winning a
wilderness, and in developing at each area of this progress out of the primitive economic and political conditions of the frontier into the complexity of
city life. Said Calhoun in 1817, "We are great, and rapidly—I was about to
say fearfully—growing!" So saying, he touched the distinguishing feature of
American life. All peoples show development; the germ theory of politics
has been sufficiently emphasized. In the case of most nations, however, the
development has occurred in a limited area; and if the nation has expanded,
it has met other growing peoples whom it has conquered. But in the case of
the United States we have a different phenomenon. Limiting our attention to
the Atlantic coast, we have the familiar phenomenon of the evolution of institutions in a limited area, such as the rise of representative government; the
differentiation of simple colonial governments into complex organs; the
progress from primitive industrial society, without division of labor, up to
manufacturing civilization. But we have in addition to this a recurrence of
the process of evolution in each western area reached in the process of expansion. Thus American development has exhibited not merely advance
along a single line, but a return to primitive conditions on a continually ad-
vancing frontier line, and a new development for that area. American social
development has been continually beginning over again on the frontier. This
perennial rebirth, this fluidity of American life, this expansion westward with
its new opportunities, its continuous touch with the simplicity of primitive society, furnish the forces dominating American character. The true point of
view in the history of this nation is not the Atlantic coast, it is the Great West.
Even the slavery struggle, which is made so exclusive an object of attention
by writers like Professor von Holst, occupies its important place in American
history because of its relation to westward expansion.

In this advance, the frontier is the outer edge of the wave—the meeting   3
point between savagery and civilization. Much has been written about the
frontier from the point of view of border warfare and the chase, but as a field
for the serious study of the economist and the historian it has been neglected.

The American frontier is sharply distinguished from the European fron-   4
tier—a fortified boundary line running through dense populations. The most
significant thing about the American frontier is that it lies at the hither edge
of free land. In the census reports it is treated as the margin of that settlement which has a density of two or more to the square mile. The term is an
elastic one, and for our purposes does not need sharp definition. We shall
consider the whole frontier belt, including the Indian country and the outer
margin of the "settled area" of the census reports. This paper will make no
attempt to treat the subject exhaustively; its aim is simply to call attention to
the frontier as a fertile field for investigation, and to suggest some of the
problems which arise in connection with it.

In the settlement of America we have to observe how European life en-   5
tered the continent, and how America modified and developed that life and
reacted on Europe. Our early history is the study of European germs developing in an American environment. Too exclusive attention has been paid
by institutional students to the Germanic origins, too little to the American
factors. The frontier is the line of most rapid and effective Americanization.
The wilderness masters the colonist. It finds him a European in dress, industries, tools, modes of travel, and thought. It takes him from the railroad
car and puts him in the birch canoe. It strips off the garments of civilization
and arrays him in the hunting shirt and the moccasin. It puts him in the log
cabin of the Cherokee and Iroquois and runs an Indian palisade around
him. Before long he has gone to planting Indian corn and plowing with a
sharp stick; he shouts the war cry and takes the scalp in orthodox Indian
fashion. In short, at the frontier the environment is at first too strong for the
man. He must accept the conditions which it furnishes, or perish, and so he
fits himself into the Indian clearings and follows the Indian trails. Little by
little he transforms the wilderness, but the outcome is not the old Europe,
not simply the development of Germanic germs, any more than the first
phenomenon was a case of reversion to the Germanic mark. The fact is that
here is a new product that is American. At first, the frontier was the Atlantic
coast. It was the frontier of Europe in a very real sense. Moving westward, the
frontier became more and more American. As successive terminal moraines
result from successive glaciations, so each frontier leaves its traces behind it,
and when it becomes a settled area the region still partakes of the frontier
characteristics. Thus the advance of the frontier has meant a steady movement away from the influence of Europe, a steady growth of independence
on American lines. And to study this advance, the men who grew up under

these conditions, and the political, economic, and social results of it, is to study the really American part of our history. . . .

But the most important effect of the frontier has been in the promotion 6 of democracy here and in Europe. As has been indicated the frontier is productive of individualism. Complex society is precipitated by the wilderness into a kind of primitive organization based on the family. The tendency is anti-social. It produces antipathy to control, and particularly to any direct control. The tax-gatherer is viewed as a representative of oppression. Professor Osgood, in an able article, has pointed out that the frontier conditions prevalent in the colonies are important factors in the explanation of the American Revolution, where individual liberty was sometimes confused with absence of all effective government. The same conditions aid in explaining the difficulty of instituting a strong government in the period of the confederacy. The frontier individualism has from the beginning promoted democracy. . . .

So long as free land exists, the opportunity for a competency exists, and 7 economic power secures political power. But the democracy born of free land, strong in selfishness and individualism, intolerant of administrative experience and education, and pressing individual liberty beyond its proper bounds, has its dangers as well as its benefits. Individualism in America has allowed a laxity in regard to governmental affairs which has rendered possible the spoils system and all the manifest evils that follow from the lack of a highly developed civic spirit. In this connection may be noted also the influence of frontier conditions in permitting lax business honor, inflated paper currency and wildcat banking. The colonial and revolutionary frontier was the region whence emanated many of the worst forms of an evil currency. The West in the War of 1812 repeated the phenomenon on the frontier of that day, while the speculation and wildcat banking of the period of the crisis of 1837 occurred on the new frontier belt of the next tier of States. Thus each one of the periods of lax financial integrity coincides with periods when a new set of frontier communities had arisen, and coincides in area with these successive frontiers, for the most part. The recent Populist agitation is a case in point. Many a State that now declines any connection with the tenets of the Populists, itself adhered to such ideas in an earlier stage of the development of the State. A primitive society can hardly be expected to show the intelligent appreciation of the complexity of business interests in a developed society. The continual recurrence of these areas of paper-money agitation is another evidence that the frontier can be isolated and studied as a factor in American history of the highest importance. . . .

From the conditions of frontier life came intellectual traits of profound 8 importance. The works of travelers along each frontier from colonial days onward describe certain common traits, and these traits have, while softening down, still persisted as survivals in the place of their origin, even with a higher social organization succeeded. The result is that to the frontier the American intellect owes its striking characteristics. That coarseness and strength combined with acuteness and inquisitiveness; that practical, inventive turn of mind, quick to find expedients; that masterful grasp of material things, lacking in the artistic but powerful to effect great ends; that restless, nervous energy; that dominant individualism, working for good and for evil, and withal that buoyancy and exuberance which comes with freedom— these are traits of the frontier, or traits called out elsewhere because of the existence of the frontier. Since the days when the fleet of Columbus sailed into the waters of the New World, America has been another name for opportunity, and the people of the United States have taken their tone from the incessant expansion which has not only been open but has even been forced upon them. He would be a rash prophet who should assert that the expansive character of American life has now entirely ceased. Movement has been its dominant fact, and, unless this training has no effect upon a people, the American energy will continually demand a wider field for its exercise. But never again will such gifts of free land offer themselves. For a moment, at the frontier, the bonds of custom are broken and unrestraint is triumphant. There is not *tabula rasa*. The stubborn American environment is there with its imperious summons to accept its conditions; the inherited ways of doing things are also there; and yet, in spite of environment, and in spite of custom, each frontier did indeed furnish a new field of opportunity, a gate of escape from the bondage of the past; and freshness, and confidence, and scorn of older society, impatience of its restraints and its ideas, and indifference to its lessons, have accompanied the frontier. What the Mediterranean Sea was to the Greeks, breaking the bond of custom, offering new experiences, calling out new institutions and activities, that, and more, the ever retreating frontier has been to the United States directly, and to the nations of Europe more remotely. And now, four centuries from the discovery of America, at the end of a hundred years of life under the Constitution, the frontier has gone, and with its going has closed the first period of American history.

Working with the Text

1. Turner makes a number of claims as to how the frontier contributes to making the United States "distinctly American." What does Turner say is "American" about the frontier experience? Do you consider these qualities distinctively American or typically American?

2. In his essay, Turner describes the frontier not only as a "place" but as a "process" of social development. What is that process? Write a paper

in which you examine his assumptions about culture, society, and civilization that lie behind the process.

3. What are the connections in Turner's essay between geography and culture? How does the physical environment (the land and wilderness itself) influence American institutions? What aspects of the American experience does his thesis limit or exclude?

Adventures of the Frontier in the Twentieth Century

PATRICIA NELSON LIMERICK

Among the generation of contemporary historians of the American West, none perhaps is more well known than Patricia Nelson Limerick. She is currently on the faculty of the University of Colorado at Boulder. Limerick's works include *Sweet Medicine: Sites of Indian Massacres, Battlefields, and Treaties* (1995), and *Something in the Soil: Legacies and Reckonings in the New West* (2000). The essay that follows is from *The Frontier in American Culture: An Exhibition at the Newberry Library, August 26, 1994–January 7, 1995*. In this book Limerick explicitly rejects Frederick Jackson Turner's influential thesis regarding the history of the West as a history of frontiers and his claim that the frontier essentially closed at the end of the 19th century. Limerick suggests that we should look at the West "as a place—as many complicated environments occupied by natives who considered their homelands to be the center, not the edge." For her, "the American West was an important meeting ground, the point where Indian America, Latin America, Anglo-America, Afro-America, and Asia intersected," and its story is one primarily of conquest. In the following essay she examines what she considers simplistic contemporary conceptions of frontier and proposes a more complicated idea of *la frontera*.

Travels in Frontierland

The year 1988 signified the fortieth anniversary of humanity's escape from   1
zippers and buttons. In May of that year a journal of science and technology
called *Discover* published an article commemorating this occasion. "Velcro,"
the headline read: "The Final Frontier."

To the specialist in Western American history, this is a title to ponder. In   2
what sense might Velcro constitute a frontier? In his 1893 essay "The Significance of the Frontier in American History," Frederick Jackson Turner left his
central term curiously befogged: The word "frontier," he said, "is an elastic
one, and for our purposes does not need sharp definition."[1] But Turner did
join the director of the United States census in offering one clear and concrete definition: the frontier was a place occupied by fewer than two people
per square mile. Thus, if the headline writer were a strict follower of Turner's
quantitative definition, then the Velcro Frontier would be a place where
fewer than two people per square mile used Velcro. The writer, on the other
hand, might have been following one of the more poetic and less precise
Turnerian definitions, finding in a society's choice of fasteners a symbolic
line of division between wilderness and human culture, backwardness and
progress, savagery and civilization. The habit-bound users of zippers would
now represent the primitive and backward people of North America, with the
hardy, adventurous users of Velcro living on the cutting edge of progress.

Historians of the American West might puzzle over the shifting defini-   3
tions of the word "frontier," but few readers experience any confusion when
they see this headline. To them, the frontier analogy says simply that makers, marketers, and users of Velcro stand on the edge of exciting possibilities. Velcro is a frontier because Velcro has thousands of still-to-be-imagined
uses. No normal reader, if one defines "normal reader" as a person who is
not a Western American historian, would even notice the peculiar implications of the analogy. For most Americans in the twentieth century, the term
"frontier" is perfectly clear, reliable, and simple in its meanings.

"Frontier," the historian David Wrobel writes, "has become a metaphor   4
for promise, progress, and ingenuity."[2] And yet, despite the accuracy of this
summation, the relation between the frontier and the American mind is not
a simple one. Clear and predictable on most occasions, the idea of the frontier is still capable of sudden twists and shifts of meaning, meanings considerably more interesting than the conventional and familiar definition of the
frontier as a zone of open opportunity.

Conventional thinking is at its most powerful, however, in twentieth-   5
century reconstructions of the nineteenth-century experience of westward
expansion, reconstructions quite explicitly designed for sale. To see this

commercialized vision of the Old Frontier in concrete, three-dimensional form, the best place to go is Disneyland in Anaheim, California. When they enter Frontierland, visitors might ask Disneyland employees for directions, but they do not have to ask for a definition of the frontier. The frontier, every tourist knows, was the edge of Anglo-American settlement, the place where white Americans struggled to master the continent. This frontier, as everything in Frontierland confirms, was populated by a colorful and romantic cast of characters—mountain men, cowboys, prospectors, pioneer wives, saloon girls, sheriffs, and outlaws. Tepees, log cabins, and false-front stores were the preferred architecture of the frontier; coonskin caps, cowboy hats, bandannas, buckskin shirts and leggings, moccasins, boots, and an occasional sunbonnet or calico dress constituted frontier fashion; canoes, keelboats, steamboats, saddle horses, covered wagons, and stagecoaches gave Americans the means to conquer the rivers, mountains, deserts, plains, and other wide-open spaces of the frontier; firearms, whether long rifles or six-shooters, were everywhere and in frequent use. These images are very well understood. Tourists do not need any assistance in defining Frontierland.

And yet, even in the tightly controlled world of Disneyland, the idea of the frontier has encountered complications. At the Golden Horseshoe, Frontierland's saloon, every show once had a "spontaneous" gunfight in which Black Bart and Sheriff Lucky blazed away at each other. In 1958, as a reporter for the *Saturday Evening Post* watched, the gunfight underwent some slippage at the joint that connects fantasy to reality: "As the sheriff advanced toward the wounded bandit," the writer said, "a tow-headed five-year-old, wearing a cowboy suit and holding a cap pistol, came running from the crowd," asking earnestly, "'Can I finish him off, sheriff, can I?'" The sheriff consented, and everyone fired.

> Black Bart shuddered, then lay deathly still.
> The lad took one look, dropped his gun and fled, screaming,
> "Mommy, mommy! I didn't mean to! I didn't mean to!"

Scholars with a penchant for interpreting signs, symbols, and signifiers could go to town with this incident, pondering the way in which the appeal to "mommy" follows hard and fast on the attempted initiation into the manly sport of gunplay. But my own attention fixes on the line, "I didn't mean to!" Since the child wanted to kill Black Bart, and, with an impressive deference to authority, asked the sheriff for permission to kill him, why would he then make the claim, "I didn't mean to"? His worries of intention and outcome were, in any case, soon ended: "His tears stopped a moment later, however, when he turned and saw Black Bart and Sheriff Lucky walking into the Golden Horseshoe to get ready for their next performance."[3] Rather than feeling soothed, another sort of child might at that moment have conceived a long-range ambition to kill *both* Black Bart and Sheriff Lucky for their complicity in tricking him.

In the twentieth century, as this boy learned, the image of the frontier balances precariously between too much reality and too little. Properly screened and edited, the doings of the Old Frontier are quite a bit of fun. But when encounters with death, or injury, or conflict, or loss become unexpectedly convincing and compelling, then fun can make an abrupt departure, while emotions considerably more troubling take its place.

The outlaw-killing lad was not the only child encountering the limits of Frontierland's fun, not the only one to stumble in the uncertain turf along the border between the imagined and the actual. As the *Saturday Evening Post* writer described it, one "seven-year-old boy was certain he could tell the real from the unreal."

> As they jogged along on the burro ride, the leathery mule-skinner warned, "Look out for them thar cactus plants. Them needles is mighty sharp."
>
> The skeptical boy leaned over and took a swipe at the cactus. On the way to the first-aid station, he decided all was not fantasy at Disneyland. The management has since moved the cactus out of reach.[4]

Moving the cactus—finding the place where its thorns could *look* sharp and scary but not *be* sharp and scary—can serve as a fine representation of the whole process of getting authenticity into the proper adjustment at Frontierland. When too many surprised innocents made visits to the first-aid stand, the frontier was clearly out of alignment, and a repositioning was in order.

And yet, in other parts of Frontierland's turf, wounds and injuries were a taken-for-granted dimension of frontier life. At Tom Sawyer's Island, as the *Saturday Evening Post* writer put it, kids "can fire air-operated, bulletless rifles at the plastic Indians."[5] A writer for the *Reader's Digest* described the same opportunity in 1960: "From the top of a log fort you can sight in with guns on a forest in which Indians lurk. The guns don't fire bullets—they're hydraulically operated—but the recoil is so realistic that you'd never guess they aren't the genuine article."[6]

The Indians of this frontier were not, however, the sort to hold a grudge. Visitors could fire away at the Indians and then move on to a voyage in "Indian canoes paddled by real Indians."[7] "Realness" was not, in this case, an easy matter to arrange. "Wanting authentic Native Americans to paddle canoes full of guests around the rivers of the theme area, Disneyland recruited employees from southwestern tribes," the historian John Findlay writes in his book *Magic Lands*. "These Indians, of course, came from the desert rather than a riverine or lakes environment, so they had to be taught how to paddle canoes by white employees of the park who had learned the skill at summer camp."[8]

Over the decades, life at Frontierland has become, if anything, more confusing for those rare individuals who stop and think about what they are seeing. There is, for instance, the question of the frontier's geographical location. On one side of a path, a roller coaster rushes through a southwestern mesa, carved into a mine. On the other side of the path, the great river, with its stately steamboat, rolls by. Where is the frontier? Evidently where New Mexico borders on the Mississippi River, where western gold and silver miners load their ore directly onto steamboats heading to New Orleans.

In recent times, even the ritualized violence between whites and Indians has become a matter of some awkwardness. On the various rides along the Rivers of America, one passes a settler's cabin, wildly in flames. In my childhood, the guides announced that the cabin was on fire because Indians had attacked it. In current times, the cabin is just on fire, usually without commentary or blame. At the further reaches of cultural change lies the recent experience of an acquaintance: the guide told his group that the cabin was on fire because the settler had been ecologically and environmentally careless.[9]

Consider, as well, the curious politics of the shooting gallery encountered at the entrance to Frontierland. Visitors can take firearm in hand and shoot at a variety of targets—including a railroad train, winding its way through a sculpted landscape. But if you are shooting at a railroad train, then *who*—in this frontier role-play—*are you?* Which side are you on? If you are firing on the train, then you seem to be either a hostile Indian or a murderous and larcenous outlaw. What is going on here? Is the visitor receiving an invitation to play with point of view, to reconsider the whole question of the identity and interests of good guys and bad guys, champions of progress and opponents of progress? Or is this casting of the railroad as target simply the product of Disneyland's designers working under the mandate to create a scene chock-full of the shapes and forms that will say "frontier," with the assumption that any visitor so stimulated visually will fall into step with the mythic patterns of frontier life, pick up a gun, and blast away at whatever is in sight?

If professional Western American historians find themselves conceptually without anchor when they visit Frontierland, the reason is clear: with the possible exception of the suggestion that environmental carelessness produced the settler's cabin fire, the work of academic historians has had virtually no impact either on Disneyland's vision of the frontier or on the thinking of Disneyland's visitors. That cheerful and complete indifference to the work of frontier historians may, in truth, be the secret of the place's success.

11

12

13

14

The Fight for the Frontier in the History Department

In recent years, academic historians have given the idea of the frontier a   15
pretty rough overhauling. Nicknamed the "f-word" and pummeled for its
ethnocentrism and vagueness, the term has from time to time landed on the
ropes, perilously close to conceding the match. But a determined group of
trainers and handlers has always trooped out to the rescue, braced up the
frontier, and gotten it back on its feet for the next round.

The academic boxing match centers on this question: how well does the   16
concept of the frontier perform the task of describing, explaining, and en-
capsulating the story of the colonization of North America? "Miserably," answers one group of historians, of which I happen to be a member.[10] "Pretty
well," responds a different set of historians, "if you make a few adjustments
and realignments in its definition."

The case for the frailty of the "f-word" is an easy one to make. First, built   17
into the idea is an inflexible point of view. For the term to have clear meaning, historians have had to hand their point of view over to the custody of
English-speaking white people. In its clearest and most concrete meaning,
as Richard White has said, the frontier was where white people got scarce—
or, with a friendly amendment, the frontier was where white people got
scared because they were scarce. This perspective has certainly been an important psychological reality in American history, and it is a psychological
reality well worth study. But using the frontier as an analytic concept puts
the historian at risk of adopting the point of view of only one of the contesting groups. Moreover, the frontier came with two sides, the Anglo-American
side and the one labeled "the other side of the frontier." Jammed into the second category were Indians of all tribes (often tribes that fought against each
other as well as against Anglo Americans), long-term Hispano settlers, and
more recent Mexican immigrants. In lived reality, the people on this "other
side of the frontier" did not form anything remotely resembling a united
team or a homogeneous society. Conceptually, neither "side" of the frontier
offered much in the way of accommodations for Asian Americans, who
came from the "wrong" direction, or for African Americans, participants in
the westward movement who encountered a full measure of restrictions and
exclusions. Trying to grasp the enormous human complexity of the American West is not easy under any circumstances, and the effort to reduce a tan-
gle of many-sided encounters to a world defined by a frontier line only
makes a tough task even tougher.

Second, the idea of the frontier runs almost entirely on an east-to-west   18
track. Indeed, to most of its users, the term "frontier" has been a synonym

for the American nation's westward movement. Can such a term do justice to the prior presence of Indian people, to the northward movement of Spanish-speaking people, or the eastward movement of Asians? The east-to-west movement of Anglo Americans and African Americans is enormously important, but so are these movements of other people. Try to wrap the term "frontier" around all these movements, and the poor idea stretches to the point of snapping.

Third, it is nearly impossible to define either the beginning or the ending of a frontier. If one cannot define the beginning or ending of a condition, it is not going to be easy to say when that condition is present and when it is *not* present. Return, for instance, to Frederick Jackson Turner's definition of a frontier, borrowed from the Census Department, as a place where the population numbers fewer than two people per square mile. Then think of a mining rush—where, as soon as the news of the gold or silver gets out, the population instantly exceeds two people per square mile, with enough people to form a camp or a town. By Turner's definition, then, one would have to declare the mining frontier closed virtually the moment it opened.

Other scholars have offered more enterprising, and certainly more colorful, definitions of the closing of the frontier. One of the best comes from the historian Paula Petrik, who studied prostitutes in Helena, Montana. In the early years of Helena, Petrik reports, the prostitutes tended to be their own employers. They were able to hold on to the rewards of their labors, and some of them saved significant amounts of money, owned real estate, and lent money at interest. But then, as the frontier phase passed, men took control of the prostitutes and their earnings. This, I thought when I first heard Petrik's evidence and argument, is the most interesting marker of the end of the frontier I am ever going to hear: the frontier ends when the pimps come to town.[11]

My own entry in the "closing" competition rests on the popularization of tourism and the quaintness of the folk. When Indian war dances became tourist spectacles, when the formerly scorned customs of the Chinese drew tourists to Chinatown, when former out-groups found that characteristics that once earned them disapproval could now earn them a living, when fearful, life-threatening deserts became charming patterns of color and light, the war was over and the frontier could be considered closed, even museumized. But this nomination comes with its own fatal flaw. Let the car break down in the desert, or let the Indians file a lawsuit to reassert an old land claim, and the quaint appeal of nature and native can abruptly vanish. The frontier is suddenly reopened, and the whole question of beginnings and endings becomes unsettled again.

Fourth, a presumption of innocence and exceptionalism is interwoven with the roots of frontier history, as Americans have understood it. The contrast becomes clearest when one thinks of a nation like South Africa. Europeans forcibly took South Africa from the natives, everyone understands, and the residents still struggle with the consequences. But the idea of the frontier permits the United States to make an appeal to innocence and exceptionalism: while South Africa underwent an invasion and a conquest, the United States had an expanding frontier of democracy, opportunity, and equality.

The term "frontier" blurs the fact of conquest and throws a veil over the similarities between the story of American westward expansion and the planetary story of the expansion of European empires. Whatever meanings historians give the term, in popular culture it carries a persistently happy affect, a tone of adventure, heroism, and even fun very much in contrast with the tough, complicated, and sometimes bloody and brutal realities of conquest. Under these conditions, the word "frontier" uses historians before historians can use it. . . .   23

Meanwhile, *La Frontera*

Anglo Americans have fixed their attention on the definition of the frontier drawn from the imaginative reconstruction of the story of the United States and its westward expansion. But North America has, in fact, had two strong traditions in the use of the term. There is the much more familiar, English, usage of the frontier as the place where white settlers entered a zone of "free" land and opportunity. But there is the much less familiar, but much more realistic, usage of *la frontera,* the borderlands between Mexico and the United States. This is not simply a place where two groups meet; Indian people have been influential players in the complicated pattern of human relations in the area. In the nineteenth century, trade, violence, conquest, and cultural exchange punctuated and shaped life in the borderlands. In the twentieth century, with conflicts over the restriction of immigration, with disputes over water flow and environmental pollution, and with a surge of industrial development and population growth from American-owned businesses (*maquiladoras*) operating in northern Mexico, conditions along the border remain far from tranquil.[12]   24

In the idea of *la frontera,* there is no illusion of vacancy, of triumphal conclusions, or of simplicity. As the writer Gloria Anzaldúa puts it, the United States–Mexican border is "where the Third World grates up against the first and bleeds."[13] It is a unique place on the planet's surface, a zone where an industrialized nation shares a long land border with a nation much troubled by poverty. "Ambivalence and unrest," Anzaldúa says, "reside there and death is no stranger."[14] Any temptation to romanticize *la frontera*—as a place of cultural syncretism, a place where the Spanish and English lan-   25 guages have learned to cohabit and even merge—runs aground on the bare misery of poverty in the border towns.[15]

The idea of the frontier is extremely well established as cultural common property. If the idea of *la frontera* had anywhere near the standing of the idea of the frontier, we would be well launched toward self-understanding, directed toward a realistic view of this nation's position in the hemisphere and in the world. "The struggle of borders is our reality still," Anzaldúa writes.[16] One can tinker a bit with that line to draw the crucial contrast: "The adventure of frontiers is our fantasy still; the struggle of borders is our reality still."

In truth, this idea of the frontier as border has made some inroads in popular thinking. If you are reading a headline for a news story set outside the United States, there is a chance that the word "frontier" will carry a meaning completely different from its usual one. References to "the Romania-Bulgaria frontier" or to "the Lebanese-Israeli frontier" are quite a different matter from references to the frontier where the pioneer stands on the edge of vacancy and opportunity. These are frontiers in the old, concrete, down-to-earth sense, much closer in meaning to *la frontera:* borders between countries, between peoples, between authorities, sometimes between armies. When "Algeria and Morocco reopen their frontier," or when the nation of Turkey decides it "will close its frontier with Bulgaria," these are references to borders that are full of possibilities for both cooperation and friction, places where the meaning of "opening" and "closing" differs dramatically from what Frederick Jackson Turner and the director of the census meant in the 1890s.[17]

In these references to international borders and boundaries, the word "frontier" takes a firmer hold on reality. In my collection of headlines, the frequent appearance of this definition of frontier caught me by surprise. Perhaps, it began to seem, there is more hope for this word than seemed possible at first; perhaps popular thinking has already dug a sizable channel for thinking about the frontier in a manner quite different from the *Star Trek* mode.

One other pattern of usage, however, struck me as equally surprising: the omnipresence in headlines of African American pioneers. Here, the usage was again closer to the *Star Trek* definition, with pioneers boldly going where no one like them had gone before. Pioneers in civil rights—"Desegregation's Pioneers"—were everywhere, from A. Philip Randolph to Rosa Parks, from Julian Bond to Charlayne Hunter-Gault. The range of African American pioneers covers a great deal of turf: a Pioneer Black Professional Golfer; a Pioneer of Black Pride; the National Football League's Pioneer Black Coach; a Pioneer Black (Theatrical) Producer; a Pioneer Black Announcer; Negro League Pioneers; a Pioneer Black Ivy League Teacher; a Black Radio Pioneer; a Black Foreign Service Pioneer; a Pioneer Black Los Angeles Judge; a Pioneer Black Journalist; a Pioneer in Black Film; and

26

27

28

29

Sidney Poitier, the winner of the "coveted Pioneer Award," bestowed at the Black Oscar Nominees dinner in 1989. As all these headlines suggest, the idea of calling African American people pioneers, as an appropriately complimentary way to refer to their dignity, courage, and determination in traveling where no black person had gone before, has established itself as part of the American cultural vocabulary. When in 1989 Secretary of Health and Human Services Louis Sullivan "told the graduating class of A. Philip Randolph Campus High School in Manhattan that they will become 'pioneers' if they meet the challenges of fighting inequality, racism, and poverty in the 21st century," Sullivan was employing the term in its standard usage.[18]

30   This usage was so well understood that it gave rise to one of the few cases where a person interviewed in a newspaper article actually engaged and questioned the meaning of the term "pioneer," and its application to him. "National League President Plays Down 'Pioneer' Talk," the headline read. The opening sentence explained, "National League President Bill White says he's getting tired of people referring to him as a black pioneer. . . . 'I'm not a pioneer,' White said. 'Jackie [Robinson] was the pioneer.'"[19] To Bill White, "pioneer" was the term reserved for the unusually courageous person who went first, and the one who faced the worst and the most intense opposition and resistance.

31   The African American applications of the pioneer analogy caught me completely by surprise. They took the ground out from under any remaining inclination I might have had simply to mock the analogy. The lesson of these references is this: the whole package of frontier and pioneer imagery has ended up as widely dispersed intellectual property. One could argue, as I probably at other times *would* have argued, that African Americans would be well advised to keep their distance from the metaphors and analogies of conquest and colonialism, that there are other, and better, ways to say that someone was a person of principle, innovation, and determination without calling him or her a pioneer. Even though they have been significant participants in the westward movement and in the life of the American West in the twentieth century, African Americans barely figured in the traditional tellings of frontier history; the history of pioneering Americans was for far too long a segregated, "whites-only" subject matter.[20] The image of the heroic pioneer was in many ways a vehicle of racial subordination, exalting the triumph of whites over Indians. Jackie Robinson, A. Philip Randolph, and Rosa Parks were people of great courage and spirit, and getting them entangled in the whole inherited myth of Manifest Destiny, nationalistic cheerleading, and justifications for conquest does not seem to be the best way to honor them.

32   But it is a bit too late to avoid that entangling. Greatly troubled by the problem of violence inflicted by blacks against blacks, Rev. Jesse Jackson

pled with people to "Stop the violence!" The campaign to end the violence, he said, is "the new frontier of the civil rights movement."[21] Logic and history say that the frontier was, in fact, a place where violence served the causes of racial subordination, but a more powerful emotional understanding says that the frontier is where people of courage have gone to take a stand for the right and the good. For people of a wide range of ethnicities, when it comes to the idea of the frontier, logic and history yield to the much greater power of inherited image.

This is the curious conclusion that these headlines forced upon me: a   33 positive image of the frontier and the pioneer is now implanted in nearly everyone's mind. It would not surprise me to see headlines referring to an American Indian lawyer as "a pioneer in the assertion of Indian legal rights," "pushing forward the frontier of tribal sovereignty"—even though it was the historical pioneers who assaulted those rights, even though it was the pioneers' historical frontier that charged head-on into tribal sovereignty. And yet Indian people have adopted any number of items introduced by whites. They wear cowboy hats, drive pickup trucks and automobiles, shop in supermarkets, study constitutional law in law schools, and remain Indian. In all sorts of ways, Indian people put Anglo-American artifacts, mental and physical, to use for Indian purposes. There is no very convincing argument for saying they must put a stop to their adopting and incorporating when it comes to the idea of the frontier and the image of the pioneer.

The historian Arthur Schlesinger, Jr., and many others have recently   34 lamented "the disuniting of America" through the expansion of multicultural history.[22] We hear frequent expressions of nostalgia for an imagined era of unity, before an emphasis on race, class, and gender divided Americans into contesting units and interests. Reading several thousand headlines about pioneers and frontiers, however, convinced me that matters are by no means as disunited as the lamenters think. When African Americans turn comfortably to the image of the pioneer, then the idea of the frontier and the pioneer have clearly become a kind of multicultural common property, a joint-stock company of the imagination. As encounters with scholars from other countries usually demonstrate, this is not just multicultural, this is international. People from the Philippines, people from Senegal, people from Thailand, people with plenty of reasons to resent the frontier and cowboy diplomacy inflicted on their nations by our nation: many of them nonetheless grew up watching western movies and yearning for life on the Old Frontier and the open range.[23]

As a mental artifact, the frontier has demonstrated an astonishing sticki-   35 ness and persistence. It is virtually the flypaper of our mental world; it attaches itself to everything—healthful diets, space shuttles, civil rights campaigns, heart transplants, industrial product development, musical innovations. Packed full of nonsense and goofiness, jammed with nationalistic self-congratulation and toxic ethnocentrism, the image of the frontier is nonetheless universally recognized, and laden with positive associations. Whether or not it suits my preference, the concept works as a cultural glue— a mental and emotional fastener that, in some very curious and unexpected ways, works to hold us together.

The frontier of an expanding and confident nation; the frontier of cultural interpenetration; the frontier of contracting rural settlement; the frontier of science, technology, and space; the frontier of civil rights where black pioneers ventured and persevered; the frontiers between nations in Europe, Asia, and Africa; *la frontera* of the Rio Grande and the deserts of the southwestern United States and northern Mexico: somewhere in this weird hodgepodge of frontier and pioneer imagery lie important lessons about the American identity, sense of history, and direction for the future. Standing in the way of a full reckoning with those lessons, however, is this fact: in the late *twentieth* century, the scholarly understanding formed in the late *nineteenth* century still governs most of the public rhetorical uses of the word "frontier"; the vision of Frederick Jackson Turner still governs the common and conventional understandings of the term. If the movement of ideas from frontier historians to popular culture maintains its velocity, sometime in the next century we might expect the popular usage of the word to begin to reckon with the complexity of the westward movement and its consequences. Somewhere in the mid-2000s the term might make a crucial shift, toward the reality of *la frontera* and away from the fantasy of the frontier. And that shift in meaning, *if* it occurs, will mark a great change in this nation's understanding of its own origins. 36

NOTES

I would like to thank Kim Gruenwald, Stephen Sturgeon, and Jon Coleman for their help in following the trail of the frontier. I would also like to thank my colleague Mark Pittenger, whose book *American Socialists and Evolutionary Thought, 1870–1920* (Madison: University of Wisconsin Press, 1993) showed me how to think about the habits, ways, and customs of analogy-users.

1. In Frederick Jackson Turner, *The Frontier in American History* (1920; rpt. Tucson: University of Arizona Press, 1986), 2.

2. David M. Wrobel, *The End of American Exceptionalism: Frontier Anxiety from the Old West to the New Deal* (Lawrence: University Press of Kansas, 1993), 145.

3. Robert Cahn, "The Intrepid Kids of Disneyland," *Saturday Evening Post,* June 18, 1958, 22–23.

4. Ibid., 120.

5. Ibid., 119.

6. Ira Wolfert, "Walt Disney's Magic Kingdom," *Reader's Digest,* April 1960, 147.

7. Ibid., 147.

8. John M. Findlay, *Magic Lands: Western Cityscapes and American Culture after 1940* (Berkeley: University of California Press, 1992), 93–94.

9. Change seems to have been equally dramatic in Disney thinking about Indians. In 1993, the Walt Disney Company announced plans for a new American history theme park in Virginia. The section called "Native America," one company representative said, would now display "the sophisticated, intelligent societies that existed here before European settlers came, and in fact wiped out their societies" (Michael Wines, "Disney Will 'Recreate' U.S. History next to a Place Where It Was Made," *New York Times,* November 12, 1993).

10. See Patricia Nelson Limerick, Clyde A. Milner II, and Charles E. Rankin, eds., *Trails: Toward a New Western History* (Lawrence: University Press of Kansas, 1991).

11. Paula Petrik, *No Step Backward* (Helena: Montana Historical Society Press, 1987), chapter 2, "Capitalists with Rooms: Prostitution in Helena, 1865–1900," 25–58. [Notes no. 12 through no. 37, which relate to a portion of the essay not printed in this text, have been omitted.]

12. See Oscar J. Martínez, *Troublesome Border* (Tucson: University of Arizona Press, 1986); Mario T. García, "La Frontera: The Border as Symbol and Reality in Mexican-American Thought," *Mexican Studies,* Summer 1985, 195–225; Alan Weisman and Jay Dusard, *La Frontera: The United States Border with Mexico* (Tucson: University of Arizona Press, 1986); Tom Miller, *On the Border: Portraits of America's Southwestern Frontier* (New York: Harper and Row, 1981).

13. Gloria Anzaldúa, *Borderlands/La Frontera: The New Mestiza* (San Francisco: Aunt Lute Books, 1987), 3.

14. Ibid., 4.

15. See Luis Alberto Urrea, *Across the Wire: Life and Hard Times on the Mexican Border* (New York: Doubleday, 1993).

16. Anzaldúa, *Borderlands/La Frontera,* 63.

17. "Thousands Form Human Chain across Romania-Bulgaria Frontier," Reuters, June 8, 1990; "Palestinian Guerrilla is Killed at Lebanese-Israeli Frontier," *New York Times,* September 6, 1989; "Algeria and Morocco Reopen their Frontier," Reuters, June 5, 1988; Jim Bodgener, "Turkey Will Close its Frontier with Bulgaria Today," *Financial Times,* August 22, 1989.

18. David Maraniss, "Memories in Black and White; Desegregation's Pioneers," *Washington Post,* June 6, 1990; "Genevieve Stuttaford Reviews *A. Philip Randolph: Pioneer of the Civil Rights Movement,*" *Publishers Weekly,* May 11, 1990; "Rights Pioneer Parks Hospitalized," *Los Angeles Times,* February 2, 1989; "City in Ohio Honors Civil Rights Pioneer," *Chicago Tribune,* May 11, 1990; Tanya Barrientos, "Civil Rights Pioneer Julian Bond Perplexed by Persistence of Racism," *Philadelphia Inquirer,* May 9, 1992; David Treadwell, "She is the First Black to Give Commencement Address: Integration Pioneer Returns to Speak at U. of Georgia," *Los Angeles Times,* June 12, 1988; "Thelma Cowans, Pioneer Black Professional Golfer, Dies," United Press International, February 7, 1990; Rosemary L. Bray, "Renaissance for a Pioneer of Black Pride," *New York Times,* February 4, 1990; G. D. Clay, "First, There Was

Fritz; Long before Art Shell, Pollard was NFL's Pioneer Black Coach," *Newsday,* December 20, 1989; "Didi Daniels Peter; Pioneer Black Producer," *Los Angeles Times,* March 2, 1989; "Joseph W. Bostic: Pioneer Black Announcer," *Los Angeles Times,* June 2, 1988; Charles Fountain, "A Baseball Historian Goes to Bat for Some Negro League Greats: Blackball Stars: Negro League Pioneers," *Christian Science Monitor,* April 15, 1988; C. Gerald Fraser, "J. Saunders Redding, 81, Is Dead; Pioneer Black Ivy League Teacher," *New York Times,* March 5, 1988; David Mills, "Tuned In to Jockey Jack; Tribute to a Black Radio Pioneer," *Washington Post,* June 23, 1990; "Clifton R. Wharton Sr. Dies; Foreign Service Pioneer," *Jet,* May 14, 1990; "Pioneer Black L.A. Judge Edwin Jefferson Dies at 84," *Jet,* September 18, 1989; "Pioneer Black Journalist Albert J. Dunsmore, 73, Praised at Detroit Rites," *Jet,* February 20, 1989; Tia Swanson, "A Pioneer in World of Black Film," *Philadelphia Inquirer,* June 4, 1992; "Black Oscar Nominees Gala Celebrates Movie Talents (Sidney Poitier Wins Pioneer Award)," *Jet,* April 17, 1989; Gene Siskel, "Poitier the Pioneer: He's Back on Screen—and Taking a Second Look at a Life Full of Firsts," *Chicago Tribune,* January 31, 1988; Nick Jesdanun, "'Pioneer' Futures," *Newsday,* June 24, 1989.

19. "NL President Plays Down 'Pioneer' Talk," *Chicago Tribune,* May 16, 1989. See also "NL Boss Won't Wear Pioneer Tag," *USA Today,* May 16, 1989.

20. The first efforts at including African Americans within Western American history left the framework of traditional frontier history unchallenged. In the introduction to the first edition of *The Black West* (1971; rpt. Seattle, Wash.: Open Hand Publishing, 1987), William Loren Katz remarked, "When historian Frederick Jackson Turner told how the frontier shaped American democracy, he ignored the black experience—not because it challenged his central thesis, but because he wrote in a tradition that had denied the existence of black people" (xii). By the time of a later edition, Katz was developing a more critical approach; consider this remark from the 1987 introduction:

> A U.S. Army that treated its Buffalo Soldiers [African American men enlisted in the post–Civil War western army] shabbily and cynically buried their military record, has accepted an image rehabilitation and trumpeted black heroism the better to recruit despairing, unemployed black youths. Will it, in the name of troopers who battled Apaches, Sioux and Commanches, train dark young men to stem Third World liberation forces? This would be a tragic misuse of the past. (xi)

See also William Leckie, *The Buffalo Soldiers* (Norman: University of Oklahoma Press, 1967). The recent issuing of a United States Post Office stamp commemorating the Buffalo Soldiers puts an unintended spotlight on the question of the African American role in conquest; see "Part of America's Past Becomes a Stamp of Tomorrow," *New York Times,* December 8, 1993.

21. Don Terry, "A Graver Jackson's Cry: Overcome the Violence!" *New York Times,* November 11, 1993.

22. Arthur Schlesinger, Jr., *The Disuniting of America: Reflections on a Multicultural Society* (New York: Whittle Books, 1991).

23. These impressions come from a number of speaking engagements with United States Information Agency tour groups, where international scholars have told me about their early encounters with the American frontier myth.

Working with the Text

1. What does the term "frontier" mean to you? What are some of the different definitions of "frontier" that Limerick explores and invokes? Which of Limerick's different definitions comes closest to the images conjured in your mind by the word "frontier"?

2. What point is Limerick trying to make in her discussion about "Frontierland" at Disneyland? What does she mean by the "uncertain turf along the border between the imagined and the actual?" How does she extend her point about Frontierland to her broader discussion of the role of the "frontier" in twentieth-century American culture?

3. What is the relationship between images of the American "frontier" and American values? Which American values or characteristics do the imagery and mythology of the frontier implicate? How are they invoked and used, for example, by American presidents and politicians?

4. Why is Limerick bothered initially by the use of the terms "pioneer" and "frontier" in African-American contexts? How does she resolve this in her own mind? Do you think that her concerns about language are legitimate? Does the historical meaning of words matter if there are popular meanings that are simpler or less problematic?

5. Near the end of the article, Limerick says, "If the idea of *la frontera* had anywhere near the standing of the idea of the frontier, we would be well launched toward self-understanding, directed toward a realistic view of this nation's position in the hemisphere and in the world." What is the difference between "the frontier" and "*la frontera*"? How in Limerick's eyes are "borders" different from the American "frontier"? In a paper, explore which ideas or assumptions are present in the traditional notion of the frontier that are not applicable or operative in an analysis of borders or the borderlands.

At the Buffalo Bill Museum— June 1988

JANE TOMPKINS

A professor of English at Duke University in North Carolina, Jane Tompkins has approached literary study from a cultural perspective. She is more interested in what novels and stories and poems tell us about the cultures that produced them than in the works as discrete artistic productions. Tompkins has also often written from a highly personal perspective, linking her own experiences to the works she studies. Rather than drawing firm conclusions, she admits her inability to resolve contradictory responses. Her books include *Sensational Designs* (1985), *A Life in School* (1996), and *West of Everything: The Inner Life of Westerns* (1992), which examines historical images of the American West as filtered through popular culture. In the following essay, which became a part of that book, she focuses on a Western icon whose legacy suggests the many contradictory images we have of the coming together of cultures in the American West.

The video at the entrance to the Buffalo Bill Historical Center tells us that   1
Buffalo Bill was the most famous American of his time, that by 1900 over a billion words had been written about him, and that he had a progressive vision of the West. Buffalo Bill had worked as a cattle driver, a wagoneer, a Pony Express rider, a buffalo hunter for the railroad, a hunting guide, an army scout and sometime Indian fighter; he wrote dime novels about himself and an autobiography at the age of thirty-three, by which time he was already famous; and then he began another set of careers—first he became an actor, performing on the urban stage in wintertime melodramatic representations of what he actually earned a living at in the summer (scouting and leading hunting expeditions), and finally he became the impresario of the Wild West show, a form of entertainment which he invented and carried on as actor, director, and all-around idea man for thirty years. Toward the end of his life he founded the town of Cody, Wyoming, to which he gave, among other things, $200,000. Strangely enough, it was as a progressive civic leader that Bill Cody wanted to be remembered. "I don't want to die," the video at the entrance tells us he said, "and have people say—oh, there

goes another old showman. . . . I would like people to say—this is the man who opened Wyoming to the best of civilization."

The best of civilization. This was the phrase that rang in my head as I 2 moved through the museum, which is one of the most disturbing places I have ever visited. It is also a wonderful place. It is four museums in one: the Whitney Gallery of Western Art, which houses art works on western subjects; the Buffalo Bill Museum proper, which memorializes Cody's life; the Plains Indian Museum, which exhibits artifacts of American Indian civilization; and the Winchester Arms Museum, a collection of firearms, historically considered.

The whole operation is extremely well designed and well run, from the 3 video program at the entrance that gives an overview of all four museums, to the fresh-faced young attendants wearing badges that say "Ask Me," to the museum shop stacked with books on western Americana, to the ladies' room—a haven of satiny marble, shining mirrors, and flattering light. Among other things, the museum is admirable for its effort to combat prevailing stereotypes about the so-called "winning of the West," a phrase it self-consciously places in quotation marks. There are placards declaring that all history is a matter of interpretation, and that the American West is a source of "myth." Everywhere except, perhaps, in the Winchester Arms Museum, where the rhetoric is different, you feel the effort of the museum staff to reach out to the public, to be clear, to be accurate, to be fair, not to condescend, in short, to educate in the best sense of the term.

On the day I went, the museum was featuring an exhibition of Frederic 4 Remington's works. There are two facts about these productions that make them different from those of artists one is used to encountering in museums. The first is that Remington's paintings and statues function as a historical record. Their chief attraction has always been that they transcribe scenes and events that have vanished from the earth. The second fact, related to this, is the brutality of their subject matter. Remington's work makes you pay attention to *what is happening* in the painting or the piece of statuary. When you look at his work you cannot escape from its subject.

Consequently, as I moved through the exhibit, the wild contortions of 5 the bucking broncos, the sinister expression invariably worn by the Indians, and the killing of animals and men made the placards discussing Remington's use of the "lost wax" process seem strangely disconnected. In the face of unusual violence, or implied violence, their message was: what is important here is technique. Except in the case of paintings showing the battle of San Juan Hill, where white Americans were being killed, the material accompanying Remington's works did not refer to the subject matter of the paintings and statues. Nevertheless, an undertone of disquiet ran beneath the explanations; at least I thought I detected one. Someone had taken the trouble to ferret out Remington's statement of horror at the slaughter on San Juan Hill; someone had also excerpted the judgment of art critics commending Remington for the lyricism, interiority, and mystery of his later canvases—pointing obliquely to the fascination with bloodshed that preoccupied his earlier work.

The uneasiness of the commentary, and my uneasiness with it, were   6
nothing compared to the blatant contradictions in the paintings themselves. A pastel palette, a sunlit stop-action haze, murderous movement arrested under a lazy sky, flattened onto canvas and fixed in azure and ocher—two opposed impulses nestle here momentarily; the tension that keeps them from splitting apart is what holds the viewer's gaze.

The most excruciating example of what I mean occurs in the first paint-   7
ing in the exhibit. Entitled *His First Lesson,* it shows a horse standing saddled but riderless while a man pierces it just below the shoulder with a sharp instrument. The white of the horse's eye signals his pain. The man who is doing the piercing is simultaneously backing away from the reaction he clearly anticipates, and the man who holds the horse's halter is doing the same. But what can they be afraid of? For the horse's right rear leg is tied a foot off the ground by a rope that is also tied around his neck. He can't move. That is the whole point.

"His First Lesson." Whose? And what lesson, exactly? How to stay still   8
and stand pain? How not to break away when they come at you with sharp instruments? How to be obedient? How to behave? It is impossible not to imagine that Remington's obsession with physical cruelty had roots somewhere in his own experience. Why else, in statue after statue, is the horse rebelling? The bucking bronco—symbol of the state of Wyoming, on every license plate, on every sign for every bar, on every belt buckle, mug, and decal—this image Remington cast in bronze over and over again. There is a wild diabolism in the bronzes; the horse and rider seem one thing, not so much rider and ridden as a single bolt of energy gone crazy and caught somehow, complicatedly, in a piece of metal.

In the paintings it is different, more subtle and bizarre. The cavalry on   9
its way to a massacre, sweetly limned, softly tinted, poetically seized in mid-career, and gently laid on the two-dimensional surface. There is about these paintings of military men in the course of their deadly duty an almost maternal tenderness. The idealization of the cavalrymen in their dusty uniforms on their gallant horses has nothing to do with patriotism; it is pure love.

Remington's paintings and statues, as shown in this exhibition, embody   10
everything that was objectionable about his era in American history. They are imperialist and racist; they glorify war and the torture and killing of animals; there are no women in them anywhere. Never the West as garden, never as pastoral, never as home. But in their aestheticizing of violent life

Remington's pictures speak (to me at least) of some other desire. The maternal tenderness is not an accident, nor the beauty of the afternoons, nor the warmth of the desert sun. In these paintings Remington plays the part of the preserver, as if by catching the figures in color and line he could save their lives, and absorb some of that life into himself.

In one painting that particularly repulsed and drew me, a moose is out-   11
lined against the evening sky at the brink of a lake. He looks expectantly into the distance. Behind him and to one side, hidden from his view, and only just revealed to ours, for it is dark there, is a hunter poised in the back of a canoe, rifle perfectly aimed. We look closer; the title of the picture is *Coming to the Call*. Ah, now we see. This is a sadistic scene. The hunter has lured the moose to his death. But wait a moment. Isn't the sadism really directed at us? First we see the glory of the animal; Remington has made it as noble as he knows how. Then we see what is going to happen. The hunter is one up on the moose but Remington is one up on us. He makes us feel the pain of the anticipated killing, and makes us want to hold it off, to preserve the moose, just as he has done. Which way does the painting cut? Does it go against the hunter—who represents us, after all—or does it go against the moose, who came to the call? Who came, to what call? Did Remington come to the West in response to it—to whatever the moose represents, or to whatever the desire to kill the moose represents? But he hasn't killed it; he has only preserved an image of a white man about to kill it. And what call do we answer when we look at this painting? Who is calling whom? What is being preserved here? That is the question that for me hung over the whole museum.

The Whitney Gallery is an art museum: its allegiance is to "art" as our   12
academic tradition has defined it. In this tradition, we come to understand a painting by having in our possession various bits of information. Something about the technical process used to produce it (pastels, watercolors, woodblock prints, etc.); something about the elements of composition—line and color and movement; something about the artist's life (where born, how educated, by whom influenced, which school belonged to or revolted against); something about his relation to this particular subject, such as how many times he painted it, or whether it contains his favorite model. Occasionally there will be some philosophizing about the themes or ideas the paintings are said to represent.

The problem is, when you're faced with a painter like Remington, these   13
bits of information, while nice to have, don't explain what is there in front of you. They don't begin to give you an account of why a person should have depicted such things. The experience of a lack of fit between the explanatory material and what is there on the wall is one I've had before in museums, when, standing in front of a painting or a piece of statuary, I've

felt a huge gap between the information on the little placard and what it is I'm seeing. I realize that "works of art," so-called, all have a subject matter, are all engaged with life, with some piece of life no less significant, no less compelling than Remington's subjects are, if we could only see its force. The idea that art is somehow separate from history, that it somehow occupies a space that is not the same as the space of life, seems out of whack here.

I wander through the gallery thinking these things because right next to   14
it, indeed all around it, in the Buffalo Bill Museum and in the Plains Indian Museum, are artifacts that stand not for someone's expertise or skill in manipulating the elements of an artistic medium, but for life itself; they are the residue of life.

The Buffalo Bill Museum envelops you in an array of textures, colors,   15
shapes, sizes, forms. The fuzzy brown bulk of a buffalo's hump, the sparkling diamonds in a stickpin, the brilliant colors of the posters—there's something about the cacophonous mixture that makes you want to walk in and be surrounded by it, as if you were going into a child's adventure story. It all appeals to the desire to be transported, to pretend for a little while that we're cowboys or cowgirls; it's a museum where fantasy can take over. In this respect, it is true to the character of Buffalo Bill's life.

As I moved through the exhibition, "the best of civilization" was the   16
phrase that rang through my head, and particularly I thought of it as I looked at certain objects on display in a section of the museum that recreates rooms from Cody's house. Ostrich and peacock feather fans, a chair and a table made entirely of antlers, a bearskin rug. Most of all, I thought of the phrase as I looked at the heads on the wall: Alaska Yukon moose, Wapiti American elk, musk-ox (the "Whitney," the "DeRham"), mountain caribou (the "Hyland"), Quebec Labrador caribou (the "Elbow"), Rocky Mountain goat (the "Haase," the "Kilto"), woodland caribou (world's record, "DeRham"), the "Rogers" freak Wapiti, the "Whitney" bison, the "Lord Rundlesham" bison. The names that appear after the animals are the names of the men who killed them. Each of the animals is scored according to measurements devised by the Boone and Crockett Club, a big-game hunters' organization. The Lord Rundlesham bison, for example, scores 124⅝, making it number 25 in the world for bison trophies. The "Reed" Alaska Yukon moose scores 247. The "Witherbee" Canada moose holds the world's record.

Next to the wall of trophies is a small enclosure where jewelry is dis-   17
played: a buffalo-head stickpin and two buffalo-head rings, the heads made entirely of diamonds, with ruby eyes, the gifts of the Russian Crown Prince; a gold and diamond stickpin from Edward VII; a gold, diamond, and garnet locket from Queen Victoria. The two kinds of trophies—animals and jew-

els—form an incongruous set, the relationship between them compelling but obscure.

If the rest of the items in the museum—the dime novels with their out-   18
rageous covers, the marvelous posters, the furniture, Cody's wife's dress, his daughter's oil painting—if these have faded in my mind, it is because I cannot forget the heads of the animals as they stared down, each with an individual expression on its face. When I think about it I realize that I don't know why these animals' heads are there. Buffalo Bill didn't kill them; perhaps they were gifts from the famous people he took on hunts. A different kind of jewelry.

After the heads, I began to notice something about the whole exhibition.   19
In one display, doghide chaps, calfskin chaps, Angora goatskin chaps, and horsehide chaps. Next to these a rawhide lariat and a horsehair quirt. Behind me, boots and saddles, all of leather. Everywhere I looked there was tooth or bone, skin or fur, hide or hair, or the animal itself entire—two full-size buffaloes (a main feature of the exhibition) and a magnificent stone sheep (a mountain sheep with beautiful curving horns). This one was another world's record. The best of civilization.

In the literature about Buffalo Bill you read that he was a conservation-   20
ist, that if it were not for the buffaloes in his Wild West shows, the species might have become extinct. (In the seventeenth century, 40 million wild buffalo roamed North America; by 1900 all the wild buffalo had been killed except for one herd in northern Alberta.) That the man who gained fame first as a buffalo hunter should have been an advocate for conservation of the buffalo is not an anomaly but typical of the period. The men who did the most to preserve America's natural wilderness and its wildlife were big-game hunters. The Boone and Crockett Club, founded by Theodore Roosevelt, George Bird Grinnell, and Owen Wister, turns out to have been one of the earliest organizations to devote itself to environmental protection in the United States. The *Readers' Encyclopaedia of the American West* says that the club "supported the national park and forest reserve movement, helped create a system of national wildlife refuges, and lobbied for the protection of threatened species, such as the buffalo and antelope." At the same time, the prerequisites for membership in the club were "the highest caliber of sportsmanship and the achievement of killing 'in fair chase' trophy specimens [which had to be adult males] from several species of North American big game."

The combination big-game hunter/conservationist suggests that these   21
men had no interest in preserving the animals for the animals' sake but simply wanted to ensure the chance to exercise their sporting pleasure. But I think this view is too simple; something further is involved here. The men

who hunted game had a kind of love for game and a kind of love for nature which led them to want to preserve the animals which they also desired to kill. That is, the desire to kill the animals was in some way related to a desire to see them live. It is not an accident, in this connection, that Theodore Roosevelt, Owen Wister, and Frederic Remington all originally went west for reasons of health. Their devotion to the West, their connection to it, their love for it, is rooted in their need to reanimate their own lives. The preservation of nature, in other words, becomes for them symbolic of their own survival.

In a sense, then, there is a relationship between the Remington exhibition in the Whitney Gallery and the animal memorabilia in the Buffalo Bill Museum. The moose in *Coming to the Call* and the moose heads on the wall are not so different as they might appear. The heads on the wall serve an aesthetic purpose; they are decorative objects, pleasing to the eye, which call forth certain associations. In this sense they are like visual works of art. The painting, on the other hand, has something of the trophy about it. The moose as Remington painted it is about to *become* a trophy, yet in another sense it already is one. Remington has simply captured the moose in another form. In both cases the subject matter, the life of a wild animal, symbolizes the life of the observer. It is the preservation of that life which both the painting and the taxidermy serve.

What are museums keeping safe for us, after all? What is it that we wish so much to preserve? The things that we put in safekeeping, that we put in our safe-deposit boxes and keep under lock and key, are always in some way intended finally as safeguards of our own existence. The money and jewelry and stock certificates are meant for a time when we can no longer earn a living. Similarly, the objects in museums preserve for us a source of life from which we need to nourish ourselves when the resources that would normally supply us have run dry.

The Buffalo Bill Historical Center, full as it is of dead bones, lets us see more clearly than we normally can what it is that museums are for. It is a kind of charnel house that houses images of living things that have passed away but whose life force still lingers around their remains and so passes itself on to us. We go and look at the objects in the glass cases and at the paintings on the wall, as if by standing there we could absorb into ourselves some of the energy that flowed once through the bodies of the live things represented. A museum, rather than being, as we normally think of it, the most civilized of places, a place most distant from our savage selves, actually caters to the urge to absorb the life of another into one's own life.

To give the idea its most extreme form, museums are a form of cannibalism made safe for polite society. If we see the Buffalo Bill Museum in this way, it is no longer possible to separate ourselves from the hunters respon-

Library Resource Center
Renton Technical College
3000 N.E. 4th St.
Renton, WA 98056

sible for the trophies with their wondering eyes or from the curators who put them there. We are not, in essence, different from Teddy Roosevelt, or Frederic Remington, or Buffalo Bill, who killed animals when they were abundant in the Wild West of the 1880s. If, in doing so, those men were practicing the ancient art of absorbing the life of an animal into their own through the act of killing it, realizing themselves through the destruction of another life, then we are not so different from them as visitors to the museum. We stand beside the bones and skins and hooves of beings that were once alive, or stare fixedly at their painted images. Indeed our visit is only a safer form of the same enterprise.

So I did not get out of the Buffalo Bill Museum unscathed, unimplicated   26
in the acts of rapine and carnage which these remains represent. And I did not get out without having had a good time, either, because however many dire thoughts I may have had, the exhibits were interesting and fun to see. I was even able to touch a piece of buffalo hide they have displayed especially for that purpose (it was coarse and springy). Everyone else had touched it, too. The hair was worn down, where people's hands had been, to a fraction of its original length.

After this, the Plains Indian Museum was a terrible letdown. I went from one   27
exhibit to another expecting to become absorbed, but nothing worked. What was the matter? I thought I was interested in Indians, had read about them, taught some Indian literature, felt drawn to their religion. I had been prepared to enter this museum as if I were going into another children's story, only this time I would be an Indian instead of a cowboy or a cowgirl. But the objects on display, most of them behind glass, seemed paltry and insignificant. They lacked visual presence somehow. The bits of leather and sticks of wood triggered no fantasies in me. I couldn't make anything of them.

At the same time, I noticed with some discomfort that almost everything   28
in those glass cases was made of feathers and claws and hide, just like the men's chaps and ladies' fans in the Buffalo Bill Museum, only there was no luxury here. Plains Indian culture, it seemed, was made entirely from animals. Their mode of life had been completely dependent on animals for food, clothing, shelter, equipment, everything. In the Buffalo Bill Museum I was able to say to myself: Well, if these men had been more sensitive, if they had had a right relation to their environment and to life itself, the atrocities that produced their trophies would never have occurred. They never would have exterminated the Indians and killed off the buffalo. But faced with the spectacle before me, it wasn't possible to say just what a right relation to the environment might be. I had expected that the Plains Indian Museum would show me how life in nature ought to be lived: not the wholesale destruction

practiced by Euro-Americans, but an ideal form of communion with animals and the land. What the museum seemed to say, on the contrary, was that both colonizer and colonized had had their hands imbrued with blood. The Indians had lived off animals and had made war against each other. Violence was simply a necessary and inevitable part of life. There was no such thing as the life lived in non-violent harmony with nature. It was all bloodshed and killing, an unending cycle, over and over again, and no one could escape.

But perhaps there was a way to understand the violence that made it   29
less terrible. Perhaps if violence was necessary, a part of nature, intended by the universe, then it could be seen as sacramental. Perhaps it was true what Calvin Martin had said in *Keepers of the Game:* that the Indians had a sacred contract with the animals they killed, that they respected them as equals and treated their remains with honor and punctilio. If so, the remains of animals in the Plains Indian Museum weren't the same as those left by Buffalo Bill and his friends. They certainly didn't look the same. All I knew for certain was that these artifacts, lifeless and shrunken, spoke to me of nothing I could understand. No more did the life-size models of Indians, with strange featureless faces, draped in costumes that didn't look like clothing. The figures, posed awkwardly in front of tepees too white to seem real, carried no sense of a life actually lived, any more than the objects in the glass cases had.

The more I read the placards on the wall, the more disaffected I be-   30
came. Plains Indian life, apparently, had been not only bloody but exceedingly tedious. All those porcupine quills painstakingly softened, flattened, dyed, then appliquéd through even more laborious methods of stitching or weaving. Four methods of attaching porcupine quills, six design groups, population statistics, patterns of migration. There wasn't any glamour here at all. No glamour in the lives the placards told about, no glamour in the objects themselves, no glamour in the experience of looking at them. Just a lot of shriveled things accompanied by some even drier information.

Could it be, then, that the problem with the exhibitions was that Plains   31
Indian culture, if representable at all, was simply not readable by someone like me? Their stick figures and abstract designs could, by definition, convey very little to a Euro-American eye trained to know what glamour is by slick magazines. One display in particular seemed to illustrate this. It was a piece of cloth, behind glass, depicting a buffalo skin with marks on it. The placard read: "Winter Count, Sioux ca. 1910, after Lone Dog's, Fort Peck, Montana, 1877." The hide with its markings, now copied onto cloth, had been a calendar, each year represented by one image, showing the most significant event in the life of the tribe. To one side of the glass case was a book-length pamphlet explaining each image, year by year: 1800–1801, the attack of the Uncapoo on a Crow Indian fort; 1802–1803, a total eclipse of the sun. The

images, once you knew what they represented, made sense, and seemed poetic interpretations of the experiences they stood for. But without explanation they were incomprehensible, empty.

The Plains Indian Museum just stopped me in my tracks. It was written in a language I had never learned. I didn't have the key. Maybe someone did, but I wasn't too sure.   32

For it may not have been just cultural difference that made the text unreadable. I began to suspect that the text itself was corrupt. That the architects of this museum were going through motions whose purpose was, even to themselves, obscure. Knowing what event a figure stands for in the calendar doesn't mean you understand an Indian year. The deeper purpose of the museum began to puzzle me. What is an Indian museum for, anyway? Why should we be bothering to preserve the vestiges of a people whose culture we had effectively extinguished? Wasn't there an air of bad faith about this? Did the museum exist to assuage our guilt and not for any educational reason? I did not and do not have an answer to these questions. All I know is that I felt I was in the presence of something pious and a little insincere. It had the aura of a failed attempt at virtue, as though the curators were trying to present, as interesting, objects whose purpose and meaning even they could not fully imagine.   33

In a last-ditch attempt to salvage something, I went up to one of the guards and asked where the movie was showing that the video had advertised, the movie about Plains Indian life. "Oh, the slide show, you mean," he said. "It's been discontinued." When I asked why, he said he didn't know. It occurred to me then that that was the message the museum was sending, if I could read it—that that was the bottom line. Discontinued, no reason given.   34

The movie in the Winchester Arms Museum, "Lock, Stock, and Barrel," was going strong. The film began with the introduction of the cannon into European warfare in the Middle Ages, and was working its way slowly toward the nineteenth century when I left. I was in a hurry. Soon my husband would be waiting for me in the lobby. Trying to get a quick impression of the objects on display, I went from room to room, but the objects in this museum repelled me even more than the artifacts in the Indian museum had. They were all the same: guns, guns, and more guns. Some large drawings and photographs on the walls tried to give a sense of the context in which the arms had been used, but the effect was nil. It was case after case of rifles and pistols, repeating themselves over and over, and even when some slight variation caught my eye the differences meant nothing to me.   35

But the statistics that accompanied a display of commemorative rifles did mean something. I saw the Antlered Game Commemorative Carbine. Date of manufacture: 1978. Number produced: 19,999. How many antlered   36 animals had each carbine killed? I saw the Canadian Centennial, 1962, 90,000; the Legendary Lawman, 1978, 19,999; the John Wayne, 1980–81, 51,600. Like the titles of the various sections of the museum, these names had a message. The message was: guns are patriotic. Associated with national celebrations, law enforcement, and cultural heroes, the firearms were made to seem inseparable from the march of American history: Firearms in Colonial America; Born in America: The Kentucky Rifle; The Era of Expansion and Invention; The Civil War: Firearms of the Conflict; The Golden Age of Hunting; Winning the West. The guns embodied phases of the history they had helped to make, and the fact that firearms had *had* a history seemed to consecrate them, to make them worth not only preserving but revering.

Awe and admiration are the attitudes the museum invites. You hear the   37
ghostly march of military music in the background; you imagine flags waving and sense the implicit reference to feats of courage in battle and glorious death. The place had the air of an enormous reliquary, or of the room off the transept of a cathedral where the vestments are kept. These guns were not there merely to be seen or even studied; they were there to be venerated.

But I did not look closely. I did not try to appreciate the guns. Uncon-   38
sciously, I said to myself, my ability to empathize, to extend myself toward the virtues of an alien craft, ends here. For here in the basement the instruments that had produced the hides and horns upstairs, and had massacred the Indians, were being lovingly displayed. And we were still making them. Fifty-one thousand six hundred John Waynes in 1980–81. Arms were going strong.

As I bought my books and postcards in the gift shop, I noticed a sign that   39
read, "Rodeo Tickets Sold Here," and something clicked into place. So that was it. *Everything* was still going strong. The whole museum was just another rodeo, only with the riders and their props stuffed, painted, sculpted, immobilized, and put under glass. Like the rodeo, the museum witnessed a desire to bring back the United States of the 1880s and 1890s. The quotation marks around the phrase "the winning of the West," the statements about myth and interpretation, were only gestures in the direction of something that had nothing to do with the museum's real purpose. The American people did not want to let go of the winning of the West. They wanted to win it all over again, in imagination. It was the ecstasy of the kill, as much as the life of the hunted, that we fed off here. The Buffalo Bill Historical Center did not repudiate the carnage that had taken place in the nineteenth century. It celebrated it. With its gleaming restrooms, cute snack bar, opulent museum shop, wooden Indians, thousand rifles, and scores of animal trophies, it helped us all reenact the dream of excitement, adventure, and conquest that was what the Wild West meant to most people in this country.

This is where my visit ended. But it had a sequel. When I left the Buf-   40
falo Bill Historical Center I was full of moral outrage, an indignation so

intense it made me almost sick, though it was pleasurable, too, as such emotions usually are. But the outrage was undermined by the knowledge that I knew nothing about Buffalo Bill, nothing of his life, nothing of the circumstances that led him to be involved in such violent events. And I began to wonder if my reaction wasn't in some way an image, however small, of the violence I had been objecting to. So I began to read about Buffalo Bill, and as I did, a whole new world opened up.

"I have seen him the very personification of grace and beauty . . . dashing   41
over the free wild prairie and riding his horse as though he and the noble animal were bounding with one life and one motion." That is the sort of thing people wrote about Buffalo Bill. They said "he was the handsomest man I ever saw." They said there "was never another man lived as popular as he was." They said there "wasn't a man, woman or child that he knew or ever met that he didn't speak to." They said he "was handsome as a god, a good rider and a crack shot." They said he "gave lots of money away. Nobody ever went hungry around him." They said he "was way above the average, physically and every other way."

These are quotes from people who knew Cody, collected by one of his   42
two most responsible biographers. She puts them in the last chapter, and by the time you get there they all ring true. Buffalo Bill was incredibly handsome. He was extremely brave and did things no other scout would do. He carried messages over rugged territory swarming with hostile Indians, riding all night in bad weather to get through, and then taking off again the next day to ride sixty miles through a blizzard. He was not a proud man. He didn't boast of his exploits. But he did do incredible things, not just once in a while but on a fairly regular basis. He had a great deal of courage; he believed in himself, in his abilities, in his strength and endurance and knowledge. He was very skilled at what he did—hunting and scouting—but he wasn't afraid to try other things. He wrote some dime novels; he wrote his autobiography at age thirty-three, without very much schooling. He wasn't afraid to try acting even though the stage terrified him and he knew so little about it that, according to his wife, he didn't even know you had to memorize lines.

Maybe it was because he grew up on the frontier, maybe it was just the   43
kind of person he was, but he was constantly finding himself in situations that required resourcefulness and courage, quick decisions and decisive action and rising to the occasion. He wasn't afraid to improvise.

He liked people, drank a lot, gave big parties, gave lots of presents,   44
and is reputed to have been a womanizer.[1] When people came to see him in his office tent on the show grounds, to shake his hand or have their picture taken with him, he never turned anyone away. "He kept a uniformed

doorman at the tent opening to announce visitors," writes a biographer. "No matter who was outside, from a mayor to a shabby woman with a baby, the Colonel would smooth his mustache, stand tall and straight, and tell the doorman to 'show 'em in.' He greeted everyone the same." "He told the damnedest stories you ever heard," writes the son of an Indian who worked in the Wild West show, "entertaining his troupe of performers for hours with Old West blood and guts make-believe. He was admired by all, including the hundreds of Indians he took along on tour. Indians love a man who can tell good stories." They also admired him for fighting well, said his bi-ographers. Though I looked for it, I could find no evidence that contradicts those claims.

As a showman, he was a genius. People don't say much about why he   45
was so successful; mostly they describe the wonderful goings-on. But I get the feeling that Cody was one of those people who was connected to his time in an uncanny way. He knew what people wanted, he knew how to entertain them, because he *liked* them, was open to them, felt kinship with them, or was so much in touch with himself at some level that he was thereby in touch with almost everybody else.

He liked to dress up and had a great sense of costume (of humor, too,   46
they say). Once he came to a fancy-dress ball, his first, in New York, wear-ing white tie and tails and a large Stetson. He knew what people wanted. He let his hair grow long and wore a mustache and beard because, he said, he wouldn't be believable as a scout otherwise. Hence his Indian name, Pa-haska, meaning "long hair," which people loved to use. Another kind of cos-tume. He invented the ten-gallon hat, which the Stetson company made to his specifications. Afterward, they made a fortune off of it. In the scores of pictures reproduced in the many books about him, he most often wears scout's clothes—usually generously fringed buckskin, sometimes a modified cavalryman's outfit—though often he's impeccably turned out in a natty-looking three-piece business suit (sometimes with overcoat, sometimes not). The photographs show him in a tuxedo, in something called a "Mexican suit," which looks like a cowboy outfit, and once he appears in Indian dress. In almost every case he is wearing a hat, usually the Stetson, at exactly the right angle. He poses deliberately, and with dignity, for the picture. Cody didn't take himself so seriously that he had to pretend to be less than he was. "Jesus / he was a handsome man," wrote e. e. cummings in "Buffalo Bill's defunct."

What made Buffalo Bill so irresistible? Why is he still so appealing, even   47
now, when we've lost, supposedly, all the illusions that once supported his popularity? There's a poster for one of his shows when he was traveling in France that gives a clue to what it is that makes him so profoundly attrac-tive. The poster consists of a huge buffalo galloping across the plains; in the

center of the buffalo's hump is a cutout circle that shows the head of Buffalo Bill, white mustachioed and bearded now, in his famous hat, and beneath, in large red letters, are the words *"Je viens."*

Je viens, I am coming, are the words of a savior. The announcement is 48
an annunciation. Buffalo Bill is a religious figure of a kind who makes sense, I think, within a specifically Christian tradition. That is, he comes in the guise of a redeemer, of someone who will save us, who will through his own actions do something for us that we cannot. He will lift us above our lives, out of the daily grind, into something larger than ourselves.

His appeal on the surface is to childish desires, the desire for glamour, 49
fame, bigness, adventure, romance. But these desires are also the sign of something more profound, and it is to something more profound in us that he also appeals. Buffalo Bill comes to the child in us, understood not as that part of ourselves which we have outgrown but the part that got left behind, of necessity, a long time ago, having been starved, bound, punished, disciplined out of existence. He promises that that part of the self can live again. He has the power to promise these things because he represents the West, that geographical space of the globe which was still the realm of exploration and discovery, which was still open, which had not yet quite been tamed when he began to play himself on the stage. He not only represented it, he *was* it. He brought the West itself with him when he came: the very Indians, the very buffaloes, the very cowboys, the very cattle, the very stagecoach itself which had been memorialized in story. He performed in front of the audience the feats that had made him famous. He shot glass balls and clay pigeons out of the air with amazing rapidity. He rode his "watersmooth-silver stallion" at full gallop.

"I am coming." The appearance of Buffalo Bill, in the flesh, was akin to 50
the apparition of a saint or of the Virgin Mary to believers. He was the incarnation of an ideal. He came to show people that what they had only imagined was really true. The West really did exist. There really were heroes who rode white horses and performed amazing feats. e. e. cummings was right to invoke the name of Jesus in his poem. Buffalo Bill was a secular messiah.

He was a messiah because people believed in him. When he died, he is 51
reputed to have said, "Let my show go on." But he had no show at the time, so he probably didn't say that. Still, the words are prophetic because the desire for what Buffalo Bill had done had not only not died but would call forth the countless reenactments of the Wild West, from the rodeo—a direct descendant of his show—to the thousands of western novels, movies, and television programs that comprise the western genre in the twentieth century, a genre that came into existence as a separate category right about the time that Bill Cody died. Don Russell maintains that the way the West exists

in our minds today is largely the result of the way Cody presented it in his show. That was where people got their ideas of what the characters looked like. Though many Indian tribes wore no feathers and fought on foot, you will never see a featherless, horseless Indian warrior in the movies because Bill employed only Sioux and other Plains tribes that had horses and traditionally wore feathered headdresses. "Similarly," he adds, "cowboys wear ten-gallon Stetsons, not because such a hat was worn in early range days, but because it was part of the costume adopted by Buffalo Bill for his show."[2]

But the deeper legacy is elsewhere. Buffalo Bill was a person who inspired other people. What they saw in him was an aspect of themselves. It really doesn't matter whether Cody was as great as people thought him or not, because what they were responding to when he rode into the arena, erect and resplendent on his charger, was something intangible, not the man himself but a possible way of being. William F. Cody and the Wild West triggered the emotions that had fueled the imaginative lives of people who flocked to see him, especially men and boys who made up the larger portion of the audience. He and his cowboys played to an inward territory: a Wild West of the psyche that hungered for exercise sprang into activity when the show appeared. *Je viens* was a promise to redeem that territory, momentarily at least, from exile and oblivion. The lost parts of the self symbolized by buffaloes and horses and wild men would live again for an hour while the show went on. 52

People adored it. Queen Victoria, who broke her custom by going to see it at all (she never went to the theater and on the rare occasions when she wanted to see a play, she had it brought to her), is supposed to have been lifted out of a twenty-five-year depression caused by the death of her husband after she saw Buffalo Bill. She liked the show so much that she saw it again, arranging for a command performance to be given at Windsor Castle the day before her Diamond Jubilee. This was the occasion when four kings rode in the Deadwood coach with the Prince of Wales on top next to Buffalo Bill, who drove. No one was proof against the appeal. Ralph Blumenfeld, the London correspondent for the *New York Herald,* wrote in his diary while the show was in London that he'd had two boyhood heroes, 53

> Robin Hood and Buffalo Bill, and delighted in Cody's stories of the Pony Express and Yellow Hand. Everything was done to make Cody conceited and unbearable, but he remained the simple, unassuming child of the plains who thought lords and ladies belonged in the picture books and that the story of Little Red Riding Hood was true. I rode in the Deadwood coach. It was a great evening in which I realized a good many of my boyhood dreams, for there was Buffalo Bill on his white rocking horse charger, and Annie Oakley behind him.[3]

Victor Weybright and Henry Blackman Sell, from whose work on the Wild West some of the foregoing information has come, dedicated their 54 book to Buffalo Bill. It was published in 1955. Nellie Irene Snyder Yost, whose 1979 biography is one of the two scholarly accounts of Cody's life, dedicates her book "to all those good people, living or dead, who knew and liked Buffalo Bill."[4] Don Russell's *Lives and Legends of Buffalo Bill* (1960), the most fact-filled scholarly biography, does not have a dedication, but in the final chapter where he steps back to assess Cody and his influence, Russell ends by exclaiming: "What more could possibly be asked of a hero? If he was not one, who was?"[5]

Let me now pose a few questions of my own. Must we throw out all the wonderful qualities that Cody had, the spirit of hope and emulation that he aroused in millions of people, because of the terrible judgment history has passed on the epoch of which he was a part? The kinds of things he stands for—courage, daring, strength, endurance, generosity, openness to other people, love of drama, love of life, the possibility of living a life that does not deny the body and the desires of the body—are these to be declared dangerous and delusional because he manifested some of them while fighting Indians, and others while representing his victories to the world? And the feelings he aroused in his audiences—the idealism, the enthusiasm, the excitement, the belief that dreams could become real—must these be declared misguided or a sham because they are associated with the imperialistic conquest of a continent, with the wholesale extermination of animals and men?

It is not so much that we cannot learn from history as that we cannot teach history how things should have been. When I set out to discover how Cody had become involved in the killing of Indians and the slaughter of buffalo, I found myself unable to sustain the outrage I had felt on leaving the museum. From his first job as an eleven-year-old herder for an army supply outfit, sole wage earner for his ailing, widowed mother, who had a new infant and other children to support, to his death in Colorado at seventy-one, there was never a time when it was possible for me to say, There, there you went wrong, Buffalo Bill, you should not have killed that Indian. You should have held your fire and quit the army and gone to work in the nineteenth-century equivalent of the Peace Corps. You should have known how it would end. My reading made me see that you can't prescribe for someone in Buffalo Bill's position—what he should have done, how things should have been—and it made me reflect on the violence of my own reaction. I saw how eager I had been to get off on being angry at the museum. The thirst for moral outrage, for self-vindication, lay pretty close to the surface.

I cannot resolve the contradictions between my experience at the Buffalo Bill Museum, with its celebration of violent conquest, and my response to the shining figure of Buffalo Bill as it emerged from the pages of books. On the one hand, a history of shame; on the other, an image of the heart's desire. But I have reached one conclusion that for a while, at least, will have to serve.

Major historical events like genocide and major acts of destruction are   58 not simply produced by impersonal historical processes or economic imperatives or ecological blunders; human intentionality is involved and human knowledge of the self. Therefore, if you're really interested in not having any more genocide or killing of animals, no matter what else you might do—condemning imperialism or shaking your finger at history—if you don't first, or also, come to recognize the violence in yourself and your own anger and your own destructiveness, whatever else you do won't work. It isn't that genocide doesn't matter. Genocide matters and it starts at home.

NOTES

1. Iron Eyes Cody, as told to Collin Perry, *Iron Eyes: My Life as a Hollywood Indian* (New York, 1982), 16.

2. Don Russell, *The Lives and Legends of Buffalo Bill* (Norman, Okla., 1960), 470.

3. Victor Weybright and Henry Blackman Sell, *Buffalo Bill and the Wild West* (New York, 1955), 172.

4. Nellie Irene Snyder Yost, *Buffalo Bill, His Family, Friends, Fame, Failures, and Fortunes* (Chicago, 1979).

5. Russell, *Lives and Legends,* 480.

Working with the Text

1. Throughout her essay, Tompkins describes her feelings and observations in terms of "contradictions"; she either points to the "blatant contradictions" in the exhibits, or to her attempts to "resolve the contradictions" in herself. Throughout the museums she senses an "undertone of disquiet" and "uneasiness of the commentary." What are the sources of these conflicting feelings and thoughts? What larger contradictions or tensions in American culture do they point to? Does she resolve these tensions in the essay, either for herself or for you, the reader?

2. Early in the essay, Tompkins points out that Buffalo Bill (according to the museum) had a "progressive vision of the West." Yet, late in the essay, Tompkins concludes that what made Buffalo Bill so attractive was the way that he embodied a frozen image of the West, a sense of what the West *was* in the 1880s and 90s and not what it could become. Moreover, she claims that the museum helps "us all reenact the dream of excitement, adventure, and conquest that was what the Wild West meant to most people in this country." Explore in an essay how this shift—from the West as progressive to the West as nostalgic—seems

contradictory or consistent to you. How might the nostalgia for the Wild West relate to America's progressive notions of itself as a national community? What characteristics of the Wild West have become part of the American psyche? How has the geographic space of the West become a part of American national culture? Explore these questions in a paper.

3. Tompkins often uses the term "the best of civilization"; she later pairs the idea of civilization with the idea of savagism or "the savage." Bridging these two ideas—civilization and savagism—is the idea of violence. How does her treatment of the violence that is part of civilization change over the course of the essay? What is the relationship between cultural violence and our personal attitudes toward violence? How is the violence and brutality represented in the museum repugnant to us, yet seems sanitized or rationalized in the context of the past, or in the context of "the West"?

4. The Buffalo Bill Museum in Cody, Wyoming has an extensive site on the World Wide Web. There are also many other Web resources on Buffalo Bill. Visit some of these resources and compare their presentation of materials on Buffalo Bill and the Wild West to Tompkins's descriptions. Do you see or feel the same kind of contradictions?

5. What do you think she means by the phrase "Genocide . . . starts at home"? Do you find that phrase startling or disturbing? How does it echo back through the essay?

Comanche Moon

JACK JACKSON

Jack Jackson first drew for a University of Texas humor magazine, the *Ranger*. Jackson's work now presents itself as adult literature, maintaining the comic book's genres and themes, and confronting the relations between history and fiction, ideology and narrative. His comic-book histories include "Nits Make Lice," biographies of southwest American history figures—*Comanche Moon* (1978) and *Los Tejanos* (1982), a narrative about Spanish Texas—and a horror-fantasy epic, "Bulto." *Comanche Moon* begins with the capture of young Cynthia Ann Parker, her upbringing by Indians, and her marriage to a Comanche chief. The narrative, covering almost a hundred years, extends to their son, Quanah Parker, his family, and the power relations among Indians and between Indians and whites. This profile of Quanah Parker shows some of the challenges and innovations that Native Americans found as they were exiled from traditional ways and besieged by the expanding white culture.

PENNED UP..

BUT NOT EVEN THE RESPECT AND GOODWILL OF YOUNG MACKENZIE CAN ALTER THE FATE THE VANQUISHED INDIANS MUST SUFFER. THEY ARE STRIPPED OF ALL THEIR POSSESSIONS AND PUT IN SQUALID CAMPS, UNDER HEAVY GUARD. SCURVY AND DYSENTERY RAVAGE THEIR SULLEN RANKS. THEY EAT IN HASTE AND SLEEP IN FEAR, UNSURE OF TOMORROW.

SOME, LIKE THE LEADERS WHO SIGNED TREATIES AND THEN BOLTED THE RESERVATION, ARE LOCKED IN AN UNFINISHED ICEHOUSE AND FED LIKE WILD ANIMALS.

LATER THE CHIEF TROUBLEMAKERS ARE SENT IN CHAINS TO THE UNHEALTHY CLIMATE OF FLORIDA PRISONS.

QUANAH, LIKE HIS WARRIORS, HAS NOTHING TO DO BUT SIT AND STARE, DREAMING OF THE DAYS WHEN REDMEN RULED.

THE QUOHADAS ARE NOT SINGLED OUT FOR HARSH TREATMENT. MANY OFFICERS SPEAK OUT ON QUANAH'S BEHALF.

HE MADE NO PROMISES, SIGNED NO TREATIES — THEREFORE, HE HAS BROKEN NONE. SURE, HE KILLED — BUT IN DEFENSE OF HIS OWN TERRITORY, AS A SOLDIER OF HIS PEOPLE — AND A VERY WORTHY ONE I MIGHT ADD..

EVEN THE HATED TEXANS' TAKE A CERTAIN PRIDE IN HIM, NOW THAT HE IS NO LONGER A THORN IN THEIR SIDE.

QUANAH ?? WAHL HIS MA WUZ A PARKER, YOU KNOW, THERE'S BLUE BLOOD IN THET BOYS VEINS. YESSIR, BLOOD WILL ALWAYS TELL, YOU CAN COUNT ON IT !!

YOU TALK ABOUT A FIGHTER, LET ME TELL YOU A-BOUT TH' TIME...

MACKENZIE, THINKING THE NOMADS MIGHT MAKE GOOD HERDSMEN, SELLS THEIR HORSES AND BRINGS IN A FLOCK OF PURE-BRED SHEEP FROM NEW MEXICO.

SHEEP ??

THE PROJECT FAILS MISERABLY...

MUTTON STEW GAGG!

WISH THEY'D BROUGHT US DOGS INSTEAD OF SHEEP!

THE CHIEFS THAT CO-OPERATED WITH THE AGENTS IN THE FINAL DAYS ARE REWARDED WITH HOUSES.

WHY DON'T YOU LIVE IN YOUR NICE NEW HOUSE, HORSEBACK?

HEAP SNAKES IN THERE !!

✳ INDIAN WORD FOR CATTLE, FROM HEARING DROVERS HOLLER "WHOA-HAW" AT STEERS

HE DETERMINES TO CONTACT SOME OF HIS WHITE KINSMEN SO THAT HE MAY LEARN MORE OF THEIR MYSTERIOUS WAYS. ARMED WITH A PASS FROM THE AGENT, HE MAKES HIS WAY THROUGH TEXAS TO SEE HIS MOTHER'S BROTHER, JOHN PARKER. HE IS CAREFUL TO AVOID THE MANY NEW CABINS THAT HAVE SPRUNG UP ALONG THE OLD WAR TRAIL TO MEXICO.

AFTER JOHN PARKER RETURNED TO THE COMANCHES, HE HAD BEEN STRICKEN WITH SMALLPOX AND LEFT TO DIE BY THE INDIANS. HOWEVER, HE WAS NURSED BACK TO HEALTH BY A MEXICAN CAPTIVE, MARRIED HER, AND WENT TO LIVE AMONG HER PEOPLE IN NORTHERN MEXICO. HIS LIFE HAS MADE HIM A CURIOUS MIXTURE OF ANGLO-COMANCHE-MEXICAN.

HOW YOU DOING, UNCLE JOHN..

SAME OLD STUFF, QUANAH — RANCHIN' AND RAISIN' HELL. YOU SHORE ARE A SIGHT FOR SORE EYES!!

NOW A WELL-TO-DO STOCKMAN, JOHN PARKER TAKES HIS NEPHEW HUNTING, COMANCHE FASHION.

YOU OUGHT TO GET INTO TH' CATTLE BUSINESS, QUANAH. IT SHORE BEATS FARMIN'..

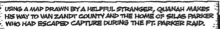

USING A MAP DRAWN BY A HELPFUL STRANGER, QUANAH MAKES HIS WAY TO VAN ZANDT COUNTY AND THE HOME OF SILAS PARKER WHO HAD ESCAPED CAPTURE DURING THE FT. PARKER RAID.

YOU...MAYBE MY MOTHER'S PEOPLE? ME, QUANAH PARKER.

LAND'S SAKES! MY DEAR, DEPARTED SISTER'S BOY! LIGHT, AND COME IN THE HOUSE, SON...

QUANAH SLEEPS IN HIS MOTHER'S OLD BED.

NADUAH, HOW STRANGE TO THINK OF YOU IN THIS... LITTLE CAGE...

ALREADY A LEGEND IN THIS PART OF TEXAS, QUANAH ASKS SILAS FOR GUIDANCE.

UNCLE, TEACH ME ABOUT "CIVILIZATION", SO THAT I MAY TELL MY PEOPLE...

FIRST THING OFF, YOU NEED TO KNOW ABOUT "MONEY"!

SEVERAL WEEKS LATER, HE RETURNS TO THE RESERVATION, ALMOST CONVINCED THE WHITEMAN'S WAY IS BEST.

THEY LIKE ME DOWN THERE. I CHURN BUTTER, LEARN ABOUT COWS, COTTON, & BLACK-EYED PEAS.

IF THEY LIKE YOU SO MUCH, WHY DIDN'T YOU STAY?

DOWN THERE, I JUST A PLAIN INJUN - HERE, I AM BIG CHIEF!

HAHA

BUT HE WANTS TO BE SURE. THE AGENT CONSENTS TO LET HIS CHARGES GO ON A FALL HUNT TO SUPPLEMENT THEIR MEAGER BEEF RATIONS. QUANAH LEADS THE GLEEFUL WARRIORS OFF TOWARD THEIR BELOVED BISON RANGE.

THE OLD MEN TELL THE YOUNG HOW IT WILL BE. THEY SIGH FOR THE TASTE OF MARROW BONES, FOR STEAMING LIVER, SPLASHED WITH GALL...

BELIEVE ME, THERE'S NOTHING LIKE IT!

BUT THE PLAINS ARE A GRAVEYARD OF BONES. SKIN HUNTERS HAVE DONE THEIR GRISLY WORK WELL. THE HERDS ARE GONE— NOT ONE BUFFALO IS FOUND!!

THE WARRIORS STARE DUMBLY INTO THEIR CAMPFIRES AS THE SHAMANS VAINLY SUMMON THE BUFFALO SPIRIT.

IN PALO DURO CANYON, JUST A FEW YEARS AGO THE LAST COMANCHE STRONGHOLD, QUANAH'S DISILLU-SIONED BRAVES — NEAR STARVATION AND SUFFERING FROM THE COLD — MEET CHARLES GOODNIGHT, PIO-NEERING FOUNDER OF THE AREA'S FIRST BIG RANCH.

THERE AIN'T NO MORE BUFFALO, QUANAH— JUST MY COWS! AND IF YOU'LL KEEP YOUR MEN FROM KILL-ING THEM, I'LL SEE THAT YOU DON'T GO HUNGRY...

AS QUANAH LEADS HIS EMPTY-HANDED BAND BACK TO THE RESERVATION, HE KNOWS THE PAST IS GONE FOREVER. THERE IS NO TURNING BACK.

THERE IS NO PATH LEFT FOR US, EXCEPT THE WHITEMAN'S ROAD...

WHITEMAN'S ROAD

QUANAH STARTS TO TAKE AN ACTIVE ROLE IN TRIBAL AFFAIRS. ALTHO HIS WHITE BLOOD KEEPS HIM FROM BEING RECOGNIZED BY SOME STRICT TRADITIONALISTS AS HEADCHIEF, MANY INDIANS LOOK TO HIM FOR LEADERSHIP *BECAUSE* OF THIS BLOOD-LINK TO THE WHITES, HOPING IT MIGHT WORK TO QUANAH'S ADVANTAGE.

PUT ON YOUR BEST BUCKSKINS AND ROBES. WE MUST SPEAK TO THE SOLDIER CHIEF.

AFTER MOW-WAY STEPS DOWN AS HEADCHIEF, QUANAH'S INFLUENCE GROWS. THE COMANCHES FOLLOW HIM BECAUSE HE IS A PROVEN LEADER AMONG THEM — AND A MAN THE WHITES SEEM TO RESPECT AND LISTEN TO.

Working with the Text

1. Our "tradition" of comic books assumes that simple drawings offer juvenile escape through exaggerations and fantasy. These pages use comic-book methods to present "real history." What specific techniques do you see being used from comics and from history? What composite effect does this create?

2. The Native Americans depicted here face challenges from whites, and from each other. Excluding Quanah, describe a specific response to each group. What new problems are created by these responses? How does the white technique of "divide and rule" operate here?

3. Both whites and Indians believe Quanah's "mixed blood" gives him special characteristics. In what ways does he gain stature through such "racialist" thinking? In what ways does his family connection offer him new perspectives?

4. From this passage, in a paper characterize the generation of Native Americans who lived traditionally, and the later one growing up on reservations. What predictions can you make of the next generation; how might it adapt traditional ways? How might a "frontier space" become a new center of Indian civilization?

5. Quanah shows characteristics that many writers (such as Turner, White, or Kamal) see in other Americans. In what ways are his experiences typical of an immigrant or member of a minority group? In what ways are the psychic borders crossed by Native Americans unique?

An Egyptian Girl in America

KARIMA KAMAL

Karima Kamal is currently the Deputy Chief Editor of *Sabah Al Kheir* in Cairo. In the 1980s she spent several years living in the United States while pursuing her doctorate at the University of Chicago. Her memoir, *An Egyptian Girl in America*, details her encounter with individual Americans and American culture at large. Her work is notable for its stringent appraisal of the difficulties inherent in American attitudes toward "freedom" in comparison to a more deterministic and traditional Egyptian culture.

America is truly a society without a mask!   1

It is a society that uncovers its face and in a moment you are able to wit-   2
ness all its shortcomings and virtues. Because it is a face without a mask, it
surprises you and shocks you. It even outrages you . . .

America is a society that does not wear a mask because the American   3
fears himself more than he fears God or other people.

The American puts his own interests a thousand times above God or   4
above what others might say. America is a society of individuals who came
from around the world and have nothing in common with one another except for a dream that fills their heads and a label for being "an immigrant."
They dug in hard and faced a tough life. They made themselves; they did
not live at the expense of others. Their experience has been a matter of life
or death, surviving or perishing, that is why the American lives his life to the
fullest. He tries to enjoy every minute. He refuses to continue in a failing
venture, because in his mind he lives once and only once! He enjoys his life
and refuses to accept old age. He tries to postpone old age as much as he
can, which is why the retirement age in America is 70 years.

Probably from the same desire to enjoy life, the Americans hate to delve   5
into anything outside their work. As a result, American culture is glossed with
superficiality to an extent that when I was speaking with a young American
man he said in amazement, "Why do you think a lot, and analyze and theorize?" I actually discovered that we Egyptians spend a lot of time thinking and
analyzing our own conduct and the conduct of others. This is strange to the
American who doesn't usually spend a lot of time thinking and analyzing. Actually he thinks while he walks, or you can say that his steps are an expression of his thinking. So he does not spend a lot of time thinking before
making his decision. The American's concept of entertainment is that it must
be of great size and great quantity. Even if that enjoyment were an ice cream
cone, or a box of popcorn, or a glass of Coca-Cola, it has to be unbelievably
gigantic. This American "large-size" concept of entertainment and fun is not
found in Europe or any other place for that matter.

This exaggerated need for pleasure is probably what glosses the Amer-   6
ican culture with superficiality. For example, American television is boring;
it rarely grabs you or stimulates your mind. The most interesting and enjoyable part of American television is the news which is covered at times live,
at much risk to the news crew, taking you to the scene of the action as
though you were living it. It does not matter what the news item is. For example, the war in Lebanon was brought live to America's living rooms. What
was happening there was not presented from a piece of paper read by
an anchorman. Instead the viewer was able to watch live scenes from the
battlefront. The reporter on television was reporting from the middle of

Lebanon while the bullets were flying about him and tanks and soldiers were around him.

American politics are similar to the movies. The politicians, local and international, are in the eyes of the American like the Hollywood stars. 7

The sitcoms and series are all detective stories or "westerns" that do not 8 appeal to you. The strangest thing is that the successful sitcoms that we import from American television are the best that appear on our television sets, albeit these programs are rare in proportion to the long hours and the many channels. There are special cable channels for which you must pay a subscription fee, and they present horror films or sex films. None of it is of good quality at all.

The way Americans enjoy their lives sometimes seems strange. One re- 9 alizes this during American national holidays. I had firsthand experience celebrating "Taste of Chicago," one way the city of Chicago celebrates the Fourth of July. In the morning, a large group of us from the International House took a train to the center of town where the festival was scheduled to take place. It was in a park that occupies a large space in the city. It is such a large space one cannot imagine that a park could be so big. Within a short amount of time the park was filled with thousands of people. The American men, women, and children crowded the park, some of them sitting on quilts while others roamed around, but with great difficulty because of the big crowds. There were many stands selling food, drinks, and balloons of different shapes, with faces, stars, and animals drawn on them. Some of the people wore headbands with stars on them, and some drew stars and other colored objects on their faces. The old as well as the young took part in the festivities.

In the amusement park there were carts that sold presents, and there 10 was a big stage on which they sang patriotic songs and the audience sang along with the small band. In the evening fireworks went off. What defines the whole event was one thing: a big crowd, so big that one was crushed in its midst.

People were moving aimlessly in every direction, bumping into each 11 other. They had trouble moving about. They turned into one huge mass that could not do anything except spend money at the food stands. You had to get tickets to buy food and you had to stand in lines to buy certain types of food or a beer. Upon our return near dawn, the street looked as if it had been taken over by mobs. The train station was filled with exhausted people dreaming of their beds, trying to get on the train. They didn't do anything all day except struggle with the crowds and eat different types of food. In conclusion, that was enjoyment à la American style.

Life in America is life on the move, action every moment, work every 12 minute, and decisions every second. You cannot sleep or do anything. What you do for work decides whether you will live or die, whether you will rise to the summit or fall to the abyss of society. In America you do not advance because of seniority or goodwill, and your work controls not only whether you will advance or not but whether you will have an income at all. Otherwise you will be fired and will not be able to go to work the next day. The worst is that you may find yourself on the street without work and without income. This lack of security is what has created all this technology, civilization, and fast progress. The security in our country is what promotes laziness, dependence on others, slow-paced life, and the lack of innovation.

America is freedom . . . progress . . . violence . . . and aggression, all at once!   13

Freedom in America gives human beings the opportunity to live as they please, and we Egyptians might feel we are deprived of this freedom. In order for us to make a decision, we need to consider a wide range of options and probably ask a lot of people. All the American has to do is search his mind, and he makes his decision without consideration to anyone else. So a lot of ideas disappear in our life and do not get translated into action because of our fear of what others might say.   14

But freedom in America often kills innocence, the innocence of the young, the innocence of social relations, the innocence of love, and the innocence of feelings. At the same time you envy America for its freedom, you pity her for the price she pays for this freedom.   15

America is civilization, progress, and technology. Those who say that technology crushes the human, are those who do not know what civilization is or have never experienced it, or do not want to be jealous of American civilization. After my stay in America, I would laugh sarcastically at those who think that civilization destroys humanity. The reality as I witnessed it in America, the country of civilization, is that civilization gives a human an increased sense of individuality, self-confidence, and his own sense of importance.   16

In this civilization, the American gets compensated unbelievably for trivial losses. It surprises you if you are from the Third World, where there is no surprise or outrage for people who happen to swallow a nail, fall into a gutter, or eat poisonous food. When civilization disappears, the value of a human dwindles. But in America, where civilization reigns, humans become very valuable. Humans are worth more than anything else. For example, if somebody slipped on a stairwell, the designer of the stairs will be sued because they were not designed well. The American gets compensation if his pool was not built the way it was designed, or if he ate in a restaurant and got indigestion. The American will return something he bought from the store, even if he bought it a while ago, because he does not like it. In the   17 store they welcome him as if he has come to buy the whole store, not as if he is there to return a single product. That might be why Americans are very friendly, because there is no pressure and stress on them. The Americans usually carry the smile of contentedness.

You can feel this friendliness in restaurants, in stores, in supermarkets, on the bus, and in the subway. The Americans always use classical expressions to express this friendliness. They always say "good day," "good evening," "have a good time," and all of these have one meaning, which is to wish someone happiness.   18

Observers of the American scene have different viewpoints about this friendliness. Some say it is a nice way to attract customers, and some say it is the nature of the people, who are united as immigrants and try to overcome their differences. Some say it is only a mask to hide the true American character and nature. Still others say it is friendliness that is not from the heart, insincere. No matter what the truth is about these explanations and analyses, this friendliness makes you feel comfortable and welcomed. You are treated with respect, whether this is out of the desire to deal wisely with others, or out of genuine sentiment.   19

This friendliness does not extend to people of other nationalities, so the Americans here are not dissimilar to the Nazis.   20

The German citizen under the Nazis felt that he was the best in the world because of his race. The American feels he is the strongest in the world because he owns the arms, the civilization, the technology, and controls the fate of the world.   21

The American feels his power and his wealth, but his only weak point is that he has no history. That is why the American is in awe of an old carpet or an antique vase. Even if the antique is of rotted wood or is a faded picture of an old person, they are interested in it. The American tries to convince himself and others that he has history. So in Disney World you find a collection of wooden statues depicting the American presidents. They beam light on these statues and have them speak about their period of governing the United States to give the illusion that the country has an old history.   22

Everything in America is big: the streets, skyscrapers, glasses of Coca-Cola, bags of popcorn, and glasses of beer. The one thing here that comes in small amounts is respect. The American does not have to respect anyone. He does what he wants, says what he wants, and moves around in the way he wants. I wonder whether it is an excessive respect for his individual freedom or a rejection of all the traditions of the Old World in the New World.   23

America is aggressive. America is a society that is used to aggression. So they listen to news about crimes in the same way they listen to the weather forecast. Most of these incidents appear strange to any foreigner. For example, one day American television reported two bizarre incidents. The first   24 one was in Miami. One of the workers in a factory did not like the work shifts, so he shot and killed nine people and wounded three others. In the second incident, a man kidnapped two young girls and raped them.

We should ask ourselves, is crime in American society more frequent and more dangerous than it is in any other society? Or does it just appear that way because everything is reported and not concealed? 25

If the crime situation in the American society appears strange, the condition of the law is stranger. The accused will not be convicted unless there is absolutely no doubt he committed the crime. If he was caught committing the crime, he gets out of it by claiming psychological insanity, as John Hinckley did when he shot President Reagan. 26

In no other country can you shoot at a president and not get sentenced to life imprisonment. Only in America, where the television cameras filmed Hinckley shooting President Reagan, could he be found not guilty and sent for psychological treatment. Who knows what he is capable of doing after he is let out. . . . 27

No matter how long your trip to America is, when it is time to leave and you gather all your belongings, your feeling of homesickness that was with you throughout your trip will be replaced with a new feeling of sadness. It is sadness for leaving a place that is dear to you, a place that has become part of your life. You are leaving an experience that filled your life for some time. You are leaving a lot of memories, moments of discovery, sadness, happiness, homesickness, and a sense of acceptance as well as repulsion. You are still searching for an answer to the question that was on your mind when you first set foot in America. A world completely different from yours and the question is, which world do you prefer? 28

Your world suffers from the lack of freedom, and this world suffers from excessive freedom. Your world suffers from being under-civilized, and this world suffers from over-civilization. Your world suffers from a lack of seriousness, and this world suffers from too much seriousness. Is it the fate of the human beings to go on comparing and complaining? It seems to me that we will continue to complain because there is no country that will give us the right solution; the only solution is the one we will find within ourselves. 29

—Translated by Dima Reda

Working with the Text

1. Kamal begins her essay with a bold set of claims on American "openness": American society wears no mask because the American "fears himself more than he fears God or other people." List some

examples of both this apparent "fear" and its consequences in American culture.

2. Kamal argues that American behavior is shaped by the "immigrant" of its residents. Name some cultural features that respond to this background; how do these features compare with the American "mindset" depicted by other essayists in this chapter (e.g., Turner, Lapham, etc.)?

3. According to Kamal, how do Americans imagine and recreate the world outside the United States? What are the pros and cons of our "re-creation" of cultural realities and events outside our country? How does Kamal reconcile American "friendliness" toward others with her view that our "friendliness does not extend to people of other nationalities"?

4. What elements of American "freedom" are compared to those in Egyptian culture? What elements of American diversity does Kamal subordinate in order to make this comparison? Does she imagine American limits and borders differently than Egyptian ones? Give your responses in a written essay.

5. Kamal finds that America's state of "over-civilization" grants very particular rights to individuals; she also proposes that Egypt is, comparatively, "under-civilized." Based on your own specific experience, how has U.S. civilization progressed in the twenty years since this essay? How would you imagine that individual life in Egypt might have progressed?

The Resistance: Ten Years of Pop Culture That Shook the World

ARMOND WHITE

Armond White, former chairman of the New York Film Critics' Circle, is a journalist and critic who has written for *The City Sun* and currently reviews films for *The New York Press*. The following essay was part of his 1995 book *The Resistance: Ten Years of Pop Culture That Shook the World* and has subsequently appeared in other collections of cultural criticism. White's latest book is a biography of the controversial rapper Tupac Shakur titled *Rebel for the Hell of It*. In this excerpt from *The Resistance: Ten Years of Pop Culture that Shook the World,* White analyzes the complicated racial dynamics of corporate-sponsored hip hop, focusing particularly on the white performer Marky Mark and related acts.

The original title of this essay, "Who Wants to See Ten Niggers Play Basketball?" is taken from *Tougher Than Leather,* the 1987 Run DMC movie written by Rick Menello and directed by former Def Jam Records president Rick Rubin. The film was released around the period Rubin was withdrawing from Def Jam and settling unspecified accounts with his partner Russell Simmons; reacting more to Rubin than to the film, the rap cognoscenti dissed the movie, making it the first victim of "reverse racism" in hip hop. The street vibe dogged Rubin and his movie even though it was and still is the funniest, shrewdest celluloid depiction of the hip hop ethos—the insecurities that make Black American boys aggress, the style that gives them charm, and their inventive derivations from existing pop culture (specifically blaxploitation flicks, booty-begging records, comic books, and mainstream action-and-adventure fantasies) that, through hip hop, gets turned into art.

Rubin admired this ethos from his white, Jewish, suburban, long-haired, metal-head perspective and helped significantly to commercialize it. *Tougher Than Leather* reveals both Rubin's love for b-boy culture and his adept assessment of its commercial and cultural potential. In contrast, *Krush Groove,* a standard, cheap bio-pic about Rubin's rise to the top produced by *House Party II, New Jack City,* and *Disorderlies* shlockmeisters George Jackson and Doug McHenry, trivialized Rubin's entrepreneurial project into make-it-rich dreams of empire. *Tougher Than Leather* got to something stranger and tougher: Rubin presented himself as an exploiter, a bizzer who held no delusions about Presley as a messiah. Acting on the plain knowledge that the American marketplace was no less a stage for class antagonism, racial bias, and sexual orthodoxy than the floor of the Congress, Rubin made Black labor work *for him.* In a venerable tradition (from slavery to sports to rock 'n' roll) Rubin developed this exploitation into *symbiotic forms.* Workers and beneficiaries traded off each other—the chance to be heard for the chance to control; the chance to be recognized for the chance to be entertained. And everybody gets paid (to varying degrees).

Founding Def Jam and breaking and entering movies via Run DMC were sincere expressions of Rubin's white advantaged condition. His big-screen, film-student wet dream about b-boys-turned-professionals-turned-movie-stars epitomized his deepest feelings about race and culture. Every scene in *Tougher Than Leather* is fascinating; it is Rubin's subconscious, diaristic account of pop as a mirror that reflects desire—for empowerment, for prowess, for fame, for money, for style, for art. Each scene mediates what draws rap listeners and artists together. And there in back of Run DMC's hijinks are Rick

Rubin's alter-ego revolutionaries, the Beastie Boys. When a *Tougher Than Leather* character asks him why he's integrating rap with these ill-mannered fuckups, Rubin responds, "Nobody wants to see ten niggers play basketball!"

Those cold words describe American pop as much as they express 4
racism—the phrase conjoins the two phenomena in a perfectly mater-of-fact expression. Rap flourished into corporate-sponsored hip hop *because* of the symbiosis that held whites enthralled to Blacks and kept Blacks indentured. Like sports, the music game needs diversity of playing style and elicits the envy of sideliners, compelling them to step into center court. As Rubin knew when he left hip hop for whiter, more rarefied metal at Def American Records (the label of Slayer and Andrew Dice Clay—also Seattle's Sir Mix-A-Lot), whites don't just want to cheer their own, *they want to play!*

Marky Mark and All-American Rap

Marky Mark Wahlberg has the best definition of any white rapper—meaning 5
not just that he has better pecs than 3rd Bass or drops his drawers with more style than the Beastie Boys drop science but that he defines hip hop as a *Black* cultural movement. His brashness, as in the song, "Just Like the Beastie Boys and 3rd Bass," does not distort the music's essence.

Alright, alright
What an odd sight
Here's another MC whose skin is white
A white kid, a white boy
With a white voice
Just like the Beastie Boys and 3rd Bass
Hmm. This looks like a topic for discussion
To build racial tension
For fussin' and cussin'.

Such honesty makes him the first white rapper to dispel derision. A Marky 6
Mark record and video proudly acknowledge their derivation from Black culture. There's a paradox here: When white artists give Black pop its proper homage, there is still a limit to how far they can take their appreciation. This isn't determined by the artists' ability or the audience's acceptance but by the artists' own imagination. They must be able to borrow without losing sight of themselves as borrowers. The secret is attitude, and the attitude must be shared (as California's Latino rappers Cypress Hill show) before any mannerism can be copied.

From the release of his initial single with the group the Funky Bunch, 7
"Good Vibrations" (featuring vocal excitement by Loleatta Holloway), Marky Mark has shown a genuine understanding of hip hop style and politics. By

giving Holloway respect (providing her the visual presence Martha Wash was denied by Black Box and C&C Music Factory), Marky Mark transcended the obvious need for street smarts and hooked up with hip hop's earlier, dance-music influence.

Since it is impossible for any white rapper to achieve originality (the axiom "Too Black, too strong" becomes "Too white, too late"), attempts at combining identification with imitation (such as 3rd Bass's "Steppin' to the A.M.") wind up disingenuous. 3rd Bass's automatic assimilation of street slang and fly rhythm is automatically suspect. But on "Good Vibrations," Holloway's sizzling, piercing growl, which reduces all listeners to stupefaction, made Marky Mark's "difference" a pertinent fact. He seemed justifiably awed yet game—a white rap boy up against the gale force of sensual Black art. Speaking between Holloway's choruses, Marky Mark played out a good-natured cartoon of the racial-sexual envy that makes whites blush. 8

Call it a secret shame perhaps, because this race-sex thing is rarely gauged properly by the mainstream without shifting the balance of cultural authority. Marky Mark's youth and callowness relative to Holloway's age and power is almost a mythical demonstration of white desire and Black fecundity. The multi-ethnic, largely Black Funky Bunch (a six-person crew that includes two women) helps maintain Marky Mark's cultural context. That's usually the first thing denied by white crossover acts and counterculture theorists like the Bears and Norman ("The White Negro") Mailer. 9

This cultural egotism is the main thing Mark learned to avoid from the example of his older brother Donnie Wahlberg of the insufferably derivative New Kids on the Block—a group that could succeed in pop but never in rap. Donnie Wahlberg produced Marky Mark's debut album, *Music for the People* (Interscope), and co-wrote most of the tracks. This funk-heavy album fulfills the hip hop ambition Wahlberg showed on "Games," the 1990 rap single from the last New Kids album. The other *Music for the People* tracks stay within proven Black pop formulas. (In 1994 the group acronymized its name to NKOTB and released a lame imitation of Snoop Doggy Dogg's sexism called "Dirty Dawg.") For instance, the second and third singles, "Wildside" and "I Need Money," were essentially cover versions of records already marked with strong ethnic referents. 10

Like many younger siblings, Mark dives into the depth of his older brother's commitment—in this case to Black pop—but the surprise on *Music for the People* is the breadth of the Wahlbergs' pop savvy, from the intense house of "Good Vibrations" to the sex rap "Make Me Say Ooh!" which uses only the revving-up bits of Marvin Gaye's "Let's Get It On." Marky Mark's whispered rap bites L.L. Cool J's loveman pose, yet he gets over, because how many white kids would know the right Gaye parts to use? This show of instinct seems impressively genuine in a third-generation pop addict. It 11 doesn't discredit Marky Mark, but it clarifies the passion for Black pop that one hears in his records.

White communion with Black style is nothing new, but Marky Mark per- 12 fects it—politically if no other way. This happens as a benefit of Marky Mark's naiveté, something that a producer as smart as Hank Shocklee can't quite manipulate. Shocklee's white rapper projects, Young Black Teenagers and Kid Panic and the Adventures of Dean Dean, are too "Black," too slick. The amazingly inventive productions for these groups (Young Black Teenagers was a test run for the soundscapes Shocklee perfected with Son of Bazerk) strained the white rappers' plausibility. A similar anxiety affects the musical inventions of writer-producer Sam Sever (3rd Bass and his own duo, Downtown Science), which can't be called innovative without choking on the word. Clunkier funk, like Marky Mark's or the Beastie Boys', would have been a more credible mode for these white rappers.

Shocklee gave his acts more sophistication than the public could recog- 13 nize—or even wanted to. Such semiadept white rap provokes a tricky de-bate about cultural authenticity. Rap performance and linguistics connote a particular social, ethnic experience. The use of this idiom is not a right to be earned but a given. For the middle-class, suburban Black kids who assume street manner and philosophy it implies a particular knowledge and empa-thy that is assiduously maintained by social circumstances if not genetics.

For the moment, rap's codes are inimitable; that's why TV and radio com- 14 mercials can parody rap without diluting its potency. White rappers who try so hard for Black style confuse the music's communication. Gerardo, JT, and even Falco may know the form but not the essence. And though their tone may get close, their intent is unclear. The issue is not whether there is good music or acceptable rapping on *Radioactive, The Cactus Album, Young Black Teenagers, Licensed to Ill,* or *Music for the People* (there is) but whether these records can give comparable pleasure and enlightenment.

It's difficult to actually *hear* some of this music because its impetus is un- 15 known, its purpose uncommunicated by the halting meter and the white voice (as Marky Mark identified) trying to pass as nothing unusual. Hip hop is such a rich culture that its audience can thrive without paying attention to white rappers. But instead of dismissing this white subgenre, it's best to understand that the audience is not indifferent; its needs (which will determine the shape of hip hop to come) simply preclude records or artists who are shams.

Hip hop has so many styles that it can't be accused of racial exclusivity, 16 but its ethnic specificity is crucial. Rap's seemingly casual expression actu-ally developed as the careful, forceful, personal articulation of social groups without access to America's dominant language and media. Even records as disparate as Young MC's "Bust A Move" and Naughty by Nature's "O.P.P." are informed by this expressive urgency. Both evince an African American yearning to claim, protest, enunciate. The significance of speaking—as an expression of identity and a form of power—gives hip hop endless fascination.

In Ed O.G. & Da Bulldogs' "Speak upon It," the Boston-based group performs the necessary function of interpreting history and recording it for the artists' sanity and the audience's awareness. "Speak upon It" retells the Charles Stuart scandal, in which a white Boston man killed his pregnant wife for an insurance settlement. Stuart's claim that a Black man murdered his wife provoked a police riot in which an innocent Black man, William Bennett, was arrested and charged with the killing. Ed O.G.'s account of this social disgrace is as serious as Scripture; his purpose is to make sense of an unjust world if only by keeping this horrible tale fresh. It is instant folklore made eternal by the rapper's intensity and a blues-righteous backing track.

"Speak upon It" is a classic example of what makes hip hop special; it contains a mythmaking, muckraking imperative about racial and social affronts that white showbizzers cannot be expected to have, an anger they dare not show. Unexpectedly, Marky Mark's "Wildside" makes the grade. Of course "Wildside" can't match the deeply pleasurable nuances of Ed O.G. & Da Bulldogs (their "Gotta Have It" and "Bugaboo" show the rich, humorous foundation for their ethnic identity), yet it is a remarkable display of empathy and a strong polemic.

On "Wildside," Marky Mark narrates several real-life tragedies, but the Stuart case is the song's center; its details are proof of Marky Mark's social consciousness. His voice isn't mature enough to sound bitter, but his sense of outrage gives this Boston Irish kid an undeniable emotional link to Ed O.G. & Da Bulldogs. Marky Mark's hip hop consciousness in "Wildside" is another form of homage, this time to the political status of African Americans that even whites are coming to share. The video begins matter-of-factly with a burning American flag—the kind of inflammatory image Marky Mark was able to get past MTV censors after 2 Black 2 Strong & the MMG's *Burn, Baby Burn* video was stopped.

Marky Mark's racially enlightened social protest is also an advance for white pop, as demonstrated by the "Wildside" bass line from Lou Reed's "Walk on the Wild Side." Bad-boy Marky purposely follows Reed's lawless example, but he stops short of Reed's bohemian white-negro tradition. "Wildside" covers Reed studiously but leaves out his chorus intro, "And the colored girls say . . ." This is intentional and smart for its implicit Afrocentric acknowledgment. There's no exoticism in Marky Mark's crossover; he maintains his own identity without circumscribing an Other. (This healthy approach to pop means he'll never have to cover Reed's masochistic-racist "I Wanna Be Black.")

"Wildside" speaks on a level of social identification that hip hop represents better than any other contemporary art form. (The video for Marky

Mark's antigreed screed "I Need Money" boldly spotlights the era's villains, starting with George Bush, Charles Keating, and Michael Milken and ending with Ronald Reagan.) Marky Mark touches realities that more adept white rappers like Jesse Jaymes or Kid Panic avoid. His empathy allows him to express the tension felt by the new, vocally empowered white working class. Songs like "Wildside," and "I Need Money" provide cross-racial, emotional solidarity; it's hip hop with a purpose, not just radio fodder. Marky Mark isn't simply in it to win it.

Young Black Teenagers' best track, "Daddy Kalled Me Niga 'Cause I Likeded   22
to Rhyme," only added to the racial static it attempted to calm. There may be no resolution to the cultural tension provoked by the class and race divisions of rock 'n' roll and hip hop, but the integration happens best when it happens unostentatiously, as in De La Soul's sampling of Wayne Fontana and the Mind Benders on "My Brother's a Basehead" or Marky Mark's "Peace."

Marky Mark relishes that hip hop salutation for more than fun. He poses   23
its ameliorating notion against the "racial tension" and "fussin' and cussin'" he knows he will provoke in some whites and Blacks. His hip hop gregariousness extends to the white b-boy image he cultivates: backwards cap, exposed muscle, peekaboo briefs, and lowriding jeans.

Since whites can't cut it vocally in hip hop, where the texture of African   24
American speech is as musical an element as the samples used, the visual image is all-important. Marky Mark knows that the white assumption of this image is the reason he and Vanilla Ice and Gerardo exist and prosper— they're the non-Black mediators of hip hop aesthetics. But he avoids this racist trap by dint of his boyish, cartoon eroticism. No match for the sexual images of L.L. Cool J, King Sun, Chuck D, Big Daddy Kane, or Treach, Marky Mark simulates their swagger and energy in a way that's as amusing as it is flattering.

Marky Mark delineates how new styles of white fashion result from cul-   25
tural transference; his hip hop–era innocence presents something new: working-class confidence that proudly maintains the source of witty behavioral innovations without trading it in for middle-class snobbery (cf. his good-sense *Interview* magazine statements on class).

If Public Enemy represents Blackness as (among its many meanings) a   26
metaphorical condition recognizable to any unempowered person, Marky Mark underscores that proposition. He says "Peace" in imitation of hip hop attitude, but it's also fellowship, his communion with homeboys as social and ideological neighbors. Marky Mark takes such honest pleasure in hip hop phrases that when his voice goes surfer-boy flat saying "Wooord!" he still demonstrates the process by which slang moves through culture from

Blacks to whites and between generations. Marky Mark himself becomes the
site of racial/cultural exchange.

Marky Mark's style may be transparent (the underwear bit suggests that   27
he knows white sexual fear and racial naïveté are inseparable from his success), but his effort is forthright. His manner and delivery capitulate to Black
style in ways that those of Vanilla Ice and Tairrie B. don't. It's flattery with
intelligence, and on "So What Chu Sayin'?" he defines the entire racial/
aesthetic complex of white rappers:

See, some do hiphop and forget how it started
They claim their white complexion
Ain't the reason why their records charted
Please!
Man, it's so easy to see
When a white dude raps
The public calls it a novelty
Even me, although I take it seriously
Some dislike me because of my r-a-c-e
But I won't quit and I won't stop
'Cuz I do hiphop just because I love hiphop
I never claim to be vanilla
I'm Irish American
And never did I claim to be African American . . .
With respect to the Old School
That created this art form
It comes from the heart
Not from critical acclaim
'Cuz that's just the same as the political game.

If hip hop can inspire a white American kid to such cogent cultural   28
analysis that shows respect for others and sees politics even in rock criticism, it surely will outlast all its detractors. Marky Mark makes the prospect
of all-American rap a little less frightening.

Whiteface Mimicry: Dissin' Race and Culture

Miles Davis asked, "When you say 'pop,' that's white, isn't it?" The answer   29
goes back to Al Jolson singing "Mammy" in blackface—the first Beastie Boy.
But an act as meretricious as Vanilla Ice is such a cynically calculated, contemporary example of pop that it destroys any optimistic delusion about
shared, democratic culture. Not only does pop put Black art under siege but
the natural function of culture and the way it perpetuates itself are all undergoing an obvious, shameless, systematic perversion. (So perverse that

even 3rd Bass can make a song and video, "Pop Goes the Weasel," that singles out Vanilla Ice's appropriation of rap as a less noxious act than their own.) The pop forces that conspired to give Vanilla Ice his ascension are disgusting; his rapping is merely rotten.

A conventional critical approach to Vanilla Ice gets us nowhere because   30 it presumes standards of judgment and competence that the whole phenomenon of whites imitating Blacks' music has always obviated. Whether it's Lisa Stansfield, Vanilla Ice, Michael Bolton, or the Beastie Boys, the disgrace of such ethnic/cultural mimicry lies in its political meaning. And that's what is hidden in the unsophisticated, indeed, racist, responses that such work solicits. When "smoothing over" a Black sound occurs, it is a moralizing act, judging the ethnic traits and meanings of a sound inferior, unbeautiful, or bad, somehow in need of white correction.

But listeners responsible for big sales must not be able to hear how   31 awkward some of these imitations look and sound—the strain, the lack of elegance and potency, pass them by or else are received kindly, as fond tics. Despite his dysfunctions, Vanilla Ice is an emblem of usurpation and suppression. The canniest thing about him—his name (replacing the legal Robert Van Winkle)—indicates the issue of taste. Racial preference is central to his existence and explains why he got TV and radio airplay. He is promoted instead of the other Ices—T, Cube, and Just—because of the fiat of marketers. The preference for vanilla sublimates chocolate as it always does in white-run industries that deem Blackness unacceptable or objectionable.

It is a perfect coincidence that what Vanilla Ice has to say—nothing—   32 leaves his representation of whiteness his only point. As mass culture's most prominent exemplar of rap, he helped suppress the music's original African American essence and expression. He even faked reggae rap on "Rostaman" to keep Black ingenuity marginalized. Vanilla Ice's primary cultural achievement is that he lays to rest Norman Mailer's fifties notion of "the white negro" as a white middle-class aspiration. By now the move is past achieving a psychic state of elegance and endurance; it's a move toward omnipotence, the hidden compulsion of white supremacy.

With better, late-eighties whiteface acts like the Beastie Boys and 3rd   33 Bass and Young Black Teenagers, the impulse is also omnivorous. The Beastie Boys' album *Licensed to Ill* offers a set of songs that, heard today, sound less like rap than like a postmodern potpourri of styles from blues-metal to sampled sounds, all borrowed, of course, from Black sources. It is inauthentic as rap because the appropriations lack the effrontery that inspired the first rap artists. The Beastie Boys end up parodying the Black artists' original subversions—and their original celebration—which expressed a special need to achieve some control (some say) over pop-culture influences and to participate in their native musical tradition.

That is why the Beastie Boys' second album, *Paul's Boutique,* sank with- 34
out a trace: The joke of the group's Black parody came from the novelty of
its accomplished white mimicry and not-so-subtle ridicule. (Before the Beastie
Boys the best rap record by a white performer was Mel Brooks's aptly titled
"It's Good to Be the King.") Like an invading army on its second offensive,
the Beasties lost the element of surprise that once startlingly announced, "I
control what I can deride."

If Black exploitation is the second-oldest profession in the West, there 35
may be significance in it as a neurotic projection of Manifest Destiny. The
pop imitation of Black music is less a suggestion of white self-denial than a
disguise of tyrant's guilt. And though the envy factor looms large, it's too late
to think that white business people appropriate Black art to flatter their
powerless dupes—or merely for profit. There is another, less obvious, compulsion to normalize their hegemony.

White appropriation (such as TV's *Murphy Brown* using Aretha Franklin 36
as I.D.) may look like a form of tribute, but it preys more than it praises. And
while the political distortion is truly horrible, the traducement of Black aesthetics can be hilariously grotesque: the Beastie Boys' bowdlerized rage,
Vanilla Ice's too tense 'tude. Eerily, when I reached to replay *Licensed to Ill*
my roughly alphabetical record collection had the Beastie boys next to Julie
Brown's *Trapped in the Body of a White Girl* and the BMOC's twelve-inch
single, "Play That Funk."

The latter 1988 curio is a one-record genre of frat rap, made by a pair of 37
white male students from Harvard and Bennington, that I held onto just because it was so gruesome and boasted the prestige of a Nile Rodgers production. These white boys show an almost embarrassing affection for rap,
yet they can't help but adulterate its musical and sexual integrity. They steal
slang and rhythm that, like the Beasties', say less about how white American
males deal with their personal culture than how they condescend to the
spontaneous actions of the less advantaged. The air of frivolity reasserts the
blithe indifference that came down on rappers in the first place. Carried
away, these Big Men on Campus expose themselves:

Sgt. Rock is my middle name
Sucker-punching Nazis is my claim to fame
I'm a Harvard undergrad
A scholarly scholar
And I use rap music
To make me dollar

The ungrammatical choice of "dollar" is an appropriately wack Black- 38
ism, portraying BMOC's truest identification with the Black underclass's urge
to make money. (Unlike Marky Mark's "I Need Money," BMOC's sentiment

is completely unironic.) The song makes a telling move from antifascism to profiteering. When the record flopped, rapper Sultan MC (John Shecter) moved on to edit the ad-rich, self-proclaimed "magazine of Hip-hop music, culture & politics," *The Source*—the dollar-making guidebook to rebel music as a simulacrum of white brattiness. *The Source* makes plain the distortion of Black ideas through white mediation. For people who hear Black art only as rhythm or attitude, not as ideas. *The Source*'s editorial bent encourages the artistic vapidity of hip hop culture. Instead of challenging the music to articulate and sustain political ferment—a real affront to the status quo—it emphasizes the tantrum, teen-idol aspect, the infantilization. This may be all white rap can ever attain—a parody of Black that, in fact, hides the self-hatred of whites (and the masochism of some Jews, such as Sandra Bernhard brought out in *Without You I'm Nothing*).

These things were more clearly understood before pop-culture machinery became so invincible. The 1927 movie *The Jazz Singer* pinpointed the ethics-and-ethnic dilemma that the talented Jewish playwright Samson Raphaelson first outlined in his original stage play about the rabbi's son who pays the price of fame singing jazz in dives. From Jolson's heartfelt minstrel-show parodies on, some form of darkie mimicking has been the strongest musical tradition in pluralized American culture. It's the love-hate link between the oppressor and the oppressed—the tension Rick Rubin used to animate *Tougher Than Leather.* 39

White appropriation attempts to erase the culture it plunders—a metaphor for the submission that dominant groups will upon others. Raphaelson was ambivalent about this, but he understood that the celebrity and fortune ethnic entertainers found through self-abnegation was balanced by a spiritual loss. Almost exactly sixty years later, three New York Jewish boys mimicked the badass attitude of rappers (eighties minstrels) and, as the Beastie Boys, broke the barriers of airplay and media promotion that had resisted the efforts of Black rap artists. The advent of Vanilla Ice does not suggest that show-biz politics have improved any. 40

But the white influence isn't all negative. The Beastie Boys were a watershed for a culture they didn't create because of the social advantages open to those in control of industry and media. The Beastie Boys' *Licensed to Ill* album, like *The Jazz Singer,* Hollywood's first sound film, made history as a technological achievement that revolutionized the art form. That may be only because Hank Shocklee was burrowing through academe at the time, although a pertinent question nags as to why Rubin, the Beasties' producer, was unable to get an equally rich-sounding mix for Def Jam's Black artists at the time. Rap wasn't waiting for the Beastie Boys to improve its earliest stages—although white listeners and critics may have been in suspense, anticipating rappers whose voices *sounded* like their own—but there's no 41 denying that the form's current prominence partly derives from their boost. As ever, the price of fame is heritage, this time Black heritage, as the music industry paves the way for an onslaught of white artists into Black musical forms—a passing parade from Vanilla Ice to Snow. The Beastie Boys hold the official record for the first number-one rap album and single. These racial anomalies are cultural facts, but they shouldn't be swallowed whole.

Me-too Acts: An Emphatic Top Ten

America disseminates Black culture much more readily than Black politics, so thank God for the particular genius of life that turns Black culture's influence into political fact. I want to comment on ten acts that would have been unthinkable without the inspiration the artists (good and bad) got from hip hop. Listening to a bunch of white rappers is as remote from the pleasure of listening to indigenous rap as reading is from dancing, but it is the particular genius of rap to bring out some intellectual spark, some musical pleasure, in almost anyone who attempts it. Among these "me-too, me-too" acts are some expected abominations but also some surprising, legitimate pop wonder. Like their Black counterparts, these white acts capture a moment in America's social-cultural-political development revealing the empathy that occurs between social groups despite the official divisions of race. 42

THE GOATS, *TRICKS OF THE SHADE* (RUFFHOUSE/COLUMBIA)

Trying too hard to copy the uncanny political fantasia of a De La Soul skit, The Goats conceived their debut album around the idea of capitalist America as a racist carnival in which spectators and performers all are "freaks." The word is a faulty imitation of the surreal hatred/affection in the term *nigger,* which no white group should feel right about using. Yet, The Goats' choice for a substitute proves them imaginatively stunted, witless. The satire here is more like a collegiate revue than Black rappers' street-rooted colloquial humor: British carny barkers . . . ("This is the Shoot-the-Black-Guy Gallery"); suburban naifs ("Scam's our uncle, he's gonna take care of us"); and fatuous ironists ("I'll be dreaming of a Black Christmas") make up The Goats' menagerie. 43

White critics celebrated The Goats, perhaps after relating to the prospect of cultural scavenging in the name but also—no doubt—approving the group's "correct" political sentiments, which are stated as dully but more straightforwardly than the implicit liberalism of most white rock criticism. The Goats' masochism (referring to their own dreaded selves as Hangerheads in several of the album's lamely enunciated pro-choice abortion songs) syncs with the way white rock critics like to identify Black victimhood. It's hard to tell if, in a song about the vengeance African Americans are entitled to, the lines "Rodney King would love [to take] a swing / if Yusuf Hawkins was 44 walkin' he'd say the same thing" are cruel or just stupid. But by concentrating on this position, The Goats willingly indulge pity rather than actual acts of Black defiance as in the great (but critically despised) Willlie D song "Rodney K."

SNOW, 12 INCHES OF SNOW (EASTWEST RECORDS AMERICA)

The most successful white rap act since Vanilla Ice, Snow has a better mon-   45
icker (which occasions the best line on the album: "Snow's getting deeper"). Plus, the benefits from the rootsy credibility of his reggae imitations. "Informer," the spring 1993 number-one single, cashed in on hip hop's borrowing from dance hall, a historically distorted certification of cultural trends that the market insists have a white signifier. (Snow gets the credit for Shabba Rank's foregone artistic impact.) While Snow is more vocally adept than your average white rap wannabe—his tongue breezily twists the raggamuffin-style fast talk—there is a sameness and lapsing intensity, despite the more musical sense of rhythm that reggae confers on anyone. (Snow's attempts at singing "Uhh in You" and "Can't Get Enough" recall the sweet-voiced, reggae-intoxicated ballads of Scritti Politti's Green Gartside.) "Informer" is actually the first hit record by New York rapper MC Shan, who produced Snow's smash and vocalizes the rap break. Shan's own savvy business maneuvering is disguised in the song's story about Snow being set up to the police by a "friend." It's classic folkart subterfuge, an updated Uncle Remus tale portraying a pretentious white's fear of being caught out.

In colonial countries struggling for independence Shan would be called   46
a native informant. He plays the almost indispensable role of Black teacher/ trainer who helps the white star successfully translate Black culture to the mass audience. There's poetic justice of a kind in Shan's biggest record's belonging to someone else while confessing, "See, this is what I had to do to get paid in the overcrowded rap field."

KID ROCK, THE POLYFUZE METHOD (CONTINUUM/TOP DOG RECORDS)

This completes the rock-to-rap metamorphosis that started with *Licensed*   47
to Ill and surpasses the Beastie Boys through the absence of a single snide line or sample. Kid Rock's recipe is rudeness + metal. Instead of imitating rap rhythms and melodies, he proceeds on its liberation of subject matter and attitude, its legitimizing of youthful disaffection that *acknowledges* racial politics.

The subtext of this album is the typical dissatisfaction of white youth in   48
the hip hop era: Kid Rock confronts the shibboleths of his white working-class (Detroit suburban) upbringing; each brazen guitar riff and profane rhyme announces the revolution that has already happened in his mind. The

centerpiece, "My Oedipus Complex," tells a better story than Body Count's "Momma's Gotta Die Tonight"—trouncing parental limitations, agonizing over their distance like primal-scream John Lennon, then recognizing the pathetic humanity of misguided parents and topping that off with a leap of faith, recalling the parents' past reckless youth. It's a coup that outdoes Springsteen's family epics.

Kid Rock's emotional range includes Slick Rick's folky raunch. ("Fuck U Blind") and the cogent alienation of seventies punk rock ("In So Deep," a worthy match for any seventies punk classic). Playing his own guitar on most of the tracks, Kid Rock is a more accomplished and expressive artist than the Beastie Boys on their single release *Check Your Head;* each form he uses has a meaning and purpose, it's not for showing off. Skeptical of this white-rock tendency, Kid Rock disses House of Pain as an example of faking the punk. 49

This is intricate business. Attitude—as seen in ex-3rd Basser Minister Pete Nice's "Rat Bastard"—isn't enough to make a rapper. Kid Rock shows an authentic feel for hip hop impudence on "Balls in Your Mouth" when he loops a macho obscenity for the dirty thrill of it, yes, but the art of it comes from exposing boyish ego. (The difference is what makes 2 Live Crew's "Me So Horny" sexist and this cut . . . well, fair.) 50

Instead of meanness, Kid Rock raps brattiness, spite rather than arrogance. When "Back from the Dead" reveals samples from both The Smiths and Public Enemy, it's plain that this is not a work of rockist privilege but of true, wide, and deep hip hop sophistication. 51

YOUNG BLACK TEENAGERS (SOUL)

The name is the only art here. Public Enemy producer Hank Shocklee's business determination obscures what truth and affection he knows about the white youth who admire rap. Except for the intensity of "My TV Went Black and White on Me"—a veritable instrumental—little truth or affection are apparent here. (YBT raps too fast; their imitator's eagerness gives the game away, just as whites, unsure of the rhythm, sometimes dance too fast to a slow groove.) The second album, *Dead Enz Kidz Doin' Lifetime Bidz,* has even less impact, except when it bites House of Pain on "Tap the Bottle" and "Outta My Head." But the group's name is the important cultural footnote: It's meant to confuse pop's racist precepts and signify the common rock 'n' rap identity. The name can be read cynically or hopefully, but, until Shocklee, Kamron, and Skribble can come up with raps that convey the complications of the white-to-Black crossover compulsion, the name conceit will just seem unfortunate. 52

CONSOLIDATED, *FRIENDLY FASCISM* (NETTWERK)

Consolidated's explosive aural environments are truly alarming. The group   53
spews out leftist doctrine so fast that it gains crazy lyricism of a kind. The
band uses a violent artifice—smart talk and rampaging sonic energy—to
combat musical inanity. This is the group the Disposable Heroes of Hiphoprisy are mistaken for. The straight-on approach to political pop music is
solidly in the tradition legitimized in America by rap, even though the band's
industrial sound is recognizable only as hip hop's extreme. That means
Public Enemy and the powerful opening riff that explodes throughout "In-
formodities '92" (from the second album, *Play More Music*) is worthy of
Shocklee's loudest, most undeniable aural dream. Consolidated go right for
the political issue—homophobia, vegetarianism, abortion—without the in-
sulting placation of cute, dumb rhymes like the Disposables use. This approach respects its audience's intelligence—the most direct method to
moving the mind and butt by white people since Gang of Four. Consolidated's impact is unrelenting except for the vox pop tracks recorded at
the band's gigs, where fans get to give a piece of their mind or just criticize
the band; it's as beautifully democratic as the neighborhood shout-outs on
the New York cable-TV rap show *Video Music Box*.

HOUSE OF PAIN (TOMMY BOY)

A B-side remix of "Put on Your Shit Kickers" is a live performance (superior   54
to the LP version) where the lead rapper begins another good-natured litany
of things Irish: "I got the corned beef." His partner Danny Boy responds in
a stoned, happily incredulous vice, "I got the matzoh?!" wonderfully sum-
ming up white rap's ethnic confusion. House of Pain's many Irish American
boasts (from shillelaghs to cladagh rings) recognize that rap's specificity isn't
simply about race but about ethnicity. The form gives America's ethnic
groups a new way to celebrate themselves, asserting the pride necessary to
maintain self-esteem in a society that otherwise oppresses and diminishes
them. Even the specific forms of loutishness that House of Pain brag on—
carousing, fighting, drinking—are more about legitimizing oneself through
subcultural habit than about defying middle-class conformity. This is the basis of House of Pain's ethnocentric hip hop—it's a complex, irresistible act
of white emulation by the group's leader, Erik Schrody, who, as a solo artist
in Ice-T's Rhyme Syndicate, first became known as Everlast (a reference to
boxing as a way out of poverty for Irish as well as African Americans). It also
derives from the social circumstances implicit in the Latino rap of the Los
Angeles group Cypress Hill, who also produced this LP.

"Jump Around," House of Pain's establishing single, is a triumph of eth-   55
nic illing—the very thing the Beastie Boys were slick enough to gainsay
but that Cypress Hill, with significantly more ethnic fortitude, used to ener-

gize their own superb eponymous debut album that mixed funk and Latin rhythms, Black and Hispanic sensibilities. (It's also indicative of the class confines that the Jewish Beastie boys have escaped.) The song's rubbery piano melody accommodates Irish step dancing, but DJ Muggs's arrangement also distorts the rhythm, first into Public Enemy–style caginess and then into a purely blunted high. And Everlast keeps us (the record debuts his sharpened rapping style), spitting out words menacingly, raising drunken barroom spiel to hip hop lyricism.

House of Pain's superiority over the Beastie Boys comes out of this intrinsic sense of fun in class attitude and behavior. Identity's the central element, and the depth of this cross-cultural Irish-Latino-African-American commiseration and comradeship can be found in one tiny but telling detail: the way House of Pain use the work *punk*—not in the British sense or the usual (white) rock-crit or Establishment sense, but as a sexist (originally homophobic) street epithet. This macho identification is a rap commonplace that House of Pain does not transcend; in fact, the group's startling command of nonwhite lingo and delinquent's attitude is disturbingly similar to the subcult toughness of white hate groups. Everlast's skinhead, tattooed image is additionally disorienting—another complication of pop semiotics that typifies the harsher, more strained political climate than what produced the Beastie Boys' mideighties appropriations. As America's poor increasingly are divided against each other, their isolation, frustration, and fury blurs. The dispossessed begin to look alike.

It turns out that the response on that live exchange is actually "I got the Motts"—the rapper's delirious consternation is, of course, applesauce. Like any good rap group, House of Pain—an excellent name for personal paranoia, as well as the general state of things (taken from the movie *The Island of Lost Souls*)—offers reasons to be cheerful and uneasy.

THE BEASTIE BOYS, *LICENSED TO ILL* (DEF JAM/COLUMBIA)

Their only good album, despite the rock-crit acclaim that mounts with each later release (the uneven hodge-podge *Paul's Boutique,* the execrable *Check Your Head,* and the unlistenable *Ill Communication*). Some of this record's impudence influenced later white artists' releases, but even those albums (by House of Pain, Kid Rock) transcended the Beastie Boys' dilettantish slumming in rap style. This first album was full of humor, making the group hip hop comedians, their posturing on a par with the Fat Boys. But subsequent records confirm the suspicion that much of the Beastie Boys' agenda was a condescending parody of rap. Their style is to do rap vocalizing over a silly mélange of metal, soul, salsa, R & B, whatever, but with decreasing vigor and wit. The 1992 track "The Biz vs. the Nuge," a Beasties-sponsored collision between Biz Markie and Ted Nugent (Black rap and white rock reduced to its inanities), was pointless except to imply that all pop is travesty. And that's what it means to those who don't care about it.

JESSE JAYMES, *THIRTY FOOTER IN YOUR FACE* (DELICIOUS VINYL)

Matt Dike and Michael Ross, the "chefs" at Delicious Vinyl, have committed the recipe for commercial hip hop to their memories and bank vault. After their big successes signing and producing Tone Loc and Young MC, they finally cooked up a white rapper. Jesse Jaymes is lo-cal rap from SoCal, with fun, not decadent, beats. 59

J.J. has a sunny disposition, like all Delicious Vinyl acts, but the suspicion builds throughout this album that Dike and Ross add sweetness only to make up for the lack of grit. The spiciest part of "Wild Thing" and "Bust a Move" was the taste of life lived hard (Blackness). J.J.'s only crisis is a cartoon escapade called "Dave the Bookie." It shows that white youth see life as fun (while Black youth see it as survival). Bleaching rap—even this well—means neutering it. Compare J.J.'s "$55 Motel" (in which he raps, "I was rocking those bells just like L.L.") to L.L. Cool J's "Bristol Hotel," and note the effort to whitewash an art form almost beyond recognition. Mission accomplished. 60

THE DISPOSABLE HEROES OF HIPHOPRISY, *HYPOCRISY IS THE GREATEST LUXURY* (4TH & BROADWAY)

If you dismiss this group, you must be cruel—or else about to have a party. This is the least fun hip hop band I can think of. Not only are rapper Michael Franti and partner Rono Tse groove stingy, but their messages are presumptuous to the point of boredom. 61

The pretentious, cumbersome monicker is a tip-off to their literal-minded seriousness. "Hiphoprisy" is not a witty coinage; it lacks the free-and-easy disregard of linguistic rules that often is evident when rappers flip meanings and tweak homonyms. (Try Chuck D's "The women make the men all pause" to describe a situation of sexual dysfunction.) 62

Franti is straining, sweating to be clever. When this kind of guy hits the books you can feel the pages cringe—just like your neck muscles. But when a rapper displays this kind of nerdy solemnity, it makes white critics all cough up their most pandering tributes. The Disposables have been called "smart" and important—the kind of assessment that most often means that the reviewer approves of what is being said. Certainly the Disposables are not musically important; they are "important" the way *Time* and *Newsweek* are considered more important than *X-Men* or *The Punisher*. 63

But reading newsmagazines doesn't make one smart, it doesn't make one a poet, and it doesn't mean one's regurgitation of "facts" matters. The Disposables have not transformed anything they read; they lyrics are cold, 64 dull, obvious. Their slogans lie inert atop even the few bumptious rhythm tracks. But in the game of pop-music politics, the Disposables are being hailed as hip hop intellectuals. The Disposables have been horribly misused by reviewers anxious to find "acceptable," "proper," "polite" rappers. In a most pathetic (and foolish) divide-and-conquer tactic, these San Francisco hip hoppers have been propped up as ideals against the unruly, disputatious Public Enemy, Ice Cube, and Sister Souljah.

Their elevation starts with the basic inability to appreciate rap as a genuine intellectual, rhythmic vocal-art form. The Disposables exemplify a made-up, bourgeois "smartness" instead of giving off the sense of a newly discovered, freshly felt idea or experience—and even when Slick Rick, DJ Quick, or Roxanne Shanté achieves that, it is the art of hard thought transformed into an *act*. Those street rappers only seem nonintellectual, while the Disposables practically wave *The Economist* in your face, hoping you'll notice everything they say has been processed from some official middlebrow source and wasn't merely felt.

This group lacks precisely the thing that is so fundamentally charming and thrilling about Sister Souljah, that unbeatable ability to convey passion. Franti is a withering, dry vocalist. He doesn't rap; he talks. And the only time he summons creative energy is to do an imitation of Chuck D that is, arguably, a dis. It's on the title track, which predictably has been praised as a brave confrontation with the "hypocrisy" of rap artists. Franti's list of career errors targets those performers with the bad taste to grow up in public. Worst of all, this gets interpreted as a defense of the moral standards that rappers ought not offend (you know, white capitalist politics). Funny thing is, the Disposables didn't do this album for charity. Sad thing is, this album isn't funny.

Only a churl could get a kick out of Chuck D vocal inflections chained to rhymes as awful as this one from "Television, the Drug of the Nation" (catchy title): "The bass, the treble / Don't make a rebel / Having your life together does."

On this song, the Disposables' first single, they come up with observations such as "breeding ignorance and feeding radiation" that weren't even news thirty years ago. These are traditional gripes, easy to take because they are not revolutionary. In fact, it *is* TV—a homogenization of what we already know.

That also goes for the words-music counterpoint. The Disposable (Franti and Tse used to be members of the West Coast thrash band The Beatnuts) use dissonance and rhythm in obvious, dull ways—as sonic effect and background noise. This is weak stuff compared to San Francisco thrash rappers Consolidated, and though the group is acknowledged on The Disposables' liner notes, there's no evidence that Consolidated's talent rubbed off.

Even the most Consolidated-like song, "Language of Violence," is an ut- 70
ter failure. It's a supposed attack on homophobia but done in the idiotic, essentially homophobic manner of Terence Trent D'Arby's "Billy Don't Fall."
In Franti's scenario, a gay basher goes to prison and gets raped: "The young
bully felt fear / He'd never been on this side of the name calling." By Franti's
effed-up logic, homo sex remains a crime. But that's just the second offense
in a song with these lines:

But dehumanizing the victim makes things simpler
It's like breathing with a respirator
It eases the conscience of even the most conscious
And calculating violator.

The best thing about the Disposables is the appropriateness of the name 71
they gave themselves.

MARKY MARK, "YOU GOTTA BELIEVE" (INTERSCOPE)

At the moment Marky Mark disgraced his rap credibility by selling it out to 72
a racist Calvin Klein ad, he released his best record. This single (again produced by brother Donnie) confirms Marky's naive rap faith, but it doesn't
take off until female vocalist Darcelle Wilson wails encouragement and
Marky delivers his most urgent, rhythmic rap. It makes a good farewell disc,
insisting on Marky's good intentions in the face of the media's backlash exposé of his juvenile court rap sheet for ethnic and gay bashing. It's pitiful
end for what should have been a happy American story, but this disc shows
it's still a classic tale.

Marky's growth out of white Boston's racist, insular environment into 73
being a frontman for an integrated rap group and a gay icon is the bil-
dungsroman that American fiction celebrated before hip hop. Now, with
new nonwhite examples of Horatio Alger (superficial) success, Marky seems
to be doing penance for nothing more than reminding the larger society of
its hypocrisies—the race baiting and gay bashing that white males indulge
in as a right of passage and big business's noxious exploitation of sexuality.
Now the insincerity includes appropriating Marky's rap bona fides (and
show-biz gimmickry) and attempting to convert it into images of white erotic
supremacy. A Black rapper's sexuality would upset the balance of trade,
whereas the nasty look of a white thug rapper like Everlast is equally threatening. Marky conveys the innocent dumbness of probably most white rap
aficionados. His very innocuousness has been turned against him. And still
he insists, for the best reasons you can imagine, "You gotta believe!"

Working with the Text

1. White begins his essay by explaining the original title of the essay,"Who Wants to See Ten Niggers Play Basketball?" was adapted from a 1987 movie about rap pioneers Run DMC. What does Rick Rubin's original statement mean? What larger significance does White find in it? What tone is set with the word "niggers," and what purposes are served by that tone? Why do you think the essay's title rephrases Rubin's line as a question?

2. Why does the author prefer Marky Mark to rappers such as the Beastie Boys, Vanilla Ice, and 3rd Bass? What is the paradox confronted by white artists working with black musical forms, and how has Marky Mark avoided its dangers and exploited its possibilities? Why does the author assert that "Marky Mark makes the prospect of all-American rap a little less frightening"?

3. Why does White believe that "ethnic specificity is crucial" to hip hop? What does he mean by the phrase "ethnic specificity" and why is it so important? Which of the ten "me-too acts" best demonstrate this specificity? Which honor other key features of hip hop, such as its "mythmaking, muckraking imperative"? Since the essay appeared in 1995, several of these artists have become famous, while others have virtually disappeared. How well do White's values predict artistic and commercial success?

 4. In the course of exploring the racial borders of hip hop, White refers to other, older "border performances," such as blackface minstrelsy. Perhaps the most specific of these references, cited several times, derives from Norman Mailer's famous essay "The White Negro," widely influential since its publication in the 1950s. Using either a library or the Internet, find out what a "white negro" is. Then discuss the author's claim that Vanilla Ice laid it to rest "as a white middle-class aspiration." Is White being ironic when he calls this interment Vanilla Ice's "primary cultural achievement"?

 5. At the time the essay was written, White saw the music industry preparing for "an onslaught of white artists into Black musical forms." White's observation was astute; the late 1990s and early 2000s saw such an onslaught, not only of white rappers, but also of white singers adopting the sound of black rhythm and blues. Choose one such artist, and use White's criteria to assess in an essay whether the artist emulates or appropriates, honors or plunders, black music. (Alternatively, choose a pair of artists representing the kind of contrast

that White found in Marky Mark and Vanilla Ice.) Though your argument will necessarily be subjective, you must support your claims with specific evidence from the artists' work. Be prepared to cite song lyrics and statements to the press, along with details of dress, manner, and appearance.

Who and What Is American?

LEWIS H. LAPHAM

Born in San Francisco in 1935, Lewis Lapham attended Yale and later worked as a reporter for a variety of newspapers and magazines. Since 1971 he has been the editor of *Harper's* magazine, for which he contributes a monthly column of ideas. One of the best known journalists and social critics in America, Lapham has written on topics ranging from environmentalism and conservation to education, politics, and class and race relations. His books include *Money and Class in America* (1988), *Imperial Masquerade* (1990), and *Hotel America: Scenes in the Lobby at the Fin-de-Siècle* (1995). In the following 1992 essay, Lapham argues that instead of focusing on a kind of identity politics based on difference, Americans should be raising serious questions about the forces that bind them together.

There may not be an American character, but there is the emotion of being American. It has many resemblances to the emotion of being Russian—that feeling of nostalgia for some undetermined future when man will have improved himself beyond recognition and when all will be well.

—V. S. Pritchett

Were I to believe what I read in the papers, I would find it easy to think that   1
I no longer can identify myself simply as an American. The noun apparently means nothing unless it is dressed up with at least one modifying adjective. As a plain American I have neither voice nor authentic proofs of existence. I acquire a presence only as an old American, a female American, a white American, a rich American, a black American, a gay American, a poor American, a native American, a dead American. The subordination of the noun to the adjectives makes a mockery of both the American premise and the democratic spirit, but it serves the purposes of the politicians as well as the news media, and throughout the rest of this election year I expect the political

campaigns to pitch their tents and slogans on the frontiers of race and class. For every benign us, the candidates will find a malignant them; for every neighboring we (no matter how eccentric or small in number), a distant and devouring they. The strategies of division sell newspapers and summon votes, and to the man who would be king (or president or governor) the popular hatred of government matters less than the atmosphere of resentment in which the people fear and distrust one another.

Democratic politics trades in only two markets—the market in expecta- 2
tion and the market in blame. A collapse in the former engenders a boom in the latter. Something goes wrong in the news—a bank swindle of genuinely spectacular size, a series of killings in Milwaukee, another disastrous assessment of the nation's schools—and suddenly the air is loud with questions about the paradox of the American character or the Puritan subtexts of the American soul. The questions arise from every quarter of the political compass—from English professors and political consultants as well as from actors, corporate vice presidents, and advertising salesmen—and the conversation is seldom polite. Too many of the people present no longer can pay the bills, and a stray remark about acid rain or a third-grade textbook can escalate within a matter of minutes into an exchange of insults. Somebody calls Jesse Helms a fascist, and somebody else says that he is sick and tired of paying ransom money to a lot of welfare criminals. People drink too much and stay too late, their voices choked with anecdote and rage, their lexicons of historical reference so passionately confused that both Jefferson and Lincoln find themselves doing thirty-second commercials for racial quotas, a capital gains tax, and the Persian Gulf War.

The failures in the nation's economy have marked up the prices for ob- 3
vious villains, and if I had a talent for merchandising I would go into the business of making dolls (black dolls, white dolls, red-necked dolls, feminist dolls, congressional dolls) that each of the candidates could distribute at fund-raising events with a supply of color-coordinated pins. Trying out their invective in the pre-season campaigns, the politicians as early as last October were attributing the cause of all our sorrows to any faction, interest, or minority that could excite in their audiences the passions of a beloved prejudice. David Duke in Louisiana denounced the subsidized beggars (i.e., black people) who had robbed the state of its birthright. At a partisan theatrical staged by the Democratic Party in New Hampshire, Senator Tom Harkin reviled the conspiracy of Republican money. President Bush went to Houston, Texas, to point a trembling and petulant finger at the United States Congress. If the country's domestic affairs had been left to him, the President said, everybody would be as prosperous and smug as Senator Phil Gramm, but the liberals in Congress (blind as mollusks and selfish as eels) had wrecked the voyage of boundless opportunity.

The politicians follow the trends, and apparently they have been told 4
by their handlers to practice the arts of the demagogue. Certainly I cannot
remember an election year in which the political discourse—among newspaper editorialists and the single-issue lobbies as well as the candidates—
relied so unashamedly on pitting rich against poor, black against white,
male against female, city against suburb, young against old. Every public
event in New York City—whether academic appointment, traffic delay, or
homicide—lends itself to both a black and a white interpretation of the
news. The arguments in the arenas of cultural opinion echo the same bitter
refrain. The ceaseless quarrels about the canon of preferred texts (about
Columbus the Bad and Columbus the Good, about the chosen company of
the politically correct, about the ice people and the sun people) pick at the
scab of the same questions. Who and what is an American? How and where
do we find an identity that is something other than a fright mask? When using the collective national pronoun ("we the people," "we happy few," etc.)
whom do we invite into the club of the we?

Maybe the confusion is a corollary to the end of the Cold War. The im- 5
age of the Soviet Union as monolithic evil held in place the image of the
United States as monolithic virtue. Break the circuit of energy transferred between negative and positive poles, and the two empires dissolve into the
waving of sectional or nationalist flags. Lacking the reassurance of a foreign
demon, we search our own neighborhoods for fiends of convincing malevolence and size.

The search is a boon for the bearers of false witness and the builders of 6
prisons. Because it's so easy to dwell on our differences, even a child of
nine can write a Sunday newspaper sermon about the centrifugal forces that
drive the society apart. The more difficult and urgent questions have to do
with the centripetal forces that bind us together. What traits of character or
temperament do we hold in common? Why is it that I can meet a black man
in a street or a Hispanic woman on a train and imagine that he and I, or she
and I, share an allied hope and a joint purpose? That last question is as
American as it is rhetorical, and a Belgian would think it the work of a
dreaming imbecile.

What we share is a unified field of emotion, but if we mistake the sources 7
of our energy and courage (i.e., if we think that our uniqueness as Americans rests with the adjectives instead of the noun) then we can be rounded
up in categories and sold the slogan of the week for the fear of the month.
Political campaigns deal in the commodity of votes, and from now until November I expect that all of them will divide the American promise into its
lesser but more marketable properties. For reasons of their own convenience, the sponsors of political campaigns (Democratic, environmental,

racial, Republican, sexual, or military-industrial) promote more or less the same false constructions of the American purpose and identity. As follows:

> That the American achieves visible and specific meaning only by reason of his or her association with the political guilds of race, gender, age, ancestry, or social class.

The assumption is as elitist as the view that only a woman endowed   8
with an income of $1 million a year can truly appreciate the beauty of money and the music of Cole Porter. Comparable theories of grace encourage the belief that only black people can know or teach black history, that no white man can play jazz piano, that blonds have a better time, and that Jews can't play basketball.

America was founded on precisely the opposite premise. We were al-   9
ways about becoming, not being; about the prospects for the future, not about the inheritance of the past. The man who rests his case on his color, like the woman who defines herself as a bright cloud of sensibility beyond the understanding of merely mortal men, makes a claim to special privilege not unlike the divine right of kings. The pretensions might buttress the cathedrals of our self-esteem, but they run counter to the lessons of our history.

We are a nation of parvenus, all bound to the hopes of tomorrow, or next   10
week, or next year. John Quincy Adams put it plainly in a letter to a German correspondent in the 1820s who had written on behalf of several prospective émigrés to ask about the requirements for their success in the New World. "They must cast off the European skin, never to resume it," Adams said. "They must look forward to their posterity rather than backward to their ancestors."

We were always a mixed and piebald company, even on the seventeenth-   11
century colonial seaboard, and we accepted our racial or cultural differences as the odds that we were obliged to overcome or correct. When John Charles Frémont (a.k.a. The Pathfinder) first descended into California from the East in 1843, he remarked on the polyglot character of the expedition accompanying him south into the San Joaquin Valley:

"Our cavalcade made a strange and grotesque appearance, and it was   12
impossible to avoid reflecting upon our position and composition in this remote solitude . . . still forced on south by a desert on one hand and a mountain range on the other; guided by a civilized Indian, attended by two wild ones from the Sierra; a Chinook from the Columbia; and our own mixture of American, French, German—all armed; four or five languages heard at once; about a hundred horses and mules, half-wild; American, Spanish and Indian dresses and equipments intermingled—such was our composition."

The theme of metamorphosis recurs throughout the whole chronicle of   13
American biography. Men and women start out in one place and end up in

another, never quite knowing how they got there, perpetually expecting the unexpected, drifting across the ocean or the plains until they lodge against a marriage, a land deal, a public office, or a jail. Speaking to the improvised character of the American experience, Daniel Boorstin, the historian and former Librarian of Congress, also summed up the case against the arithmetic of the political pollster's zip codes: "No prudent man dared to be too certain of exactly who he was or what he was about; everyone had to be prepared to become someone else. To be ready for such perilous transmigrations was to become an American."

That the American people aspire to become more nearly alike.

The hope is that of the ad salesman and the prison warden, but it has   14
become depressingly familiar among the managers of political campaigns. Apparently they think that no matter how different the native songs and dances in different parts of the country, all the tribes and factions want the same beads, the same trinkets, the same prizes. As I listen to operatives from Washington talk about their prospects in the Iowa or New Hampshire primary, I understand that they have in mind the figure of a perfect or ideal American whom everybody in the country would wish to resemble if only everybody could afford to dress like the dummies in the windows of Bloomingdale's or Saks Fifth Avenue. The public opinion polls frame questions in the alphabet of name recognitions and standard brands. The simplicity of the results supports the belief that the American citizen or the American family can be construed as a product, and that with only a little more time and a little more money for research and development all of us will conform to the preferred images seen in a commercial for Miller beer.

The apologists for the theory of the uniform American success some-   15
times present the example of Abraham Lincoln, and as I listen to their sentimental after-dinner speeches about the poor country grown to greatness, I often wonder what they would say if they had met the man instead of the statue. Throughout most of his life Lincoln displayed the character of a man destined for failure—a man who drank too much and told too many jokes (most of them in bad taste), who was habitually late for meetings and always borrowing money, who never seized a business opportunity and missed his own wedding.

The spirit of liberty is never far from anarchy, and the ur-American is apt   16
to look a good deal more like one of the contestants on *Let's Make a Deal* (i.e., somebody dressed like Madonna, or Wyatt Earp, or a giant iguana) than any of the yachtsmen standing around on the dock of Kennebunkport. If America is about nothing else, it is about the invention of the self. Because we have little use for history, and because we refuse the comforts of a society established on the blueprint of class privilege, we find ourselves set

adrift at birth in an existential void, inheriting nothing except the obligation to construct a plausible self, to build a raft of identity on which (with a few grains of luck and a cheap bank loan) maybe we can float south to Memphis or the imaginary islands of the blessed. We set ourselves the tasks of making and remaking our destinies with whatever lumber we happen to find lying around on the banks of the Snake or Pecos River.

Who else is the American hero if not a wandering pilgrim who goes forth on a perpetual quest? Melville sent Ahab across the world's oceans in search of a fabulous beast, and Thoreau followed the unicorn of his conscience into the silence of the Maine woods. Between them they marked out the trail of American literature as well as the lines of speculation in American real estate. To a greater or a lesser extent, we are all confidence men, actors playing the characters of our own invention and hoping that the audience—fortunately consisting of impostors as fanciful or synthetic as ourselves—will accept the performance at par value and suspend the judgments of ridicule.

The settled peoples of the earth seldom recognize the American as both a chronic revolutionary and a born pilgrim. The American is always on the way to someplace else (i.e., toward some undetermined future in which all will be well), and when he meets a stranger on the road he begins at once to recite the summary of the story so far—his youth and early sorrows, the sequence of his exits and entrances, his last divorce and his next marriage, the point of his financial departure and the estimated time of his spiritual arrival, the bad news noted and accounted for, the good news still to come. Invariably it is a pilgrim's tale, and the narrator, being American, assumes that he is addressing a fellow pilgrim. He means to exchange notes and compare maps. His newfound companion might be bound toward a completely different dream of Eden (a boat marina in Naples, Florida, instead of a garden in Vermont; a career as a Broadway dancer as opposed to the vice presidency of the Wells Fargo bank), but the destination doesn't matter as much as the common hope of coming safely home to the land of the heart's desire. For the time being, and until something better turns up, we find ourselves embarked on the same voyage, gazing west into the same blue distance.

> That the American people share a common code of moral
> behavior and subscribe to identical theories of the true,
> the good, and the beautiful.

Senator Jesse Helms would like to think so, and so would the enforcers of ideological discipline on the vocabulary of the doctrinaire left. The country swarms with people making rules about what we can say or read or study or smoke, and they imagine that we should be grateful for the moral guidelines (market-tested and government-inspected) imposed (for our own good) by a centralized bureau of temporal health and spiritual safety. The would-be reformers of the national character confuse the American sense of equality with the rule of conformity that governs a police state. It isn't that we believe that every American is as perceptive or as accomplished as any other, but we insist on the preservation of a decent and mutual respect across the lines of age, race, gender, and social class. No citizen is allowed to use another citizen as if he or she were a means to an end; no master can treat his servant as if he or she were only a servant; no government can deal with the governed as if they were nothing more than a mob of votes. The American loathing for the arrogant or self-important man follows from the belief that all present have bet their fortunes (some of them bigger than others, and some of them counterfeit or stolen) on the same hypothesis.

The American premise is an existential one, and our moral code is political, its object being to allow for the widest horizons of sight and the broadest range of expression. We protect the other person's liberty in the interest of protecting our own and our virtues conform to the terms and conditions of an arduous and speculative journey. If we look into even so coarse a mirror as the one held up to us by the situation comedies on prime-time television, we see that we value the companionable virtues—helpfulness, forgiveness, kindliness, and, above all, tolerance.   20

The passenger standing next to me at the rail might be balancing a parrot on his head, but that doesn't mean that he has invented a theory of the self any less implausible than the one I ordered from a department-store catalogue or assembled with the tag lines of a two-year college course on the great books of Western civilization. If the traveler at the port rail can balance a parrot on his head, then I can continue my discussion with Madame Bovary and Mr. Pickwick, and the two gentlemen standing aft of the rum barrels can get on with the business of rigging the price of rifles or barbed wire. The American equation rests on the habit of holding our fellow citizens in thoughtful regard not because they are exceptional (or famous, or beautiful, or rich) but simply because they are our fellow citizens. If we abandon the sense of mutual respect, we abandon the premise as well as the machinery of the American enterprise.   21

> That the triumph of America corresponds to its prowess
> as a nation-state.

The pretension serves the purposes of the people who talk about "the national security" and "the vital interest of the American people" when what they mean is the power and privilege of government. The oligarchy resident in Washington assumes that all Americans own the same property instead of taking part in the same idea, that we share a joint geopolitical program in-   22 stead of a common temperament and habit of mind. Even so faithful a servant of the monied interests as Daniel Webster understood the distinction: "The public happiness is to be the aggregate of individuals. Our system begins with the individual man."

The Constitution was made for the uses of the individual (an implement   23
on the order of a plow, an ax, or a surveyor's plumb line), and the institutions of American government were meant to support the liberties of the people, not the ambitions of the state. Given any ambiguity about the order of priority or precedence, it was the law that had to give way to the citizen's freedom of thought and action, not the citizen's freedom of thought and action that had to give way to the law. The Bill of Rights stresses the distinction in the two final amendments, the ninth ("The enumeration in the Constitution, of certain rights, shall not be construed to deny or disparage others retained by the people") and the tenth ("The powers not delegated to the United States by the Constitution, nor prohibited by it to the States, are reserved to the States, respectively, or to the people").

What joins the Americans one to another is not a common nationality,   24
language, race, or ancestry (all of which testify to the burdens of the past) but rather their complicity in a shared work of the imagination. My love of country follows from my love of its freedoms, not from my pride in its fleets or its armies or its gross national product. Construed as a means and not an end, the Constitution stands as the premise for a narrative rather than a plan for an invasion or a monument. The narrative was always plural. Not one story but many stories.

That it is easy to be an American.

I can understand why the politicians like to pretend that America is   25
mostly about going shopping, but I never know why anybody believes the ad copy. Grant the existential terms and conditions of the American enterprise (i.e., that we are all bound to invent ourselves), and the position is both solitary and probably lost. I know a good many people who would rather be British or Nigerian or Swiss.

Lately I've been reading the accounts of the nineteenth-century adven-   26
turers and pioneers who traveled west from Missouri under circumstances almost always adverse. Most of them didn't find whatever it was they expected to find behind the next range of mountains or around the next bend in the river. They were looking for a garden in a country that was mostly desert, and the record of their passage is largely one of sorrow and failure. Travelers making their way across the Great Plains in the 1850s reported great numbers of dead horses and abandoned wagons on the trail, the echo of the hopes that so recently preceded them lingering in an empty chair or in the scent of flowers on a new grave.

Reading the diaries and letters, especially those of the women in the car-   27
avans, I think of the would-be settlers lost in an immense wilderness, looking into the mirrors of their loneliness and measuring their capacity for
self-knowledge against the vastness of the wide and indifferent sky.

Too often we forget the proofs of our courage. If we wish to live in the   28
state of freedom that allows us to make and think and build, then we must
accustom ourselves to the shadows on the walls and the wind in trees. The
climate of anxiety is the cost of doing business. Just as a monarchy places
far fewer burdens on its subjects than a democracy places on its citizens, so
also bigotry is easier than tolerance. When something goes wrong with the
currency or the schools, it's always comforting to know that the faults can
be easily found in something as obvious as a color, or a number, or the
sound of a strange language. The multiple adjectives qualifying the American noun enrich the vocabulary of blame, and if the election year continues
as it has begun I expect that by next summer we will discover that it is not
only middle-aged Protestant males who have been making a wreck of the
culture but also (operating secretly and sometimes in disguise) adolescent,
sallow, Buddhist females.

Among all the American political virtues, candor is probably the one   29
most necessary to the success of our mutual enterprise. Unless we try to tell
each other the truth about what we know and think and see (i.e., the story
so far as it appears to the travelers on the voyage out) we might as well
amuse ourselves (for as long as somebody else allows us to do so) with fairy
tales. The vitality of the American democracy always has rested on the capacity of its citizens to speak and think without cant. As long ago as 1838,
addressing the topic of *The American Democrat,* James Fenimore Cooper argued that the word "American" was synonymous with the habit of telling the
truth: "By candor we are not to understand trifling and uncalled for exposi-
tions of truth; but a sentiment that proves a conviction of the necessity of
speaking truth, when speaking at all; a contempt for all designing evasions
of our real opinions.

"In all the general concerns, the public has a right to be treated with   30
candor. Without this manly and truly republican quality . . . the institutions
are converted into a stupendous fraud."

If we indulge ourselves with evasions and the pleasure of telling lies, we   31
speak to our fears and our weaknesses instead of to our courage and our
strength. We can speak plainly about our differences only if we know and
value what we hold in common. Like the weather and third-rate journalism,
bigotry in all its declensions is likely to be with us for a long time (certainly
as long as the next hundred years), but unless we can draw distinctions and
make jokes about our racial or cultural baggage, the work of our shared
imagination must vanish in the mist of lies. The lies might win elections (or

sell newspapers and economic theories) but they bind us to the theaters of wish and dream. If I must like or admire a fellow citizen for his or her costume of modifying adjectives (because he or she is black or gay or rich), then I might as well believe that the lost continent of Atlantis will rise next summer from the sea and that the Japanese will continue to make the payments—now and forever, world without end—on all our mortgages and battleships.

Among all the nations of the earth, America is the one that has come 32 most triumphantly to terms with the mixtures of blood and caste, and maybe it is another of history's ironic jokes that we should wish to repudiate our talent for assimilation at precisely the moment in time when so many other nations in the world (in Africa and Western Europe as well as the Soviet Union) look to the promise of the American example. The jumble of confused or mistaken identities that was the story of nineteenth-century America has become the story of a late-twentieth-century world defined by a vast migration of peoples across seven continents and as many oceans. Why, then, do we lose confidence in ourselves and grow fearful of our mongrel freedoms?

The politician who would lift us to a more courageous understanding of 33 ourselves might begin by saying that we are all, each and every one of us, as much at fault as anybody else, that no matter whom we blame for our troubles (whether George Bush, or Al Sharpton, or David Duke) or how pleasant the invective (racist, sexist, imperialist pig), we still have to rebuild our cities and revise our laws. We can do the work together, or we can stand around making strong statements about each other's clothes.

Working with the Text

1. Lapham claims that "The subordination of the noun [American] to the adjectives makes a mockery of both the American premise and the democratic spirit. . ." Do you agree? Is the modification of "American" with something in front of it in the democratic spirit or in opposition to it? How could you argue it one way or the other?

2. A couple of pages into the essay, Lapham asks some big questions: "Who and what is an American? How and where do we find an identity that is something other than a fright mask? When using the collective national pronoun ('we the people,' 'we happy few,' etc.) whom do we invite into the club of the we?" Does he answer these questions in the course of the essay? How does he negotiate the central tension of his essay: the conflict between the desire for identity and the historical tendency of immigrants toward metamorphosis? Do you find his conclusions satisfying?

3. In your opinion, do you think this is an optimistic or pessimistic essay? If it is optimistic, where do you locate his reasons for being optimistic? Do you think he considers the "shared work of the imagination" that holds Americans together a reality or an ideal? Does he characterize that "shared work" as a solution to the divisiveness of the politics of identity that are at the heart of his essay? Give your response in an essay.

4. Working together in a group, look at the list of "false constructions" that structures the middle part of the essay. Do you agree that they are "false constructions"? Where do these constructions come from? Are they merely the invention of politicians, as Lapham claims? Are they linked at all to American ideals?

A Different Mirror

RONALD TAKAKI

Historian Ronald Takaki was born in Honolulu in 1939. A graduate of the College of Wooster, he later earned his M.A. and Ph.D. at the University of California at Berkeley, where he is now a professor of history. He has written frequently on historical issues of race and multiculturalism. His works include *A Different Mirror: A History of Multicultural America* (1993); *The Asian-American Experience* (1994), a fourteen-volume history for young adult readers; and *Hiroshima: Why America Dropped the Atomic Bomb* (1995). He also edited the anthology *From Different Shores: Perspectives on Race and Ethnicity in America* (1994). In the following chapter from *A Different Mirror*, Takaki argues that it is time Americans started viewing their history through "a different mirror," one that can enable "the people of America's diverse groups . . . to see themselves and each other in our common past."

I had flown from San Francisco to Norfolk and was riding in a taxi to my hotel to attend a conference on multiculturalism. Hundreds of educators from across the country were meeting to discuss the need for greater cultural diversity in the curriculum. My driver and I chatted about the weather and the tourists. The sky was cloudy, and Virginia Beach was twenty minutes away.

The rearview mirror reflected a white man in his forties. "How long have you been in this country?" he asked. "All my life," I replied, wincing. "I was born in the United States." With a strong southern drawl, he remarked: "I was wondering because your English is excellent!" Then, as I had many times before, I explained: "My grandfather came here from Japan in the 1880s. My family has been here, in America, for over a hundred years." He glanced at me in the mirror. Somehow I did not look "American" to him; my eyes and complexion looked foreign.

Suddenly, we both became uncomfortably conscious of a racial divide 2
separating us. An awkward silence turned my gaze from the mirror to the passing landscape, the shore where the English and the Powhatan Indians first encountered each other. Our highway was on land that Sir Walter Raleigh had renamed "Virginia" in honor of Elizabeth I, the Virgin Queen. In the English cultural appropriation of America, the indigenous peoples themselves would become outsiders in their native land. Here, at the eastern edge of the continent, I mused, was the site of the beginning of multicultural America. Jamestown, the English settlement founded in 1607, was nearby: the first twenty Africans were brought here a year before the Pilgrims arrived at Plymouth Rock. Several hundred miles offshore was Bermuda, the "Bermoothes" where William Shakespeare's Prospero had landed and met the native Caliban in *The Tempest*. Earlier, another voyager had made an Atlantic crossing and unexpectedly bumped into some islands to the south. Thinking he had reached Asia, Christopher Columbus mistakenly identified one of the islands as "Cipango" (Japan). In the wake of the admiral, many peoples would come to America from different shores, not only from Europe but also Africa and Asia. One of them would be my grandfather. My mental wandering across terrain and time ended abruptly as we arrived at my destination. I said goodbye to my driver and went into the hotel, carrying a vivid reminder of why I was attending this conference.

Questions like the one my taxi driver asked me are always jarring, but I can 3
understand why he could not see me as an American. He had a narrow but widely shared sense of the past—a history that has viewed American as European in ancestry. "Race," Toni Morrison explained, has functioned as a "metaphor" necessary to the "construction of Americanness": in the creation of our national identity, "American" has been defined as "white."

But America has been racially diverse since our very beginning on the 4
Virginia shore, and this reality is increasingly becoming visible and ubiquitous. Currently, one-third of the American people do not trace their origins to Europe; in California, minorities are fast becoming a majority. They already predominate in major cities across the country—New York, Chicago, Atlanta, Detroit, Philadelphia, San Francisco, and Los Angeles.

This emerging demographic diversity has raised fundamental questions about America's identity and culture. In 1990, *Time* published a cover story on "America's Changing Colors." "Someday soon," the magazine announced, "white Americans will become a minority group." How soon? By 2056, most Americans will trace their descent to "Africa, Asia, the Hispanic world, the Pacific Islands, Arabia—almost anywhere but white Europe." This dramatic change in our nation's ethnic composition is altering the way we think about ourselves. "The deeper significance of America's becoming a majority nonwhite society is what it means to the national psyche, to individuals' sense of themselves and their nation—their idea of what it is to be American."

Indeed, more than ever before, as we approach the time when whites become a minority, many of us are perplexed about our national identity and our future as one people. This uncertainty has provoked Allan Bloom to reaffirm the preeminence of Western civilization. Author of *The Closing of the American Mind,* he has emerged as a leader of an intellectual backlash against cultural diversity. In his view, students entering the university are "uncivilized," and the university has the responsibility to "civilize" them. Bloom claims he knows what their "hungers" are and "what they can digest." Eating is one of his favorite metaphors. Noting the "large black presence" in major universities, he laments the "one failure" in race relations—black students have proven to be "indigestible." They do not "melt as have *all* other groups." The problem, he contends, is that "blacks have become blacks": they have become "ethnic." This separatism has been reinforced by an academic permissiveness that has befouled the curriculum with "Black Studies" along with "Learn Another Culture." The only solution, Bloom insists, is "the good old Great Books approach."

Similarly, E. D. Hirsch worries that America is becoming a "tower of Babel," and that this multiplicity of cultures is threatening to rend our social fabric. He, too, longs for a more cohesive culture and a more homogeneous America: "If we *had* to make a choice between the *one* and the *many,* most Americans would choose the principle of unity, since we cannot function as a nation without it." The way to correct this fragmentization, Hirsch argues, is to acculturate "disadvantaged children." What do they need to know? "Only by accumulating shared symbols, and the shared information that symbols represent," Hirsch answers, "can we learn to communicate effectively with one another in our national community." Though he concedes the value of multicultural education, he quickly dismisses it by insisting that it "should not be allowed to supplant or interfere with our schools' responsibility to ensure our children's mastery of American literate culture." In *Cultural Literacy: What Every American Needs to Know,* Hirsch offers a long list of terms that excludes much of the history of minority groups.

While Bloom and Hirsch are reacting defensively to what they regard as 8
a vexatious balkanization of America, many other educators are responding
to our diversity as an opportunity to open American minds. In 1990, the
Task Force on Minorities for New York emphasized the importance of a culturally diverse education. "Essentially," the *New York Times* commented, "the
issue is how to deal with both dimensions of the nation's motto: 'E pluribus
unum'—'Out of many, one.'" Universities from New Hampshire to Berkeley
have established American cultural diversity graduation requirements. "Every
student needs to know," explained University of Wisconsin's chancellor
Donna Shalala, "much more about the origins and history of the particular
cultures which, as Americans, we will encounter during our lives." Even the
University of Minnesota, located in a state that is 98 percent white, requires
its students to take ethnic studies courses. Asked why multiculturalism is so
important, Dean Fred Lukermann answered: As a national university, Minnesota has to offer a national curriculum—one that includes all of the peoples of America. He added that after graduation many students move to
cities like Chicago and Los Angeles and thus need to know about racial diversity. Moreover, many educators stress, multiculturalism has an intellectual
purpose. By allowing us to see events from the viewpoints of different groups,
a multicultural curriculum enables us to reach toward a more comprehensive understanding of American history.

What is fueling this debate over our national identity and the content of 9
our curriculum is America's intensifying racial crisis. The alarming signs and
symptoms seem to be everywhere—the killing of Vincent Chin in Detroit, the
black boycott of a Korean grocery store in Flatbush, the hysteria in Boston
over the Carol Stuart murder, the battle between white sportsmen and Indians over tribal fishing rights in Wisconsin, the Jewish-black clashes in Brooklyn's Crown Heights, the black-Hispanic competition for jobs and educational
resources in Dallas, which *Newsweek* described as "a conflict of the have-
nots," and the Willie Horton campaign commercials, which widened the divide between the suburbs and the inner cities.

This reality of racial tension rudely woke America like a fire bell in the 10
night on April 29, 1992. Immediately after four Los Angeles police officers
were found not guilty of brutality against Rodney King, rage exploded in Los
Angeles. Race relations reached a new nadir. During the nightmarish ram-
page, scores of people were killed, over two thousand injured, twelve thousand arrested, and almost a billion dollars' worth of property destroyed. The
live televised images mesmerized America. The rioting and the murderous
melee on the streets resembled the fighting in Beirut and the West Bank.
The thousands of fires burning out of control and the dark smoke filling the
skies brought back images of the burning oil fields of Kuwait during Desert

Storm. Entire sections of Los Angeles looked like a bombed city. "Is this America?" many shocked viewers asked. "Please, can we get along here," pleaded Rodney King, calling for calm. "We all can get along. I mean, we're all stuck here for a while. Let's try to work it out."

But how should "we" be defined? Who are the people "stuck here" in America? One of the lessons of the Los Angeles explosion is the recognition of the fact that we are a multiracial society and that race can no longer be defined in the binary terms of white and black. "We" will have to include Hispanics and Asians. While blacks currently constitute 13 percent of the Los Angeles population, Hispanics represent 40 percent. The 1990 census revealed that South Central Los Angeles, which was predominantly black in 1965 when the Watts rebellion occurred, is now 45 percent Hispanic. A majority of the first 5,438 people arrested were Hispanic, while 37 percent were black. Of the fifty-eight people who died in the riot, more than a third were Hispanic, and about 40 percent of the businesses destroyed were Hispanic-owned. Most of the other shops and stores were Korean-owned. The dreams of many Korean immigrants went up in smoke during the riot: two thousand Korean-owned businesses were damaged or demolished, totaling about $400 million in losses. There is evidence indicating they were targeted. "After all," explained a black gang member, "we didn't burn our community, just *their* stores." 11

"I don't feel like I'm in America anymore," said Denisse Bustamente as she watched the police protecting the firefighters. "I feel like I am far away." Indeed, Americans have been witnessing ethnic strife erupting around the world—the rise of neo-Nazism and the murder of Turks in Germany, the ugly "ethnic cleansing" in Bosnia, the terrible and bloody clashes between Muslims and Hindus in India. Is the situation here different, we have been nervously wondering, or do ethnic conflicts elsewhere represent a prologue for America? What is the nature of malevolence? Is there a deep, perhaps primordial, need for group identity rooted in hatred for the other? Is ethnic pluralism possible for America? But answers have been limited. Television reports have been little more than thirty-second sound bites. Newspaper articles have been mostly superficial descriptions of racial antagonisms and the current urban malaise. What is lacking is historical context; consequently, we are left feeling bewildered. 12

How did we get to this point, Americans everywhere are anxiously asking. What does our diversity mean, and where is it leading us? *How* do we work it out in the post–Rodney King era? 13

Certainly one crucial way is for our society's various ethnic groups to develop a greater understanding of each other. For example, how can African Americans and Korean Americans work it out unless they learn about each other's cultures, histories, and also economic situations? This need to share 14 knowledge about our ethnic diversity has acquired new importance and has given new urgency to the pursuit for a more accurate history.

More than ever before, there is a growing realization that the established 15 scholarship has tended to define America too narrowly. For example, in his prize-winning study *The Uprooted,* Harvard historian Oscar Handlin presented—to use the book's subtitle—"the Epic Story of the Great Migrations That Made the American People." But Handlin's "epic story" excluded the "uprooted" from Africa, Asia, and Latin America—the other "Great Migrations" that also helped to make "the American People." Similarly, in *The Age of Jackson,* Arthur M. Schlesinger, Jr., left out blacks and Indians. There is not even a mention of two marker events—the Nat Turner insurrection and Indian removal, which Andrew Jackson himself would have been surprised to find omitted from a history of his era.

Still, Schlesinger and Handlin offered us a refreshing revisionism, paving 16 the way for the study of common people rather than princes and presidents. They inspired the next generation of historians to examine groups such as the artisan laborers of Philadelphia and the Irish immigrants of Boston. "Once I thought to write a history of the immigrants in America," Handlin confided in his introduction to *The Uprooted.* "I discovered that the immigrants *were* American history." This door, once opened, led to the flowering of a more inclusive scholarship as we began to recognize that ethnic history was American history. Suddenly, there was a proliferation of seminal works such as Irving Howe's *World of Our Fathers: The Journey of the East European Jews to America,* Dee Brown's *Bury My Heart at Wounded Knee: An Indian History of the American West,* Albert Camarillo's *Chicanos in a Changing Society,* Lawrence Levine's *Black Culture and Black Consciousness,* Yuji Ichioka's *The Issei: The World of the First Generation Japanese Immigrants,* and Kerby Miller's *Emigrants and Exiles: Ireland and the Irish Exodus to North America.*

But even this new scholarship, while it has given us a more expanded 17 understanding of the mosaic called America, does not address our needs in the post–Rodney King era. These books and others like them fragment American society, studying each group separately, in isolation from the other groups and the whole. While scrutinizing our specific pieces, we have to step back in order to see the rich and complex portrait they compose. What is needed is a fresh angle, a study of the American past from a comparative perspective. . . .

The signs of America's ethnic diversity can be discerned across the con- 18 tinent—Ellis Island, Angel Island, Chinatown, Harlem, South Boston, the Lower East Side, places with Spanish names like Los Angeles and San Antonio or Indian names like Massachusetts and Iowa. Much of what is familiar in America's cultural landscape actually has ethnic origins. The Bing cherry was developed by an early Chinese immigrant named Ah Bing. American Indians were cultivating corn, tomatoes, and tobacco long before the arrival of Columbus. The term *okay* was derived from the Choctaw word *oke,* meaning "it is so." There is evidence indicating that the name *Yankee* came from Indian terms for the English—from *eankke* in Cherokee and *Yankwis* in Delaware. Jazz and blues as well as rock and roll have African-American origins. The "Forty-Niners" of the Gold Rush learned mining techniques from the Mexicans; American cowboys acquired herding skills from Mexican *vaqueros* and adopted their range terms—such as *lariat* from *la reata, lasso* from *lazo,* and *stampede* from *estampida.* Songs like "God Bless America," "Easter Parade," and "White Christmas" were written by a Russian-Jewish immigrant named Israel Baline, more popularly known as Irving Berlin.

Furthermore, many diverse ethnic groups have contributed to the building of the American economy, forming what Walt Whitman saluted as "a vast, surging, hopeful army of workers." They worked in the South's cotton fields, New England's textile mills, Hawaii's canefields, New York's garment factories, California's orchards, Washington's salmon canneries, and Arizona's copper mines. They built the railroad, the great symbol of America's industrial triumph. Laying railroad ties, black laborers sang:

Down the railroad, um-huh
Well, raise the iron, um-huh
Raise the iron, um-huh.

Irish railroad workers shouted as they stretched an iron ribbon across the continent:

Then drill, my Paddies, drill—
Drill, my heroes, drill,
Drill all day, no sugar in your tay
Workin' on the U.P. railway.

Japanese laborers in the Northwest chorused as their bodies fought the fickle weather:

A railroad worker—
That's me!
I am great.
Yes, I am a railroad worker.
Complaining:
"It is too hot!"
"It is too cold!"
"It rains too often!"
"It snows too much!"
They all ran off.

I alone remained.
I am a railroad worker!

Chicano workers in the Southwest joined in as they swore at the punishing work:

Some unloaded rails
Others unloaded ties,
And others of my companions
Threw out thousands of curses.

Moreover, our diversity was tied to America's most serious crisis: the Civil War was fought over a racial issue—slavery. In his "First Inaugural Address," presented on March 4, 1861, President Abraham Lincoln declared: "One section of our country believes slavery is *right* and ought to be extended, while the other believes it is *wrong* and ought not to be extended." Southern secession, he argued, would be anarchy. Lincoln sternly warned the South that he had a solemn oath to defend and preserve the Union. Americans were one people, he explained, bound together by "the mystic chords of memory, stretching from every battlefield and patriot grave to every living heart and hearthstone all over this broad land." The struggle and sacrifices of the War for Independence had enabled Americans to create a new nation out of thirteen separate colonies. But Lincoln's appeal for unity fell on deaf ears in the South. And the war came. Two and a half years later, at Gettysburg, President Lincoln declared that "brave men" had fought and "consecrated" the ground of this battlefield in order to preserve the Union. Among the brave were black men. Shortly after this bloody battle, Lincoln acknowledged the military contributions of blacks. "There will be some black men," he wrote in a letter to an old friend, James C. Conkling, "who can remember that with silent tongue, and clenched teeth, and steady eye, and well-poised bayonet, they have helped mankind on to this great consummation. . . ." Indeed, 186,000 blacks served in the Union Army, and one-third of them were listed as missing or dead. Black men in blue, Frederick Douglass pointed out, were "on the battlefield mingling their blood with that of white men in one common effort to save the country." Now the mystic chords of memory stretched across the new battlefields of the Civil War, and black soldiers were buried in "patriot graves." They, too, had given their lives to ensure that the "government of the people, by the people, for the people shall not perish from the earth." . . .

In his recent study of Spain and the New World, *The Buried Mirror,* Carlos Fuentes points out that mirrors have been found in the tombs of ancient Mexico, placed there to guide the dead through the underworld. He also tells us about the legend of Quetzalcoatl, the Plumed Serpent: when this god was given a mirror by the Toltec deity Tezcatlipoca, he saw a man's face in the mirror and realized his own humanity. For us, the "mirror" of history can guide the living and also help us recognize who we have been and hence are. In *A Distant Mirror,* Barbara W. Tuchman finds "phenomenal parallels" between the "calamitous 14th century" of European society and our own era. We can, she observes, have "greater fellow-feeling for a distraught age" as we painfully recognize the "similar disarray," "collapsing assumptions," and "unusual discomfort."

But what is needed in our own perplexing times is not so much a "dis-   22
tant" mirror, as one that is "different." While the study of the past can provide collective self-knowledge, it often reflects the scholar's particular perspective or view of the world. What happens when historians leave out many of America's peoples? What happens, to borrow the words of Adrienne Rich, "when someone with the authority of a teacher" describes our society, and "you are not in it"? Such an experience can be disorienting—"a moment of psychic disequilibrium, as if you looked into a mirror and saw nothing."

Through their narratives about their lives and circumstances, the people   23
of America's diverse groups are able to see themselves and each other in our common past. They celebrate what Ishmael Reed has described as a society "unique" in the world because "the world is here"—a place "where the cultures of the world crisscross." Much of America's past, they point out, has been riddled with racism. At the same time, these people offer hope, affirming the struggle for equality as a central theme in our country's history. At its conception, our nation was dedicated to the proposition of equality. What has given concreteness to this powerful national principle has been our coming together in the creation of a new society. "Stuck here" together, workers of different backgrounds have attempted to get along with each other.

People harvesting
Work together unaware
Of racial problems,

wrote a Japanese immigrant describing a lesson learned by Mexican and Asian farm laborers in California.

Finally, how do we see our prospects for "working out" America's racial   24
crisis? Do we see it as through a glass darkly? Do the televised images of racial hatred and violence that riveted us in 1992 during the days of rage in Los Angeles frame a future of divisive race relations—what Arthur Schlesinger, Jr., has fearfully denounced as the "disuniting of America"? Or will Americans of diverse races and ethnicities be able to connect themselves to a larger narrative? Whatever happens, we can be certain that much of our society's future will be influenced by which "mirror" we choose to see ourselves. America does not belong to one race or one group, the people in this study remind us, and Americans have been constantly redefining their

national identity from the moment of first contact on the Virginia shore. By sharing their stories, they invite us to see ourselves in a different mirror.

Working with the Text

1. Toward the end of his essay, Takaki quotes the writer Ishmael Reed as describing America as a "society 'unique' in the world because 'the world is here'—a place 'where the cultures of the world crisscross'." How does Takaki discuss America as a global crossroads? What are some of the details that he invokes in outlining a global context for American multiculturalism?

2. Why are the Los Angeles "riots" of 1992 a key event for Takaki? What does he think they tell us about the current state of race relations in the United States? What are your memories of the event? Do you think that it has endured as a meaningful event in our recent past? Do you remember it very well or at all? How do you recall the riots being portrayed in the media? What aspects do you recall being emphasized? Do your memories ring true with Takaki's descriptions?

3. Takaki implies that there has always been a central tension at the heart of American development and history: the tension between group identity and national identity. In an essay discuss how this tension is raised in Takaki's essay. Is there an essential relationship between commonality and difference, as well as a tension? What is the balance of importance in the United States between group identity and national identity? What kinds of group identity are allowed or compatible with national identity and which are at odds?

4. What makes Takaki's "different mirror" different? What are the most important differences that are derived from "looking back" at history with "a different mirror?" How would history look differently and how should our response to it differ? How, does he imply, would a different mirror on the past shed a different light on our present and future? Explore these questions in an essay.

The Correspondent

AGHA SHAHID ALI

Agha Shahid Ali, who called himself a "multiple-exile," was born in New Delhi in 1949. He grew up Muslim in Kashmir, the border territory between India and Pakistan, graduated from the University of Delhi, and earned a doctorate at Penn State. His many books of poetry include *The Beloved Witness: Selected Poems* and *The Country Without a Post Office*, from which the following poem is taken; he is also the author of *T. S. Eliot as Editor* and translator of *The Rebel's Silhouette: Selected Poems by Faiz Ahmed Faiz*. A widely respected teacher, he directed the MFA program at the University of Massachusetts—Amherst until his death in 2001. This poem, "The Correspondent," offers a fantasy sequence in which the "real world"—a history of exile, loss, and fractures due to wars—is shown as a documentary film.

I say "There's no way back to your country,"
I tell him he must never leave. He cites
the world: his schedule. I set up barricades:
the mountain routes are damp;
there, dead dervishes damascene   5
the dark. "I must leave now," his voice ablaze.
I take off—it's my last resort—my shadow.

And he walks—there's no electricity—
back into my dark, murmurs *Kashmir!*, lights
(to a soundtrack of exploding grenades)   10
a dim kerosene lamp.
"We must give back the hour its sheen,
or this spell will never end. . . . Quick," he says,
"I've just come—with videos—from Sarajevo."

His footage is priceless with sympathy,   15
close-ups in slow motion: from bombed sites
to the dissolve of mosques in colonnades.
Then, wheelchairs on a ramp,
burning. He fast-forwards: the scene:
the sun: a man in formal wear: he plays   20
on the sidewalk his unaccompanied cello,

the hour turned, dusk-slowed, to Albinoni,
only the *Adagio* as funeral rites
before the stars dazzle, polished to blades
above a barbed-wire camp.   25
The cellist disappears. The screen
fills—first with soldiers, then the dead, their gaze
fractured white with subtitles. Whose echo

inhabits the night? The phone rings. I think he
will leave. I ask: "When will the satellites   30
transmit my songs, carry Kashmir, aubades
always for dawns to stamp
True! across seas?" The stars careen
down, the lamp dies. He hangs up. A haze
settles over us. He opens the window,   35

points to convoys in the mountains, army
trucks with dimmed lights. He wants exclusive rights
to this dream, its fused quartz of furtive shades.
He's been told to revamp
his stories, reincarnadine   40
their gloss. I light a candle. He'll erase
Bosnia, I feel. He will rewind to zero,

film from there a way back to his country,
bypassing graves that in blacks and whites
climb ever up the hills. The wax cascades   45
down the stand, silver clamp
to fasten this dream, end it unseen.
In the faltering light, he surveys
what's left. He zooms madly into my shadow.

Working with the Text

1. The speaker and a film-making "correspondent" undergo a strange
   interview: the speaker's shadow—the past—becomes a dark passage
   or screen on which the correspondent shows wreckage of the Bosnian
   war of the early 1990s, and then other scenes. Yet the speaker and
   correspondent have different motives. What does each of them hope
   for? What does each of them offer the other? And how do the "films"
   offer each of them still other responses?

2. The poem moves quickly from scene to scene: can you mark the
   sequence of different places we encounter from the second stanza to
   the end of the poem? Besides these sudden glimpses of history, there

is a local "here" where the two speakers are located. What happens to the film when a phone rings or a candle is lit?

3. In the poem, the need to return to one's country is at first denied, then provided through fantasy, vision, art, and reimagined history. What subsequent desires do they each manifest in the fifth and sixth stanza? How do they express the fantasies to get back to one's country?

4. Write a very brief description of a cherished place you will never return to. What details appear? Can your depiction become an imaginative "replacement" for the place, and for your past experience, or are the details, and some sense of your present nostalgia, left out? From your experience and from reading the poem, what unfulfilled desires does each speaker carry at the poem's end?

Critical Questions Revisited: From Reading to Writing

Essay Topic 1: How has the imagined and actual frontier shaped the U.S. national identity?

YOUR PAPER: Explore the ways that "the frontier" contributes to the cultural construction of America's identity. In what ways has the American frontier stood as both an idea (an "inward territory" based on images, narratives, memory, etc.) and as an actual, physical place? From evidence in your readings, trace the role of these different senses of the frontier in forming and underpinning an American identity.

SUGGESTED STRATEGIES

- Identify places in the readings that describe "characteristic American values"—such as individualism, democracy, equality—and link them to specific physical places in the United States. How does the synthesis of place and idea help fashion certain folk myths we hold, and archetypal visions of America?

- List two or three moments from the readings that portray these "mythic" constructions as being at odds with historical reality.

- What synthesis of these "materials"—ideas, images, historical facts— makes up our sense of the frontier?

Essay Topic 2: What is a frontier: an "edge" or a "zone"?

YOUR PAPER: Working from some of the definitions in this chapter, and elsewhere in the book, compare the conceptions of the frontier as a stable and defined boundary—an "edge"—and as a "borderland" or "zone."

SUGGESTED STRATEGIES

- In the readings, mark several definitions of the frontier (e.g see Limerick in this chapter, Pratt in Chapter 3, Anzaldúa in Chapter 5).
- Write out both the traditional notion of the American frontier, and one of these other, more flexible, versions.
- How does each provide a different sense of a controversial American issue (such as bilingual education, gun control, new state holidays, the "other," etc.)?
- How does each conception allow for negotiations between value systems and cultural perspectives? What advantages does each conception provide?

Essay Topic 3: In what ways does an allegiance to group identity conflict with and/or contribute to a U.S. national identity?

YOUR PAPER: Analyze and build an argument as to how *group identity* conflicts with and/or contributes to a U.S. national identity, and the functioning of democracy. Some commentators, such as Lewis Lapham (in this chapter) claim that our tendency to qualify the noun *American* with adjectives like *gay*, *African*, or *Jewish* mocks our "democratic spirit"? Others propose that our capacity to identify with an American 'sub-group' is itself a distinctively "American" quality, and part of U.S. national identity.

SUGGESTED STRATEGIES

- In the readings, identify passages in which authors argue for a diverse, multifaceted definition of U.S. culture and society, and passages where the opposite position is advocated—that the U.S. identity needs to be coherent, more homogenous, or unified. What would be gained and lost by adopting each position?
- What forms of *group consciousness* does each vision prefer? What consequences for public and private life does each vision offer?
- In which ways do you identify with a "subgroup," and with a national group? In terms of both your reading and your own experience, how might we negotiate or work to resolve these seemingly contrary ideals?

Essay Topic 4: How does the United States' *internal* diversity affect its role and image in global culture?

YOUR PAPER: The United States' multicultural character defines its national self-image, and helps define its international image as well. How does its internal diversity shape its relationship to global culture? How does the cluster of U.S. images projected worldwide show our diversity—and hide it?

SUGGESTED STRATEGIES

- In the readings, what tensions do authors describe between American diversity and international conceptions of U.S. culture?
- How do our diversity and our energy for change—expressed by cross-cultural interaction, free enterprise, upward mobility—make U.S. culture difficult for foreign observers to define?
- How are forms of global culture altered by entering the U.S.? How do American forms of culture change when leaving the U.S.? Using a very specific "test case," depict the relation between our internal diversity and our role in world culture.

CHAPTER 5

THE WORLD'S NEW BORDERS:
Beyond Nation, Beyond Place

Critical Questions

Before reading: How has the contemporary concept of place and borders changed for the United States and throughout the world?

Taking it Further: The Internet and cyberspace seem to change the ways people form communities. How do virtual communities exist? How do they differ from local or physical communities? Do such communities make the concept of "nation" less important than that of a global culture? Or do they emphasize the need for smaller and more focused communities? What representations of outside cultures are offered by American media (print, visual, online)?

IMAGINED COMMUNITIES AND THE VIRTUAL FRONTIER

Ever since the Internet came into its first wave of popularity, its users have imagined it as a new, empty space waiting to be filled, akin to the American frontier. We think of electronic environments in spatial terms, and represent the *process* of developing them as parallel to the settlement of the American West. Cyberspace first appeared as a vast and open country that was essentially vacant, a place where no one initially "owned" anything. This anarchy of open spaces quickly subsides as people settle the space and set up their own communities and societies. Something has been both lost and gained in the settlement. In the end, people may well be nostalgic for the "good old days" of Wild Cyberspace in the same ways that American culture endlessly relives, revises, and often rejoices in the days of pioneers and the Wild West. Perhaps one of the features that attracted people to the Internet during its early, idealistic phase was the supposed unfettered "space" it gave them to explore and call their own. It was not, however, inevitable that the Internet would be conceived as a space, or that people would speak of electronic environments as new "worlds" and alternative, constructed "realities." After all, the very thing a virtual world is *not* is tangible and inhabitable. However, these traditional terms of understanding seem to be the most compelling and attractive, whether in the context of pure romantic speculation about technology's potential, or in the media campaigns of cyber-capitalism.

Cyberspace then, is a nonphysical place built by analogies to physical things: property lines, homes, sites, bodies, communities. Cyberspace and the Internet are the ultimate meeting place of *border texts* and *place*; after all, what are the places on the Internet but texts? As a place built out of texts, cyberspace may be understood as imaginative realities with made-up structures, representations of people, and simulated environments with new kinds of rules and limits.

This chapter raises some of the book's most abstract questions. In Chapters 2 and 3, we looked at how communities and cultures define a sense of "otherness" that often has the impact of excluding or denigrating certain groups of people. In the course of examining American culture, we find that our sense of difference and otherness often relates to space and place. How people regard the homeless, how one neighborhood perceives its own borders, or how natives perceive immigrants are all real social phenomena that are rooted in the imaginative and perceptive qualities of physical space and geography. It would be incomplete, then, to think about the nature of identity and difference without considering these spatial and environmental dimensions. Watching the development and spread of cyberspace and the Internet gives us an easy window into how physical and imaginative components interact to construct a reality. In this sense, however, electronic spaces are not unique, but just one version of the interaction of the physical and the nonphysical, of real and symbolic dimensions of the worlds we inhabit—whether an electronic community, a neighborhood community, a group identity that transcends physical space, or even a nation.

THE RISE OF GROUP IDENTITY

In this chapter, one force posited against national identity is *group identity*. In the early chapters of *Beyond Borders* we explored the ways in which individuals developed their sense of identity in light of cultural institutions and community structures. In the later chapters we have been examining the dynamics of difference and otherness—what happens when individuals interact in zones where their differences come together.

This final chapter continues many of those same concerns but looks at group identity from the perspective of national and global society. Inasmuch as America has always been a global crossroads, the context for this phenomenon is global as well. Central to this chapter is the idea that the intensification of group identity politics is in no way unique to America, and in fact the rise of "group consciousness" in the United States is in many ways part of a larger global pattern. International politics for the last two decades, especially since the breakup of the Soviet Union in the late 1980s, has been defined by the reassertion of "group identity," largely along ethnic and, in some cases, religious lines.

GROUP SOLIDARITY OR GLOBAL THEME PARK?

The rise of "group consciousness" in the United States and around the world is not the only major pattern of world development. It has taken place at the same time when the world is becoming increasingly connected, when aspects of global culture are becoming increasingly homogenous. The paradox of this situation is that these two contrary tendencies are occurring simultaneously; the world seems to be both coming together and to be dividing into smaller pieces at the same time. This complex of tensions, ones that are different in every local context, forms an important context for this chapter, and for taking our final look at the borders of American culture. America is often taken as a "model" of "benign multiculturalism" where differences are noted and respected, but subsumed into a higher allegiance or identity, i.e., a sense of national belonging, as a citizen of a democracy. Several of the selections in this chapter explore the paradox of a world of increasing unity and fragmentation in terms of the idea of a single nation and the pronounced diversity of separate peoples and cultures. How related, they ask, is the rising tide of group identities in the United States to the worldwide tendency toward tribalism, or what we might call subnational or transnational identities?

The complexity of these issues—which are only partially touched upon here—is relevant to this book in that it ultimately bears on the borders of American cultural identity. As inhabitants of the United States, *who* we think we are is significantly influenced by our sense of our place in the world. As you will see in the final readings in this chapter and in the additional materials in *Beyond Borders* online, the internationalization of economies and the global export of American culture might look very different in other countries. Yet, as we saw in Chapter 4, *differences* are rarely negotiated on equal terms.

Writers who focus on the new global economy, such as William Grieder and Benjamin Barber, discuss a number of ways that global economic forces can both drive cultural values and structures, and conflict with local customs and culture. One persistent question in these readings is whether the new globalism of interdependent economies makes capitalism and democracy interdependent. Though Howard Rheingold urges us to consider the "democratizing potential of virtual communities," one of the fallacies of the new globalism, as Barber notes, is the tendency to mistake "the right to shop" (free-market capitalism) for the "right to vote" (democracy).

All this suggests an idea of electronic frontiers and a construction of cyberspace based on the values and emotions associated with the Western frontier: open space and opportunity, progress, mobility, democracy, and even adventure and discovery. To what extent do the Internet and cyberspace play to America's "inward territory"? William Mitchell, one of the first people to explore the modes of communication on this frontier, heralds the development of cyberspace as an important community development project that will provide the economically disadvantaged with a new social and political voice. Allocquére Rosanne Stone also celebrates the new social possibilities that virtual interactions provide, by analyzing the various ways that people online take on and play with different personae and genders. In stark contrast,

Stephen Doheny-Farina turns a skeptical eye toward notions of cyberspace as expanding human potential. Doheny-Farina is troubled by the allure of "transcending our messy, indeterminate, complex physical existence through the technotopia of the net."

Other writers in this chapter focus on the interrelationship between identity and economic and cultural concerns. In considering the United States and its border, Guillermo Gómez-Peña notes the ways that cultural mixing in the borderlands becomes an outward manifestation of economic interdependence. For Gómez-Peña, our profound interdependence leads to a call for a "more fluid and tolerant" understanding of personal and national identity, one that in effect forgoes the "saving" of individual cultures. The tension between mixing (or hybrid culture) and cultural purity underlies many of the selections in this chapter. Gloria Anzaldúa, alarmed by an increasing cultural fragmentation experienced by Chicanos/Chicanas, appeals to a past lineage of "Indianness" as the basis of an independent "*mestizaje*" identity, a strategy Benjamin Alire Sáenz, in turn, flatly rejects as a "politics and an identity centered on 'loss.'" Salman Rushdie examines the dangerous blurring of modes of identification in the Middle East between the politically charged notion of "Islamic identity" versus the "politically neutral" Muslim and questions the very possibility of a modern world that can peacefully contain Islam and the West unless less radical Muslims begin to speak of the need for a Reformation in the Muslim world. The necessity for the politically marginalized to speak up literally in order to survive is shared by Audre Lorde in her poem of individual perseverance.

Disturbed by the ease with which we refer to people simply in terms of a "feature" of their cultural group, K. Anthony Appiah challenges the very term "cultural diversity," suggesting that our insistent appeal to "cultural difference" "obscures rather than illuminates" the cultural content of identities. Wen Shu Lee deconstructs hierarchical color codes, demonstrating the various criteria by which different cultures designate people as "white." The tension between what may be historically "lost" in order to gain a new conception of shared identity prompts bell hooks to propose a much-needed ethics of love in order to counter the prevailing ethic of domination and in so doing recover personal and political self-recovery. Like hooks, Ian Frazier envisions a world in which multiple identities converge into a congenial communal whole. Whereas hooks's world lies in the future, Frazier discovers an existing model of harmonious diversity among the many different peoples that constitutes the community of Queens.

The questions of this chapter, as broad and global as they are, bring us full circle to the most central questions of the book. How do individuals see themselves in the world? How do we see ourselves in relation to others? How does our sense of individual identity relate to other kinds of identity:

our family, our community, our region, our nation, our ethnicity or race? How does *where we are* determine *who we are?* In the end, these are questions about borders: borders that we live with, borders that we resist, borders that define us and that we help to reinforce. And no questions will be more important for the next century than these.

Soft Cities

WILLIAM MITCHELL

Australian-born architect William Mitchell holds degrees from the University of Melbourne, Yale, and Cambridge. For sixteen years he was on the faculty of the School of Architecture at the University of California, Los Angeles, and in 1986 he joined the School of Architecture and Planning at the Massachusetts Institute of Technology, where he is currently dean. He was also a founding partner of the Computer-Aided Design Group in Marina del Rey, California. His publications include *Computer-Aided Architectural Design* (1977), *The Logic of Architecture* (1990), *E-topia: Urban Life, Jim—But Not As We Know It* (1999), and *City of Bits: Space, Place, and the Infobahn* (1995), in which the following essay appears. In *City of Bits,* Mitchell looks at the early "frontier days" of cyberspace and its potential development into "public space" for communication much like the public squares of ancient Rome.

Real Estate / Cyberspace

I was there at the almost-unnoticed Big Bang—the silent blast of bits that be-   1
gat the new communities of the digital era. It was UCLA, fall 1969, and I was a very young assistant professor writing primitive CAD software and trying to imagine the role that designers might play in the emerging electronic future. In a back room just down the hallway from the monster mainframe on which I worked, some Bolt Beranek and Newman engineers installed a considerably smaller machine that booted up to become the very first node of ARPANET—the computer network that was destined to evolve into the worldwide Internet.

From this inconspicuous point of origin, network tentacles grew like   2
kudzu to blanket the globe. By December there were four ARPANET nodes.

In April 1971 there were 23, in June 1974 there were 62, and in March 1977 there were 111. Soon, cyberspace was busting out all over: two more important networks, CSnet (funded by the National Science Foundation) and BITNET (funded by IBM) developed in the early 1980s. A high-speed backbone (NSFnet) was in place by July 1988; this connected thirteen regional networks scattered across the United States—much as the interstate highway system linked local road networks—and the whole loosely organized system became known as the Internet. During the late 1980s and early 1990s more and more networks connected to the Internet, and by 1993 it included nearly two million host computers in more than 130 countries. In the first six months of 1994 more than a million additional machines were hooked up.

In the United States, by that point, there was one Internet host for every   3
couple of hundred people. (Take care in interpreting these figures, though; the actual density is likely to be much higher in affluent, computer-literate places like Cambridge, Massachusetts, and Palo Alto, California, and much lower in inner-city Detroit or East Los Angeles.) According to the best estimates—but in truth, nobody really knew—there were more than thirty million active users.

While the Internet community was evolving into something analogous   4
to a ramshackle Roman Empire of the entire computer world, numerous smaller, independent colonies and confederations were also developing. Dial-in bulletin board systems such as the Sausalito-based WELL—much like independent city-states—appeared in many locations to link home computers. Commercial online services such as Compuserve, Prodigy, and America Online emerged in parallel to the government-sponsored, education- and research-oriented Internet. Before long, though, most of these erstwhile rivals found it necessary to join forces with the Internet.

There would not have been a great deal to connect if computers had re-   5
mained as large and expensive as they were when ARPANET began in 1969. But as networks developed, so did inexpensive personal computers and mass-marketed software to run on them. The very first, the Altair, showed up in 1974, and it was followed in the early 1980s by the first IBM PCs and Apple Macintoshes. Each one that rolled off the assembly line had its complement of RAM and a disk drive, and it expanded the potential domain of cyberspace by a few more megabytes of memory.

Somewhere along the line, our conception of what a computer *is* began   6
to change fundamentally. It turns out that these electronic boxes are not just big, fast, centralized calculating and data-sorting machines, as ENIAC, UNIVAC, and their mainframe successors had led us to believe. No, they are primarily *communication* devices—not dumb ones like telephone handsets, that merely encode and decode electronic information, but smart ones that can organize, interpret, filter, and present vast amounts of information. Their

real role is to construct cyberspace—a new kind of place for human interactions and transactions.

Wild West / Electronic Frontier

The early days of cyberspace were like those of the western frontier. Paral- 7
lel, breakneck development of the Internet and of consumer computing
devices and software quickly created an astonishing new condition; a vast,
hitherto-unimagined territory began to open up for exploration. Early computers had been like isolated mountain valleys ruled by programmer-kings;
the archaic digital world was a far-flung range in which narrow, unreliable
trails provided only tenuous connections among the multitudinous tiny realms.
An occasional floppy disk or tape would migrate from one to the other,
bringing the makings of colonies and perhaps a few unnoticed viruses. But
networking fundamentally changed things—as clipper ships and railroads
changed the preindustrial world—by linking the increasingly numerous individual fragments of cyberturf into one huge, expanding system.

By the 1990s the digital electronics and telecommunications industries 8
had configured themselves into an immense machine for the ongoing production of cyberspace. We found ourselves rapidly approaching a condition
in which every last bit of computer memory in the world would be electronically linked to every other. And those links will last forever. Because its
electronic underpinnings are so modular, geographically dispersed, and re-
dundant, cyberspace is essentially indestructible. You can't demolish it by
cutting links with backhoes or sending commandos to blow up electronic
installations, and you can't even nuke it. (The original ARPANET was, in fact,
explicitly designed to withstand nuclear attack.) If big chunks of the network were to be wiped out, messages would automatically reroute themselves around the damaged parts. If some memory or processing power
were to be lost, it could quickly be replaced. Since copies of digital data are
absolutely exact replicas of the originals, it doesn't matter if the originals get
lost or destroyed. And since multiple copies of files and programs can be
stored at widely scattered locations, eliminating them all with certainty is as
hard as lopping Hydra heads.

Cyberspace is still tough territory to travel, though, and we are just be- 9
ginning to glimpse what it may hold. "In its present condition," Mitch Kapor
and John Perry Barlow noted in 1990, "cyberspace is a frontier region, populated by the few hardy technologists who can tolerate the austerity of its
savage computer interfaces, incompatible communications protocols, pro-
prietary barricades, cultural and legal ambiguities, and general lack of useful
maps or metaphors." And they warned, "Certainly, the old concepts of property, expression, identity, movement, and context, based as they are on

physical manifestation, do not apply succinctly in a world where there can be none."

This vast grid is the new land beyond the horizon, the place that beck-   10
ons the colonists, cowboys, con artists, and would-be conquerors of the twenty-first century. And there are those who would be King.

Human Laws / Coded Conditionals

Out there on the electronic frontier, code is the law. The rules governing any   11
computer-constructed microworld—of a video game, your personal computer desktop, a word processor window, an automated teller machine, or a chat room on the network—are precisely and rigorously defined in the text of the program that constructs it on your screen. Just as Aristotle, in *Politics,* contemplated alternative constitutions for city-states (those proposed by the theorists Plato, Phaleas, and Hippodamos, and the actual Lacedae-monian, Cretan, and Carthaginian ones), so denizens of the digital world should pay the closest of critical attention to programmed polity. Is it just and humane? Does it protect our privacy, our property, and our freedoms? Does it constrain us unnecessarily or does it allow us to act as we may wish?

At a technical level, it's all a matter of the software's conditionals—those   12
coded rules that specify *if* some condition holds, *then* some action follows. Consider, for example, the familiar ritual of withdrawing some cash from an ATM. The software running the machine has some gatekeeper conditionals; *if* you have an account and *if* you enter the correct PIN number (the one that matches up, in a database somewhere, with the information magnetically encoded on your ATM card), *then* you can enter the virtual bank. (Otherwise you are stopped at the door. You may have your card confiscated as well.) Next the program presents you with a menu of possible actions—just as a more traditional bank building might present you with an array of appropriately labeled teller windows or (on a larger scale) a directory pointing you to different rooms: *if* you indicate that you want to make a withdrawal, *then* it asks you to specify the amount; *if* you want to check your balance, *then* it prints out a slip with the amount; *if* you want to make a deposit, *then* yet another sequence of actions is initiated. Finally, the program applies a banker's rule; *if* the balance of your account is sufficient (determined by checking a database), *then* it physically dispenses the cash and appropriately debits the account.

To enter the space constructed by the ATM system's software you have to   13
submit to a potentially humiliating examination—worse than being given the once-over by some snotty and immovable receptionist. You are either embraced by the system (if you have the right credentials) or excluded and marginalized by it right there in the street. You cannot argue with it. You cannot

ask it to exercise discretion. You cannot plead with it, cajole it, or bribe it. The field of possible interactions is totally delimited by the formally stated rules.

So control of code is power. For citizens of cyberspace, computer code—   14 arcane text in highly formalized language, typically accessible to only a few privileged high-priests—is the medium in which intentions are enacted and designs are realized, and it is becoming a crucial focus of political contest. Who shall write the software that increasingly structures our daily lives? What shall that software allow and proscribe? Who shall be privileged by it and who marginalized? How shall the writers of the rules be answerable?

Face-To-Face / Interface

The most basic built-in rules of virtual places control when you can act,   15 what kinds of actions you can take, and who or what you can affect by your actions. Old computer graphics hackers, for example, fondly remember *Spacewar,* the first computer game; it provided a diagrammatically depicted, deep-space battlefield in which players could take turns moving simulated spaceships, launching missiles, and amiably attempting to blow each other to bits. On timesharing systems, players did not have to share a single console but could operate individually from their own. And when networks began to develop, so did remote *Spacewar* between players who might be hundreds of miles apart. But the game stayed the same. The relationships that mattered were not those of the players' bodies in physical space (as, for example, in a pistol duel) but those of their surrogates in cyberspace, and the rules that counted were the coded-in ones of the virtual place in which the surrogates met.

On the early bulletin boards and commercial networks, "forums" or   16 "rooms" that allowed participants to "chat" quickly became a main attraction. Here the rules structured not a shoot-'em-up arena but a space for (mostly) risk-free, multiparticipant conversation. The place that you entered was presented as a scrolling text window. It had a descriptive or evocative name (like a bar, coffee shop, or other such hangout), and you could survey the scene by looking at a list of current participants. At any point, you could type in a short text comment; this appeared in the window, preceded by your chosen online handle, so that a stream of comments scrolled by on each participant's screen—a geographically distributed, highly stylized, cocktail party with electronically masked participants and a mouse in your hand instead of a drink.

Forum habitués would often bar crawl from room to room until they   17 found one that seemed to have the right buzz. If they struck up an interesting conversation, they could agree to go off into private rooms to continue, and eventually might even contemplate the big step of choosing times and physical locations to go face-to-face with new-found friends. So these virtual places performed, in a vivid new way, the traditional urban function of creating opportunities for chance encounters between strangers. And the associated conventions allowed those encounters to evolve, step by step, toward friendship and intimacy. Not surprisingly, some of these convivial spots became hot hangouts in cyberspace.

In the early days of computer networks it seemed a slightly far-fetched 18 metaphor to describe these sorts of interaction sites as "places," since bandwidth was narrow and communication was mostly restricted to typing and receiving text. But SIMNET changed that. A military project dating from the interregnum when ARPA was DARPA, SIMNET first came online in 1986 as a network of M-1 tank simulators, and it has since been elaborated to include other types of vehicles. The viewports of the "tanks" are video screens displaying simulated three-dimensional terrain over which a mock tank battle takes place. Since the computer-generated display is updated in real time as controls are manipulated, dozens of widely scattered tank crews have the vivid impression of maneuvering around the same patch of countryside. Perhaps fittingly, this prototypical electronic landscape—this Garden of Eden of cyberspace—is a realistically simulated battlefield.

The technology of distributed interactive simulation (DIS) systems grew 19 out of SIMNET, and by the early 1990s it was being hyped as the latest thing for the theme park industry. Pretty soon you could line up to play *Battle Tech, Virtuality,* or *Fightertown*—interactive games unfolding in networked simulator pods that immerse you in tacky but fairly convincing virtual worlds.

As bandwidth burgeons and computing muscle continues to grow, cy- 20 berspace places will present themselves in increasingly multisensory and engaging ways. They will look, sound, and feel more realistic, they will enable richer self-representations of their users, they will respond to user actions in real time and in complex ways, and they will be increasingly elaborate and artfully designed. We will not just look *at* them; we will feel present *in* them. We can expect them to evolve into the elements of cyberspace construction—constituents of a new architecture without tectonics and a new urbanism freed from the constraints of physical space.

On The Spot / On The Net

Why do some places attract people? Often, it is because being on the spot 21 puts you in the know. The merchants' coffeehouses of eighteenth-century New York, for instance, provided opportunities to get the latest shipping information, to meet potential trading partners, and to exchange other important commercial information. Depending on your trade, you might find the need to locate in the financial district, the garment district, or SoHo, on Harley Street, Fleet Street, or Lincoln's Inn Fields, in Hollywood, Silicon Val-

ley, or Detroit. You might be attracted to the literary salon, the corner saloon, or the Cambridge high table. It's not just a matter of where the jobs
are, but of where you can exchange the most up-to-date, specialized information with the most savvy people; you may be able to do the same work
and pursue similar interests if you are out in the sticks, but you are likely to
feel cut off and far from the center of things.

In cyberspace, list servers soon evolved to perform some of the same   22
functions. These are programs for broadcasting e-mail messages to all the
"subscribers" on specified address lists. They are like electronic Hyde Park
Corners—places in which anybody can stand up and speak to the assembled crowd. Lists may assemble formal groups such as the employees of a
business, or the students enrolled in a class, or they may be constructed
through some informal, self-selection process. As with physical assemblies,
some lists are public and some secret, some are open to anybody and some
are rigorously exclusive.

Electronic "newsgroups" were also quick to develop. Newsgroup soft-   23
ware allows participants to "post" text messages (and sometimes other sorts
of files), much as you might pin printed notices to a physical bulletin board.
The notices—queries, requests, responses, news items, announcements, tips,
warnings, bits of gossip, jokes, or whatever—stay there until they are deleted,
and anyone who enters the place can read them. Usually there is a host—a
sort of Cyber de Staël or Virtual Gertrude presiding over an online rue de
Fleury—who sets topics, coaxes the exchanges along when they flag, and
occasionally kicks out an unruly or objectionable participant. By the 1990s
there were countless thousands of these places, advertising every interest
you might imagine and some that you surely would not. If you wanted to be
in touch and up with the latest in your field, it was increasingly important to
have ready access to the right newsgroups. And your physical location no
longer mattered so much.

When there is a sudden need, ad-hoc newsgroups can spring almost in-   24
stantly into existence. Within hours of the January 1994 Los Angeles earthquake, there was a Usenet newsgroup called *alt.current-events.la.quake.*
Long before the rubble had been swept from Wilshire Boulevard and before
telephone service had unjammed, it was providing a place to post damage
reports and find news about friends and relatives. It was the best place to be
if you wanted to know what was going on.

The virtual communities that networks bring together are often defined   25
by common interests rather than by common location: Unix hackers, Amiga
enthusiasts, Trekkies, and Deadheads are scattered everywhere. But the opposite can also be true. When networks and servers are organized to deal
with information and issues of local concern to the people of a town or to
the students, staff, and faculty of a university, they act to maintain more tra-

ditional, site-specific communities. So, for example, the City of Santa Monica's pioneering Public Electronic Network (PEN) is available only to residents of Santa Monica, to people who work in the city, or at thirty-five public-access terminals located within the city boundaries. And the Athena educational network was put in place on MIT's Cambridge campus to serve the MIT community.

Street Networks / World Wide Web

Ever since Ur, urban places have been linked by movement channels of various kinds: doorways and passageways have joined together the rooms of buildings, street grids have connected buildings to each other, and road and rail networks have allowed communication between distant cities. These familiar sorts of physical connections have provided access to the places where people lived, worked, worshipped, and entertained themselves.   26

Now there is a powerful alternative. Ever since the winter of 1994, I have had a remarkable piece of software called Mosaic on the modest desktop machine that I'm using to write this paragraph. (Right now, Mosaic is open in another window.) Mosaic is a "client" program that provides convenient access to World Wide Web (WWW) servers located throughout the Internet. These servers present "pages" of information, which may be in the form of text, graphics, video, or sound. Pages typically have "hyperlinks" pointing to related pages elsewhere in the Web, allowing me to jump from page to page by clicking on highlighted text or images.   27

The "home page" of any WWW server invites me to step, like Alice through the looking glass, into the vast information flea market of the Web— a cyberspace zone now consisting of countless millions of interconnected pages. The astonishing thing is that a WWW page displayed on my screen may originate from a machine located *anywhere* on the Internet. In fact, as I move from page to page, I am logging into computers scattered around the world. But as I see it, I jump almost instantaneously from virtual place to virtual place by following the hyperlinks that programmers have established— much as I might trace a path from station to station through the London Underground. If I were to diagram these connections, I would have a kind of subway map of cyberspace.   28

Neighborhoods / MUDs

MUD crawling is another way to go. Software constructions known as MUDs, Multi-User Dungeons, have burned up countless thousands of log-in hours since the early 1980s. These provide settings—often very large and elaborately detailed ones—for online, interactive, role-playing games, and they   29 often attract vast numbers of participants scattered all over the Internet. They are cyberspace equivalents of urban neighborhoods.

The particular joy of MUDville is the striking way that it foregrounds is-   30
sues of personal identity and self-representation; as newcomers learn at old MUDders' knees, your first task as a MUD initiate is to construct an online persona for yourself by choosing a name and writing a description that others will see when they encounter you. It's like dressing up for a masked ball, and the irresistible thing is that you can experiment freely with shifts, slippages, and reversals in social and sexual roles and even try on entirely fantastic guises. You can discover how it *really* feels to be a *complete* unknown.

Once you have created your MUD character, you can enter a virtual place   31
populated with other characters and objects. This place has exits—hyperlinks connecting it to other such settings, which have in turn their own exits. Some heavily frequented MUDs are almost incomprehensibly vast, allowing you to wander among thousands of distinct settings, all with their own special characteristics, like Baudelaire strolling through the buzzing complexity of nineteenth-century Paris. You can examine the settings and objects that you encounter, and you can interact with the characters that you meet.

But as you quickly discover, the most interesting and provocative thing   32
about a MUD is its constitution—the programmed-in rules specifying the sorts of interactions that can take place and shaping the culture that evolves. Many are based on popular fantasy narratives such as *Star Trek,* Frank Herbert's *Dune,* C. S. Lewis's *Chronicles of Narnia,* the Japanese animated television series *Speed Racer,* and even more doubtful products of the literary imagination; these are communities held together, as in many traditional societies, by shared myths. Some are set up as hack-'n-slash combat games in which bad MUDders will try to "kill" your character; these, of course, are violent, Darwinian places in which you have to be aggressive and constantly on your guard. Others, like many of the TinyMUDs, stress ideals of constructive social interaction, egalitarianism, and nonviolence—MUDderhood and apple pie. Yet others are organized like high-minded lyceums, with places for serious discussion of different scientific and technical topics. The MIT-based *Cyberion City* encourages young hackers—MUDders of invention—to write MUSE code that adds new settings to the environment and creates new characters and objects. And some are populated by out-of-control, crazy MUDders who will try to engage your character in TinySex—the one-handed keyboard equivalent of phone sex.

Early MUDs—much like text-based adventure video games such as *Zork*—   33
relied entirely on typed descriptions of characters, objects, scenes, and actions. (James Joyce surely would have been impressed; city as text and text as city. Every journey constructs a narrative.) But greater bandwidth, faster computers, and fancier programming can shift them into pictorial and spatial

formats. Lucasfilm's *Habitat,* for example, was an early example of a graphic MUD that had its first incarnation, in North America, on the QuantumLink Club Caribe network (a precursor of America Online) and Commodore 64 computers. Later, it spawned a colony, *Populopolis,* that reputedly attracted a lot more paying customers on the NIFtyServe network in Japan.

As a citizen of *Habitat,* you could customize your character, known as your Avatar, by selecting from a menu of body parts and choosing a sex. (That was a one-bit choice, since *Habitat* was marketed as fairly conservative family entertainment.) Players conversed with one another in comic strip speech balloons. A region—one of as many as 20,000 similar ones in the original *Habitat* at its zenith—was a place that you can walk your character around, and it had doors and passages to other regions. These regions were filled with functional objects such as ATM machines to provide cash, bags and boxes to carry things in, books and newspapers to read, weapons, flashlights, and garbage cans. You could walk, take elevators, or teleport to other regions and explore them; you could exchange conversation, buy and sell goods, and even swap body parts. And, if you got tired of your character, you could reconfigure it, give it some drugs, or take it to the Change-o-matic sex-change machine.

As the creators of *Habitat* soon found, their task became one of reinventing architecture and urban design for cyberspace. They commented:

> For 20,000 Avatars we needed 20,000 "houses" organized into towns and cities with associated traffic arteries and shopping and recreational areas. We needed wilderness areas between the towns so that everyone would not be jammed together into the same place. Most of all, we needed things for 20,000 people to do. They needed interesting places to visit—and since they can't all be in the same place at the same time, they needed a *lot* of interesting places to visit—and things to do in those places. Each of those houses, towns, roads, shops, forests, theaters, arenas, and other places is a distinct entity that someone needs to design and create.

Only limitations in bandwidth and processing power inhibit taking the next step—the realization of whizzier World Wide Webs, superMUDs, and other multiparticipant, urban-scale structures consisting of hyperlinked, three-dimensional, sensorily immersive spaces. And these limitations are temporary. The online environments of the future will increasingly resemble traditional cities in their variety of distinct places, in the extent and complexity of the "street networks" and "transportation systems" linking these places, in their capacity to engage our senses, and in their social and cultural richness.

But no matter how extensive a virtual environment or how it is presented, it has an underlying structure of places where you meet people and find things and links connecting those places. This is the organizing framework from which all else grows. In cyberspace, the hyperplan is the generator.

Enclosure / Encryption

You don't get to go just anywhere in a city, and the same is true of cyber-   38
space. In both domains, barriers and thresholds play crucial roles.

In the built fabric of a city, the enclosing surfaces of the constituent   39
spaces—walls, floors, ceilings, and roofs—provide not only shelter, but also
privacy. Breaches in these surfaces—gates, doors, and windows—incorporate mechanisms to control access and maintain privacy; you can lock your
doors or leave them open, lower the window shades or raise them. Spatial
divisions and access-control devices are carefully deployed to organize places
into hierarchies grading from completely public to utterly private. Sometimes you have to flip your ID to a bouncer, take off your shoes, pay admission, dress to a doorman's taste, slip a bribe, submit to a search, speak
into a microphone and wait for the buzzer, smile at a receptionist, placate a
watchdog, or act out some other ritual to cross a threshold into a more private space. Traditions and laws recognize these hierarchies and generally
take a dim view of illicit boundary crossing by trespassers, intruders, and
Peeping Toms.

Different societies have distinguished between public and private do-   40
mains (and the activities appropriate to them) in differing ways, and urban
form has reflected those distinctions. According to Lewis Mumford, domestic privacy was "a luxury of the well-to-do" up until the seventeenth century
in the West. The rich were the people who could do pretty much what they
wanted, as long as they didn't do it in the street and frighten the horses. As
privacy rights trickled down to the less advantaged classes, the modern "private house" emerged, acquired increasingly rigorous protections of constitutional law and public policy, and eventually became the cellular unit of
suburban tissue. Within the modern Western house itself—in contrast to
some of its ancient and medieval predecessors—there is a staged gradation
from relatively public verandahs, entry halls, living rooms, and parlors to
more private, enclosed bedrooms and bathrooms, where you can shut and
lock the doors and draw down the shades against the outside world.

It doesn't rain in cyberspace, so shelter is not an architectural issue. But   41
privacy certainly is. So the construction technology for virtual cities—just
like that of bricks-and-mortar ones—must provide for putting up boundaries
and erecting access controls, and it must allow cyberspace architects and urban designers to organize virtual places into public-to-private hierarchies.

Fortunately, some of the necessary technology does exist. Most obvi-   42
ously, in cyberspace construction the rough equivalent of a locked gate or
door is an authentication system. This controls access to virtual places (such
as your e-mail inbox) by asking for identification and a password from those

who request entry. If you give the correct password, you're in. The trouble, of course, is that passwords, like keys, can be stolen and copied. And they can sometimes be guessed, systematically enumerated until one that works is found, or somehow extorted from the system manager who knows them all. So password protection—like putting a lock on a door—discourages illicit entry but does not block the most determined break-in artists.

Just as you can put the valuables that you *really* want to protect in   43
a sturdy vault or crypt, though, you can build the strongest of enclosures around digital information by encrypting it—scrambling it in a complex way so that it can be decoded only by someone with the correct secret numerical key. The trick is not only to have a code that is difficult to crack, but also to manage keys so that they don't fall into the wrong hands. The cleverest known way to do this is to use a technique called RSA public-key encryption. In this system, which derives its power from the fundamental properties of large prime numbers, each user has both a secret "private" key and a "public" key that can be distributed freely. If you want to send a secure message, you obtain the intended recipient's public key and use it to encode the information. Then the recipient decodes the message using the private key.

Under pressure from cops and cold warriors, who anticipate being   44
thwarted by impregnable fortresses in cyberspace, the U.S. federal government has doggedly tried to restrict the availability of strong encryption software. But in June 1991, hacker folk hero Philip Zimmerman released his soon-to-be-famous, RSA-based Pretty Good Privacy (PGP) encryption program. By May 1994 commercial versions had been licensed to over four million users, and MIT had released a free, noncommercial version that anybody could legally download from the Internet. From that moment, you could securely fence off your private turf in cyberspace. . . .

So the technological *means* to create private places in cyberspace are   45
available, but the *right* to create these places remains a fiercely contested issue. Can you always keep your bits to yourself? Is your home page your castle? These are still open questions.

Public Space / Public Access

Once public and private spaces are distinguished from each other, they can   46
begin to play complementary roles in urban life; a well-organized city needs both. And so it is in cyberspace. At the very least, this means that some part of our emerging electronic habitat should be set aside for public uses—just as city planners have traditionally designated land for public squares, parks, and civic institutions. Public pressure for this grew in the 1990s as the importance of cyberspace became increasingly clear. In 1994, for example,

Senator Inouye of Hawaii introduced to the U.S. Senate a bill that would reserve 20 percent of all new telecommunication capacity for free, public uses (noncommercial educational and informational services and civic discourse) and would provide funding for those uses.

But urban public space is not merely un-private—what's left over when everyone walls off their private domains. A space is genuinely public, as Kevin Lynch once pointed out, only to the extent that it really is openly accessible and welcoming to members of the community that it serves. It must also allow users considerable freedom of assembly and action. And there must be some kind of public control of its use and its transformation over time. The same goes for public cyberspace, so creators and maintainers of public, semipublic, and pseudopublic parts of the online world—like the makers of city squares, public parks, office building lobbies, shopping mall atriums, and Disneyland Main Streets—must consider who gets in and who gets excluded, what can and cannot be done there, whose norms are enforced, and who exerts control. These questions, like the complementary ones of privacy and encryption, have become the foci of crucial policy debates. 47

The Internet and commercial online services like America Online and Compuserve have to date provided only semipublic cyberspace at best, since they are widely but not universally accessible; you have to belong to a subscribing organization or have to pay to get in. This begs the question of how truly public cyberspace—the equivalent, say, of the Piazza San Marco in Venice—might be constructed. The community networks that emerged in the 1980s and 1990s—Santa Monica Public Electronic Network, Blacksburg Electronic Village, Telluride InfoZone, Smart Valley, and Cambridge Civic Network, for example—sought answers by trying to make network access openly available to entire communities in the same way that city hall and the local public parks traditionally have been. 48

Many of these community networks are structured as so-called free-nets, in which a "city" metaphor is explicitly used to structure information access: you go to the appropriate "building" to find the information or services that you want. Thus the "welcome" screen of the Cleveland Free-Net (one of the oldest and largest, with more than 35,000 registered users and over 10,000 log-ins per day) presents the following quotidian directory: 49

1. The Administration Building
2. The Post Office
3. Public Square
4. The Courthouse and Government Center
5. The Arts Building
6. Science and Technology Center

7. The Medical Arts Building
8. The Schoolhouse (Academy One)
9. The Community Center and Recreation Area
10. The Business and Industrial Park
11. The Library
12. University Circle
13. The Teleport
14. The Communications Center
15. NPTN / USA Today Headline News

On the free-net model, then, the new, virtual city becomes a kind of electronic shadow of the existing physical one. In many (though not all) cases, a citizen can choose between going to an actual public building or to the corresponding virtual one.

Being There / Getting Connected

But a free-net's superimposition of the virtual onto the physical, while sensible enough, is not a logical or technical necessity. In fact, one of the most interesting questions for twenty-first-century urban designers to ask is, "How *should* virtual and physical public space relate to one another?"

Consider the obvious options. There is complete dissociation of the two if the electronic public space is accessible only from personal computers in homes and businesses. Another possibility is to associate access points with civic architecture: put an electronic information kiosk in the lobby of city hall or in the public library, for example. The Berkeley Community Memory and Santa Monica PEN systems have demonstrated a more radical strategy by placing rugged workstations in places like laundromats and at congregation points for the homeless; these workstations thus begin to play a public role much like the traditional one of fountains in the public places of Rome. The artist Krzysztof Wodiczko has gone a step further by suggesting that the physically homeless and displaced might carry electronic "alien staffs"—personal devices that connect them to cyberspace and sometimes construct public representations of self by providing information to others about who they are and where they come from. These are public rather than personal digital assistants.

Since physical distance means little in cyberspace, the possibility also exists to "condense" scattered rural communities by creating public spaces that serve large, thinly populated areas. The Big Sky Telegraph, which has been running in Montana since 1988, successfully pioneered this idea. It began

50

51

52

by linking one-room and two-room rural schoolhouses across the state, and it has focused on education, economic opportunity, and economic self-sufficiency. In economically disadvantaged communities, where adequate public facilities of a traditional kind do not exist, the possibility of providing public cyberspace may become an important community development issue. Increasingly, communities and their planners will have to consider tradeoffs between investing scarce resources in creating or upgrading parks and community buildings and putting the money into effective electronic networks.

Whatever approach is taken to deploying network capacity for public purposes, though, simply making computers available and providing some kind of electronic access to civic information and discourse is not enough to create successful public cyberspace. Just as parks and squares must be pleasant and welcoming to a diverse population in order to function effectively, so must the interfaces to public areas of cyberspace; an interface that depends on cryptic commands and arcane knowledge of computer technology is as much a barrier to most people as is a flight of steps to a park user in a wheelchair. People must also feel secure and comfortable—not subject to hostility, abuse, or attack. And more subtly, but just as importantly, the cultural presumptions and cues that are built into an interface must not discourage potential users. Think of important physical public spaces like New York's Central Park and consider the extent to which both their successes and their failures depend on these sorts of things; designers of public cyberspace will have to deal with them as well.

53

Community Customs / Network Norms

Where public cyberspace exists, how can and should it be used? Do the customs and laws that govern physical public space still make sense in this new context?

54

As usage of the Internet and commercial online services has grown, there have been increasingly frequent disputes that have tested the limits of acceptable behavior in electronic public places and raised the question of how these limits might reasonably be enforced. In April 1994, for example, some particularly thick-skinned lawyers from Phoenix spammed the Internet by indiscriminately spraying a commercial advertisement for the services of their firm into thousands of newsgroups. This blast of unwanted bits had the same effect as driving a blaring sound truck into a public park. The Internet community reacted with outrage and disdain, and flamed back tens of thousands of complaints. One of the unrepentant perpetrators proclaimed his right to be a pain and threatened to do it again. Eventually—to cries of "censorship!" from some quarters—a young Norwegian programmer wrote and unleashed

55

an effective piece of "cancelbot" software that sniffed out and automatically removed the offending advertisements wherever they showed up.

In another widely publicized incident that unfolded almost simultane-   56
ously, a graduate student at MIT was busted by the FBI for operating an Internet bulletin board that had become a very active site for illegal activity—much
like a bar in which drug deals were going down. Copies of commercial software were being posted, then downloaded without payment by users who
logged in from all over the world. Was the operator of this openly accessible
place responsible for knowing and controlling what was going on there? Or
could he rightfully claim that it was just none of his business?

Like the proprietors of shopping malls and Disneylands, the operators of   57
commercial online services must struggle with the inherently contradictory
nature of the semipublic places they create. On the one hand, these places
need lots of paying customers to support them, so they have to seem as welcoming, open, and inclusive as possible. On the other hand, though, the operators want to stay in firm control of what goes on. (The question is often
framed as one of whether these services should be regarded as common car-
riers, like the telephone companies, and therefore not responsible for any li-
belous, obscene, or criminal information that they might carry or whether
they should be in control and therefore held responsible like book and
newspaper publishers and television broadcasters.) The last time I peeked
at Prodigy, for example, I found the following notice from the management
(a bit like the "Do not spit" signs that used to appear in railway stations):
"And please remember that PRODIGY is for people of all ages and backgrounds. Notes containing obscene, profane or sexually explicit language
(including descriptions of sexual acts, and whether or not masked with 'x's
and the like) are not allowed. A good test is whether the language in your
note would be acceptable at a public meeting."

Prodigy explicitly aims at a family audience, so it remorselessly enforces   58
the norms of Middle America. Its competitors Compuserve and Genie have
different sorts of constituencies, but their operators also take care to remove
messages they consider obscene or illegal. And America Online has shut
down some feminist discussion forums because, according to a spokesperson, kids might see the word "girl" in the forum's headline and "go in there
looking for information about their Barbies." The excluded feminists might
be forgiven for responding in not-for-prime-time language. And forget the
'x's. These places have found a useful role to play, but don't mistake them
for genuine, open-to-all, watch-out-for-yourself spaces for unconstrained
public discourse.

Some institutions are even more restrictive. My daughter's high school   59
treats its corner of public cyberspace as a schoolyard where teachers

enforce discipline. When the kids first got e-mail addresses, they were asked to sign contracts banning "sexually explicit speech." Then, when the inevitable happened, and some students complained about receiving obscene messages, the e-mail system was temporarily shut down as punishment.

But then, there will always be a Berkeley! The Berkeley Community   60
Memory system is a radical political invention—a transposition of the Free Speech Movement and People's Park into cyberspace. All information on the system is community generated, postings can be anonymous, and no central authority controls the content of postings. Funding is decentralized as well: there are coin-operated terminals on which postings can be read without charge, but it costs a quarter to post an opinion and a dollar to open up a new forum.

Nolli And The Net

The story of virtual communities, so far, is that of urban history replayed in   61
fast forward—but with computer resource use playing the part of land use, and network navigation systems standing in for streets and transportation systems. The WELL, the World Wide Web, MUDs, and Free Nets are—like Hippodamos's gridded layout for Miletos, Baron Haussmann's radial patterning of Paris, or Daniel Burnham's grand plan for Chicago—large-scale structures of places and connections organized to meet the needs of their inhabitants.

And the parallels don't stop there. As traditional cities have evolved, so   62
have customs, norms, and laws governing rights to privacy, access to public and semipublic places, what can be done where, and exertion of control. The organization of built space into public-to-private hierarchies, with gates and doors to control boundary crossings, has reflected this. Nolli's famous map of Rome vividly depicted it. Now, as cyberspace cities emerge, a similar framework of distinctions and expectations is—with much argument— being constructed, and electronic plazas, forums, lobbies, walls, doors, locks, members-only clubs, and private rooms are being invented and deployed. Perhaps some electronic cartographer of the future will produce an appropriately nuanced Nolli map of the Net.

Working with the Text

1. This chapter from Mitchell's book *City of Bits* is titled "Soft Cities." Is it inevitable that "cyberspace" be described as a city? He speaks of electronic environments as providing "a new urbanism freed from the constraints of physical space." In what ways does he argue that cyberspace is like an "urban" environment? What constraints (if not physical) does he say are present even in these new environments?

2. Mitchell makes the distinction between "virtual communities" (imaginary places constructed entirely on the Internet) and "site-specific communities" (physical places served by an electronic network). What are some of the characteristics of each? What are their differences? What kind of impact might an electronic community network (for a site-specific community) have on the actual physical community? What might an electronic dimension to a local place add or take away? On the World Wide Web, find an example of a community network, like the Cleveland Free-Net that he describes. How is the local place represented electronically? What kinds of groups, activities, or relationships are represented there?

3. A significant portion of Mitchell's discussion is about "public cyberspace"—the need to create and preserve "public" spaces on the Internet that people can share. Here, he sees a lot of parallels with urban planning. What are some of these parallels? Do you agree with him that "some part of our emerging electronic habitat should be set aside for public uses"? Where are those public spaces in your physical community now? Could they be replaced, created, or enhanced with public electronic spaces?

4. How do Mitchell's metaphors of "cities" for cyberspace compare to the tendency of early Internet theorists to refer to cyberspace as a frontier? Do "soft cities" retain any of the frontier qualities, or do they represent the "civilized" version of cyberspace?

5. Toward the conclusion of his essay, Mitchell says: "In economically disadvantaged communities, where adequate public facilities of a traditional kind do not exist, the possibility of providing public cyberspace may become an important community development issue. Increasingly, communities and their planners will have to consider tradeoffs between investing scarce resources in creating or upgrading parks and community buildings and putting the money into effective electronic networks." Write an essay that considers these questions: Do you agree with Mitchell that this is a "tradeoff"? Would significant electronic resources providing "public cyberspace" substitute for "upgrading parks and community buildings"? Could "public cyberspace" provide alternative space for the economically disadvantaged?

Sex, Death, and Machinery, or How I Fell in Love with My Prosthesis

ALLUCQUÈRE ROSANNE STONE

In the following introduction to her 1996 book, *The War of Desire and Technology at the Close of the Mechanical Age*, Allucquère Rosanne Stone posits that we are passing from a "mechanical age" to a "virtual age." This new age is characterized by a "gradual change that has come over the relationship between sense of self and the body, and the relationship between individual and group." As computers become, as Stone puts it, "arenas for social experience," our notions of selfhood, space, and communication may well undergo drastic changes. Stone teaches at the University of Texas, Austin.

It started this afternoon when I looked down at my boots. I was emerging from a stall in the women's room in my department. The university was closed for the holidays. The room was quite silent except for the distant rush of the air conditioning, imparting to the cramped institutional space the mechanical qualities of a submarine. I was idly adjusting my clothing, thinking of nothing in particular, when I happened to look down, and there they were: My boots. Two completely unremarkable boots. They were right where they belonged, on the ends of my legs. Presumably my feet were inside.

I felt a sudden thrill of terror. 2

Maybe, I suppose, the boots could have reminded me of some long-buried trauma, of the sort that Freudians believe leads to shoe fetishism. But my sudden fear was caused by something quite different. What was driving me was not the extraordinariness of the sight of my own boots, but the ordinariness of them. They were common as grass. In fact, I realized that I hadn't even thought about putting them on. They were *just there*. If you wanted to "get real ugly about it"—as they say in Austin—you might call it a moment of radical existential *Dasein,* in the same way you might say déjà vu again. I had become transparent to myself. Or rather, the *I* that I customarily express and that reflexively defines me through my chosen personal style had become part of the wallpaper.

This is hardly a serious problem for some. But I tend to see myself as an 4 entity that has chosen to make its life career out of playing with identity. It

606

sometimes seems as though everything in my past has been a kind of extended excuse for experiments with subject position and interaction. After all, what material is better to experiment with than one's self? Academically speaking, it's not exactly breaking new ground to say that any subject position is a mask. That's well and good, but still most people take some primary subject position for granted. When pressed, they may give lip service to the idea that perhaps even their current "root" persona is also a mask, but nobody really believes it. For all intents and purposes, your "root" persona is *you.* Take that one away, and there's nobody home.

Perhaps someone with training in drama already perceives this, but it was a revelation to me. In the social sciences, symbolic interactionists believe that the root persona is always a momentary expression of ongoing negotiations among a horde of subidentities, but this process is invisible both to the onlooker and to the persona within whom the negotiations are taking place. For me this has never been particularly true. My current *I* has been as palpably a mask to me as any of my other *I's* have been. Perceiving that which is generally invisible as really a kind of capital has been more than a passing asset (as it were); it has been a continual education, a source of endless challenge, not to mention fear, and certainly not least, an ongoing celebration of the sacred nature of the universe of passing forms. It was for these reasons, then, that I found looking down rather complacently at my boots and not really seeing them to be so terrifying. Like an athlete who has begun to flub a long-polished series of moves, I began to wonder if I was losing my edge.

Going through life with this outlook has been a terrific asset in my chosen work, and the current rise in the number of people who engage in social interactions without ever meeting in the customary sense of the term—that is, engaging in social intercourse by means of communication technologies—has given me increasing opportunities to watch others try on their own alternative personae. And although most still see those personae as just that—alternatives to a customary "root" identity—there are some out at the margins who have always lived comfortably with the idea of floating identities, and inward from the margins there are a few who are beginning, just a bit, to question. What it is they are questioning is a good part of what this essay is about.

A bit of background may be appropriate here.

I have bad history: I am a person who fell in love with her own prostheses. Not once, but twice. Then I fell in love with somebody *else's* prosthesis.

The first time love struck was in 1950. I was hunkered down in the dark late at night, on my bed with the big iron bedstead on the second floor, listening absently to the crickets singing and helping a friend scratch around on the surface of a galena crystal that was part of a primitive radio. We were looking for one of the hot spots, places where the crystal had active sites that worked like diodes and could detect radio waves. There was nothing but silence for a long, long time, and then suddenly the earphones burst into life, and a whole new universe was raging in our heads—the ranting voice of Jean Shepherd, boiling into the atmosphere from the massive transmitter of WOR-AM, 50 kilowatts strong and only a few miles away. At that distance we could have heard the signal in our tooth fillings if we'd had any, but the transmitter might as well have been in Rangoon, for all the fragrant breath of exotic worlds it suggested. I was hooked. Hooked on technology. I could take a couple of coils of wire and a hunk of galena and send a whole part of myself out into the ether. An extension of my will, of my instrumentality . . . that's a prosthesis, all right.

The second time happened in 1955, while I was peering over the edge　10 of a 24 × 24 recording console. As I stood on tiptoe, my nose just clearing the top of the console, from my age and vantage point the massive thing looked as wide as a football field. Knobs and switches from hell, all the way to the horizon . . . there was something about the vast forest of controls that suggested the same breath of exotic worlds that the simple coil of wire and the rickety crystal did. I was hooked again. I looked on even bigger technology, on another extension of my instrumentality. I could create whole oceans of sound, universes of sound, could at last begin on my life's path of learning how to make people laugh, cry, and throw up in dark rooms. And I hadn't even heard it turned *on*.

But the third time . . .　11

The third time was when Hawking came to town.　12

Stephen Hawking, the world-famous physicist, was giving a lecture at　13 UC Santa Cruz. The auditorium was jammed, and the overflow crowd was being accommodated outside on the lawn. The lawn looked like a medieval fair, with people sitting on blankets and towels, others standing or milling around, all ears cocked toward the loudspeakers that were broadcasting Hawking's address across the landscape.

If you haven't seen Stephen Hawking give a talk, let me give you a quick　14 background. Hawking has amyotrophic lateral sclerosis, which makes it virtually impossible for him to move anything more than his fingers or to speak. A friendly computer engineer put together a nice little system for him, a program that displays a menu of words, a storage buffer, and a Votrax allophone generator—that is, an artificial speech device. He selects words and phrases, the word processor stores them until he forms a paragraph, and the Votrax says it. Or he calls up a prepared file, and the Votrax says that.

So I and a zillion other people are on the lawn, listening to Hawking's　15 speech, when I get the idea that I don't want to be outside with the PA system—what I really want to do is sneak into the auditorium, so I can actually hear Hawking give the talk.

In practice this maneuver proves not too hard. The lecture is under way, security is light—after all, it's a *physicist,* dammit, not the UC Board of Regents, for which they would have had armed guards with two-way radios—so it doesn't take long for me to worm my way into the first row. | 16

And there is Hawking. Sitting, as he always does, in his wheelchair, utterly motionless, except for his fingers on the joystick of the laptop; and on the floor to one side of him is the PA system microphone, nuzzling into the Votrax's tiny loudspeaker. | 17

And a thing happens in my head. Exactly where, I say to myself, *is* Hawking? Am I any closer to him now than I was outside? Who is it doing the talking up there on stage? In an important sense, Hawking doesn't stop being Hawking at the edge of his visible body. There is the obvious physical Hawking, vividly outlined by the way our social conditioning teaches us to see a person as a person. But a serious part of Hawking extends into the box in his lap. In mirror image, a serious part of that silicon and plastic assemblage in his lap extends into him as well . . . not to mention the invisible ways, displaced in time and space, in which discourses of medical technology and their physical accretions already permeate him and us. No box, no discourse; in the absence of the prosthetic, Hawking's intellect becomes a tree falling in the forest with nobody around to hear it. On the other hand, with the box his voice is auditory and simultaneously electric, in a radically different way from that of a person *speaking* into a microphone. Where *does* he stop? Where are his edges? The issues his person and his communication prostheses raise are boundary debates, borderland/*frontera* questions. Here at the close of the mechanical age, they are the things that occupy a lot of my attention. | 18

Flashback: I Was Idly Looking

I was idly looking out my window, taking a break from some nasty piece of academic writing, when up the dusty, rutted hill that constitutes my driveway and bastion against the world there abruptly rode, on a nasty little Suzuki Virago, a brusque, sharp-tongued person of questionable sexuality. Doffing her helmet, she revealed herself, both verbally and physically, as Valkyrie, a postoperative m/f transgender with dark hair and piercing black eyes who evinced a pronounced affinity for black leather. She announced that there were things we had to do and places we had to go, and before I could mutter "science fiction" we were off on her bike. | 19

Valkyrie proceeded to introduce me to a small community of women in the San Francisco Bay area. Women's collectives were not new to me; I had | 20 recently studied a group of women who ran a business, housed themselves under one roof, and lived their lives according to the principles of a canonically undefined but quite powerful idea known as lesbian separatism. But the group to which my new friend now introduced me did not at all fit the model I had painstakingly learned to recognize. This collective ran a business, and the business was hetero phone sex . . . not something of which my other research community, immured in radical lesbian orthodoxy, would have approved.

I was instantly entranced, and also oddly repelled. After all, I had broken bread with one of the most episcopal of women's collectives for five years, and any deviation from group norms would have been punishable in fairly horrid ways. To imagine that hetero sex could be enjoyable, not to mention profitable, was playing into the hands of the gentiles, and even to spend time with a group that supported itself in such a manner (and even joked about it) could have had mortal consequences.   21

For reasons best described as kismet, the phone sex workers and I became good friends. We found each other endlessly fascinating. They were intrigued by my odd history and by what I'd managed to make out of it. In turn, I was intrigued by the way they negotiated the mine fields of ethics and personal integrity while maintaining a lifestyle that my other research community considered unthinkable.   22

After a while, we sorted out two main threads of our mutual attraction. From my point of view, the more I observed phone sex the more I realized I was observing very practical applications of data compression. Usually sex involves as many of the senses as possible. Taste, touch, smell, sight, hearing—and, for all I know, short-range psychic interactions—all work together to heighten the erotic sense. Consciously or unconsciously phone sex workers translate all the modalities of experience into audible form. In doing so they have reinvented the art of radio drama, complete down to its sound effects, including the fact that some sounds were best represented by *other* improbable sounds that they resembled only in certain iconic ways. On the radio, for example, the soundmen (they were always literally men) represented fire by crumpling cellophane, because to the audience it sounded *more like* fire than holding a microphone to a real fire did.   23

The sex workers did similar stuff. I made a little mental model out of this: The sex workers took an extremely complex, highly detailed set of behaviors, translated them into a single sense modality, then further boiled them down to a series of highly compressed tokens. They then squirted those tokens down a voice-grade phone line. At the other end of the line the recipient of all this effort added boiling water, so to speak, and reconstituted the tokens into a fully detailed set of images and interactions in multiple sensory modes.   24

Library Resource Center
Renton Technical College
3000 N.E. 4th St.
Renton, WA 98056

Further, what was being sent back and forth over the wires wasn't just information, it was *bodies*. The majority of people assume that erotics implies bodies; a body is part of the idea of erotic interaction and its concomitants, and the erotic sensibilities are mobilized and organized around the idea of a physical body which is the seat of the whole thing. The sex workers' descriptions were invariably and quite directly about physical bodies and what they were doing or what was being done to them. . . .   25

A recent but fairly broad area of inquiry in the social sciences into the nature and character of human-computer interaction is known as the study of computer-supported cooperative work (CSCW). Part of the informing philosophy of this discipline is the idea that all human activity can be usefully interpreted as a kind of work, and that work is the quintessential defining human capacity. This, too, I think, misses some of the most important qualities of human-computer interaction just as it does when applied to broader elements of human experience. By this I mean that a significant part of the time that humans spend in developing interactional skills is devoted not to work but to what by common understanding would be called play. Definitions of what counts as play are many and varied, generally revolving around the idea of purposive activities that do not appear to be directly goal oriented. "Goal orientation" is, of course, a problematic phrase. There is a fine body of research addressed to the topic of play versus work activities, but it doesn't appear to have had a deep effect on CSCW and its allied disciplines. From the standpoint of cultural criticism, the issue is not one of definitions of work or play, but of how the meanings of those terms are produced and maintained. Both work and play have culture-specific meanings and purposes, and I am conducting a quite culture-specific discussion when I talk about the primacy of play in human-computer interaction (HCI, or for our purposes just "interaction") as I do here.   26

In order to clarify this point, let me mention that there are many definitions of interaction and many opinions about what interaction is for. As I write, large industry consortiums are finalizing their standards for what they call interactive multimedia platforms. These devices usually consist of a computer, color monitor, mouse, CD-ROM drive, sound card, and pair of speakers. This electronic instantiation of a particular definition freezes the conceptual framework of interaction in a form most suitable for commercial development—the user moves the cursor to the appropriate place and clicks the mouse, which causes something to happen—or what the interactivist Michael Naimark would call, more pejoratively, poke-and-see technology. This definition of interaction has been in the wind for so long now that few researchers say much about it. It is possible to play within the constraints of such a system, but the potential for *interaction* is limited, because the machine can only respond to an on-off situation: that is, to the click of the   27 mouse. Computer games offer a few more input modes, usually in the form of a joystick, which has two or three degrees of freedom. However, from the standpoint of kind and gentle instruction, what the game companies do with this greater potential is not very inspiring. Technologically speaking, Sega's *Sewer Shark* (1993), for example, was an amazing exercise in game design for its time, but it reinforced the feeling that interaction in a commercial frame is still a medium like television, in which the most advanced product of the technological genius of an entire species conveys Geraldo Rivera to millions of homes in breathtaking color.

28   I don't want to make this a paradise-lost story, but the truth is that the definitions of interactivity used by the early researchers at MIT possessed a certain poignancy that seems to have become lost in the commercial translation. One of the best definitions was set forth by Andy Lippman, who described interaction as mutual and simultaneous activity on the part of both participants, usually working toward some goal—but, he added, not necessarily. Note that from the beginning of interaction research the idea of a common goal was already in question, and in that fact inheres interaction's vast ludic dimension.

29   There are five corollaries to Lippman's definition. One is *mutual interruptibility,* which means that each participant must be able to interrupt the other, mutually and simultaneously. Interaction, therefore, implies conversation, a complex back-and-forth exchange, the goal of which may change as the conversation unfolds.

30   The second is *graceful degradation,* which means that unanswerable questions must be handled in a way that doesn't halt the conversation: "I'll come back to that in a minute," for example.

31   The third is *limited look-ahead,* which means that because both parties can be interrupted there is a limit to how much of the shape of the conversation can be anticipated by either party.

32   The fourth is *no-default,* which means that the conversation must not have a preplanned path; it must develop fully in the interaction.

33   The fifth, which applies more directly to immersive environments (in which the human participant is surrounded by the simulation of a world), is that the participants should have *the impression of an infinite database.* This principle means that an immersive interactional world should give the illusion of not being much more limiting in the choices it offers than an actual world would be. In a nonimmersive context, the machine should give the impression of having about as much knowledge of the world as you do, but not necessarily more. This limitation is intended to deal with the Spock phenomenon, in which more information is sometimes offered than is conversationally appropriate.

Thus interactivity implies two conscious agencies in conversation, play-   34
fully and spontaneously developing a mutual discourse, taking cues and
suggestions from each other as they proceed.

In order to better draw this out let me briefly review the origins and uses   35
of computers. Afterward I will return to the subject of play from a slightly
different perspective.

The first devices that are usually called computers were built as part of   36
a series of projects mandated by the military during World War II. For many
years, computers were large and extremely costly. They were also cranky
and prone to continual breakdown, which had to do with the primitive nature of their components. They required continual maintenance by highly
skilled technicians. The factors of cost, unreliability, and the need for skilled
and continual attention, not to mention the undeniable aura of power that
surrounded the new machines like some heady smell, combined to keep
computers available only to large corporations and government organizations.
These entities came already equipped with their own ideas of efficiency, with
the concepts of time and motion study then in vogue in industry (of which my
colleagues have written at length), and of course with the cultural abstraction
known as the work ethic perpetually running in the background. Even
within the organizations themselves, access to the new machines was restricted to a technological elite which, though by no means monolithic in its
view of technological achievement, had not had enough time to develop
much of a sense, not to mention a sensibility, of the scope and potential of
the new devices.

These factors combined to keep attention focused on the uses of com-   37
puters as rather gross instrumentalities of human will—that is, as number
crunchers and databases. Computers could extend human abilities, physically and conceptually. That is, computers were tools, like crowbars and
screwdrivers, except that they primarily extended the mind rather than the
muscles. Even Vannevar Bush's astonishingly prophetic "As We May Think"
(1949) treated computers as a kind of superswitch. In this frame of understanding, computers were prosthetic in the specific sense of the Greek term
prosthenos—extension. Computers assisted or augmented human intelligence
and capabilities in much the same way that a machine or even another human being would; that is, as separate, discrete agencies or tools that occupied physical or conceptual spaces separate from those of the human. . . .

All this changed in the 1960s, but the change was largely invisible both   38
physically and conceptually. Deleuze and Guattari and Manuel De Landa and
the eerie concept of the machinic phylum would not arrive on the scene for
some 30 years. In 1962, the young hackers at Project MAC, deep in the bowels of MIT, made hardly a ripple in corporate arenas with their invention of

a peculiarly engrossing computational diversion that they called *SpaceWar.* This first computer game was still firmly identified with the military, even down to its name and playing style, but in that moment something quite new and (dare I say it) completely different had happened to the idea of computation. Still, it would not be until the 1970s that two kids in a garage in Mountain View, California, rather than a corporate giant like Sperry Rand or IBM or a government entity like the Bureau of Vital Statistics, would knock the props out from under the idea of computation-as-tool for all time.

Let me return to the discussion of work versus play once again, from the standpoint of computation and instrumentality. Viewing computers as calculatory devices that assist or mediate human work seems to be part of a Kuhnian paradigm that consists of two main elements. The first is a primary *human work ethic;* the second is a particularized view of *computers as tools.* The emergence of the work ethic has been the subject of innumerable essays, but the view of computers as tools has been so totally pervasive among those with the power to determine meaning in such forums as school policy and corporate ethics that only recently has the idea begun to be seriously challenged. The paradigm of computers as tools burst into existence, more or less, out of the allied victory in World War II (although the Nazis were working on their own computers). A paradigm of computers as something other than number crunchers does not have a similar launching platform, but the signs of such an imminent upheaval are perspicuous. Let me provide an example.

One of the most perceptive scholars currently studying the emergent computer societies is the anthropologist Barbara Joans. She describes the community of cyberspace workers as composed of two groups that she calls Creative Outlaw Visionaries and Law and Order Practitioners. One group has the visions; the other group knows how to build stuff and get it sold. One group fools around with technology and designs fantastic stuff; the other group gets things done and keeps the wheels turning. They talk to each other, if they talk to each other, across a vast conceptual gulf. These groups are invisible to each other, I think, because one is operating out of the older paradigm of computers as tools and the other out of the newer paradigm of computers as something else. Instead of carrying on an established work ethic, the beliefs and practices of the cultures I observe incorporate a *play* ethic—not to displace the corporate agendas that produce their paychecks, but to complexify them. This play ethic is manifest in many of the communities and situations I study. It is visible in the northern California Forth community, a group of radical programmers who have adopted for their own an unusual and controversial programming language; in the CommuniTree community, an early text-based virtual discussion group that adopted such mottos as "If you meet the electronic avatar on the road, laserblast Hir"; and in the Atari Research Lab, where a group of hackers created an artificial person who became real enough to become pro tem lab director. The people who play at these technosocial games do not do so out of any specific transformative agenda, but they have seized upon advantages afforded by differences of skill, education, and income to make space for play in the very belly of the monster that is the communication industry.

This production and insertion of a play ethic like a mutation into the corporate genome is a specifically situated activity, one that is only possible for workers of a certain type and at a certain job level. In specific, it is only possible to the communities who are perhaps best described as hackers—mostly young (although the demographic changes as the first- and second-generation hackers age), mostly educated (although the field is rife with exceptions, perhaps indicating the incapability of U.S. public schools to deal with talented individuals), mostly white (and exceptions are quite rare in the United States), and mostly male (although a truly egregious exception is part of this study). They create and use a broad variety of technological prosthetics to manifest a different view of the purpose of communication technology, and their continual and casual association with the cutting edge of that technology has molded them and their machines—separately and jointly—in novel and promising ways. In particular, because they are thoroughly accustomed to engaging in nontrivial social interactions through the use of their computers—social interactions in which they change and are changed, in which commitments are made, kept, and broken, in which they may engage in intellectual discussions, arguments, and even sex—they view computers not only as tools but also as *arenas for social experience.* 41

The result is a multiple view of the state of the art in communication technology. When addressing the question of what's new about networking, it's possible to give at least two answers. Let's stick with two for now. 42

Answer 1: Nothing   The tools of networking are essentially the same as they have been since the telephone, which was the first electronic network prosthesis. Computers are engines of calculation, and their output is used for quantitative analysis. Inside the little box is information. I recently had a discussion with a colleague in which he maintained that there was nothing new about virtual reality. "When you sit and read a book," he said, "you create characters and action in your head. That's the same thing as VR, without all the electronics." Missing the point, of course, but understandably. 43

Answer 2: Everything   Computers are arenas for social experience and dramatic interaction, a type of media more like public theater, and their 44 output is used for qualitative interaction, dialogue, and conversation. Inside the little box are *other people*.

In order for this second answer to be true, we have to rethink some as-   45
sumptions about presence. Presence is currently a word that means many different things to many different people. One meaning is the sense that we are direct witnesses to something or that we ourselves are being directly ap-prehended. This is what we might call the straightforward meaning, the one used by many sober virtual reality researchers. Another meaning is related to agency, to the proximity of intentionality. The changes that the concept of presence is currently undergoing are embedded in much larger shifts in cultural beliefs and practices. These include repeated transgressions of the traditional concept of the body's physical envelope and of the locus of hu-man agency. . . .

My first organized piece of research in the field of virtual systems in-   46
volved studying a group of phone sex workers in the early 1980s. In this study I was doing two things. On one hand, I was beginning to develop some of the ideas I set forth here and, on the other, also discovering in mi-crocosm the fascinating interplays between communication technology, the human body, and the uses of pleasure. If I were to frame some of the ques-tions that occurred to me during that time, they might be these: How are bodies represented through technology? How is desire constructed through representation? What is the relationship of the body to self-awareness? What is the role of play in an emergent paradigm of human-computer interaction? And overall: What is happening to sociality and desire at the close of the mechanical age?

If I'm going to give in to the temptation to periodize—which I do again   47
and again, though frequently with tongue in cheek—then I might as well take the period that follows the mechanical age and call it the virtual age. By the virtual age I don't mean the hype of virtual reality technology, which is certainly interesting enough in its own ways. Rather, I refer to the gradual change that has come over the relationship between sense of self and the body, and the relationship between individual and group, during a particu-lar span of time. I characterize this relationship as virtual because the ac-customed grounding of social interaction in the physical facticity of human bodies is changing. Partly this change seems good, and partly it seems bad. There are palpable advantages to the virtual mode in relation to the ways that the structure of cities and expectations of travel have changed with the advent of the telephone, the rise of large corporations, the invention and marketing of inexpensive tract housing, the development of the shopping mall, the commercial development and exploitation of electronic mass me-dia, the development of the personal computer, the greening of large-scale

information networks (which can be coopted for social interaction), and the increasing miniaturization of electronic components (eventually perhaps to be extended to mechanical devices, that is, Drexler and others). There are equally palpable disadvantages to each of these deep changes in our lives. I don't want this perhaps too-familiar list to be read as either extolling or condemnation. They are the manifestations, as well as causative agents, of the social changes, ruptures, and reorganizations that they accompany. . . .

Just as textual technologies—cheap paper, the typewriter, printing— 48 accompanied new discourse networks and social formations, so electronic communication technologies—radio, television, computer networks— accompany the discourse networks and social formations now coming into being. These technologies, discourse networks, and social formations continue the trend toward increasing awareness of a sense of self; toward increasing physical isolation of individuals in Western and Western-influenced societies; and toward displacement of shared physical space, both public and private, by textuality and prosthetic communication—in brief, the constellation of events that define the close of the mechanical age and the unfolding or revealing of what, for lack of a better term, we might call the virtual age.

Working with the Text

1. Stone subtitles her essay "How I Fell in Love with My Prosthesis," and in fact describes falling in love with three "prostheses": a crystal radio, a massive recording console, and the Votrax generator physicist Stephen Hawking uses to communicate orally. Later she suggests that we all view computers as prosthetic devices. What does she mean by *prosthesis*? How does the example of Hawking (which she compares to "boundary debates, borderland/*frontera* questions") serve her effort to reconceptualize computers as "arenas for social experience"? Similarly, how does her discussion of phone sex relate to this point?

2. Computer technology is referred to as "interactive," but Stone writes that because of current standards that freeze the "conceptual framework of interaction in a form most suitable for commercial development . . . the potential for *interaction* is limited." How does Stone, summarizing Andy Lippman, define *interactive*? Can you imagine human-computer interaction (HCI) of this sort?

3. Stone suggests that we are at the beginning of a "virtual age" (as the "mechanical age" ends). She characterizes this as redefining "the relationship between sense of self and the body, and the relationship between individual and group," and claims that "the accustomed grounding of social interaction in the physical facticity of human bodies is changing." What is she getting at? How do you respond to

her picture of those "on the cutting edge" of computer technology? Here she describes people who are "thoroughly accustomed to engaging in nontrivial social interactions through the use of their computers—social interactions in which they change and are changed, in which commitments are made, kept, and broken, in which they may engage in intellectual discussions, arguments, and even sex." How might this virtual environment alter our conception of individual—and group—identity?

 4. At the conclusion of this excerpt, Stone says that "the discourse networks and social formations coming into being" as a result of new electronic communication technologies will lead toward the "displacement of shared physical space, both public and private, by textuality and prosthetic communication." How drastic do you think this "displacement" might be over the course of your lifetime and beyond? Can you describe a world in which, as Stone seems to suggest, people will rarely be together in physical space? What might this developing virtual space ultimately "look" and "feel" like? Explore these questions in an essay.

Real Cold, Simulated Heat: Virtual Reality at the Roxy

STEPHEN DOHENY-FARINA

Stephen Doheny-Farina is Professor of Technical Communications at Clarkson University in Potsdam, New York. An influential critic of electronic culture, Doheny-Farina contributes to the "Last Link" column of the online magazine *Computer-Mediated Communication*. He is the author of several books on the social and organizational effects of emerging technologies, including *Rhetoric, Innovation, Technology* and the book excerpted in the following essay, "Real Cold, Simulated Heat: Virtual Reality at the Roxy." That book, *The Wired Neighborhood*, challenges both "cyber-utopian" and "Luddite" thinking about the tightening embrace of virtual culture, arguing that a geophysical sense of place is essential to the wise use of virtual technologies. "Real Cold, Simulated Heat" analyzes the conflict between place and cyberspace, particularly as it engages the American archetypes of the individual and the frontier.

The storm door slammed, rattling its window and echoing across the frozen   1
yard. As soon as the door left my hand, we knew how cold it had gotten that
evening. The gauge was the automatic door closer—the hydraulic tube and
shaft designed to enable aluminum storm doors to glide to a close. We had
long since discovered that this closer ceased to operate whenever the temperature dropped below zero degrees Fahrenheit. We had learned how to
read the information provided by this technology because it had been sending us the same simple message for weeks. Night after night the temperature
dropped into negative digits. It was January 1994, and our north country, the
northern-most region of New York State, was in the middle of a record-
breaking stretch of frigid weather. On the coldest night the temperature fell
to forty below; some days it never rose above minus ten.

I let the door slam that night because my wife and I were in a hurry, as   2
usual. It was the first night of the Cinema 10 film series at the Roxy, our
town's lone theater, and we expected a crowd. Ten Monday nights in the fall
and another ten in the winter gave the locals a chance to see movies that
would never come to town otherwise. Tonight it was Kenneth Branagh's
production of *Much Ado about Nothing.*

In this cold, the snow crunches and squeaks beneath your boots, the   3
slightest breeze threatens to freeze exposed skin, and the car heater takes
forever to get warm. But none of it mattered this night. We were bundled up
enough to withstand the elements for the five-minute ride into town. When
we arrived, a line was forming down the street. Everyone was battling the
cold. Some huddled with their companions; some stood hunched, arms
crossed, trying to hide mitten-clad hands beneath each arm; some bounced
from foot to foot. Our collective breaths hovered visibly above us. Finally
the doors opened, and we all shuffled inside.

My town is small, and I saw many familiar faces: college students and   4
faculty, some local joggers—people I knew from Frozen Foote, a series of
winter road races in a neighboring town—and a few members of the local
bicycle club and the local chapter of the Adirondack Mountain Club. In retrospect, I wonder if everyone there was seeking psychic help in preparation
for the long dark expanse of the real winter, the winter that stretches on and
on after the holidays, the winter that isn't over when you proclaim it over
(as I did that year by deciding to do no more cross-country skiing after a
warm day in early April even though weeks of good skiing were left in the
woods; I was trying to will the end of winter after being seduced by the false
spring of the north country).

There was escape for all of us in the theater that night. The film reveled   5
in warmth. It showed sun and sweat and golden, tanned limbs. It bathed us
in oranges and yellows and reds. We waded through the lush green of
the ripe Italian vineyards, and the sunshine washed over and through

everyone. I can still see myself sitting there, dazed by the virtual heat. And the opposition between that heat and the real cold of the night paralleled a number of tensions in the film: the camaraderie within the group versus the alienation of the individual; the celebrations of a community in the wake of its victory over an external necessity; a simple, unassuming, blind love versus a skeptical, complex but ardent love; trust and faith versus cynicism and lies.

When it ended and the houselights came up, I recall that others looked   6
the way I felt: smiling, sunstruck, and warm as we all began to fumble with scarves and hats and gloves. On my way out, I saw one of the organizers of the series still sitting as she pulled on her coat. I told her I had just spent a couple of hours in Italy. She nodded "me too."

The meaning of this intense experience of virtual reality must be assessed   7
in terms of that night in that place among those people. For me, a seemingly individualizing experience—watching a screen in a darkened theater—became a small communal act because it was situated in and spoke to a common necessity: the need to get through this long, dark, unremitting winter.

(I am troubled by my recollections. The weather was real, I know, but   8
was the community? Did I experience community only because I saw a depthless reflection of it on the screen? Am I constructing a community in the act of describing it?)

This was an unusual cinematic experience, not because the film was un-   9
usual—it wasn't—but because it was so connected to an extraordinary communal constraint. This happens rarely. I can remember only one other such experience: in the last week of March 1979 I was teaching school about fifteen miles from the Three Mile Island nuclear power plant when the plant suffered its infamous partial core meltdown. The incident happened midweek and became known to the local population through a small news item of little note. On Friday morning, however, it suddenly became a crisis. The governor announced a state of emergency. We heard that Harrisburg Hospital was evacuating patients. We were told that a radioactive bubble of pressure was developing within the reactor containment building. No one was sure whether the structure would hold. Within twenty-four hours, tens of thousands of area residents voluntarily evacuated. Schools, banks, businesses, restaurants, and most bars closed.

I had grown up in the area, and while my immediate and extended fam-   10
ily headed out of town, a buddy of mine, Bill Weiss, and I decided to stay. (We loaded his van with food, water, and sleeping bags nonetheless. "Just in case it blows," we said.) Coincidence of coincidences: the just-released movie *The China Syndrome* came to the area that weekend. One local theater remained open to show it, and Bill and I went that first night. It may

have been my earliest postmodern experience. Although the theater was packed (NBC News was there, covering the opening), every other business nearby was dark, and the streets were empty except for the traffic of the couple hundred moviegoers. We seemed to be wandering through a ghost community, accompanied only by those of us compelled to seek our reflections on the screen.

Indeed, throughout the movie there were murmurs, bouts of nervous laughter, and moments of vocal recognition among us. At one point, when we finally came to understand exactly what had happened to the nuclear plant (run by a sweating, nervous Jack Lemmon), Bill leaned over to me and whispered, "That's not as serious as what happened here!" At another point, we all roared when a character representing a nuclear power expert stated that a meltdown could wipe out an area "the size of Pennsylvania." Yes, there we were, cheering out doom in unison, bound by an external necessity so vast and so terrible that we could do little but laugh at it. After all, we were coming to realize that we might need to evacuate the area permanently at any moment. So, regardless of the technical hindsight that validated the strength of the containment system, that night we faced the possibility that nuclear technology would destroy, forever, our community.

The two cinematic experiences I've described represent ephemeral moments of social bonding—borne out, yes, through media images; nonetheless, these were communal experiences made rich by place, the particular physical, geographic locations in which they occurred. Yet these moments are wholly insignificant compared with the powerful forces of electronic communication and electronic media that both individuate and globalize—forces that work to isolate individuals by exalting individuality, while making those individuals dependent on mass markets and globalized communication networks.

This is a subtle but devastating finesse: we become the globalized individuals, focusing on our individuality while becoming ever more reliant on large-scale markets and technologies. Further, in response to our isolation, we attempt to buoy our fragmented selves through artificial means of commitment and community. This is the result of the virtualization of everyday life and the concurrent demise of geographically bound, physical communities.

In *Habits of the Heart* Robert Bellah and his co-authors discuss Alexis de Tocqueville's examination of America in the nineteenth century. According to Tocqueville, Americans place the rights of the individual above the rights of the collective. Yet the collective, the democracy, can thrive as long as individuals subscribe to a set of social mores, the "habits of the heart" that ensure the survival of society. Tocqueville nevertheless cautions about this powerful individuating tendency in the American character. He warns that this democracy enables a dangerous inward turn through which citizens forget their history and ignore their communities. Such individualists

> owe no man anything and hardly expect anything from anybody. They form the habit of thinking of themselves in isolation and imagine that their whole destiny is in their own hands.
>
> Thus, not only does democracy make men forget their ancestors, but also clouds their view of their descendants and isolates them from their contemporaries. Each man is forever thrown back on himself alone, and there is danger that he may be shut up in the *solitude of his own heart*.

It is no longer American democracy that isolates the individual; it is the simulacrum of democracy, the electronic democracy, the virtual culture, the society of the net that isolates individuals while seducing them with mere appearances of communication and collectivity. Once we begin to divorce ourselves from geographic place and start investing ourselves in virtual geographies, we further the dissolution of our physical communities.

Clearly, much in our society convinces us to do just that. The message is   15
current and pervasive, John Markoff, for example, describes the phenomenon of climbing a peak in the Adirondacks while talking business on a cellular phone. He tries to make us feel good about how electronic communication enables us to be separated from the constraints of physical location:

> In the 1950's the sociologist David Riesman wrote in his book *The Lonely Crowd* that the death of community meant that one could be surrounded by people yet still be profoundly alone and isolated. Wireless communications technologies are turning his original vision inside out. With cellular phones and wireless E-mail, one can be physically alone yet still in the midst of a clamoring invisible crowd.
>
> "The community has triumphed over the individual," said Michael Schrage, a research associate at the Sloan School of Management at the Massachusetts Institute of Technology and a technology columnist for the *Los Angeles Times*.

But, in reality, electronic communication pushes in exactly the opposite direction—toward the shadow we call virtual community. In immersing ourselves in the electronic net, we are ignoring our real, dying communities. The cinematic events I described illustrate how my geographic place impinged on and gave meaning to virtual experiences. But more than I may ever realize, the virtual mediates my understanding of my local, physical experience.

I am drenched in virtual worlds. One day I walked into a small open-air   16
courtyard within a university building complex. As I moved through the archway into the courtyard, I could see that I was alone; no one was sitting on the benches among the trees and ornamental shrubs; no one was meandering through the sculpture garden. At the instant I stepped into the space, I heard a noise and looked up. A flock of birds flew over the courtyard, cov-

ering entirely its skyward opening. They were silhouetted against the sky and framed by four walls, and I heard the beating of their wings and then they were gone. My god, I thought, that was like an advertisement for Obsession perfume. Clearly, I see the world through a veil of images constructed through artificial media. This veil permeates all of my perception.

It is fall as I write this, and the birds in the north country are mustering 17 like troops, soon to fly south. Recently, as I walked along my road, I passed beneath a tall maple, about eighty feet high. Hundreds of birds perched, chirping, among its yellowing leaves. I don't often hear so many birds vocalizing at once at such close range. But I am so embedded in virtual worlds that it reminded me of the sounds I've heard at the Nature Company in the Carousel Centre Mall in Syracuse. On the few occasions when I've been to that mall I have visited the store because it markets its products through the use of sounds, images, and space to create a virtual atmosphere of nature: a rushing stream, its waters cascading down a rocky bed only to disappear into an unseen and silent pumping system behind a wall; CD's playing the cries of loons, wolves, or whales, or the gusting howls of the wind. On display are large posters of plants, animals, and mountains so clear and grand that they would appear real if framed within faux windows. A few strolls through this simulated natural environment have apparently informed the ways I experience the world. And this is merely a store at the mall. Imagine the impact of an immersion like the one envisioned by Steve Pruitt and Tom Barrett in their anticipation of a future workplace bound by virtual reality.

Pruitt and Barrett derive a fictional account of work in Corporate Virtual 18 Workspaces (cvws) in order to better understand the capabilities of networked virtual realities. In their story, a man named Austin enters a Personal Virtual Workspace (pvw) in a room of his California home, where he puts on computerized clothing and connects via fiber-optic network to the cvw "where" he works. The room and clothing interfaces enable him to see, hear, and feel everything in the virtual work environment. He is one of many employees connecting to the cvw from their "home reality engines." But the cvw is not exactly like an office building. Inside the cvw, Austin can design his own work space and tools to meet the needs of his current project and to suit his tastes.

At one point in his day, Austin must meet with a man named Johann 19 who lives in Bonn, Germany, and who also connects to the cvw from his home. Austin virtually walks down the hallway to Johann's office, sees the door ajar, knocks, and walks in.

> The office is quite dramatic. Johann is obviously an avid mountain climber. One entire wall of the eight-sided office sports a lifelike panorama of El Capitan from Austin's home state of California. At first glance, it appears that the wall is just a

still photograph of the majestic climbing magnet, but as Austin investigates it more closely, he notices that the leaves on the trees in the foreground are fluttering as if the wind were blowing. Upon still closer inspection, he notices brilliantly colored objects about halfway up the side of El Capitan. By invoking the zoom feature with a gesture toward a telescope icon in the lower-right corner of the wall, Austin brings the scene progressively closer. With another gesture toward a stop sign icon, he stabilizes the picture at about 50 yards from the band of hearty climbers that are making their ascent.

The event is visually exciting and so is the audio content. By gesturing again at the wall's icon controls, the sounds of the scene are now audible via the directional sound receptors in Austin's computerized clothing. He hears the calls of "belay on" and "on belay" as the second climber clad in a burnt orange rugby shirt, dark brown knickers, and sky blue climbing shoes makes his way toward the lead climber positioned some 25 feet above at the next pitch. The wind whistles behind Austin as he hears the calls of a distant songbird.

Suddenly, Austin's serenity is partially broken, as Johann reenters the cvw and appears between him and the El Capitan experience.

After reading this passage, I'm left with a few questions: In his spare time is Johann a climber? Or is Johann a virtual climber? And if he is a virtual climber, does he actually don the computer suit and simulate the visual, aural, and tactile elements of the climb by scaling some structure that enables the simulated trek up El Capitan? Or does he merely watch the projection of himself climbing El Capitan while his suit and pvw provide stimulations, making him feel as if he is moving his body while he is actually sitting on the couch? Can Johann climb virtual El Capitan by himself with some sort of intelligent agent—a simulated partner—as his companion? More important, does Johann still know the difference between his virtual El Capitan and the rock geographically located in Yosemite? Most important, does it even matter? Does anyone need or want to travel to Yosemite to do the climb, and how is that climbing experience different after doing the virtual climb? Can Johann see the natural world anymore?   20

Because Johann is a fictional character, I'm going to supply some plausible answers: Johann is a virtual climber because all the real climbs are impossible now that poor air quality makes real climbing too dangerous. Johann's father did real climbs until his death at an early age from cancer. Johann tried several outdoor climbs during his reckless youth but finally wised up. Now he works out in the gym so he can continue to move his body during the virtual climbs. But he knows that he won't have the strength and agility to keep at it for many more years, and he expects to move into the sedentary "mind-climbing" phase of the sport soon. Johann hasn't climbed with another real human for several years. In fact, Johann hasn't had much contact with other humans since a year or so after he became involved in his pvw. He and his wife, Marta, and their grown children virtually meet every   21

Christmas, but lately they have been at odds over which communal scenario should be the setting for the event. Marta would like a traditional old German winter, while Johann likes the Alpine ski chalet simulation. The children? Their simulations are so strange that Johann can't understand them. They don't seem to relate at all to the natural world Johann knows.

As for Johann's understanding of the real El Capitan, he began to cus- 22
tomize his simulation several years ago. At that time he wanted to vary the event structure so he could practice a greater variety of climbing techniques on each ascent. Can Johann see the natural world anymore? If I have trouble seeing the natural world merely after going to the mall, I think it is reasonable to conclude that Johann's understanding of nature has been radically altered. After all, for me nature is more mediated by virtuality than it was for my pre-television forebears; for subsequent, fully virtualized generations, nature will be far more artificially mediated than I can imagine.

And we are already getting gee-whiz glimpses of this future. A *USA To-* 23
day feature breathlessly tells us about the CAVE, the Cave Automatic Virtual Environment, under development at the Argonne National Laboratory: "It is astonishing. The system can make computer-animated fish swim around your legs, then rush to nibble cartoon food dropped from a hand-held wand. It can let people thousands of miles apart design a full-scale car together, walk around it, look under the hood. Someday, systems like this may let a grandfather play with his grandchild who lives in another city. Both would interact with full-size, three-dimensional images of the other—like a whole-person video phone call." Wearing only "what looks like oversize Ray Ban sunglasses," one can walk through a room completely engaged in three-dimensional VR. As remotely located CAVE sites become linked through high-speed networks, interactions as complex as those of Johann and Austin can begin to be developed. To a population just starting to get used to the Internet, immersive VR will require a further shift in perception. "Says Argonne Labs' Ian Foster. 'We need to get people thinking bigger than they ever have before.'" Start thinking big; the transformation has already begun.

Until recently my life has been virtualized through powerful but blunt 24
mass-communication technologies: radio, television, magazines, newspapers. But now I face a far more powerful engine of individuation and virtualization: networked virtual realities. Moving far beyond the interactivty of telephony and the immersive capabilities of books, radio, television, and movies, NVRS can seduce us completely.

The two key terms here are interactivity and immersion. Johann and 25
Austin are immersed in simulated environments, and they can interact with anyone connected to the network. But Johann and Austin are virtual characters. Pruitt and Barrett have engaged, among other things, their readers' knowledge of virtuality—regardless of whether their readers ever used that

word to describe the willing (or unwitting) suspension of disbelief—to conjure up visions of these characters and their CVWS.

Technologically there is a chasm between, say, television, on one hand, and fully immersive, broadband networks, on the other. Despite the hype and the energetic visions of the future, CAVES and CVWS and the like may not be fully realized in our lifetimes. But it doesn't really matter whether scenarios like Pruitt and Barrett's become reality. We are already capable of powerfully immersive, interactive technologies. They may not be as totalizing as CVWS, but they are seductive nonetheless. 26

Let us examine the primitive (by comparison) combination of the Internet and network television that is operating around the clock today. Already the two technologies are combined in a kind of people's broadband, interactive virtual community development project, as James Barron describes: 27

> Christopher Fusco watches his favorite television show from a chrome-legged swivel chair he bought at a yard sale. The moment a commercial comes on, he whirls around to his I.B.M.-compatible personal computer, dials up an on-line service and types out messages to other fans who are also tuned in to "The X-Files," the Fox network's New Age answer to "The Twilight Zone" or "The Outer Limits."
> . . . Mr. Fusco is the newest kind of couch potato. When not staring at one video screen (his television), he is staring at another (his computer monitor). When the closing credits roll on one, the show is just beginning on the other.

Thousands (soon to be millions) of Fuscoesque Internauts, unable to interact within the virtual reality of the television shows, can at least interact with each other, one step removed from the shows themselves. And the hype-mongers are calling discussion groups like this the new virtual communities (for example, the *X-Files* Community, the *Star Trek* Community, the Wolf Blitzer Community). But online discussion groups are not the only type of seductive NVR. Imagine an *X-Files* MUD; that is, imagine a multi-user dimension—a network environment through which participants all over the world can interact simultaneously—where all those connected are role-playing within the thematic confines of the *X-Files,* or *Star Trek,* or the CNN Newsroom in a post-apocalyptic war zone, or whatever scenarios, rules, and aesthetics you can imagine. Even if it is all merely text-based, even if the only thing you can do is type into your computer and watch your words and the words of others scroll up the screen, you can quickly become entwined in a complex and compelling virtual world.

The most famous such world is LambdaMOO, a virtual house to which participants can connect (or "telnet") via their computers, "where" they can assume online identities, where they meet, communicate, get to know one another, develop social groups, social strata, social structures and policies—in short, where participants create virtual community. And all this is done via relatively primitive computers using only text. Most people seem quite 28

excited by the wondrous possibilities of these networked virtual realities—
and in later chapters I discuss these enterprises in more detail—but my point
is that networked virtual realities individuate us. They encourage us to ignore, forget, or become blind to our sense of geographic place and community, and they direct our focus toward the self in relation to the mythologies
and promises of virtual communities.

The force behind NVRs and behind projections like Pruitt and Barrett's is   29
what Kroker and Weinstein call the "will to virtuality." This evolution into
the virtual is promulgated by a "virtual class" of people who benefit from the
promotion and development of techno-utopianism, or "technotopia": the
complete belief in and acceptance of the "medianet," the digital information
highway. The purpose of the medianet is not to enhance communication
among individuals but to propel individuals toward virtuality: "The digital
superhighway always means its opposite: not an open telematic autoroute
for fast circulation across the electronic galaxy, but an immensely seductive
harvesting machine for delivering bodies, culture, and labor to virtualization."
This harvest underlies Kroker and Weinstein's theory of the virtual class: "Cultural accommodation to technotopia is its goal, political consolidation (around
the aims of the virtual class) its methods, multimedia nervous systems its re-
lay, and (our) disappearance into pure virtualities its ecstatic destiny."

Given this evolution to virtuality, we must consider what is lost in our   30
immersion. Let's go back to that moment when I stood beneath the maple
tree on my road. If you allow me, for the sake of argument, the technological power that Pruitt and Barrett envision, the question becomes, What
could be incorporated into a virtual reality simulation of that experience? I
assume that the following elements could be simulated: the light from the
sun and the sky, the tree in all its golden brilliance, the feel of the cool October breezes, the bird droppings falling onto the road, the ramshackle
house beneath the tree, the sensation of walking toward the tree and the increasing noise of the birds, the leaves flying in the air, the road, the view of
cars and pickup trucks occasionally passing.

I'll even accept that an amazing variety of contingencies can be virtual-   31
ized, such as the possibility of birds flying to and from the tree, or the possibility of getting hit by bird droppings as I stand there in awe. Add to these
all the contingencies that come with a networked system in which remotely
located others are entering the simulation. But virtuality becomes less plausible as local contingencies become more complex, for example, the possibility of getting killed when one of the pickups driven by a local teenage
drunk runs me over; the possibility that my neighbor will drive past and
wave, stop her car, back up, and tell me that her husband discovered two
pieces of my mail left mistakenly in their mailbox; the possibility that the elderly woman who lives in the house beneath the tree is heading toward her

mailbox to send off the town taxes that she and I and our neighbors pay to provide crews to plow the road all winter; the web of relations in town that connect her to me; the difficulties that all of us encounter in keeping an eye on vacationers' places, in baby-sitting, in dog-sitting, in picking up garbage dumped on the side of the road by local jerks, in taking care of the kittens dumped on this country road by other jerks; and on and on. In short, try as we might, via the medianet we cannot live a life. The difference between reality and the infinitely realistic irreality of VR, notes Michael Heim, are the biological imperatives of bodies—imperatives, I would add, that include all the biologies of the ecosystem and the vast web of social relations fused to those imperatives. Regardless, we are increasingly attracted by the possibility of transcending our messy, indeterminate, complex physical existence through the technotopia of the net.

In physical communities we are forced to live with people who may dif-   32
fer from us in many ways. But virtual communities offer us the opportunity to construct utopian collectivities—communities of interest, education, tastes, beliefs, and skills. In cyberspace we can remake the world out of an unsettled landscape. The natural frontier has been long since tamed. Leave it behind, say the cybernetic hypemeisters, and settle the wild electronic frontier.

This metaphor conjures up traditional American images of the individ-   33
ual lighting out for the territories, independent and hopeful, to make a life. It fools us into thinking that as natural frontiers become ever more remote from our lives, there is another kind of nature, another kind of wild place, where we can develop and express our human potential. For example, after having considered the Adirondack hiker with the cellular phone, Markoff speculates about future frontiers:

> If wilderness plays an important part in kindling the human spirit, perhaps as it vanishes people are reinventing it in different ways.
>
> In the future with the earth encircled by satellites and everyone wired together by digital links, the new back country may become the world of artificial computer networks known as cyberspace. One can already become lost for hours in the neck of the Internet called the World Wide Web, pointing and clicking a trail through a maze of hypertext documents and digital pictures.

Markoff goes on to quote John Perry Barlow, one of the founders of the Electronic Frontier Foundation, an organization that promotes citizens' rights in cyberspace. "That's the thing about cyberspace," notes Barlow. "It's the last frontier and it will be a permanent frontier. It's infinite and it's continuously changing." Unfortunately, what is silent is our emigration into this so-called frontier is our utter dependence on technology created, provided, and sustained by others. This is a sign not of frontier but of containment, not of our independence but of our domestication.

Humans are the most domesticated of all animals, argues Canadian nat-   34
uralist John Livingston, because we have become completely dependent on
ideas—nurture, technology—over nature.

> There are many viable earmarks of domestication. One, however, must be
> stressed above all others, and that is the matter of dependence. All domesticated
> animals depend for their day-to-day survival upon their owners. . . . The human
> domesticate has become equally dependent, not upon a proprietor, but upon
> storable, retrievable, transmissible technique. Technology provides us with every-
> thing we require. Knowledge of how-to-do-it sustains us utterly. And since none
> of us knows how to do everything, we are further dependent upon the exper-
> tise of countless others to provide even the most basic of daily necessities. . . .
> Without knowledge of how-to-do-it, or access to someone else who does know
> how, we are irretrievably helpless.

Networked virtual realities are shining examples of "storable, retrievable,
transmissible technique." They are quintessential domesticating engines hiding beneath frontier-like facades. The domesticates of the net are like domesticates in Livingston's view of the natural world: placeless. "Nowhere
may the human presence be seen as fully integrated and 'natural' because
wherever we may be, or however long we may have been there, we are still
domesticates. Domesticates have no ecologic place, and they show it consistently and universally." And in achieving our domestication, we strike a
bargain. We get protection from natural enemies while giving up our place
in nature. "Domestication confers special gifts, the most important of which
is relative freedom from the pressure of natural selection, meaning at least
temporary immunity to many normal ecological constraints," says Livingston.
"In return for these gifts, we have handed back, as it were, the quality of natural, integrated belongingness." The further we surrender ourselves to this
ersatz frontier, the greater our placelessness.

Working with the Text

1. Relationships between the individual and the community are very
   complicated in this essay, beginning with Doheny-Farina's recognition
   that the "individualizing" experience of watching *Much Ado about
   Nothing* on a frigid winter night was, in reality, "communal." What
   factors—physical and social, real and conceptual—made it so? How
   does the author's second cinematic example develop the tension
   between individual and community? Why does he regard watching *The
   China Syndrome* as perhaps his "earliest postmodern experience"?

2. According to Doheny-Farina, what are the chief differences between
   community and "virtual community"? Using your response to the

previous question as a basis for comparison, describe the relationship of individuals to virtual communities, as the author sees it. What happens to the individual in cyberspace? Why does Doheny-Farina reject the conventional designation of cyberspace as a "frontier"? On the basis of your own experience of Internet community (newsgroup, listserv, IRC discussion group, MUD, or other), evaluate the author's claims.

3. Doheny-Farina devotes much of his essay to technology that is projected but not yet available—and not likely to be available for some time. Why does he juxtapose real and hypothetical scenarios—for example, following a description of the Nature Company store in Syracuse with a detailed fantasy of Pruitt and Barrett's virtual office with its simulation of El Capitan? Why does he offer such a wealth of imagined detail, then assert that "it doesn't really matter" whether such scenarios ever materialize?

4. What are the primary differences between the tall maple tree that Doheny-Farina recalls midway through the essay and the simulated maple he envisages at the end? In what sense is the existing maple already "virtual"? How does the simulated maple function in the essay— does it supply essential evidence for an important claim or merely illustrate a claim already substantiated? Does this distinction matter?

5. Reflect on your own movie-going experience. Can you recall films that produced moments of social bonding, such as those Doheny-Farina recounts? Choose one such screening, and write a brief essay describing in detail the local conditions that made the film into a catalyst for community. Note: Do not narrate the full plot of the movie; supply only those elements relevant to its social role.

Disinformocracy

HOWARD RHEINGOLD

Author of books on science and technology, as well science fiction novels, Howard Rheingold has been praised for his ability to translate scientific and technological concepts into language lay readers can understand. His *Talking Tech: A Conversational Guide to Science and Technology* (1982, co-authored with Howard Levine) defines seventy scientific terms current in popular usage and explains each in a brief, accessible, scientifically accurate essay. An early writer on computer technology, Rheingold has also published *The Cognitive Connection: Thought and Language in Man and Machine* (1987), *Virtual Reality* (1991), *The Virtual Community: Homesteading on the Electronic Frontier* (1993), and *Tools for Thought* (2000). His science fiction includes the "Sisterhood Trilogy" and the "Savage Report" series. In the following essay from *The Virtual Community*, Rheingold considers the fears of some critics that computer-mediated communication (CMC) could ultimately stifle public discourse both nationally and internationally.

Virtual communities could help citizens revitalize democracy, or they could 1 be luring us into an attractively packaged substitute for democratic discourse. A few true believers in electronic democracy have had their say. It's time to hear from the other side. We owe it to ourselves and future generations to look closely at what the enthusiasts fail to tell us, and to listen attentively to what the skeptics fear. . . .

Three different kinds of social criticisms of technology are relevant to 2 claims of CMC as a means of enhancing democracy. One school of criticism emerges from the longer-term history of communications media, and focuses on the way electronic communications media already have preempted public discussions by turning more and more of the content of the media into advertisements for various commodities—a process these critics call commodification. Even the political process, according to this school of critics, has been turned into a commodity. The formal name for this criticism is "the commodification of the public sphere." The public sphere is what these social critics claim we used to have as citizens of a democracy, but have lost to the tide of commodization. The public sphere is also the focus of the hopes of online activists, who see CMC as a way of revitalizing the open and wide-spread discussions among citizens that feed the roots of democratic societies.

The second school of criticism focuses on the fact that high-bandwidth   3
interactive networks could be used in conjunction with other technologies
as a means of surveillance, control, and disinformation as well as a conduit
for useful information. This direct assault on personal liberty is compounded
by a more diffuse erosion of old social values due to the capabilities of new
technologies; the most problematic example is the way traditional notions
of privacy are challenged on several fronts by the ease of collecting and
disseminating detailed information about individuals via cyberspace technologies. When people use the convenience of electronic communication or
transaction, we leave invisible digital trails; now that technologies for track-
ing those trails are maturing, there is cause to worry. The spreading use of
computer matching to piece together the digital trails we all leave in cyberspace is one indication of privacy problems to come.

Along with all the person-to-person communications exchanged on the   4
world's telecommunications networks are vast flows of other kinds of personal information—credit information, transaction processing, health information. Most people take it for granted that no one can search through all
the electronic transactions that move through the world's networks in order
to pin down an individual for marketing—or political—motives. Remember
the "knowbots" that would act as personal servants, swimming in the info-
tides, fishing for information to suit your interests? What if people could turn
loose knowbots to collect all the information digitally linked to *you*? What if
the Net and cheap, powerful computers give that power not only to governments and large corporations but to everyone?

Every time we travel or shop or communicate, citizens of the credit-card   5
society contribute to streams of information that travel between point of purchase, remote credit bureaus, municipal and federal information systems,
crime information databases, central transaction databases. And all these other
forms of cyberspace interaction take place via the same packet-switched,
high-bandwidth network technology—those packets can contain transactions as well as video clips and text files. When these streams of information
begin to connect together, the unscrupulous or would-be tyrants can use the
Net to catch citizens in a more ominous kind of net.

The same channels of communication that enable citizens around the   6
world to communicate with one another also allow government and private
interests to gather information about them. This school of criticism is known
as Panoptic in reference to the perfect prison proposed in the eighteenth
century by Jeremy Bentham—a theoretical model that happens to fit the real
capabilities of today's technologies.

Another category of critical claim deserves mention, despite the rather   7
bizarre and incredible imagery used by its most well known spokesmen—
the hyper-realist school. These critics believe that information technologies
have already changed what used to pass for reality into a slicked-up electronic simulation. Twenty years before the United States elected a Hollywood actor as president, the first hyper-realists pointed out how politics had
become a movie, a spectacle that raised the old Roman tactic of bread and
circuses to the level of mass hypnotism. We live in a hyper-reality that was
carefully constructed to mimic the real world and extract money from the
pockets of consumers: the forests around the Matterhorn might be dying,
but the Disneyland version continues to rake in the dollars. The television
programs, movie stars, and theme parks work together to create global industry devoted to maintaining a web of illusion that grows more lifelike as
more people buy into it and as technologies grow more powerful.

Many other social scientists have intellectual suspicions of the hyper-   8
realist critiques, because so many are abstract and theoretical, based on little
or no direct knowledge of technology itself. Nevertheless, this perspective
does capture something about the way the effects of communications technologies have changed our modes of thought. One good reason for paying
attention to the claims of the hyper-realists is that the society they predicted
decades ago bears a disturbingly closer resemblance to real life than do the
forecasts of the rosier-visioned technological utopians. While McLuhan's image of the global village has taken on a certain irony in light of what has
happened since his predictions of the 1960s, "the society of the spectacle"—
another prediction from the 1960s, based on the advent of electronic media—
offered a far less rosy and, as events have proved, more realistic portrayal of
the way information technologies have changed social customs.

The Selling of Democracy:
Commodification and the Public Sphere

There is an intimate connection between informal conversations, the kind   9
that take place in communities and virtual communities, in the coffee shops
and computer conferences, and the ability of large social groups to govern
themselves without monarchs or dictators. This social-political connection
shares a metaphor with the idea of cyberspace, for it takes place in a kind of
virtual space that has come to be known by specialists as the public sphere.

Here is what the preeminent contemporary writer about the public   10
sphere, social critic and philosopher Jurgen Habermas, had to say about the
meaning of this abstraction:

By "public sphere," we mean first of all a domain of our social life in which such a thing as public opinion can be formed. Access to the public sphere is open in principle to all citizens. A portion of the public sphere is constituted in every conversation in which private persons come together to form a public. They are then acting neither as business or professional people conducting their private affairs, nor as legal consociates subject to the legal regulations of a state bureaucracy and obligated to obedience. Citizens act as a public when they deal with matters of general interest without being subject to coercion; thus with the guarantee that they may assemble and unite freely, and express and publicize their opinions freely.

In this definition, Habermas formalized what people in free societies 11
mean when we say "The public wouldn't stand for that" or "It depends on public opinion." And he drew attention to the intimate connection between this web of free, informal, personal communications and the foundations of democratic society. People can govern themselves only if they communicate widely, freely, and in groups—publicly. The First Amendment of the U.S. Constitution's Bill of Rights protects citizens from government interference in their communications—the rights of speech, press, and assembly are communication rights. Without those rights, there is no public sphere. Ask any citizen of Prague, Budapest, or Moscow.

Because the public sphere depends on free communication and discus- 12
sion of ideas, as soon as your political entity grows larger than the number of citizens you can fit into a modest town hall, this vital marketplace for political ideas can be powerfully influenced by changes in communications technology. According to Habermas,

When the public is large, this kind of communication requires certain means of dissemination and influence; today, newspapers and periodicals, radio and television are the media of the public sphere. . . . The term "public opinion" refers to the functions of criticism and control or organized state authority that the public exercises informally, as well as formally during periodic elections. Regulations concerning the publicness (or publicity [Publizitat] in its original meaning) of state-related activities, as, for instance, the public accessibility required of legal proceedings, are also connected with this function of public opinion. To the public sphere as a sphere mediating between state and society, a sphere in which the public as the vehicle of publicness—the publicness that once had to win out against the secret politics of monarchs and that since then has permitted democratic control of state activity.

Ask anybody in China about the right to talk freely among friends and 13
neighbors, to own a printing press, to call a meeting to protest government policy, or to run a BBS. But brute totalitarian seizure of communications technology is not the only way that political powers can neutralize the

ability of citizens to talk freely. It is also possible to alter the nature of discourse by inventing a kind of paid fake discourse. If a few people have control of what goes into the daily reporting of the news, and those people are in the business of selling advertising, all kinds of things become possible for those who can afford to pay.

Habermas had this to say about the corrupting influence of ersatz public opinion: 14

> Whereas at one time publicness was intended to subject persons or things to the public use of reason and to make political decisions subject to revision before the tribunal of public opinion, today it has often enough already been enlisted in the aid of the secret policies of interest groups; in the form of "publicity" it now acquires public prestige for persons or things and renders them capable of acclamation in a climate of nonpublic opinion. The term "public relations" itself indicates how a public sphere that formerly emerged from the structure of society must now be produced circumstantially on a case-by-case basis.

The idea that public opinion can be manufactured and the fact that electronic spectacles can capture the attention of a majority of the citizenry damaged the foundations of democracy. According to Habermas, 15

> It is no accident that these concepts of the public sphere and public opinion were not formed until the eighteenth century. They derive their specific meaning from a concrete historical situation. It was then that one learned to distinguish between opinion and public opinion. . . . Public opinion, in terms of its very idea, can be formed only if a public that engages in rational discussion exists. Public discussions that are institutionally protected and that take, with critical intent, the exercise of political authority as their theme have not existed since time immemorial.

The public sphere and democracy were born at the same time, from the same sources. Now that the public sphere, cut off from its roots, seems to be dying, democracy is in danger, too.

The concept of the public sphere as discussed by Habermas and others includes several requirements for authenticity that people who live in democratic societies would recognize: open access, voluntary participation, participation outside institutional roles, the generation of public opinion through assemblies of citizens who engage in rational argument, the freedom to express opinions, and the freedom to discuss matters of the state and criticize the way state power is organized. Acts of speech and publication that specifically discuss the state are perhaps the most important kind protected by the First Amendment of the U.S. Constitution and similar civil guarantees elsewhere in the world. Former Soviets and Eastern Europeans who regained it after decades of censorship offer testimony that the most important freedom of speech is the freedom to speak about freedoms. 16

In eighteenth-century America, the Committees of Correspondence were   17
one of the most important loci of the public sphere in the years of revolution
and constitution-building. If you look closely at the roots of the American
Revolution, it becomes evident that a text-based, horseback-transported version of networking was an old American tradition. In their book *Networking,*
Jessica Lipnack and Jeffrey Stamps describe these committees as

> a communications forum where homespun political and economic thinkers
> hammered out their ideological differences, sculpting the form of a separate
> and independent country in North America. Writing to one another and sharing
> letters with neighbors, this revolutionary generation nurtured its adolescent
> ideas into a mature politics. Both men and women participated in the debate
> over independence from England and the desirable shape of the American
> future. . . .
>
> During the years in which the American Revolution was percolating, letters,
> news-sheets, and pamphlets carried from one village to another were the means
> by which ideas about democracy were refined. Eventually, the correspondents
> agreed that the next step in their idea exchange was to hold a face-to-face meet-
> ing. The ideas of independence and government had been debated, discussed,
> discarded, and reformulated literally hundreds of times by the time people in
> the revolutionary network met in Philadelphia.
>
> Thus, a network of correspondence and printed broadsides led to the for-
> mation of an organization after the writers met in a series of conferences and
> worked out a statement of purpose—which they called a "Declaration of Inde-
> pendence." Little did our early networking grandparents realize that the result of
> their youthful idealism, less than two centuries later, would be a global super-
> power with an unparalleled ability to influence the survival of life on the planet.

As the United States grew and technology changed, the ways in which   18
these public discussions of "matters of general interest," as Habermas called
them—slavery and the rights of the states versus the power of the federal
government were two such matters that loomed large—began to change as
well. The text-based media that served as the channel for discourse gained
more and more power to reshape the nature of that discourse. The communications media of the nineteenth century were the newspapers, the penny
press, the first generation of what has come to be known as the mass media.
At the same time, the birth of advertising and the beginnings of the public-
relations industry began to undermine the public sphere by inventing a kind
of buyable and sellable phony discourse that displaced the genuine kind.

The simulation (and therefore destruction) of authentic discourse, first in   19
the United States, and then spreading to the rest of the world, is what Guy
Debord would call the first quantum leap into the "society of the spectacle"
and what Jean Baudrillard would recognize as a milestone in the world's
slide into hyper-reality. Mass media's colonization of civil society turned into

a quasi-political campaign promoting technology itself when the image-making technology of television came along. ("Progress is our most important product," said General Electric spokesman Ronald Reagan, in the early years of television.) And in the twentieth century, as the telephone, radio, and television became vehicles for public discourse, the nature of political discussion has mutated into something quite different from anything the framers of the Constitution could have foreseen.

A politician is now a commodity, citizens are consumers, and issues are   20
decided via sound-bites and staged events. The television camera is the only spectator that counts at a political demonstration or convention. According to Habermas and others, the way the new media have been commoditized through this evolutionary process from hand-printed broadside to telegraph to penny press to mass media has led to the radical deterioration of the public sphere. The consumer society has become the accepted model both for individual behavior and political decision making. Discourse degenerated into publicity, and publicity used the increasing power of electronic media to alter perceptions and shape beliefs.

The consumer society, the most powerful vehicle for generating short-   21
term wealth ever invented, ensures economic growth by first promoting the idea that the way to be is to buy. The engines of wealth depend on a fresh stream of tabloids sold at convenience markets and television programs to tell us what we have to buy next in order to justify our existence. What used to be a channel for authentic communication has become a channel for the updating of commercial desire.

Money plus politics plus network television equals an effective system.   22
It works. When the same packaging skills that were honed on automobile tail fins and fast foods are applied to political ideas, the highest bidder can influence public policy to great effect. What dies in the process is the rational discourse at the base of civil society. That death manifests itself in longings that aren't fulfilled by the right kind of shoes in this month's color or the hot new prime-time candidate everybody is talking about. Some media scholars are claiming a direct causal connection between the success of commercial television and the loss of citizen interest in the political process.

Another media critic, Neal Postman, in his book *Amusing Ourselves to*   23
Death, pointed out that Tom Paine's *Common Sense* sold three hundred thousand copies in five months in 1776. The most successful democratic revolution in history was made possible by a citizenry that read and debated widely among themselves. Postman pointed out that the mass media, and television in particular, had changed the mode of discourse itself, by substituting fast cuts, special effects, and sound-bites for reasoned discussion or even genuine argument.

The various hypotheses about commodification and mode of discourse   24
focus on an area of apparent agreement among social observers who have
a long history of heated disagreements.

When people who have become fascinated by BBSs or networks start   25
spreading the idea that such networks are inherently democratic in some magical way, without specifying the hard work that must be done in real life to
harvest the fruits of that democratizing power, they run the danger of becoming unwitting agents of commodification. First, it pays to understand how old
the idea really is. Next, it is important to realize that the hopes of technophiles
have often been used to sell technology for commercial gain. In this sense,
CMC enthusiasts run the risk of becoming unpaid, unwitting advertisers for
those who stand to gain financially from adoption of new technology.

The critics of the idea of electronic democracy have unearthed examples   26
from a long tradition of utopian rhetoric that James Carey has called "the
rhetoric of the 'technological sublime.'" He put it this way:

> Despite the manifest failure of technology to resolve pressing social issues over
> the last century, contemporary intellectuals continue to see revolutionary po-
> tential in the latest technological gadgets that are pictured as a force outside
> history and politics. . . . In modern futurism, it is the machines that possess tele-
> ological insight. Despite the shortcomings of town meetings, newspaper, tele-
> graph, wireless, and television to create the conditions of a new Athens,
> contemporary advocates of technological liberation regularly describe a new
> postmodern age of instantaneous daily plebiscitory democracy through a com-
> puterized system of electronic voting and opinion polling.

Carey was prophetic in at least one regard—he wrote this years before   27
Ross Perot and William Clinton both started talking about their versions of
electronic democracy during the 1992 U.S. presidential campaign. If the
United States is on the road to a version of electronic democracy in which
the president will have electronic town hall meetings, including instant
voting-by-telephone to "go directly to the people" (and perhaps bypass Congress?) on key issues, it is important for American citizens to understand
the potential pitfalls of decision making by plebiscite. Media-manipulated
plebiscites as political tools go back to Joseph Goebbels, who used radio so
effectively in the Third Reich. Previous experiments in instant home polling
and voting had been carried out by Warners, with their Qube service, in the
early 1980s. One critic, political scientist Jean Bethke Elshtain, called the
television-voting model an

> interactive shell game [that] cons us into believing that we are participating
> when we are really simply performing as the responding "end" of a prefabri-
> cated system of external stimuli. . . . In a plebiscitary system, the views of the
> majority . . . swamp minority or unpopular views. Plebiscitism is compatible
> with authoritarian politics carried out under the guise of, or with the connivance

of, majority views. That opinion can be registered by easily manipulated, ritualistic plebiscites, so there is no need for debate on substantive questions.

What does it mean that the same hopes, described in the same words, 28
for a decentralization of power, a deeper and more widespread citizen involvement in matters of state, a great equalizer for ordinary citizens to counter the forces of central control, have been voiced in the popular press for two centuries in reference to steam, electricity, and television? We've had enough time to live with steam, electricity, and television to recognize that they did indeed change the world, and to recognize that the utopia of technological millenarians has not yet materialized.

An entire worldview and sales job are packed into the word *progress,* 29
which links the notion of improvement with the notion of innovation, highlights the benefits of innovation while hiding the toxic side-effects of extractive and lucrative technologies, and then sells more of it to people via television as a cure for the stress of living in a technology-dominated world. The hope that the next technology will solve the problems created by the way the last technology was used is a kind of millennial, even messianic, hope, apparently ever-latent in the breasts of the citizenry. The myth of technological progress emerged out of the same Age of Reason that gave us the myth of representative democracy, a new organizing vision that still works pretty well, despite the decline in vigor of the old democratic institutions. It's hard to give up on one Enlightenment ideal while clinging to another.

I believe it is too early to judge which set of claims will prove to be ac- 30
curate. I also believe that those who would prefer the more democratic vision of the future have an opportunity to influence the outcome, which is precisely why online activists should delve into the criticisms that have been leveled against them. If electronic democracy advocates can address these critiques successfully, their claims might have a chance. If they cannot, perhaps it would be better not to raise people's hopes. Those who are not aware of the history of dead ends are doomed to replay them, hopes high, again and again.

The idea that putting powerful computers in the hands of citizens will 31
shield the citizenry against totalitarian authorities echoes similar, older beliefs about citizen-empowering technology. As Langdon Winner (an author every computer revolutionary ought to read) put it in his essay "Mythinformation,"

> Of all the computer enthusiasts' political ideas, there is none more poignant than the faith that the computer is destined to become a potent equalizer in modern society. . . . Presumably, ordinary citizens equipped with microcomputers will be able to counter the influence of large, computer-based organizations.
>
> Notions of this kind echo beliefs of eighteenth-century revolutionaries that placing fire arms in the hands of the people was crucial to overthrowing entrenched authority. In the American Revolution, French Revolution, Paris Com-

mune, and Russian Revolution the role of "the people armed" was central to the revolutionary program. As the military defeat of the Paris Commune made clear, however, the fact that the popular forces have guns may not be decisive. In a contest of force against force, the larger, more sophisticated, more ruthless, better equipped competitor often has the upper hand. Hence, the availability of low-cost computing power may move the baseline that defines electronic dimensions of social influence, but it does not necessarily alter the relative balance of power. Using a personal computer makes one no more powerful vis-à-vis, say, the National Security Agency than flying a hang glider establishes a person as a match for the U.S. Air Force.

The great power of the idea of electronic democracy is that technical   32
trends in communications technologies can help citizens break the monopoly on their attention that has been enjoyed by the powers behind the broadcast paradigm—the owners of television networks, newspaper syndicates, and publishing conglomerates. The great weakness of the idea of electronic democracy is that it can be more easily commodified than explained. . . .

What should those of us who believe in the democratizing potential of   33
virtual communities do about the technological critics? I believe we should invite them to the table and help them see the flaws in our dreams, the bugs in our designs. I believe we should study what the historians and social scientists have to say about the illusions and power shifts that accompanied the diffusion of previous technologies. CMC and technology in general [have] real limits; it's best to continue to listen to those who understand the limits, even as we continue to explore the technologies' positive capabilities. Failing to fall under the spell of the "rhetoric of the technological sublime," actively questioning and examining social assumptions about the effects of new technologies, [and] reminding ourselves that electronic communication has powerful illusory capabilities are all good steps to take to prevent disasters.

If electronic democracy is to succeed, however, in the face of all the ob-   34
stacles, activists must do more than avoid mistakes. Those who would use computer networks as political tools must go forward and actively apply their theories to more and different kinds of communities. If there is a last good hope, a bulwark against the hyper-reality of Baudrillard or Forster, it will come from a new way of looking at technology. Instead of falling under the spell of a sales pitch, or rejecting new technologies as instruments of illusion, we need to look closely at new technologies and ask how they can help build stronger, more humane communities—and ask how they might be obstacles to that goal. The late 1990s may eventually be seen in retrospect as a narrow window of historical opportunity, when people either acted or failed to act effectively to regain control over communications technologies. Armed with knowledge, guided by a clear, human-centered vision,

governed by a commitment to civil discourse, we the citizens hold the key levers at a pivotal time. What happens next is largely up to us.

Working with the Text

1. Which aspects of cyberspace (or CMC, computer-mediated communication) does Rheingold claim might enhance personal liberty and democracy, and which inhibit it? What are the major arguments against the "democratizing" effects of the 'Net that Rheingold summarizes? Which do you find most compelling? Which are supported by your experience of online communication?

2. Rheingold spends a good deal of time explaining the concept of the "public sphere" (which is not in itself an easy concept to comprehend). Based on his description and definitions, would you say that you experience a version of "the public sphere" in your participation in politics, government, and democracy in the United States, at either the national or local levels? What, if anywhere, constitutes a "public sphere" in which you participate? What defines for you what we might call the *"marketplace of political ideas"*? Do you agree with those critics who see that "public sphere" as commodified and commercialized? Does the Internet seem an extension of these tendencies or a possible opposition to them?

3. Rheingold quotes James Carey's use of the term "technological sublime." Where do you see evidence of that in media images of new network technologies, such as commercials for personal computers and the Internet? How do media images of new technologies invoke connections between individuals and cultures around the world? How do media images bring together ideals of participatory democracy, community values, and international networking and understanding?

4. What do you think is the value of the Internet for democracy? Can you find examples of participatory democracy online? Do you think that the Internet and online technologies will enhance democracy, civic participation, and the First Amendment? Explore these questions in an essay.

One World: Ready Or Not

WILLIAM GREIDER

A graduate of Princeton University, journalist William Greider (born 1936) worked as a reporter for the *Washington Post* from 1968 to 1982 and has since then served as the Washington columnist and national affairs editor for *Rolling Stone* magazine. He has also written for periodicals such as *Ramparts, Esquire,* and *The Atlantic Monthly* and has published a number of books on political issues, including *Who Will Tell the People?: The Betrayal of American Democracy* (1992), about America's decaying political process, and *One World, Ready or Not: The Manic Logic of Global Capitalism* (1997). In the following adaptation from that book, which originally appeared in *Rolling Stone,* Greider reports on working conditions in American-owned factories in Southeast Asia and poses "the gut question for any citizen of the new world": "Do you believe that every human being has a thirst for self-realization and is entitled . . . to the opportunity? Or are those others who make our products really lesser beings, incapable of an expanding self-awareness and larger ideas of themselves?"

1. Motorola's Ladies

In the industrial zone at Petaling Jaya, outside of Kuala Lumpur, Malaysia, the dingy blue buses drop off workers for the 2 P.M. shift at the Motorola plant. Though it is visible from the highway, Motorola's blue logo is not the only familiar sign in this compound of global commerce—Canon, Sanyo, Panasonic, and Minolta also maintain large manufacturing plants here. Motorola's factory, like many other U.S. semiconductor companies located nearby, looks like a low-slung office-type building. It faces an asphalt parking lot that is neatly bordered by palms and giant yews. The building's white façade is decorated with red paper lanterns and gilded banners in honor of the Chinese New Year. Above the front entrance, a billboard invites employees to enter the Motorola 10K Run. The winners will get a chance to compete in a marathon in Austin, Texas.

The building's glass entry leads to a long, gleaming corridor that takes Motorola's 2 P.M. shift, all of them young, delicate-looking women, past the company library, a health center and an automatic banking machine. The women dress in the modest garb of Islam: flowing ankle-length dresses, and silk scarves of pale blue, orange and brown that are called *tundjung*. A few of the women wear the more conservative black veils that shape their faces into pale brown hearts.

"Good afternoon, ladies," says Roger Bertelson, Motorola's national manager for Malaysia, who is showing me around. The two of us tower above the stream of women who pass by, eyes lowered, barely nodding. With his brush cut and sunny American forwardness, Bertelson comes off like a taller version of Ross Perot. He's explaining the I RECOMMEND board, a wall display covered with snapshots of employees who have made successful suggestions. 3

"We had to change the culture," Bertelson says, "because the Malay home does not encourage women to speak out. The daughter is supposed to have babies and take care of the husband. The idea was to break down the resistance to speaking out." 4

Here at what is one of Motorola's largest plants outside the U.S. (5,000 employees, 80 percent Malay, 3,900 of them "ladies," as they are called), the main hallway is decorated with a series of Norman Rockwell paintings— warm, nostalgic scenes of American life—each accompanied by an inspirational aphorism in English: PEOPLE WILL TAKE NOTE OF EXCELLENT WORK; YOU'LL BE PREPARED FOR ANYTHING WITH ENTHUSIASM; WHAT WE SAY IS AS IMPORTANT AS HOW WE SAY IT. 5

The women pass these paintings each day on their way to the changing room where they prepare for work. They remove their shoes and veils before proceeding to the "gowning room" across the hall. A few minutes later they emerge, cloaked in ghostly white jumpsuits, surgical masks and hooded bonnets. Dressed for their high-tech work, they appear even more chaste than they would in the most traditional Islamic garments. But there's one more step. The hooded, masked women step into an "air shower," which blasts away any remaining particles of dust. Only then are they ready to enter the sealed operations room, where rows of complex machines and monitors await their gloved touch. 6

Once inside, the 2 P.M. shift begins the exacting daily routine of manufacturing semiconductor chips. The women work in a realm of submicrons, attaching leads to components too small to see without the aid of electronic monitors. It is likely that the silicon wafers they bend over are designed and fabricated back in the United States (or in Scotland) and flown by 747 here (or to Singapore, the Philippines or elsewhere in Asia) for final assembly— sawed into individual boards, wired, tested and packaged. The finished chips are shipped back to North America, Asia and Europe, where they will function as the brains and memories—the functional guts—of cars, televi- 7 sions, computers, portable phones, missile control systems and countless other products.

The one-world spectacle of Motorola's Petaling Jaya plant is quite rou-   8
tine—three shifts a day, seven days a week—but watching it up close conveyed to me something of the high human drama of intertwining cultures. Our partners in high technology are now shy young women from the *kampong,* the rural Malaysian villages where, not long ago, a girl's future was limited to helping her father or husband with the rice harvest. Now she stares at electronic monitors for hours at a time and must try to explain to the men back home how her pay comes out of an automatic teller machine in the hallway at the electronics plant.

This cultural exchange, as profound as it is, constitutes a single transac-   9
tion in a great, unfolding economic story. To find out what else the increasingly global nature of finance and business might mean for us, I spent three months visiting factories, plants and communities on three continents. Among the contradictions and surprising juxtapositions I encountered, I also found out firsthand that people from the most unpromising circumstances are now producing the most highly advanced artifacts of our daily lives. The notion that only certain populations—specifically, white people from Europe or America—are capable of producing goods of world-class quality is simply wrong. A great leveling has begun, I've found, and the tools of advanced industrial civilization are being shared with other tribes. Ironically, it is the multinational corporations, imperious, aloof and powerful, that are the vehicles for this historical act of generosity.

At a small house in a working-class neighborhood in Kuala Lumpur, I spent   10
time talking to six young women who live together and work at Motorola and the other electronics factories of Petaling Jaya. Some had just arrived at this union-subsidized hostel after evening prayers at a mosque; others would depart later for the 11 P.M. shift. They spoke of the details of their lives, their modest ambitions, their mild complaints, the stories of how they had come to join the global work force.

"The company came to my *kampong* and approached my father, and he   11
suggested that I work," says Rosita. "The basic pay was 270 ringgit [$108 a month]; now it is 300."

A 24-year-old woman named Raziah says she changed jobs three times   12
because at each one, the salary was less than what she was promised. She says that the Japanese-owned factory was "not a happy place, and my supervisors were very rude and pressured me. . . . I want to better myself, but I've got no money for classes."

I ask what brought them here. Some of them answer that they were   13
bored at home. Others say that they are saving for something. Still others fol-

lowed their friends. A 25-year-old named Rakimah says, "I have put away some savings. I might even start a small business—like a nursery for children. That is my plan. I love to cook, so if not a nursery, I will open a restaurant."

Dutiful daughters all, each woman sends some money home every   14 month to her father and mother. One girl is getting married and will soon quit the factory. Another talks about a friend who was overwhelmed by the fast life of Kuala Lumpur and returned home to her village. They discuss the relative merits of the foreign employers and agree that Koreans are the worst, Americans are the best, and Motorola is the best among the Americans.

The frank discussion, which could have taken place in any company   15 cafeteria in the States, reminds me of Roger Bertelson's I RECOMMEND board. "The government would like to maintain Islamic principles and protect people from Western values," he says, "but whether the government likes it or not, the people are becoming Westernized."

2. A Visit to Boeing's Itch

Boeing's assembly plant in Everett, Wash., is one of the great wonders of the   16 industrial world. The cavernous factory, located north of Seattle on the Puget Sound, encompasses 98 acres of manufacturing activity under a single roof and is said to be the largest building on earth. Ten stories above the factory floor, an intricate grid of pale green girders covers the ceiling like a steel spider web. Yellow cranes creep silently through this network, dangling pieces of a wing or tail section beneath them on long, slender threads. To orchestrate the construction of the wide-body aircraft known as the 747, 767 and 777, the Boeing plant keeps 40 such cranes in motion—so many that an air-traffic control center is required to coordinate their movements.

The dimensions of the place are overwhelming. From an observation   17 loft near the ceiling, the dangling, disconnected shells of fuselages, nose cones, tails and wings resemble pieces from a fabulous model-airplane kit fastidiously arranged by a precocious child. Every seven days these pieces are methodically, miraculously brought together by the yellow cranes, then fitted and fastened by the people down below. Wings and center section are joined to fuselage, electronics wired in, jet engines attached, and every week a finished airplane, weighing as much as 400 tons, emerges from the Everett plant.

On the shop floor, the perspectives are reversed, and the workers are   18 dwarfed by what they are making. People bicycle from one behemoth to another, carrying plans from the dozens of computerized design stations. The nose section of a 777, its delicate aluminum skin protected by an iridescent blue coating, floats down on cables. To the rear, a wing surface is being walked into place by four machinists, who gently coax it back and forth into a snug fit with its frame. An automatic riveting machine, two stories high and mounted on railed track, moves patiently along the wing, punching out precision stitches almost noiselessly. Not counting the millions of rivets that hold it together, the "Triple Seven" has 132,000 parts.

In some circumstances, a display of technology may approach the power   19
of art in its ability to inspire. One could not observe the majesty of the Everett factory without experiencing such exultation—or, at the least, a momentary joy—at the beauty of things actually working. The making of one of these planes requires the fusing of sensitive touch and Gargantuan strength, computerized tolerances with the human gentleness of assembly workers.

The Everett plant likewise demonstrates, perhaps even more tangi-   20
bly, the international character of advanced manufacturing. On the shop floor, wooden crates marked BELFAST, IRELAND contain nose landing-gear doors. Stacked on a metal rack are outboard wing flaps, their tags labeled ALENIA OF ITALY.

The 777's entire fuselage arrives in quarter sections from Japan, shipped   21
by Mitsubishi from Nagoya to Washington's Puget Sound, where the pieces are barged from Tacoma to the port of Everett, then hauled by railcars up the steep grade to the factory. The wingtip assembly comes from Korea, rudders from Australia, dorsal fins from Brazil, main landing gear from Canada and France. Flight computers are made in the United Kingdom. And so on.

"I am scratching their itch," says Lawrence W. Clarkson, Boeing's senior   22
vice president for planning and international development, of his many international vendors. Clarkson explains: "I have to create some jobs in those countries to get those markets. But what we're trying to do in the net equation is to protect the jobs here. I think I can show that happened with China or with Japan. But overall, it's a tougher problem as I look at the future. Will I have a lot of U.S. suppliers, or will I have more international suppliers? I don't know, but it's clear the U.S. suppliers don't bring me any market."

A few months later, I visit a small Chinese village that hopes to provide   23
the answer to Clarkson's question. The village of Sanyuan, in the Shaanxi province, is a settlement of worn, brown-brick dwellings located in a narrow river valley. A steep ridge, gullied and desiccated by erosion, rises behind the village, and the pale walls in the center of town have the same tired, washed-out look. The houses here are small, with dark tile or thatched roofs, and for the most part are clustered together, though several newer ones stand apart, their doorways decorated with dramatic floral designs. Behind the courtyard wall of one home, a family's possessions are scattered about on the hard-baked ground: a two-wheeled farm cart, a bicycle and tools, jumbled rows of unused bricks, mounds of darkening cornstalks, a tethered cow for plowing and two white goats for milk.

I came to this place at the suggestion of a Boeing manager who thought   24
I should see the other end of the global aircraft industry. Sanyuan is like
10,000 other villages in China—poor and primitive, removed from the rest
of the world. But this farm village is also home to the Hongyuan Aviation
Forging & Casting Industry Company, a state-owned enterprise that manufactures a titanium-alloy jet-engine mount for Boeing's world-class aircraft.

In Sanyuan there are no streetlights along the paved road that leads   25
through the village. At night the blackness is broken only by the occasional
glow of a TV set seen through an open doorway. People, bicycles, handcarts
appear abruptly from the thick darkness, then seem to evaporate. The night
strollers are indifferent to the speeding, honking trucks that flash through
the village with loads of crushed stone or steel rods.

In the morning the peasant farmers open up their daily market at the   26
center of the village. They squat back on their heels in the universal manner
of plain country folk, behind abundant piles of produce—carrots, greens,
cauliflower, scallions and cabbages spread out on white muslin. A young
man in a blue sweater jabbers self-importantly through a bullhorn. He is
selling lotus flour, a milky white powder that he has packaged in clear plastic bags and weighed on a crude, hand-held scale.

At the north end of town, the Hongyuan Forging plant sits behind high   27
fences, its gates guarded by young soldiers wearing the olive-green jackets
of the People's Liberation Army. Inside, the shop floors are soiled and pitted, and casually littered with scrap metal. The towering green Weingarten
screw press from Germany and a few other advanced machine tools look
out of place in the factory's gloom. I watch four workers wrestle with a large
steel plate that elsewhere in the world might have been handled by a heavy
crane. A row of solemn young machinists standing at their lathes looks like
a sepia photograph from a bygone industrial era.

Hongyuan Forging is itself rising from the dead past, a surviving legacy   28
of China's Cold War paranoia. In the 1960s, Mao Tse-tung became convinced that either Russia or the United States was about to launch a pre-
emptive nuclear strike against China, so he ordered China's heavy industries
to relocate to the country's interior—the so-called Third Front. Factories
were hidden in obscure places like Sanyuan so that China might survive a
nuclear first strike and fight on. It might have been a lunatic defense strategy, but it brought industrial development to some very poor places.

In Sanyuan, scores of caves were dug in the narrow ravines of the valley   29
wall. These broad tunnels run several hundred feet into the mountainside,
and within them the company placed its laboratories and most valuable technical equipment. Thirty years later, Hongyuan's technicians are still operating
in these caves, running the high-tech machines that test alloys or monitor

quality control in the forgings. The company officials who show me around seem slightly embarrassed by these primitive aspects of their enterprise.

In the village, some families still live in the man-made caves—quite   30
comfortably, it seems. A farmer invited me to inspect one of them, a cool, cluttered dwelling lit by a single light bulb. Walls curve into ceilings and are whitewashed, decorated with colorful travel posters and his daughter's school certificates. We sat in the coolness and drank tea from glass jars. Times are good, he says. Soon he expects to build a new house, above ground. Prosperity, Chinese style.

It feels like an impossible distance from the dazzling factory of Puget   31
Sound, yet Hongyuan Forging is a Boeing subcontractor in good standing— ambitious, in fact, to become a world-class producer of advanced industrial goods. The company already makes precision turbine blades for Siemens of Germany and ABB of Switzerland and is pursuing business deals with General Electric. Hongyuan Forging has opened sales offices on three continents. Its general manager, Kang Feng Xiao, a gray-haired engineer who came to the city 29 years earlier to build Mao's Third Front, seems confident of the new vision.

"Since we have business with Boeing," Kang says, "this makes us up-   32
grade our forgings so our technology is very close to world standards. Also, we learned the quality-control system. Our purpose is to push into the world market, mainly aerospace, steam turbines, car forgings. We intend to develop our company as the biggest in China, the biggest in East Asia. I think in this way—the way of the market—it won't be long before China will have great changes."

In Hongyuan Forging's showroom are displayed the wheels, joints, rings,   33
rods and axles that go out from this small village to customers in Germany, Japan, Korea and the United States. An honored place is reserved for the American aircraft company that has shared its precious knowledge. Displayed on a blue felt drape are five of the titanium-alloy support struts that Hongyuan Forging manufactures for the engine mounts of the Boeing 747.

3. A Toy-Factory Fire in Thailand

On May 10, 1993, the worst industrial fire in the history of capitalism deci-   34
mated a toy factory on the outskirts of Bangkok, Thailand. The news was reported on Page 25 of the *Washington Post*. The *Financial Times* of London, which styles itself as the daily newspaper of the global economy, ran a brief item on Page 5. The *Wall Street Journal* followed a day later with an account on Page 11. The *New York Times* also put the story inside but printed a dramatic photo on its front page: rows of small, shrouded bodies on bamboo pallets—dozens of them—lined along the damp pavement,

while dazed rescue workers stood awkwardly among the corpses. In the background, one could see the collapsed, smoldering structure of the mammoth factory where the Kader Industrial toy company of Thailand had employed 3,000 workers, manufacturing stuffed toys and plastic dolls, playthings destined for American children.

The official count was 188 dead, 469 injured, but the actual toll was undoubtedly higher, since the four-story buildings had collapsed swiftly in the intense heat, and many bodies were incinerated. Some of the missing were never found; others fled home to their villages. All but 14 of the dead were women, most of them young, some as young as 13 years old. Hundreds of workers had been trapped on upper floors of the burning building and were forced to jump from third- and fourth-floor windows because the main exit doors were kept locked by the managers and the narrow stairways collapsed or became clotted with trampled bodies.

When I visit Bangkok about nine months later, physical evidence of the disaster is gone—the site was scraped clean by bulldozers—and Kader is already resuming production at a new toy factory, built far from the city in a rural province of northeastern Thailand. When I talk with Thai labor leaders and civic activists, the people who had rallied to the cause of the fire victims, some of them are under the impression that a worldwide boycott of Kader products is under way, organized by conscience-stricken Americans and Europeans. I have to inform them that the civilized world barely noticed their tragedy.

As news accounts pointed out, the Kader fire surpassed what was previously the worst industrial fire in history, the Triangle Shirtwaist Company fire of 1911, in which 146 young immigrant women died in similar circumstances at a garment factory in Lower Manhattan. The Triangle factory fire became a pivotal event in American politics. It was a public scandal that provoked citizen reform and energized the growth of the International Ladies' Garment Workers' Union. The fire in Thailand produced no such response or even a sign of shame among consumers. The indifference of the powerful newspapers merely reflects the tastes of their readers, who might be moved by human suffering in their own communities but are inured to news of recurring calamities in distant places. A fire in Bangkok was like a typhoon in Bangladesh or an earthquake in Turkey.

The Kader fire might have become more meaningful for Americans if they could have seen the thousands of soot-stained dolls that spilled from the wreckage, the macabre litter scattered among the dead: Bugs Bunny, Bart Simpson, Big Bird and other *Sesame Street* dolls, Playskool Water Pets, Santa Claus dolls. What the initial news accounts did not mention was that Kader's Thai factory had produced most of its toys for American companies— Toys "R" Us, Fisher-Price, Hasbro, Tyco, Arco, Kenner, Gund and J.C. Penney.

Americans worry obsessively over the everyday safety of their children,   39
and the U.S. government's regulators diligently police the design of toys. Yet
neither American citizens nor their government took any interest in the brutal and dangerous conditions imposed on the toy makers, many of whom
were mere adolescents themselves.

The toy industry, not surprisingly, felt the same way. Hasbro Industries,   40
maker of Playskool, subsequently told the *Boston Globe* that it would no
longer do business with Kader, but in general, the U.S. companies shrugged
off responsibility. Kader, a major toy manufacturer based in Hong Kong, is
"extremely reputable, not sleazebags," David Miller, president of the Toy
Manufacturers of America, assured *USA Today*. "The responsibility for those
factories," Miller told ABC News, "is in the hands of those who are there and
managing the factory."

The grisly details of what occurred reveal the casual irresponsibility of   41
both companies and governments. The Kader factory compound consisted
of four interconnected, four-story industrial barns on a three-acre lot on
Buddhamondhol VI Road in the Sampran district, west of Bangkok. It is only
one among Thailand's many thriving new industrial zones for garments, tex-
tiles, electronics and toys. More than 50,000 people, most of them migrants
from the Thai countryside, work in the Sampran district at 7,500 large and
small firms. Thailand's economic boom is based on places such as this, and
Bangkok is almost choking on its own fantastic growth, dizzily erecting luxury hotels and office towers.

The fire started late on a Monday afternoon on the ground floor in the   42
first building and spread rapidly upward, jumping to two adjoining buildings, all three of which swiftly collapsed. Investigators noted afterward that
the structures had been cheaply built, without adequate reinforcement, so
steel girders and stairways crumpled easily in the heat. Thai law requires
that in such a large factory, fire-escape stairways must be 16 to 33 feet wide,
but Kader's stairways measured only 4½ feet. The factory's main doors were
locked, and many windows were barred to prevent pilfering by the employees. Flammable raw materials—fabric, stuffing, animal fibers—were
stacked everywhere, on walkways and next to electrical boxes. Neither
safety drills nor fire alarms and sprinkler systems had been provided.

A young woman named Lampan Taptim who survived the fire remem-   43
bers "the sound of yelling about a fire. I tried to leave the section, but my
supervisor told me to get back to work. My sister, who worked on the fourth
floor with me, pulled me away and insisted we try to get out. We tried to go
down the stairs and go to the second floor; we found that the stairs had already caved in. There was a lot of yelling and confusion. . . . In desperation,
I went back up to the windows, and went back and forth, looking down be-

low. The smoke was thick, and I picked the best place to jump in a pile of boxes. My sister jumped, too. She died."

Another young woman, a survivor named Cheng, recalls: "[People were 44 shouting], 'There is no way out. The security guard has locked the main door out!' It was horrifying. I thought I would die. I took off my gold ring and kept it in my pocket, and put on my name tag so that my body could be identifiable. I had to decide [whether] to die in the fire or from jumping down from a three stories' height."

An older textile worker named Vilaiwa Satieti, who sewed shirts and 45 pants at a neighboring factory, describes to me the carnage she encountered: "I got off work about 5 and passed by Kader, and saw many dead bodies lying around uncovered. They had broken legs and broken arms and broken heads. We tried to keep them alive until they got to the hospital— that's all you could do. Oh, they were teenagers, 15 to 20 years, no more than that, and so many of them, so many."

Similar tragedies, large and small, are now commonplace across develop- 46 ing Asia and elsewhere. Two months after Kader, another fire at a Bangkok shirt factory killed 10 women. Three months after Kader, a six-story hotel collapsed and killed 133 people, injuring 351. The embarrassed minister of industry ordered special inspections of 244 large factories in the Bangkok region and found that 60 percent of them had basic violations similar to Kader's. Just as Thai industry is growing explosively—12 to 15 percent a year—workplace injuries and illnesses are growing even faster, from 37,000 victims in 1987 to more than 150,000 in 1992 and an estimated 200,000 in 1994.

Which brings up these questions: Why does global commerce, with its 47 wondrous technologies and sophisticated economics, restore barbaric conditions that were long ago forbidden by law? If the Information Age has enabled corporations to become truly multinational—managing production and distribution spread across continents—why are their managers unable or unwilling to manage such mundane matters as fire prevention?

4. Shoes and Power in Indonesia

The young Indonesian factory workers gathered around the table steal 48 glances at one another and at me like embarrassed teenagers not sure they are dressed properly for the occasion. My questions in English draw them forward in their chairs. When they hear the translation in Bahasa, they sink back, wearing nervous smiles.

"Why did you come here from your villages?" I ask. 49

"To earn money . . . to be independent," says a worker. 50

"Were your hopes fulfilled?" 51

"Not really."   52

"Why?"   53

"The costs are very big; the pay is very small." Each answer is accom-   54
panied by scattered giggles and nodding heads.

It is a Sunday afternoon in the dim front room of a small house in the   55
Tangerang district, an hour or so outside Jakarta. The house is maintained
by YAKOMA, a church-supported social foundation that uses it as an informal training center. It is a place for young workers to come on their days off
for frank discussions about working conditions in this industrial zone, where
famous American brands like Nike shoes, Arrow shirts and Levi's jeans are
manufactured. The young men and women in the room with me make the
shoes and the jeans, though they work for contractor concerns with less familiar names like Sung Hwa Dunia, Nasa and Hasi.

YAKOMA is prominent among the dozens of nongovernmental organi-   56
zations that have taken hold in Indonesia during the last 10 years as advocates for civil rights, environmental issues and women. Inevitably, many of
these groups converged on the core issue of labor rights, since the outcome
of that struggle would determine almost everything else—personal dignity
and civic democracy, economic justice and individual freedom.

"This is a paternalistic culture," explains Indera Nababan, the YAKOMA   57
leader who arranged the session for me. "It teaches the people that all that
comes from above is good, that you never raise your voice. Some do resist,
but most of the workers are rural girls and unsure of themselves. It's only
through experience that they learn they must take their destiny in their own
hands."

Their names are Sadisah, Cicih, Sugeng, Suprato, Hazimah, Eva, Enaf,   58
among others. Most of them are in their late teens or early 20s, but their hesitant manner makes them seem much younger than their American counterparts. The young women are unmarried—still girls in Indonesian social
status. They have sweetly beautiful Javanese faces with rich, loosely flowing
black hair. They are simply dressed in slacks and bright print blouses or
striped cotton shirts. One of the boys, Suprato, wears a crisp T-shirt that declares in English: FOLLOW THE FLAG.

What do you expect for the future, I want to know. A blank pause, then   59
tentative and unfocused answers: "We hope to improve ourselves," one of
them says.

Can you do that? No. . . . Yes. . . . Possibly. . . . "If we struggle. . . ." There   60
is something painfully innocent in their mien. They seem so young and un-
equipped, too frail and vulnerable to be caught up by such heavy questions.
Still, they lean earnestly into the conversation, chins up, trying to answer
correctly, bravely.

"If we fight, things may be different," Eva Novitasari offers slowly at last. 61
"I think we will fight."

"We are hopeful," Suprato says. "Right now, we accept what we have, 62
but we would like to change that."

They are well aware of the risks of organizing against their companies, 63
since a new national heroine has arisen in Indonesia as a courageous symbol of their aspirations. Marsinah, a 23-year-old worker, tried to organize her
fellow workers at a watch factory in East Java. She was abducted, raped
and murdered. The brutal details of her death have become a national scandal, and though the military itself was implicated in her murder, President
Suharto's regime has anointed Marsinah posthumously as a "worker hero."
Her story inspires these young workers in Tangerang and also reminds them
of the dangers of asserting themselves.

Cicih and Sadisah themselves organized a strike at one of Nike's con- 64
tractor plants, demanding the legal minimum wage and other improve-
ments. They were fired, along with 20 others (suspended, the company said,
for damaging the plant. Nike insists that it has since taken steps to ensure
that contractors comply with prevailing labor legislation). "I was scared because we were fighting for our rights," Cicih says. What about losing your
job? "No, I wasn't afraid of that," she says. "The pay is very poor."

"I expected much higher wages, but I was new," Sadisah says. "I ex- 65
pected to rise, then I found it was not true. It's no good going back home
without success; you don't feel satisfied."

Sadisah signed on with YAKOMA as a community organizer, living in an 66
impoverished settlement near the factories and trying to engage the workers
in dialogue about their conditions. Progress is slow and difficult. "The community is too close; they won't take advice," she grumbles. "The women
workers, I hope, will be independent and brave enough to fight for their
rights. But, you know, in Indonesia, the women are the weak ones, not
strong, not brave."

Beyond the question of courage, the young workers lack even the most 67
basic knowledge about how the industrial world works and how they might
cope with it. What is a union? What rights do they possess to complain? "We
have a union at Hasi," Enaf says, "but it is not the union that told us to strike.
[That was] the workers. The union is all from the company." Eva adds: "The
company told us to choose our union leader from the company staff. We
didn't know about the union or what it was."

Our meeting adjourns, and the kids rush out to find their friends, to 68
stroll along the dusty streets or to hang out at shops for the few hours that
remain of their day off. On the long ride back to Jakarta, I try to imagine
what young Americans would say to the young people from Tangerang,

what commonality they might discover if they were ever brought together in the same room.

Here in Indonesia, kids assemble the basketball shoes and brand-name   69
jeans so valued back in the United States, the goods that are expensive symbols of style and grace for American youth. In their advertising messages, the most successful athletic-shoe manufacturers have concocted an artful fantasy of power that status-conscious young Americans eagerly consume: the idea of magical shoes that embody superhuman athletic prowess.

The young Indonesians who actually make the shoes are still trying to   70
understand real power, even as it buffets their lives in the real world. They thought, perhaps naively, that if the American kids would stop buying Nike shoes, their own grievances might be heard, and some of them have signed a petition asking other young people around the world to boycott a company that the workers maintain collaborates in their oppression.

Though Americans seldom read about it, thousands of wildcat strikes   71
are launched against the new factories of developing Asia, staged by brave young people like the ones I met. They want better pay and working conditions, but they also want a voice in their own destiny. An infant labor movement is struggling to be born in these countries and faces extraordinary obstacles. It is not simply the multinational companies standing in the way but, usually, the workers' own governments.

5. An Emerging Dignity

Several months after my visit to Indonesia, I meet with a group of commu-   72
nity leaders in Texas. I recount some of what I have seen in Southeast Asia—the bewilderment of the young workers, the terrible conditions imposed on the powerless. One of the community leaders, a Mexican-American woman named Dora Olivo from the Rio Grande Valley, responds with her own story.

"When I was a kid and we used to pick cotton," Olivo says. "Our fam-   73
ily lived in a barracks, all of us in one room, and we didn't have water or toilets or anything. We were very poor; we didn't know to expect anything else. Then Cesar Chavez came and told us we had dignity. And that started to change things. People began to recognize their dignity—that they have a right to dignity—and we began to expect something better for ourselves."

Olivo's eloquent comment sounds disarmingly simple, yet she is ex-   74
pressing the vital, universal core of human experience—the possibilities of self-realization. Across vastly disparate cultures, people in different places define the search in wildly various terms, from material accumulation to spiritual awareness, but the unifying thread of mortal existence is the search for self-discovery. Who am I? What is my purpose here on earth, my true po-

tential? Where do I fit in the larger scheme of things? Part of the human struggle, in every time and place, among wealthy and poor, is to seek answers to those questions.

When all the economic complexities are set aside, the question before the world is really about that word—*dignity*—and the possibilities for individual self-realization. It cannot be only about money. It must begin from the understanding that the human potential is vast, unfathomable and largely unrealized. The unknown is what makes the future so interesting, so promising in every age, especially in this one.

Some Asian political leaders belittle the Western understanding of individualism and assure us that their cultures do not share in these assumptions. These smug politicians, I think, are in for a rude surprise. They may dismiss the concept of personal identity, but ultimately their prospering societies will be unable to hold back the tide of individualism that is carried in on the waves of capitalist enterprise.

Japanese culture has already been changed by Western-style capitalism's impact and wrestles now with the social and economic implications. In Malaysia, the young Muslim women working for Motorola gain personal control over their own wages for the first time by using ATMs. In Indonesia or China, it is self-realization that is present in the courage to aspire to make great products or even to contemplate a strike against powerful employers. Commerce invades with revolutionary ideas and challenges. Once the concepts are implanted, a regime will need enormous force to keep them down.

So the gut question for any citizen of the new world is: Do you believe that every human being has a thirst for self-realization and is entitled, in his or her own terms, to the opportunity? Or are those others who make our products really lesser beings, incapable of an expanding self-awareness and larger ideas of themselves? The human struggles and aspirations that I encountered around the world make the answer seem obvious to me.

Working with the Text

1. Greider says that watching the operation of the Motorola plant in Malaysia conveyed to him something of the "high human drama of intertwining cultures." What are some of the details of that drama as he describes them in his article? Who are the players? What are the tensions? Why do you think he calls it "high human drama"?

2. What are the key issues raised in the story about the "Toy-Factory Fire" in Thailand? How does it reveal certain changing realities in relations between "First World" and "Third World" nations? How does it represent the continuation of values?

3. Greider compares the "Toy-Factory Fire" in Thailand to the "Triangle Shirtwaist Company Fire" in 1911, which he says was a signal moment in American industrial history. There is a good site on the World Wide Web about the "Triangle Shirtwaist Company Fire." Read around the site and find at least one document that raises some of the issues that Greider does about the international workforce. Are there similarities and differences in attitude about women, work, and culture?

4. Greider says near the end of the essay, "When all the economic complexities are set aside, the question before the world is really about that word—*dignity*—and the possibilities for individual self-realization." And then later, "So the gut question for any citizen of the new world is: Do you believe that every human being has a thirst for self-realization and is entitled, in his or her own terms, to the opportunity?" How are the world's new borders, especially as they are shaped by new global economic realities, affecting individual quests for "dignity" and self-fulfillment? How can the new globalism advance the cause of individual rights and opportunities?

Jihad vs. McWorld

BENJAMIN R. BARBER

A professor of political science at Rutgers University, Benjamin Barber was born in New York City and attended the London School of Economics and Grinnell College, receiving his master's and doctoral degrees from Harvard. His research and writing have focused on a wide variety of topics, and his books include *Liberating Feminism* (1975), *The Artist and Political Vision* (1982), *Strong Democracy: Participatory Politics for a New Age* (1984), and *An Aristocracy of Everyone* (1992). The author of a novel as well as a number of plays, Barber also collaborated on the prize-winning television series and companion book, *The Struggle for Democracy* (1988). The following essay is the introduction to his 1995 *Jihad vs. McWorld*, in which Barber focuses on two competing forces in global culture: "the one driven by parochial hatreds, the other by universalizing markets, the one re-creating ancient subnational and ethnic borders from within, the other making national borders porous from without."

History is not over. Nor are we arrived in the wondrous land of techné 1
promised by the futurologists. The collapse of state communism has not delivered people to a safe democratic haven, and the past, fratricide and civil
discord perduring, still clouds the horizon just behind us. Those who look
back see all of the horrors of the ancient slaughterbench reenacted in disintegral nations like Bosnia, Sri Lanka, Ossetia, and Rwanda and they declare
that nothing has changed. Those who look forward prophesize commercial
and technological interdependence—a virtual paradise made possible by
spreading markets and global technology—and they proclaim that everything is or soon will be different. The rival observers seem to consult different almanacs drawn from the libraries of contrarian planets.

Yet anyone who reads the daily papers carefully, taking in the front 2
page accounts of civil carnage as well as the business page stories on the
mechanics of the information superhighway and the economics of communication mergers, anyone who turns deliberately to take in the whole 360-
degree horizon, knows that our world and our lives are caught between
what William Butler Yeats called the two eternities of race and soul: that of
race reflecting the tribal past, that of soul anticipating the cosmopolitan future. Our secular eternities are corrupted, however, race reduced to an insignia of resentment, and soul sized down to fit the demanding body by
which it now measures its needs. Neither race nor soul offers us a future that
is other than bleak, neither promises a polity that is remotely democratic.

The first scenario rooted in race holds out the grim prospect of a retrib- 3
alization of large swaths of humankind by war and bloodshed: a threatened
balkanization of nation-states in which culture is pitted against culture, people against people, tribe against tribe, a Jihad in the name of a hundred narrowly conceived faiths against every kind of interdependence, every kind of
artificial social cooperation and mutuality: against technology, against pop
culture, and against integrated markets; against modernity itself as well as
the future in which modernity issues. The second paints that future in shim-
mering pastels, a busy portrait of onrushing economic, technological, and
ecological forces that demand integration and uniformity and that mesmer-
ize peoples everywhere with fast music, fast computers, and fast food—
MTV, Macintosh, and McDonald's—pressing nations into one homogenous
global theme park, one McWorld tied together by communications, information, entertainment, and commerce. Caught between Babel and Disneyland, the planet is falling precipitously apart and coming reluctantly together
at the very same moment.

Some stunned observers notice only Babel, complaining about the thou- 4
sand newly sundered "peoples" who prefer to address their neighbors with
sniper rifles and mortars; others—zealots in Disneyland—seize on futuro-

logical platitudes and the promise of virtuality, exclaiming "It's a small world after all!" Both are right, but how can that be?

We are compelled to choose between what passes as "the twilight of sovereignty" and an entropic end of all history; or a return to the past's most fractious and demoralizing discord; to "the menace of global anarchy," to Milton's capital of hell, Pandaemonium; to a world totally "out of control."

The apparent truth, which speaks to the paradox at the core of this book, is that the tendencies of both Jihad *and* McWorld are at work, both visible sometimes in the same country at the very same instant. Iranian zealots keep one ear tuned to the mullahs urging holy war and the other cocked to Rupert Murdoch's Star television beaming in *Dynasty, Donahue,* and *The Simpsons* from hovering satellites. Chinese entrepreneurs vie for the attention of party cadres in Beijing and simultaneously pursue KFC franchises in cities like Nanjing, Hangzhou, and Xian where twenty-eight outlets serve over 100,000 customers a day. The Russian Orthodox church, even as it struggles to renew the ancient faith, has entered a joint venture with California businessmen to bottle and sell natural waters under the rubric Saint Springs Water Company. Serbian assassins wear Adidas sneakers and listen to Madonna on Walkman headphones as they take aim through their gun-scopes at scurrying Sarajevo civilians looking to fill family watercans. Orthodox Hasids and brooding neo-Nazis have both turned to rock music to get their traditional messages out to the new generation, while fundamentalists plot virtual conspiracies on the Internet.

Now neither Jihad nor McWorld is in itself novel. History ending in the triumph of science and reason or some monstrous perversion thereof (Mary Shelley's Doctor Frankenstein) has been the leitmotiv of every philosopher and poet who has regretted the Age of Reason since the Enlightenment. Yeats lamented "the center will not hold, mere anarchy is loosed upon the world," and observers of Jihad today have little but historical detail to add. The Christian parable of the Fall and of the possibilities of redemption that it makes possible captures the eighteenth-century ambivalence—and our own—about past and future. I want, however, to do more than dress up the central paradox of human history in modern clothes. It is not Jihad and McWorld but the relationship between them that most interests me. For, squeezed between their opposing forces, the world has been sent spinning out of control. Can it be that what Jihad and McWorld have in common is anarchy: the absence of common will and that conscious and collective human control under the guidance of law we call democracy?

Progress moves in steps that sometimes lurch backwards; in history's twisting maze, Jihad not only revolts against but abets McWorld, while McWorld not only imperils but re-creates and reinforces Jihad. They produce their contraries and need one another. My object here then is not simply to offer sequential portraits of McWorld and Jihad, but while examining McWorld, to keep Jihad in my field of vision, and while dissecting Jihad, never to forget the context of McWorld. Call it a dialectic of McWorld: a study in the cunning of reason that does honor to the radical differences that distinguish Jihad and McWorld yet that acknowledges their powerful and paradoxical interdependence.

There is a crucial difference, however, between my modest attempt at dialectic and that of the masters of the nineteenth century. Still seduced by the Enlightenment's faith in progress, both Hegel and Marx believed reason's cunning was on the side of progress. But it is harder to believe that the clash of Jihad and McWorld will issue in some overriding good. The outcome seems more likely to pervert than to nurture human liberty. The two may, in opposing each other, work to the same ends, work in apparent tension yet in covert harmony, but democracy is not their beneficiary. In East Berlin, tribal communism has yielded to capitalism. In Marx-Engelsplatz, the stolid, overbearing statues of Marx and Engels face east, as if seeking distant solace from Moscow: but now, circling them along the streets that surround the park that is their prison are chain eateries like T.G.I. Friday's, international hotels like the Radisson, and a circle of neon billboards mocking them with brand names like Panasonic, Coke, and GoldStar. New gods, yes, but more liberty? 9

What then does it mean in concrete terms to view Jihad and McWorld dialectically when the tendencies of the two sets of forces initially appear so intractably antithetical? After all, Jihad and McWorld operate with equal strength in opposite directions, the one driven by parochial hatreds, the other by universalizing markets, the one re-creating ancient subnational and ethnic borders from within, the other making national borders porous from without. Yet Jihad and McWorld have this in common: they both make war on the sovereign nation-state and thus undermine the nation-state's democratic institutions. Each eschews civil society and belittles democratic citizenship, neither seeks alternative democratic institutions. Their common thread is indifference to civil liberty. Jihad forges communities of blood rooted in exclusion and hatred, communities that slight democracy in favor of tyrannical paternalism or consensual tribalism. McWorld forges global markets rooted in consumption and profit, leaving to an untrustworthy, if not altogether fictitious, invisible hand issues of public interest and common good that once might have been nurtured by democratic citizenries and their watchful governments. Such governments, intimidated by market ideology, are actually pulling back at the very moment they ought to be aggressively intervening. What was once understood as protecting the public interest is now excoriated as heavy-handed regulatory browbeating. Justice yields to markets, even though, as Felix Rohatyn has bluntly confessed, "there is a 10 brutal Darwinian logic to these markets. They are nervous and greedy. They look for stability and transparency, but what they reward is not always our preferred form of democracy." If the traditional conservators of freedom were democratic constitutions and Bills of Rights, "the new temples to liberty," George Steiner suggests, "will be McDonald's and Kentucky Fried Chicken."

In being reduced to a choice between the market's universal church and   11
a retribalizing politics of particularist identities, peoples around the globe are threatened with an atavistic return to medieval politics where local tribes and ambitious emperors together ruled the world entire, women and men united by the universal abstraction of Christianity even as they lived out isolated lives in warring fiefdoms defined by involuntary (ascriptive) forms of identity. This was a world in which princes and kings had little real power until they conceived the ideology of nationalism. Nationalism established government on a scale greater than the tribe yet less cosmopolitan than the universal church and in time gave birth to those intermediate, gradually more democratic institutions that would come to constitute the nation-state. Today, at the far end of this history, we seem intent on re-creating a world in which our only choices are the secular universalism of the cosmopolitan market and the everyday particularism of the fractious tribe.

In the tumult of the confrontation between global commerce and   12
parochial ethnicity, the virtues of the democratic nation are lost and the instrumentalities by which it permitted peoples to transform themselves into nations and seize sovereign power in the name of liberty and the commonweal are put at risk. Neither Jihad nor McWorld aspires to resecure the civic virtues undermined by its denationalizing practices; neither global markets nor blood communities service public goods or pursue equality and justice. Impartial judiciaries and deliberative assemblies play no role in the roving killer bands that speak on behalf of newly liberated "peoples," and such democratic institutions have at best only marginal influence on the roving multinational corporations that speak on behalf of newly liberated markets. Jihad pursues a bloody politics of identity, McWorld a bloodless economics of profit. Belonging by default to McWorld, everyone is a consumer; seeking a repository for identity, everyone belongs to some tribe. But no one is a citizen. Without citizens, how can there be democracy?

From Self-Determination to Jihad

Not long ago, Daniel Patrick Moynihan predicted that the next half hundred   13
states likely to come into existence over the next fifty years will all be defined by ethnic conflict: that is to say, by civil war. The Soviet Union and Yugoslavia have together already produced twenty or more new (old) "nations" or national fragments. In the most egregious cases, the United Nations sends

peacekeeping forces, although its member nations are increasingly loath to put their soldiers at risk. Currently, it has stationed troops in eighteen countries—in nearly every case, arrayed against forces of domestic insurrection and civil discord. The Carter Center in Atlanta has a still more nuanced and thus expansive list that is more or less mirrored in the forty-eight trouble spots charted by the *New York Times* at the beginning of 1993. Amnesty International reports political prisoners and political executions in more than sixty countries.

In this tumultuous world, the real players are not nations at all but   14
tribes, many of them at war with one another. Their aim is precisely to redraw boundaries in order to divide—say in Kurdish Iraq or Muslim Sudan or Serbian-populated sections of Croatia. Countries like Afghanistan, recently fighting a foreign invader in the name of its national independence, have been effectively dismembered: divided among Panthans, Hazaras, Uzbeks, and Tajiks. This is ethnic membership enhanced via national dismemberment—or by expulsion or expunction of unwanted contaminators, as has occurred in slaughter-happy Rwanda. Is this pandaemonium just an extension of benign efforts at multiculturalism? A natural consequence of a centuries-old impulse to self-determination? Or the appearance of a new disease that has corrupted integral nationalism and opened the way to ethnic and religious Jihad?

Jihad is, I recognize, a strong term. In its mildest form, it betokens reli-   15
gious struggle on behalf of faith, a kind of Islamic zeal. In its strongest political manifestation, it means bloody holy war on behalf of partisan identity that is metaphysically defined and fanatically defended. Thus, while for many Muslims it may signify only ardor in the name of a religion that can properly be regarded as universalizing (if not quite ecumenical), I borrow its meaning from those militants who make the slaughter of the "other" a higher duty. I use the term in its militant construction to suggest dogmatic and violent particularism of a kind known to Christians no less than Muslims, to Germans and Hindis as well as to Arabs. The phenomena to which I apply the phrase have innocent enough beginnings: identity politics and multicultural diversity can represent strategies of a free society trying to give expression to its diversity. What ends as Jihad may begin as a simple search for a local identity, some set of common personal attributes to hold out against the numbing and neutering uniformities of industrial modernization and the colonizing culture of McWorld.

America is often taken as the model for this kind of benign multicultur-   16
alism, although we too have our critics like Arthur Schlesinger, Jr., for whom multiculturalism is never benign and for whom it signals the inaugural logic of a long-term disintegration. Indeed, I will have occasion below to write about an "American Jihad" being waged by the radical Right. The startling

fact is that less than 10 percent (about twenty) of the modern world's states are truly homogenous and thus, like Denmark or the Netherlands, can't get smaller unless they fracture into tribes or clans. In only half is there a single ethnic group that comprises even 75 percent of the population. As in the United States, multiculturalism is the rule, homogeneity the exception. Nations like Japan or Spain that appear to the outside world as integral turn out to be remarkably multicultural. And even if language alone, the nation's essential attribute, is made the condition for self-determination, a count of the number of languages spoken around the world suggests the community of nations could grow to over six thousand members.

The modern nation-state has actually acted as a cultural integrator and   17 has adapted well to pluralist ideals: civic ideologies and constitutional faiths around which their many clans and tribes can rally. It has not been too difficult to contrive a civil religion for Americans or French or Swiss, since these "peoples" actually contain multitudes of subnational factions and ethnic tribes earnestly seeking common ground. But for Basques and Normans? What need have they for anything but blood and memory? And what of Alsatians, Bavarians, and East Prussians? Kurds, Ossetians, East Timorese, Quebecois, Abkhazians, Catalonians, Tamils, Inkatha Zulus, Kurile Islander Japanese—peoples without countries inhabiting nations they cannot call their own? Peoples trying to seal themselves off not just from others but from modernity? These are frightened tribes running not to but from civic faith in search of something more palpable and electrifying. How will peoples who define themselves by the slaughter of tribal neighbors be persuaded to subscribe to some flimsy artificial faith organized around abstract civic ideals or commercial markets? Can advertising divert warriors of blood from the genocide required by their ancient grievances?

Like McWorld, Jihad can of course be painted in bright as well as dark   18 colors. Just as McWorld's sometimes rapacious markets have been advanced in the name of democratic free choice, so Jihad's combative interests can be touted in the name of self-determination. Indeed, the ideology of self-determination may be the source of more than a few of Jihad's pathologies. President Woodrow Wilson's own secretary of state, Robert L. Lansing, failed to share his chief's enthusiasm for the idea, asking would not self-determination "breed discontent, disorder and rebellion? The phrase is simply loaded with dynamite. It will raise hopes which can never be realized. It will, I fear, cost thousands of lives. What a calamity that the phrase was ever uttered! What misery it will cause!"

Lansing's anxieties seem well justified. In Wilson's own time, the politics   19 of self-determination balkanized Europe, fanned nationalist wildfires, and created instabilities that contributed to the rise of fascism. Today there is no tribe, no faction or splinter group or neighborhood gang, that does not aspire to self-determination. "Don't dis me!" shouts the gangsta rapper, "I gotta get some respect." The futile Owen-Vance map for the partition of Bosnia, multiplying boundaries as it narrowed the compass of ethnic communities, finally seemed to give respectability to a gang logic, trying to write into law the absurdity of treating nearly each city block as a nation, almost every housing unit a potential sovereign. In other times, this bankrupt political arrangement, sanctioned for a considerable time by a desperate United Nations Security Council, would carry the name anarchy.

One cannot really blame the cartographers or peacemakers for Jihad's 20 absurdity, however. They do not rearrange the scene, they just take snapshots of it. Multiculturalism has in some places conjured anarchy. Self-determination has at times amounted to little more than other-extermination. Colonial masters did still worse in their time, drawing arbitrary lines across maps they could not read with consequences still being endured throughout the ex-colonial world, above all in Africa and the Middle East. Jihad is then a rabid response to colonialism and imperialism and their economic children, capitalism and modernity; it is diversity run amok, multiculturalism turned cancerous so that the cells keep dividing long after their division has ceased to serve the healthy corpus.

Even traditionally homogenous integral nations have reason to feel anx- 21 ious about the prospect of Jihad. The rising economic and communications interdependence of the world means that such nations, however unified internally, must nonetheless operate in an increasingly multicultural global environment. Ironically, a world that is coming together pop culturally and commercially is a world whose discrete subnational ethnic and religious and racial parts are also far more in evidence, in no small part as a reaction to McWorld. Forced into incessant contact, postmodern nations cannot sequester their idiosyncracies. Post-Maastricht Europe, while it falls well short of earlier ambitions, has become integrated enough to force a continent-wide multicultural awareness whose consequences have by no means been happy, let alone unifying. The more "Europe" hoves into view, the more reluctant and self-aware its national constituents become. What Günter Grass said of Germany—"unified, the Germans were more disunited than ever"— applies in spades to Europe and the world beyond: integrated, it is more disintegral than ever.

Responding to McWorld, parochial forces defend and deny, reject and 22 repel modernity wherever they find it. But they also absorb and assimilate, utilizing the native's strategy against every colonizer to have crossed a border since the Romans came to Gaul. When the Hilton came to the Hills of Buda, a local architect grafted the new structure onto a thirteenth-century monastery. When the French restored the Champs Élysées to its former glory, they banished the arch from McDonald's. When American music

invaded the Caribbean, Orlando Patterson reminds us, the Caribbean reacted with enormous music production of its own, of which reggae is only
one well-known example. Yet to think that indigenization and globalization
are entirely coequal forces that put Jihad and McWorld on an equal footing
is to vastly underestimate the force of the new planetary markets. The Budapest Hilton's "monastery" houses a casino; Paris's McDonald's serves Big
Macs and fries with or without the arch; reggae gets only a tiny percentage
of MTV play time even in Latin markets. It's no contest.

A pattern of feudal relations does, however, persist. And so we are re-   23
turned to the metaphor of feudalism, that puzzling world of fragments knit
together by the abstraction of Christianity. Today's abstraction is the consumers' market, no less universal for all its insistent materialist secularism.
Following McDonald's golden arch from country to country, the market
traces a trajectory of dollars and bonds and ads and yen and stocks and currency transactions that reaches right around the globe. Grass's observation
works the other way around as well: disunited, pulled apart by Jihad, the
world is more united than ever. And more interdependent as well.

The Smalling World of McWorld

Even the most developed, supposedly self-sufficient nations can no longer   24
pretend to genuine sovereignty. That is the meaning of *ecology,* a term that
marks the final obsolescence of all man-made boundaries. When it comes to
acid rain or oil spills or depleted fisheries or tainted groundwater or fluoro-
carbon propellants or radiation leaks or toxic wastes or sexually transmitted
diseases, national frontiers are simply irrelevant. Toxins don't stop for customs inspections and microbes don't carry passports. North America became
a water and air free-trade zone long before NAFTA loosened up the market
in goods.

The environmental tocsin has been sounded, loudly and often, and   25
there is little to add here to the prodigious literature warning of a biospher-
ical Armageddon. We have learned well enough how easily the German
forests can be devastated by Swiss and Italians driving gas-guzzling road-
sters fueled by leaded gas (the Europeans are far behind the Americans in controlling lead). We know that the planet can be asphyxiated by
greenhouse gases because Brazilian farmers want to be part of the twentieth century and are burning down their tropical rain forests to clear a little
land to plow, and because many Indonesians make a living out of convert-
ing their lush jungles into toothpicks for fastidious Japanese diners, upset-
ting the delicate oxygen balance and puncturing our global lungs.

Ecological interdependence is, however, reactive: a consequence of nat-   26
ural forces we cannot predict or fully control. But McWorld's interdepen-

dence and the limits it places on sovereignty is more a matter of positive economic forces that have globalism as their conscious object. It is these economic and commercial forces—the latest round in capitalism's long-standing search for world markets and global consumers—that are the primary subject of this book.

Every demarcated national economy and every kind of public good is   27 today vulnerable to the inroads of transnational commerce. Markets abhor frontiers as nature abhors a vacuum. Within their expansive and permeable domains, interests are private, trade is free, currencies are convertible, access to banking is open, contracts are enforceable (the state's sole legitimate economic function), and the laws of production and consumption are sovereign, trumping the laws of legislatures and courts. In Europe, Asia, and the Americas such markets have already eroded national sovereignty and given birth to a new class of institutions—international banks, trade associations, transnational lobbies like OPEC, world news services like CNN and the BBC, and multinational corporations—institutions that lack distinctive national identities and neither reflect nor respect nationhood as an organizing or a regulative principle. While mills and factories sit somewhere on sovereign territory under the eye and potential regulation of nation-states, currency markets and the Internet exist everywhere, but nowhere in particular. Without an address or a national affiliation, they are altogether beyond the devices of sovereignty. Even products are becoming anonymous: whose national workforce do you fault on a defective integrated circuit labeled:

> Made in one or more of the following countries: Korea, Hong Kong, Malaysia, Singapore, Taiwan, Mauritius, Thailand, Indonesia, Mexico, Philippines. The exact country of origin is unknown.

How are the social and political demands of responsibility preserved under such remarkable circumstances?

The market imperative has in fact reinforced the quest for international   28 peace and stability, requisites of an efficient international economy, without improving the chances for civic responsibility, accountability, or democracy, which may or may not benefit from commerce and free markets and which, although it depends on peace, is not synonymous with it. The claim that democracy and markets are twins has become a commonplace of statesmanship, especially in light of the demise of state socialism, which has left capitalism's zealots free to regard themselves not only as victors in the Cold War but as the true champions of a democracy that (they are certain) markets alone make possible. Thus have they managed to parlay the already controversial claim that markets are free into the even more controversial claim that market freedom entails and even defines democracy. President Clinton employed the phrase *democratic markets* as a mantra during his historic visit to Eastern Europe and Russia at the beginning of 1994. His foreign policy aides have consistently done the same.

This stealth rhetoric that assumes capitalist interests are not only compatible with but actively advance democratic ideals, translated into policy, is difficult to reconcile with the international realities of the last fifty years. Market economies have shown a remarkable adaptability and have flourished in many tyrannical states from Chile to South Korea, from Panama to Singapore. Indeed, the state with one of the world's least democratic governments—the People's Republic of China—possesses one of the world's fastest-growing market economies. "Communist" Vietnam is not far behind, and was opened to American trade recently, presumably on the strength of the belief that markets ultimately defeat ideology. Capitalism requires consumers with access to markets and a stable political climate in order to succeed: such conditions may or may not be fostered by democracy, which can be disorderly and even anarchic, especially in its early stages, and which often pursues public goods costly to or at odds with private-market imperatives—environmentalism or full employment for example. On the level of the individual, capitalism seeks consumers susceptible to the shaping of their needs and the manipulation of their wants while democracy needs citizens autonomous in their thoughts and independent in their deliberative judgments. Aleksandr Solzhenitsyn wishes to "tame savage capitalism," but capitalism wishes to tame anarchic democracy and appears to have little problem tolerating tyranny as long as it secures stability.

Certainly the hurried pursuit of free markets regardless of social consequences has put democratic development in jeopardy in many nations recently liberated from communism. Social insecurity and rampant unemployment for peoples accustomed to the cradle-to-the-grave ministrations of paternalistic socialist bureaucracies are unlikely to convert them to a system of democracy for which they have otherwise had no preparation. This is perhaps why majorities in all but a handful of ex-Soviet lands have been busy reelecting former Communist officials (usually wearing new party labels and carrying new ideological doctrines) to their new democratic legislatures. In economist Robert McIntyre's blunt words: "Communists and former Communists are winning because the Western economic advice has led to pointless, dysfunctional pain, while failing to set the foundations for politically and socially viable future growth." The right to choose between nine VCR models or a dozen automobile brands does not necessarily feel like freedom to workers whose monthly salaries can hardly keep up with the rising price of bread, let alone to women and men with no jobs at all. Capitalists may be democrats but capitalism does not need or entail democracy. And capitalism certainly does not need the nation-state that has been democracy's most promising host.

This is not to criticize capitalism in and of itself: joint-stock, limited- 31
liability corporations are quite properly interested primarily in profits and
pursue civic liberty and social justice only where they do not interfere with
the bottom line. Indeed, they have certain conspicuous virtues beyond their
intrinsic economic utilities like efficiency, productivity, elasticity, profitabil-
ity. They are enemies of parochialism, isolation, fractiousness, and war and
are hostile to constraints on economic choice and social mobility, although
this hardly makes them friends of justice. Market psychology also can attenuate the psychology of ideological and religious cleavages and nurture
concord among producers and consumers, identities that ill-suit Jihad's narrowly conceived ethnic or religious cultures. But it also undermines the psychology of skeptical inquiry upon which autonomous judgment and
resistance to manipulation are founded. In the world of McWorld, the alternative to dogmatic traditionalism may turn out to be materialist consumerism
or relativistic secularism or merely a profitable corruption. Democracy's ties
to McWorld are at best contingent. Shopping, it is true, has little tolerance for
blue laws, whether dictated by pub-closing British paternalism, Sabbath-
observing Jewish Orthodoxy, or no-Sunday-liquor-sales Massachusetts Puri-
tanism; but intolerance for blue laws is hardly a condition for constitutional
faith or a respect for due process. In the context of common markets, international law has largely ceased to be a vision of justice and has become a
workaday framework for getting things done: enforcing contracts, certifying
deals, regulating trade and currency relations, and supervising mergers or
bankruptcies. Moralists used to complain that international law was impo-
tent in curbing the injustices of nation-states, but it has shown even less capacity to rein in markets that, after all, do not even have an address to which
subpoenas can be sent. As the product of a host of individual choices or singular corporate acts, markets offer no collective responsibility. Yet responsibility is the first obligation of both citizens and civic institutions.

While they produce neither common interests nor common law, com- 32
mon markets do demand, along with a common currency, a common language; moreover, they produce common behaviors of the kind bred by
cosmopolitan city life everywhere. Commercial pilots, computer programmers, film directors, international bankers, media specialists, oil riggers, entertainment celebrities, ecology experts, movie producers, demographers,
accountants, professors, lawyers, athletes—these compose a new breed of
men and women for whom religion, culture, and ethnic nationality are marginal elements in a working identity. Although sociologists of everyday life
will continue to distinguish a Japanese from an American mode, shopping
has a common signature throughout the world. Cynics might even suggest
that some of the recent revolutions in Eastern Europe had as their true goal
not liberty and the right to vote but well-paying jobs and the right to shop.

Shopping means consumption and consumption depends on the fabrication of needs as well as of goods in what I will call the infotainment telesector of the service economy.

McWorld is a product of popular culture driven by expansionist com-　　33 merce. Its template is American, its form style. Its goods are as much images as matériel, an aesthetic as well as a product line. It is about culture as commodity, apparel as ideology. Its symbols are Harley-Davidson motorcycles and Cadillac motorcars hoisted from the roadways, where they once represented a mode of transportation, to the marquees of global market cafés like Harley-Davidson's and the Hard Rock where they become icons of lifestyle. You don't drive them, you feel their vibes and rock to the images they conjure up from old movies and new celebrities, whose personal appearances are the key to the wildly popular international café chain Planet Hollywood. Music, video, theater, books, and theme parks—the new churches of a commercial civilization in which malls are the public squares and suburbs the neighborless neighborhoods—are all constructed as image exports creating a common world taste around common logos, advertising slogans, stars, songs, brand names, jingles, and trademarks. Hard power yields to soft, while ideology is transmuted into a kind of videology that works through sound bites and film clips. Videology is fuzzier and less dogmatic than traditional political ideology: it may as a consequence be far more successful in instilling the novel values required for global markets to succeed.

McWorld's videology remains Jihad's most formidable rival, and in the　　34 long run it may attenuate the force of Jihad's recidivist tribalisms. Yet the information revolution's instrumentalities are also Jihad's favored weapons. Hutu or Bosnian Serb identity was less a matter of real historical memory than of media propaganda by a leadership set on liquidating rival clans. In both Rwanda and Bosnia, radio broadcasts whipped listeners into a killing frenzy. As *New York Times* rock critic Jon Pareles has noticed, "regionalism in pop music has become as trendy as microbrewery beer and narrowcasting cable channels, and for the same reasons." The global culture is what gives the local culture its medium, its audience, and its aspirations. Fascist pop and Hasid rock are not oxymorons; rather they manifest the dialectics of McWorld in particularly dramatic ways. Belgrade's radio includes stations that broadcast Western pop music as a rebuke to hard-liner Milosevic's supernationalist government and stations that broadcast native folk tunes laced with antiforeign and anti-Semitic sentiments. Even the Internet has its neo-Nazi bulletin boards and Turk-trashing Armenian "flamers" (who assail every use of the word *turkey,* fair and fowl alike, so to speak), so that the abstractions of cyberspace too are infected with a peculiar and rabid cultural territoriality all their own.

The dynamics of the Jihad-McWorld linkage are deeply dialectical. Japan has, for example, become more culturally insistent on its own traditions in recent years even as its people seek an ever greater purchase on McWorld. In 1992, the number-one restaurant in Japan measured by volume of customers was McDonald's, followed in the number-two spot by the Colonel's Kentucky Fried Chicken. In France, where cultural purists complain bitterly of a looming Sixième République ("la République Américaine"), the government attacks "franglais" even as it funds EuroDisney park just outside of Paris. In the same spirit, the cinema industry makes war on American film imports while it bestows upon Sylvester Stallone one of France's highest honors, the Chevalier des arts et lettres. Ambivalence also stalks India. Just outside of Bombay, cheek by jowl with villages still immersed in poverty and notorious for the informal execution of unwanted female babies or, even, wives, can be found a new town known as SCEEPZ—the Santa Cruz Electronic Export Processing Zone—where Hindi-, Tamil-, and Mahratti-speaking computer programmers write software for Swissair, AT&T, and other labor-cost-conscious multinationals. India is thus at once a major exemplar of ancient ethnic and religious tensions and "an emerging power in the international software industry." To go to work at SCEEPZ, says an employee, is "like crossing an international border." Not into another country, but into the virtual nowhere-land of McWorld.

More dramatic even than in India, is the strange interplay of Jihad and McWorld in the remnants of Yugoslavia. In an affecting *New Republic* report, Slavenka Drakulic recently told the brief tragic love story of Admira and Bosko, two young star-crossed lovers from Sarajevo: "They were born in the late 1960's," she writes. "They watched Spielberg movies; they listened to Iggy Pop; they read John le Carré; they went to a disco every Saturday night and fantasized about traveling to Paris or London." Longing for safety, it seems they finally negotiated with all sides for safe passage, and readied their departure from Sarajevo. Before they could cross the magical border that separates their impoverished land from the seeming sanctuary of McWorld, Jihad caught up to them. Their bodies lay along the riverbank, riddled with bullets from anonymous snipers for whom safe passage signaled an invitation to target practice. The murdered young lovers, as befits émigrés to McWorld, were clothed in jeans and sneakers. So too, one imagines, were their murderers.

Further east, tourists seeking a piece of old Russia that does not take them too far from MTV can find traditional Matryoshka nesting dolls (that fit one inside the other) featuring the nontraditional visages of (from largest to smallest) Bruce Springsteen, Madonna, Boy George, Dave Stewart, and Annie Lennox.

In Russia, in India, in Bosnia, in Japan, and in France too, modern his-   38
tory then leans both ways: toward the meretricious inevitability of McWorld,
but also into Jihad's stiff winds, heaving to and fro and giving heart both to
the Panglossians and the Pandoras, sometimes for the very same reasons.
The Panglossians bank on EuroDisney and Microsoft, while the Pandoras
await nihilism and a world in Pandaemonium. Yet McWorld and Jihad do
not really force a choice between such polarized scenarios. Together, they
are likely to produce some stifling amalgam of the two suspended in chaos.
Antithetical in every detail, Jihad and McWorld nonetheless conspire to undermine our hard-won (if only half-won) civil liberties and the possibility of
a global democratic future. In the short run the forces of Jihad, noisier and
more obviously nihilistic than those of McWorld, are likely to dominate the
near future, etching small stories of local tragedy and regional genocide on
the face of our times and creating a climate of instability marked by multi-
microwars inimical to global integration. But in the long run, the forces of
McWorld are the forces underlying the slow certain thrust of Western civilization and as such may be unstoppable. Jihad's microwars will hold the
headlines well into the next century, making predictions of the end of history look terminally dumb. But McWorld's homogenization is likely to establish a macropeace that favors the triumph of commerce and its markets
and to give to those who control information, communication, and entertainment ultimate (if inadvertent) control over human destiny. Unless we
can offer an alternative to the struggle between Jihad and McWorld, the
epoch on whose threshold we stand—postcommunist, postindustrial, post-
national, yet sectarian, fearful, and bigoted—is likely also to be terminally
postdemocratic.

Working with the Text

1. The two basic forces that Barber speaks about—Jihad vs. McWorld—
   are not separate or exclusive, but rather interdependent in many ways.
   What are at least two ways that he talks about their interdependence?
   He talks about their relationship as a "dialectic" one: What does he
   mean by that? Is it possible for one to exist without the other?

2. In a number of places Barber focuses on distinctions between capitalism and democracy, critiquing the claims of "capitalism's zealots" that
   "market freedom entails and even defines democracy." For example,
   he discusses differing tendencies between capitalism and democracy in
   saying that "On the level of the individual, capitalism seeks consumers
   susceptible to the shaping of their needs and the manipulation of their
   wants while democracy needs citizens autonomous in their thoughts
   and independent in their deliberative judgments." Elsewhere he para-

phrases some "cynics" who suggest that "freedom" and "democracy" are less about the "right to vote" than the "right to shop." What are the possible conflicts and alliances between democracy and capitalism as he describes them and as you see them? We tend to think of them as going hand in hand, but are there contradictions? How do the factors of capitalism and consumerism influence the two tendencies of Jihad and McWorld (tribalism and globalism)? Barber claims McWorld is all about "global markets." In what ways do these global markets enhance freedom and in what ways do they not?

3. How do the two forces of Jihad and McWorld relate to the issue of freedom and rights? Barber argues that both tribal communities and global markets share an "indifference to civil liberty"—that civil liberties, like citizenship, are the property of nations, and both Jihad and McWorld are hostile to nations and nationalism. Yet, both forces also seem to bear on individual liberties as well. Which of these two forces leads to more or less liberty? What different kinds of freedoms or liberties are implied by Barber's discussion? What is the relationship between group identity and self-determination and individual liberty and freedom?

4. It is possible to see the Internet and the World Wide Web as embodying and facilitating both of these tendencies. That is, the network of the World Wide Web makes possible both global and tribal connections. In pairs, do some research on the Web and locate one example for each tendency. What would you consider a "tribal" tendency of the Web, and a "global" one? What about "national" interests (the cultural force left out in the tension between Jihad and McWorld)? Are there any ways that the WWW fosters national identity? Or are the identifications one finds on the Web either bigger or smaller than the "national"?

Yes, This Is About Islam

SALMAN RUSHDIE

Born in Bombay, Salman Rushdie is an author, novelist, essayist, and critic; he currently lives in New York City. He is the author of over a dozen books, including *Shame, Midnight's Children*, and *The Ground Beneath her Feet*. His controversial 1989 book, *Satanic Verses*, was awarded the Whitbread Prize but was condemned by orthodox Muslims around the world and banned from many countries including India. The Ayatollah Khomeini issued a "fatwah" against Rushdie, calling for his immediate assassination. Forced to go into hiding, Rushdie's whereabouts remained unknown for several years. During that period, he granted an interview to David Frost for PBS in which he stated, "I do not envy people who think they have a complete explanation of the world, for the simple reason that they are obviously wrong." Rushdie has emerged from hiding, but must constantly be accompanied by bodyguards. As is evident in the following op-ed piece he recently wrote for the *New York Times*, Rushdie remains an outspoken critic of Islam.

LONDON—"This isn't about Islam." The world's leaders have been repeating this mantra for weeks, partly in the virtuous hope of deterring reprisal attacks on innocent Muslims living in the West, partly because if the United States is to maintain its coalition against terror it can't afford to suggest that Islam and terrorism are in any way related.

The trouble with this necessary disclaimer is that it isn't true. If this isn't about Islam, why the worldwide Muslim demonstrations in support of Osama bin Laden and Al Qaeda? Why did those 10,000 men armed with swords and axes mass on the Pakistan-Afghanistan frontier, answering some mullah's call to jihad? Why are the war's first British casualties three Muslim men who died fighting on the Taliban side?

Why the routine anti-Semitism of the much-repeated Islamic slander that "the Jews" arranged the hits on the World Trade Center and the Pentagon, with the oddly self-deprecating explanation offered by the Taliban leadership, among others, that Muslims could not have the technological know-how or organizational sophistication to pull off such a feat? Why does Imran Khan, the Pakistani ex-sports star turned politician, demand to be shown the evidence of Al Qaeda's guilt while apparently turning a deaf ear to the self-incriminating statements of Al Qaeda's own spokesmen (there will be a rain of aircraft from the skies, Muslims in the West are warned not to live or work in tall buildings)? Why all the talk about American military infidels desecrating the sacred soil of Saudi Arabia if some sort of definition of what is sacred is not at the heart of the present discontents?

Of course this is "about Islam." The question is, what exactly does that   4
mean? After all, most religious belief isn't very theological. Most Muslims are not profound Koranic analysts. For a vast number of "believing" Muslim men, "Islam" stands, in a jumbled, half-examined way, not only for the fear of God—the fear more than the love, one suspects—but also for a cluster of customs, opinions and prejudices that include their dietary practices; the sequestration or near-sequestration of "their" women; the sermons delivered by their mullahs of choice; a loathing of modern society in general, riddled as it is with music, godlessness and sex; and a more particularized loathing (and fear) of the prospect that their own immediate surroundings could be taken over—"Westoxicated"—by the liberal Western-style way of life.

Highly motivated organizations of Muslim men (oh, for the voices of   5
Muslim women to be heard!) have been engaged over the last 30 years or so in growing radical political movements out of this mulch of "belief." These Islamists—we must get used to this word, "Islamists," meaning those who are engaged upon such political projects, and learn to distinguish it from the more general and politically neutral "Muslim"—include the Muslim Brotherhood in Egypt, the blood-soaked combatants of the Islamic Salvation Front and Armed Islamic Group in Algeria, the Shiite revolutionaries of Iran, and the Taliban. Poverty is their great helper, and the fruit of their efforts is paranoia. This paranoid Islam, which blames outsiders, "infidels," for all the ills of Muslim societies, and whose proposed remedy is the closing of those societies to the rival project of modernity, is presently the fastest growing version of Islam in the world.

This is not wholly to go along with Samuel Huntington's thesis about the   6
clash of civilizations, for the simple reason that the Islamists' project is turned not only against the West and "the Jews," but also against their fellow Islamists. Whatever the public rhetoric, there's little love lost between the Taliban and Iranian regimes. Dissensions between Muslim nations run at least as deep, if not deeper, than those nations' resentment of the West. Nevertheless, it would be absurd to deny that this self-exculpatory, paranoiac Islam is an ideology with widespread appeal.

Twenty years ago, when I was writing a novel about power struggles in   7
a fictionalized Pakistan, it was already de rigueur in the Muslim world to blame all its troubles on the West and, in particular, the United States. Then as now, some of these criticisms were well-founded; no room here to

rehearse the geopolitics of the cold war and America's frequently damaging foreign policy "tilts," to use the Kissinger term, toward (or away from) this or that temporarily useful (or disapproved-of) nation-state, or America's role in the installation and deposition of sundry unsavory leaders and regimes. But I wanted them to ask a question that is no less important now: Suppose we say that the ills of our societies are not primarily America's fault, that we are to blame for our own failings? How would we understand them then? Might we not, by accepting our own responsibility for our problems, begin to learn to solve them for ourselves?

Many Muslims, as well as secularist analysts with roots in the Muslim world, are beginning to ask such questions now. In recent weeks Muslim voices have everywhere been raised against the obscurantist hijacking of their religion. Yesterday's hotheads (among them Yusuf Islam, aka Cat Stevens) are improbably repackaging themselves as today's pussycats.   8

An Iraqi writer quotes an earlier Iraqi satirist: "The disease that is in us, is from us." A British Muslim writes, "Islam has become its own enemy." A Lebanese friend, returning from Beirut, tells me that in the aftermath of the attacks on Sept. 11, public criticism of Islamism has become much more outspoken. Many commentators have spoken of the need for a Reformation in the Muslim world.   9

I'm reminded of the way noncommunist socialists used to distance themselves from the tyrannical socialism of the Soviets; nevertheless, the first stirrings of this counterproject are of great significance. If Islam is to be reconciled with modernity, these voices must be encouraged until they swell into a roar. Many of them speak of another Islam, their personal, private faith.   10

The restoration of religion to the sphere of the personal, its depoliticization, is the nettle that all Muslim societies must grasp in order to become modern. The only aspect of modernity interesting to the terrorists is technology, which they see as a weapon that can be turned on its makers. If terrorism is to be defeated, the world of Islam must take on board the secularist-humanist principles on which the modern is based, and without which Muslim countries' freedom will remain a distant dream.   11

Working with the Text

1. What distinction does Rushdie make between "Muslims" and "Islamists"? Why is the difference significant to our understanding of current international tensions between the East and the West?

2. What are the conditions that contribute to the emergence of collectivities around religious identification? Are ethnic, religious,

and national identifications one and the same or are they seen as analytically distinct phenomena in this text?

3. What does Rushdie propose as the *proper* role of religion in what we might call a "post-national" and globalized age? How does he understand the relationship between religion and freedom? Between religion and modernity?

4. "Dissensions between Muslim nations run at least as deep, if not deeper, than those nations' resentment of the West," argues Rushdie. How does he account for this? What does this imply in terms of the Muslim world's responsibility for current acts of terrorism?

5. In order for the Islamic world to enter into the modern world, it needs to undergo a "Reformation" in which religion is separated from politics, suggests Rushdie. Some might see this imposed separation of church and state as in effect an attempt to take over and "Westoxicate" the East. What do you think? Answer in an essay.

One Whiteness Veils Three Uglinesses

From Border-Crossing to a Womanist Interrogation of Gendered Colorism
WEN SHU LEE

A native of Taiwan, Wen Shu Lee earned her Ph.D. at the University of Southern California. She is currently a professor in Communications Studies at San Jose State University. Lee's work on gender and interpersonal and intercultural communication has appeared in *Communication and Identity Across Cultures* (1998), the *Quarterly Journal of Speech* (1998), and *The Public Voice in a Democracy at Risk*. She has also written on humor and idiom, "translating" taken-for-granted knowledge across cultural borders for *The American Communications Review*. Much of Lee's recent work is in the field of whiteness studies. In the following essay from the anthology *Whiteness Identity* (1999), Lee illuminates a number of the theoretical foundations underlying whiteness studies and analyzes constructions of whiteness in domestic and international contexts. Specifically, Lee explores the color codes of American culture, performing what she describes in the subtitle as "a womanist interrogation of colorism."

For when what is given as natural needs to be torn apart, language be-comes as vulnerable as skin, and the body, quivering in its newness, must lay itself open to fresh forms of otherness.

—*Meena Alexander,* The Shock of Arrival *(1996, p. 171)*

Womanist is to feminist as purple to lavender.

—*Alice Walker,* In Search of Our Mothers' Gardens *(1983, p. xii)*

Whiteness, if held "naturally" as a transparent, colorless term, marks a race-free world from a world occupied by people of color—black, brown, red, and yellow. At the same time, this marking corresponds to real social gains, what David Roediger (1991), following W. E. B. DuBois, calls the "wages" of whiteness (p. 12). Put differently, in the United States, color words, red, white, yellow, black, and brown, not only *racialize* people, but rank order them hierarchically to parcel out different social and material interests.

The Many Hues of "Blackness"

I was surprised to read about the many colors used by Alice Walker (1983) to describe black people.[1] A black woman who is halfway between light and dark is a "brown" person (p. 291) or a "yellow-skinned" person (p. 303, see footnote). Then, there are "black black women" and "light-skinned" or "cream-colored" black women. These differently color-coded black women have been historically arranged by the "color-struck black society" (p. 299) into "light as right" and "dark as problem."

When Walker was growing up during the 1950s, color codes also dictated different compliments, a form of social capital. "Beautiful" was reserved for white women. Light-skinned black women might receive a few "handsomes" and "pretty." "Medium browns like me," says Walker, "might evoke 'good-looking' or 'fine.'" (p. 292). In addition to compliments, black women of light skin are more likely to be the "prizes" sought after by both black and white men (often of greater means). "Superiority" is bestowed on them rather than on black black women. But black women of light skin are merely "co-opted" into a colorism encouraged by a racist, sexist, and classicist society.

It was black black women (women kidnapped from Africa) who were raped and had their children sold by white masters many years ago. Yet many years later, black black skin still occupies the bottom of a colorist hierarchy even within black communities. To tear away such inequity, we need to begin with ourselves, and we need to go to black black women. But such a process is not easy! "A necessary act of liberation within myself was to acknowledge the beauty of black black women," writes Walker (1983), "but I was always aware I was swimming against the tide" (p. 292). Reading Walker's criticism of gendered colorism within black communities in the United States opened up an old wound in me, one that had been written out of my consciousness. Forgotten! It is to my "swimming against the tide" in Taiwan that I will now turn.

The Many Hues of "Yellowness"

In Taiwan, I rarely label myself as an Asian or Oriental. When Chinese, a label more specific than Asian, is used, it is invariably in a plural form—"we Chinese." This plurality marks the difference between us "Chinese" and the "Japanese," who are derogatorily named as "devils from the Eastern ocean" (*Dong Yang Guei Zi*). "Chinese" also differentiates us from Europeans and Euro-Americans, who are called "devils from across the ocean" (*Yang Guei Zi*). "The yellow race" (*Huang Zhong Ren*) is seldom brought up in daily conversations, and we certainly never think of ourselves as a "peril." On rare occasions is "the yellow race" used to mark foreign imperialists' racial discrimination against us Chinese in the 19th and 20th centuries. 5

At the same time, there is a color line within Taiwanese (and Chinese) cultures, and in some ways, it is just as brutal as the one I discussed earlier. To "tear apart" the colorism in my culture, I shall introduce the Chinese words associated with blackness and whiteness below. This is made necessary by the different associations connected with black and white as color in my culture. 6

BLACKNESS AND WHITENESS IN CHINESE EXPRESSIONS

There are two words to denote "blackness" in Mandarin, *Wu* and *Hei*. The first word, *Wu* (烏), literally refers to the crow. It is used in classical texts. I will offer two examples. The first is *Wu Yi Men Di* (烏衣門第). Literally, it means the crow-clothing residence. It marks families that are aristocratic, wealthy, and established rather than common and poor. We may trace this expression back to the Dong Jing period when Crow-Clothing Alley was the area where the Wang and Sheh, two extremely influential families, resided. Another expression, *Wu He Zhi Zhong* (烏合之眾) refers to an expediently and hastily organized group of people, like the crows. Such a group differs from groups that are organized by an established order or via shared ideology and values. Next, let me share with you another Mandarin word that refers to blackness, *Hei* (黑). 7

BOX 14.1: Chinese Expressions Related to Blackness, "Hei"

I. The First Set of Expressions Related to *Hei,* Blackness
Hei Shih, the black market—unofficially regulated places where people can exchange things not approved by the government
Hei Huah, black talk—secret codes used among secret society members
Hei Mu, black curtain—secrets or conspiracy violating rules and regulations
Hei Ming Dan, black list—a list of names of those officially under surveillance by the government or the status quo

II. The Second Set of Expressions Related to *Hei,* Blackness
Hei Xing, the black heart/mind—ferocious and poisonous mind
Hei An Shih Jei, black and dark world—a world of no justice, of oppression
Hei Bai Feng Ming, differentiating blackness from whiteness—knowing the difference between right and wrong
Hei Bai Feng Ming, differentiating blackness from whiteness—knowing the difference between right and wrong

III. The Third Set of Expressions Related to *Hei,* Blackness
Hei Ma, black horse—a person who is not expected to win or is not in the running yet wins the contest
Bei Hei Guo, carrying a black wok—a person who is chosen to bear the brunt of blame (black wok) even though he or she is innocent

---

Hei is both a classical and contemporary word, and is used more frequently than *Wu* in daily conversations. To facilitate my discussion, I will group expressions related to *Hei* into three different sets (see Box 14.1). The first set pertains to a world that is unofficial and secretive, as opposed to a world that is authorized and endorsed by the government. Let me elaborate further. *Hei Shi* or black market refers to the market where one may buy and sell items illegally. *Hei Huah* or black talk, the second expression in this set, refers to coded talk in the "black" (i.e., underworld) society as opposed to the talk used by law-abiding citizens. The third expression in this set, *Hei Mu,* black curtain, refers to a situation where one does not accomplish one's goals as expected because of one's failure to gauge layers of conspiracy and behind-the-scene maneuvering. Finally, *Hei Ming Dan,* black list, refers to a secret list of individuals (i.e., rebels or dissenters) who are under surveillance by those in power. Next, let me discuss the second set of expressions related to *Hei.*

Hei in this set refers to the wrong, the poisonous, and the unjust. It is the opposite of the right, the good, and the just. For example, *Hei Xing,* black heart/mind, refers to an individual who takes pleasure in framing people, setting people up for a downfall, and taking advantage of the innocent and the virtuous. *Hei An Shih Jei* refers to a world where people suffer from oppression and injustice. Finally, *Hei Bai Feng Ming,* the ability to differentiate wrong from right, is usually used by Chinese elders and teachers to caution their juniors against immoral conduct. 9

Finally, the meanings of *Hei* in the last set are miscellaneous. They have to do with an unexpected winning force as in *Hei Ma,* the black horse. For example, in 1948, Harry Truman was a *Hei Ma* when he won the presidential election against Thomas Dewey. *Bei Hei Guo,* carrying a black wok, refers to an individual who bears the brunt of blame for something she or he did not do. I have shared with you three sets of Chinese expressions related to *Hei* (blackness). I now turn to *Bai* (白), which means whiteness in Mandarin. 10

Like *Hei, Bai* is used in both contemporary and classical Chinese. I will list two sets of expressions related to *Bai* (see Box 14.2). *Bai* in the first set carries negative meanings. *Bai Zhi,* white word/s, refers to incorrect words. It is often used by school teachers to scold pupils for not using the correct Chinese characters in their homework. *Bai Chai,* white eating, refers to a situation in which an individual does not pay for what she or he eats/consumes. Parents often use this expression (white eating and white drinking) to refer to their adult children who live at home without paying for food and rent. It may also refer to a friend who comes to visit without bringing a 11

BOX 14.2: Chinese Expressions Related to Whiteness, "Bai"

I. The First Set of Expressions Related to *Bai,* Whiteness
Bai Zi, white word—incorrect word
Bai Chi or *Bai Shi,* white eating—to eat without paying
Bai Shuo, white speaking—speaking in vain
Bai Chi, white dumbness—idiot or a person who is dumb, unintelligent

II. The Second Set of Expressions Related to *Bai,* Whitness
Bai Sheng, white body—ordinary people who did not obtain official rank through the civil examination system during the dynastic periods
Bai Yi Gong Qing or *Bai Yi Zai Xiang,* white attired high officials—people who have no official rank but are as capable and distinguished as the high officials

gift and who has the habit of overstaying for dinner. The third expression in this set, *Bai Shuo,* white speaking, means speaking in vain. It marks the feeling of frustration, futility. A person who repeatedly tries to convince an individual to do things without success often complains, "I have done white speaking. I have said lots of useless words!" The last expression, *Bai Chi,* means white dumbness. It may refer to a mentally retarded person or to a person who is clueless or unintelligent. For example, scolding a student who fails to follow the most basic instruction for an assignment, a teacher may say, "You are really a white dumbness." An individual who fails to notice the most obvious sign of romantic advancement from an eager suitor may be called " a big white dumbness!" by his or her friend. Now, let me discuss the second set of expressions related to *Bai.*

Bai in the second set refers to ordinary people who do not have official 12 titles or ranks, in contrast to those who are in office. The expression *Bai Yi Gong Qing* affirms an observation that those who do not have official ranks can be just as intelligent and distinguished. This is an implicit criticism of the centuries-old Chinese bureaucracy, which awards those who have mastered the art of ingratiation. Regardless of their learnedness and competence, those who are critical of governmental practices are often exiles.

The above commonly used Chinese terms associated with *Hei* (black- 13 ness) and *Bai* (whiteness) do not reflect a discursive world in which blackness is *invariably* bad, unjust, negative, and inferior while whiteness is *invariably* pure, good, innocent, positive, and superior. The differences marked by these two concepts are in fact mixed, ambiguous, and on the border between the good and the bad, the official and the secretive, the dynastic and the ordinary.

GENDERED COLORISM IN CHINESE CULTURE

Bai and *Hei* take a different meaning when related to skin tones. Skin in Man- 14 darin is *Pifu* (皮膚). Skin tone is marked discursively into *Hei Pifu* (黑皮膚), literally translated as "black skin," and *Bai Pifu* (白皮膚), translated as "white skin." However, *Hei Pifu* does not refer to black skin as defined in the United States, and *Bai Pifu* does not refer to white skin, either. Translated more appropriately, *Hei Pifu* means dark skin and *Bai Pifu* light skin.

Colorism in Chinese society is like the hierarchy of skin tones in black 15 communities discussed by Alice Walker. For Chinese girls and women, *Bai Pifu* is linked to beauty, while *Hei Pifu* is interpreted as something undesirable. For a girl who has relatively "black" skin, the best redeeming feature for her looks is found in the expression, "She is red sugar year cake" *(Hong Tang Nien Gao).* "Red sugar" in Mandarin refers to "brown sugar" in English. This expression indicates that her skin is unfortunately as dark as "red" sugar, but she is like the sugar year cake, a sought-after dessert specially made for Chinese Lunar New Year. Her sweetness—being cheerful and adorable—is a saving grace because it can compensate a little bit for her darkness/blackness.

The affirmation of whiteness is embodied in a common saying, *Yi Bai Zhe Xian Chow* (一白遮三醜), which translates as "One whiteness veils three uglinesses." I chose this saying for the title of the chapter because it captures the essence of an unjust practice collectively endorsed for centuries by many Chinese women and men. In classical Chinese, three means many. A woman's looks are important. If she has "many uglinesses" (i.e., if she is unbearably ugly), her *Bai Pifu* can veil them, compensate for them. This saying trumpets the social advantage of whiteness for Chinese *women*. It is gendered—it is not applied in Chinese men's physical appearance.

Hei Pifu in My Border Crossing

I was born into a "mixed" family. My mother, Chen Shujen, is a Taiwanese. Her maternal grandmother (my great grandmother) was an aborigine of the Ping Pu tribe, a very smart woman of natural feet.[2] She was good at mathematics. Because of this, she was often asked by neighbors to preside over business transactions, for example, selling pigs, exchanging crops. In her tribe, she was a princess. She was said to have dark skin or *Hei Pifu*.

To understand the sociopolitical meaning attached to aborigine people in Taiwan, we need to know the power differences among the aborigine, the Taiwanese, and the Mainlanders. Taiwan is dominated by Chinese people of the Han ethnicity. Han Chinese in Taiwan are further divided into two main groups—the Taiwanese and the Mainlanders. The Taiwanese are those whose ancestors came from Fu-Jien Province in China about two or three hundred years ago.[3] The Mainlanders are non-Fu-Jien Han people who came to Taiwan with Chiang Kai-shek's nationalist troops around 1949. The natives of Taiwan are aboriginal people. They are of darker skin[4] and non-Han ethnicity. There are different tribes, and they speak different languages. When the Fu-Jien people came, they stole the aboriginal people's lands and forced them into the less fertile mountain areas. The aboriginal people came to be called "the mountain people" (*Shang Di Ren*). When the Mainlanders came, they in turn stole Taiwanese people's lands and forced them into lesser positions in the private and public sectors.

During the Chiang family's semiautocratic rule from 1949 through 1988, the Mainlanders stood at the top of the political hierarchy, next were the Taiwanese, and at the bottom were the aborigines. After 1988, with multiple voices competing for a hearing in public (e.g., the Taiwanese independence movement, the labor movement, the women's movement, and the Tong Zhi[5] or queer movement), the Taiwanese gained more power and are displacing the Mainlanders. However, the aborigine people are still powerless. In the eyes of the Han-centric ruling class, aborigines are people who are poorly educated and "naturally" inclined to alcoholism and prostitution. The government locates nuclear waste dumps on their land. Their plight is analogous to that of Native Americans in the United States.

As a little girl, I used to watch my maternal grandmother sitting in front   20
of a polished red wood mirror, massaging a white powder cake onto her face. It never occurred to me that she was half aborigine and half Taiwanese, because her face was always painted white! I remember overhearing conversations among my mother and her four sisters:

> Because of the "aborigine princess" in our family [referring to my maternal great grandmother], we are cursed with *Hei Pifu*. There is nothing we can wear to be pretty. It's a shame not to be able to wear colorful dresses!

But what about my great grandmother's great intelligence? her math skills despite her illiteracy? her generosity of spirit? Only silence, a silence I have finally broken. A silence I have to break in order to come to terms with my own "color."

As far back as I can remember, my mother often reminded me, "Color-   21
ful dresses look awful on you. You should only wear plain-colored outfits. Avoid purple and other light colors. They make you look very black!" The impact was profound. I wonder now if one reason I studied so hard to become an excellent student had to do with my *Hei Pifu,* an unconscious need to find a means of advancement in society to avoid my "fate"!

When I came to the United States, I thought about myself as a *Hei Pifu*   22
Taiwanese woman. I was glad that Americans treated me and other *Bai Pifu* Taiwanese women in the same way—we all became "Asian women." Border-crossing caused a "color revolution" in my life. I bought dresses of different shades of purple, pink, yellow, and white. I often received compliments, and my mother's harsh words receded into the dark unreflecting pool. Nobody seemed to be bothered by my *Hei Pifu*. My American friends could not even name it, let alone criticize it!

My escape was momentary. I began to read about how women of color   23
had to struggle to become heard in the feminist movement. Suddenly it dawned on me that Asian women are also "women of color." I escaped gendered colorism in Taiwan only to join another form of discrimination, gendered racism in the United States—a historically subjugated position shared with my red, brown, and black sisters. My newfound delight and freedom in choosing what colors to wear has been replaced by the desire to end oppression in its multiple forms in the United States and in Taiwan.

This focus has personal implications. What would I want my mother and   24
her sisters to have said differently? They were all "strong women" in their

own families. They ran the business! This seemed to have come from the great intelligence and mathematical skills of their "aborigine princess" grand-mother. In working this out, I recalled an important family story—my mother and father's marriage.

My mother asked her father if he would approve of her marrying my fa-   25
ther, a Mainlander of no financial means. "Absolutely not!" he replied. At that time, Taiwanese people harbored a deep resentment against Mainland-ers because of their political and economic exploitation, and my grandfather was no exception. However, my mother did not flinch. She patiently waited for her father's approval.

For over a year, my grandfather did not speak to my mother. Finally, my   26
great grandmother, the *Hei Pifu,* dark-skinned aboriginal woman, came to her rescue. She reasoned with her son-in-law,

> If your child has decided on her mate, you should not stand in the way. Is he a good man? reliable man? Will he treat your daughter well? These are more im-portant questions. Plus, we do not want to have tragedies in the family.

My grandfather reluctantly agreed to the marriage, though he and my grand-mother did not attend the wedding, held in 1958. Mother told this story many times as I grew up, and in telling this part her voice always quavered.

My great grandmother got my grandfather, a stubborn, polygamous, and   27
powerful patriarch, to look into my father's character as an individual rather than as a Mainlander. I had almost forgotten this story. Had my great grand-mother been Taiwanese and male, we would I think, have celebrated her in-telligence and wisdom. Yet because she was aboriginal and female, we only remember the color of her skin.

Reflections

Border crossing challenges the ideological meaning of color codes. The crit-   28
ical link drawn between the black black women in the United States and the *Hei Pifu* women in Taiwan may exist in many people's border-crossing ex-periences. Unlike my case, where I moved from gendered colorism to gen-dered racism, the following tells a story of social gain:

> A young doctor, recently graduated from medical school in England, went to the former British colony of Jamaica to study the effects of sickle-cell anemia. With her English accent, she was received as English and white by the Jamaicans. This surprised her, as she had a distinctly Persian name and "complexion," hav-ing been born in Iran though she had migrated to England with her parents when only four years old. In contrast, in England, despite being a British citi-zen, she was never considered English by the English but as a woman of color. In England, she was the subjugated Other who would always be from "some-where else," even though England was the only home she knew. In Jamaica,

however, she had suddenly become a member of a privileged class of Other. Whether seen as a privileged white woman or as a woman of color, the young doctor was reduced by both societies to the place and role of an Other because of social hierarchies and prejudices and denied her full and unique personal history. (O'Connell et al., 1995, pp. 787–788)

This story pushes two classification schemes and their corresponding hierarchies into my consciousness, one in England and another in Jamaica. The same person could be a woman of color *and* a white woman, depending on where she was located and in relation to whom.

For me, border crossing changed me from a *Hei Pifu* woman in Taiwan   29
to a woman of color (or an Asian woman or a yellow woman) in California. Both are oppressive and in need of change. Whether one moves up or down the colorist hierarchy when one crosses a border, colorism denies a full and unique understanding of people.

From the above, I learn that color codes cannot be used to racialize   30
people neatly. People from different communities use color codes to name different things, as in black communities and Taiwanese communities. These words carry meanings different from those authorized in the white communities—a yellow-skinned Asian woman may become a white-skinned Taiwanese woman. This speaks to the bankruptcy of a purely biological interpretation of skin colors. In its place, I argue that skin codes are politically constructed to create and justify hierarchies (now benignly called "cultural differences") that parcel out real social gain and loss. Because skin colors are constructed, they can also be deconstructed and transformed.

In deconstructing color codes and ending a colorist hierarchy, we need   31
to keep in mind that inequalities are multifaceted. This requires a stance that is also multifaceted. Recalling Alice Walker, I urge the use of a womanist perspective to work against colorism, to understand that it is often gendered, class based, and imperialistic. *Fighting against "whiteness" alone is not enough;* we need to take a more complex, a womanist view to change the "gendered whiteness" treasured by elitist ruling classes in different global communities.

Whiteness and blackness become the fate of Chinese women rather than   32
that of Chinese men. One whiteness can indeed veil three uglinesses for a Chinese woman, but it cannot veil her infertility, her sonlessness, and her desire to be herself, to love other women, to have a career! Perhaps, whiteness in *Bai Pifu* can take on the meaning of whiteness in the expression "white speaking" (*Bai Shou,* speaking in vain) to mean *skin in vain.* That is, "white skin" does not do much for you, and valuing it is in vain, futile. Along the same line, blackness in *Hei Pifu* can take on the meaning of blackness in the expression "black list" (*Hei Ming Dan*), to mean *skin under surveillance* by a patrilineal, elitist ruling class. Writing and rewriting blackness and

whiteness into yellowness from a womanist perspective. I have shared with you and, hopefully, my Taiwanese fellow women and men, the importance of "tearing apart" gendered colorism, the ways in which color codes have been used as fate to mark people, especially women, denying their potentials as whole human beings. Swimming against the tide, I can now say that I am proud of my *Hei Pifu* great grandmother. She did not leave me with a fate that is beyond my efforts. It is her generosity of spirit and her wisdom that gave me the courage to break the silence in my family and my culture, to rethink the meanings of whiteness and blackness, and ultimately to come to terms with my own color as a Taiwanese woman.

NOTES

1. This made me reflect on the fact that I had been indoctrinated into the use of color codes from a "white" perspective. There was only one word, "black," in my vocabulary to describe "black people." I held a very general, undifferentiated view. I did not know the gendered colorism within black communities.

2. Footbinding was practiced by Han women from the nonlaborer classes for about eight hundred years in China. It evolved into a sign signifying feminine beauty, elitist standing, and Han-centric pride. During Japan's colonization of Taiwan from 1895 through 1945, Japanese authorities formally called an end to footbinding. This, in their view, terminated a backward cultural practice. My great grandmother lived from the 1870s through the 1960s. Because of her aboriginal culture, her feet were not bound. My paternal great grandmother, of Han ethnicity, had 3-inch lotus feet. For a brief history of Chinese footbinding and the critique of antifootbinding discourse leading to the abolition of footbinding, see Lee (1998a).

3. Haka people are also part of the Taiwanese population, but "Taiwanese" often excludes Haka people. Many Fu-Jien Taiwanese discriminate against Haka Taiwanese. Related to footbinding, Haka Taiwanese women, because they often worked with Haka men in the fields, did not practice footbinding as much as Fu-Jien Taiwanese women.

4. Because of interracial relationships with Portuguese invaders, some Taiwanese aboriginal people have *Bai Pifu* or white/light skin and European facial features.

5. *Tong Zhi* means comrade; it is used in Communist China as a common title for both men and women. For example, Mrs. Chen is called Comrade Chen. In the late 1980s, gays and lesbians in Hong Kong and Taiwan appropriated "comrade" or *Tong Zhi* to refer to people who love same-sex companions. So, queer theory in English can be translated as Tong Zhi theory in Chinese, and the gay/lesbian/bisexual/transgendered rights movement is the Tong Zhi movement in Hong Kong and Taiwan.

REFERENCES

Alexander, M. (1996), *The shock of arrival: Reflections on postcolonial experience.* Boston: South End.

Brown, E. B. (1989). Womanist consciousness: Maggie Lena Walker and the independent order of Saint Luke. *Signs: Journal of Women in Culture and Society, 14,* 610–633.

Higginbotham, E. B. (1992). African-American women's history and the metalanguage of race. *Signs: Journal of Women in Culture and Society, 21,* 251–274.

hooks, b. (1981). *Ain't I a woman: Black women and feminism.* Boston: South End.

hooks, b. (1989). *Talking back: Thinking feminist, thinking black.* Boston: South End.

hooks, b. (1990) *Yearning: Race, gender and cultural politics.* Boston: South End.

hooks, b. (1992). *Black looks: Race and representation.* Boston: South End.

Lee, W. S. (1998a). Patriotic breeders or colonized converts? A postcolonial feminist approach to antifootbinding discourse in China. In D. Tanno & A. Gonzalez (Eds.), *Communication and identity across cultures* (International & Intercultural Communication Annual, Vol. 21, pp. 11–33). Thousand Oaks, CA: Sage.

Lee, W. S. (1998b). In the names of Chinese women. *Quarterly Journal of Speech, 84,* 283–302.

O'Connell, J., Reyes, A., Berger, I., Chaney, E. M., Clark, V. A., Lionnet, F., & Shiha, M. (1995). Editorial: Postcolonial, emergent, and indigenous feminisms. *Signs: Journal of Women in Culture and Society, 20,* 787–796.

Ogunyemi, C. O. (1985). Womanism: The dynamics of the contemporary black female novel in English. *Signs: Journal of Women in Culture and Society, 11,* 63–80.

Phillips, L., & McCaskill, B. (1995). Who's schooling who? Black women and the bringing of the everyday into academe, or why we started *The Womanist. Signs: Journal of Women in Culture and Society, 20,* 1007–1018.

Qiong, Y. (1964). *Lio Ge Meng* [Six dreams]. Taipei: Crown.

Roediger, D. R. (1991). *The wages of whiteness: Race and the making of the American working class.* New York: Verso.

Walker, A. (1983). *In search of our mothers' gardens: Womanist prose.* New York: Harcourt Brace Jovanovich.

Working with the Text

1. What does the title, a common Taiwanese saying, mean? What values and attitudes does it convey?

2. What, exactly, is the difference between a feminist and a womanist? Between color and colorism? How do these terms shape the arguments that Wen Shu Lee makes about race and gender? Could the arguments be made without them?

3. The author devotes considerable attention to nonracial uses of Taiwanese words for "black" and "white," grouping different idioms in different categories and noting the positive or negative valence of each term. What purposes do these lists serve? Why are selected entries recalled at the end of the essay?

4. According to the author, it was crossing borders that first revealed to her the constructedness of skin color. Which borders, literal and figurative, did Wen Shu Lee cross? Which was most important to the understanding that shaped her argument?

5. Think of a legend, fairy tale, or other story you learned in childhood, one that you recall well but one whose underlying meaning you now question or reject. Briefly narrate the story, then explain how it promotes values that trouble you. It is not necessary to justify your objection to the values themselves; instead, concentrate on demonstrating how they emerge through plot, character, dialogue, and other narrative strategies. Finally, reflect for a moment upon features of the story that seem to pull in a *different* thematic direction. Does anything about the tale challenge its dominant meaning, however subtly?

The '90s Culture of Xenophobia: Beyond the Tortilla Curtain

GUILLERMO GÓMEZ-PEÑA

Born in Mexico City in 1955, Guillermo Gómez-Peña later immigrated to California and earned an M.F.A. degree from the California Institute of the Arts. An interdisciplinary writer, artist, and performer, Gómez-Peña has created a number of solo theater pieces that he has performed throughout the United States and abroad, including *Border Brujo*, later turned into a film. He has also created the experimental radio works *Norte/Sur* and *Border Notebooks* and for five years edited the journal *Broken Line/La Linea Quebrada*. A 1991 McArthur fellow, Gómez-Peña has published *Warrior for Gringostroika: Essays, Performance Texts, and Poetry* (1993), *The New World Border: Prophesies, Poems, and Loqueras for the End of the Century* (1996), and *Temple of Confessions: Mexican Beasts and Living Santos* (1997), which includes an audio compact disk. In the following selection from *The New World Border*, Gómez-Peña argues that current anti-immigration sentiments, particularly those directed at Mexicans and Latinos, are ultimately motivated by xenophobia.

Americans never remember; Mexicans never forget.

—popular Mexican saying

The Capital of the American Crisis

From 1978 to 1991, I lived and worked in and among the cities of Tijuana, 1
San Diego, and Los Angeles. Like hundreds of thousands of Mexicans living
at the border, I was a binational commuter. I crossed that dangerous border
regularly, by plane, by car, and on foot. The border became my home, my
base of operations, and my laboratory for social and artistic experimentation. My art, my dreams, my family and friends, and my psyche were literally and conceptually divided by the border. But the border was not a
straight line; it was more like a Möbius strip. No matter where I was, I was
always on "the other side," feeling ruptured and incomplete, ever longing
for my other selves, my other home and tribe.

Thanks to my Chicano colleagues and border accomplices, I learned to 2
perceive California as an extension of Mexico; and the city of Los Angeles
as the northernmost barrio of Mexico City. And despite many Californians'
denial of their state's Mexican past and their bittersweet relationship with
contemporary Mexicans, I never quite felt like an immigrant. As a mestizo
with a thick accent and an even thicker mustache, I knew I wasn't exactly
welcome, but I also knew that millions of Latinos, "legal" and "illegal," Mexican or not, shared that border experience with me.

Then in 1991, I moved to New York City, and my umbilical cord was fi- 3
nally snapped. For the first time in my life, I felt like a true immigrant. From
my Brooklyn apartment, Mexico and Chicanolandia seemed a million light
years away. (The republic of Mexa York was still a project yet to be realized.)

I decided to return to Southern California in 1993. Since the riots, Los 4
Angeles had become the epicenter of America's social, racial, and cultural
crisis. It was, unwillingly, the capital of a growing Third World within the
shrinking First World. I wanted to be both a witness and a chronicler of this
wonderful madness.

I found a city at war with itself; a city gravely punished by natural and 5
social forces; a city whose experience is a concentrated version of the crises
confronting the entire country. Its political structures are dysfunctional and
its economy is in shambles; cutbacks in the defense budget have resulted in
increased unemployment; and racial tensions are the focus of daily news
reports. Crime rates and poverty levels can be compared with those of any
Third World city. All this coincides with an unprecedented crisis of national
identity: post–Cold War America is having a very hard time shedding its im-

perial nostalgia, embracing its multiracial soul, and accepting its new status as the first "developed" country to become a member of the Third World.

Perhaps what scared me most was to realize who was being blamed for all the turmoil. The Mexican/Latino immigrant community was the scapegoat, singled out by politicians (both Republicans and Democrats), fanatic citizen groups like SOS [Save Our State], and by sectors of the mainstream media as the main cause of California's social ills. The racist Proposition 187, which denies nonemergency medical services and education to "illegal aliens," passed with 60 percent of the vote on November 8, 1994, turning every doctor, nurse, pharmacist, policeman, schoolteacher and "concerned citizen" into a de facto border patrolman. Furthermore, the very same people who supported Prop. 187 (which is now being challenged in the courts) also opposed women's and gay rights, affirmative action, bilingual education, freedom of speech, and the existence of the National Endowment for the Arts and the Corporation for Public Broadcasting. Why? What does this all mean? What are we all losing?

You are the posse and 187 is the rope.

—Orange County rightwinger

Godzilla With A Mariachi Hat

Despite the fact that the United States has been a nation of immigrants and border crossers ever since its violent foundation, nativism has periodically reared its head. American identity has historically depended on opposing an "other," be it cultural, racial, or ideological. Americans need enemies against whom to define their personal and national boundaries. From the original indigenous inhabitants of this continent to the former Soviets, an evil "other" has always been stalking and ready to strike.

Now, it is the "illegal aliens" who are to take the blame for everything that American citizens and their incompetent politicians have been unable (or unwilling) to solve. Undocumented immigrants are being stripped of their humanity and individuality, becoming blank screens for the projection of Americans' fear, anxiety, and rage. In California and other southwestern states, this threatening otherness comes in a huge package that includes Mexicans, Latinos (including U.S.-born Latinos), Mexican-looking people (whatever this means), Mexican and Chicano culture, and the Spanish language. This horrible menace is here, inside of "our" country, within "our" borders, not only threatening "our" jobs and neighborhoods, but also "our" ideals of justice and order.

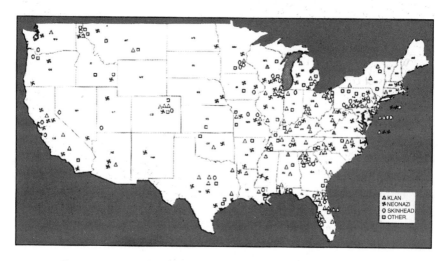

Documented hate groups in the United States in 1994.
From the *Klanwatch Intelligence Report,* March 1995

Anti-immigration has become a galvanizing force behind the resurgence   9
of a phony form of patriotism. "True" Americans (as opposed to the dark-skinned invaders) perceive themselves as the victims of immigration: "If it wasn't for *them,* everything would be all right." Of all the current arguments against immigration, perhaps the one most often used is that the United States is not as able to absorb immigrants as it was in the past; the Statue of Liberty is exhausted, and she needs a break. What is not stated openly is that she needs a break mainly from immigrants of color; the most "different" ones; those who are less willing or able to assimilate. Sadly, sectors of the Latino and African American communities also subscribe to these bizarre nativist beliefs, forgetting that they themselves are perceived as part of the problem. In the eyes of the xenophobes, any person with visibly different features, skin color, accent, clothes, or social or sexual behavior is an alien.

> *Illegal aliens are a category of criminal, not a category of ethnic group.*
>
> —Proposition 187 advocate Ron Prince

The Blurring of the Border

Fear is always at the core of xenophobia. This fear is particularly disturbing   10
when directed at the most vulnerable victims: migrant workers. They become the "invaders" from the South, the human incarnation of the Mexican fly, subhuman "wetbacks," the "alien" from another (cultural) planet. They are

accused of stealing "our jobs," of shrinking "our budget," of taking advantage of the welfare system, of not paying taxes, and of bringing disease, drugs, street violence, foreign thoughts, pagan rites, primitive customs, and alien sounds. Their indigenous features and rough clothes conjure images of an unpleasant pre-European American past, and of the mythical lands to the south immersed in poverty and political turmoil, where innocent gringos could be attacked for no apparent reason. Yet, these invaders no longer inhabit the remote past, some banana republic, or a Hollywood film. They actually live down the block, and their children attend the same schools as the Anglo kids.

Nothing is scarier than the blurring of the border between them and us;   11
between the Dantesque South and the prosperous North; between paganism and Christianity. For many Americans, the border has failed to stop chaos and crisis from creeping in (the origin of crisis and chaos is somehow always located outside). Their worst nightmare is finally coming true: The United States is no longer a fictional extension of Europe, or the wholesome suburb imagined by the screenwriter of *Lassie*. It is rapidly becoming a huge border zone, a hybrid society, a mestizo race, and worst of all, this process seems to be irreversible. America shrinks day by day, as the pungent smell of enchiladas fills the air and the volume of quebradita music rises.

Both the anti-immigration activists and the conservative media have uti-   12
lized extremely charged metaphors to describe this process of "Mexicanization." It is described as a Christian nightmare ("hell at our doorsteps"); a natural disaster ("the brown wave"); a fatal disease or an incurable virus; a form of demographic rape; a cultural invasion; or the scary beginning of a process of secession or "Quebequization" of the entire Southwest.

Paradoxically, the country allegedly responsible for all of these anxieties   13
is now an intimate business partner of the United States. But NAFTA only regulates the exchange of consumer products; human beings are not part of the deal. Our new economic community advocates open markets and closed borders, and as NAFTA goes into effect, the Tortilla Curtain is being replaced by a metallic wall that resembles the one that "fell" in Berlin.

If you catch 'em [Mexicans], skin 'em and fry 'em yourself.

—Harold Ezell, head of SOS and
   Western Regional Commissioner of the INS

The Contradictions of Utopia

Many Americans easily forget that thanks to "illegal" Mexicans hired by   14
other Americans, the food, garment, tourist, and construction industries of

California and the rest of the Southwest survive. They forget that the straw-berries, apples, grapes, oranges, tomatoes, lettuce, and avocadoes that they eat were harvested, prepared, and served by Mexican hands. And that these very same "illegal" hands clean up after them in restaurants and bars, fix their broken cars, paint and mop their homes, and manicure their gardens. They also forget that their babies and elderly are being cared for by Mexican nannies. The list of underpaid contributions by "illegal aliens" is so long that the lifestyle of many Americans couldn't possibly be sustained without them. Yet the Americans who are against illegal immigration prefer to believe that their cities and neighborhoods are less safe, and that their cultural and edu-cational institutions have lowered their standards since we were allowed in.

What begins as inflammatory rhetoric eventually becomes accepted dic-tum, justifying racial violence against suspected illegal immigrants. What Operation Gatekeeper, Proposition 187, and SOS have done is to send a very frightening message to society: The governor is behind you; let those "aliens" have it. Since they are here "illegally," they are expendable. Since they have no "legal residency," they lack both human and civil rights. To hurt, attack, or offend a faceless and nameless "criminal" doesn't seem to have any legal or moral implications. Precisely because of their undocu-mented condition, the "aliens" are not protected if they talk back, or decide to organize politically. If they demonstrate or engage in direct political ac-tions, or if they report a crime to the police, they risk deportation. When the police or the border patrol abuse their human rights, there is nowhere to go for help. They are the easy targets of state violence, economic exploitation, and civilian vigilantism. And quite often, neither the police nor the citizenry can differentiate between an "illegal alien" and a U.S.-born Latino.

Suicidal Measures and Enlightened Proposals

Authoritarian solutions to "the problem" of immigration can only make things worse. Further militarizing the border while dismantling the social, medical, and educational support systems that serve the immigrant population will only worsen social tensions. Denying medical services to undocumented im-migrants will result in more disease and more teenage pregnancy. Throwing 300,000 kids out of the schools and into the streets will only contribute to crime and social disintegration. Not only will these proposals backfire, but they will also contribute to a growing nationalism in the Chicano/Latino communities, repoliticizing entire communities that were dormant in the past decade—any community under attack tends to be more defiant.

So, what to do with "the problem" of immigration? First of all, we need to stop characterizing it as a unilateral "problem." Let's be honest: The end of the century appears scary to both Anglos and Latinos; to legal and illegal immigrants. Both sides feel threatened, uprooted, and displaced, to different degrees and for different reasons. We all fear deep inside that there won't be enough jobs, food, air, and housing for everybody. Yet we cannot deny the processes of interdependence that define our contemporary experience as North Americans. In a post-NAFTA/post–Cold War America, the binary models of us/them, North/South, and Third World/First World are no longer useful in understanding our complicated border dynamics, our transnational identities and our multiracial communities.

It is time to face the facts: Anglos won't go back to Europe, and Mexicans and Latinos (legal or illegal) won't go back to Latin America. We are all here to stay. For better or for worse, our destinies and aspirations are in one another's hands. For me, the only solution lies in a paradigm shift: the recognition that we all are the protagonists in the creation of a new cultural topography and a new social order, one in which we all are "others," and we need the other "others" to exist. Hybridity is no longer up for discussion. It is a demographic, racial, social, and cultural fact. 18

The real tasks ahead of us are to embrace more fluid and tolerant notions of personal and national identity, and to develop models of peaceful 19

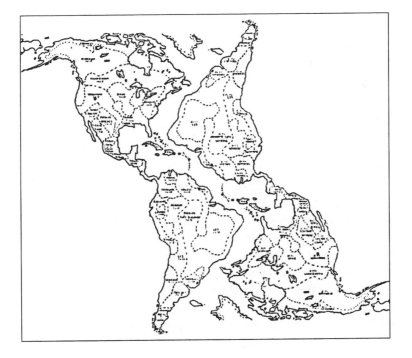

coexistence and multilateral cooperation across nationality, race, gender, and religion. To attain this, rather than more border patrols, border walls, and punitive laws, we need more and better information about one another. Culture and education are at the core of the solution. We need to learn each others' languages, histories, art, and cultural traditions. We need to educate our children and teenagers about the dangers of racism and the complexities of living in a multiracial, borderless society—the inevitable society of the next century.

Working with the Text

1. Do you agree with Gómez-Peña's assertions that "American identity has historically depended on opposing an 'other,' be it cultural, racial, or ideological," that "Americans need enemies against whom to define their personal and national boundaries"? In what ways do you think that recent efforts to curb illegal immigration, and responses to immigration in general, are tied to issues of personal and national identity?

2. How are economics and culture interrelated in Peña's discussion of the border? What are the ironies he points out regarding America's growing disdain for "illegal aliens?" In what ways is the "lifestyle of many Americans" dependent on an underpaid underclass? Do you agree that it is ironic?

3. In speaking about such legislative restrictions as Proposition 187, Gómez-Peña claims, "Not only will these proposals backfire, but they will also contribute to a growing nationalism in the Chicano/Latino communities, repoliticizing entire communities that were dormant in the past decade—any community under attack tends to be more defiant." In that claim, how is he using the term "nationalism"? Are nation and community synonymous in his usage? How are they defined? Look at his usage of nationalism next to Benjamin Barber's usage in the essay in this chapter, "Jihad vs. McWorld." Do the two men use the word nationalism the same way?

4. What new way of seeing does Gómez-Peña propose at the end of the essay? What might it mean to grapple with the "processes of interdependence that define our contemporary experience as North Americans," as he puts it at the end of the essay? To what extent do you agree that the "inevitable society of the next century" will be a "multiracial, borderless" one? How might his proposals practically be put into effect? Do you think that his proposals would actually serve the purposes he advocates? Answer these questions in an essay.

The Multicultural Mistake

K. ANTHONY APPIAH

K. Anthony Appiah was born in London in 1954, his father a Ghanian diplomat, his mother an English artist; and he spent much of his childhood in both England and Ghana. Educated at Cambridge University, Appiah taught in Ghana, as well as at Yale, Cornell, Duke and Harvard universities. He is currently professor of African-American studies at Princeton. His books include *Necessary Questions: An Introduction to Philosophy* (1989) and *In My Father's House: Africa in the Philosophy of Culture* (1992), as well as *Avenging Angel* (1990), a novel; and he has co-edited *Color Conscious: A Political Morality of Race* (1995) and a series of critical studies of African-American writers, including *Africana: The Encyclopedia of the African and African American Experience* (1999). He has said "most of my publications have grown out of my philosophical training, my upbringing in Europe and Africa, my explorations of African-American culture and history, and my love of reading." In the following essay, Appiah suggests that he finds "the broad cultural homogeneity of America more striking than its much-vaunted variety."

Have you noticed that *culture*—the word—has been getting a heavy work-out recently? Anthropologists, of course, have used it zealously for over a century, though the term's active life in literature and politics began long be-fore that. But some current ways in which the concept of culture has been put to use would have surprised even midcentury readers, especially the idea that everything from anorexia to zydeco is illuminated by being dis-played as the product of some group's culture. 1

Culture's main competitor in its kudzu-like proliferation is *diversity*, a fa-vorite now of corporate and educational CEOs, politicians, and pundits. And *cultural diversity* brings the two together. Is it not, indeed, one of the most pious of the pieties of our age that the United States is a society of enormous cultural diversity? And isn't Nathan Glazer right to say, in his new book, *We Are All Multiculturalists Now* (Harvard, 1997), that "multiculturalism is just the latest in [a] sequence of terms describing how American society, partic-ularly American education, should respond to its diversity"? 2

Well, yes, American diversity is easily granted, and so is the need for a   3
response to that diversity. But what isn't so clear is that it's our *cultural* diversity that deserves attention.

When Jews from the *shtetl* and Italians from the *villaggio* arrived at Ellis   4
Island, they brought with them a rich mixture of what we call culture. That
is, they brought a language and stories and songs and sayings; they trans-
planted a religion with specific rituals, beliefs, and traditions, a cuisine of a
certain hearty peasant quality, and distinctive modes of dress; and they came
with particular ideas about family life. It was often reasonable for their new
neighbors to ask what these first-generation immigrants were doing, and
why; and a sensible answer would frequently have been, "It's an Italian
thing" or "a Jewish thing," or, simply, "It's their culture."

It's striking how much of this form of difference has disappeared. There   5
are still seders and nuptial masses, still gefilte fish and spaghetti, but how
much does an Italian name tell you these days about church attendance, or
knowledge of Italian, or taste in food or spouses? Even Jews, whose status
as a small non-Christian group in an overwhelmingly Christian society might
have been expected to keep their "difference" in focus, are getting harder to
identify as a cultural group. (At the seder I go to every Passover, nearly half
of those in attendance are gentiles.)

One way—the old way—of describing what has happened would be to   6
say that the families that arrived during the turn-of-the-century wave of immigration have assimilated, become American. But, from another perspective, we might say that they became white. When the Italians and the Jews
of Eastern Europe arrived, they were thought of as racially different both
from African Americans and from the white Protestant majority. Now hardly
anybody thinks of their descendants this way. They are Americans, but unless their ancestors include people from Africa or Asia, they are also white.
And nobody, except perhaps a few oddballs in the Aryan Nation, thinks
white people share a culture different from everybody else's.

The contrast between blacks and whites seems very evident, of course.   7
White people rarely think of anything in their culture as white: normal, no
doubt, middle-class, maybe, and even, sometimes, American; but not white.
Black Americans, by contrast, do think of much in their lives in racial terms;
they may speak black English (which some respectfully call Ebonics), go to
black churches, listen and dance to black music. (And this isn't just how
black people think; other people think that way about them.)

Yet to contrast black and white stories is to neglect much that they have   8
in common. There are, indeed, forms of English speech that are black, even
if there are also large regional and class variations in black, as in white,
speech. But these are all forms of English we're talking about. Indeed, de-

spite the vast waves of immigration of the past few decades, something like 97 percent of adult Americans, whatever their color, speak English "like a native"; and, with the occasional adjustment for an accent here and there, those 97 percent can all understand one another. Leave out recent immigrants and the number gets close to 100 percent.

Language is only one of many things most Americans share. This is, for example, a country where almost every citizen knows something about baseball and basketball. Americans also share a familiarity with the consumer culture. They shop American style and know a good deal about the same consumer goods: Coca-Cola, Nike, Levi's, Ford, Nissan, GE. They have seen Hollywood movies and know the names of some stars; and even the few who watch little or no television can probably tell you the names of some of its personalities. Even the supposedly persisting differences of religion turn out to be shallower than you might think. American Judaism is, as is often observed, extraordinarily American. Catholics in this country are a nuisance for Rome just because they are . . . well, so Protestant. 9

Coming as I do from Ghana, I find the broad cultural homogeneity of America more striking than its much-vaunted variety. So why, in this society, which has less diversity of culture than most others, are we so preoccupied with diversity and so inclined to conceive of it as cultural? 10

Let me offer a name—not an explanation, just a piece of terminology for our much-vaunted diversity. Let's say that we are creatures of *diverse social identities.* The cozy truism that we are a diverse society reflects the fact that many people now insist that they are profoundly shaped by the groups to which they belong, that their social identity—their membership in these groups—is central to who they are. Moreover, they go on to pursue what the Canadian philosopher Charles Taylor calls a "politics of recognition"; they ask the rest of us to acknowledge publicly their "authentic" identities. 11

The identities that demand recognition are multifarious. Some groups have the names of the earlier ethnic cultures: Italian, Jewish, Polish. Some correspond to the old races (black, Asian, Indian) or to religions (Baptist, Catholic, Jewish). Some are basically regional (Southern, Western, Puerto Rican). Yet others are new groups modeled on the old ethnicities (Hispanic, Asian American) or are social categories (woman, gay, bisexual, disabled, deaf) that are none of these. 12

Nowadays, we are not the slightest bit surprised when someone remarks upon a feature of the "culture" of groups like these. Gay culture, deaf culture, Chicano culture, Jewish culture—see how these phrases trip off the tongue. But if you ask what distinctively marks off gay people or deaf people or Jews from others, it is not obviously the fact that to each identity there corresponds a distinct culture. *Hispanic* sounds like the name of a cultural 13 group defined by sharing the cultural trait of speaking Spanish, but half the second-generation Hispanics in California don't speak Spanish fluently, and in the next generation the proportion will fall even further.

You may wonder, in fact, whether there isn't a connection between the   14 thinning of the cultural content of identities and the rising stridency of their claims. Those European immigrants who lived in their rich ethnic cultures were busy demanding the linguistic Americanization of their children, making sure they learned America's official culture. One suspects that they didn't need to insist on the public recognition of their culture, because— whether or not they were happy with it—they simply took it for granted. Their middle-class descendants, whose domestic lives are conducted in English and extend eclectically from *Seinfeld* to Chinese takeout, are discomfited by a sense that their identities are shallow by comparison with those of their grandparents; some of them fear that unless the rest of us acknowledge the importance of their difference, there soon won't be anything worth acknowledging.

For many middle-class Americans, families have changed. Grandparents   15 have moved into retirement communities, cousins no longer live down the street, parents have separated. In sum, many of the social preconditions of that extended intergenerational family life have disappeared, and, for many Americans, the will to live that way has vanished too. Given the connection between the old family life and the old cultural identities, it is not surprising that the loss of the former has produced nostalgia for the latter.

The trouble with appealing to cultural difference is that it obscures   16 rather than illuminates this situation. It's not black culture that the racist disdains, but blacks. No amount of knowledge of the architectural achievements of Nubia or Kush guarantees respect for African Americans. No African American is entitled to greater concern because he is descended from a people who created jazz or produced Toni Morrison. Culture is not the problem, and it is not the solution.

So maybe we should conduct our discussions of education and citizen-   17 ship, toleration and social peace, without the talk of cultures. Long ago, in the mists of prehistory, our ancestors learned that it is sometimes good to let a field lie fallow.

Working with the Text

1. What is the definition of "culture" that Appiah is working with in this essay? How does it compare to other uses of "culture" in this reader or that you have explored across the course of the semester? Would you define culture differently? More broadly? More narrowly?

2. How do you respond, based on your own experience, to his statement, "I find the broad cultural homogeneity of America more striking
   than its much-vaunted variety"?

3. Write a paper in which you explore the meanings and differences between the two main phrases at the heart of Appiah's essay: "cultural
   diversity" and "diverse social identities." What is the difference between the two? Which do you think is most applicable to America?
   What are the consequences of paying attention to one over the other?

Someplace in Queens

IAN FRAZIER

Originally from Ohio, Ian Frazier attended Harvard, where he wrote for the
Lampoon and earned national attention with a parody of *Cosmo*, featuring
Henry Kissinger as centerfold. After graduation in 1973, Frazier became a
staffer at *The New Yorker*, where his pieces appeared for two decades. He
has published several collections of humorous essays, including *Dating
Your Mom (1986)* and *Coyote v. Acme* (1996), whose title essay imagines
the cartoon character Wile E. Coyote in a product liability suit against Acme
Company, a supplier of unpredictable rocket sleds and faulty spring-
powered shoes. Frazier's nonfiction debut, *Great Plains* (1994), an account
of his 25,000-mile expedition through western America, became an immediate bestseller. His latest book, *On the Rez* (2000), considers Indian ideas
of freedom and community and equality that are basic to how we view ourselves. Frazier has also appeared in cameo roles in Wayne Wang's films
Smoke and *Blue in the Face*. The following essay originally appeared in
Doubletake magazine and was included in *Best American Essays 1998*.

Off and on, I get a thing for walking in Queens. One morning, I strayed into   1
that borough from my more usual routes in Brooklyn, and I just kept rambling. I think what drew me on was the phrase "someplace in Queens." This
phrase is often used by people who live in Manhattan to describe a Queens
location. They don't say the location is simply "in Queens"; they say it is
"someplace in Queens," or "in Queens someplace": "All the records are

stored in a warehouse someplace in Queens," "His ex-wife lives in Queens someplace." The swooning, overwhelmed quality that the word "someplace" gives to such descriptions is no doubt a result of the fact that people who don't live in Queens see it mostly from the windows of airplanes landing there, at La Guardia or Kennedy airports. They look out at the mile after mile of apparently identical row houses coming up at them and swoon back in their seats at the unknowability of it all. When I find myself among those houses, with their weightlifting trophies or floral displays in the front windows, with their green lawns and nasturtium borders and rose bushes and sidewalks stained blotchy purple by crushed berries from the overhanging mulberry trees, and a scent of curry is in the air, and a plane roars above so close I think I could almost recognize someone at a window, I am happy to be someplace in Queens.

Queens is shaped sort of like a brain. The top, or northern border, is furrowed with bays and coves and salt marshes and creeks extending inland from the East River and Long Island Sound. To the west, its frontal lobe adjoins the roughly diagonal line running southeast that separates it from Brooklyn. At its stem is the large, solid mass of Kennedy Airport, at its east the mostly flat back part that borders Nassau County, Long Island. To the south stretches the long narrow peninsula of Rockaway Beach, which does not really fit my analogy. Queens is the largest New York City borough. It has the longest and widest avenues, the most freeways, and the most crowded subway stations. It has more ethnic groups and nationalities than any other borough; observers say that it has more ethnic diversity than any other place its size on earth. Some of its schools are the city's most overcrowded. In one Queens school district, a dozen or more new pupils enroll every week during the school year, many speaking little English. Classes meet in bathrooms and on stairways; kids use stairs as desks when they practice their spelling and teachers go home hoarse every night from trying to make themselves heard. Immigrants open stores along the avenues beneath the elevated-train tracks in Queens, the way they used to under the old Second Avenue El on the Lower East Side. Queens has more miles of elevated tracks than any borough, and the streets below them teem.

I like to walk under the elevated tracks early on summer mornings, before people are up. At six-thirty, a steeply pitched shaft of sunlight falls between each pair of dark iron pillars. On down the avenue you see the shafts of light, each tinted with haze, receding after each other into the distance. Sun here is secondary, like sun in a forest or on a reef. Some of the shadows of the El on the empty pavement are solid blocks, some are sun-and-shadow plaid. Traffic lights overhang the intersections from the El's beams and run through their cycles at this hour for no one. Security gates on all the stores are down. There's a sharp tapping as an Asian man turns a corner hitting the top of a fresh pack of cigarettes against his palm. He tears off the cellophane, throws it on the ground, opens the pack, hurries up the steps to the station. Each metallic footstep is distinct. When the noise of the train comes, it's a ringing, clattering pounding that fills this space like a rioting throng. The sound pulses as if the train were bouncing on its rails, and, in fact, if you stand in the station the floor does seem to trampoline slightly beneath your feet. Then there's the hiss of the air brakes, a moment of quiet, the two notes of the signal for the closing doors, and the racket begins again. In the world under the El, speech-drowning noise comes and goes every few minutes.

Queens specializes in neighborhoods that nonresidents have heard of 4 but could never place on a map. Long Island City, for example, is not someplace out on Long Island but on Queens's East River side, across from midtown Manhattan. High-society families had estates there when that side of the river was New York's Gold Coast. Today, it is Con Ed property, warehouses, and movie-equipment supply places. You can buy a used police car there for a third off the book price. Astoria is near La Guardia Airport, just across the river from Rikers Island, which is in the Bronx. Sunnyside is southeast of Long Island City, and below Sunnyside is Maspeth, and below Maspeth is Ridgewood, one of the most solidly blue-collar neighborhoods in the city. Springfield Gardens, in Southeast Queens, has many wood-frame houses, and that general area has the city's highest fire-fatality rate. Queens used to be the city's vegetable garden and orchard, and in certain places the old farmland still bulges through the borough's concrete lacings. In Fresh Meadows, in the east middle of the borough, a cherry tree survives that was planted in about 1790. It stands on a small triangular relic of field now strewn with Chinese-restaurant flyers and abutted by the back of a beverage store, a row of small businesses, and some row houses. This year, the tree bore a crop of cherries, just as it did when it was out in the country and Lincoln was a boy.

In Forest Hills, in the middle of the borough, flight attendants in blue 5 uniforms with red scarves wheel suitcase caddies up its sloping sidewalks. Woodside, on the northwest border, is the city's most integrated neighborhood. St. Albans and Cambria Heights, on the east of the borough, are almost all black and middle class. In Queens, the median black household income is higher than the median white household income—$34,300 a year compared to $34,000 a year. Howard Beach is just west of Kennedy Airport. It became famous some years ago when a white mob killed a black man there. Ozone Park, just north of it, has houses in rows so snug you can hardly see the seams between them, and each house has a lawn the size of a living room rug: some of the lawns are bordered by brick fences with statuettes of elephants raising their trunks, some are thick with flowers, some with ornamental shrubs in rows. People water in the mornings there, and get down on all fours to pick pieces of detritus from the grass. In front of 107-44 110th Street, a house with gray siding and black trim and a picture window, several men came up to the owner, Joseph Scopo, as he got out of a car one night in 1993, and they shot him a number of times. He made it across the street and died near the stone-front house at 107-35. The front yard of Mr. Scopo's former house is all cement; for many years, he was the vice president of Local 6A of the Cement and Concrete Workers of New York City.

On Kissena Boulevard, in Flushing, I passed a two-story brick row   7
house with a dentist's office on the first floor and the sign "D. D. Dong, D.M.D." By now, my feet were hurting and my legs were chafed and I was walking oddly. At the end of a sunlit alley, a pink turban leaned under the hood of a yellow cab. A yellow-and-black butterfly flew over a muffler-repair shop. A red rose grew through coils of razor wire and chain-link fence. At a juicing machine on the street, I bought an almost-cool Styrofoam cup of sugarcane juice, grassy-tasting and sweet. Then I was among the Cold War ruins of Flushing Meadow Park, site of the 1964–65 World's Fair, which is now a mostly empty expanse coexisting with about half a dozen freeways at the borough's heart. No place I know of in America looks more like Moscow than Flushing Meadow Park: the heroic, forgotten statuary, all flexed muscle and straining toes; the littered grounds buffed by feet to smooth dirt; the vast broken fountains, with their twisted pipes and puddles of olive-colored water. I leaned on the railing of a large, unexplained concrete pool thick with floating trash and watched a sparrow on a soda can do a quick logrolling number to stay on top. No matter what, I could not get out of my mind "D. D. Dong, D.M.D."

Legally, you can buy wigs made of human hair in Queens, and two-   8
hundred-volt appliances designed to work in the outlets in foreign countries, and T-shirts that say "If you can't get enough, get a Guyanese," and extra-extra-large bulletproof vests with side panels, and pink bikini underwear with the New York Police Department shield and "New York's Hottest" printed on the front, and pepper-spray personal-defense canisters with ultraviolet identifying dye added, and twenty-ounce bottles of Laser Malt Liquor, whose slogan is "Beam me up," and a cut-rate ten-minute phone call to just about any place on earth, and a viewing of the Indian movie *Sabse Bade Khiladi*, featuring "the hottest song of 1995, 'Muqubla Muqubla.'" Illegally, if you know how, you can buy drugs in bulk, especially cocaine. Drug enforcement officers say that Queens is one of the main entry points for cocaine in the United States, and that much of the trade is engineered by Colombians in the neighborhoods of Elmhurst and Jackson Heights, a dis-

trict called Little Colombia. On the Elmhurst–Jackson Heights border, at Eighty-third Street just below the Roosevelt Avenue El, is a pocket-sized park of trees and benches called Manuel de Dios Unanue Triangle. It is named for a journalist killed in Queens in 1992 by agents of a Colombian drug cartel.

Manuel de Dios Unanue was born in Cuba, graduated from the University of Puerto Rico, and worked as a newspaper reporter in New York. In 1984, he became the editor of *El Diario–La Prensa,* the city's largest Spanish-language newspaper. At *El Diario,* he was, according to various accounts, obsessive, crusading, blindly self-righteous, possessed of a brilliant news sense, delusional, uncompromising, vain. He chain-smoked. He believed that the United States should open political discussions with Castro, a view that angered anti-Communist terrorist groups, and he printed many articles about the drug trade. He received death threats with a regularity that became a joke between him and his colleagues. Once, someone painted black zebra stripes on his white car and left a note saying he would "get it."

In the eighties and the early nineties, drug money flowed into Queens. Police said that check-cashing places and travel agencies and other businesses in Elmhurst and Jackson Heights were laundering it. Steamer trunks full of submachine guns traced to a realty company on Queens Boulevard led to the discovery of apartments with stashes of drugs and money elsewhere in the city. Colombians died by violence in Queens all the time. One year, 44 of the borough's 357 homicide victims were Colombians. Pedro Méndez, a political figure who had raised money for the 1990 campaign of Colombia's new antidrug president, was shot to death near his home in Jackson Heights the night before that president's inauguration. At a pay telephone by a florist's shop on Northern Boulevard, police arrested a man named Dandeny Muñoz-Mosquera, who they said was an assassin wanted for crimes that included the murders of at least forty police officers in Colombia. Although the authorities believed he had come to Queens to kill somebody, at his arrest they could hold him only for giving a false name to a federal officer. In prison, he requested that Manuel de Dios do an interview with him.

Manuel de Dios had left *El Diario* by then, fired in 1989 for reckless reporting, according to some accounts. On his own, he wrote (and published) a book called *The Secrets of the Medellín Cartel,* an antidrug exposé. He began to publish two magazines, *Cambio XXI* and *Crimen,* in which he identified alleged drug traffickers and dealers and the local places where they did business, with big photographs. In Colombia, some people—according to federal agents, José Santacruz Londono and Gilberto Rodriguez-Orejula, of the Cali drug cartel, among others—decided to have him killed. Someone hired someone and his wife, who hired someone, who hired Wilson Alejandro Mejia Vélez, a sixteen-year-old employee of a chair factory in Staten

Island. One afternoon the boy put on a hood, walked into the Mesón Asturias restaurant in Queens, and shot Manuel de Dios twice in the back of
the head as he finished a beer at the bar.

The *Times, The New Yorker,* Salman Rushdie, and others decried the mur-   12
der. Police said they would solve it soon, and sixteen months after the killing, on a tip from an informant, they caught the killer and some of the
conspirators, not including the higher-ups in Colombia. The killer and four
others stood trial, were convicted, and went to jail. The triggerboy got life
without parole. Manuel de Dios's magazines ceased publication after his
death. His book cannot be found in the Spanish-language bookstores in
Elmhurst, or *Books in Print.* People in Elmhurst know the name of the book,
and they say the name of its author in a familiar rush, but they cannot tell
you where you might find a copy. Recently, the number of local drug-
related murders has gone down; people say this is because the victory of
one big drug cartel over another has brought stability to the trade.

The Mesón Asturias restaurant is just across Eighty-third Street from the   13
Manuel de Dios Unanue Triangle. On a hot July afternoon, I went into the
restaurant, sat down at the bar, and had a beer. The bartender, a short, trim
man with dark hair, put a bowl of peanuts by me and cut some slices of
chorizo sausage. We watched Spanish TV on cable and commented on a
piece about the running of the bulls at Pamplona. The bartender said that an
American had been killed and that you had to know how to be with the
bulls. I paid for the beer and got up to leave. I asked, "Is this where the journalist was killed?"

"Oh, yes," the bartender said.   14

"Were you here?"   15

"No, I was outside."   16

"Did you know him?"   17

"Yes, he was a regular."   18

"He must have been a brave man," I said.   19

The bartender stood not facing me and not facing away. He pushed the   20
dollar I had left for a tip across the bar, and I pushed it back at him. For a
while the bartender looked off toward the dim, gated window. "Well," he
said, "You never know your luck."

The oldest house in Queens—perhaps in the city—is a frame farmhouse   21
built in 1661 by a man who later suffered banishment for letting Quakers
meet there. His neighbors in the town of Flushing sent the Dutch governor
a Remonstrance stating their belief in religious freedom not only for Quakers and other Christians but also for "Jews, Turks, and Egyptians." Today, the
house, called the Bowne House, sits on a small patch of lawn between a
four-story apartment building and a city playground. The theoretical Jews,

Turks, and Egyptians are now real and living nearby, but nearest are the Koreans. Almost all the signs you see in downtown Flushing are in Korean, and the neighborhood has a Quaker meetinghouse, Korean Buddhist temples, and Korean Catholic and Protestant churches. At the end of the No. 7 Flushing subway line, pamphleteers for a city council person hand you fliers saying that the line is going to hell, while other people hand you fundamentalist Christian tracts saying that you are. Pentecostal churches in storefronts all over Queens have signs in the window advising, for example, "Do nothing you would not like to be doing when Jesus comes," in Spanish and English. A multimillion-dollar Hindu temple, the largest in the city, recently went up in Flushing. Many Hindus, Buddhists, and Sikhs have recently added small celebrations of Christmas to their traditional worship calendars. Groups of Gnostics meet in Queens, and Romanian Baptists, and followers of the guru Sri Chinmoy, who sometimes express their faith by doing enough somersaults to get into the *Guinness Book of World Records*. When summer comes, big striped tents rise on outlying vacant lots with billboards advertising tent meeting revivals led by Pastor John H. Boyd.

In Douglaston, a far Queens neighborhood that still has the feel of a town, I sat on the lawn of an Episcopal church at the crest of a hill. The ancient gravestones in the churchyard leaned, the daylilies along the driveway bloomed, and the white wooden church panted discreetly in the heat through its high open windows. In Astoria, I visited St. Irene's of Chrysovalantou Greek Orthodox Church, home of the icon of Saint Irene, which witnesses say wept on the eve of the Persian Gulf War. A short woman all in black said, "Why not? Why not?" when I asked if I could see the icon, and she led me slowly up the aisle in fragrant, dusky church light. The icon, a six-by-eight-inch painting, is in a large frame made of gold bracelets, jeweled wristwatches, and rows of wedding rings donated by parishioners. On a wooden rail below it are inhalers left by asthma sufferers whose breath Saint Irene has restored. In Richmond Hill, I stopped in at Familiar Pharmacy, managed and co-owned by Mohammad Tayyab, who knows the Koran by heart. He is thirty-nine, has a neatly trimmed beard, and wears his baseball cap backward. He told me that, growing up in Multan, Pakistan, he memorized verses from the Koran almost every day, morning to night, from when he was six until he was twelve. The Koran is about the length of the New Testament. A person who knows the Koran by heart is called a *haviz*. Mohammad Tayyab recites the whole Koran once a year in a mosque during the fast of Ramadan, and reviews three chapters every night, to keep fresh. The stored-up energy of his knowledge causes him to radiate, like a person who has just been to a spa. 22

In Montefiore Cemetery, in another far part of Queens, the Grand Rebbe of the Lubavitcher Hasidim, Menachem Schneerson, lies in a coffin made of 23 boards from his lectern. By the time of Rebbe Schneerson's death, in 1994, at the age of ninety-three, some of his followers had come to believe he was the Messiah. Tens of thousands of Lubavitchers from around the world have visited his grave, sometimes annoying the black families who own homes nearby. Neighbors complained that the Lubavitchers were singing loudly, drinking beer, trespassing, and asking to use their bathrooms. The sect has since bought a house near the grave for the convenience of visitors. I went to see the grave myself, on an anniversary of the Rebbe's death. Cars with out-of-state plates lined the boulevard by the cemetery gate; some cars had their doors open to the curb, and shoeless Lubavitchers lay asleep on the seats. Along the paths to the gravesite ran that orange-webbed plastic security fence in which we now routinely wrap important public events. Some of the Lubavitchers were pink-cheeked teens with blond sidecurls. Cops not much older leaned against the cemetery gate and smoked, thumbs hooked in their belts, cigarettes between their first two fingers.

Black-clad Lubavitchers in black hats were coming and going. In the patio behind the nearby Lubavitcher house, many were reciting prayers. Occasionally, an impassioned voice would rise like a firework, bursting higher than the others. A man about my age who pointed the way to the grave suggested that I remove my shoes before approaching it: "Remember, this is a holy place," he said. My running shoes looked as bright as a television ad on top of the pile of functional black brogans of many sizes already there. I ducked through a low door to an anteroom filled with candles. It led into an enclosure of walls maybe twelve feet high, and open to the sky. At the center of the enclosure was a knee-high wall around the grave itself. Men were standing at the graveside wall and praying, chanting, flipping expertly through small prayer books in their palms, rocking from side to side with the words. Heaped on top of the grave like raked-up leaves, spilling onto the smooth pebbles next to it, drifting into the anteroom, were hundreds or thousands of small square pieces of paper on which people had written prayers for special intercessions. There are so many hopes in the world. Just out of the line of sight past the higher wall, 747s descended slowly to Kennedy Airport like local elevators stopping at every floor. Across the street just out of earshot, long-legged girls jumped double-Dutch jump rope, superfast.

Working with the Text

1. "Someplace in Queens" is everywhere concerned—often literally concerned—with point of view. Frazier frames his essay with a contrast between the view of Queens afforded by flight and the view of Queens afforded by walking, reminding us periodically of his physical passage through the borough—and others' passage over it.

What is the purpose of this contrast? Does it simply rehearse the familiar point that proximity enhances detail or does it have more complicated purposes? What kinds of things are visible from each perspective? What other perspectives, spatial and temporal, does the essay go on to develop?

2. What is the relationship between physical and cultural geography in the essay? Where does Frazier find borders, and what kinds of borders are they? Who or what comes into contact there—and what kinds of contact are visible?

3. Though most essays are descriptive at some point, few use description as their primary mode, and few offer the depth and variety of detail that Frazier musters for "Someplace in Queens." What types of detail do you find surprising or compelling—and why? Consider, for example, the essay's use of superlatives or buildings or goods for sale. Where does Frazier cluster such details in a catalogue or list, and where does he disperse them? To what effects? Why does he describe some persons collectively and others individually?

4. How is the essay organized? With no conspicuous argumentative or narrative axis, how does the essay's wealth of detail cohere? Why is such a large, central segment devoted to the murder of Manuel de Dios Unanue? How does the episode relate to other parts of the essay?

5. Write a description of a place you know well, launching your description by confronting a phrase or term commonly used by outsiders. The outsiders' term need not offend but should somehow be limited, if only by habitual users' failure to appreciate its true significance. As always, descriptive detail should be concrete and revealing.

La conciencia de la mestiza/Towards a New Consciousness

GLORIA ANZALDÚA

Gloria Anzaldúa was born in southwest Texas in 1942 into a farmworking family that had been U.S. citizens for generations. A *mestiza* (that is, a person of mixed Mexican, Indian, and Anglo ancestry), Anzaldúa early in life rebelled against the limited role assigned females in Chicano culture. As a writer and lecturer, she has explored issues of feminism and lesbianism, as well as Mexican and Mexican-American culture. In 1983 she co-edited with Cherríe Moraga the groundbreaking collection *The Bridge Called My Back: Writings by Radical Women of Color.* She also edited *Haciendo Caras: Making Face, Making Soul: Creative and Critical Perspectives by Feminists of Color* (1990) and has written two children's books, *Amigos del Otro Lado/ Friends from the Other Side* (1994) and *Prietia y la Llorena/Prietia and the Ghost Woman* (1996). The following is an excerpt from her most well-known work, *Borderlands/La Frontera* (1987), a sort of cultural and political autobiography. In it Anzaldúa argues that, in straddling contradictory cultures, the "new *mestiza*" must achieve a new consciousness that tolerates ambiguity and "includes rather than excludes." Though many applaud the political agenda of the book, Anzaldúa's methods and arguments have recently come under sharp critique, often within the Chicano/Chicana community itself. Many now feel, as Benjamin Alire Sáenz notes in a later essay, that "the pastoral tradition that she reproduces is overstated, reductive, and offensive."

Por la mujer de mi raza
hablará el espíritu.[1]

Jose Vascocelos, Mexican philosopher, envisaged *una raza mestiza, una*   1
mezcla de razas afines, una raza de color—la primera raza síntesis del globo. He called it a cosmic race, *la raza cósmica,* a fifth race embracing the four major races of the world.[2] Opposite to the theory of the pure Aryan, and to the policy of racial purity that white America practices, his theory is

one of inclusivity. At the confluence of two or more genetic streams, with chromosomes constantly "crossing over," this mixture of races, rather than resulting in an inferior being, provides hybrid progeny, a mutable, more malleable species with a rich gene pool. From this racial, ideological, cultural and biological cross-pollinization, an "alien" consciousness is presently in the making—a new *mestiza* consciousness, *una conciencia de mujer.* It is a consciousness of the Borderlands.

Una lucha de fronteras / A Struggle of Borders

Because I, a *mestiza,*
continually walk out of one culture
and into another,
because I am in all cultures at the same time,
alma entre dos mundos, tres, cuatro,
me zumba la cabeza con lo contradictorio.
Estoy norteada por todas las voces que me hablan
simultáneamente.

The ambivalence from the clash of voices results in mental and emotional   2
states of perplexity. Internal strife results in insecurity and indecisiveness. The mestiza's dual or multiple personality is plagued by psychic restlessness.

In a constant state of mental nepantilism, an Aztec word meaning torn   3
between ways, *la mestiza* is a product of the transfer of the cultural and spiritual values of one group to another. Being tricultural, monolingual, bilingual, or multilingual, speaking a patois, and in a state of perpetual transition, the *mestiza* faces the dilemma of the mixed breed: which collectivity does the daughter of a darkskinned mother listen to?

El choque de un alma atrapado entre el mundo del espíritu y el mundo   4
de la técnica a veces la deja entullada. Cradled in one culture, sandwiched between two cultures, straddling all three cultures and their value systems, *la mestiza* undergoes a struggle of flesh, a struggle of borders, an inner war. Like all people, we perceive the version of reality that our culture communicates. Like others having or living in more than one culture, we get multiple, often opposing messages. The coming together of two self-consistent but habitually incompatible frames of reference[3] causes *un choque,* a cultural collision.

Within us and within *la cultura chicana,* commonly held beliefs of the   5
white culture attack commonly held beliefs of the Mexican culture, and both attack commonly held beliefs of the indigenous culture. Subconsciously, we see an attack on ourselves and our beliefs as a threat and we attempt to block with a counterstance.

But it is not enough to stand on the opposite river bank, shouting ques-   6
tions, challenging patriarchal, white conventions. A counterstance locks one
into a duel of oppressor and oppressed; locked in mortal combat, like the
cop and the criminal, both are reduced to a common denominator of violence. The counterstance refutes the dominant culture's views and beliefs,
and, for this, it is proudly defiant. All reaction is limited by, and dependent
on, what it is reacting against. Because the counterstance stems from a problem with authority—outer as well as inner—it's a step towards liberation
from cultural domination. But it is not a way of life. At some point, on our
way to a new consciousness, we will have to leave the opposite bank, the
split between the two mortal combatants somehow healed so that we are on
both shores at once and, at once, see through serpent and eagle eyes. Or
perhaps we will decide to disengage from the dominant culture, write it off
altogether as a lost cause, and cross the border into a wholly new and separate territory. Or we might go another route. The possibilities are numerous once we decide to act and not react.

A Tolerance For Ambiguity

These numerous possibilities leave *la mestiza* floundering in uncharted seas.   7
In perceiving conflicting information and points of view, she is subjected to
a swamping of her psychological borders. She has discovered that she can't
hold concepts or ideas in rigid boundaries. The borders and walls that are
supposed to keep the undesirable ideas out are entrenched habits and patterns of behavior; these habits and patterns are the enemy within. Rigidity
means death. Only by remaining flexible is she able to stretch the psyche hor-
izontally and vertically. *La mestiza* constantly has to shift out of habitual formations; from convergent thinking, analytical reasoning that tends to use
rationality to move toward a single goal (a Western mode), to divergent thinking,[4] characterized by movement away from set patterns and goals and toward a more whole perspective, one that includes rather than excludes.

The new *mestiza* copes by developing a tolerance for contradictions, a   8
tolerance for ambiguity. She learns to be an Indian in Mexican culture, to be
Mexican from an Anglo point of view. She learns to juggle cultures. She has
a plural personality, she operates in a pluralistic mode—nothing is thrust
out, the good, the bad and the ugly, nothing rejected, nothing abandoned.
Not only does she sustain contradictions, she turns the ambivalence into
something else.

She can be jarred out of ambivalence by an intense, and often painful,   9
emotional event which inverts or resolves the ambivalence. I'm not sure
exactly how. The work takes place underground—subconsciously. It is work
that the soul performs. That focal point or fulcrum, that juncture where the

mestiza stands, is where phenomena tend to collide. It is where the possibility of uniting all that is separate occurs. This assembly is not one where severed or separated pieces merely come together. Nor is it a balancing of opposing powers. In attempting to work out a synthesis, the self has added a third element which is greater than the sum of its severed parts. That third element is a new consciousness—a *mestiza* consciousness—and though it is a source of intense pain, its energy comes from continual creative motion that keeps breaking down the unitary aspect of each new paradigm.

En unas pocas centurias, the future will belong to the *mestiza.* Because   10 the future depends on the breaking down of paradigms, it depends on the straddling of two or more cultures. By creating a new mythos—that is, a change in the way we perceive reality, the way we see ourselves, and the ways we behave—*la mestiza* creates a new consciousness.

The work of *mestiza* consciousness is to break down the subject-object   11 duality that keeps her a prisoner and to show in the flesh and through the images in her work how duality is transcended. The answer to the problem between the white race and the colored, between males and females, lies in healing the split that originates in the very foundation of our lives, our culture, our languages, our thoughts. A massive uprooting of dualistic thinking in the individual and collective consciousness is the beginning of a long struggle, but one that could, in our best hopes, bring us to the end of rape, of violence, of war.

La encrucijada / The Crossroads

A chicken is being sacrificed
    at a crossroads, a simple mound of earth
a mud shrine for *Eshu,*
    Yoruba god of indeterminacy,
who blesses her choice of path.
    She begins her journey.

Su cuerpo es una bocacalle. La mestiza has gone from being the sacrifi-   12 cial goat to becoming the officiating priestess at the crossroads.

As a *mestiza* I have no country, my homeland cast me out; yet all coun-   13 tries are mine because I am every woman's sister or potential lover. (As a lesbian I have no race, my own people disclaim me; but I am all races because there is the queer of me in all races.) I am cultureless because, as a feminist, I challenge the collective cultural/religious male-derived beliefs of Indo-Hispanics and Anglos; yet I am cultured because I am participating in the creation of yet another culture, a new story to explain the world and our participation in it, a new value system with images and symbols that connect

Library Resource Center
Renton Technical College
3000 N.E. 4th St.
Renton WA 98056

us to each other and to the planet. *Soy un amasamiento,* I am an act of kneading, of uniting and joining that not only has produced both a creature of darkness and a creature of light, but also a creature that questions the definitions of light and dark and gives them new meanings.

We are the people who leap in the dark, we are the people on the knees   14
of the gods. In our very flesh, (r)evolution works out the clash of cultures. It makes us crazy constantly, but if the center holds, we've made some kind of evolutionary step forward. *Nuestra alma el trabajo,* the opus, the great alchemical work; spiritual *mestizaje,* a "morphogenesis,"[5] an inevitable unfolding. We have become the quickening serpent movement.

Indigenous like corn, like corn, the *mestiza* is a product of crossbreed-   15
ing, designed for preservation under a variety of conditions. Like an ear of corn—a female seed-bearing organ—the *mestiza* is tenacious, tightly wrapped in the husks of her culture. Like kernels she clings to the cob; with thick stalks and strong brace roots, she holds tight to the earth—she will survive the crossroads.

Lavando y remojando el maíz en agua de cal, despojando el pellejo.   16
Moliendo, mixteando, amasando, haciendo tortillas de masa.[6] She steeps the corn in lime, it swells, softens. With stone roller on *metate,* she grinds the corn, then grinds again. She kneads and moulds the dough, pats the round balls into *tortillas.*

We are the porous rock in the stone *metate*
squatting on the ground.
We are the rolling pin, *el maíz y agua,*
la masa harina. Somos el amasijo.
Somos lo molido en el metate.
We are the *comal* sizzling hot,
the hot *tortilla,* the hungry mouth.
We are the coarse rock.
We are the grinding motion,
the mixed potion, *somos el molcajete.*
We are the pestle, the *comino, ajo, pimienta,*
We are the *chile colorado,*
the green shoot that cracks the rock.
We will abide.

El camino de la mestiza / The Mestiza Way

Caught between the sudden contraction, the breath sucked in and the endless space, the brown woman stands still, looks at the sky. She decides to go down, digging her way along the roots of trees. Sifting through the bones, she shakes them to see if there is any marrow in them. Then, touching the dirt to her forehead, to her tongue, she takes a few bones, leaves the rest in their burial place.

She goes through her backpack, keeps her journal and address book, throws away the muni-bart metromaps. The coins are heavy and they go next, then the greenbacks flutter through the air. She keeps her knife, can opener and eyebrow pencil. She puts bones, pieces of bark, *hierbas,* eagle feather, snakeskin, tape recorder, the rattle and drum in her pack and she sets out to become the complete *tolteca.*[7]

Her first step is to take inventory. *Despojando, desgranando, quitando* 17 *paja.* Just what did she inherit from her ancestors? This weight on her back—which is the baggage from the Indian mother, which the baggage from the Spanish father, which the baggage from the Anglo?

Pero es difícil differentiating between *lo heredado, lo adquirido, lo im-* 18 *puesto.* She puts history through a sieve, winnows out the lies, looks at the forces that we as a race, as women, have been a part of. *Luego bota lo que no vale, los desmientos, los desencuentros, el embrutecimiento. Aguarda el juicio, hondo y enraízado, de la gente antigua.* This step is a conscious rupture with all oppressive traditions of all cultures and religions. She communicates that rupture, documents the struggle. She reinterprets history and, using new symbols, she shapes new myths. She adopts new perspectives toward the darkskinned, women and queers. She strengthens her tolerance (and intolerance) for ambiguity. She is willing to share, to make herself vulnerable to foreign ways of seeing and thinking. She surrenders all notions of safety, of the familiar. Deconstruct, construct. She becomes a *nahual,* able to transform herself into a tree, a coyote, into another person. She learns to transform the small "I" into the total Self. *Se hace moldeadora de su alma. Según la concepción que tiene de sí misma, así será.*

Que no se nos olvide los hombres

"Tú no sirves pa' nada—
you're good for nothing.
Eres pura vieja."

"You're nothing but a woman" means you are defective. Its opposite is to be 19 *un macho.* The modern meaning of the word "machismo," as well as the concept, is actually an Anglo invention. For men like my father, being "macho" meant being strong enough to protect and support my mother and us, yet being able to show love. Today's macho has doubts about his ability to feed and protect his family. His "machismo" is an adaptation to oppression and poverty and low self-esteem. It is the result of hierarchical male dominance. The Anglo, feeling inadequate and inferior and powerless, displaces or transfers these feelings to the Chicano by shaming him. In the Gringo world, the Chicano suffers from excessive humility and self-effacement, shame of self and self-deprecation. Around Latinos he suffers from a sense of language inadequacy and its accompanying discomfort; with Native Americans he suffers from a racial amnesia which ignores our common blood, and from guilt because the Spanish part of him took their land and oppressed them. He has an excessive compensatory hubris when around Mexicans from the other side. It overlays a deep sense of racial shame.

The loss of a sense of dignity and respect in the macho breeds a false 　20 machismo which leads him to put down women and even to brutalize them. Coexisting with his sexist behavior is a love for the mother which takes precedence over that of all others. Devoted son, macho pig. To wash down the shame of his acts, of his very being, and to handle the brute in the mirror, he takes to the bottle, the snort, the needle, and the fist.

Though we "understand" the root causes of male hatred and fear, and 　21 the subsequent wounding of women, we do not excuse, we do not condone, and we will no longer put up with it. From the men of our race, we demand the admission/acknowledgment/disclosure/testimony that they wound us, violate us, are afraid of us and of our power. We need them to say they will begin to eliminate their hurtful put-down ways. But more than the words, we demand acts. We say to them: We will develop equal power with you and those who have shamed us.

It is imperative that mestizas support each other in changing the sexist el- 　22 ements in the Mexican-Indian culture. As long as woman is put down, the Indian and the Black in all of us is put down. The struggle of the mestiza is above all a feminist one. As long as *los hombres* think they have to *chingar mujeres* and each other to be men, as long as men are taught that they are superior and therefore culturally favored over *la mujer,* as long as to be a *vieja* is a thing of derision, there can be no real healing of our psyches. We're halfway there—we have such love of the Mother, the good mother. The first step is to unlearn the *puta/virgen* dichotomy and to see *Coatlapopeuh-Coatlicue* in the Mother, *Guadalupe.*

Tenderness, a sign of vulnerability, is so feared that it is showered on 　23 women with verbal abuse and blows. Men, even more than women, are fettered to gender roles. Women at least have had the guts to break out of bondage. Only gay men have had the courage to expose themselves to the woman inside them and to challenge the current masculinity. I've encountered a few scattered and isolated gentle straight men, the beginnings of a new breed, but they are confused, and entangled with sexist behaviors that they have not been able to eradicate. We need a new masculinity and the new man needs a movement.

Lumping the males who deviate from the general norm with man, the oppressor, is a gross injustice. *Asombra pensar que nos hemos quedado en ese pozo oscuro donde el mundo encierra a las lesbianas. Asombra pensar que hemos, como femenistas y lesbianas, cerrado nuestros corazónes a los hombres, a nuestros hermanos los jotos, desheredados y marginales como nosotros.* Being the supreme crossers of cultures, homosexuals have strong bonds with the queer white, Black, Asian, Native American, Latino, and with the queer in Italy, Australia and the rest of the planet. We come from all colors, all classes, all races, all time periods. Our role is to link people with each other—the Blacks with Jews with Indians with Asians with whites with extraterrestrials. It is to transfer ideas and information from one culture to another. Colored homosexuals have more knowledge of other cultures; have always been at the forefront (although sometimes in the closet) of all liberation struggles in this country; have suffered more injustices and have survived them despite all odds. Chicanos need to acknowledge the political and artistic contributions of their queer. People, listen to what your *jotería* is saying.   24

The mestizo and the queer exist at this time and point on the evolutionary continuum for a purpose. We are a blending that proves that all blood is intricately woven together, and that we are spawned out of similar souls.   25

Somos una gente

> *Hay tantísimas fronteras*
> *que dividen a la gente,*
> *pero por cada frontera*
> *existe también un puente.*

—GINA VALDÉS[8]

Divided Loyalties. Many women and men of color do not want to have any dealings with white people. It takes too much time and energy to explain to the downwardly mobile, white middle-class women that it's okay for us to want to own "possessions," never having had any nice furniture on our dirt floors or "luxuries" like washing machines. Many feel that whites should help their own people rid themselves of race hatred and fear first. I, for one, choose to use some of my energy to serve as mediator. I think we need to allow whites to be our allies. Through our literature, art, *corridos,* and folktales we must share our history with them so when they set up   26 committees to help Big Mountain Navajos or the Chicano farmworkers or *los Nicaragüenses* they won't turn people away because of their racial fears and ignorances. They will come to see that they are not helping us but following our lead.

Individually, but also as a racial entity, we need to voice our needs. We   27
need to say to white society: We need you to accept the fact that Chicanos are different, to acknowledge your rejection and negation of us. We need you to own the fact that you looked upon us as less than human, that you stole our lands, our personhood, our self-respect. We need you to make public restitution: to say that, to compensate for your own sense of defectiveness, you strive for power over us, you erase our history and our experience because it makes you feel guilty—you'd rather forget your brutish acts. To say you've split yourself from minority groups, that you disown us, that your dual consciousness splits off parts of yourself, transferring the "negative" parts onto us. (Where there is persecution of minorities, there is shadow projection. Where there is violence and war, there is repression of shadow.) To say that you are afraid of us, that to put distance between us, you wear the mask of contempt. Admit that Mexico is your double, that she exists in the shadow of this country, that we are irrevocably tied to her. Gringo, accept the doppelganger in your psyche. By taking back your collective shadow the intracultural split will heal. And finally, tell us what you need from us.

By Your True Faces We Will Know You

I am visible—see this Indian face—yet I am invisible. I both blind them with   28
my beak nose and am their blind spot. But I exist, we exist. They'd like to think I have melted in the pot. But I haven't, we haven't.

The dominant white culture is killing us slowly with its ignorance. By   29
taking away our self-determination, it has made us weak and empty. As a people we have resisted and we have taken expedient positions, but we have never been allowed to develop unencumbered—we have never been allowed to be fully ourselves. The whites in power want us people of color to barricade ourselves behind our separate tribal walls so they can pick us off one at a time with their hidden weapons; so they can whitewash and distort history. Ignorance splits people, creates prejudices. A misinformed people is a subjugated people.

Before the Chicano and the undocumented worker and the Mexican   30
from the other side can come together, before the Chicano can have unity with Native Americans and other groups, we need to know the history of

their struggle and they need to know ours. Our mothers, our sisters and brothers, the guys who hang out on street corners, the children in the playgrounds, each of us must know our Indian lineage, our afro-*mestisaje,* our history of resistance.

To the immigrant *mexicano* and the recent arrivals we must teach our   31
history. The 80 million *mexicanos* and the Latinos from Central and South America must know of our struggles. Each one of us must know basic facts about Nicaragua, Chile and the rest of Latin America. The Latinoist movement (Chicanos, Puerto Ricans, Cubans and other Spanish-speaking people working together to combat racial discrimination in the market place) is good but it is not enough. Other than a common culture we will have nothing to hold us together. We need to meet on a broader communal ground.

The struggle is inner: Chicano, *indio,* American Indian, *mojado, mexi-*   32
cano, immigrant Latino, Anglo in power, working class Anglo, Black, Asian—our psyches resemble the border-towns and are populated by the same people. The struggle has always been inner, and is played out in the outer terrains. Awareness of our situation must come before inner changes, which in turn come before changes in society. Nothing happens in the "real" world unless it first happens in the images in our heads.

El Día de la Chicana

I will not be shamed again
Nor will I shame myself.

I am possessed by a vision: that we Chicanas and Chicanos have taken back   33
or uncovered our true faces, our dignity and self-respect. It's a validation vision.

Seeing the Chicana anew in light of her history. I seek an exoneration,   34
a seeing through the fictions of white supremacy, a seeing of ourselves in our true guises and not as the false racial personality that has been given to us and that we have given to ourselves. I seek our woman's face, our true features, the positive and the negative seen clearly, free of the tainted biases of male dominance. I seek new images of identity, new beliefs about ourselves, our humanity and worth no longer in question.

Estamos viviendo en la noche de la Raza, un tiempo cuando el trabajo se   35
hace a lo quieto, en el oscuro. El día cuando aceptamos tal y como somos y para en donde vamos y porque—ese día será el día de la Raza. Yo tengo el compromiso de expresar mi visión, mi sensibilidad, mi percepción de la revalidación de la gente mexicana, su mérito, estimación, honra, aprecio, y validez.

On December 2nd when my sun goes into my first house, I celebrate *el*   36
día de la Chicana y el Chicano. On that day I clean my altars, light my *Coat-*
lalopeuh candle, burn sage and copal, take *el baño para espantar basura,*
sweep my house. On that day I bare my soul, make myself vulnerable to
friends and family by expressing my feelings. On that day I affirm who we are.

On that day I look inside our conflicts and our basic introverted racial   37
temperament. I identify our needs, voice them. I acknowledge that the self
and the race have been wounded. I recognize the need to take care of our
personhood, of our racial self. On that day I gather the splintered and dis-
owned parts of *la gente mexicana* and hold them in my arms. *Todas las*
partes de nosotros valen.

On that day I say, "Yes, all you people wound us when you reject us. Re-   38
jection strips us of self-worth; our vulnerability exposes us to shame. It is our
innate identity you find wanting. We are ashamed that we need your good
opinion, that we need your acceptance. We can no longer camouflage our
needs, can no longer let defenses and fences sprout around us. We can no
longer withdraw. To rage and look upon you with contempt is to rage and
be contemptuous of ourselves. We can no longer blame you, nor disown the
white parts, the male parts, the pathological parts, the queer parts, the vulnerable parts. Here we are weaponless with open arms, with only our magic.
Let's try it our way, the mestiza way, the Chicana way, the woman way.

On that day, I search for our essential dignity as a people, a people with   39
a sense of purpose—to belong and contribute to something greater than our
pueblo. On that day I seek to recover and reshape my spiritual identity.
¡Anímate! Raza, a celebrar el día de la Chicana.

El retorno

All movements are accomplished in six stages,
and the seventh brings return.

—*I Ching*[9]

Tanto tiempo sin verte casa mía,
mi cuna, mi hondo nido de la huerta.

— *"Soledad"*[10]

I stand at the river, watch the curving, twisting serpent, a serpent nailed to   40
the fence where the mouth of the Rio Grande empties into the Gulf.

I have come back. *Tanto dolor me costó el alejamiento*. I shade my eyes   41
and look up. The bone beak of a hawk slowly circling over me, checking
me out as potential carrion. In its wake a little bird flickering its wings,
swimming sporadically like a fish. In the distance the expressway and the

slough of traffic like an irritated sow. The sudden pull in my gut, *la tierra, los aguaceros.* My land, *el viento soplando la arena, el lagartijo debajo de un nopalito. Me acuerdo como era antes. Una región desértica de vasta llanuras, costeras de baja altura, de escasa lluvia, de chaparrales formados por mesquites y huizaches.* If I look real hard I can almost see the Spanish fathers who were called "the cavalry of Christ" enter this valley riding their burros, see the clash of cultures commence.

Tierra natal. This is home, the small towns in the Valley, *los pueblitos* 42
with chicken pens and goats picketed to mesquite shrubs. *En las colonias* on the other side of the tracks, junk cars line the front yards of hot pink and lavender-trimmed houses—Chicano architecture we call it, self-consciously. I have missed the TV shows where hosts speak in half and half, and where awards are given in the category of Tex-Mex music. I have missed the Mexican cemeteries blooming with artificial flowers, the fields of aloe vera and red pepper, rows of sugar cane, of corn hanging on the stalks, the cloud of *polvareda* in the dirt roads behind a speeding pickup truck, *el sabor de tamales de rez y venado.* I have missed *la yegua colorada* gnawing the wooden gate of her stall, the smell of horse flesh from Carito's corrals. *He hecho menos las noches calientes sin aire, noches de linternas y lechuzas* making holes in the night.

I still feel the old despair when I look at the unpainted, dilapidated, 43
scrap lumber houses consisting mostly of corrugated aluminum. Some of the poorest people in the U.S. live in the Lower Rio Grande Valley, an arid and semi-arid land of irrigated farming, intense sunlight and heat, citrus groves next to chaparral and cactus. I walk through the elementary school I attended so long ago, that remained segregated until recently. I remember how the white teachers used to punish us for being Mexican.

How I love this tragic valley of South Texas, as Ricardo Sánchez calls it; 44
this borderland between the Nueces and the Rio Grande. This land has survived possession and ill-use by five countries: Spain, Mexico, the Republic of Texas, the U.S., the Confederacy, and the U.S. again. It has survived Anglo-Mexican blood feuds, lynchings, burnings, rapes, pillage.

Today I see the Valley still struggling to survive. Whether it does or not, 45
it will never be as I remember it. The borderlands depression that was set off by the 1982 peso devaluation in Mexico resulted in the closure of hundreds of Valley businesses. Many people lost their homes, cars, land. Prior to 1982, U.S. store owners thrived on retail sales to Mexicans who came across the border for groceries and clothes and appliances. While goods on the U.S. side have become 10, 100, 1000 times more expensive for Mexican buyers, goods on the Mexican side have become 10, 100, 1000 times cheaper

for Americans. Because the Valley is heavily dependent on agriculture and Mexican retail trade, it has the highest unemployment rates along the entire border region; it is the Valley that has been hardest hit.[11]

"It's been a bad year for corn," my brother, Nune, says. As he talks, I re- 46
member my father scanning the sky for a rain that would end the drought, looking up into the sky, day after day, while the corn withered on its stalk. My father has been dead for 29 years, having worked himself to death. The life span of a Mexican farm laborer is 56—he lived to be 38. It shocks me that I am older than he. I, too, search the sky for rain. Like the ancients, I worship the rain god and the maize goddess, but unlike my father I have recovered their names. Now for rain (irrigation) one offers not a sacrifice of blood, but of money.

"Farming is in a bad way," my brother says. "Two or three thousand 47
small and big farmers went bankrupt in this country last year. Six years ago the price of corn was $8.00 per hundred pounds," he goes on. "This year it is $3.90 per hundred pounds." And, I think to myself, after taking inflation into account, not planting anything puts you ahead.

I walk out to the back yard, stare at *los rosales de mamá*. She wants me 48
to help her prune the rose bushes, dig out the carpet grass that is choking them. *Mamagrande Ramona también tenía rosales.* Here every Mexican grows flowers. If they don't have a piece of dirt, they use car tires, jars, cans, shoe boxes. Roses are the Mexican's favorite flower. I think, how symbolic—thorns and all.

Yes, the Chicano and Chicana have always taken care of growing things 49
and the land. Again I see the four of us kids getting off the school bus, changing into our work clothes, walking into the field with Papí and Mamí, all six of us bending to the ground. Below our feet, under the earth lie the watermelon seeds. We cover them with paper plates, putting *terremotes* on top of the plates to keep them from being blown away by the wind. The paper plates keep the freeze away. Next day or the next, we remove the plates, bare the tiny green shoots to the elements. They survive and grow, give fruit hundreds of times the size of the seed. We water them and hoe them. We harvest them. The vines dry, rot, are plowed under. Growth, death, decay, birth. The soil prepared again and again, impregnated, worked on. A constant changing of forms, *renacimientos de la tierra madre.*

This land was Mexican once
    was Indian always
        and is.
            And will be again.

NOTES

1. This is my own "take off" on Jose Vasconcelos' idea. Jose Vasconcelos, *La Raza Cósmica: Misión de la Raza Ibero-Americana* (México: Aguilar S.A. de Ediciones, 1961).

2. Vasconcelos.

3. Arthur Koestler termed this "bisociation." Albert Rothenberg, *The Creative Process in Art, Science, and Other Fields* (Chicago, IL: University of Chicago Press, 1979), 12.

4. In part, I derive my definitions for "convergent" and "divergent" thinking from Rothenberg, 12–13.

5. To borrow chemist Ilya Prigogine's theory of "dissipative structures." Prigogine discovered that substances interact not in predictable ways as it was taught in science, but in different and fluctuating ways to produce new and more complex structures, a kind of birth he called "morphogenesis," which created unpredictable innovations. Harold Gilliam, "Searching for a New World View," *This World* (January, 1981), 23.

6. *Tortillas de masa harina:* corn tortillas are of two types, the smooth uniform ones made in a tortilla press and usually bought at a tortilla factory or supermarket, and *gorditas,* made by mixing *masa* with lard or shortening or butter (my mother sometimes puts in bits of bacon or *chicharrones*).

7., 8. Gina Valdés, *Puentes y Fronteras: Coplas Chicanas* (Los Angeles, CA: Castle Lithograph, 1982), 2.

9. Richard Wilhelm, *The I Ching or Book of Changes,* trans. Cary F. Baynes (Princeton, NJ: Princeton University Press, 1950), 98.

10. *"Soledad"* is sung by the group, Haciendo Punto en Otro Son.

11. Out of the twenty-two border counties in the four border states, Hidalgo County (named for Father Hidalgo who was shot in 1810 after instigating Mexico's revolt against Spanish rule under the banner of *la Virgen de Guadalupe*) is the most poverty-stricken county in the nation as well as the largest home base (along with Imperial in California) for migrant farm-workers. It was here that I was born and raised. I am amazed that both it and I have survived.

Working with the Text

1. What is *"mestiza* consciousness"? What characterizes it? How is it different from being Mexican or from the United States?

2. Throughout her essay Anzaldúa engages in what she calls "code switching" between English and Spanish. How does her use of language contribute to her argument about cultural hybridization? In what ways is language integral to the new *mestiza* consciousness? How did you feel reading the essay, with the two languages? Do you read enough Spanish to follow both? Was the Spanish alienating to you? If so, how do you analyze that response?

3. Clearly, an important aspect of Anzaldúa's argument is based on issues of gender and sexuality. What are some of the connections between sexuality, gender, and culture? To what, for example, does she attribute the prevailing attitudes of machismo in Mexican culture? How are current constructions of masculinity important to the future of the new race consciousness? How does homosexuality fit into her argument? In what ways does her position as a lesbian woman of color shape her vision of the new *mestiza* consciousness?

4. Near the end of the essay, she describes a vision she has of the first Christian missionaries entering the Rio Grande valley. What does she see in this vision of the valley. What conflicts does she foresee? In the subsequent paragraph she shifts to a series of memories she recalls from her own childhood in this same valley. What does she remember from her upbringing? How do these memories influence her vision of the "Borderlands" as a cultural crossroads?

5. In what ways is her essay about "tribal" consciousness? Does it emphasize "tribalism" over "nationalism"? She calls the new *mestiza* consciousness a new "race" consciousness: Is this racial consciousness as you understand it? Does her essay uphold traditional racial constructions or try to reconstruct them? Explore these questions in an essay.

In the Borderlands of Chicano Identity, There Are Only Fragments

BENJAMIN ALIRE SÁENZ

Benjamin Alire Sáenz teaches creative writing at the University of Texas at El Paso (UTEP). He earned an M.A. in theology from the University of Louvain in Belgium, an M.A. in creative writing from UTEP, and a Ph.D. at Stanford University, where he was a Wallace E. Stegner Fellow. Sáenz was a recipient of the Lannan Poetry Prize in 1993. His first book of poems, *Calendar of Dust,* won the Before Columbus Foundation's American Book Award in 1992. Other books include a collection of poems, *Dark and Perfect Angel, Flowers for the Broken, Carry Me Like Water, Vatos,* and *Finding Your Literary Voice.* In the following essay, Sáenz reflects upon the celebration of ethnic identification, specifically Chicano identity, as a source of a multicultural and a pluralist society.

A bill is coming in that I fear America is not prepared to pay.
JAMES BALDWIN

The time for undiscriminating racial unity has passed.
TONI MORRISON

My wife and I go to an opening reception at the newly opened Barnes & Noble bookstore. We are disappointed because it looks like a mall. What did we expect? The store is full of people who gather around food tables and gawk through the aisles. People visit and chat with one another. My wife and I look at each other and finally whisper: *"There's no one here but white people."* El Paso is 70 percent "Hispanic" (I hate that word). The West Side, where the bookstore was built, is the whitest part of El Paso. The clientele assembled here tonight is decidedly white. My wife and I become uncomfortable. We drink a cup of coffee. We leave. We drive to a book reception—Texas Western Press is celebrating the publication of its latest book. I feel obliged to attend because I am on the editorial board. My wife and I again notice that everyone there is white. "What is this?" I ask myself. "White Night?" I remembered living in Lafayette, Louisiana. There was a blues joint where Black people hung out, but on Tuesdays the "Blacks" would clear out and the place would fill up with "white" people. The locals referred to Tuesdays at that place as "White Night." I never knew if the term was used ironically or not. Tonight, I remember that place. We make small talk (there is no "big" talk at such events). My wife, Patricia, is an associate judge. I am used to attending events with her where many (if not most) of the people are "Hispanics." At the reception, my wife and I keep looking around then nod at each other knowingly. We leave. Why do Patricia and I notice that we are the only Chicanos at these events when nobody else around us seems to notice—or care? Why do *we* notice? And them— why don't *they* notice?

In response to one of my assignments, one of my undergraduate students casually announced, with no discernible rage in his voice, "I don't read gringo poets." His absolute separatist stance appalled me. I confess, I experienced a moment of complete outrage, and I reacted more out of spontaneous reflex than reflective intelligence. My anger was evident, and I made no attempt to hide it. "I'm not about to put up with racist discourse in this class, got that? You *will* read Anglo poets or you will drop my course." He looked at me quietly. Later, I tell myself that I overreacted. I know what lies behind his words: *I have been erased. Ergo, I will erase. I have been hated. I will hate.* There is a compelling logic here.

Later, he wrote me a poem in which my person was represented. I was   3
not exactly the hero. I asked him to visit my office. We talked. But we came to no real solutions. The student (a very dark, Indian-looking Chicano) was disappointed by my response. He was completely disillusioned with me. *What kind of a role model was I, anyway?* Not that he said that, not outright, but his eyes accused. I told him I was not the enemy. But there he was—in my office, and he was staring at me and his eyes kept saying: very definitely not the real thing—not a *real Chicano.* I hate playing the game of "who is more Chicano than whom." (It's a variation on a game currently played in Washington between Newt Gingrich and Bill Clinton: Who is more middle-class than whom?) I detest pissing contests.

I think about this student. It is tempting to dismiss him. But his rage is   4
very real and it is a dangerous thing to dismiss rage. Rage never just disappears—it boomerangs back, and if it doesn't hit me, it will hit someone else. I cannot allow myself to forget that I have felt what he feels. I am not free of hate. I am not free of rage with regard to the subject of identity, and I do not really believe anybody else in that classroom is free of rage either. Most of us merely carry our race-based mistrust in a more acceptable manner (especially those of us who are holding very serious dialogues with a "dominant culture" and have a great deal invested in those dialogues). Some of us deny the relevance of race- or ethnicity-based identities simply by invoking a democracy-based identity that is supposed to supersede all other arguments and discourses: "We are all Americans. We are all equal." This particular strategy is facile, lazy, and anti-intellectual, and has more to do with denial and erasure than with examining our material culture and how that material culture is decidedly built upon inequalities.

I think about this "radical" student later in the day. His argument is de-   5
cidedly unsubtle, unnuanced, superficial, reactionary. But the possibility exists that his attitude really offended me because I am embarrassed by the way he handles his rage (which has everything to do with his identity). Why do I find his position unacceptable? *Bad politics. Very bad politics. And the premises behind his politics? Well, those are bad, too.* I chew on this. I am not so unlike him. I too have been formed by racist discourse—and yet I have just demanded that he not engage in that discourse in my class because I find the way he talks about this disagreeable. Knowing, as I do, the very real reasons behind his rage and knowing, as I do, the way most of my colleagues ignore the material circumstances of our student population, why should he play the role of the accommodationist? Should I shoot the messenger because he has articulated an attitude we all know is just beneath the surface? He did not produce himself. He is a product. And the word *prod-*

uct here should not be confused with *victim*. Though we may all occupy different positions in the material world, *we are all* the products of the cumulative discourses around us. None of us is as much an "active subject" as we'd like to imagine. We are all contained by these discourses—especially the discourse of capitalism—and few of us are able to break through to a "radical" talk that is outside of these discourses. All of us make feeble attempts. And isn't this student trying?

Some would say that this young man's rage was produced by an inflammatory separatist Chicano rhetoric that does nothing but produce a climate of hatred and mistrust—and this is partially true. *Partially true.* But this is too easy an answer—too easy because it masks more complex issues and protects a plethora of guilty parties. When faced with the "in your face" talk of some African Americans, Chicanos, "radical" feminists, or members of Queer Nation, we would do well to remember that one of the reasons this kind of talk bothers us has a great deal to do with the "talk" we have adopted. We are trained to use a certain discourse, have grown accustomed to using a different kind of grammar. Most of us who teach in universities have been reproduced by tamer, more genteel rhetorics, but it is disingenuous to pretend we are free of violence simply because we appear to have more control over our actions. The pretense of civility in our places of employment (especially in universities) is just that—a pretense.

I cannot forget this one important thing: this man has something very real invested in his "identity politics." This is serious business. He is fighting back. *Maybe I am the enemy.*

> I have a curious relationship with the word *Chicano*. I don't mind being called a "Chicana," but I have problems using the label to describe myself. It's not that I don't feel like a Chicana, or I'm embarrassed by my culture or even by the word itself. I usually end up calling myself a Mexican American. The word Chicana inevitably stumbles out of my mouth clumsily like I'm pronouncing a foreign word. I don't know why. I'm not offended by it, I just can't seem to get used to using that word.

The evening's conversation is easygoing, not too provocative, light, something you would expect from a dinner party held in honor of a visiting lecturer. Near the end of the evening, the woman seated next to me asks: "Why do you insist on calling yourself a Chicano writer? Why not simply call yourself a writer?" She does not ask the question belligerently, but there is a firm tone behind her question that demands an answer, a challenge perhaps. And yet I know that no answer I give will satisfy the questioner. I take a sip of wine. A series of answers run through my mind: "If I called myself a Jewish writer, would you ask me the same question? Would you ask why I insisted on my Jewishness? If I called myself an 'American' writer, would you ask why I insisted on my Americanness?" Too aggressive. Another

possible answer—one more mysterious, subtle, more suggestive, more worthy of the writer she imagines me to be: "I don't want to call myself anything." I see myself smiling at her. What would she do with *that* answer? But
the answer doesn't suit me—I don't like being in the wisdom business. Far
too many poets have bored me with their humanistic wisdom that under serious scrutiny turns out to be as thoughtful as *The Bridges of Madison
County*. Another answer races through my mind. "Exactly what about the
term Chicano bothers you? Clearly the label of *writer* (an identity label if
there ever was one) doesn't bother you a bit. Why riot? Isn't *writer* a problematic identity for you? Why not?" But I don't want to get into an argument,
and *that* answer sounds too much like an ambush. "Well," I say, "I'm comfortable with that identity. I choose it." I say this partially because it's true
and partially because people are comfortable when anything that is being
discussed is framed in terms of "choice"—part of a democratic rhetoric we
are all steeped in.

   She doesn't skip a beat. "But doesn't calling yourself that limit you? Why   9
would you want to be so limited?"

   "Why does it limit me?" I ask. *Of course it limits me. It limits me because*   10
when many whites see that word, they won't pick up the book. Serious read-
ers want to read "universal literature," "world literature." "All writers have
their limitations." I say. I'm angry now, and I know it. And I know why I am
angry, but I also know that I will not go into any diatribes. I do speak passionately, though I am very bad at hiding my emotions. I suggest to her—
and by now the entire table—that I have no wish to distance myself from
the history of a people I consider to be my community. I tell her that I am
unapologetically political. I tell her that this country has no right to demand
historical amnesia from its citizens. I praise the memory of my parents, who
were seasonal cotton pickers. I am romanticizing the image of the farm-
worker shamelessly. She nods her head. But I see she is not completely satisfied by my answer. I have, however, managed to silence her. Does this
mean I have won the argument? She is suspicious of my "choice"—finds my
"identity" false, though she does not say it. She feels *Chicano* is divisive, an
unnecessary and inappropriate political intrusion. *Yes, yes, we all come from
immigrant stock. Just be a writer and cut the crap.* Writer, now there's an
identity. The conversation is lively, but she is not convinced of anything I
have said. I assume that *Chicano* threatens her because it asserts—and insists upon—difference. Difference for difference's sake? Is that what she
imagines? And I am equally suspicious of her assumptions. She does not
have to discuss *her* identity. She does not have to hold it up for public debate, for "intellectual" scrutiny. Doesn't she have an identity? *Tell me, what
is it like to be white?* What are the politics of her "chosen" identity? I imagine

her answer would sound something like this: "Come, come, we are educated and civil. We are all the same. We all love, we all hate, we all dream, we all will die. We feel. We all feel." I imagine that she tells me this, and I imagine my response: "Yes. And some die sooner than others, and some live better than others, and some work harder than others, and some have a great deal more than others. *Work makes freedom.* Clearly work makes some freer than others."

As I drive home with my wife, I tell her that "gringos" just don't get it. 11

Catholicism. Marxism. Capitalism. Humanism. Chicanismo. I find it impossible to live without organizing principles. I need to organize my identity around certain narratives. I reject certain discourses, certain kinds of talks that do their work on me despite my protestations—which makes me resent those discourses even more ("nationalism" immediately comes to mind). For the good or for the bad, I find it impossible to live without an identity. *No one can live without an identity.* The day of the "posthuman" has not yet arrived, and anyone who thinks it has arrived had better go back and do some serious analysis of the discourses that have (de)formed and shaped our "selves." The debate surrounding identity and identity formations cannot be reduced to obsessions "invented" by academic people of color and sympathetic white progressives who have no real interest in "knowledge" or "standards" or "academic discipline" or "scholarship." The "identity wars" did not begin in 1968, did not begin with Gloria Steinem, did not begin with Malcom X, did not begin with Langston Hughes, did not begin with Toni Morrison, did not begin with César Chávez, did not begin with Gloria Anzaldúa, did not begin with Rigoberta Menchú, did not begin with Maxine Hong Kingston, did not begin even with Harold Bloom. The West's obsession with identity began with Plato and Aristotle and was extended by (among others) Thomas Aquinas, Augustine, Descartes, Locke, Hume, Heidegger, and Marx. 12

"Identity" cannot exist without an attendant politics—and everybody engages in identity politics. *Everybody.* We all privilege certain categories or discourses over others and organize ourselves around these discourses, some of us organize our identities around the vague term *human.* Some of us organize our identities around our sexuality. Some of us organize our identities around the countries of our origins. Some of us organize our identities around our genders. I am often enraged when Chicanos (and other "colorful" people) are accused of playing "identity politics." It is like accusing someone of breathing. 13

It is fair to say that many people (inside academia as well as outside it) resent *the way* people who call themselves Chicanos (and Indians and African Americans and Asian Americans) have played identity politics (at 14 white people's expense, no doubt—at *everybody* else's expense). I recall a passage in Richard Rodriguez's *Hunger of Memory:*

"Damn!" he said, and his chair rasped the floor as he pushed himself back. Suddenly it was to *me* that he was complaining. "It's just not right, Richard. None of this is fair. You've done some good work, but so have I. I'll bet our records are just about even. But when we go looking for jobs this year, it's a very different story. You're the one who gets all the breaks."

To evade his criticism, I wanted to side with him. I was about to admit the injustice of affirmative action. "Oh, it's all very simple this year. You're a Chicano. And I am a Jew. That's really the only difference between us."

His words stung anger alive. In a voice deceptively calm I replied that he oversimplified the whole issue. Phrases came quickly: the importance of cultural diversity; new blood; the goal of racial integration. They were all the old arguments I had proposed years before—long since abandoned. After a minute or two, as I heard myself talking, I felt self-disgust. The job offers I was receiving were indeed unjustified. I knew that. All I was saying amounted to a frantic self-defense. It all was a lie. I tried to find an end to my sentence; my voice faltered to a stop.

"Yeah, yeah sure," he said. "I've heard all that stuff before. Nothing you can say, though, really changes the fact that affirmative action is unfair. You can see that, can't you? There isn't any way for me to compete with you. Once there were quotas to keep my parents out of schools like Yale. Now there are quotas to get you in. And the effect on me is the same as it was for them . . . ."

At the edge of hearing, I listened to every word he spoke. But behind my eyes my mind reared—spooked and turning—then broke toward a reckless idea: Leave the university. Leave. Immediately the idea sprang again in my bowels and began to climb. Rent money. I pictured myself having to borrow. Get a job as a waiter somewhere? I had come to depend on the intellectual companionship of students—bright students—to relieve the scholar's loneliness. I remembered the British Museum, a year in silence. I wanted to teach; I wanted to read; I wanted this life. But I had to protest. How? Disqualify myself from the profession as long as affirmative action continued? Romantic exile? But I had to. Yes. I found the horizon again. It was calm.

The graduate student across the room had stopped talking; he was staring out the window. I said nothing. My decision was final. No, I would say to them all. Finally, simply, no.

I wrote a note to all the chairmen of English departments who had offered me jobs. I left a note for the professor in my own department at Berkeley who was in charge of helping graduate students look for teaching positions. (The contradictions of affirmative action have finally caught up with me. Please remove my name from the list of teaching job applicants.)

I telephoned my mother and father. My mother did not seem to hear exactly what I was trying to tell her. She let the subject pass without comment. (Was I still planning on coming for dinner this Sunday?) My father, however, clearly understood. Silent for a moment, he seemed uncertain of what I expected to hear. Finally, troubled, he said hesitantly, "I don't know why you feel this way. We have never had any of the chances before."

We, he said. But he was wrong. It was *he* who had never had any chance before.[1]

As I recall this passage, I open the book to that page and reread it. Ahh, Richard, I sometimes wonder what your friend would have said to *you* if *you* had said: "You're a Jew. And I am a Chicano. That's really the only difference between us." It was only *you* who was playing the affirmative action identity politics game, not him. Not him. He was just a talented individual. And you, you were a member of a group. And he (unlike you) lived in the best of all possible worlds—where there were nothing but "individuals" who always got jobs according to objective criteria and merit. So there was nothing left for you to do but divorce yourself from the "We." "Romantic exile." Isn't that how you self-consciously referred to it? In the face of "contradictions" you simply take yourself out of the game. And yet you insert. yourself back into it by writing a book—a "public" book, about what?—*about identity.*

You say you have become a public man—self-made in a public language—English. But isn't Spanish a public language? All languages are public, Richard. But the talented "individual" wants only to be an "individual"—insists on it. You have become middle-class without so much as analyzing and critiquing that powerful and complex word: "But I write of one life only. My own. If my story is true, I trust it will resonate with significance for other lives. Finally, my history deserves public notice as no more than this: a parable for the life of its reader. Here is the life of a middle class man" (7). The romance of it is too much for me to bear. You have exchanged one identity for another and cloaked yourself in a rhetoric that denies the complex and unequal positions we occupy in this very complicated material world. Escape is not possible. But you are enamored of the image of escape and you embrace the long literary traditions in which you base your aesthetic: "The world is too much with us," the world is only the place where "ignorant armies clash by night" (especially the ignorant armies that battle for bilingual education and affirmative action). There is no community possible for you. There is only exile. There is only that aesthetic gesture that valorizes the alienation of the enlightened individual. This is an old story, Richard. It will not save you. It will not save anyone.

Like Rodriguez, many Chicanos have come to the conclusion that identity politics is the only game in town. (The conservatives who have appropriated Rodriguez's writing must be reminded at every turn that Mr. Rodriguez has built a career around identity politics.) Why is identity politics inescapable? Because we live in a shitty, disgusting world that produces and reproduces appalling inequalities, a society that helps to create suspicions of "others." The politics of identity cannot be separated from these inequalities. Identity politics in the workplace, for all its disturbing problematics, is at least a recognition that we live in a racist society and a demonstration of a willingness to meet and confront that racist society with solutions. I cannot take opponents of affirmative action seriously, not because affirmative action is so delightfully free of "prejudice" and "discrimination," and not because I seriously believe that affirmative action is going to usher in the just world order we have all been awaiting since the day Adam and Eve were exiled from the garden, but because opponents of affirmative action offer no real solutions to those inequalities (which are undeniably, but not exclusively, race and gender based). We ought to have at least learned by now that an objective merit system does not exist. Trying to hire the best person for the job is like judging a literary contest: for every judge, there is a different deserving winner, and each judge will insist that his or her only criterion is "good writing."

When I call myself a Chicano, I do not do so unproblematically. Do I 18 privilege the culture to which I was born? Yes. Do I do so out of nostalgia? No. Do I overprivilege my culture? Sometimes. Do I resent gringos? Sometimes. Do I *hate* gringos? No. Do I realize that white or light skin is overprivileged in the country in which I live? Yes. Am I enraged by people who refuse to acknowledge that fact? Absolutely. Am I an essentialist? No.

I live on a border between Mexico and the United States. I sometimes 19 sneer (perhaps unfairly) at Latinos who think the border is only a metaphor. What is so radical about using a very material culture as a literary device to describe an individual's psychological state? I know border culture intimately, the anxieties and mistrust that the very fact of living here raises in people. But I refuse to romanticize my culture. I am fond of saying that I don't do hat dances. In my writings, there is no nostalgia—the people represented there are not poor but happy and they do not lean on cacti. I am not ignorant of other cultures, other traditions, other ways of talking. I am neither provincial nor insulated nor blind to the other discourses that have formed me. I am not a separatist. I am not an extremist. If I wear *Chicano* as if it were a badge, I do so because "to live is to take sides" and it does not seem an unreasonable thing to side with the class and the ethnic group that produced me. On the other hand, Chicano identity has nothing to do with particular cultural characteristics that an individual must have (or attain) in order to be that thing called Chicano. *I am not a neo-Platonist, I am not an essentialist, I am not a cultural purist.* I realize the pitfalls of identity labels (though I reject such easy metaphors that imply an identity—any identity—is something that is facile, put on like a shirt and just as easily exchanged depending on the weather, the mood, or the occasion).

It's a curious thing that I don't consider myself "white." I'm clearly some   20
kind of Caucasian—to look at me. I don't look like an Indian. Where is my
mestizaje? Does my *mestizaje* reside on my skin? In my blood? In my heart?
In the way that I think? In the way that I speak? I have a brother who is
darker. I have another brother who has blue eyes and light-brown hair. I
have European blood. Is there such a thing as European blood? And if there
is, is it pure? I never asked these questions when I was a boy. In southern
New Mexico, the world where I grew up, my ethnic/racial identity was not
questioned. We were *Mexicanos.* The gringos were *Americanos.* Ours was
a rural, insular, poor community. Food on the table was more important
than arguing identities. All we knew was the world did not belong to us. It
belonged to someone else.

A graduate student (white) asked me one day how my seminar on Chi-   21
cano literature was going. "Are you making good little Chicanos?" A joke. A
bad joke. I said nothing. He noticed I wasn't laughing. He changed the subject. He is an intelligent man, serious, well-read, thoughtful about many things.

My Chicano literature class that semester was full: twelve Mexican Amer-   22
icans, two non-Mexican Americans (both women, one of whom was British
and had grown up in Africa and had immigrated to the United States and the
other of whom had grown up in Latin America), no white males. The title of
the class was "Chicano Literature, Culture and Identity." I was frustrated by
the ethnic and racial makeup of the class. Don't "white" people who live
quite literally on the border and who live in a city where 70 percent of the
population is Mexican American and attend a university whose Mexican
American student population is greater than 60 percent read Chicano literature? Don't they need to know anything about Chicano culture? Chicano
identity? *I don't read gringo poets. You will read gringo poets or you will drop
the course.*

I often thumb through Gloria Anzaldúa's book *Borderlands/La Frontera.*[2]   23
Ever since I first read this book, I have had a running battle with Anzaldú. I
applaud her political agenda. Unlike that of Richard Rodriguez, her writing
cannot be easily appropriated by the Right. She comprehends that identity
is formed by a multiplicity of discourses that conflict with one another. That
conflict takes root in our bodies. Like W. E. B. Du Bois, Anzaldúa intuits a
split consciousness, and she scrutinizes that (self) consciousness. She confronts her sexuality, she confronts a male-dominated world, she confronts a
racist society. She challenges an academic discourse by insisting on a more
personal-poetic discourse. She speaks unapologetically with the voice of a
woman, and it is not surprising that so many women (though her audience
is not exclusively female) have championed her work. Hers is the voice of
a strong feminist who seeks to empower, but her voice is not the voice of a
separatist. I have no quarrels with Anzaldúa's politics. We are on the same

side—she is an ally. If Richard Rodriguez is completely mortgaged to an ideology that privileges the category of "individual," than Gloria Anzaldúa is on the other end of the pole: she is the champion of communitarian thinking—something I am reticent to criticize. But ultimately, the basis for the formation of that "community" is unsettling. I find her book engaging, unsatisfying, overly optimistic, and mired in contradictions that cannot easily be overlooked.

In foraging for a usable past, she fetishizes Aztec and Indian culture.   24 Finding solutions (and identities) by appropriating indigenous mythologies is disturbing and very problematic—but even if this were not so, Anzaldúa's project offers very little to Chicanos and Chicanas who live in mostly urban settings. At the very least, her "solutions" are inappropriate for a late-twentieth-century audience. Added to that, appropriating Aztec and/ or any Indian culture in order to create a new identity is not so different from Englishmen appropriating the "classical" culture of the ancient Greeks as their own. To be sure, Anzaldúa is more closely related to indigenous culture and history than any Englishman ever was to the culture and history of the ancient Greeks. I, like Anzaldúa, have a mixed ancestry. My great-grandmother was a Tahurumaran Indian from Mexico. But for me to claim her material culture as mine rings hollow. I was raised in a far different environment, and I was formed by that environment. It is too late for me to forge a return to my great-grandmother's culture. This does not mean that I am unconcerned about the deforestation that is destroying the Tahurumaran people of northern Mexico, but I cannot mistake myself for them. I occupy a different position from indigenous peoples and I cannot borrow their identities. In wanting to distance herself from dominant European discourses, which she views as dualistic, oppressive, and racist, Anzaldúa gestures toward mythologies and cultures that I cannot believe are truly her own. Acknowledgment of mixed ancestry is not in itself problematic; it is far better to acknowledge the competing cultures we literally inherit than to base our identities on ridiculous (and dangerous) notions of "purity" and "pedigree" such as those that gave rise to Nazi Germany and the current wars of ethnic cleansing in Eastern Europe. I sympathize with Anzaldúa and I understand very well the impulse that lies behind Anzaldúa's strategy. The subtitle of her book is *The New Mestiza*. By calling herself a mestiza, she takes herself out of a European mind-set. She refuses to refer to herself as "Hispanic"—to do so would be to embrace an identity that admits no competing discourses, that admits only a European history and erases any indigenous consciousness. Her impulse is to defy that her "Indianness" has been destroyed. But her "Indianness" has been destroyed—just as mine has. I do not find it productive to build a politics and an identity centered on "loss."

Anzaldúa, unfortunately, falls into the dualistic thinking she so elo- 25
quently critiques. To categorize the world into "European" and "indigenous"
and try to bridge those two worlds under *mestiaje* is to fall squarely into "dualistic" thinking that does not do justice to the complex society in which we
live.

"Consciousness" is ultimately what Anzaldúa's project is all about. If we 26
but immerse ourselves in a particular mythology (a non-European, nonlin-
ear discourse), then our sick body politic will be healed (*healing* is a totem
word for Anzaldúa).

It begins where it ends.
I descend into black earth,
dark primordial slime,
no longer repellent to me,
nor confining.
The four winds
fire welds splinter with splinter.
I find my kindred spirits.

The moon eclipses the sun.
La diosa lifts us.
  We don the feathered mantle
    and change our fate. (198–99)

This is how Anzaldúa ends her book, her final solution. I can hardly disagree with Anzaldúa that we live in a society desperately in need of healing—though I would not choose to use that language. She firmly believes
that *La diosa,* her goddess figure (whose identity remains vague but is based
on the Aztec goddess Coatlicue), will "lift us." She suggests that a return to
indigenous ways of thinking will "change our fate." But I find it impossible
to appreciate this solution even while I understand the gesture. This is no
solution. This is an escape, not a *confrontation*. To return to the "traditional"
spiritualities that were in place before the arrival of Cortés and company
makes very little sense. The material conditions that gave rise to the Aztec's
religion no longer exist. Anzaldúa's language, her grammar, her talk are ultimately completely mortgaged to a nostalgia that I find unacceptable. The
resurrection of the old gods (be they "white" or "indigenous") is a futile and
impossible task. To invoke old gods as a tool against oppression and capitalism is to choose the wrong weapon.

    Yes, the Chicano and the Chicana have always taken care of growing things and
    the land. Again I see the four of us kids getting off the school bus, changing into
    our work clothes, walking into the field with Papi and Mami, all six of us bend-
    ing to the ground. Below our feet, under the earth lie the watermelon seeds. We

cover them with paper plates, putting *terremotes* on top of the plates to keep them from being blown away. Next day or the next, we remove the plates, bare the tiny green shoots to the elements. They survive and grow, give fruit hundreds of times the size of the seed. We water them and hoe them. We harvest them. The vines dry, rot, are plowed under. Growth, decay, birth. The soil prepared again and again, impregnated, worked on. A constant changing of forms, *renacimientos de la tierra madre.*

This land was Mexican once
   was Indian always
      and is.
         And will be again. (91)

This passage, which ends a section in Anzaldúa's book titled "La conciencia de la mestiza/Towards a New Consciousness," is deeply disturbing to me. The pastoral tradition that she reproduces is overstated, reductive, and offensive. Like Anzaldúa, I, too, worked the land while I was growing up. Alongside my family, I picked cotton and onions, and I have no wish to represent that particular part of my life romantically in the way Anzaldúa does. The politics of "picking seasons" in this country is disgusting, and the entire system it is based on is certainly indecent, and almost entirely corrupt. The phrase "the Chicano and Chicana have always taken care of growing things" turns us into rural peasants with a deep consciousness with regard to our relationship to Mother Earth. The statement needn't be deconstructed because it deconstructs itself. More disturbingly, Anzaldúa engages in an imperialist discourse of ownership over the land with her ending "poem." The "land," whatever it was, was never "Indian," was never "Mexican." And in terms of ownership, the land will never be returned to the indigenous peoples who lived on it before the conquest. It will *never* be again. The conquest was cruel, harsh, and irrevocable. Whatever the future looks like, it will not resemble the past.

Like Richard Rodriguez, I have become "middle-class." I do not wear 27
that identity with honor. I am almost ashamed of it—given my background, it would be surprising if I wore that label without wincing. I was recently speaking to a reading club about my novel. I mentioned something about my ambivalence toward money—I am sometimes ashamed of having some. "Is that a Hispanic thing?" a woman asked. "No," I said, "it's a class thing." But there is no denying the way I live my material existence. I do not live a peasant's lifestyle—nor do I wish to. I do not believe anybody should live *that* lifestyle. But when I admit to being middle-class, I do not mean that I am middle-class in the same way as someone who was born into it—or someone who stepped "down" into it. And I certainly do not privilege that particular identity over others. *Chicano,* for some, is a class label—and because they associate that word with an "underclass," they cannot flee fast enough from

it. But I refuse to associate *Chicano* with a particular class (though I must confess, I know no rich persons who refer to themselves as Chicanos).

In the Lone Star State, *Hopwood v. the University of Texas* threatens to end any "race"-based scholarships in the state of Texas. Reverse discrimination—that's what they call it. If people without jobs resent people who are rich, is that reverse discrimination? If the worker resents the landowner, is that reverse discrimination? If a woman who is raped detests the man who raped her, is that reverse discrimination? Why is it we refuse to acknowledge that the affirmative action debate is based on position and entitlements? Who exactly is entitled to what—and who is positioned (regardless of merit) to receive those entitlements? There is a group of people (mostly white and always upper- and middle-class) who firmly believe that they are the true heirs—that they are entitled to the riches of America. When the entitled are threatened, they fight back. They call the rest of us racists because we, too, want a piece of the inheritance. 28

I did not grow up with that sense of entitlement. I was one of the barbarians at the gate. I have to laugh at the anxiety caused by affirmative action, refuse this hateful accusation that I hold a job only because I am a Chicano: in the fall of 1992, I became the second "Chicano" to be hired in the English Department at the University of Texas at El Paso—this in a university where more than 60 percent of the students are "Hispanic." Call me cynical, but if our M.F.A. program in creative writing had not had a bilingual dimension attached, I doubt very seriously that I would have landed this job. I have nothing to base this on *except our past hiring practices.* 29

Once, after a reading, a young woman gave me a note in which she pleaded with me to stop "criticizing" the United States. "Criticize Mexico instead—criticize your own country." The young woman must have been confused as to the country of my genesis. Mexico is not my place—the United States is *my* place (and I resent having to make that point). It is perhaps too easy for me to criticize the country in which I was born and in which I live, easy because I detest "nationalisms" (though I will not pretend to be free of all nationalist discourses and influences). But isn't it true that it is a nationalist discourse that is most offended by the name *Chicano?* A nationalist discourse demands complete acquiescence. You are allowed only one name: American. We are all so sure we know what that label means. To some it means erasure. 30

No one is born with an "essential" identity. Identities are produced, and they make sense, they have meaning, only in the cultural context of their production. I spent the summer of 1985 in Tanzania. Tanzanians referred to me as *Mzungu* (the word in Swahili for European). I was not differentiated from the other *Mzungus*. To them, I was as white as my "white" friends from 31

Oklahoma and Kansas. And, living there for a summer, I felt "white." I felt European. *I was European.* It was a painful and difficult thing to admit to myself. I studied for four years at the University of Louvain in Belgium. I never felt very "American" when I was growing up in southern New Mexico, but in Belgium, I felt American. *I was American.* That, too, was a painful and difficult thing to admit to myself. *Chicano* in those years meant nothing. There was no context, no social or political necessity for that identity. But it was my time in Europe and my summer in Africa that taught me that I did not belong in those places. I was a foreigner there—and would always be a foreigner. I came to the conclusion that I had a people—that I belonged to a people, a community. When I returned to the United States, *Chicano* became important again because in the place to which I had returned, the inequalities of my society were everywhere to be found. My aim as a person, as a citizen, as a writer, as a teacher, as a Chicano, as a critic, has had, at least for the past ten years, a political project: to help create a "radical democracy." Like my students, I would like to live in a world where "we are all equal," a world where fragmentation isn't the operative modus operandi. I know this is utopian thinking (but I was one of those people who loved Karl Marx precisely because he was a utopian thinker—in 1996 are we allowed to invoke his name?). If I were to let go of my "Chicano" identity, then I would be complicit in the lie that we have arrived at the day of equality. Chicano—the word echoes with a particular history, but that word also exists to condemn our social and political failures. Chicano—it is an identity that waits for the day that it is no longer necessary.

NOTES

1. Richard Rodriguez, *Hunger of Memory: The Education of Richard Rodriguez* (New York: Bantam, 1983), 170–72. Page numbers for further quotations from this work appear in parentheses in the text.

2. Gloria Anzaldúa, *Borderlands/La Frontera: The New Mestiza* (San Francisco: Aunt Lute, 1987). Page numbers for further quotations from this work appear in parentheses in the text.

Working with the Text

1. Though many argumentative essays begin with an anecdote, Sáenz's essay begins with *two*, the first about the paucity of Chicanos at El Paso literary gatherings, and the second about the refusal of a Chicano undergraduate to read "gringo" poets. Compare and contrast the two anecdotes, then comment on the relationship between them. How do they serve the rest of the essay, both separately and together?

2. "*No one can live without an identity,*" Sáenz writes, italicizing the statement for emphasis. What is identity, and how is it constituted?

How does the author distinguish features of identity (and identity politics) that are true for him from those that are true for everybody? Why is this distinction essential to the essay's primary argument?

3. Sáenz offers detailed critiques of two Mexican-American writers, quoting each at length, explaining how each understands identity, and disputing key elements of each writer's major work. What is Sáenz's argument with Richard Rodriguez? Does it seem reasonable, fair, and well-substantiated? Why, do you think, does Sáenz address Rodriguez directly, as "you"? What is Sáenz's argument with Anzaldúa? Is it reasonable, fair, and well-substantiated? Why isn't she a "you" as well? Why, given that Sáenz considers Rodriguez an opponent and Anzaldúa an ally, does he charge both with seeking to "escape" the problems posed by Chicano identity?

4. In addition to its direct engagement with Rodriguez and Anzaldúa, the essay subtly acknowledges its participation in a complicated, long-running, occasionally vociferous debate. What are some of the ways it does so? In other words, what special rhetorical challenges confront Sáenz, and how does he meet them?

5. Affirmative action remains a controversial means of addressing historical inequality in business, government, and education; several major universities, for example, have recently abolished affirmative action in college admissions. Working in groups of four to six students, research *one* local affirmative action law or policy. Find out its history, its wording, its original goals, and any amendments. Then research its effectiveness—and any dispute about that effectiveness. Start with back issues of local or campus newspapers, but be prepared to supplement that research with interviews. Next, imagine that your group has been charged with making a recommendation to retain, revise, or abolish the existing policy. Vote, then draft a five-page statement explaining why you voted as you did, citing specific evidence for your conclusion. If you vote to abolish, respond to Sáenz's charge that "opponents of affirmative action offer no real solutions to [race- and gender-based] inequalities" by offering an alternative solution.

Love as the Practice of Freedom

bell hooks

Social commentator, essayist, memoirist, and poet bell hooks (née Gloria Jean Watkins) is a feminist theorist who speaks on contemporary issues of race, gender, and media representation in America. Her many books include *Ain't I a Woman* (1981), *Talking Back* (1989), *Killing Rage: Ending Racism* (1995), *Outlaw Culture* (1994), and *Remembered Rapture* (1999). In *Black Looks* (1994), she writes, "It struck me that for black people, the pain of learning that we cannot control our images, how we see ourselves (if our vision is not decolonized), or how we are seen is so intense that it rends us. It rips and tears at the seams of our efforts to construct self and identify." In *Outlaw Culture: Resisting Representations* (1994), hooks advocates a "progressive cultural revolution" by means of repudiating all forms of domination in a "holistic manner." In order to decolonize our minds, suggests hooks, we must begin to " surrender participation in whatever sphere of coercive hierarchical domination we enjoy individual and group privilege." In the essay that follows from that book, hooks proposes and "ethic of love" as the means by which we might be guided to turn away from an ethic of domination.

In this society, there is no powerful discourse on love emerging either from politically progressive radicals or from the Left. The absence of a sustained focus on love in progressive circles arises from a collective failure to acknowledge the needs of the spirit and an overdetermined emphasis on material concerns. Without love, our efforts to liberate ourselves and our world community from oppression and exploitation are doomed. As long as we refuse to address fully the place of love in struggles for liberation we will not be able to create a culture of conversion where there is a mass turning away from an ethic of domination.

Without an ethic of love shaping the direction of our political vision and our radical aspirations, we are often seduced, in one way or the other, into continued allegiance to systems of domination—imperialism, sexism, racism, classism. It has always puzzled me that women and men who spend a lifetime working to resist and oppose one form of domination can be systematically supporting another. I have been puzzled by powerful vision-ary black male leaders who can speak and act passionately in resistance to racial domination and accept and embrace sexist domination of women, by feminist white women who work daily to eradicate sexism but who have major blind spots when it comes to acknowledging and resisting racism and white supremacist domination of the planet. Critically examining these blind spots, I conclude that many of us are motivated to move against domination solely when we feel our self-interest directly threatened. Often, then, the longing is not for a collective transformation of society, an end to politics of dominations, but rather simply for an end to what we feel is hurting us. This is why we desperately need an ethic of love to intervene in our self-centered longing for change. Fundamentally, if we are only committed to an im-provement in that politic of domination that we feel leads directly to our in-dividual exploitation or oppression, we not only remain attached to the status quo but act in complicity with it, nurturing and maintaining those very sys-tems of domination. Until we are all able to accept the interlocking, inter-dependent nature of systems of domination and recognize specific ways each system is maintained, we will continue to act in ways that undermine our individual quest for freedom and collective liberation struggle.

The ability to acknowledge blind spots can emerge only as we expand 3 our concern about politics of domination and our capacity to care about the oppression and exploitation of others. A love ethic makes this expansion possible. The civil rights movement transformed society in the United States because it was fundamentally rooted in a love ethic. No leader has empha-sized this ethic more than Martin Luther King, Jr. He had the prophetic in-sight to recognize that a revolution built on any other foundation would fail. Again and again, King testified that he had "decided to love" because he be-lieved deeply that if we are "seeking the highest good" we "find it through love" because this is "the key that unlocks the door to the meaning of ulti-mate reality." And the point of being in touch with a transcendent reality is that we struggle for justice, all the while realizing that we are always more than our race, class, or sex. When I look back at the civil rights movement which was in many ways limited because it was a reformist effort, I see that it had the power to move masses of people to act in the interest of racial justice—and because it was profoundly rooted in a love ethic.

The sixties Black Power movement shifted away from that love ethic. 4 The emphasis was now more on power. And it is not surprising that the sex-ism that had always undermined the black liberation struggle intensified, that a misogynist approach to women became central as the equation of freedom with patriarchal manhood became a norm among black political leaders, almost all of whom were male. Indeed, the new militancy of mas-culinist black power equated love with weakness, announcing that the quintessential expression of freedom would be the willingness to coerce, do violence, terrorize, indeed utilize the weapons of domination. This was the crudest embodiment of Malcolm X's bold credo "by any means necessary."

On the positive side, Black Power movement shifted the focus of black 5 liberation struggle from reform to revolution. This was an important political development, bringing with it a stronger anti-imperialist, global perspective. However, masculinist sexist biases in leadership led to the suppression of the love ethic. Hence progress was made even as something valuable was lost. While King had focused on loving our enemies, Malcolm called us back to ourselves, acknowledging that taking care of blackness was our central responsibility. Even though King talked about the importance of black self-love, he talked more about loving our enemies. Ultimately, neither he nor Malcolm lived long enough to fully integrate the love ethic into a vision of political decolonization that would provide a blueprint for the eradication of black self-hatred.

Black folks entering the realm of racially integrated, American life be- 6 cause of the success of civil rights and black power movement suddenly found we were grappling with an intensification of internalized racism. The deaths of these important leaders (as well as liberal white leaders who were major allies in the struggle for racial equality) ushered in tremendous feelings of hopelessness, powerlessness, and despair. Wounded in that space where we would know love, black people collectively experienced intense pain and anguish about our future. The absence of public spaces where that pain could be articulated, expressed, shared meant that it was held in—festering, suppressing the possibility that this collective grief would be reconciled in community even as ways to move beyond it and continue resistance struggle would be envisioned. Feeling as though "the world had really come to an end," in the sense that a hope had died that racial justice would become the norm, a life-threatening despair took hold in black life. We will never know to what extent the black masculinist focus on hardness and toughness served as a barrier preventing sustained public acknowledgment of the enormous grief and pain in black life. In *World as Lover, World as Self,* Joanna Macy emphasizes in her chapter on "Despair Work" that

> the refusal to feel takes a heavy toll. Not only is there an impoverishment of our emotional and sensory life . . . but this psychic numbing also impedes our capacity to process and respond to information. The energy expended in pushing down despair is diverted from more creative uses, depleting the resilience and imagination needed for fresh visions and strategies.

If black folks are to move forward in our struggle for liberation, we must confront the legacy of this unreconciled grief, for it has been the breeding ground for profound nihilistic despair. We must collectively return to a radical political vision of social change rooted in a love ethic and seek once again to convert masses of people, black and nonblack.

A culture of domination is anti-love. It requires violence to sustain itself. To choose love is to go against the prevailing values of the culture. Many people feel unable to love either themselves or others because they do not know what love is. Contemporary songs like Tina Turner's "What's Love Got To Do With It" advocate a system of exchange around desire, mirroring the economics of capitalism: the idea that love is important is mocked. In his essay "Love and Need: Is Love a Package or a Message?" Thomas Merton argues that we are taught within the framework of competitive consumer capitalism to see love as a business deal: "This concept of love assumes that the machinery of buying and selling of needs is what makes everything run. It regards life as a market and love as a variation on free enterprise." Though many folks recognize and critique the commercialization of love, they see no alternative. Not knowing how to love or even what love is, many people feel emotionally lost; others search for definitions, for ways to sustain a love ethic in a culture that negates human value and valorizes materialism.

The sales of books focusing on recovery, books that seek to teach folks ways to improve self-esteem, self-love, and our ability to be intimate in relationships, affirm that there is public awareness of a lack in most people's lives. M. Scott Peck's self-help book *The Road Less Traveled* is enormously popular because it addresses that lack.

Peck offers a working definition for love that is useful for those of us who would like to make a love ethic the core of all human interaction. He defines love as "the will to extend one's self for the purpose of nurturing one's own or another's spiritual growth." Commenting on prevailing cultural attitudes about love, Peck writes:

> Everyone in our culture desires to some extent to be loving, yet many are in fact not loving. I therefore conclude that the desire to love is not itself love. Love is as love does. Love is an act of will—namely both an intention and an action. Will also implies choice. We do not have to love. We choose to love.

His words echo Martin Luther King's declaration, "I have decided to love," which also emphasizes choice. King believed that love is "ultimately the only answer" to the problems facing this nation and the entire planet. I share that belief and the conviction that it is in choosing love, and beginning with love as the ethical foundation for politics, that we are best positioned to transform society in ways that enhance the collective good.

It is truly amazing that King had the courage to speak as much as he did about the transformative power of love in a culture where such talk is often seen as merely sentimental. In progressive political circles, to speak of love is to guarantee that one will be dismissed or considered naive. But outside those circles there are many people who openly acknowledge that they are consumed by feelings of self-hatred, who feel worthless, who want a way out. Often they are too trapped by paralyzing despair to be able to engage effectively in any movement for social change. However, if the leaders of such movements refuse to address the anguish and pain of their lives, they will never be motivated to consider personal and political recovery. Any political movement that can effectively address these needs of the spirit in the context of liberation struggle will succeed.

In the past, most folks both learned about and tended the needs of the   11
spirit in the context of religious experience. The institutionalization and commercialization of the church has undermined the power of religious community to transform souls, to intervene politically. Commenting on the collective sense of spiritual loss in modern society, Cornel West asserts:

> There is a pervasive impoverishment of the spirit in American society, and especially among Black people. Historically, there have been cultural forces and traditions, like the church, that held cold-heartedness and mean-spiritedness at bay. However, today's impoverishment of the spirit means that this coldness and meanness is becoming more and more pervasive. The church kept these forces at bay by promoting a sense of respect for others, a sense of solidarity, a sense of meaning and value which would usher in the strength to battle against evil.

Life-sustaining political communities can provide a similar space for the renewal of the spirit. That can happen only if we address the needs of the spirit in progressive political theory and practice.

Often when Cornel West and I speak with large groups of black folks   12
about the impoverishment of spirit in black life, the lovelessness, sharing that we can collectively recover ourselves in love, the response is overwhelming. Folks want to know how to begin the practice of loving. For me that is where education for critical consciousness has to enter. When I look at my life, searching it for a blueprint that aided me in the process of decolonization, of personal and political self-recovery, I know that it was learning the truth about how systems of domination operate that helped, learning to look both inward and outward with a critical eye. Awareness is central to the process of love as the practice of freedom. Whenever those of us who are members of exploited and oppressed groups dare to critically interrogate our locations, the identities and allegiances that inform how we live our lives, we begin the process of decolonization. If we discover in ourselves self-hatred, low self-esteem, or internalized white supremacist thinking and we face it, we can begin to heal. Acknowledging the truth of our reality, both individual and collective, is a necessary stage for personal and political growth. This is usually the most painful stage in the process of learning to love—the one many of us seek to avoid. Again, once we choose love, we instinctively possess the inner resources to confront that pain. Moving through

the pain to the other side we find the joy, the freedom of spirit that a love ethic brings.

Choosing love we also choose to live in community, and that means that we do not have to change by ourselves. We can count on critical affirmation and dialogue with comrades walking a similar path. African American theologian Howard Thurman believed that we best learn love as the practice of freedom in the context of community. Commenting on this aspect of his work in the essay "Spirituality out on The Deep," Luther Smith reminds us that Thurman felt the United States was given to diverse groups of people by the universal life force as a location for the building of community. Paraphrasing Thurman, he writes: "Truth becomes true in community. The social order hungers for a center (i.e. spirit, soul) that gives it identity, power, and purpose. America, and all cultural entities, are in search of a soul." Working within community, whether it be sharing a project with another person, or with a larger group, we are able to experience joy in struggle. That joy needs to be documented. For if we only focus on the pain, the difficulties which are surely real in any process of transformation, we only show a partial picture. 13

A love ethic emphasizes the importance of service to others. Within the value system of the United States any task or job that is related to "service" is devalued. Service strengthens our capacity to know compassion and deepens our insight. To serve another I cannot see them as an object, I must see their subjecthood. Sharing the teaching of Shambala warriors, Buddhist Joanna Macy writes that we need weapons of compassion and insight. 14

> You have to have compassion because it gives you the juice, the power, the passion to move. When you open to the pain of the world you move, you act. But that weapon is not enough. It can burn you out, so you need the other—you need insight into the radical interdependence of all phenomena. With that wisdom you know that it is not a battle between good guys and bad guys, but that the line between good and evil runs through the landscape of every human heart. With insight into our profound interrelatedness, you know that actions undertaken with pure intent have repercussions throughout the web of life, beyond what you can measure or discern.

Macy shares that compassion and insight can "sustain us as agents of wholesome change" for they are "gifts for us to claim now in the healing of our world." In part, we learn to love by giving service. This is again a dimension of what Peck means when he speaks of extending ourselves for another.

The civil rights movement had the power to transform society because the individuals who struggle alone and in community for freedom and justice wanted these gifts to be for all, not just the suffering and the oppressed. Visionary black leaders such as Septima Clark, Fannie Lou Hamer, Martin Luther King, Jr., and Howard Thurman warned against isolationism. They encouraged black people to look beyond our own circumstances and 15 assume responsibility for the planet. This call for communion with a world beyond the self, the tribe, the race, the nation, was a constant invitation for personal expansion and growth. When masses of black folks starting thinking solely in terms of "us and them," internalizing the value system of white supremacist capitalist patriarchy, blind spots developed, the capacity for empathy needed for the building of community was diminished. To heal our wounded body politic we must reaffirm our commitment to a vision of what King referred to in the essay "Facing the Challenge of a New Age" as a genuine commitment to "freedom and justice for all." My heart is uplifted when I read King's essay; I am reminded where true liberation leads us. It leads us beyond resistance to transformation. King tells us that "the end is reconciliation, the end is redemption, the end is the creation of the beloved community." The moment we choose to love we begin to move against domination, against oppression. The moment we choose to love we begin to move towards freedom, to act in ways that liberate ourselves and others. That action is the testimony of love as the practice of freedom.

Working with the Text

1. Why does progressive politics "desperately need an ethic of love," according to bell hooks? How does she explain its disappearance from contemporary political discourse? Why is it particularly important in the struggle for racial justice?

2. What *is* "love"? Where does the essay find a working definition of this famously elusive term? What sort of politics derives ideas from the literature of self-help? In other words, does the essay make claims—overt or implied—about where political theory should look for inspiration? What other nonpolitical disciplines furnish ideas to "Love as the Practice of Freedom"?

3. Why does the essay stress love as a "practice"? Consult a good dictionary (the *Oxford English Dictionary*, if you can) to see which meanings of the word "practice" may be relevant; then consider the relationships among the various definitions. According to bell hooks, what does the practice of love require people to do? And what does it do for them, both collectively and individually?

4. The essay features a number of exemplary characters, from Martin Luther King, who illustrates the vast political efficacy of love, to Tina Turner, whose 1984 hit "What's Love Got To Do With It" expresses a contrasting cynicism. Why do you suppose the author introduces these figures? What do they have in common, and where do they differ? Given the essay's topic and approach, did any of them surprise you?

5. Identify another ideal not normally associated with politics—possibly one from a completely different value system. You may wish to brainstorm with classmates or look up lists of unusual virtues, such as those embraced by crusaders or geisha. In a timed-writing exercise (20 to 30 minutes), consider the possible benefits of your irregular ideal to the specific branch of politics that you know best. The branch need not be national; it can be extremely local—the politics of your college sorority, for example. Write for the allotted time without stopping to reflect or reread.

A *Litany for Survival*

AUDRE LORDE

Audre Lorde once detailed her many, simultaneous identities: "black, lesbian, feminist, mother, lover, poet." Born in New York City (1934), she went to Catholic schools and attended New York's Hunter College. Shy, rarely speaking, she later earned an M.A. in library science, was married, and bore a daughter and a son. By 1970, though, during the rise of black cultural nationalism, the now-divorced Lorde began to publish poems that would establish her reputation as a leading African-American voice, in books such as *From a Land Where Other People Live, Coal,* and *The Black Unicorn.* Her topics ranged from marital life and child-rearing to African mythology and culture, and her own battle with cancer. Lorde was as well a powerful theorist on issues of poetics, feminism, marginalized voices, and the political power of eros in literature. Her final book of poems, written just before her death, is entitled *Undersong: Chosen Poems Old and New* (1992).

For those of us who live at the shoreline
standing upon the constant edges of decision
crucial and alone
for those of us who cannot indulge
the passing dreams of choice   5
who love in doorways coming and going
in the hours between dawns

looking inward and outward
at once before and after
seeking a now that can breed   10
futures
like bread in our children's mouths
so their dreams will not reflect
the death of ours;

For those of us   15
who were imprinted with fear
like a faint line in the center of our foreheads
learning to be afraid with our mother's milk
for by this weapon
this illusion of some safety to be found   20
the heavy-footed hoped to silence us
For all of us
this instant and this triumph
We were never meant to survive.

And when the sun rises we are afraid   25
it might not remain
when the sun sets we are afraid
it might not rise in the morning
when our stomachs are full we are afraid
of indigestion   30
when our stomachs are empty we are afraid
we may never eat again
when we are loved we are afraid
love will vanish
when we are alone we are afraid   35
love will never return
and when we speak we are afraid
our words will not be heard
nor welcomed
but when we are silent   40
we are still afraid.

So it is better to speak
remembering
we were never meant to survive.

Working with the Text

1. The poem depicts people "imprinted with fear," who stand upon the "constant edges of decision," and "cannot indulge / the passing dreams

of choice." What do they fear? What decisions do they face? List some examples that Lorde provides—both specific references and more abstract ones. Is there a pattern to these examples?

2. A traditional litany offers a "call and response" medley, a cleric's invocations and supplications, and the congregation's answers. This poem provides a refrain about survival: does this last statement supply comfort or support to "those of us" living in fear and indecision? What is the tone and effect of this refrain?

3. Many poems achieve a fullness of perspective by embracing paradoxes and contradictions—as if the poem were a place of competing forces. In the second stanza, fear is proposed as a "weapon" that brings "an illusion of some safety": Can you explicate or paraphrase this passage?

4. Why, in the third stanza, are "we" afraid the setting sun won't rise again, or that "when we are loved" that love might "vanish"? What claims is Lorde making about the workings of the imagination, how it provides opposites and absences for whatever our lives hold? What kinds of borders does our imagination bring us across?

5. Audre Lorde's poems have been praised for making her distinctive voice—African American, feminist, lesbian—audible and public. This poem, however, does not specifically make reference to these features of identity. In what ways does the poem seek to dramatize a dilemma not specific to Lorde? In what ways is her distinctiveness shown by a poem in which race, sexual orientation, or one's place in culture is not spoken of directly? In what ways might anyone be understood to "live at the shoreline"? Explore these questions in an essay.

Critical Questions Revisited: From Reading to Writing

Essay Topic 1: In what ways is an online community a community?

YOUR PAPER: Write a paper analyzing how an online community functions. Begin by describing one you know well or have observed. What factors define, promote, or threaten it? How are bonds established, and borders crossed? How will these groups and spaces alter how we view physical communities?

SUGGESTED STRATEGIES

- Describe a virtual community (e.g., MUD, an interactive Web site, chat group, etc.) in terms of its purpose, "shape," and individual character.
- In terms of a physical, social community, how does this function? What traits and differences bring its members together? What needs or desires are fulfilled?
- How is authority or hierarchy established in this community?
- Indicate how your observations are confirmed or contradicted by the perspectives represented in the readings in this chapter. Based on your observations and the readings, what role will virtual communities play in the future?

Essay Topic 2: How are cultural images of the Other shaped by economic forces?

YOUR PAPER: Working with readings in this chapter, analyze how American representations of other cultures are shaped by economic forces. How do American attitudes and biases about "developing" countries reflect a level of economic interdependence? How do writers such as Anzaldúa or Gómez-Peña (who focus on the U.S.-Mexico border) or Greider and Barber (who focus on global and local identities) frame the relationship of economics and culture?

SUGGESTED STRATEGIES

- Analyze passages in which the writers describe an interrelationship between economic and cultural forces. Does one side predominate?
- How does economic interdependence influence the ways "other" cultures are represented and stereotyped in the media?
- What values that we normally consider cultural and social values have resulted from global economic culture? What specific consequences come from the conflict of global economics and local cultures?

Essay Topic 3: How do cultural perspectives on individual identity differ?

YOUR PAPER: Explore the distinctions between cultural perspectives on individual identity and rights. The readings of this chapter question the fate of individual liberty, civil rights, and local, community values. When do cultural values take precedence over individual ones? What assumptions might we make about the *universality* of certain rights (for example, the U.S. bias toward individual liberty)?

SUGGESTED STRATEGIES:

- Depict a couple of examples of conflicts between individual rights and some form of community rights—look for these outside the U.S., or between the U.S. and other countries.
- In these examples, what are the most compelling differences between other cultures' values and dominant U.S. values?
- What are the consequences of these differences? What difficulties come from applying American perspectives to other countries?
- How can conversation on "values" continue without universal acceptance of certain rights?

Essay Topic 4: In an increasingly interconnected world, which differences are visible and which are invisible?

YOUR PAPER: Your paper should explore how, in an interconnected world, cultural differences and diversity become visible and/or invisible. Consider the readings on globalization: What are the tensions between diversity and coherence? How are they expressed within the United States or outside of it? In a world of new borders, what differences still make a difference?

SUGGESTED STRATEGIES

- Analyze some passages where writers depict an increasingly globalized economic culture, and media culture. What tensions develop between cultural diversity and cultural sameness?
- Which visions of culture present "plural" or "multiple" differences as not melting into one culture, society, or economy?
- What underlying causes or perspectives make such a vision possible?
- Does visibility serve to protect difference? How might difference survive as an invisible element in a coherent culture?

TEXT CREDITS

Adrienne Rich. Part II "Here is a map of our country" from "An Atlas of the Difficult World," from *An Atlas of the Difficult World: Poems 1988–1991* by Adrienne Rich. Copyright © 1991 by Adrienne Rich. Used by permission of the author and W.W. Norton & Company, Inc.

Anonymous. "The Hopi Boy and The Sun" From *American Myths and Legends* edited by Richard Erdoes and Alfonso Ortiz, copyright © 1984. Used by permission of Pantheon Books, a division of Random House, Inc.

Anna Deavere Smith. From *Fires in the Mirror,* copyright © 1993 by Anna Deavere Smith. Used by permission of Doubleday, a division of Random House, Inc.

Robert Hass. "About the Body" From *Human Wishes* by Robert Hass. Copyright 1990 by Robert Hass. Reprinted by permission of HarperCollins Publishers Inc.

Thomas King. "Borders" by Thomas King originally published in *One Good Story, that one,* HarperCollins Canada. 1993. Reprinted by permission of the author.

Noel Ignatiev and John Garvey. "Who Lost an American? by Joel Gilbert as told to Noel Ignatiev Copyright 1996 from *Race Traitor* by Noel Ignatiev and John Garvey. Reproduced by permission of Routledge, Inc., part of The Taylor & Francis Group.

Eden Abigail Trooboff. "The Gravity of Pink" by Eden Abigail Trooboff. Reprinted by permission.

Amy Tan. "Mother Tongue" Copyright © 1990 by Amy Tan. "Mother Tongue" first appeared in *The Three Penny Review*. Reprinted by permission of the author and the Sandra Dijkstra Literary Agency.

Jim Mince. "The Begenning of the End" from *American Mosaic*, edited by Robert Wolf, pp. 64–68, copyright © 1999 by Free River Press, Inc. Used by permission of Oxford University Press, Inc.

Evelyn Lau. From *Runaway, Diary of a Streetkid,* by Evelyn Lau, pp. 99–105. Published by HarperCollins Publishers Ltd. Copyright © 1989 by Evelyn Lau. All rights reserved.

Tara L. Masih. "Exotic, or 'What Beach Do You Hang Out On?" by Tara L. Masih. From *Two Worlds Walking: Short Stories, Essays, & Poetry by Writers with Mixed Heritages*. Diana Glancy and C.W. Truesdale, eds. Minneapolis: New Rivers Press, 1994. Copyright 1994 by Tara L. Masih. Reprinted by permission of the author.

Frank Bidart. "Ellen West" from *In The Western Night: Collected Poems 1965–1990* by Frank Bidart. Copyright © 1990 by Frank Bidart. Reprinted by permission of Farrar, Straus and Giroux, LLC.

Ruben Martinez. "Going Up in L.A." from *The Other Side: Notes from the New L.A., Mexico City, and Beyond*. Copyright © 1992 by Verso. Reprinted with permission.

Leonard Kriegel. "Graffiti: Tunnel Notes of a New Yorker" by Leonard Kriegel. From *The American Scholar*, Vol. 67, Summer 1993, pp. 431–436. Reprinted with permission from *The American Scholar* and the author.

Kai T. Erikson. Reprinted with the permission of Simon & Schuster from *Everything In Its Path* by Kai T. Erikson. Copyright © 1976 by Kai T. Erikson.

Daniel Kemmis. "The Last Best Place: How Hardship and Limits Build Community" first published in *A Society to Match the Scenery* by University Press of Colorado, 1991. Copyright 1991 by Daniel Kemmis. Reprinted with permission of the author.

Randall Balmer "Georgia Charismatics" from *Mine Eyes Have Seen the Glory: A Journey into the Evangelical Subculture in America*, Third Edition, by Randall Balmer, copyright © 1989, 1993, 2000 by Oxford University Press, Inc. Used by permission of Oxford University Press, Inc.

Jacob Riis. "How the Other Half Lives" from *How the Other Half Lives* by Jacob Riis. Copyright © 1990 by Dover Publications. Reprinted with permission.

Peter Marin. "Helping and Hating the Homeless" Copyright © 1986 by Harper's Magazine. All rights reserved. Reproduced from the January 1987 issue by special permission.

David Sibley. "Feelings About Difference" from *Geographics of Exclusion: Society and Difference in the West* by David Sibley. Reprinted with permission from Taylor & Francis, U.K. and the author.

See credit line above.

Elizabeth Bishop. "In the Waiting Room" from *The Complete Poems 1927–1929* by Elizabeth Bishop. Copyright © 1979, 1983 by Alice Helen Methfessel. Reprinted by permission of Farrar, Straus and Giroux, LLC.

Margorie Garber. "Vested Interests" Copyright 1992 from *Vested Interests: Cross-Dressing and Cultural Anxiety* by Margorie Garber. Reproduced by permission of Routledge, Inc., part of The Taylor and Francis Group.

John Hartigan. "The Baseball Game" from *Racial Situations*. Copyright © 1999 by Princeton University Press. Reprinted by permission of Princeton University Press.

Robert Berkhofer, Jr. *The White Man's Indian* from *The White Man's Indian* by Robert Berkhofer, Jr., copyright © 1978 by Robert F. Berkhofer, Jr. Used by permission of Alfred A. Knopf, a division of Random House, Inc.

Stuart Hall. "Ethnicity: Identity and Difference" by Stuart Hall was first printed in *Radical America*, Volume 23, No. 4. Reprinted with permission.

Gwendolyn Brooks. "We Real Cool" Reprinted by permission of The Estate of Gwendolyn Brooks.

Mary Louise Pratt. "Arts of the Contact Zone" Reprinted by permission of the Modern Association from *Profession 91*.

Richard White. From *The Middle Ground: Indians, Empires and Republics in the Great Lakes Region, 1650–1815* by Richard White, pp. IX–10. Copyright © 1991 by Cambridge University Press. Reprinted with the permission of Cambridge University Press.

Roger Williams. "A Key into the Language of America" by Roger Williams. © 1643.

Jeffery Paul Chan, Frank Chin, Lawson Fusao Inada and Shawn Wong. Introduction to "An English-Chinese Phrasebook" by Wong Sam and Assistants, from *The Big Aiiieeeee!* by Jeffery Paul Chan, Frank Chin, Lawson Fusao Inada and Shawn Wong, copyright © 1991 by Jeffery Paul Chan, Frank Chin, Lawson Fusao Inada and Shawn Wong. Used by permission of Dutton Signet, a division of Penguin Putnam Inc.

Robert Blauner. "Talking Past Each Other: Black and White Languages of Race" Reprinted with permission from *The American Prospect* Volume 3, Number 10: June 23, 1992. The American Prospect, 5 Broad Street, Boston, MA 02109. All rights reserved. Robert Blauner is the author of a new book, Still the Big News: Racial Oppression in America, Temple University Press, 2001.

Rita Dove. "Arrow" from *Grace Notes* by Rita Dove. Copyright © 1989 by Rita Dove. Used by permission of the author and W.W. Norton & Company, Inc.

Martin Luther King Jr. Reprinted by arrangement with the Estate of Martin Luther King Jr., c/o Writers House as agent for the proprietor, New York, NY. Copyright 1963 Dr. Martin Luther King Jr., copyright renewed 1991 Coretta Scott King.

Tim O'Brien. "Sweetheart of the Song Tra Bong" from *The Things They Carried* by Tim O'Brien. Copyright © 1990 by Tim O'Brien. Reprinted by permission of Houghton Mifflin Company. All rights reserved.

Luis Alberto Urrea. From *Across the Wire: Life & Hard Times* by Luis Alberto Urrea, copyright © 1993 by Luis Alberto Urrea. Photographs © 1993 by John Lueders-Booth. Used by permission of Doubleday, a division of Random House, Inc.

Mary Gaitskill. "On Not Being a Victim" Copyright © 1994 by Harper's Magazine. All rights reserved. Reproduced from the March issue by special permission.

Lester Bangs. "The White Noise Supremacists" From *Psychotic Reactions and Carburetor Dung* by Lester Bangs, edited by Greil Marcus, copyright © 1987 by The Estate of Lester Bangs. Used by permission of Alfred A. Knopf, a division of Random House, Inc.

Sherry Turkle. "TinySex and Gender Trouble" Reprinted with the permission of Simon & Schuster from *Life on the Screen: Identity in the Age of the Internet* by Sherry Turkle. Copyright © 1995 by Sherry Turkle.

Frantz Fanon. "The Fact of Blackness" From *Black Skin, White Masks* by Frantz Fanon, translated by Charles Lam Markmann. Copyright © 1962 by Grove Press, Inc. Used by permission of Grove/Atlantic, Inc.

Art Spiegelman. "MAUS: A Survivor's Tale" From *MAUS I: A Survivor's Tale/My Father Bleeds History* by Art Spiegelman, copyright © 1973, 1980, 1981, 1982, 1984, 1985, 1986 by Art Spiegelman. Used by permission of Pantheon Books, a division of Random House, Inc.

Andrea Freus Lowenstein. "Confronting Stereotypes: MAUS in Crown Heights" (excluding artwork) by Andrea Freus Lowenstein. From *College English*, Volume 60, Number 4, April 1998, pp. 396–419. Copyright 1998 by the National Council of Teachers of English. Reprinted with permission.

Myra Jehlen. "Papers of Empire" Excerpted from "The Literature of Colonization" by Myra Jehlen. From *The Cambridge History of American Literature* by Sevan Bercovitch and

Cyrus R.K. Patell, eds, pp. 26–36. Copyright © 1994 by Cambridge University Press. Reprinted with permission.

Alan Thomas. "Maps, Projections and Ethnocentricity" from *Third World Atlas* by Alan Thomas with Ben Crow et al, 2nd ed. Bristol, PA: Taylor & Frances, 1994. Reprinted with the permission of the publisher.

Benedict Anderson. "The Concept of "Nation": A Definition" From *Imagined Communities: Reflections on the Origins and Spread of Nationalism* by Benedict Anderson, pp. 5–7. Copyright © 1983 by Verso. Reprinted with permission.

Frederick Jackson Turner. "The Significance of the Frontier in American History" by Frederick Jackson Turner from George Rogers Taylor ed. *The Turner Thesis: Concerning the Role of the American Frontier in History*, Lexington, MA: D.C. Heath and Company, 1972.

Patricia Limerick. "Adventures of the Frontier in the Twentieth Century" from *Frontier in American Culture*, edited by James Grossman. Copyright © 1994 The Regents of the University of California. Reprinted with permission.

Jane Tompkins. "At the Buffalo Bill Museum—June 1988" from *West of Everything* by Jane Tompkins, copyright © 1992 by Jane Tompkins. Used by permission of Oxford University Press, Inc.

Kamal Abdul-Malek. "An Egyptian Girl in America" from *American in an Arab Mirror* by Kamal Abdul-Malek. Copyright © 2000. Reprinted with permission from Palgrave Global Publishing.

Armond White. "The Resistance: Ten Years of Pop Culture That Shook the World" by Armond White. Copyright © 1995 by The Overlook Press. Reprinted with permission.

Lewis Lapham. "Who and What is an American?" Copyright © 1992 by Harper's Magazine. All rights reserved. Reproduced from the January issue by special permission.

Ronald Takaki. "A Different Mirror" by Ronald Takaki from *A Different Mirror*, Little, Brown & Company, 1993. Reprinted by permission of the Balkin Agency, Inc.

Agha Shahid Ali. "The Correspondent" from *The Country without a Post Office* by Agha Shahid Ali. Copyright © 1997 by Agha Shahid Ali. Used by permission of W.W. Norton & Company, Inc.

William Mitchell. "Soft Cities" by William Mitchell from *City of Bits: Space, Place, and the Infobahn*. Copyright © 1995 The MIT Press. Reprinted by permission of the publisher.

Allucquère Roseanne Stone. "Sex, Death and Machinery, or How I Fell in Love with My Prothesis" from *The War of Desire and Technology at the Close of the Mechanical Age* Copyright © 1995 The MIT Press. Reprinted by permission of the publisher.

Stephen Doheny-Farina. "Real Cold, Simulated Heat: Virtual Reality at the Roxy" From *The Wired Neighborhood* by Stephen Doheny-Farina, pp. 3–18. Copyright © 1996 by Yale University Press. Reprinted with permission.

Howard Rheingold. "Disinformocracy" From *The Virtual Community* by Howard Rheingold. Copyright © 1993 by Howard Rheingold. Reprinted by permission of Perseus Books Publishers, a member of Perseus Books, L.L.C.

William Greidler. "One World: Ready Or Not" Adapted with the permission of Simon & Schuster, Inc., from *One World, Ready or Not: The Manic Logic of Global Capitalism* by William Greidler. Copyright © 1997 by William Greidler. Originally appeared in the February 6, 1997 issue of *Rolling Stone.*

Benjamin R. Barber. "Jihad vs. McWorld" From *Jihad vs. McWorld* by Benjamin R. Barber, copyright © 1995 by Benjamin R. Barber. Used by permission of Times Books, a division of Random House, Inc.

Salman Rushdie. "Yes, This Is About Islam" Copyright © 2001 Salman Rushdie. Distributed by The New York Times Special Features/Syndication Sales.

Wen Shu Lee. "One Whiteness Veils Three Uglinesses" From *Whiteness Identity*, edited by Thomas N. Nakayama and Judith N. Martin. pp. 279–298, copyright © 1999 by Sage Publications, Inc. Reprinted by Permission of Sage Publications, Inc.

Guillermo Gomez-Pena. "The '90s Culture of Xenophobia: Beyond the Tortilla Curtain" by Guillermo Gomez-Pena. Copyright © 1996 by Guillermo Gomez-Pena. Reprinted by permission of City Lights Books.

K. Anthony Appiah. "The Multicultural Mistake" Reprinted with permission from The New York Review of Books. Copyright © 1997 NYREV, Inc.

Ian Frazier. "Someplace in Queens" © 1997 by Ian Frazier, permission of the Wylie Agency.

Gloria Anzaldua. "La conciencia de la mestiza/Towards a New Consciousness" From *Borderlands/La Frontera: The New Mestiza.* Coypright © 1987, 1999 by Gloria Anzaldua. Reprinted by permission of Aunt Lute Books.

Benjamin Alire Saenz. "In the Borderlands of Chicano Identity, There Are Only Fragments" by Benjamin Alire Saenz. From *Border Theory: The Limits of Cultural Politics* by Scott Michaelsen and David E. Johnson. Copyright 1997 by the Regents of the University of Minnesota. Reprinted with permission.

bell hooks. Copyright 1994 from *Outlaw Culture: Resisting Representations* by bell hooks. Reproduced by permission of Routledge, Inc., part of The Taylor & Francis Group.

Audre Lorde. "A Litany for Survival." Copyright © 1978 by Audre Lorde, from *Collected Poems* by Audre Lorde. Used by permission of W.W. Norton & Company, Inc.

INDEX